C0-BPH-998

Technology, Investment, and Trade

Kimio Uno
Keio University at Shonan Fujisawa
Fujisawa, 252 Japan

Theodore Lownik Library
Illinois Benedictine College
Lisle, IL 60532

Elsevier
New York • Amsterdam • London • Tokyo

337.52
U58t

No responsibility is assumed by the Publisher for any injury and/or damage to persons or property as a matter of products liability, negligence or otherwise, or from any use or operation of any methods, products, instructions, or ideas contained in the material herein.

Elsevier Science Publishing Co., Inc.
655 Avenue of the Americas
New York, New York 10010

Distributors outside the United States and Canada:

Elsevier Science Publishers B.V.
P.O. Box 211, 1000 AE Amsterdam, The Netherlands

© 1991 by Elsevier Science Publishing Co., Inc.

This book has been registered with the Copyright Clearance Center, Inc. For further information, please contact the Copyright Clearance Center, Inc., Salem, Massachusetts.

All inquiries regarding copyrighted material from this publication, other than reproduction through the Copyright Clearance Center, Inc., should be directed to: Rights and Permissions Department, Elsevier Science Publishing Co., Inc., 655 Avenue of the Americas, New York, New York 10010. Fax 212-633-3977.

Library of Congress Cataloging-in-Publication Data
Uno, Kimio.
Technology, investment, and trade/Kimio Uno.
p. cm.
Includes bibliographical references and index.
ISBN 0-444-01615-5 (alk. paper)
1. Japan–Foreign economic relations. 2. Investments, Japanese.
3. Technological innovations–Japan. 4. International trade.
5. International finance. I. Title.
HF1602.15.J3U56 1991
337.52–dc20 91-16517
CIP

This book is printed on acid-free paper.

Current printing (last digit):
10 9 8 7 6 5 4 3 2 1

Manufactured in the United States of America

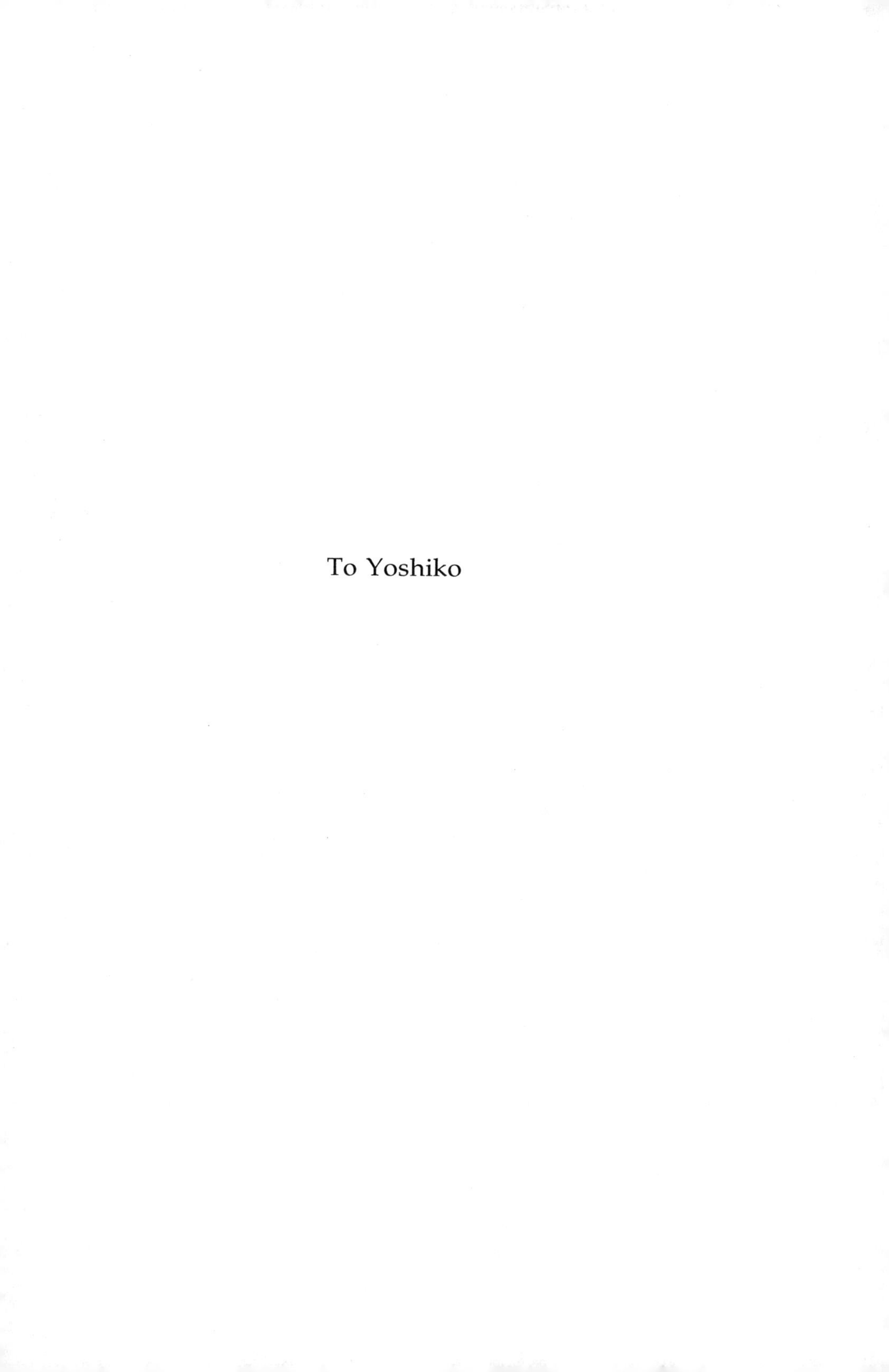

To Yoshiko

Preface

This book looks into the new trends in international relations from three aspects, namely (a) technology, (b) investment, and (c) foreign trade. Even when one limits the scope to an economic sphere, it is obvious that today's international relations do not merely evolve around exports and imports. The world economy today is going through a structural change of a very fundamental nature and we may attribute this to technological shift due to widespread application of electronics which is only achieved through investment at home and abroad. And the magnitude of the change is well reflected in the changing structure of the world economy. It is recognized that Japan has emerged not only as a successful exporter of high-technology products but also as a major innovator as well as the largest supplier of investment fund. Thus, we draw heavily on the changes that are taking place in Japan in innovative activities, capital formation, and foreign trade and investment, which are compared with the experiences in other countries wherever deemed relevant.

Our approach in this book is to let the data tell the story. In order to shed light on these emerging issues, a series of analysis has been carried out. The methodology is quite transparent so that it allows room for cross examination and alternative scientific experiments. The analytical tools have been made fully open in previous publications, including a multisectoral industry model, input-output tables, and industry-occupation matrices, each covering the last 30 years. Interested readers are referred to *Japanese Industrial Performance* (1987) and *Measurement of Services in an Input-Output Framework* (1989), both from the North-Holland. Thus, current work is an "outward" extension of the analysis provided in previous publications. The scope of the analysis has been expanded to capture emerging new trends in Japan's international economic relations and technological aspects in the industry.

Managing the process of structural change of the world economy could turn out to be turbulent and may well constitute a major policy problem. Here is a list of questions:

(1) Technology is the key factor in today's industrial activity. Japan's success must be due to imported technology, or even to outright copying of technology, software and design. More stringent regulation of industrial property right should be the answer to stop Japan.

(2) How is R&D linked to actual technological progress and to the success in exports? Japan may be a major exporter of high-technology products, but she must be lagging when it comes to research and developed.

(3) What is the diffusion of high technology such as computers, indus-

trial robots, and NC metalworking machines? What is the impact on society, especially on employment?
(4) Industrial policy is one of the peculiarities of Japanese economic system. What is behind the continued technological progress and capital formation in Japan as compared to US, EC and elsewhere? Is not this due to targetting under the leadership of the Japanese government, namely MITI? If so, other countries should have industrial policy to coordinate the private effort with that of the government and to pour in more public fund.
(5) New inventions in laboratories and their actual implementation in factories are two different things. Why are the Japanese more apt to accept high technology even when it involves considerable risks and labor displacement? Why do Japanese have longer time horizon, whereas in the West management is pressed to perform in the short run?
(6) What are the pros and cons of direct foreign investment? Japan is using trade surplus to finance foreign investment, thereby buying up industry and real estate overseas. Japan has turned out to be the largest creditor nation, but what would be the benefit to the host countries? Is not Japan only exploiting profitable markets overseas?
(7) Are not less developed countries suffering from turbulent world economy as witnessed by the fact that they are heavily indebted? How about Japan's posture in foreign economic assistance? Her investment is now directed mainly to developed world, and the Japanese ratio of economic assistance to GNP has been among the lowest among major industrial countries.
(8) What is the cause of persistent trade imbalance? Why does Japan keep recording export surplus in the face of continued appreciation of the yen currency? Is not this due to import restriction, explicit or implicit, and other unfair practices on the part of Japan?
(9) After all, is not Japan's increased role in technology, investment, and trade a destabilizing factor in the world economy? Should not we erect protective barriers to seal off the disturbing "Japan problem"? Granting that she has now become not only a major exporter of high-tech products but also a major innovator and an investor, is there a way of turning her strength to the benefit of the world community? Or, as the Soviet Union has become less of an enemy, has Japan emerged as the "public enemy No.1?"
(10) In a borderless world economy, we have observed that the emergence of multinational or global firms and their planning sphere is not bound by the national borders, whereas the governments are constrained to conceive the issues only from the view point of a nation state and their policies are formulated from that perspective. What should be the proper roles of the national governments in an open economy?

In a world which consists of democratic societies, no policy can be formulated devoid of public opinion if it is meant to be realistic. At the basis of public opinion, there lies a series of judgement, some of which are based on solid fact, some of them are imaginary. And problem arises when public opinion is ill founded and policy formulation is confined by such biases. There are cases when policy authorities are inclined to appease such opinion by attacking a straw man, for instance.

It is extremely important in this context to update the common understanding of the functions of the world community, of which Japan is a part. Quite often, Japan is considered to be a trouble maker because she undergoes rapid changes and this triggers adjustment elsewhere. This book addresses itself to the new stage of the world economy. It analyzes the emerging role of Japan in a world which is evolving around new technology. New technology is being defused through investment at home and abroad, giving new impetus to international relations.

The analysis is carried out on a disaggregated industry level rather than macroeconomic level. This standpoint is important because on a macro level we lose sight of structural changes that are affecting various segments of the economy with different pace and intensity. It does not intend to introduce various case studies, either. The cases of successful firms are interesting, but we try to avoid the "fallacy of aggregation": what is good for an individual firm may not be sustainable economy-wide.

It is slightly different in its orientation from conventional approach to international economic relations in that it explicitly treats technology factor and flow of funds. As for technology, the main data source includes world patent application matrix and research and development data. As for foreign investment, the main data sources include flow of funds statistics as well as direct foreign investment data. As for trade, world trade matrix and internationally linked input-output tables are utilized. In view of the importance of trade in services, implication of international technology flow and capital transactions is extensively sought.

It is also different from conventional approach to international relations in that it highlights domestic aspects as well as international aspects. This is based on the belief that international performance has its domestic roots.

The exchange rate alignment in 1985 and after has changed the foreign economic relations in a fundamental way. For one thing, the structure of the Japanese imports which hitherto consisted mainly of raw materials, has shifted toward importation of finished products. In the process, Japan has emerged as a major absorber of industrial outputs, which was beneficial in adding a new dimension to her economic relationship with the newly industrializing countries in Asia. It also worked toward reducing the mounting trade surplus which had reached an unacceptable proportions to the trade partners including the United States and the EC. Direct foreign investment was also prompted by the appreciation of the yen, reducing exports of industrial goods from Japan by shifting production sites overseas, and by the introduction of foreign-produced goods into the home market. In addition, activated portfolio investment filled the shortage of fund overseas while balancing the saving-investment equilibrium domestically.

Despite such success in structural adjustment, the efficacy of exchange rate adjustment in restoring bilateral trade balance has been a limited one. And this delay cannot be solely attributed to the J curve effect which results from lagged response of the economic system to exchange rate adjustment. One may suspect more structural factors, and technology is one such factor, and indeed, a very important one. In longer terms, technological factor exerts powerful influence on trade and investment pattern.

At the same time, one has to take the financial mechanism into consideration. In our context, this includes everything from a very high saving rate of the household sector to "keiretsu" (within-firm-group) financing. Research and development expenditures are being financed out of ample financial resources, together with capital formation embodying new technology. Technological advance is creating an absolute advantage in favor of Japan whereby certain products are only available from this particular source. Japan's position in this sense is somewhat analogous to producers of natural resources, only that in Japan's case the advantage has been created by deliberate research and investment effort. It is hoped that increased outward direct investment, which is also facilitated by the supply of financial resources and exchange rate adjustment, will work toward lessening the technological gap through technology transfers and will strengthen the economic ties in the world community in the long run.

The structure of the book is as follows. Part 1 provides an overview of the economic policy issues unfolding before us. Chapter 1 describes the dilemma emerging between private enterprises on the one hand which have become multinational in their operation and nation states on the other which are confined within national boundaries. Increased market orientation of the private sector seems to have contributed to increased efficiency. This, however, had an unintended result of leaving behind those who cannot effectively participate in the world economic network. At the same time, even among the advanced industrial countries, macroeconomic imbalance and structural adjustment have posed a formidable task for policy makers, industrial circles, and working population alike. Chapter 2 describes the growth of Pacific rim countries as the growth axis. The newly industrializing economies (NIES) in Asia has been one of the most energetic participants in the global society. The new factor is the emergence of Japan as an absorber of exports from these countries. As is widely known, Japanese imports mainly consisted of raw materials, but after the exchange rate adjustment in the mid 1980s her imports of finished goods have been increasing at a rapid pace. Japan's direct foreign investment in Asia and North America is, and will continue to be, an important vehicle of technology transfer and will promote exports from these areas. Thus, despite economic integration in North America and Europe, Pacific rim countries will tend toward a more open economic regime. Chapter 3 takes up the economic relation between the Soviet Union and Japan. Despite their economic size and geographical proximity, international trade between the two countries remained relatively small. Given the fact that Japan's demand for raw materials has tapered off in recent years due to economy-wide technological change and a shift of industrial structure toward electronics and services, this chapter looks into the possibility of increased trade in machinery. The conclusion is that there exists fundamental mismatch in trade structure which will have to be overcome through direct investment and technology transfer.

Part 2 includes two chapters dealing with technology aspect. Chapter 4 looks into the production of technological knowledge. Research and development (R&D) has become an increasingly important economic activity besides production of goods and services in conventional sense. The number of patents will serve as an output indicator of such endeavor, of course with many limitations. Thus, this chapter examines R&D trends and the world patent application statistics. Finally, an attempt is made to identify the benefits of R&D received by individual sectors as well as final demand such as private consumption and exports. Chapter 5 takes up a particular segment of new technology which is of vital importance, namely the ones embodying electronics represented by computer, communication, and control (C-C-C) technology. Their diffusion brought about new modes of production. Application of triple-C technology in manufacturing is changing the logistic sectors. Not only that, it has wide implication on occupational requirement.

Part 3 includes two chapters concerning investment. Capital formation is the vehicle of new technology, and bears particular importance in preparing the production basis for the future society. Chapter 6 discusses the changing pattern of flow of funds in Japan and how it relates to financing of new investment. New trends in capital formation are then analyzed, revealing the rising importance of the C-C-C technology. Chapter 7 provides an analysis of capital stock vintage and how it is related to growth potentials. Output growth of individual industrial sectors is explained in terms of number of workers, working hours, capital stock, the rate of capacity utilization, technological progress embodied in capital, and the changes in capital stock vintage, enabling us to establish direct links between technology, capital stock, and output growth. Results are reported focusing on sectors which are closely related to C-C-C technology.

Part 4 is devoted to international trade. The focal point in chapter 8 is the world trade structure. Based on trade matrices by commodity, it is demonstrated that the direction of trade has undergone considerable change in the recent past. Apparently, this is attributable to increased importance of triple-C technology in international trade. The differential rate of diffusion of this technology also has given rise to new suppliers. Chapter 9 examines the balance of payments for Japan which provides a summary view on the structural change which is taking place in various aspects of the economy. The case in question concerns merchandise trade, trade in services including technology, and capital transactions.

The analyses in this book are based on an econometric model named COMPASS (*co*mprehensive *m*odel for *p*olicy *ass*essment), which is described briefly in Part 5. The model has 25 sectors and is designed to serve as a testbed for various policy simulations. After brief description of the model, the parts of the model which have direct bearing on the interaction among technology, investment, and trade are explained.

I have benefitted from a great deal of support and stimulus from a large number of people. I would particularly like to thank the participants to the international symposium on "the State and the Private Enterprise in a Global Society" organized by the Japan Association for Planning Administration and supported by the National Institute for Research Advancement (NIRA) for raising relevant issues. My appreciation also goes to the Japan Forum on International Relations headed by Saburo Okita and coordinated by Kenichi Ito, where the economic task force led by Toshio Watanabe looked into new economic relations in the Pacific. Related to this project, Michael Aho of the Council on Foreign Affairs gave me an opportunity to discuss Japan's international relations in depth with leading scholars and government officials in the United States. Phil Trezise and Edward Lincoln of the Brookings Institution provided, on numerous occasions, information about economic policies on both sides of the Pacific. The Japan-U.S. specialist meeting on Japan-Soviet relations organized by Hiroshi Kimura of the Slavic Research Center of Hokkaido University was another occasion to reconsider Japan's international posture. Kazuo Ogawa of Japan Association for Trade with Soviet Union and Socialist Countries of Europe provided me with information at the time of my participation in the American

Association for Advancement of Slavic Studies (AAASS) in 1988. The Social Council of Japan gave me opportunity to conduct research trips during 1986–1988 in the U.S., Canada, and E.C. The Canadian government granted Japan-Canadian Study Award to a research team, headed by Hideo Sato, of which I was a member. My earlier experience as coordinator at the Japan Economic Research Center under Hisao Kanamori and for a joint research project between Keio University and Fletcher School of Law and Diplomacy was also helpful. The session on potential growth in the 1989 conference of the International Association for Research in Income and Wealth (IARIW) was stimulating, and this is where I was able to discuss some of the key issues with Angus Maddison, John W. Kendrick, Zoltan Kenessey, and Graham Pyatt, among others. My exposure to Technology Economy Society (TES) project at the International Institute for Applied Systems Analysis (IIASA) provided me an added stimulus to combine technological aspects into economic framework, and my special thanks go to Friedrich Schmidt-Bleek, Jukka Ranta, and Robert Ayres. A research group headed by Yoichi Kaya under the auspices of the Science and Technology Agency of the Japanese Government facilitated me to expand the scope of the research. I also thank participants to the Multiple-Use Socio-Economic Data Bank (MUSE) project, especially Akihiro Amano, Toshihisa Toyoda, Iwao Ozaki, Fumimasa Hamada, Masahiro Kuroda, and Masahiko Shimizu for various suggestions.

As always, my appreciation goes to research assistants for their help at various stages of data collection and simulation experiment. All possible errors and omissions are the sole responsibility of the present author.

Publication of this volume was supported by Grant-in-Aid for Publication of Scientific Research Result by the Ministry of Education, Science, and Culture (application number 2039). Part of the research was supported by Grant-in-Aid for Scientific Research entitled "Technological Change in Japan and the United States and the Structure of Trade and Industry" (grant number 02451073), and Keio Gijuku Fukuzawa Memorial Fund for the Education and Research.

Shonan Fujisawa Campus

August 12, 1990

Kimio Uno

Contents

Part 3. Investment

Part 4. International trade

Part 5. Analytical framework

List of tables

List of figures

First appearance of the chapters

Chapter 1: "The State and Private Enterprise in a Global Society: Points at Issue and Their Future Outlook," National Institute for Research Advancement, September 1988. Summary of a symposium held by the Japan Association for Planning Administration, entitled International Symposium on the State and the Private Enterprise in a Global Society, Tokyo, September 5 and 6, 1987.

Chapter 2: "The Policy Recommendation on the Structural Adjustment of Economies of Japan, U.S., and Asian NICs," written by a task force composed of Toshio Watanabe, Takeshi Aoki, Mitsuhiko Morimoto, and the present author, Japan Forum on International Relations, March 1988.

Chapter 3: "An Overview of Soviet Exports to Japan—A Japanese Perspective." Paper presented at the US-Japan Joint Study on the Soviet Union, organized by the Slavic Center, Hokkaido University, Sapporo, June 15-17, 1989. An earlier version of the paper was presented at the 20th National Convention, American Association for the Advancement of Slavic Studies (AAASS), Honolulu, November 18-21, 1988.

Chapter 4: "Fixed Capital Formation Matrix and R&D Benefit," Institute of Socio-Economic Planning, the University of Tsukuba, February 1990, and "International Flow of Patents (Release 2)," Institute of Socio-Economic Planning, the University of Tsukuba, March 1990.

Chapter 5: Summary was presented as "CIM and the Economy: Clues for Empirical Analysis," Computer Integrated Manufacturing (CIM) project under Technology, Economy, and Society (TEP) program at International Institute for Applied Systems Analysis (IIASA), The Final IIASA Conference on Computer Integrated Manufacturing: Technology, Organization and People in Transition, July 1–4, 1990, Laxenburg Austria. Reproduced in *CIM: Revolution in Progress,* WP-90-32, IIASA, August 1990.

Chapter 6: "Innovation and Finance," presented at the Institute of Statistical Research, Tokyo, November 24, 1989.

Chapter 7: "Potential output: conceptual problems and empirical measurement," paper presented at the 21st General Conference, International Association for Research in Income and Wealth (IARIW), Lahnstein, Germany, August 20–25, 1989.

Chapter 10: "Framework of the Model COMPASS (Comprehensive Model for Policy ASSessment)—Dealing with Technological Change—," paper presented at the International Symposium on Economic Modelling, University of Urbino, Italy, 23–25 July, 1990.

Part 1

Economic policy in changing international environment

Chapter 1. New perspectives in international relations

1-1 Introduction

The world economy is changing at a rapid pace in many respects. It is a formidable task to try to identify new forces which are behind the transformation of interrelationship among countries and various economic agents, and no single person can be solely responsible for that kind of an endeavor. It is in this context that I believe interchange of opinion is extremely important. And such interchange should take place among different disciplines and among people from different parts of the world.

Such rare occasion was provided by an international symposium on "The State and Private Enterprise in a Global Society" held in Tokyo.[1] The present author was entrusted to publish a summary of the discussions, which I reproduce here. The general summary is based on nine papers and discussions based upon them, and is intended to sum up the views expressed and questions to be explored.

The following six topics have emerged as points-of-issue:
(1) Trends towards a supply-side policy.
(2) Appropriate roles of government in a borderless economy.
(3) Effectiveness of structural adjustment through exchange rate policy.
(4) National policy management with special reference to US savings-investment balance and Japan's trade balance.
(5) Emergence of Japan as a key player in the international scene.
(6) De-industrialization, service orientation of the economy, and international economic rules.

These items do not correspond directly to the papers presented, but are intended to span the various points raised in the papers or emerged during the discussion.

1-2 Emphasis on supply side

In the wake of the 1970s oil crisis, world economic policy was focused on restraining aggregate demand. At that time, many countries were faced with constraints on growth such as energy availability, inflation, balance of international payments deficits, and cumulative debt. At any rate, many governments were faced with fiscal deficit reflecting declined revenues under slower growth on the one hand and fixed expenditures which were already committed and institutionalized on the other. In contrast, the symposium suggested that there has been a recent shift to supply-oriented policy. This is true in both developed and developing economies.

It was significant that both the French and German papers were concerned with potential economic growth.[2] This is an extremely important shift in viewpoint, despite the fact that the speakers did not approach the question directly. They both noted that, whereas policy intervention in the past had placed emphasis upon adjustments on the demand-side, the weight has now been shifted to the supply-side. Restrictive measures were adopted after the oil crisis because of inflation, but changes in the conditions of supply and demand in 1986 undermined these restrictions, thereby producing a shift to the supply-side.

The question is, what will happen if we rely on a demand-oriented policy, particularly if it depends on increased government spending. World-wide inflation will undoubtedly result if countries such as Germany and Japan try to stimulate their economies by increasing their budget deficit, while the U.S. fails to reduce its budget deficit. Germany and Japan, after initially adopting an expansionist policy, will then ultimately be forced to adopt tightening policies.

On the national level, supply-oriented policies have become more important. There has been a shift in business circles from real investment to portfolio investment. At the same time, the manufacturing sector is trying to ensure its survival under appreciated currencies by moving production sites overseas. "Hollowing out" may be a rational behavior for individual firms, but is not necessarily desirable for a nation. Because of liberalization of trade and capital transactions, a dilemma arises when governments lose the policy tools through which they could influence business behavior.

C. Sauter's paper entitled "A Social Compromise for Competitive Growth: French Socialist Economic Policy 1981–1986" outlines the French experience. Like other countries, France has suffered for the last five years from a depressed environment resulting from the strong dollar, expensive oil and low OECD growth. Under the pre-1982 system, wages were fully indexed to prices. With international competition, business was unable to pass cost increases entirely to price increase and, as a result, manufacturing profits were reduced and investment declined. From 1982 onwards, wage adjustments for inflation were made only partially, as a part of an implicit social compromise, resulting in recovery of the economy to the 1973 level. In order to realize growth potentials, efforts were made in two directions: stimulating competition and fostering investment. To stimulate competition, Spain and Portugal were allowed to join the EC, expanding potential market. The EC diversified its interests in such areas as telecommunications. Furthermore, the government encouraged an influx of foreign capital, and the financial market was partially liberalized. To foster investment, the government nationalized five groups of industries. In addition, more funds were devoted to research and development, while investments were reduced in structurally-depressed industries.

There are, however, some problems. The financial returns from securities and bonds are much higher than those from real investment, and manufacturing centers are being moved overseas.

Leibfritz's paper discusses the situation in Germany. As is suggestd by its title "Demand Management and Supply Side Policies in West Germany, Past Experience and Prospects for the Future", this paper explains the reasons for the shift to the supply-side in Germany. The basic principle underlying traditional policy in Germany has been to encourage market forces to operate freely on a microeconomic level, while demand management assists in balancing extreme period of business activity on the macroeconomic level. Amidst the recession resulting from the first oil crisis, however, a major tax reform was implemented in 1975, and temporary investment grants were made available. These measures mark the beginning of development towards a supply-sided policy. In the early 1980s, in order to improve investment conditions and reduce fiscal drag, various other tax measures followed, such as income tax and business tax reductions including improvements in depreciation allowances.

Since the early 1980s, according to Leibfritz, Germany, France, Britain, and the United States have all been inclined toward placing more emphasis upon stimulating the supply-side. The discussants noted that this shift has important implications for developing countries. During periods of economic strength, developing countries were eager to borrow funds for domestic investment, but, when a period of adjustment set in after the oil crisis, they had to face a rise in interest rates and falling commodity prices. Consequently, their debt-service capacity had to fall drastically. Under these circumstances, developing countries adopted tight money policies in the hopes of reducing imports and improving their balance of trade. This kind of policy, however, leads to a fall in real investment. Curbed investment naturally invites a fall in future supply capacity and a delay in the improvement of their industrial structure, since the demand for primary products is unlikely to recover for some time. A solution to the debt problem in developing countries is not yet in sight, except for some Asian NICs and ASEAN countries.

Taking up the economic problems in the developing countries, Sakurai and Sadahiro paper brings out two points concerning recent economic scene.[3] The first is a reversal of previous capital flow patterns. Since 1983, the net transfer from developed to developing countries has dramatically decreased. The total amount of money flows to developing countries by the private sector amounted to only 3 billion dollars in 1986, down 90 billion dollars from 1981, while at the same time, the interest payments of developing countries have increased reflecting higher rate of interest. This situation is particularly acute for heavily-indebted countries and one of their options is to run down their foreign exchange reserves. Since this measure has its limits for an obvious reason, they have no other alternative but to resort to cutting imports. This will ultimately damage their economy since this leads to a reduction in investments and then to a curbing of their growth potentials.

The difficulty of solving the debt problem through reliance on a tightening policy became clear. Thus, industrialized nations are being pressed to change their policies towards developing countries. These new policies include: fostering the growth of developing countries; providing new money through private banks; and the direct reduction of debts. In contrast to conventional tight macroeconomic policy which is inclined to short-term demand management, policies for lowering the capital-output ratio (i.e., raising the capital productivity) in the long-term should be encouraged.

Snoh Unakul of Thailand does not necessarily believe that developing countries should operate an open economy under the market mechanism.[4] While efficiency of their economies will definitely improve, disadvantages such as hazardous development of resources, the deterioration of the environmental quality, and increasing income inequalities will accompany the process. There may also be a clash of interests between multinational corporations and local interests, the latter seeking local participation and technology transfer.

Thus, there is a need to skillfully combine business activities with economic assistance plans. Japan's plans to recycle some 20 billion dollars is intended to revitalize the economy of developing countries by effectively utilizing her trade surplus. Japan's annual budget for development assistance has never been fully utilized due to a lack of adequate local projects. From a worldwide point of view, however, America's need to reduce her financial deficit has diminished her aid-giving capabilities, making it necessary for Japan to respond more actively in increasing ODA. Pouring unlimited amount of offical development aid into developing countries, however, will not solve the problem. The repaying capacity itself must be strengthened. The existing liabilities pose no problem if they become part of real investment and create an increased productive capacity. It is necessary to provide developing countries with assistance in 'soft' technology and know-how, so that they will be able to effectively absorb ODA. There is also a shift to supply-oriented policies. Those countries that have been able to free themselves from debt problems are invariably the ones that have been able to adapt themselves to changes in the world economy by changing their industrial structures.

There is an emerging new relationship developing in the division of labor between some ASEAN countries and the Asian NICs (Korea, Taiwan, Hong Kong, and Singapore) on the one hand and Japan on the other. These countries had previously adopted an export-oriented (mainly to the U.S.) industrialization strategy, but, with the appreciation of the yen since the G-5 agreement of September 1985, new economic and trade relations have rapidly developed between these countries and Japan. During the first half of the 1980s, Japan's direct overseas investments were made mainly in industrialized countries such as the United States where large market exists and the investment environment is stable. With the appreciation of the yen, however, direct overseas investment to the NICs of Asia and some ASEAN countries has rapidly increased. This will promote an intra-industry division of labor, and also alter Japan's trade structure substantially.

The points Yu Yonding of the Chinese Academy of Social Sciences makes in his paper is similar to Sakurai and Sadahiro's, although it differs somewhat in terms of the policy implications arrived at.[5] Yu argues that international organizations such as GATT and UNCTAD should be strengthened in order to avoid trade wars and protectionism. He also believes that concerted government intervention is necessary in order to arrest the decline in commodity prices.

Contrary to his expectations, however, developed countries have become extremely skeptical of adjustments made by international organizations, as well as market intervention by governments. The idealistic macroeconomic approach of earlier days which favored such intervention has virtually disappeared. This probably reflects the growing realization that government policy should not, or, as a matter of fact, cannot ignore economic realities.

On the other hand, there are probably many who share Yu's belief that tightening policy alone will not solve the debt problem. Developed countries are being asked to create an economic environment that will enable indebted countries to export, as well as formulating policies for bringing down interest rates. He also believes that Japan, with her ample capital and technology, should play a more important role in helping developing countries to achieve a horizontal division of labor.

What should be done in macroeconomic terms, however, may not necessarily suit business interests. It is too optimistic to assume that government emphasis on supply-side alone will lead to desirable investment, domestically and internationally. When trade in services and overseas investment are liberalized, policy makers are limited in their ability to create an appropriate economic environment. The economic environment consists of too many factors: consistency in foreign capital policy, recognition of the autonomy of business activities, improvement of the infrastructure, easing of restrictions on employment, importation and production of parts and intermediate materials, and repatriation of earned profits.

Thus, capital tends to flow more toward developed countries than to developing countries, and among the developed countries, to those with a stable investment environment consisting of a large market and limited number of transparent restrictions on business behavior. Among developing countries, investment tends to be limited to a few countries with good performance records. If this is the case, and I believe it is, the flow of private capital may even increase the inter-country economic differentials. It may therefore be necessary to ensure that any country receiving investments, regardless of its ideological orientation, make its policy compatible with the market mechanism.

The world economy currently faces significant technological changes. It is not possible to argue for strengthening the supply-side without paying due attention to these changes. In this context, private direct investments are important to the international flow of technology as a carrier of technology. The business community will play an increasingly critical role in the development and transfer of technology through its overseas investments.

Business behavior is based primarily on efficiency, and the direction of investment is determined by the expected earnings. If the investment involves any risk, a risk premium is added. It is natural that the flow of investment and the accompanying flow of technology thus tends towards those areas where the rate of return of investment is high and the risk small. In addition, investment capital is not necessarily directed to real investment. If the rate of return of portfolio investment is higher than that of real investment, then capital will naturally take the form of the former. Even manufacturing firms nowadays take advantage of portfolio investment.

There is no guarantee that rational business behavior in microeconomic terms would bring about desirable outcome on the macroeconomic level, either on national or world economic terms. The oil crisis of the 1970s provoked substantial international differences in economic performance, not only among industrial countries but among LDCs as well. Even within a single country, there are marked differences between growing industries and stagnant ones. Such patterns will likely to continue. Differences in microeconomic behavior in adjusting to new economic environment, especially in adopting to new technology, and differences in industrial structure which can be seen as a bundle of different sectors, seem to explain differentials in economic performance.

1-3 The roles of national governments in a multinational corporate economy

Economic policy is formulated by the governments which represent national economies. Since the general acceptance of Keynesian policy in earliy post-WWII era, economic policy makers have exerted greater efforts towards macroeconomic decisions. As is widely known, a question was raised from the rational expectation school as to the theoretical validity of macroeconomic policy. The rational expectation theory stands and fall with the validity of their assumptions when it comes to policy implication. At the symposium, problems concerning the limited roles of government were addressed in the light of today's economic reality, a standpoint entirely different from that of rational expectations.

First, with the liberalization of trade and capital transfers, the influence any one government can exercise on industry has to be limited. In other words, a conflict has developed between the multinational business world and the nation states. The American government has turned to protectionism since American-based multinational businesses have carried out efficient overseas production. Their exports into the U.S. have resulted in the decline of domestic industries. This has at least partially contributed to creating the trade imbalance and unemployment. For multinational businesses, there is no impediment to profit-making interests and future development.

Second, the government, caught between the microeconomic basis of businesses and pressure from special interest groups, has become increasingly subject to political restrictions. Businesses do not feel that they are in any need of protection from the government. Rather, as Onoe who chaired the First Session pointed out, they feel that policy intervention is undesirable. This explains the warm support which Japanese business circles gave to the Provisional Commission for Administrative Reform (Rincho, or Rinji Gyosei Chosakai). Small- to medium-sized business and agriculture, alongside labor, however, demand protection. In keeping with the theme for the symposium, "the State and the Private Enterprise in a Global Society", we must realize that the increased politicization is bound to undermine sensible policy decision when the government deals with domestic or world issues. And this is not simply limited to the Japanese government.

In Sautter's evaluation of the situation in France, he remarked that "the state is now squeezed between the continental and regional interests." He also pointed out that while society is not global, technology is. Even though the EC's 320 million people form a single market for the big business, he believes, it is desirable to leave small- to medium-sized business, education, research and technological development at the regional level. According to Sautter, "decentralization, and the reduction of Paris' administrative power, allows for diversity. This is an asset in France (and in Europe) in a rapidly changing world." He points out that France is trying to find a solution, through various public and private initiatives, with the hope that progressives will carry conservatives through reforms.

The state will have to develop in two directions: internationalization and regionalization. Tajima of NIRA pointed out the following factors of development:
(1) Key industries have declined in Japan and other developed countries, and are moving to the ASEAN countries and the NICs. In addition, with the development of service industries, it has become almost impossible for central government agencies to exercise control.
(2) Though multi national businesses move freely among countries, the state has neither the desire nor the means to control them.
(3) The state has no creativity. Valuable resources in creativity exist in the individuals, the regions, and business firms.
As a result, no country can free itself from market principles in terms of economic policy, including, perhaps, even socialist ones.

In Aoki's paper, the relationship between the government and the market is examined on the basis of game theory. In contrast to the conventional, neoclassical concept of the government as a neutral policy maker, the game theory model assumes that the government and private corporations play a bargaining game. A pluralistic or corporate model and a developmental state model are presented as opposing models. The former assumes that horizontal labor organizations and business organizations permeate the state, and take part in economic planning and policy making. From this standpoint, the state is seen as a mechanism through which conflicting interests are rectified. Policy is regarded as the result of bargaining between interest groups. In contrast, the latter assumes that the state, and the powerful central economic agency in particular, constantly formulate measures on its own initiative to foster the economy. Government creates and develops new markets, autonomously performing functions beyond its role as an intermediary. Policies are formulated according to priorities set by the state.

Aoki's conclusion is that the equilibrium brought about by strategically-motivated players is equal to that brought about by state-conducted democratic weighting. Here, 'democratic weighting' refers to an attempt to equalize the interests of citizens through policy means. Judging from this viewpoint, the two models are not opposed to each other. According to the developmental state model, however, there is the possibility that the state will not reflect democratic values.

What is the situation in Japan today? There has been an increasing tendency for Japan's big business, which in fact is a coalition of labor and capital, to reject government intervention and rely instead on the market decisions. According to Aoki, this is clear from the expectations of business circles for the administrative reform. On the other hand, he writes, "special interest groups such as farmers and traditional small businesses tend to become more dependent on the state, which simply encourages the state itself to become more conservative and inert." In fact, conservative inertia has weakened market functions in Japan. It is questionable whether the consumer has benefited from a strong yen which should have brought about merits through reduced import prices. In macroeconomic terms, when compared internationally, Japan's labor force in the wholesale and retail trade is 2 percentage points too many than those in OECD countries. This may be because of rigid restrictions imposed by the government on the new opening of large-scale retail stores, requiring prior agreement with small-sized local owners who have established themselves and enjoy fat profit at the expense of consumers.

Unless rationalization occurs at the distribution channels, the appreciation of the yen currency cannot benefit the consumer. Nor can there be any expansion of imports of manufactured products. The time has come for us to realize that the preservation of an inefficient system of distribution will inherently lead the state to misinterpret its international role. Multi-national businesses are leaving Japan because of numerous restrictions imposed by the state, and are shifting their emphasis to overseas activities. The proposed administrative reform does not touch public finance, and the mobility of business is still restricted due to politically-motivated government interventions. In many cases, inefficient policies are still in force, despite the fact that the needs of the society have changed.[6]

In Miyachi's comments regarding this point, he assumes that the market function will increase in Japan, fostered by factors such as the continuing appreciation of the yen on a medium- to long-term basis; the increasing sense of being isolated internationally amidst trade friction; and the global expansion of the market. Moreover, with the participation of foreign businesses in the Japanese market, foreign governments have become more interested in Japan. Japan's increasing international presence will inevitably force her to function as an important global player.

1-4 Effectiveness of adjustment through the exchange rate

Has the appreciation of the yen since the 1985 G-5 meeting had a sufficient adjustment effect on the imbalance of trade between Japan and the United States? Or, are the adjustment effects of the exchange rate limited? What is the appropriate level of the dollar? The view that the dollar has depreciated excessively and that the appropriate rate is around ¥170 to a dollar, is held both in the United States and in Japan. Yet, there is also the view that the rate of ¥140 to ¥150 to a dollar will currently be maintained. A third view holds that the dollar should depreciate further, and that only then will the U.S. balance of trade move toward an equilibrium.[7]

W. Buiter's paper employs a theoretical model to question whether or not a fall in the dollar exchange rate is necessary to improve the balance of current accounts or the balance of trade in the United States. He points out that the ratio of imports in total abosorption varies according to the contents of policy measures (in contrast to generally accepted hypothesis that the propensity to import remains constant). Also, since the exchange rate and the balance of trade are both endogenous variables, their movement depends on the nature of the shocks that they experience.

He further notes that short-term effects limited to price changes should not be confused with long-term effects due to changes in the exchange rate, with the influence of direct overseas investment and imports from there taken into consideration.

It is not possible to determine an appropriate level for the exchange rate only from this theoretical model. However, this paper is illuminating in that the 'common sense' point of view, which sees a continued fall in the exchange rate as necessary to correcting the trade imbalance, is not always valid.

Although Buiter's paper is theoretical, his own view on the exchange rate is that the dollar has already depreciated excessively. He is thus a proponent of the first view outlined above. In response to questions in the symposium, he has stated definitely that the a depreciation of the dollar was unnecessary for the following two reasons. First, the dollar has already depreciated to the required level, and what remains now is to wait for the process of adjustment to work itself out. Second, a further depreciation of the dollar means the exportation of America's unemployment to Japan and West Germany.

One of the contributions Buiter made in his paper was to stress the importance of making a distinction between short-term effects and long-term effects of adjustments through the exchange rate realignment. As Shinohara pointed out in his comment, Japan's direct foreign investment has rapidly increased from 1985 into 1986, registering an increase of 82.7% on a dollar basis. On a yen basis, it was an increase of 41.5% (16.5% in manufacturing), because of the appreciation of the exchange rate in favor of the yen. If this pace is maintained, overseas production will rapidly increase, and Japan's exports must decrease so that Japan's balance of trade will move towards equilibrium. This effect has not yet occurred, but when it does, the effect of adjustment will be further reinforced.

Commenting on another paper, Yoshitomi of the Economic Planning Agency argued that America's remaining deficit in its balance of trade reflects past conditions, so that it would be absurd to turn protectionist on that basis alone. In other words, in the past, even businesses with comparative advantage were inclined to protectionism, but this situation has improved with the depreciation of the dollar. On a quantity basis, while the rate of increase is 11% for U.S. exports, that of imports is under 4%. This indicates clearly that the exchange rate adjustment has already shown sufficient results.

Speaking from a different standpoint, Shinohara dismissed the argument for the free fall of the dollar, and mentioned the five points listed below as necessary factors for America to maintain the current rate.
(1) The fall of the dollar will result in inflation. Since it will be the United States itself that will suffer from inflation, she should be making efforts to avoid such situation from happening.
(2) The depreciation of the dollar will lead to the withdrawal of foreign capital from the United States, and a rise in interest will result.
(3) A rise in the interest rate and a shortage of funds will be disadvantgeous to the United States.
(4) As the depreciation of the dollar will have an adverse effect on the world economy, the American pressure on other countries to stimulate their domestic demands will not produce good results.
(5) The experience of the depression in the 1920s and 1930s is a cogent example of dangers posed by withdrawal of foreign capital.

In short, America will not benefit from the fall of the dollar. In view of these factors, the current exchange rate is maturing, and the ¥140–150 level is likely to be maintained.

It should be remembered that, as far as we can judge from their observations, the symposium participants were of the view that adjustments through the exchange rate have already been effective, and that it is desirable that the effects of direct investment to surface.

1-5 National policy management with special reference to the U.S. saving-investment balance and Japan's trade balance

In his paper, Yu from China comments that America's policy management is ".... both unfair and ridiculous that, at the expense of poor countries, the richest country in the world heavily borrows money around the world in order to spend more than it produces." Yoshitomi, too, raises the question why the second richest country in the world (i.e., Japan) continues to supply a stupendous amount of funds to the richest (i.e., the United States). Kawai also points out that if money flow is left to the market forces, more funds will flow into America, already rich in capital, while it is the developing countries that require the investment funds.

We have become used to the view that funds are strictly claim on resources. However, is not this an arrogant view? To acquire resources with funds directly affects the welfare of the people. In addition, when capital is scarce in relation to labor, the owners of capital has a dictating power. This is the reason why national governments are serious about policy coordination. Yu's argument refers to this point.

The German paper in the first session suggests how serious Germans are about maintaining macroeconomic balance in the face of American pressure to increase domestic demand. After pointing out that "there are some reasons to believe that the present imbalance in the balance of payments can be attributed, to a large extent, to differing fiscal policy stances in various countries, and especially to overly expansionary fiscal policy in the United States after the 1981 tax reforms," Leibfritz expresses his concern that "if in the surplus countries like Japan and Germany, the consideration for the international adjustment process were to lead to an exaggeration of deficit-financing through their tax reforms and other fiscal measures, then the high U.S. fiscal deficit would finally be 'exported' to those countries. International policy coordination means that problems have to be tackled particularly in the countries where they were created, while the other countries can only assist to a limited extent."

Yoshitomi also raised the question, "what is the international responsibility of a country?" What kind of position does macroecnomic policy occupy in terms of international responsibility? Is it not sufficient to maintain growth and keep prices stable? Has it ever been one of America's policy objective to maintain world demand? Are Japan and Germany obliged to bear such a responsibility?

To sum up the view on American economic management, the U.S. stance on public finance poses no problem, as it is not different from those of the EC and Japan. The problem is that investment is at a high level while savings are low.

In his comment, Marumo agreed on the point that America's financial deficit had been assessed excessively. However, he pointed out that the financial deficit poses a problem because of the low level of savings. Investment is certainly at a high level compared with savings. But, since the ratio of investment to the GNP is low, investment should not be curbed.

Iwata argues in his paper that it is necessary to alter the saving-investment ratio in the private sector in the U.S. in order to solve America's external imbalance. At the same time, while Japan gives preferential treatment to savings at present, America tends to foster investment, resulting in an asymmetry of taxation. Moreover, since foreign investment is active, international arbitration in taxation develops. Therefore, Iwata argues, international convergence is required for taxation policies. However, Cooper pointed out that such arbitration had not actually developed, and uneven tax rates were being adjusted by national taxation authorities in the form of tax credit, etc.

The problem boils down to the fact that the savings rate fell in the United States, contrary to expectations under Reagan's supply-side oriented policy, from 6% prior to the Reagan Administration to about 2% recently. All the symposium participants, except those from the United States, felt that with the falling saving rate, it would be necessary to reduce the financial deficit.

In view of these arguments, the general conclusion seems to be that, while the necessity for international policy coordination decreases with a shift in policy from demand management to the supply-side, fiscal policy continues to affect the domestic demand, which in turn affects exchange rates, the balance of trade, and the balance of capital account, thus making policy coordination a continuing necessity.

There is a suggestion that Japan should carry out large-scale transfers such as those similar to America's Marshall Plan, as a means of reducing Japan's trade surplus. Shinohara, who chaired the Second Session, referred to this point in the form of comment on Iwata's paper. The reason why Japan does not carry out such a "Marshall Plan" is that there is a difference in the fundamental conditions between the United States at that time and Japan today. Without providing such assistance, America's public finance would have been in the black, and so would have been its balance of trade. In contrast, although Japan's trade balance today is in the black, its public finance is in the red. With surplus funds in the private sector, what is needed is to effect transfer from the private to the government sector.

Kanamori, who chaired the Tenth Conference of the Japan Association for Planning Administration under the auspices of which this symposium was organized, commented in his speech that macroeconomic planning had not been effectively carried out in Japan, leading to the collapse of the savings-investment balance and the trade imbalance, and at the same time intensified the problem of overcrowding in cities and depopulation of rural areas. In the case of Japan, macroeconomic planning by the Economnic Planning Agency, adjustment of industrial structure under the auspices of the Ministry of International

Trade and Industry, and regional planning by the National Land Agency existed until recently, with mutual but loose feedback among them. This played a major role in coordinating different fields and provided direction to private activities. While it is true that the difficulty of planning is increasing in an age of rapid technological and social change, blind policy management cannot be good for the Japanese economy nor for the world. How to recover the savings-investment balance of the Japanese economy is an important task with both domestic and international implications. It will thus be necessary to reconstruct efficient systems for information exchange and decision making. This is probably Japan's responsibility, now that its economic influence has extended, and this will also benefit Japan as it is trying to become a welcome member of the world economy by restructuring its industrial structure to center around high technology.

1-6 Emergence of Japan as a key player

Neo-classical concepts have hitherto formed the main-stream of economic theories, and it has been assumed that an atomistic economic agents would act under a set of given market parameters and thus form an automatic adjustment mechanism. One of the features of the symposium was that an argument was made where in Japan is to emerge as a key player based on what is implied by game theory. Moreover, the argument covered so-called macroeconomic aspects, including general economic policy and adjustment in the exchange market as well as the microeconomic aspect of individual business behavior.

Summing up for the session, Shinohara commented on the macroeconomic condition. According to him, the process of Japan's internationalization can be divided into three stages. The first stage was based on Japan's international attitude as was expressed in the slogan "do not become an orphan of the world." In the second stage, Japan's attitude was passive throughout the period when it was under pressure from other countries while the Japanese economy expanded in scale. The third stage is that of a frank exchange of opinions. It is wrong to remain passive to outrageous demands made by America. Speaking frankly does not constitute nationalism. The correct behavior is to present a just argument and to negotiate by speaking up before trying to reach a consensus through compromise.

Canada's concerns in her economic relations with the U.S. are many, which made her enter into U.S.-Canada negotiations on free trade. First is the fact that external demands by the U.S. government are directly linked with those of domestic U.S. industries. Second, American argument and decision making are of an ad-hoc and unpredictable nature. Third, the mechanism for solving conflicts has not been established, and is subject to political climate. Fourth, backed up by superiority in the services and electronics industries, the U.S. tends to rely on bilateral consultation, rather than on multilateral arrangement. Finally, the U.S. tries to achieve the abolishment of foreign laws restricting American overseas business activities. In fact, this situation seems to have made Canada feel the great need for free trade agreement with her neighbor, in which the solution to conflicts was to be clearly institutionalized. If such is the case between two countries that are closely related to each other politically, economically, racially, and linguistically, the situation must be even more serious for countries such as Japan, who have only the economic basis as a common denominator from which to negotiate.

These views urging Japan to grow as a key player clarify the point that there are limits to relying on the automatic adjustment mechanism of the market. At the same time, they also urge Japan to realize that external intervention in the market, be it by government or business, has increased in importance. Moreover, they reflected on the passive attitude of the Japanese government and business firms, and pointed out strongly that such an attitude also has its limits. Furthermore, a constantly passive stance without explicit statement of the intentions and code of conduct would lead to misunderstandings, from which not only Japan but the entire world would suffer, ultimately leading to the malfunctioning of the world economic and political system. In the future, both policy actions and business operations will be required to be more aware of the world around them, so that they can promptly and correctly realize the situation, and systematically convey their arguments to the other party.

Iwata's paper suggests that turning the yen into an international currency may be one of the contributions Japan can make to the world economy. The international currency system, based on the dollar, became unstable as America's hegemony declined. According to Iwata, it is possible to stabilize it under an oligopoly, by the inclusion of the yen and other currencies, and its effectivity as a means of last resort may be secured by reinforcing the IMF and the BIS.

Commenting on this, Cooper pointed out that Japan would probably not welcome it, if financial factors rather than trade begin to influence the yen. He also noted that the fewer the international currencies, the better for stability and policy adjustments. Yu pointed out that in order for the yen to become an international currency, it should be based on a further integration of the Asian and Japanese economies with the yen as the means of settling transactions. As long as Japan's import structure is inclined to natural resources, while the expansion of the import of finished products remains as a future task, the yen is still not very widely used as a currency of settlement. In short, the general response from the U.S. and Asian neighbors was that it is still premature to transform the yen into an international currency.

Ishiguro's paper, which questioned the approach Japan has adopted so far from the viewpoint of business activities, invited lively responses from the participants. According to him, the legal environment for international transactions can be summed up as 'extraterritorial application vs. blocking statutes'. To start with, there are the extraterritorial applications of the U.S. Anti-Trust Law and the Long Arm Statute, which places foreign businesses under restrictions imposed by U.S. law. In opposition to this, various countries have taken countermeasures. The United States, in turn, has been taking steps to offset the effect of the measures adopted by other countries. There is, therefore, a real danger that the market will continue to be closed, a process justified, ironically, on basis of reciprocity and fairness.

Obsessed by "the idea that the only true approach to international operation is to avoid irritating foreign countries as much as possible," Japan has found itself in a quandary amidst these changes. Ishiguro's paper discusses actual examples, such as preferential treatment given to foreign creditors under the Company Reorganization Law, the IBM incident regarding plug-compatible computers made in Japan (which began with the FBI's investigation using entrapment techniques), Japan's Anti-Trust Law without extraterritorial application, the problem of COCOM regulations (the case of Toshiba Machinery exporting numerically-controlled metalworking machines which surfaced by the U.S. informing Japan on the allegation that this made the Soviet submarines quieter than before, an evidence which cannot be substantiated on this side of the Pacific), America's logic and Japan's poor response concerning the Japan-U.S. friction over semi-conductors (subdued by the American pressure, Japan yielded to keep an eye on Japanese semi-conductor prices not only in the U.S. but world-wide, only to be detected by an informant in Hong Kong of violation there), and others. IBM employs laws as a strategic business weapon, leaving Japanese business behind in this respect, Ishiguro said.

Ishiguro asked, "the question is, why has Japan failed to put forward a just argument in concluding the Japan-U.S. agreement on semi-conductors, which was, after all, hardly possible to comply with. Why didn't Japan bring the matter up with GATT from the very beginning? Japan did so only when the U.S. began retaliatory measures based on Article 301 of the Trade Act, on the grounds that Japan had violated the agreement. In fact, the EC countries reacted strongly against the U.S.-Japan agreement on semiconductors, regarding it as a cartel between the two major producing countries. Japan should have tackled it as a problem of global significance from the very beginning. Japan should no longer take the servile attitude of "looking at the world through American eyes."

Ishiguro argued that Japan should acquire a form of positive international cooperation whereby what has to be said is said to the United States, the EC, and developing countries, from a global perspective. The problem does not lie solely with the government. The poor response of Japanese business was repeated with the COCOM regulations (the company president resigned while claiming the case was ill-founded). The business sector must also realize that it is a key player within the global economy.

1-7 Hollowing out and trade in services

As regards the future of the world economy, some de-industrialization had been pointed out in Japan, the United States, and West European countries such as Germany and France. Recently, however, it has assumed a clear form with advances in information orientation. This was pointed out also by Shimokobe, chairman of the third session. Will this lead to the globalization of the economy? Will it invite a balanced development of the world economy?

No paper submitted to the symposium fully discussed this point. However, it cannot be overlooked when future government and business are viewed in an international milieu. In this sense, Ishiguro's paper provides ample suggestions. Devoting one chapter to the service trade, Ishiguro discusses the attitude Japan should take in connection with Section 301 of the Trade Act and GATT negotiations.

Section 301 of the Trade Act symbolizes American logic, i.e., demand other countries open their markets on the basis of reciprocity and fairness, and taking retaliatory measures when it judges other countries' efforts to be insufficient or unfair. When revised in 1984, the Trade Act included the service trade under its jurisdiction. Among the advanced countries which are already in the process of de-industrialization, international relations in the service sector, including finance, investment, real estate, distribution, transport, telecommunications, patents, copyrights, databases and other services for business establishments, are bound to assume more importance than those involving goods.

This trend naturally extends to the developing countries. For instance, a 24-hour market has become a global reality in finance, centering around London, New York, and Tokyo. At present, the United States is ahead of other countries in utilizing this new trend, taking advantage of the fact that she is most advanced in the service economy and information technology. At the same time, this speaks for America's aim to regain the initiative in the next phase of the world economy, pushed hard by other countries including Japan.

Meanwhile, GATT is scheduled to discuss the trade in services in general at its Uruguay Round. The framework of GATT itself focuses on trade in hard goods, and is intended to realize free trade by removing various restrictions on visible trade. However, the liberalization of trade has made considerable progress through several rounds of negotiations, and a number of problems, including the problem of government procurement and that of agricultural subsidies, still remain to be resolved. They are, however, difficult problems, and are probably too difficult for agreement to be reached through multilateral negotiation, in which a concensus has to be reached by every participant. It appears that America intends to come to a solution through bilateral negotiations. By this approach, the United States will be able to effectively utilize the full weight of its importance of its market on each of the trading partners.

On the other hand, no rules have been formulated so far for the service trade. The United States intends to proceed with the formulation of rules for the services, in which its own international competitiveness will remain strong, by utilizing the GATT framework. The U.S.-Canada free trade negotiations are regarded for the time being as a prototype for international agreements that fully cover the service industry. U.S. specialists regard the U.S.-Canada negotiations as 'homework' for the Uruguay Round of GATT. As is well known, America's strong interests have prompted GATT's decisions to take up the service trade.

In this light, Ishiguro noted, "it is Japan's industry that poses a major threat to the international competitiveness of American industry," even in the sphere of the service industry. Under such circumstances, "Japan seems to be America's good partner in GATT service trade negotiations." But will this be sufficient?

Even when GATT rules cover the service industry, there is a good possibility of solving problems outside GATT, as in the case of Article 301 of the U.S. Trade Act. If so, Ishiguro argues, Japan should aim at strengthening the functions of GATT from a global point of view which differs from America's intentions. He maintains that while consultations are in progress through GATT, a safety valve should be provided so that no one country can invoke one-sided measures.

The service orientation on a global scale is not simply a market phenomena as the market begins to function only after international rules have been formulated. It was the same with visible trade, though we are no longer aware of its rules now that we have come to be used to them. International transactions in services have not had the same importance as visible trade, and this is said to have been due to the very nature of services. Services cannot be stored, with the result that production and demand occur at the same time.

However, it has now become possible to store and transport services through 'industrializing', or turning services into hardware, and through the development of computer and communication technologies in those fields centering on information and intellectual property rights.[8] The service sector is growing fast, owing especially to the increase of intermediate input of business services into industrial activities.[9] The service industry is of extreme importance for Japanese business that have reached the stage of de-industrialization and entered the stage of information orientation.

Is Japan then prepared to positively contribute to the formation of international rules for the services? Regrettably, the answer is "no", at least at present. This is fundamentally due to rigidities in the institutional setting in this country. Since decision-making takes place 'from the bottom up' in Japanese business and government, they are not suitable for quickly responding to a fundamentally new situation, such as the service orientation of the economy. Quick (and correct) response apparently requires 'top down' decision-making process with more than adequate foresight on the part of the leading personnel. In the case of industrial orgnizations such as Keidanren (Federation of Economic Organizations), however, those businesses represented are the ones which have supported Japan's industrialization, with its peak in the 1960s. They tend to respond slowly to interests in new fields.

The government should have had the foresight in such a situation. However, the service trade is new and is characterized by diversity. Since it involves numerous ministries and agencies within the vertical division of responsibility of the government, there is some concern that it cannot formulate a consistent policy which requires horizontal coordination.[10] Moreoever, since the political mechanism in Japan operates on a consensus basis, it lags fearfully behind emerging social needs. In such a situation, leadership may go to the American model, whereby management or the administration conducts decision-making 'from the top-down'. We have to begin by correctly recognizing this new situation.

All this does not mean that international rules should be formulated to suit Japan's interests. Japan is too big to have free ride on international rules, and its interests are much too involved. Japan's existence, even when every other country argues directly for its national interests, probably lies in formulating rules from a global point of view, and Japan's real national interests probably depends on the sound development of the resulting world economy.

Footnotes:

1 The symposium was held in Tokyo on September 5 and 6, 1987 on the occasion of the annual meeting of the Japan Association for Planning Administration, backed up by the National Institute for Research Advancement. The participating members were 24 experts and nearly 200 general audience, and the present author was entrusted the role of summarizing the two-day discussion for the final reports in both Japanese and English. The English version is contained in a proceeding volume entitled *International Symposium on the State and the Private Enterprise in a Global Society*, National Institute for Research Advancement (NIRA), Tokyo, 1988.
Contributors and paper titles are as follows.
Christian Sautter, "A Social Compromise for Competitive Growth, French Socialist Economic Policy 1981–1986."
Willi Leibfritz, "Demand Management and Supply Side Policies in West Germany, Past Experience and Prospects for the Future."
Masahiko, Aoki, "The State and the Markets: A Bargaining Game Theoretic Implication."
Willem H. Buiter, "Does an Improvement in the Current Account or the Trade Balance at Full Employment Require a Depreciation of the Real Exchange Rate?"
Kazumasa Iwata, "Post Venice Summit Policy Coordination—Convergence of Tax System and Establishment of Multiple Key Currency System."
Kazunori Ishiguro, "Expansion of Global Business Activities and Intensified International Economic Friction—Their Legal Aspect."
Yu Yongding, "International Imbalance and International Cooperation."
Makoto Sakurai and Akira Sadahiro, "Developing Countries' Economic Issues and International Coordination."
C. Samuel Craig and Susan P. Douglas, "Formulating Global Marketing Strategy."

2 Sauter [1987], Leibfritz [1987].

3 Sakurai and Sadahiro [1987].

4 His verbal comment in the symposium.

5 Yu [1987].

6 The cases in question include such sectors as agriculture, retail trade, finance, insurance, communication, transportation, construction, and government procurement. Privatization of the Japan Tobaccco and Salt Public Corporation (JTS) and the Nippon Telegraph and Telephone Public Corporation (NTT) occured in 1985, and that of Japanese National Railway (JNR) came in 1987.

7 The article was written in fall 1987. In retrspect, the dollar exchange rate (basic rates of the Ministry of Finance) has moved as follows.
1985 254.00 yen per US dollar
1986 185.00
1987 151.00
1988 127.00
1989 130.00
1990 (August) 150.0
Source: Bank of Japan, *Monthly Economic Statistics*.

8 For industrialization of services, see Levitt [1976].

9 The case in Japan is explored in Uno [1989a], pp.23-74.

10 The Ministry of International Trade and Industry vs. the Ministry of Posts and Telecommunications is a case in question regarding information activities. The production of hardware and upbringing of the communication industry (such as software and database, in addition to the electronics industry which produces the equipment) falls under the jurisdiction of the former whereas telecommunication, which of course is the core of communication activity, had been under state monopoly until quite recently and is still tightly guided by the latter.

Chapter 2. The U.S., Asian NICs, and Japan

2-1 The background

The United States has been the sole net absorber of exports in a triangular economic relations involving the U.S., Japan, and Asian newly industrializing economies (NIEs, i.e., NICs including Korea, Taiwan, Hong Kong, and Singapore plus ASEAN countries including Thailand, Malaysia, Indonesia, and the Philippines). This has resulted in a huge U.S. trade deficit. After the exchange rate adjustments in 1985 and with the increased effort to bring down trade barriers, Japan has emerged as a major absorber in the Pacific rim. Increased Japanese direct investment has worked as an important vehicle in technology transfer. At the same time, products from overseas facilities in Asia and North America have found their way into Japanese home market. This chapter discusses the growth axis emerging in the Pacific triangle and its impact on a global context.

We consider the recent appreciation of the yen and the structural adjustment of the economy as a desirable development not only to Japan but also to the world as a whole. There is no denying the fact that the continuing appreciation of the yen since the G5 meeting in 1985 has brought about a new round of challenges for the Japanese economy, including rapid increase of finished goods imports, relocation of manufacturing plants overseas, streamlining of domestic industries, and worsening of the labor market situation. The Japanese economy has successfully gone through a series of difficulties in the postwar period. Among them were trade liberalization in the mid-1960s when the Japanese industry moved away from protectionism and was confronted with international competition. In the early 1970s, the Japanese industry had to adjust to new and fluctuating exchange rate. By 1980, the economy had experienced two consecutive oil crises. The appreciation of the yen since 1985 is undoubtedly a major policy issue comparable to these past challenges. We may say the situation is even worse because we are now experiencing a severe economic strain with the United States, the single most important trading partner and political ally. We are lucky if the situation does not develop into a political strain. There is a growing tendency to politicize the issue in order to obtain concession in economic matters, and this inherently involves the risk of causing irreversible damages in international relations.

We believe that the recent appreciation of the yen against the U.S. dollar and the accompanying structural adjustment of the economy will not only help solve the trade imbalance with the United States but also contribute to construct a mutually supporting growth center in the Asia Pacific region. We are yet to see the entire range of the adjustment process.

Initially, the majority of the people in Japan were concerned with the "excessive" appreciation of the yen and hope for the return to the "normal" level of the exchange rate. The people were also concerned with hollowing-out of the industry. We believe, however, that the structural adjustment called for by the appreciation of the yen is desirable for the future course of development of the economies in the Pacific triangle including the United States, Japan, and the Asian NIEs.

2-2 Policy recommendation by Japan Forum

Against this background, Japan Forum on International Relations published policy recommendations entitled "The Structural Adjustment of Economies of Japan, U.S., and Asian NICs" in March 1988. The document was signed by Saburo Okita and a host of prominent Japanese economists and political scientists.[1] The Forum spent a year for deliberations and research works, including discussion with C. Michael Aho of the Council on Foreign Relations. Four-men task force headed by Toshio Watanabe was in charge of preparing the document, of which the present author was a member.[2]

The policy recommendation says in essence that Japan, the United States and Asian NIEs should adjust their economic structures so that their economies would become mutually supportive. "Japan so far acted as an efficient supplier of capital goods to the Western Pacific developing countries and has supported their industrialization and export promotion from supply side. In addition, Japan should make further efforts to act as an absorber of the finished products of these countries and to increase investment and economic cooperation to those countries."

To that end, the document lists 13-item policy recommendations addressed to the countries involved, which include the following.

(1) Adjustment of macroeconomic structure between the United States and Japan
(2) Maintaining a trade regime which is free, multilateral and indiscriminatory
(3) Normalization of flow of funds on an international level
(4) Strengthening support for the Western Pacific developing countries
(5) Strengthening the role of "absorber" by Japan
(6) Acceleration of the acceptance of foreign nationals into the Japanese labor market
(7) Interindustry and intraindustry division of labor in the Western

Pacific
(8) Correction of full-set principle in the economic structure of Japan
(9) Relocation of production sites overseas
(10) Implementation of emergency measures for the expansion of domestic demand in Japan
(11) Expansion of the roles of Asian NICs in the New Growth Axis
(12) Inducement of efforts of ASEAN countries to expand exports
(13) Inclusion of China into the Asia-Pacific Sphere

The details of the policy prescription are as follows. In order to convery the mood of the time, we chose not to modify the wording of the original text.

(1) *Adjustment of macroeconomic structure between the United States and Japan*: Both the United States and Japan should strengthen their effort to make their economic structure mutually acceptable. This is especially true for the United States where a policy package aimed at curtailing fiscal deficit must be seriously sought and implemented, thereby arresting excess demand unsustainable by the domestic supply capacity. In the meantime, Japan should continue efforts to stimulate her domestic demand.

The economic frictions between the United States and Japan are in a crisis situation. The solution to this problem is a prerequisite for the smooth operation of the world economy, not to speak of sound relations between the two countries. The U.S.-Japan economic frictions are attributable to the magnitude of imbalance in the trade account, which has resulted from the differences in macroeconomic structure reflecting policy stances in the two countries.

More precisely, the major tax reduction in the U.S. since 1982 created a large fiscal deficit as well as an increase in private expenditures such as consumption and housing investment, while failing to achieve its policy objective to increase domestic saving. This invited a situation where demand exceeded domestic supply capacity, resulting in huge trade account deficit.

In contrast to excess demand and shortage of saving in the U.S., deficient demand and saving surplus persisted in Japan. Contributing factors included stagnation of private investment in plant and equipment after the Second Oil Crisis in the face of a traditionally high saving ratio in the household sector, deferred increase in government expenditure in accordance with the Administrative Reform and inactive private consumption. Thus, Japanese growth in the first half of the 1980s is mainly due to growth in exports, especially to the United States.

We should remember that the trade account imbalance reached a major magnitude only after 1980. In the 1980s, the United States is experiencing mounting deficit not only with Japan but also with Asian NICs and EC countries. This undoubtedly reveals the fact that the direct cause of the U.S. trade account deficit is the economic policy under the Reagan administration. Therefore, the U.S. itself should take the initiative in curbing the imbalance by implementing a series of policy measures, including attainment of fiscal balance, aimed at rectifying the macroeconomic structure which currently suffers from excess demand and shortage of saving. We appreciate the fact that in the United States the efforts in this direction has been finally started to be implemented.

The U.S. fiscal deficit for 1987 is indicated to decrease considerably, from $221.1 billion last year to the current $148 billion. The October Crash, coming on top of the drop in bond prices in early 1987, forced the United States to realize the necessity of urgent fiscal improvement and this resulted in the enactment of a comprehensive budget bill in December 1987. The bill stipulates curtailment of $30.2 billion for FY 1988 and $45.9 billion for FY 1989. Though the start was rather late, the U.S. effort has come to full swing. The U.S. Government has no choice but to continue this policy.

The depreciation of the dollar has caused steady expansion of exports on the U.S. side, restoring its international competitiveness. While imports are still increasing at a high rate, in terms of quantity, their increasing rate has been slowing down. Furthermore it is hoped that reduction in the budget deficit will help to improve the state of American deficit.

Meanwhile, Japan is in a position where it needs to drastically expand domestic demand in the hope of decreasing its reliance on foreign demand. This has in fact been happening since the end of 1985 due to the rapid appreciation of the yen. Exports for 1986 and 1987 (Jan.–Oct.) showed negative growth in terms of quantity (note: 1985=100.0, 1986=99.4, 1987=99.7, 1988=104.8), while imports maintained an upward trend (note: 1985=100.0, 1986=109.5, 1987=119.7, 1988=139.7). The import of finished goods in particular has increased rapidly, 34.6% and 19.4% for 1986 and 1987 respectively (note: 1985=100.0, 1986=122.6, 1987=137.9, 1988=180.0). Consequently, import ratio of finished goods in total import rose to 44.1% in 1986 and 45.1% for 1987.

The conversion of Japan's economic structure from foreign demand-oriented and manufacturing-centered industries to domestic demand-oriented and service-centered industries is taking place more smoothly than expected. As a result, the economic growth rates since the beginning of 1987 has been 4.1% for the 1st quarter, 3.0% for the 2nd quarter and 4.3% for the 3rd quarter. Having troughed at the end of 1986, the Japanese economy seems to have entered a convalescent stage since the beginning of 1987, especially in the area of domestic demand, though at a slow pace.

As shown above, the extreme macroeconomic contrast between Japan and the United States is being narrowed down to a favorable direction through mutual adjustment. In order to reaffirm this trend, Japan should adopt the following policies: (a) maintenance of its positive fiscal policies aimed at furthering the improvement of its domestic demand even after 1988; (b) thorough opening of the domestic market to stimulate imports; (c) shift of the economic structure from foreign demand-oriented industries to domestic demand-oriented industries.

(2) *Maintaining a trade regime which is free, multilateral and indiscriminatory*: Japan and the United States, which weigh heavily in the world trade, should take full responsibility for maintaining a trade regime which is free, multilateral and indiscriminatory. It can be counterproductive to emphasize reciprocity and appeal to bilateral negotiations.

The United States and Japan should share the responsibility in the smooth expansion of world trade, in recognition of the fact that the combined economic size of the two countries reaches about 30% of the world total.

We should not blame interested countries for entering into bilateral negotiations in order to adjujst mutual interests, especially in area where there are no appropriate rules on international trade. However, there would be cause for concern if the United States conducts bilateral trade negotiations, stressing too much on the "reciprocity principle."

The United States should recognize the content of its own investment in plant and equipment if it wants to strengthen international competitiveness. Of the business investment in the 1980s, the growth of machinery and equipment is almost exclusively attributed to information processing equipment, and the growth contribution of industrial machinery remained at a few percentage points. As for investment in building (excluding housing), the major portion of which is comprised of commercial buildings and factories, comprise less than 10%. Such trend signifies service orientation of the U.S. industry. At the same time, it does show the lack of investment which directly improve production and export of the manufacturing sector. Unless accompanied by the American effort to promote industrial production domestically, exchange rate adjustment between the United States and Japan would only help shift the exporting countries, with no effect on the levels of imports. It is of no use to accuse Japan for failing to correct the U.S. balance of trade.

As for Japan, it should promote orderly marketing by recognizing the root of U.S. protectionism. At the same time, the two countries should learn a lesson from the experience of their bilateral semiconductor agreement which invited criticism from EC as being a de facto formation of cartel for the division of the world market. Retaliatory measures have been taken by the Unites States in accordance with Article 301 of the Trade Law on the ground that Japan failed to observe the rules concerning the improvement of the access to Japanese market. Regardless of such measures' legitimacy in terms of GATT, this case indicates dangerous aspect of bilateral negotiations. Any agreement between the United States and Japan should be transparent and acceptable to third parties.

(3) *Normalization of flow of funds on an international level*: It is imperative to correct the unilateral flow of funds from Japan to the United States, thereby restoring a mechanism under which investment fund would flow into LDCs where growth potentials remain uncultivated. Furthermore, it is necessary for Japan to make more of an effort to channel her trade surplus to developing countries.

The correction of macroeconomic imbalance in the U.S. and Japan is indispensable in rectifying the bilateral flow of funds and releasing such funds for use in LDCs.

From long-term perspectives, it is expected that the funds should flow from mature countries to late-comer countries where growth potentials abound and profit margin is high and it will facilitate the dynamic expansion of the world economy through releasing their growth potentials. In reality, however, the high interest rate in the United States as a result of fiscal deficit worked to attract investment funds which originally was to be directed to LDCs. In other words, the LDCs have been crowded out from the international flow of funds.

Japan has been the major supplier of funds to the United States. Its savings, which used to be abosrbed by investment in plant and equipment, could no longer be invested when slower growth after the mid-1970s set in. The government is another sector in the economy which can absorb excess savings, but mounting fiscal deficit since the 1970s prohibited the government to enlarge its expenditure. Such excess savings naturally led to low interest rate in Japan in contrast to high interest rate in the United States. It was quite natural that the excess savings in Japan was invested to the U.S. security market through institutional investors to profit from the differentials in the interest rates.

The demand for foreign funds in LDCs is potentially abundant and the rate of profit from such investment is high. However, interest rate in the United States exceeds rate of profit of investment to the LDCs and it is difficult to change the flow of funds from Japan to the Uniated States. Such flow of funds naturally squeezed the supply of funds to LDCs and closed the way toward balanced expansion of the world economy.

Although it is logically possible to correct the direction of the flow of funds by direct government intervention, prohibiting the outflow of private funds from Japan would only invite confusion in international financial market. Appropriate policy would be to adjust macroeconomic structure in both countries in order to narrow the differentials in interest rates and correct the direction of international flow of money.

We should envisage policy measures aimed at activating recycling of Japanese private funds into the Western Pacific LDCs. The announcement of Emergency Economic Measures in May 1987 is a significant step forward. The measures consist of untied aid of public and private funds into developing countries through bilateral and international agencies for a three-year period. This aid is in addition to the $10 billion which the Japanese Government has already committed to the World Bank as Japan Special Fund and other international agencies.

However, we should not forget the importance of cooperation in order that the funds recycled are to be put to the best use possible. Japan should take the initiative in uncovering viable projects in recipient countries and establish institutions to support their financial and technological operations. It is presently planned by the Overseas Economic Cooperation Fund, together with the Federation of Economic Organizations to set up the "Fund for Economic Activation of Developing Countries," aimed at effective distribution of the $30 billion fund. It is expected that the establishment of such an institution will facilitate the above-mentioned type of cooperation.

The so-called "two-step-loans" are considered to be the most effective means in upbringing export capabilities. This is a scheme by which aid fund is loaned to financial institutions in the recipient countries, which in turn provide loans to private firms. This is a flexible way of providing development fund. It is hoped that this scheme will be widely used for the promotion of export-oriented firms including smaller ones.

It is necessary to provide a comprehensive technological collaboration including (a) dispatch of specialists in production technology, managerial technology, and product development technology; (b) acceptance of trainees and other forms of manpower training; and (c) market survey, sales promotion and improvement of retail channels. Provision of infrastructure in export-oriented industrial complexes will also become important.

It is noteworthy that the Overseas Economic Cooperation Fund and a group of private enterprises in the security and banking fields have made a joint decision to establish the "Japan ASEAN Investment Company." This project aims to facilitate private investment in ASEAN countries. Although such efforts have just started, it is hoped that they would be further strengthened.

Japanese direct investment in the Western Pacific developing countries will continue to increase at a rapid pace in the years to come and is expected to facilitate transfer to recipient countries. It is the responsibility of Japanese private business to systematically transfer technology for mutual benefit while taking into consideration the various cultural backgrounds of respective recipient countries. The direction of direct foreign investment is largely dictated by the market forces. At the same time, the international flow of funds need be stabilized and promoted by the host countries by guaranteeing favorable environment for investment. Government efforts in aid-giving countries and the recipients alike are required for the provision of overseas investment insurance, investment guarantee agreement, etc.

(4) *Strengthening support for the Western Pacific developing countries*: The developing countries in the Western Pacific form the most promising region to lead off the expansion of the world economy in the 1990s. Japan should further strengthen her support of this region in order to release the dynamism of these economies. This region is expected to become the growth frontier of the world economy in the very near future.

The world economy has the potential to continue balanced expansion after several years of adjustment period from now on. Judging from their growth record in the recent past and growth potentials, we envisage that the most promising region to lead-off the world's next economic expansion would be the Western Pacific developing economies including Asian NICs, ASEAN countries and China.

To this end, policy effort is indispensable to release the economic vitality of the countries in this region to the fullest extent and to direct it as a contributing factor in the revitalization of the world economy. We should recognize the sound economic growth in the less-developed world is the most fundamental condition for the long-term balanced growth of the world economy.

The economic growth rates of Asian NICs from the early 1960s to the present was the highest among the economic regions in the world. In fact, the growth rates of ASEAN countries accelerated in the 1970s while the world economy stagnated in the aftermath of two Oil Crises. China also showed a sign of change in the late 1970s.

The growth rates of industrial production were particularly marked in these countries. They have gained productive capacity in the manufacturing sector in a short period of time, and have strengthened competitive edge in their export. Nine Western Pacific countries including Japan, Asian NICs (Hong Kong, Korea, Singapore, and Taiwan) and ASEAN countries (Indonesia, Malaysia, the Philippines, and Thailand) have rapidly expanded their share in the world industrial export from about 10% in the mid-1960s to 23% in mid-1980s.[3] We have witnessed relocation of industrial production on a global scale.

Expanded export implies increase import capability and the countries in the Western Pacific are supporting the world economy from the demand side. In fact, the Western Pacific countries boosted their share in the total world import from 8.5% in 1965 to 13.4% in 1986. These countries have been strengthening their presence in the world economy not only by creating competition through their export but also by making their economy more complementary to other economies.

The profit margin in the industrial sector in the vigorous Western Pacific economies is particularly high, and is attracting direct foreign investment of advanced countries to this region. According to the Research Division of the Japan Industrial Bank (Nihon Kogyo Ginko), 23.1% of the world real GNP gains and 41.9% of the world trade expansion would be attributable to ten countries in the Western Pacific including Asian NICs, ASEAN countries, and China between 1986 and 1990.

However, we are concerned that a full scale effort on the part of the U.S. to deal with the budget deficit will cause a wave of deflation to sweep over Western Pacific countries. Because of the upswing in domestic demand in the United States, the developing countries of the Western Pacific have built up their economic strength along export oriented policy. Korea and Taiwan in particular achieved outstanding economic growth and the contribution ratio of their exports to the United States in their economic growth reached 42% and 74% respectively for the 1981–86 period. It is likely that policy changes in the United States would endanger the economic potential of the developing Western Pacific countries. If this happens, the world economy will shut off itself off from the path to its balanced growth.

In this respect, Japan is expected to play a major role as a new "absorber" for these countries. With its huge trade surplus, Japan should neutralize the deflationary effects that are expected to occur in the course of structural adjustment of the U.S. economy, thereby protecting the world economy from slipping into spiral shrinkage.

(5) *Strengthening the role of "absorber" by Japan*: In addition to being a supplier of capital and intermediate goods to the Western Pacific developing countries, Japan should also strengthen her role as an absorber of goods produced in this region, including agricultural products.

Japan keeps close economic ties with each of the Western Pacific developing countries and is in a position among the advanced countries to exert strong influence in the course of development of these countries. Japan should therefore contribute to the promotion of growth of these countries and thereby realize balanced expansion of the world economy.

Japan has so far acted as an efficient supplier of capital goods to the Western Pacific developing countries and has supported their industrialization and export promotion from the supply side. In addition, Japan's future contribution lies in acting as an absorber of the finished goods produced in these countries. It is also necessary to increase direct investment and economic cooperation further in order to release the economic potentials of these countries. The series of events described above will all work toward correcting trade imbalance between Japan and these countries, and make available the foreign reserves which they need. The Western Pacific developing countries would then be able to increase imports from the United States with which they currently run considerable surplus.

Recent appreciation of the yen is expected to facilitate the required adjustment on the Japanese side. The lowering of import prices which resulted from the appreciation of the yen is already inviting quantum jumps in Japanese import of finished industrial products, especially from the Western Pacific developing countries where price competitiveness is particularly being strengthened. Furthermore, Japanese imports of finished goods showed remarkable increase during the 1986–1987 (Jan.–Oct.) period. Import of finished products accounted for 30% and 40% of total Japanese imports, respectively. The largest increase observed was that from the Asian NICs, which reached 59.0% in 1987. At the same time the imported products have also diversified, i.e., from the labor-intensive goods in the past to more technology-intensive parts and semi-finished goods. We have also witnessed a shift toward capital goods and to high-tech products such as semiconductors, computer parts, etc.

The Japanese role as an absorber will be enlarged in the coming years as Japanese private firms shift their production sites overseas and out-sourcing by Japanese business firmly establishes a set-up where exports of Japanese subsidiaries find their way into the home market. As a matter of fact, Japanese direct investment in Asian countries increased dramatically in 1986, 74.9% over the previous year, the electric machinery industry actually increasing 500%. This trend continued in 1987.

Besides, it is now common for Japanese corporations to relocate their production sites outside Japan, producing parts and finished goods locally and then exporting them to the home market. According to a survey conducted by the Ministry of International Trade and Industry, products imported from assembly industries in Asian countries increased during 1986 from 10.1% to 12.4%, while the products in other industrial branches rose from 5.1% to 7.2%.

As the Japanese firms become accustomed to out-sourcing, their overseas production will become an integral part of Japanese industrial activities. Imported parts, intermediate products as well as capital goods can be built into the Japanese industrial structure. In other words, Japanese producers themselves are in need of products from the Western Pacific developing countries.

Shift of production sites overseas then increases Japanese import by out- sourcing and has "export substitution effect." Namely, it will decrease Japanese exports by allowing the new producer countries to export their products to the third country instead of export from Japan. Thus, direct investment by Japan should have a strong effect on the curtailment of its trade surplus in the future.

To fulfill the role as an absorber, Japan should make the domestic market more accessible to foreign suppliers. It is true that the Japanese market is already liberalized judging from the tariff rates and the remaining import restrictions. However, with her large trade surplus, Japan should continue her efforts for further liberalization. The complicated standards and inspection system peculiar to Japan have been simplified through Action Program, but there is still room for further reduction of listed items and re-examination of trade and industrial standards themselves.

Japan should improve market accessibility to foreign suppliers by eliminating invisible barriers such as peculiarities in the retail channel, government regulation on the new location of large-scale retail stores, closed procurement practices, various standards peculiar to Japan and closedness of the construction industry.

As for agricultural products, there remain 22 items which are subject to regulation, a a situation peculiar to Japan among industrialized countries. In addition, as is typified in the case of rice, price differentials are very large when domestic prices are compared to the international level. The only way to correct such situation is to liberalize gradually agricultural trade. Trade liberalization would also facilitate productivity improvement in Japanese agriculture. It is appreciated that the Japanese Government finally shows a positive attitude to the liberalization, requested by GATT, of agricultural import quota categories. However, due attention should be paid to the domestic policies such as tariff quota system, import surcharge and price support system which might be strengthened or introduced in response to the liberalization. In such cases, care should be taken in order not to provoke a new trade frictions due to these measures. It is also necessary to pay due considerations to the requests on agricultural imports from LDCs. In this regard, it is hoped to completely abolish tariffs for the export items of interest to ASEAN countries and China and expand import ceiling quota of preferential tariff treatment in the Generalized System of Preferences to products imported from those countries and liberalize completely the import of tropical fruits.

(6) *Acceleration of the acceptance of foreign nationals into the Japanese labor market*: The Japanese Government should form policies for the admission of foreign nationals into her domestic labor market and provide more job opportunities, relaxing her immigration laws. This should be duly considered by the Japanese Government as quickly as possible.

So far, Japan has put stiff restrictions on the entry of foreign nationals for the purpose of working in Japan. A limited number of foreign nationals have been allowed to enter the Japanese labor market under the condition that they have special skills or expertise not possessed by Japanese nationals or they are trained in the areas still unavailable in the domestic labor market. Meanwhile, unskilled foreign nationals have been given no access. However, rising economic standing in general, and raising wages and continued appreciation of the yen in particular, have made the Japanese labor market increasingly attractive to people in Asian countries. It is quite natural that we have witnessed the existence of illegal aliens in Japan, entering the country under the pretext of sightseeing from Asian countries or without proper visas and in reality finding jobs in construction and manufacturing industries, or staying illegally after the expiration of their visas.

Unlike West Germany and other advanced countries where LDC workers were introduced for cheap manual labor, Japan has developed robotics and other means of automation to improve productivity. It is also true that Japanese public opinion is in general against, or at least skeptical to, the introduction of foreign manual workers who are thought of damaging to the high integrity of the Japanese society and can lower the productivity which otherwise could be improved by technology.

Time has come, however, when we can no longer resist the inflow of foreign workers who enter the country despite tight immigration control. This has to be accepted as a matter of fact for a country which has come to share a seat in an international community, whether we like it or not. At the same time, we have to pay due consideration to the segment of the Japanese industry where young workers cannot be attracted in sufficient numbers due to hard manual work. This is particularly true for small-sized firms and traditional occupations.

We should not overlook the negative side of putting severe legal constraints on foreign workers such as inferior working conditions and cheap wages which can be avoided if their legal status is established. The current situation does not in any way facilitate friendly relations with our Asian neighbors.

It is time to reconsider the strict immigration law and to ease the conditions under which foreign nationals are allowed to enter the

Japanese labor market.

Therefore, it is necessary to ease the "specific skills or expertise not possessed by Japanese nationals" clause in the entry regulations and provide more job opportunities to foreign nationals. Further efforts should be made to guarantee that, in the case of foreign nationals whose abilities are on par with their Japanese counterparts, the same wage scale be applied as far as possible. Some limitations may also be required as to the length of stay of foreign workers. Equally important is the acceptance of foreign students and trainees after finishing education in Japan.

It is the responsibility of the Japanese Government to tackle these problems and help form a national consensus in the above-mentioned direction.

(7) *Interindustry and intraindustry division of labor in the Western Pacific*: Japan should recognize the emergence of a new form of division of labor in the Western Pacific and regard it as the new growth frontiers for her economy. Current trade pattern under which the United States singly plays the role of an absorber is untenable. By expanding trade relations with the countries in this region, in particular by becoming an absorber of finished goods produced in this region, Japan should take the initiative in reorganizing and balancing the trilateral trade flows among Japan, the United States and the Western Pacific countries.

We may anticipate a formation of dynamic interregional industrial linkages by international transaction of parts and intermediate products within individual industrial sectors. Japanese industrial activity would then enhance the development of the Western Pacific developing countries and vice versa. Unlike interindustry trade where the transactions are limited to finished goods, intraindustry trade involves transactions of parts and semi-finished goods and accompanies more direct linkages of economic repercussions.

This is particularly marked in the case of machinery sector. As can be witnessed in EC, the machinery sector is the central core of intraindustry division of labor. In almost all advanced countries, we observe a fact that they engage in import as well as in export of machinery due to the fact that it is not profitable to try to be self-sufficient in a variety of machinery. Thus, we may say that this sector is promising in expanding multilateral trade flows.

The share of machinery (electric and electronic machinery, transport machinery, precision instrument and general machinery) in total exports of the Asian NICs has exhibited a sharp increase. In 1985, the share stood at 36% for Korea, 32% for Singapore, 30% for Taiwan, and 24% for Hong Kong and is approaching the 40% level which is the average for the industrial countries. Such trend in Asian NICs, followed by ASEAN countries, is facilitated by the Japanese direct investment in this region and is indicative of penetration of their products into the Japanese market.

Thus, such trend would not only correct trade imbalance between Japan and developing countries in the Western Pacific, but also reorganize the production and trade structure involving the United States which hitherto singly played the role of an absorber.

(8) *Correction of full-set principle in the economic structure*: Japan should accept division of labor with the developing countries in the Western Pacific region. This inevitably leads to the abolition of full-set and self-sufficient scheme in industrial structure that would enhance the compatibility of her economy in a global context.

The advance in intratrade division of labor would almost inevitably give a strong impact to the structure of the Japanese industry. Japan has to break away from the past adherence to "full-set principle" in the industrial structure through increased division of labor with the Western Pacific developing countries, particularly the Asian NICs. Japan must be prepared to adjust its own industrial structure to facilitate the new development in international transactions. In fact, the newly established trade pattern is mutually benefitting.

It is a well-known fact that the Japanese industry has so far maintained a closed integral structure. Because of this peculiarity, expansion of productive activity in Japan contributed to increase purchases from domestic sources for parts, intermediate products and capital goods, and induced very little imports. The income elasticity of Japanese exports in the early 1980s stood at 2.2, while that for imports stood at a mere 0.7. These parameters make strong contrast with the U.S. and German cases. The closed nature of the industry has resulted in structural imbalance in the Japanese trade.

Intraindustry division of labor with the Western Pacific developing countries would give an impetus whereby Japanese industrial structure would be modified to meke it compatible with the world economic community. At the center of the machinery industry are huge assembly firms, which, through various independent suppliers, purchase all parts and intermediate goods as well as capital goods that they require. This is very different from the American and European arrangement where related divisions are integrated in a vertical hierarchy. With the appreciation of the yen, however, Japanese assembly firms, particularly those in automobiles and electric and electronic industries, are actively engaged in imports of parts and intermediate goods and out-sourcing through direct foreign investment.

Such shift inevitably will be a severe blow to the Japanese suppliers, which in turn are beginning to relocate themselves overseas. When large firms and smaller ones alike try to find production sites overseas, traditional pattern of Japanese industrial organization, where smaller ones are harbored under the umbrella of larger ones, would certainly come to an end. This necessitates reorganization of the industrial structure at a magnitude which we have not experienced in the past.

The structural adjustment, though with pains, is an inevitable cost that we have to pay in order to make our economy more harmonious with the world economy and have to be duly accepted.

(9) *Relocation of production sites overseas*: Japan should not regard the relocation of production sites as "hollowing out." An increase in direct foreign investment, especially in the countries of the Western Pacific region, is an inevitable process in the course of reshaping the Japanese industrial structure.

Large firms in advanced countries are engaged in business activities across national boundaries without exception and have to form a diversified business network which may be termed "a global business network." As a result of business activities of the multinationals, the world economy today has become truly an integrated one. The business conduct is motivated by profit-seeking which is inherent in market economies and, in fact, we may expect the realization of optimal resource allocation on a global scale. It would not be wise to regulate business behavior from the viewpoint of a national economy when one considers the contribution of multinationals to the promotion of growth in LDCs. The hollowing-out of an economy has occurred in the United States and there is a rising concern that the same process would be repeated in Japan. However, we should remember that the only way to arrest the decline of the economy is to vitalize the home market through technological progress.

The relocation of production sites overseas is often interpreted as hollowing-out. In the case of Japan, however, it is too early to talk about hollowing-out of its economy. It is not only due to the fact that the ratio of overseas production is still rather low. More importantly, the relocation is observed in sectors which are relatively weak, losing competitive edge with the appreciation of the yen, and not in the most advanced sectors. High-tech sectors intend to remain in Japan. If this is so, relocation of production sites overseas is nothing but a shift of the industrial structure toward high value added, high-tech sectors.

In 10 years time, however, we should anticipate that the ratio of overseas production is to reach today's American level and that even high-tech industries would begin establishing overseas production facilities. The products from these facilities would penetrate into the home market and would compete with the Japanese products in a third market.

Such trend is a matter of course for private business which tries to maximize profit in a rational manner. In other words, business firms would survive only through such behavior in a changing world economic environment. The problem, however, emerges when the same trend is observed from the national economic point of view, because relocation of productive facilities could imply loss of employment opportunity at home. For the economy as a whole, there are gains to be drawn from the relocation of certain industries abroad because the world economy would became more dynamic due to accelerated growth in the LDCs.

(10) *Implementation of emergency measures for the expansion of domestic demand in Japan*: The policy package which has already been announced by the Japanese Government should be actually implemented without delay and efforts be made to achieve further expansion. It is imperative to supplement the decrease in export demand accompanying appreciation of the yen and to soften the adjustment costs. Especially important are the measures to safeguard employment opportunity.

Appreciation of the yen and the accompanying relative price factor coupled with relocation of production sites overseas and the resultant out-sourcing and export substitution are working toward increasing imports and curtailing exports. In fact, of the 2.6% real economic growth for 1986, domestic demand accounted for 4.1% and foreign demand minus 1.5%. This was also true in 1987. The year saw actual economic growth rates of 4.1%, 3.0%, and 4.3% for its 1st, 2nd and 3rd quarters, respectively. The dependency on domestic demand for each quarter remained at the relatively high levels of 4.6%, 3.8% and 4.8%. Minus growth was seen throughout the year for the dependency on foreign demand, minus 0.5%, minus 0.7%, and minus 0.5%, respectively, for each quarter.

However, it would be a mistake to believe that promotion of domestic demand itself would reduce trade surplus. The working of the market mechanism triggered by the appreciation of the yen would in the near future reduce Japan's trade surplus through increased imports from overseas production facilities and export substitution. In this respect, promotion of domestic demand is not a particularly powerful tool in bringing about reduction of Japanese trade surplus.

The domestic demand need be stimulated in order to maintain aggregate demand and to keep the growth rate from falling. Main reason for this is that the contribution of export demand would be inevitably smaller and may even be negative in the near future.

According to our analysis in which potential supply was compared to the expected demand for each industry, almost all sectors would suffer from demand shortage toward 1990. Thus, there is less concern for demand-pull inflation. It is advisable to shift to a positive fiscal policy and extreme restraint imposed upon government expenditure has to be relaxed. It is natural that continued attention be paid to improving efficiency in government disbursement. In addition, promotion of urban renewal and increased provision of social capital, not to speak of stimulus to private investment in plant and equipment, need be advocated. Expansion of the domestic economy will also contribute to the restoration of fiscal balance through increased government revenues. In this regard, we should see that the announced Comprehensive Economic Plans, which aims at expanding public investment, stimulating housing construction and business investment and releasing of private initiative through deregulation and increased provision of incentive, be carried out promptly. At the same time, expansion of the government expenditure amounting to 6 trillion yen contained in the Emergency Economic Measures need be implemented.

Such policy package is needed to soften the economic cost which accompany the structural adjustment. Particularly, it is important to avoid unemployment. The loss of employment opportunity accompanying the structural adjustment cannot be adequately compensated by newly emerging employment opportunity in services and information-related sectors because of mismatch in the skill category, region, and age bracket. As a result, the Japanese economy would suffer from unemployment rate of about 5% (presently less than 3%), while facing overall labor shortage. It is necessary to implement retraining of the workforce and to increase labor mobility among occupations and regions.

(11) *Expansion of the role of Asian NICs and the new growth axis*: Through liberalization of their trade and adjustment of exchange rates, Asian NICs are expected to emerge as a new growth axis comparable to Japan and enhance growth of ASEAN countries and China.

In the Western Pacific region today, we have seen multiple chase process in progress where Japan is chased by Asian NICs and Asian NICs in turn are chased by ASEAN countries. In this process, the competitive edge of Asian NICs has been weakened for low value-added products while that of high value-added products has gradually strengthened. In contrast, ASEAN countries have gained competitiveness in low value-added products, thereby chasing the Asian NICs. The dynamic multiple chase process has thus created a competitive and yet complementary trade relations among the Western Pacific countries.

In this context, Asian NICs are expected to recognize their role as absorbers by liberalizing import and adjusting exchange rates, thereby providing rooms for growth for the late-comers. In other words, Asian NICs should become another growth axis in Asia comparable to Japan. The Asia-Pacific region will then have two growth poles instead of one and become a region where growth of one country stimulate growth in another.

ASEAN countries are now host to not only American and Japanese investment but also to investment by Asian NICs. Asian NICs are beginning to relocate production facilities in ASEAN countries. One contributing factor is the fact that Chinese population in Taiwan, Hong Kong, and Singapore keep close ties with Chinese in the ASEAN. This trend has to be encouraged further.

Another point worth particular attention is the rapproachment of Asian NICs and China. One should note the strong complementarity which exists in their industrial structures. Their trade and investment relations would intensify in the years to come with considerable pace, although subject to political and diplomatic turbulances at times.

Asian NICs have come to establish themselves through export-oriented industrialization. In the process, they have benefitted most from the free trade regime of the world economy. Today, they have become major exporters in the world and have to be prepared to assume greater responsibility on their part to maintain the free trade. In this respect, they should openly commit themselves to trade liberalization through removal of tariffs and non-tariff barriers alike, exchange rate adjustment, graduation from preferential tariff treatment, and protection of intellectual property rights.

Industrialized countries should facilitate continued growth of the developing countries in Asia by admitting Asian NICs (Korea) to accept Article 8 of the IMF, inducing them to be active participants in the new round in GATT, and accepting them into the OECD. Increased absorption of NICs' products especially in the Japanese market would smoothen the trade liberalization and exchange rate adjustment in these countries.

(12) *Inducement of efforts of ASEAN countries to expand exports*: It is necessary for ASEAN countries to develop export-oriented industries and their peripheral industries as well, by introducing foreign funds into those sectors. Their efforts should also be directed toward relaxing various restraints in order to create favorable conditions for foreign funds.

Recent industrial achievement in the ASEAN countries is noteworthy, while their dependence on primary products is still high compared with Asian NICs. The drop in the international price for primary products started in the early 1980s and has negatively affected their economic growth. Further efforts towards industrialization are desirable.

The industrialization of ASEAN countries has been accomplished through import substitution, protected by careful government policies. However, recent observations show that they are moving on into export-oriented fields. This is especially true in labor-intensive industries which are actively entering the international market due to their strong competitiveness. NICs are losing their edge in labor-intensive product exports because of import restrictions in the advanced countries and soaring wages at home. Now is the time for ASEAN countries to expand their exports to catch up with NICs. ASEAN countries are recently announcing their export development programs. Along with its sixth Five Year Economic and Social Development Program, Thailand announced a plan to nurture its export industry through quality and productivity improvements, and efforts on marketing. Malaysia launched a new strategy to develop resource export-oriented industries based on its Comprehensive Program for Industrial Development. However, there are many problems to be solved before these countries will be able to export industrial products on a full scale basis, namely, (a) construction of infrastructures for their export industries; and (b) assistance of the peripheral industries which manufacture parts and intermediate products. Acceptance of direct foreign investments and loans for their export related infrastructures, export-oriented industries and their peripheral industries are expected to supplement these domestic efforts.

With the appreciation of the yen, Japanese business has been branching out into the ASEAN countries on an unprecedented scale while Asian NICs on their part have made efforts to directly finance those countries. ASEAN countries should prepare themselves for an influx of foreign funds. It has been our experience that ASEAN countries have had strong restraints on foreign investments and that they still exist, especially in such fields as foreign ownership, export obligations, use of local resources, employment of local labor, etc. The current investment procedure need be simplified and restrictions on manufacturing and export licenses need be relaxed.

ASEAN countries own a large number of state and/or public corporations not only in the fields of land, marine, and air transportation, communication, petroleum, and banking, but also in manufacturing industries. Such public corporations have quite often played a negative role in the course of industrialization. Privatization of these corporations and relaxation of restraints are imperative to further activate ASEAN countries.

(13) *Inclusion of China into the Asia-Pacific Sphere*: Designated special economic districts in China form a part of the regional linkages comprising the Western Pacific growth center. The parties concerned should

recognize the concept of China being an indispensable member of the Asia Pacific sphere.

China seems to have found a viable model in the market mechanism and foreign economic policies which lead to the development of Asian NICs and ASEAN countries. Chinese economic reform initiated after the 1978 National Congress was based on three pillars including agricultural reforms emphasizing individual initiative and responsibility, enlargement of autonomy of enterprises in the industrial sector and open-door policy comprised of introduction of foreign capital, and establishment of designated trade areas. The last of these is particularly noteworthy because it gave rise in 1980 to four economic districts where considerable freedom of action is exercised. In addition, 14 cities and Hainan Island were designated in April 1984 as preferential districts enjoying similar freedom of action as the four economic districts. Recently a new attempt has been made in China to interpret "preferential districts" comprehensively. The new interpretation makes it possible to include large units such as entire provinces or delta regions under the economic and preferential districts by designating the entire area as "coastal economic district."

These development is closely related to Chinese Government's intention to secure the safe return of Hong Kong and, in the near future, of Taiwan. China intends to invite capital from advanced countries, Hong Kong and South East Asia to these districts and establish joint ventures. China may even envisage establishing Chinese joint ventures in Hong Kong. In essence, China intends to internalize the dynamism by incorporating capital from advanced countries, Hong Kong, and, in the near future, Taiwan.

It is too early to say that the economic reform in China is firmly established or that open-door policy would continue without disruption. Even with temporary setbacks, however, Chinese foreign economic policy is expected to maintain its current course toward increased openness. Eventually, designated free trade areas in China will come to establish strong economic ties with the Western Pacific countries. Such economic links would release the potentials of the Chinese economy and China will find it difficult to sever its ties with the Pacific economic community. We should therefore aim at long-term gains from having an open China.

China on her turn should clearly state that the open door policy would not be subject to short-sighted manipulation and should ease state control of foreign trade and investment. This will be a prerequisite in establishing credibility among the Western Pacific countries and the Chinese population residing outside China.

2-3 The debate

The policy recommendation is a result of extensive discussions in Japan and in the United States. Japanese participants included members of the Japan Forum, and in drawing-up the document, consultation was made with relevant government ministries on informal basis. On the U.S. side, the participants included those who attended the meeting with the present author at the Council on Foreign Relations in order to exchange views on the draft proposal. In addition, a series of meetings were arranged with government officials and economists from research institutions. I should perhaps not cite particular persons for what they had to say. Rather, I would like to digest the discussion and try to highlight the views which I think are illuminating in understanding different perspectives in dealing with the global economic problems of which the emergence of the Pacific economies is a part. On the whole, the debate fulfilled a constructive role in sorting out the differences in the mind set on both sides of the Pacific.

In particular, we believe that by forming a triangular economic relations involving the United States, Asian NIEs, and Japan, and using Japanese direct foreign investment as the leverage to supplement local investment, we may be able to solve the bilateral economic conflicts which have plagued the countries involved in the recent past. There was no opportunity for participants in the U.S. and Japan to directly engage in discussion. The Japanese views were presented during the regular meetings, and some of the points were reflected in the policy proposal itself. There remain, however, some points which are worth-mentioning.

First, the most fundamental point is that the proposal should not sound like proposing a new economic block in Asia. Implicit in this statement is that we are not proposing a new "Greater East Asian Co-Prosperity Sphere", a concept which in the 1930s justified Japan's expansion in Asia which at that time was mostly colonies of the Western powers. Such concept is absolutely out of question either to Japan's neighbors or at home. Rather, in view of the fact that economic strain (which is increasingly being politicized) between the United States and Japan is the major stumbling block not only in the bilateral relations but also toward a sound functioning of the world economy, the proposal attempts to come up with a more consistent scenario. And our finding is that, by forming a triangular economic relations in the Pacific involving the United States, Asian NIEs, and Japan, and the latter playing the role of an absorber of exports from other regions, we could form a mutually supporting growth mechanism. Rather than Japan and the Asian NIEs trying to sell to the United States, thereby aggravating trade imbalance, Japan will emerge as an absorber and the trade flow will be a more balaced one. If Japanese final demand can be met by imports from Asian countries, this will take some pressure off the American market and help improve the U.S. trade balance. The Japanese plan to recycle foreign reserves via official development assistance and private loans will strengthen the effect. At any rate, it is imperative for Japan to increase import dependency rate, it was suggested. Thus, even when the proposed document mainly discusses the Pacific rim countries, improved economic relations in this area will be beneficial in a global context.

Second, regarding the scope of the proposal, some Japanese participants believed that the policy prescription is heavily geared toward Japanese side. In the United States, it may prove too optimistic to assume that fiscal balance will be restored in the near future. If this is the case, accumulated foreign debt will be a problem in the long run, and may trigger a whole issue concerning the dollar as a key currency. At the same time, to treat the U.S. fiscal deficit as if it is the only source of American problem is not warranted. For example, continued and increasing American dependence on imported oil may invite next round of oil crisis. Among Asian countries, there is a widely-held concern about political situation, for example, in Korea, the Philippines, and Taiwan. The proposal sounds excessively optimistic about the growth potential of China, particularly in the Southern part. Chine runs considerable trade deficit. China also runs a risk of inflation due to uncoordinated development policy.

Third, concerning the liberalization effort in Japan, it was pointed out that the Japanese system is not transparent. In the United Sates or in Europe, countries adopt comparable systems on the ground of mutuality in order to safeguard internationally uniform rules regarding the flow of goods and services. In Japan, liberalization is meant to provide equal treatment as the Japanese nationals, but still maintains the existing distribution channels which are rather complex reflecting multilayers of wholesale and retail network and cumbersome government regulations. Many agreed that there are needless tariffs especially on agricultural goods. Many also agreed that government-induced regulation on large-scale retail stores should be abolished. However, there exists strong sentiment among the Japanese specialists that there is much to be desired as to the American and European sales effort in the Japanese market. The Japanese effort in foreign markets, for example, when measured by number of personnel, is ten times as much as American and European counterparts here. It should be noted in addition that the American demand to open the market has passed the stage of tariff reduction and liberalization and has come to request changes in Japanese customs, which to the Japanese sounds like asking to change the Japanese culture itself.

Incidentally, it sounds rather strange when the Americans complain about Japanese preference to domestic products. Traditionally, people appreciated imports. The term "hakurai" (literally, 'arrived via ship', meaning imports) meant high-class commodity. It is only in the last two decades or so that imported consumer goods became less attractive except for high quality products from Europe. In capital goods, too, high-precision metalworking machinery used to be predominantly imports.

Fourth, some participants questioned to whom the proposal was addressed. If it is meant for Japanese business, participants from the business circle said, they are doing what they are supposed to already, including out-sourcing, direct foreign investment, and modification of full set principle. They suspected that, in the end, rapid shift of production site overseas could be hollowing-out of industry.

To the American eyes, this kind of policy proposals from Japan have been numerous such as the Maekawa Report.[4] The effectiveness of such recommedation is seen as skeptical among the American audience. And this proposal was seen as "no different from previous Japanese approaches." Is not this another set of empty proposal? One observer bluntly put it; "Japan should stop issuing external policy packages" because negative impact of empty promises is more damaging if nothing is done after the announcement.

To be sure, there are some merits in this document. According to one observer, there are several Japanese commitment implicit in the document proposed by the Forum. First, Japan intends to be internationally open. Second, there is a shift of perception from bilateral relations to global relations. Third, by avoiding a discussion on security issues, Japan seems to intend a continued free-ride on the American defense commitment in Asia. Fourth, Japan will accept Korea as an equal partner. These points, however new and important to the Japanese mind, are not particularly worth noting for the Americans. Nevertheless, the fact that the Japanese are beginning to view the world differently should be noted.

On the other hand, most American participants did not hide their "negative feeling" toward this kind of document, although it is "hard to disagree" from its content. One major source of such feeling stems from the implicit assumption on the U.S. role in Asia. To the American eyes, the document fails to appreciate the U.S. presence. That is, Japan would intensify economic ties with the South-East Asian countries, help them develop, and obtain economic benefits, whereas the U.S. would solely bear the defense burden. If the U.S. presence results only in Japanese profits, the U.S. public opinion would not tolerate such burden.

The Japanese side has never been explicit about security issue in the proposed document. On security issue, American observers were more keen, and the difference became more apparent in the discussion. One big reason is perhaps that to Japanese, the American presence in Asia is taken for granted. It is partly because the proposal is addressed to economic issues, and security issue, especially concerning Korean Peninsula, is to be taken up by the Forum as a next topic. Also, it is partly attributable to a well-known fact that Japan has recently abolished the one-percent ceiling (as the share of GNP) on defense spending. Together with the fact that its economy is growing at a faster pace than other major powers, and successive government plans are aiming at upgrading equipment, Japanese presence in the security sphere is far from negligible.

From the U.S. side, it was proposed to envisage a "security tax" on a global scale. Japan's contribution in this sense would be 1.3% of GNP, consisting of 0.3% of ODA and 1.0% of military expenditures. A comparable figure for the U.S. is 6.2%, comprised of 0.2% of ODA and 6% of defense. Judged in this context, Japan's contribution to this "international public goods" must be tripled.

In this regard, some observers felt that the scope of the proposal, with its focus on South-East Asia, was rather too narrow and pointed out the lack of discussion on LDCs located in other parts of the world. One observer felt that the proposal is "disturbing" in its limited scope to Asian context. Others felt that Japan's proposed relations with Asian countries was "outrageous." For one thing, by praising excessively the growth potentials of South-East Asian countries and China, Japan intends to establish an economic empire in the region. The same thing can be said about the rate of profit which is described as high in LDCs in the region, a point made for appeasing the Asian countries. Many suggested that the proposal concerning investment should be addressed to all LDCs, and not limited to the ones in Asia. On this point, the proposal by Okita et al. made in Helsinki should be viewed as a model framework.[5]

Many American participants had difficulty in understanding to whom the policy proposal is addressed. Is this intended for the Japanese people, business, or government? Or is it to be read by the Americans? And, what policy tools going to be used in achieving the goals? Unless these points are made explicit, the proposal remains a "wish list," as one commentator puts it. Especially for the American audience, a concrete strategy has to be explained. Examples are how to eliminate fiscal deficit (in the U.S.) or how to stimulate housing investment (in Japan). For the latter case, one economist pointed out, 10% of land in Tokyo itself is devoted to agriculture, partly because holding land is an assured way of obtaining capital gains. Similar point can be made regarding government-imposed restriction on large-scale retail stores, explicit purpose of which is to protect the vested interest of small merchants who are less competitive. Implicitly, the policy is intended to protect small merchants who are usually conservative. Thus, the policy serves political goals as well. There are political problems and the Liberal Democratic Party would have to change if they are to be solved. How does this happen?

Coming back to the economic issue, the U.S. committed itself in the 1950s and 1960s to the smooth operation of the world economy. Today's Japan should assume a similar role, it was pointed out. This is so in the fields of trade, technology, and investment.

In the field of trade, there has been discussion of structural change in Japan, but in reality nothing has been achieved. The U.S. has experienced extremely painful adjustment, gone through it, and incredible reorganization occurred within its economy. The Japanese accuse the Americans for producing the wrong products, being lazy and less competitive, but it is not so any more. But in Japan, nothing comparable occurred to her economy, it was alleged. Examples are forest products and agriculture. In this sense, industrial adjustment is a future problem in Japan.

In the field of technology, there has been no case where Japan transferred technology and improved the productivity of the recipient. The U.S. came to a record deficit in high-tech trade since 1986, and it is necessary to obtain some concrete evidence of progress in individual fields to remedy the present situation.

In the field of investment, there is only limited investment opportunity left in Japan (presumably due to the matured stage of its manufacturing sector and institutional rigidities in such fields as housing and urban redevelopment). Japan has no chance in LDCs either because discriminatory barriers exist against Japanese investment. Thus, the Japanese found that the U.S. is the only recipient of its investment.

The word "structural adjustment" is used repeatedly without precise definition, it was pointed out. As far as I am concerned, the most appropriate definition of structural adjustment is deliberate change of interindustry relations. Unlike conventional macroeconomic policy which concentrates on the appropriate levels of final demand and manipulation of government demand in managing aggregate demand, industrial adjustment policy refers to the policy aimed at input structure of an industry (which is the production technology itself) including labor, capital, and intermediate inputs. It also tries to influence the way one sector is related to the other through interindustry repercussion, and how the demand is met by different sectors and by imports. The lack of mention of specific measures to be taken in the proposal is, unlike the past industrial policy, because much depends on automatic adjustment through the market mechanism which originates from the exchange rate realignment. Government's role is probably to implement policy package aimed at urban redevelopment.

In discussing the structural adjustment, Europe should be included explicitly so that positive adjustment can be discussed on a global scale. In addition, whereas the proposed document implies lack of progress in the U.S., the American structural adjustment was initiated much earlier than in Europe, and more effectively. Industrial adjustment is keenly related to industrial policy and/or protectionism.

Whether the adjustment should be conducted through government policy or should be left to the market mechanism is an important policy issue. Also, how to achieve the adjustment on a global scale is another question to which due attention should be paid. In the United States, reorganization of industry has shown considerable progress to the point its industry regained competitiveness. In contrast, Japan maintains protectionism policy and trade barriers erected against U.S. remain intact, it is alleged.

One informed government official pointed out three levels of trade barriers in Japan. First is the trade barriers on the official level, including industrial standards and quantitative import restrictions. There remains no unresolved problem in this sphere, it was admitted. Second is the barriers of structural nature, or the ones related to business practice or organizational characteristics such as distribution channel and "keiretsu."[6] Third obstacle concerns Japanese attitudes and habits. Governments can negotiate as to the obstacles of the first kind, but they cannot be effective in the case of the second and the third. In addition, it is extremely costly to conduct business in Japan, due to high rental cost, etc., which is made doubly expensive by the recent appreciation of the yen.

Regarding the effectiveness of exchange rate adjustment, it was pointed out that business response in the two countries are different and that Japanese firms were becoming more efficient in order to survive under the appreciated yen, whereas U.S. firms were raising prices to take advantage of more expensive imports. The behavior of consumers is also different. Consumers who buy Japanese products were less sensitive to price hikes. In fact, Japanese products became only 20% more expensive in the face of 60% appreciation of the yen. They only had to slash fat profit margin created by trade restrictions imposed upon them.

Some American firms started to withdraw investment from LDCs. Semiconductor is an example. One contributing factor is the increased competitiveness in the United States due to decline in the dollar exchange rate which made the U.S. wage rate relatively inexpensive. Another factor is the recognition that the strength of the Japanese firms can be attributed to the fact that they kept production domestically, and that the past American way of producing offshore has to be amended from an industrial policy point of view.

In the financial field, the Japanese Ministry of Finance kept purchasing U.S. treasury bill and a question was raised as to the future Japanese attitude regarding such bills. Even when the yen was being appreciated rapidly, which necessarily means capital loss when the Japanese invest in the U.S., the Ministry of Finance successfully persuaded private institutional investors to keep investing in the U.S. Some argued that the Japanese had no other place to put their money. Others argued that Japanese investment in the U.S. will result in higher "visibility" in the long run. In the eyes of the Americans, this is being interpreted as "buying-up America." On the other hand, if Japan stops investing in the U.S. abruptly, although it makes a good economic sense to avoid capital loss, such a move will be interpreted as Japan's uncooperativeness. It is a well-known fact that the inflow of capital from Japan was financing U.S. government deficit and in filling the saving shortage there. According to one economist, this may be a preferred solution because the American feeling will be, while unhappy for the moment, that foreign investors are leaving the U.S. market for lack of effective policy on the U.S. side regarding, for example, budget deficit. Lack of effort in this respect is blamed for causing "Black Monday" by creating depreciated dollar and high interest rates, which pulled the stock price down. This in turn will penalize manufacturing investment (as opposed to portfolio investment), hampering the recovery of U.S. competitiveness in the future.

In concluding the debate which took place in the United States, one impressively notices the following point. In many instances, the American participants did not hide their concern over the U.S. becoming "a diminishing giant." The United States ceased to be the world's No. 1 in many fields including high-tech and finance. But, in the words of an American observer, the U.S. will be a "bad loser" and will "start pointing fingers." Japan should be prepared for all the nasty things the United States can do to it. Even the most well-informed people do not want to admit a strong Japan. They believe in the renaissance of the American industry and believe this is what is actually happening.

One American observer pointed out Japanese "negativism" towards the U.S., but I can not help noticing growing impatience and negativism among the American people. I take this seriously because such tendency is more widespread among specialists on Japan.

At the same time, and perhaps more importantly, the United States is seeking the way for "shared responsibility" and "joint decision making." It is in this sense that the responsible Americans are asking how the Japanese perceive their roles. They question whether the current regime in Japan can come up with a clear vision as true Japan's leaders.

The lack of clear response from Japan has made the Americans impatient. Even among specialists on Japanese economy and international relations, concerned voices are heard that the Japanese might "deceive" the Americans "again." These are harsh words to be thrown at an economic and political ally, but very well represent the reality.

Participating in drawing up of the policy recommendations and having opportunities to participate in discussions in the United States and in Japan concerning the draft, I feel that the debate was very useful. We notice a considerable divergence of opinion even among the Japanese participants. It is no wonder that the response of American participants were more widespread. My impression is that the Japanese participants tried to come up with a consistent scenario devoid of their individual stand point as an academician, a government official, or a business man. Implicit assumption was that it was up to each individual to interpret the scenario to fit his position and power. This way, the importance of individual issues was conveyed to the participating members. In contrast, American response was the expression of individual views. This, of course, reflects the nature of the discussion which took place only once. I believe it will be very useful if the American side can come up with a parallel survey. Because, as it stands now, American policy prescription tend to be individualistic and ad hoc, and the negotiations tend to be yes-or-no type, lacking a consistent scenario to back up the steps they are actually taking. In the process, issues are excessively politicized, usually from the American side. Excercising external political pressure even in economic sphere may be effective in the short-run when dealing with individual issues, but may prove counter productive in the long-run when we have to safeguard sound bilateral economic relations. It would be much better if internal and external consistency of envisaged policy packages could be analyzed prior to their implementation . It is a hard fact that policy implementation is up to the national governments, and even there, the viability of policy manipulation is becoming limited due to multinational corporations and flow of financial resources across national boundaries. Precisely because of this, systematic analysis on the international implication of development on national level has to be undertaken.

2-4 Postscript

Here I attempt to update the factual development concerning the policy recommendation.

Adjustment of macroeconomic structure: Japanese economy continued to

Table 2-1 Financial surplus and deficit by sector, per cent of GNP

(unit: %)

		Public	Business	Household	Overseas
Japan	1984	− 5.8	− 1.7	9.8	− 2.8
	1985	− 4.2	− 1.9	9.8	− 3.6
	1986	− 4.2	− 1.3	10.2	− 4.3
	1987	− 1.4	− 2.2	7.9	− 3.6
	1988	0.6	− 4.6	7.6	− 2.8
	1989	0.6	− 6.9	9.2	− 2.0
U.S.	1984	− 4.7	− 0.6	4.7	1.9
	1985	− 4.8	− 0.3	2.7	2.6
	1986	− 5.2	− 0.9	3.3	3.2
	1987	− 4.1	− 1.2	2.4	3.4
	1988	− 4.1	− 0.7	2.6	2.8
	1989	− 3.9	− 1.0	3.8	1.3
Germany	1984	− 1.9	− 1.6	6.3	− 0.9
	1985	− 1.1	− 1.8	6.2	− 2.1
	1986	− 1.2	− 1.9	6.6	− 4.1
	1987	− 1.8	− 1.5	6.4	− 3.8
	1988	− 2.1	− 1.6	6.7	− 4.0
	1989	0.0	− 3.1	6.6	− 4.3

Notes: The data are based on flow of funds statistics in respective countries. Financial surplus corresponds to excess saving and financial deficit to excess investment in the real side. Overseas sector indicates the balance as seen from the rest of the world. Thus, negative figures indicate current accont surplus for the reporting country.

Source: Calculated from Bank of Japan, *Comparative Economic and Financial Statistics, Japan and Other Major Countries.*

expand in the recent past. As a result, in terms of flow of funds statistics, the public sector turned into a record surplus for the first time in 27 years. Whereas this sector recorded deficit amounting to 1.4% of GNP in 1987, a surplus of 2,180 billion yen was recorded in 1988, or approximately 0.6% of GNP (Table 2-1).

This is a reflection of fiscal austerity on the one hand and increased tax revenues at national and local levels due to sound business profit and personal income on the other. Surplus in current account (which is recorded in the flow of funds statistics as the fund shortage of "the rest of the world" sector) was reduced to 2.8% of GNP in 1988 from 3.6% in the previous year. In the household sector, fund surplus (or, excess savings) was reduced due to increased housing construction and consumption. Thus, in Japan, we have witnessed a favorable development toward restoring saving-investment balance, represented by liquidation of fiscal deficit, narrowing trade surplus, and revitalized business and housing investment abosorbing surplus household savings.

A parallel development has been observed in the United States, although the pace of improvement was slower. According to flow of funds statistics, the deficit in the public sector has been at least arrested. The 1988 deficit of 194.6 billion dollars was not larger than in 1985 and 1986. When compared to GNP (current prices), the relative size has been narrowed from around 5% to 4%. Likewise, the trade deficit, which had expanded through 1987, seems to have been reversed in 1988. It should be noted that the table presents the balance as seen from overseas point of view. That is, positive figures means a surplus for countries outside of the U.S. and a deficit for the U.S.

Maintaining a free trade regime: Perhaps the single most important item under this heading is the U.S. activation of the 1988 trade act's "super-301" procedure which was announced on May 25, 1989. The United States Trade Representative Carla Hills published a list of "unfair traders" which included Japan, India, and Brazil. The announcement also demands U.S. retaliation if trade barriers are not removed through negotiation.[7] In addition, the USTR listed 8 countries (Brazil, Mexico, Thailand, Korea, Taiwan, India, China, and Saudi Arabia) on a priority watch list and 17 (including Japan and Italy, among others) on a watch list regarding intellectual property rights.

The Japan's leading newspaper *Japan Economic Journal* reported as follows. "The USTR....specified Japan as an unfair trader, while listing three items including supercomputers, satellites, and the timber industry as subjects for inquiry and negotiation. As for intellectual property rights, the USTR decided to put Japanese patent system under watch list and to follow up Japan's response closely. At the same time, the U.S. government specified, among others, business network (keiretsu), prior negotiations (dango), pricing mechanism, market division, distribution channels, and land use, as structural impediments or noncompetitive factors, and suggested that the U.S. should enter into negotiation with the Japanese government. As a matter of fact, the announcement targetted Japan, and the U.S.-Japan trade friction entered a new stage."[8]

They were not exaggerating. In response, main Japanese cabinet members reportedly commented that "the U.S. is being unfair," and that "we will not negotiate with a country which unilaterally labels an ally as unfair trader." The American ambassador in Tokyo was summoned to the Foreign Ministry and was conveyed a government message referring to the decision as "extremely regrettable." It should be noted that, within the 30 year history of U.S.-Japan trade friction, this was the first time that the Foreign Ministry summoned the American ambassador to convey a feeling of grievance. Japan openly appealed the maximum degree of displeasure to the U.S. decision regarding the "super-301".[9]

According to a press report, application of "super-301" to Japan is "equal to pinpointing Japan as the root of the world's trade frictions."[10] The shock this has given to the Japanese government stems from the prospect that this country will be viewed as an unfair trader. The same paper, which enjoys high reputation in non-emotional, factual reporting of economic affairs, wrote, "The world's free trade regime had been organized with U.S. liberalism as its guiding principle, and Japan achieved growth as a major exporter under the regime. But now, the U.S. has fallen into the position of the world's largest debtor nation, and, finding the pressure of the balance of payments deficit unbearable, turned to retaliation. The Americans began to take the attitude that the key to the solution of this impasse lies 'in the Japanese hands, and not in the U.S.'"

In Japanese eyes, they have been cooperative in the past conflicts involving textiles, color television, steel, and automobile, all of which were put under "voluntary" restraint at one time or the other. They went along in the case of electronics. They are in the process of opening up the agricultural market (this in addition to the fact that Japan is the world's largest importer of agricultural products already, and despite the recent experience of U.S. embargo on soybean which was already purchased and ready for shipment). The tariffs are already the world's lowest. They have been cooperative in the purchase of fighter planes from the U.S. (only to find themselves being accused of stealing American technology), which Japan planned to design and produce by themselves as they have done in the past. The decision by the USTR came on top of all this.

The U.S. view must be quite different. At least, Japan was not the only country which was accused. Supercomputers and satellites are already among the list of "emergency procurement program" on the Japanese side. The fact that the government itself is a customer for such products makes political solution feasible. The bilateral nature of the "super-301" may be interpreted as an effort to overcome deadlocks vis-a-vis major trading partners through more specialized negotiation. Such bilateral negotiations, it is hoped, could facilitate the GATT negotiation process.

The trade deficit with Japan will be discussed in the proposed framework of "structural impediments initiative" which accompanied the announcement of the super-301 list. The U.S. has come to mistrust Japanese economic structure and institutions which they see as the deep root of American inability to penetrate the Japanese market. The Japanese side tends to blame American heavy dependence on imports and persistent fiscal imbalance, and disagrees to enter into negotiations unless structural problems on the U.S. side are also addressed. But politicalization of economic issues in this fashion may work to obscure the American mind regarding the real cause of the problem, which is the macroeconomic imbalance in the U.S. to which the past and present administrations have done very little.

At any rate, Korea and Taiwan have given in to American pressure in order to avoid being included in the list of unfair traders. The EC and its members were also excluded reflecting active lobbying and, presumably,

Table 2-2 Outstanding external debt in Asian countries

(unit: billion dollars)

	1981	1985	1986	1987	1988	1989	1990
NIEs	42.4	58.7	57.7	46.8	35.4	32.6	28.1
Hong Kong	2.2	3.4	3.8	...	...	...	...
Korea	33.0	47.2	46.7	40.5	31.4	28.9	24.5
Singapore	2.3	3.4	3.9	4.5	2.3	2.0	2.0
Taiwan	4.9	4.8	3.2	1.9	1.8	1.7	1.6
Southeat Asia	62.2	105.2	118.8	136.5	139.0	147.4	156.1
Indonesia	22.7	36.0	43.0	52.6	55.6	57.6	59.2
Malaysia	7.5	18.3	20.0	21.7	18.4	17.7	16.9
Philippines	20.8	26.2	28.9	30.0	30.0	32.3	33.7
Thailand	10.8	17.5	18.5	20.7	22.0	25.0	29.8
South Asia	40.3	63.8	72.6	82.2	88.7	96.3	104.1
China	5.8	16.7	21.9	30.2	37.9	44.3	51.1

Note: 1989 and 1990 figures are estimates.
South Asia includes Bangladesh, Burma, India, Nepal, Pakistan, and Sri Lanka.
Source: Asian Development Bank, *Asian Development Outlook.*

political judgment on the American side. There is a danger that the current Uruguay Round of GATT negotiations will become a place to seek universal application of what is gained in bilateral application of pressure and individual negotiations. The world's largest trading country seems to be self-rightiously and unilaterally taking that course already, undermining the multilateral principle. Domestically, this will lead to a web of vested interests of various groups rather than transparent industrial policy, a situation very far removed from free trade principle, which the U.S. had advocated in spirit in forming the world economic regime and to which it has adhered to in recent years at least in words.

International flow of funds: According to the World Bank, outstanding debt totaled 1170 billion dollars at the end of 1987 and 1200 billion dollars by the year end 1988.[11] Although the outstanding debt is still increasing, debt-service ratio for all of the reporting countries has been improving from 24.6% in 1986 and 22.6% in 1987 to 21.5% in 1988. This is attributable to, first, increased exports of the developing countries due to expansion of the industrialized countries and rising trend in primary commodity prices and, second, due to declining interest rate in the world financial market which helped lighten their interest payment.

However, a situation continued where repayment exceeded capital inflow. Such a reversal in international flow of funds emerged in mid-1980s and amounted to 43 billion dollars in 1988.

The situation differs according to region. Whereas the debt-service ratio in Latin America and Africa stood at 42.8% and 26.2% in 1988, respectively, Asian countries as a whole recorded a ratio of 10.6%, showing a decline from a 13% level a few years ago.[12] The table below shows outstanding external debt among Asian countries. Although there are countries such as Indonesia and the Philippines which are heavily

Figure 2-1 Official development assistance of major countries

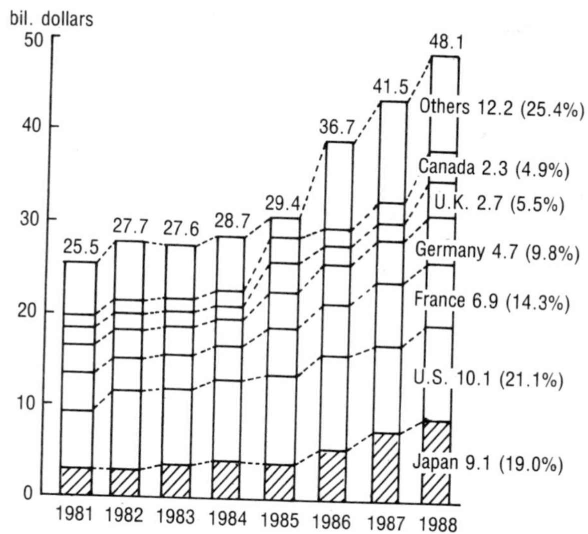

Note: Figures are net disbursement basis.
Source: DAC, *Development Cooperation.*

indebted, the situation as a whole has clearly been alleviated.[13]

During fiscal 1987–1989, Japan implemented a "30 billion dollar recycling plan" for LDCs. The plan was visioned after the Marshall Plan in order to recycle the international liquidity which accumulated in Japan reflecting the current account surplus. Ten billion dollars were commited at the time of the 1986 IMF-World Bank meeting, and 20 billion dollars at the time of the Venetian Summit in 1987. The actual disbursement already reached 90.1% at the end of April 1989, although original plan extends up to the end of March 1990. The recycling plan and disbursement is shown below.

	Plan billion	Actual (April 1989) U.S.$
Capital subscription and other forms of financial cooperation to international development funding organizations	12.00	8.68
Lendings to IMF	6.66	6.66
Yen credit through the Japan's Overseas Economic Cooperation Fund	3.00	4.54
Joint loans and direct loans by the Export-Import Bank	9.00	6.99
Others	0.15	0.15
Total about	30.00	27.02

To make the current plan succeed, the government prepared a new recycling plan to cover the next three years beginning 1989 amountint to 40 billion dollars. The official announcement was made during the Paris Summit in July 1989. The plan aims at expanding the share of the fund going into Latin American countries. In response to recent focus on global environmental problem, the Japan Overseas Cooperation Fund will put emphasis on providing low-interest credit to finance protection of tropical rain forest, water resources control, and other environment-related projects. Direct lending by the Export-Import Bank will focus on export-related sectors in LDCs in order to promote exports, particularly to Japan.

Reflecting such efforts, annual ODA has increased rapidly. The 1988 ODA recorded 9.1 billion dollars, which is an increase of 22.5% over the previous year (8.6% in yen terms). The U.S. figure for 1988 is estimated to be 10 billion dollars. The 1987 figures stood at 8.94 billion dollars for the U.S. and 7.45 billion dollars for Japan. This was followed by France which provided 6.52 billion dollars.[14]

Japan as an absorber, increased international division of labor, and correction of full-set principle: Yoshitomi, who heads the Economic Resarch Institute of the Economic Planning Agency, recently wrote that the pessimism as to the effectiveness of the exchange rate adjustment is ill founded.[15] "First of all, quantitative adjustment of trade has progressed at a rapid pace. The table below sheds light on the point. It shows the changes in Japanese trade that has taken place during the 1985–1988 period (1985=100).

exports		imports		finished goods imports
quantity	unit price	quantity	unit price	quantity
104.8	144.0	139.4	103.9	178.3

Taking 1985 as the base year when the rapid appreciation of the yen occured, Japanese exports increased only 4.8% in three years in terms of quantity. In contrast, import quantity has increased 39.4%. If one looks at the imports of finished goods, an increase of 78.3% was observed. The fact that Japanese exports practically stagnated through 1988 and that its imports, particularly that of finished goods, have increased rapidly should not cause any protectionist sentiments abroad. In fact, the U.S. exports have increased 40.1% in the two years preceding 1988 and imports, 13.9%, in quantity terms. When exports are growing at a comparatively higher pace, why one is tempted into protectionism? Because people are dazzled by nominal figures. True, the Japanese trade surplus remained at the 80 billion dollar level in the past three years. Why

Figure 2-2 Import of final consumer goods

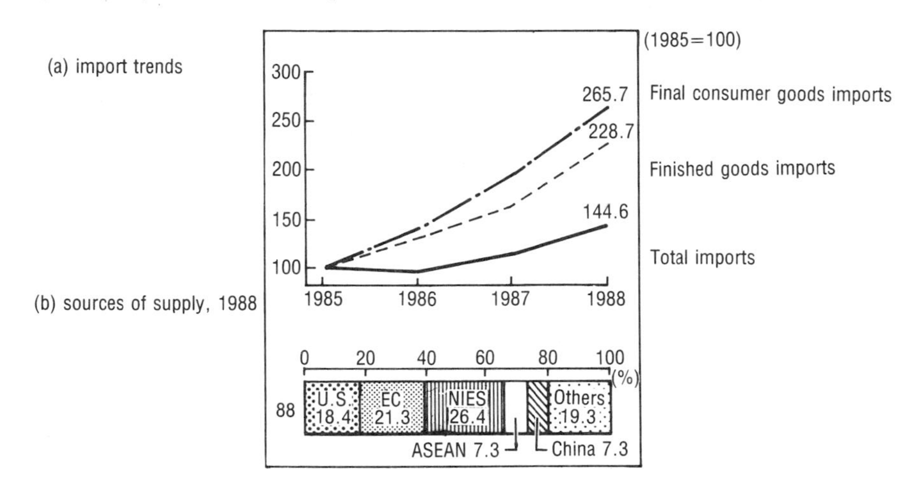

Source: Data compiled by the Economic Planning Agency. *Japan Economic Journal* (in Japanese), June 27, 1989.

is this? Because unit export price in dollar terms has risen an astonishing 44% during the 1985–1988 period. This means that, of the yen appreciation during the period of nearly 100%, about 1/2 has been passed on to export prices. ...When Japan's exports stagnate in quantity terms and export prices keep rising, how can one imagine that the U.S. firms which compete with imports from Japan are being hardpressed managerially?"

The Economic Planning Agency also compiled data concerning the imports of finished consumer goods.[16] "Final consumer goods" include foods, clothes, furniture, electric durable goods, etc. which are purchased by consumers. (In contrast, the more generally used term "finished goods" includes industrial raw materials (intermediate goods) and capital goods which are purchased by the business sector and excludes foods.) According to the report, importation of "final consumer goods" in 1988 amounted to 53.1 billion dollars, which is 2.6 times larger than the 1985 level. As can be seen in figure 2-2, this expansion exceeds finished goods imports and total imports. The share of final consumer goods in total imports expanded from 15.4% in 1985 to 28.3% in 1988. The expansion has been particularly high for furniture (55.4% increase over 1987), clothing (55.2%), automobiles (50.1%), audio-visual equipment (87.7%), watches, calculators, sporting goods, shrimps, pork, grapefruit, whisky, eels, among others. Among the supplying countries, the U.S. keeps the No. 1 position, but the shares of Asian and EC countries are growing faster, it is reported.

Figure 2-3 Direct foreign investment

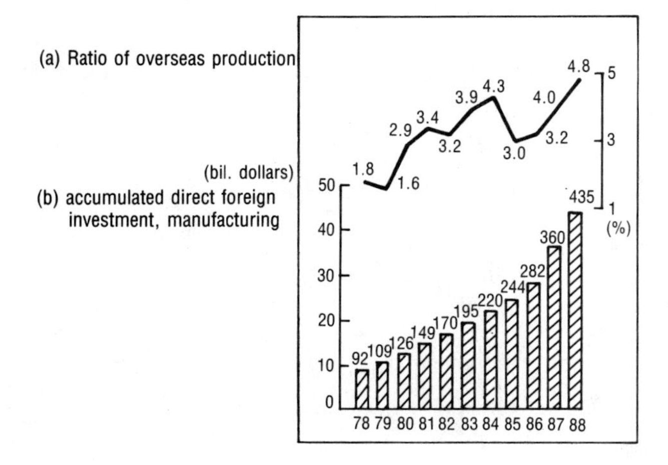

Note: Fiscal year basis.
Source: Data compiled by the Ministry of Finance.
Japan Economic Journal (in Japanese), May 11, 1989.

Relocation of production sites overseas: Direct foreign investment is the vehicle to achieve increased finished goods imports, leading to increased intraindustry division of labor, and correction of the Japanese industrial structure. At the same time, inward direct investment facilitates international integration of the economies. According to the Ministry Finance, Japan's outward direct investment in fiscal 1988 amounted to 47.022 billion dollars, up 40.9% over the previous year.

Particularly marked was the expansion of direct investment flows in manufacturing, which increased 76.3% over the previous year to reach 13.805 billion dollars. Sector-wise, growth of general machinery sector ($1.432 bil., 110% increase), ferrous and nonferrous metals ($1.367 bil, 73.9%), chemicals ($1.293 bil., 42.1%), and electric machinery ($3.041 bil., 25.6%) has been outstanding. Among the non-manufacturing sectors, finance and insurance ($13.104 billion, 22.8%), real estate ($8.641 billion, 59.2%), wholesale and retail trade ($3.204 billion, 41.2%), and services ($3.732 billion, 34.2%) were recorded for fiscal 1988.

Regional breakdown reveals that the bulk is directed toward North America. The 1988 figure stood at 22.328 billion dollars (45.4% increase over fiscal 1987), of which 21.701 billion dollars (47.6% increase) were invested in the United States. Direct divestment to Europe stood at 9.116 billion dollars (38.6% increase) and to Asia, 5.569 billion dollars (14.4% increase). Among European countries, high rates of increase were observed for the United Kingdom and the Netherlands.

Inward direct investment totaled 3.243 billion dollars, which is an increase of 46.5% over the previous year. The investment from the United States stood at 1.774 billion dollars, which is an increase of 89.1% over the previous year and has come to share 54.7% of the total inward flow.[17]

In terms of the stock amount, total outstanding direct investment is estimated at 43.5 billion dollars at the end of September 1988. Reflecting the changing pattern of direct foreign investment, 43.9% of the total is attributed to manufacturing.

The Council on Industrial Structure affiliated with the Ministry of International Trade and Industry reported in May 1989 that, by the year 2000, Japan's outstanding direct foreign investment will continue to grow at an annual rate of 16% and that the overseas production will climb to 12% of domestic production. The ratio in fiscal 1988 stood at 4.8%. The Council's "Structural Adjustment Vision", published in December 1987, predicted an annual growth of 14% for outstanding direct foreign investment towards 1995, but this has now been revised upward. In the 1987 prediction, increased overseas production was predicted to result in a net reduction of Japan's trade surplus by 46.8 billion dollars in 1995, but this is now predicted to be 70.0 billion dollars. Direct investment accompanies exports of raw materials, parts, and capital goods from Japan, but this is more than offset by export substitution by local production and increased imports, it is explained.[18]

As for hollowing out of the industry, the report contends that there will be no problem since a certain level of domestic production will be maintained and new technology is developed through R&D. There may arise mismatch in employment on regional and/or sectoral basis, which can be accomodated by appropriate policy measures.

Actually, Japan's labor market in the past few years is characterized by labor shortage. Continued economic expansion (see below) and structural change brought about extreme shortage of skilled workers. The Ministry of Labor published a survey result as of November 1988 saying that the shortage amounts to 2.06 million workers, nearly double the figure in the previous year. This amounts to 11.1% of the currently employed skilled workers (about 18.48 million), the highest level since 1974. The situation by major job categories is as follows.

	Labor shortage, (%)	
	1987	1988
Sales	4.6	10.0
Metalworking and machinery	6.5	12.5
Construction	18.9	34.1
Services	6.5	10.7
Information processing	15.9	18.3
Total	6.1	11.1

Figure 2-4 Economic growth and its sources

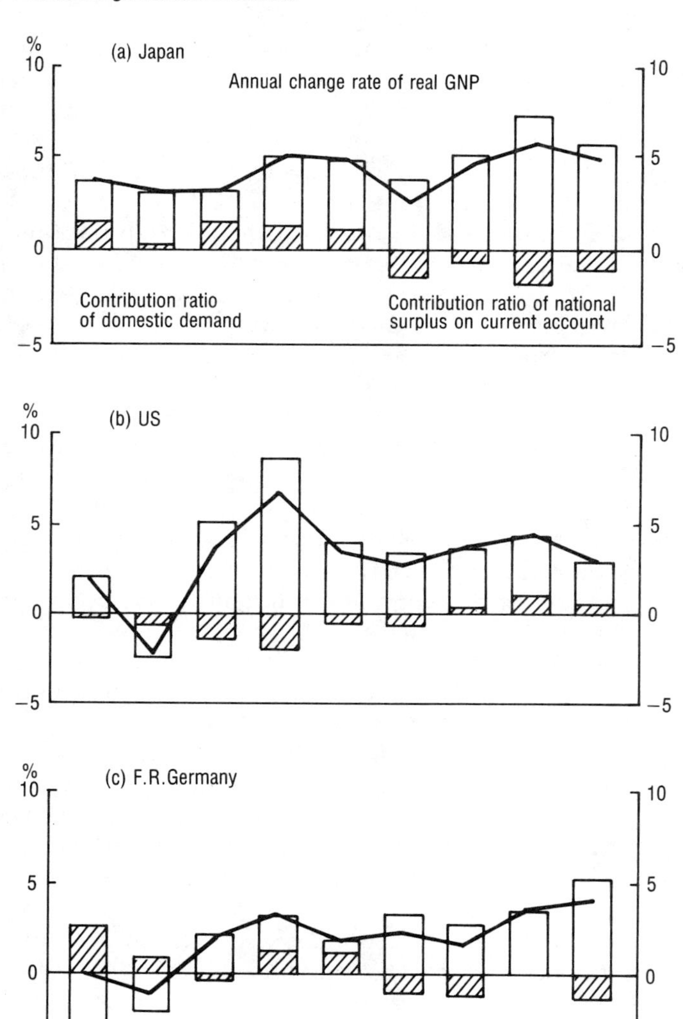

Note: The shaded area shows the contribution ratio of current account surplus. Annual growth of real GNP, shown by a solid lilne, is the sum of contribution ratio of domestic demand and foreign demand.

Source: The Bank of Japan, *Comparative Economic and Financial Statistics,* Japan and Other Major Countrries.

Of the establishments surveyed, about 52% complained of labor shortage, of which 60% said they are experiencing unfavorable effects on production plans and labor cost.[19]

Labor shortage will be a problem in the long-run. The Ministry of Labor predicts that, assuming growth rates of 4% up to 1995 and 3% thereafter, labor shortage will amount to more than one million in the year 2000. This takes into account positive factors such as increased labor force participation of female population and the old aged people and negative factors such as shortening working hours.[20]

Thus, compared to the rather severe outlook which prevailed in the 1986–1987 period when the policy recommendation in section 2 was drawn up, the Japanese tend to have a more relaxed attitude as to the future of the economy.

Expansion of domestic demand in Japan: This was of course a policy recommendation in order to neutralize the negative effect which would stem from deceleration of the U.S. economy when fiscal austerity was to be implemented. We all know by now that this did not happen. What happened actually was a simultaneous, continued expansion of the industrialized developed economies. It is very likely that this round of sustained growth is largely attributable to technological change of a fundamental nature, stemming from diffusion of computer-communication-control technology. Active investment in plant and equipment also had favorable effect on the expansion of exports, private consumption, and housing investment. As a result, tax revenues began to rise, narrowing fiscal imbalance in many countries including Japan.

The Japanese economy plunged into a recession following the appreciation of the yen in the latter half of 1985, and the real growth rate in 1986 declined to mere 2.4%. Whereas net export contributed 1.1 percentage point in 1985 to bring about overall growth of 4.9%, contribution of net export turned to minus 1.4 percentage point. Instead, domestic demand had grown 3.8%.

In 1987, domestic demand increased by 5.0%, while net export contributed minus 0.7%, largely due to increased imports, resulting in annual growth of 4.3%. Contributing factors were policy stimulus of about 6 trillion yen, lower interest rate, and improved terms of trade. In 1988, the economy continued strong growth pulled by personal consumption and private investment in plant and equipment. The contribution of external demand was negative for the three consecutive years. Thus, we may say that the Japanese economy succeeded in shifting the growth engine to domestic demand.

Asian NIEs: Asian NICs have succeeded in shifting the structure of

Figure 2-5 The share of industrial products in the exports of Asian NIEs and ASEAN countries

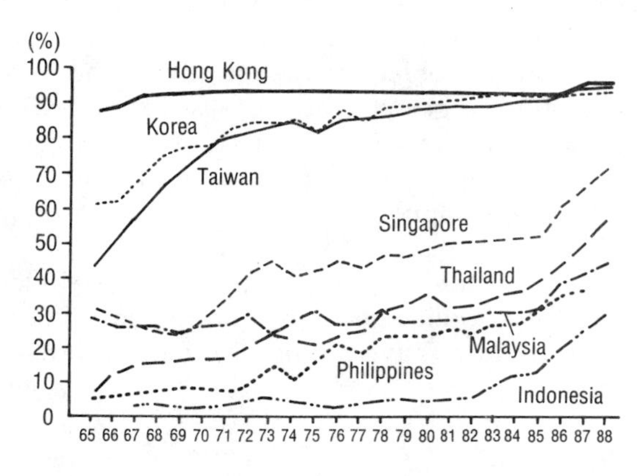

Source: Ministry of International Trade and Industry, *International Trade Whitepaper*, 1989, p.275.

exports to industrial products already in the 1970s. ASEAN countries have also entered the same stage after 1985 and their share of industrial products in total exports are growing rapidly. In 1988, for example, the share of industrial products in Thailand and Malaysia stood at 57% and 44%, respectively. Heavy reliance on primary products and petroleum have become a past story. By shifting to industrial products where income elasticity of demand is generally high, these countries will be able to take advantage of the expanding world market.

The export market for these countries are also changing. The largest market for Asian NIEs is still the United States absorbing more than 60 billion dollar worth of products in 1988. Japan's imports from these countries approached 30 billion dollars in the same year. In terms of contribution to export growth (that is, as the share of annual increment), however, the picture is very different. Japan's contribution is steadily increasing, reflecting the advanced stage of its structural adjustment and economic growth. The United States, on the other hand, is trying to reduce external deficit, and imports from these countries did not grow much in 1988. As a result, American contribution was surpassed by Japan's. Another important change in the market structure is the expanding trade wihin Asian NIEs and with ASEAN. That is to say, horizontal division of labor is taking place in this area.[21]

China: In a political declaration adopted at the Paris Summit meeting, the leaders of the seven major industrial countries urged China to stop

Figure 2-6 Contribution of major markets to annual increase in NIEs exports

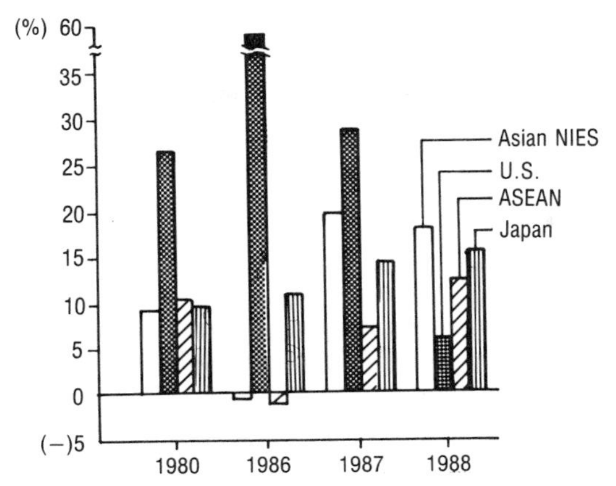

Source: Ministry of International Trade and Industry, *International Trade Whitepaper*, 1989, p.271.

repression against pro-democracy dissidents and resume movement toward political and economic reform.

"We have already condemned the violent repression in China in defiance of human rights. We urge the Chinese authorities to cease action against those who have done no more than claim their legitimate rights to democracy and liberty.

"This repression has led each of us to take appropriate measures to express our deep sense of condemnation to suspend bilateral ministerial and high-level contacts, and also to suspend arms trade with China, where it exists. Furthermore, each of us has agreed that, in view of current economic uncertainties, the examination of new loans by the World Bank be postponed. We have also decided to extend the stay of those Chinese student who so desire."

"We look to the Chinese authorities to create conditions which will avoid their isolation and provide for a return to cooperation based upon the resumption of movement towards political and economic reform and openness. We understand and share the grave concern felt by the people of Hong Kong following these events. We call on the government of the People's Republic of China to do what is necessary to restore confidence in Hong Kong. We recognize that the continuing support of the international community will be an important element in the maintenance of confidence in Hong Kong."

The world watched China emerge from the aftermath of the 1966–1976 Cultural Revolution. Rather favorable chain of events which followed during the decade of hope led us to believe secular gains in economic reform and open door policies. We were hopeful but rather cautious about the course of development in China which has undergone a series of "political cycle" in the past. In the policy recommendation we wrote, "It is too early to say that the economic reform in China is firmly established or that open door policy would continue without disruption. ... China on her turn should clearly state that the open door policy would not be subject to short-sighted manipulation. ..." The June 4, 1989 Massacre in Beijing has changed the outlook.

Chinese authorities may assume that the Western capital will come back charmed by the mere size of the Chinese market. Inexpensive wage level would be an additional factor. However, market mechanism requires rather transparent political and economic settings. It cannot be forced to function under extreme uncertainty. Moreover, Chinese government seems to have lost moral stand point which it managed to sustain ever since it came to existence. Low wage is less of an importance today due to increased automation which is made possible by electronics revolution. For business firms operating in mass consumption societies in the West, smell of blood in the products is not particularly welcome.

China's economic reform was entering a crucial period. As a Chinese economist wrote, "...the country's economic environment has become increasingly grim over the past few years, resulting most prominently in an over-expansion of the total social demand. Between 1978 and 1987, China achieved a three-fold increase in GNP. During the same 10 year period, however, the disequilibrium between the total social supply and demand in favor of demand was widened four times."[22] "Tangible inflation constitutes an indicator to the deterioration of the economic environment and one major factor responsible for the disruption of the normal economic order. It exerts a corrosive influence on the mind of people, enabling some to turn from lawful, honest labor to lawless profiteering speculation."[23] "Computed on the basis of the retail sale price index, prices have soared at an annual rate of no less than 6% since 1985. (It was) 13% higher in the first half of 1988 than in the same period of 1987. As a matter of fact, price increases are expected to reach anywhere between 15% and 18% by the end of 1988 and in some cities, have already reached the 20% mark."[24]

Hence, the economic reform. However, political repression almost certainly cause severe blow to the economic reform. Instead of economic reform, the China's political hardliners will have to resort to subsidies in state-run factories and outright rationing of energy and raw materials for strategic sectors in an effort to avoid creating bottle-necks. They may have to try to restrain wage hikes, and may be obliged to abandon needed price adjustment in order not to antagonize the people further.

Judged against this background, the postponement of the World Bank loans amounting to 1.2 billion dollars and Japan's suspension of 5.7

billion dollar loan program over a six-year period can be rather serious. Commercial banks have stopped providing long-term loans in the face of new risk in China, and short-term interest rates are also higher due to risk premium. China is yet to learn the rules of the game in a market economy. Thus, our hope for having China participating in the world economic community, first by strengthening ties in the Pacific rim context, has grown grim, pending political change in China itself.

Footnotes:

1 Japan Forum on International Relations, Inc., The Policy Recommendations on "the Structural Adjustment of Economies of Japan, U.S. and Asian NICs", March 1988. The forum was formed in 1987 under the initiative of Kenichiro Ito, and strong support by Saburo Okita and late Ichiro Hattori.

2 The task force included Toshio Watanabe (the University of Tsukuba), Takeshi Aoki (Japan External Trade Organization), Mitsuhiko Morimoto (The Yomiuri), and the present author.

3 Nowadays, a term newly industrializing economies (NIES) is preferred because this area includes economic areas rather than countries in a legal sense.

4 For Maekawa Report prepared in 1986, see Advisory Group on Economic Structural Adjustment for Economic Structural Adjustment for International Harmony [1986].

5 World Institute for Development Economics Research (WIDER), [1986] and [1987].

6 Keiretsu, which literally means corporate groups or corporate network, refers to established business relations involving parent firm and subsidiaries, often extending to different branches of manufacturing industry, and usually involving a particular bank and trading firm in order to take care of financial aspects and distribution channels, respectively.

7 The time schedule is as follows. After submission of the report on May 25, 1989, the USTR will start negotiation with the "unfair traders" within 21 days, which is June 20. The time limit for the negotiation is set at 12 months (6 months for intellectual property). On June 20, 1990, the USTR will decide on the retaliation, and this has to be implemented within 30 days, which is July 9, 1990.

8 *Japan Economic Journal* (Japanese), May 26, 1989, evening.

9 ibid., May 28, 1989.

10 ibid., May 28, 1989.

11 International Bank for Reconstruction and Development, *World Debt Tables*.

12 Ministry of International Trade and Industry, *Current Status and Problems of Economic Cooperation*, 1988, p.46.

13 Asian Development Bank, *Asian Development Outlook*, 1989.

14 *Japan Economic Journal* (Japanese), May 16, 1989 and June 11, 1989.

15 ibid., June 21, 1989.

16 ibid., June 27, 1989. The 1988 figures in this report are based on actual figures

during January–November period, converted to annual estimates.

17 ibid., May 31, 1989.

18 ibid., May 11, 1989.

19 ibid., July 3, 1989.

20 ibid., June 14, 1989.

21 Ministry of International Trade and Industry, *International Trade White Paper*, 1989, pp.271–276.

22 Jia Pei Wu, "A Crucial Period for China's Reforms—1989–1990," Mitsuru Hida, ed, *Japan-China Link Model*, Tokyo: Institute of Developing Economies, 1989, p.102.

23 ibid., p.104.

24 ibid., p.105.

Chapter 3. The Soviet Union and Japan

3-1 Introduction

The trends in Japanese-Soviet trade deserves careful scrutiny today for several reasons, which include the following:

First, four years after Gorbachev came to power, we may expect a new trend vis-a-vis Japan unfolding in foreign economic policy spheres, if there is one at all. Judging from Gorvachev's initiative demonstrated in other parts of the world, we can anticipate a renewal of Soviet trade policy toward Japan.

Second, with the continued decline of crude oil prices and general stagnation of trade in resources in the world economy, the Soviets may find themselves under pressure to shift their trade structure from a traditional position of raw material exporter to one of manufactured goods. It should be remembered that, even without a price decline, the Soviets are faced with declining production efficiency in energy resources including oil and gas, and traditional pattern of exports may be becoming 'expensive' in terms of real resource claims.[1]

Third, with the completion of long-term cooperative projects which were signed in the 1970s, renewed effort is called for from both the Soviet Union and Japan to promote trade between the two countries if they find it mutually beneficial.[2]

Fourth, on the Japanese side, changing economic structure toward 'soft' activities such as services and information processing as opposed to 'hard' goods calls for a trade structure which is distinctly different from the one which prevailed during the high-growth era. More specifically, the Japanese requirement for imported raw materials has tapered off in the 1980s. Coupled with the appreciation of the yen in recent years, Japan is now importing finished goods at an accelerated pace. It is interesting to empirically examine the structure of the Japanese-Soviet trade in this respect. In this paper, we shall look into the determining factors of Soviet exports to Japan and discuss mainly the Japanese side, focusing on economic factors.

In the early 1980s, there were 4 scenarios being envisaged among Western observers as to the future course of the Soviet economy.[3]

(a) collapse of the "Evil Empire", secession of territory, and abrupt changes in political regime.
(b) relative decline, economy first, followed by military obsolescence, and leading to loss of political power.
(c) military effort to retain and/or regain influence.
(d) fundamental change, price mechanism reinstalled, leading to

improved efficiency.

Although scenario (a) was a favorite one among Western observers, not many economists envisage complete collapse of an economic system of which the Soviet regime is one. An economis system continues to operate even under serious economic disturbance such as war or an inflationary period. (b) is thought to be more likely. This view was strengthened after consecutive attempts of economic reforms since mid-1960s, all of which ended without much tangible results, and deaths of ailing Soviet leaders which left the country immobile. (c) is a danger accompanying (b).[4] Scenario (d) is a desirable one, but may prove hard to implement because, currently being a centralized command economy where resources are allocated by the planning authority in a predetermined way, producing units have relatively small leeway as to disposal of products, and have vested interest in fulfilling the production targets under known and proven technology rather than to risk new ones. Efficiency improvement, especially in the case of electronics-related technology, has to be achieved from bottom up, rather than top down. One of the reasons is that this is a new technology potentials of which are unfamiliar to central planners. In addition, application of this particular technology requires interaction between the producers and the users to a much larger degree than was the case previously. Application has to be carried out at the production level, based on the accumulated experience of the producing personnel. This implies that the flow of information and decision-making has to be made upside down in the Soviet economy.

There seems to be three elements in scenario (d), introduction of many market elements, technology import, and expansion of the second economy.[5] Peter Wiles observed that "for USSR, 'export-led growth in the bracing atmosphere of the world market' would simply mean more gas, gold, timber and oil. It would not subject her manufacturers to this treatment, much though they undoubtedly need it." As for the second, he observed that "foreign technology proves unexpectedly difficult and expensive to assimilate." The same observer wrote that the second economy is "merely a prop to the system, a way of letting it stagger on without bogging down completely."

To the surprise of Western observers, Gorbachev emerged to the top of the Soviet power structure. As an energetic and imaginative leader, he has changed much of the Soviet political scene. In economic spheres, he seems to be heading for scenario (d), but how successful he can be in this aspect is yet to be seen even for most optimistic observers. True, there have been changes in planning priorities from investment to consumption. The Soviet curtailment in defense spending is taking place, but the real economic gains from such resource reallocation has not materialized in the form of increased supply of household goods. The intention of the Soviet regime is clear, but it is easier to make political declaration than to actually implement the restructuring, more so to achieve any concrete outcome when it comes to economic aspects. Will this be another NEP in the 1920s, a liberalization to be reversed after achieving some success in easing the acute economic difficulties? Will this be a convinced shift out of central planning?

Whichever the case may be, the Soviets in carrying out the reform need tranquil and if possible cooperative world economic and political environment.

3-2 Recent Trends in the Japanese-Soviet Trade

Recent trends in Japanese trade with the Soviet Union are shown in Table 3-1 and 2. The figures in Table 3-1 represent trade data in terms of U.S. dollars and the ones in Table 3-2 in terms of Japanese yen. One should keep in mind that the two sets of figures tend to diverge after 1985 due to apprecation of the yen.

In dollar terms, total of exports and imports between the two countries amounted to 4.9 billion dollars in 1987. This figure is not very different from the 1980 level which was 4.6 billion dollars and is about 12 percentage points lower than the peak figure in 1982. In 1988, trade volume reached a new peak at 5.9 billion dollars.

Japanese exports to the Soviet Union tended to decrease in the 1980s whereas imports tended to increase. This was particularly marked between 1986 and 1987. Compared to the previous year, 1987 exports were nearly 20% lower and imports 19% higher, bringing about near equilibrium in the trade balance. Actually, Japanese exports exceeded imports only by 0.2 billion dollars. In 1988, Japan recorded annual trade surplus of 0.4 billion dollars.

It is noted here that Japanese trade statistics record the transaction based on the country of origin. This results in inclusion of gold of Soviet origin among Japanese imports from the Soviet Union, whereas physical transportation usually takes place from European market to Japan.

In terms of the yen, the declines in Japanese exports look even more drastic. According to Table 3-2, the 1987 level is about 31% smaller than the previous year and 62% smaller than the peak figure in 1982. Japanese imports from the Sovet Union have exhibited a slight decline throughout the 1980s, and the 1987 figure is only 1.4% larger than the previous year. In 1988, we observed a reversal of this declining trend.

Table 3-3 shows the share of the Soviet Union in total Japanese trade. It indicates that the Soviet shares 1.2% in total exports and 1.5% in total

Table 3-1 Japanese trade with the Soviet Union in dollar terms

(unit: million dollars)

	Exports	Imports	Total
	ratio to previous year (%)	ratio to previous year (%)	ratio to previous year (%)
1980	2,778.2 (112.9)	1,859.9 (97.3)	4,638.1 (106.1)
1981	3,259.4 (117.3)	2,020.7 (108.6)	5,280.1 (113.8)
1982	3,898.8 (119.6)	1,682.0 (83.2)	5,580.8 (105.7)
1983	2,821.2 (72.4)	1,456.0 (86.6)	4,277.3 (76.6)
1984	2,518.3 (89.3)	1,394.0 (95.7)	3,912.3 (91.5)
1985	2,750.6 (109.2)	1,429.3 (102.5)	4,179.8 (106.8)
1986	3,149.5 (114.5)	1,972.0 (138.0)	5,121.6 (122.5)
1987	2,563.3 (81.4)	2,351.9 (119.3)	4,915.1 (96.0)
1988	3,129.9 (122.1)	2,765.8 (117.6)	5,895.7 (120.0)

Source: Ministry of Finance, *Foreign Trade Statistics.*

Tabled 3-2 Japanese trade with the Soviet Union in yen terms

(unit: million yen)

	Exports	Imports	Total
	ratio to previous year (%)	ratio to previous year (%)	ratio to previous year (%)
1980	628,748 (117.5)	423,635 (101.1)	1,052,383 (110.3)
1981	713,719 (113.5)	443,745 (104.7)	1,157,464 (110.0)
1982	967,852 (135.6)	412,635 (93.0)	1,380,487 (119.3)
1983	669,505 (69.2)	345,661 (83.8)	1,015,166 (73.6)
1984	596,073 (89.0)	329,492 (95.3)	925,565 (91.6)
1985	661,267 (110.9)	339,513 (103.9)	1,000,780 (108.1)
1986	537,602 (81.3)	336,223 (99.0)	873,825 (87.3)
1987	371,952 (69.2)	340,768 (101.4)	712,720 (81.6)
1988	401,470 (107.9)	355,247 (104.2)	756,717 (106.2)

Sourced: Same as Table 3-1.

imports, levels which are rather minimal considering that both countries are the second and third largest economies in the world. The Soviet share in exports has exhibited a considerable decline recently compared to the early 1980s when it exceeded 2%. By contrast, the Soviet share in imports has shown some gains in the 1980s. However, the recent share of 1.5% is lower than the 1.8% recorded in the late 1970s.

Finally, we should look at the levels of Japanese trade with the Soviet Union in a global context. Table 3-4 serves that purpose. The table shows the values of exports and imports of the individual OECD countries in recent years. The 1988 figures for OECD total and for some countries refer to the January–September period. Thus, we calculated the country share based on 1987 statistics. In absolute terms, Japanese imports from the Soviet Union amounted to 1,987 million dollars in 1986 and 2,368 million dollars in 1987. The Japanese share in 1986 stood at 9.8% of the OECD total and ranks fourth after West Germany, France, and Italy. The picture in 1987 was not particularly different in terms of country ranking.

Table 3-3 The share of Soviet Union in total Japanese trade

(unit: million dollars, %)

Year	Total	U.S.S.R	U.S.A.	U.K.	China
Exports					
1980	129,807	2,778 (2.14)	31,367	3,781	5,078
1981	152,030	3,259 (2.14)	38,609	4,879	5,095
1982	138,854	3,902 (2.81)	36,341	4,815	3,511
1983	146,927	2,821 (1.92)	42,829	4,982	4,912
1984	170,114	2,518 (1.48)	59,937	4,675	7,217
1985	175,638	2,751 (1.57)	65,278	4,723	12,477
1986	209,151	3,150 (1.51)	80,456	6,647	9,856
1987	229,221	2,563 (1.12)	83,580	8,400	8,250
1988	264,917	3,130 (1.18)	89,634	10,632	9,476
Imports					
1980	170,527	1,860 (1.32)	24,408	1,954	4,323
1981	143,290	2,021 (1.41)	25,297	2,694	5,292
1982	131,970	1,677 (1.27)	24,162	1,873	5,352
1983	126,393	1,456 (1.15)	24,647	1,940	5,087
1984	136,503	1,394 (1.02)	26,862	2,267	5,958
1985	129,539	1,429 (1.10)	27,793	1,817	6,483
1986	126,408	1,972 (1.56)	29,054	3,573	5,652
1987	149,515	2,352 (1.57)	31,490	3,057	7,401
1988	187,354	2,766 (1.48)	42,037	4,193	9,859

Source: Same as Table 3-1.

3-3 The commodity composition of Soviet exports to Japan

Next, we turn to a closer examinatioin of the commodities which the Soviets are selling to Japan. In order to examine detailed information at disaggregated level when required, and to be consistent with the observation in section 2 above, we continue to rely on Japanese trade statistics.

Table 3-5 lists total Japanese imports of major commodities for 1988 in column 1, which are compared to imports from the Soviet Union in column 2. The share of imports from the Soviet for each commodity is shown in column 3 in percentage. Needless to say, this indicates the relative importance of the Soviet Union as a supplier for Japan. Column 4 shows the structure of the purchases from the Soviet Union, also in percentage terms taking total imports from the Soviet Union as 100%.

According to the Japanese source, Japanese dependence on the Soviet Union as a supplier was 1.48% in 1988. As for major commodity categories, the Soviets are supplying 0.9% of foodstuffs, 1.4% of textile raw materials, 0.5% of metallic raw materials, 4.0% of chemicals, less than 0.1% of machinery, and 1.9% of other manufactured goods such as nonferrous metals. On the aggregate level, therefore, we may say that the Soviets are supplying rather limited portions of Japanese purchases from abroad.

On an individual commodity level, the Soviet shares stand at 6.9%

Table 3-4 OECD trade with the Soviet Union

(unit: million dollars, %)

	Exports			Imports		
Country	1986	1987	1988	1986	1987	1988
OECD total	20,592.0 (100.0)	20,616.0 (100.0)	*17,709.0	20,352.0 (100.0)	22,884.0 (100.0)	*17,361.0
OECD Europe	14,592.0 (70.9)	15,456.0 (75.0)	*12,291.0	17,784.0 (87.4)	20,052.0 (87.6)	*14,805.0
EC total	9,708.0 (47.1)	10,608.0 (51.5)	*8,574.0	13,164.0 (64.7)	14,964.0 (65.4)	*11,331.0
Denmark	184.3 (0.9)	120.6 (0.6)	161.8	205.0 (1.0)	211.0 (0.9)	177.2
U.K.	790.8 (3.8)	802.8 (3.9)	909.6	1,018.8 (5.0)	1,430.4 (6.3)	1,302.0
Ireland	60.7 (0.3)	32.2 (0.2)	24.5	41.5 (0.2)	48.5 (0.2)	51.4
Netherlands	333.6 (1.6)	410.4 (2.0)	476.4	1,045.2 (5.7)	1,364.4 (6.0)	1,130.4
Belgium	495.6 (2.4)	490.8 (2.4)	*419.4	1,047.6 (5.1)	1,281.6 (5.6)	*960.3
France	1,532.4 (7.4)	1,752.0 (8.5)	1,948.8	2,647.2 (13.0)	2,539.2 (11.1)	2,809.2
Germany	4,320.0 (21.0)	4,378.8 (21.2)	5,366.4	4,203.6 (20.7)	3,998.4 (17.5)	3,913.2
Italy	1,618.8 (7.9)	2,197.2 (10.7)	*1,561.2	2,323.2 (11.4)	2,836.8 (12.4)	*2,261.7
Portugal	51.2 (0.2)	56.9 (0.3)	*28.0	51.2 (0.3)	48.7 (0.2)	*31.6
Spain	237.8 (1.2)	294.7 (1.4)	267.0	299.4 (1.4)	883.7 (3.9)	1,111.7
Greece	77.6 (0.4)	76.0 (0.4)	—	284.5 (1.4)	324.8 (1.4)	—
OECD outside Europe	6,003.6 (29.2)	5,160.0 (25.0)	*5,418.0	2,574.0 (12.6)	2,832.0 (12.4)	*2,556.0
Canada	880.8 (4.3)	606.0 (2.9)	933.6	18.0 (0.0)	26.4 (0.1)	128.4
U.S.A.	1,248.0 (6.1)	1,479.6 (7.2)	2,767.2	558.0 (2.7)	424.8 (1.9)	578.4
Japan	3,178.8 (15.4)	2,587.2 (12.5)	*2,438.1	1,987.2 (9.8)	2,367.6 (10.3)	*2,091.6

Notes: Some of the 1988 figures (marked by an asterisk) are provisional, referring only to the January-September period.
Source: Organisation for Economic Cooperation and Development, Statistics of Foreign Tradaı (A). Cited from MITI, *International Trade White Paper, 1988*, p. 718.

for nonferrous metals, 7.6% for heavy fuel oils, 8.5% for wood, and 7.2% for coal (7.1% for coking coal and 6.3% for oradinary coal). A share of 6.4% is recorded for iron and steel scrap, but total amount is rather limited at 28 million dollars.

Let us look at the commodity structure of Soviet exports to Japan. As we see in column 4 of Table 3-5, major items are wood, mineral fuels (coals and petroleum products), and nonferrous metals. The share of wood in 1988 stood at 21.8%. Mineral fuels have kept their share at about 18.1%, which is comparable to the previous year. In 1987, considerable gains were noted in the share of heavy fuel oils which increased more than 57% over the 1986 level despite the fact that other commodities in this category more or less remained at the same level. 1988 figure was slightly lower, though. Fish and shellfish now account for 9.7% of total Soviet sales to Japan. This item also recorded considerable gains in 1987, and the growth rate over the previous year reached about 37%, which tapered off in 1988.

One important development is the gain in nonferrous metals. The annual rate of increase of this category amounted to 76.9% in 1987. On an individual commodity level, for instance, Soviet exports of platinum increased 3.1 fold, nickel and its alloy 3.0 fold, palladium 32.8%, and aluminum 37.1%. Gold (for non-coin use) is recorded among the "transactions n.e.c.", and of the 440 million dollars worth of transactions which are entered in this item, 430 million dollars are attributed to gold.[6] The Soviet sales of gold, which increased 2.5 fold during the previous year, increased by 11.0% in 1987. The Soviet exported 335 million dollars worth gold in 1988.

Thus, as for the commodity composition of the Soviet exports to Japan, we may say that it is still concentrated on primary commodities. The share of manufactured goods has jumped from 23.0% in 1986 to 31.9% in 1987 and to 32.9% in 1988, but, even here, the share of chemical goods and machinery remain limited, and the bulk is composed of various metals and, to a smaller degree, to wood chips, which also are closely related to primary commodities.

3-4 Soviet machinery exports to Japan

Apart from the overall structure of Soviet exports to Japan, it is interesting to examine the trends in technology-intensive items. It is widely known that recent expansion of world trade is largely attributable to increased demand in this category. This is a reflection of the world economy which is becoming increasingly intertwined in the international division of labor, not only in a vertical fashion, but, more impor-

Table 3-5 Composition of imports from the Soviet Union, 1988

(unit: million dollars, %)

	Total imports of commodity	from Soviet Union	(% of commodity category total)	(% of Soviet total
Grand total	187,357	2,766	(1.48)	(100.00)
Foodstuffs	29,120	286	(0.98)	(10.34)
Meat	4,313	275	(6.37)	(9.94)
Fish & shellfish	10,461	269	(2.5)	(9.73)
Cereals & cereal preparations	4,241			
Feedstuffs	1,225	9	(0.73)	(0.32)
Spirituous beverages	855	1	(0.11)	(0.04)
Tobacco	1,150	0	(0)	(0)
(Raw materials)	28,040	731	(2.61)	(26.43)
Textile raw materials	3,309	45	(1.36)	(1.63)
Wool	1,447	1	(0.06)	(0.04)
Cotton	1,318	34	(2.58)	(1.23)
Metallic raw materials	8,488	38	(0.45)	(1.37)
Iron ore	2,853			
Iron & steel scrap	436	28	(6.42)	(1.01)
Nonferrous metal ore	4,104	4	(0.10)	(0.14)
Other raw materials	16,243	647	(3.98)	(23.39)
Raw hides & skins	760	0	(0.07)	(0)
Soy beans	1,426			
Wood	7,122	604	(8.48)	(21.84)
Salt	167			
Animal & vegetable oils & fats	407	2	(0.49)	(0.07)
Pulp	1,980	4	(0.20)	(0.14)
Mineral fuels	38,356	500	(1.30)	(18.08)
Coal	5,421	389	(7.18)	(14.06)
Coking coal	4,123	294	(7.13)	(10.63)
Ordinary coal	1,143	72	(6.30)	(2.60)
Crude & partly refined oils	18,852	6	(0.03)	(0.22)
Petroleum products	6.955	104	(1.50)	(3.76)
Petroleum spirits	2,922			
Hevy fuel oils	1,165	88	(7.55)	(3.18)
Liguefied gases	7,128			
(Manufactured goods)	85,599	910	(1.06)	(32.90)
Chemical goods	14,830	57	(0.38)	(2.06)
Organic compounds	4,555	14	(0.31)	(0.51)
Medical & pharmaceutical prod.	2,658	4	(0.14)	(0.14)
Plastic materials	1,474	3	(0.20)	(0.11)
Machinery	26,661	11	(0.04)	(0.40)
General machinery	9,322	9	(0.10)	(0.33)
Electrical machinery	9,289	1	(0.01)	(0.04)
Transportation equipment	6,117	1	(0.01)	(0.04)
Precision instruments	1,934	1	(0.04)	(0.04)
Scientific & optical inst.	1,310	1	(0.06)	(0.04)
Other manufactured goods	44,108	843	(1.91)	(30.48)
Wood chips	1,069	28	(2.62)	(1.01)
Texile products	10,632	4	(0.04)	(0.14)
Clothing	6,702	0	(0)	(0)
Iron & Steel	4,624	104	(2.25)	(3.76)
Nonferrous metals	9,312	641	(6.88)	(23.17)
Furniture	1,032	0	(0)	(0)
Transactions n.e.c.	6,240	339	(5.43)	(12.26)
Gold	4,101	335	(8.17)	(12.11)

Source: Ministry of Finance, *Foreign Trade Statistics*. Compiled here from commodity by country table in MITI's *International Trade White Paper*.

Note: Only major items are listed; therefore, the sum of the individual items does not add up to total. Zeros in the table indicate small numbers. Blanks indicate no transactions. The percentages have been calculated based on statistics in terms of thousand dollars.

tantly, in a horizontal fashion. Such trend is further facilitated in the case of Japan due to rapid appreciation of the yen since 1985, and Japan has emerged as a major importer of technology-intensive items of various kinds. We have seen in previous sections that Japan's import demand is no exception despite the fact that Japan itself is a major exporter of technology-intensive items. In this regard, we intend to provide a brief description on Soviet machinery exports to Japan.

Table 3-6 provides recent trend in Japan's machinery imports (upper half) which is compared to machinery imports from the Soviet Union (lower half). Looking at the table, we realize that total Japanese machinery import is increasing quite rapidly and that the pace seems to have accelerated since 1985. Total machinery imports amounted to 12.4 billion dollars in 1985 and 26.7 billion dollars in 1988. Among the major items listed, office machinery, power-generating machinery, and precision instrument are the items of imports which have increased rather rapidly. Textile machinery also increased, but its absolute value is less than the items listed above.

As for imports from the Soviet Union, total value has not changed very much since 1984. Actual figure stood at 12 million dollars in 1984 and 10.7 million dollars in 1988. This amounts to only 0.10% and 0.04% of total Japanese machinery imports respecitively. It should be noted that the Soviet share has actually declined during this period. Soviet is not among the suppliers to Japan regarding the major items which are growing raidly. Metalworking machinery is the only exception and we have witnessed a steady increase from 4.3 million dollars in 1983 to 7.2 million dollars in 1987. This amounts to 2.3% and 2.6% of Japanese imports in respective years.

Our trade statistics seem to indicate that Soviet competitiveness in office machinery and precision instrument is a very limited one. Statistics also indicate that the Soviet producers retain relative strength in the case of metalworking machinery.

3-5 The structural mismatch

Our observation points to the fact that the Soviet Union has not fared well in the Japanese market in the recent past. The question to be asked is whether the structure of Soviet exports to Japan is suited for future expansion. We now turn to this issue.

It is perhaps appropriate here to briefly review the structural change that is taking place in the Japanese economy. Import demand is closely related to such trends. The fact that the Japanese economy is tending toward production of services is widely recognized. Services are defined here to include not only personal services but also business services, public services, wholesale and retail trade; finance, insurance, and real estate; transportation; communication; and public administration.

Employing the framework of input-output analysis, we can point out that this new trend is attributable to (1) shift of final demand to private consumption and government consumption which includes more service component, (2) changes in converters, which represent the sectoral shares in a given final demand category, which are also tending toward more services, and (3) changes in production technology, described by the input structure of each industrial sector, which is also tending toward more services as opposed to hard goods.

The third factor, when aggregated for the entire economy, indicates that the intermediate demand of industry is becoming more service-intensive and, for that matter, less resource-intensive. The share of services, widely defined, stood at 14.1% in 1960, 18.5% in 1970, 24.8% in 1980, and 26.4% in 1985.[7] It should be added that the input share of such sectors as general machinery, electrical machinery, and motor vehicles has been on the increase, also. Taking total intermediate input as 100%, the input shares increased between 1970 and 1985 from 4.2% to 5.1% for general machinery, from 4.1% to 5.1% for electrical machinery, and from 1.7% to 2.4% for motor vehicles. The sectors that require large amounts of resource inputs have become less important in the economic structure. One typical example is the primary metals including iron and steel and nonferrous metals. Their combined share in 1970 stood at 15.0%, which has now declined to 9.8%.

In order to reveal the macroeconomic relationship between economic growth and raw material requirements, we have plotted the two variables in Figure 3-1. It shows real GNE (1970 as the base year) on the horizontal axis and consumption of raw materials (also with 1970 as the base year) on the vertical axis. Since both variables are expressed as indexes, the relationship between the two variables should be plotted along the 45 degree line if the economy and resource requirement grow at the same rate, or, in economists' jargon, if the elasticity is unity. According to the figure, such a situation actually prevailed in Japan before 1973. Even after the Oil Crisis, we may say that the relation between the two variables more or less stayed on the 45 degree line although it has somehow shifted downward. In other word, this period saw a once-and-for-all type shift in resource requirement, which is presumably attributable to various conservation measures. In the 1980s, we are perhaps in an entirely new phase where economic expansion, which is represented by a continued rightward movement of the line, does not necessarily require increased resource inputs, which are represented by lack of upward movement of the line. We have witnessed a situation where the

Figure 3-1 Raw material inputs in the Japanese industry

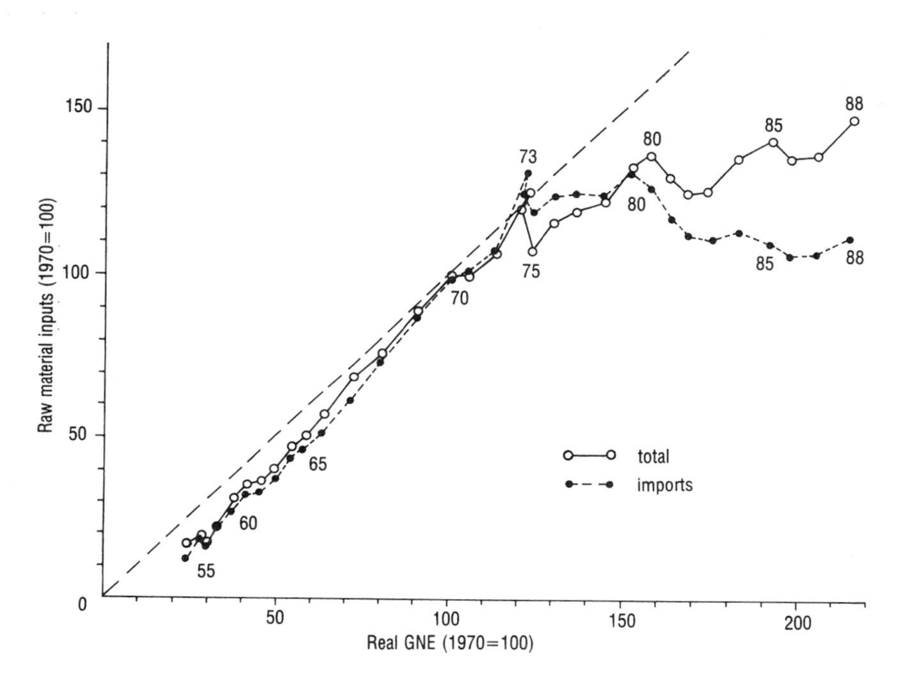

Source: Ministry of International Trade and Industry, *Indexes on Mining and Manufacturing;* Economic Planning Agency, *Annual Report on National Accounts.*

economy is expanding without increased resource inputs. It should be noted in addition that input of imported resources, which is shown by a dotted line in the figure, has been more stagnant than resources as a whole.

We can confirm the magnitude of the effect on the import trends. Table 3-7 shows quantum indexes (i.e., net of price change) of imports in recent years (with 1980 as the base year). The commodity classification follows that in Table 3-5 except that information on individual commodity level is not given here. According to the table, the growth of "other manufactured goods" surpasses all other items, and the index reached 311.3 in 1988, while "chemicals'" reached 195.8 and "machinery" 214.6. "foodstuff" imports also continued a rather rapid expansion to reach 180.2. By contrast, imports of metallic raw materials and mineral fuels stagnated and remained at 99.7 and 105.9 in 1988.[8]

It seems that the major components of Soviet export to Japan are not among the items exhibiting rapid growth. We may even say that there

Table 3-6 Soviet machinery exports to Japan

(unit: million US$)

Year	Total	Office machinery	Power generating machinery	Metal working machinery	Textile machinery	Air crafts	Vessels	Precision instrument
Total of Japanese imports								
1983	10,409	1,025	670	184	86	1,472	390	1,025
1984	12,066	1,362	939	192	114	928	665	1,257
1985	12,371	1,545	896	233	113	1,484	286	1,265
1986	14,699	1,706	897	295	134	1,777	231	1,416
1987	19,123	2,218	1,136	277	216	1,742	269	1,634
1988	26,661	3,279	1,291	436	308	2,024	256	1,934
of which imports from the Soviet Union								
1983	8.2	—	0.3	4.3	—	0.0	2.7	0.3
1984	12.0	—	0.3	4.0	—	0.0	3.7	0.4
1985	11.7	0.0	0.2	6.5	0.3	0.0	2.6	0.4
1986	10.4	0.0	0.0	6.0	0.0	—	1.8	0.4
1987	10.8	—	0.3	7.2	0.0	0.2	0.7	0.9
1988	10.7			n.a.				

Note: The figures do not add up to total because only selected items are listed. Zeros in the table indicate small numbers; — indicates no entries.
Source: Same as Table 3-5.

Table 3-7 Quantum index of imports

(unit: index, 1980 = 100)

	Total	Food stuff	Textile materials	Metallic materials	Other raw materials	Mineral fuels	Chemicals	Machinery	Other manufactured goods
1980	100.0	100.0	100.0	100.0	100.0	100.0	100.0	100.0	100.0
1981	97.8	104.8	96.3	90.5	85.4	93.3	103.6	101.2	123.0
1982	97.3	109.4	110.4	90.6	89.3	90.0	113.1	88.1	130.1
1983	98.5	112.9	99.4	87.4	93.8	89.9	124.1	94.0	127.7
1984	109.1	121.1	110.6	94.3	93.2	97.2	141.4	115.0	155.1
1985	109.5	126.0	109.5	95.5	99.3	93.7	144.0	115.7	159.4
1986	119.9	140.7	107.1	91.1	101.4	94.9	158.0	128.4	217.3
1987	131.1	161.4	128.8	90.2	112.5	98.6	177.6	150.6	238.6
1988	153.0	180.2	113.7	99.7	115.4	105.9	195.8	214.6	311.3

Source: Japan Tariff Association, *The Summary Report, Trade of Japan.*

exists a structural mismatch in the Soviet trade pattern.

Although Japanese market is rapidly expanding its importation of finished manufactured goods such as machinery and electronic products, it is unlikely that expansion of export of these items is among the realistic options for the Soviets. A most likely scenario would be continued expansion of nonferrous metals and fish products. For both items, the Soviet Union has demonstrated competence in recent years, and we can expect that the trend will continue into the future, considering both demand conditions on the Japanese side and supply conditions on the Soviet side.

3-6 Further remarks

Despite structural mismatch in Soviet exports to Japan, the potential for future expansion in economic relations between the two countries is abound. Sheer size of the two economies is enough to convince us that the absolute magnitude of trade and investment can be increased tremendously. Although in the short run, Japan's resource needs are met by existing long-term contracts with the Western and the LDC supply sources, in the long run there will be chances of shifting to new supply sources. This is particularly true for rare metals supply of which is being shifted from South Africa. In addition, there will be ample opportunities for direct investment involving consumer goods, electronics and telecommunication equipment, NC machines, etc. which the Soviets need to meet the domestic demand.

In order for the potentials to become a reality, we should examine the political and economic environment surrounding the Soviet-Japanese ties.

One is of course the prospects of the *perestroika* itself. We have pointed out that, in contrast to major changes in the political sphere, nothing tangible has been achieved in the economic front. It is not that we do not want the Soviet efforts to succeed, We are merely pointing out the difficulties in reshaping a command economy into a demand-based, incentive-oriented one. In this regard, political scientists in general tend to be more optimistic than economists. In the economists' eyes, it is an extremely difficult evolution to give decision-making power to micro-level firms. In the process, price mechanism has to be restored in goods and services market, labor market, and capital market. Whereas the Soviet economy suffers from supply shortage, serious bottlenecks have to be prevented from developing to avoid inflation and production stoppages. Planning from below has to be implemented in a system where planning from above was the rule.

On the part of the West, it is possible to facilitate the transition by supplying consumer goods in order to supplement Soviet effort to improve living standards. This will be a direct response to the will of the public in the Eastern bloc and will secure stability to the new Soviet regime. The Western industrial countries can also promote technological progress in the Soviet economy by exporting high technology equipment. Joint ventures or other forms of direct investment may work as a vehicle in technology transfer. Already there are reports of COCOM regulation being relaxed, and there have been efforts to relieve Eastern debt service.

Japanese role, in this context, is potentially quite large. There is no reason why Japan should not provide much needed capital together with technology. Japan herself is at the juncture of rediscovering her role in the world economic and political scene, and the relationship with the leader of the socialist camp is important.

Options for Japan include the following:

(a) take initiative ahead of US and EC.
(b) follow US and European moves.
(c) wait for US and EC; perhaps even wait for Korean and Chinese move.

The actual course of development is very likely the last one. Here are some reasons for my judgment.

Japan is ready to go along with her allies in a concerted effort to improve East-West relationship and facilitate economic and political transition in the Soviet Union and East European nations. But Japan has tended to shy away from any political involvement in the world scene, and have tried to limit her role in economic spheres. This is not to say that the Japanese interest lied only in business: rather, this is a reflection of the constraints within which Japan has acted since WWII. Precisely because taking initiative inevitably involves political motives, it is unlikely that she will take the lead in improving the relations with the Soviet Union. This precludes (a).

The question then is the degree of economic motives to strengthen the relations between the two countries. Here again, one cannot be overly optimistic. First, there is no direct interest involved on the part of Japan. Resource requirement has been lowered, as we have seen earlier, and the Japanese appetite for Siberian development has cooled off likewise. Reflecting structural change of the Japanese industry toward services and electronics, *Keidanren* (the Federation of Economic Organizations which mainly represents big business in heavy industry) has become less influential in a relative sense. Japan is not in a position to take the lead in relaxing COCOM regulations. This has to be done by the US and major West European countries. Partly reflecting stalement over Northern territories, public support for increased economic ties with the Soviet Union is almost nonexistent in Japan.

On top of this, the Japanese and the Soviets have been doing everything possible to keep the bilateral relations cool, if not openly hostile. Territorial issue is one. The establishment of Sino-Japanese relations which followed U.S. recognition of China added complexity. The latest development which hamper improvement of the bilateral relationship is mutual military buildup in the area. This may sound strange to the people in the U.S. or in Europe who have observed considerable change in political atmosphere. However, their impression is attributable to the fact that they are preoccupied with the development in Europe and other stages such as Afghanistan. In the Far East, however, considerable Soviet military buildup for air and sea is reported, including deployment of SS-20 and ground attack helicopters removed from Afganistan and Europe together with considerable strengthening of naval power. Japan in its turn is increasing defense spending in line with the policy of keeping it within 1% of GNP. This ceiling has been removed in recent years, but, due to strong economic growth, the debate on the 1% constraint became rather academic than real. In the Pacific, the Soviets are confronted with the U.S., China, and Korea, in addition to Japan, and they try to have adequate military capabilities to counter them. Particularly important in their eyes is Japan-U.S. joint capabilities. The Japanese in their turn interpret that the Soviet capabilities are directed at them. In addition, Japan is asked by the U.S. to share the burden, which is another factor for Japan to be spending more for defense.

How to define Japan's international economic relations with explicit recognition of Soviet presence in the Pacific is a hard question. The area is not well defined in terms of power balance. The point is that, unlike Europe where the NATO and the Warsaw Pact nations achieved some sort of power balance with precise knowledge of the intention of the other side, we still have perception gap as well as (actual or perceived) disequilibrium in military capabilities.

Adding to the difficulty is the fact that the Japanese leadership not very imaginative. This may have been traditionally so after the WWII. In order to stay merely an economic power and avoid being a political or military power, the mindset of the Japanese leadership has been confined to the commercial field. This means that political decision has to be imposed upon the Japanese leadership. The popular support has dwindled due to the Recruit scandal (bribe taking or misconduct very close to it) and the introduction of a new sales tax (this contrary to election campaign). The power base of the Japanese leading political party has been weakened in recent years because of the urbanization of the population. Their platform is generally understood to be intended for farming population and small merchants, and not for urban dwellers.

On the part of Korea, which is in the process of industrial expansion, while at the same time seeking diplomatic gains against North Korea, there is every reason to establish economic ties with the Soviet Union. In fact, these two countries have agreed to mutually establish trade offices. Korean expectation is to develop and import raw materials and energy from Siberia.[9]

After easing of tension, both China and the Soviet Union are to gain from border trade. China can sell consumer goods while importing parts etc. for the machinery and equipment bought from the Soviet Union in the 1950s and 1960s.

Despite all the foreseeable difficulties, however, there is a sign of improvement in the Soviet-Japanese relations. The signal seems to be coming mainly from the Soviet side. The Soviets are hopeful to obtain capital and technology from Japan in order to accelerate economic development in the Far East. In December 1988, the Soviets have revised the law concerning joint ventures, the main points being that the share of the foreign participants can be determined by mutual agreement, foreign managers can be accepted in the venture, wages and employment can be determined by the firm, and profit can be paid in foreign currencies and can be remitted overseas.[10] According to a press report, there are 705 joint ventures in the Soviet Union as of August 4, 1989, of which about 80 are from West Germany, about 70 from Finland, 50 from the United States, and only 15 from Japan.[11] The Soviets are also hopeful about establishing a special trade zone in the Far East where joint venture firms can be accomodated. Preferential treatment for imports, such as lower tariffs, may be envisaged under such arrangements. Unlike the Chinese case, the joint ventures with the Soviet Union is intended to satisfy domestic demand rather than export.

In discussing the Soviet-Japanese economic relations, it has long been believed that resource endowment for the two neighboring countries is complimentary. Japan, which lacks natural resources but has become increasingly competitive in machinery production, seems to be an ideal trading partner for the Soviets. Actually, however, it has been proven that merely looking at each other across virtually empty terrain was not much help in promoting trade. The national boundaries are very far from the political and economic power centers in the two countries. Long-distance inland transportation of bulky resources is not particularly desirable.

Japan continues to be a major importer of raw materials but the market for this category is not expanding. For some commodities, the market is even shrinking in quantitative terms.

An added problem for the Soviet Union is the general decline of raw material prices in the 1980s. By 1985, unit value of mineral fuels had declined to about 90% of the 1980 level in the world market.[12] By 1987, the average was further reduced to about 50%. The Soviet Union cannot be immune to such world-wide trends.

However, the fact remains that Japan and the Soviet Union rank second and third in economic size, respectively. Given a regime in Moscow that is possibly tilting its foreign policy, we need to point out some of the issues which are left out ot this purely economic discussion.

(1) The Northern Territories: The term refers to four islands including Kunashiri, Etorofu, Shikotan, and the Habomais which lie south of the Kurils. The continued Soviet occupation of the Northern Territories constitutes a major stumbling block in developing economic ties between the two countries. As Kenichi Ito puts it, "the possibility of a

linkage beetween the Northern Territories and economic cooperation is discussed often in Japan."[13] There are two approaches to the issue in Japan, one being the "entrance theory" which sees the territorial issue as the entrance to Japan-Soviet relations, a position shared by the Japanese government, and the other the "exit theory" which claims that the issue will be solved as a result of improved relations between the two countries.

In October 1988, it was reported that the Japanese Foreign Ministry had decided to suspend a planned economic mission organized by both government and business circles.[14] According to the press report, the Japanese side refrained from discussing timing and members of the mission unless some concrete progress is made on the territorial issue by Shevardnaze's visit to Japan in December. The mission was to consist of higher level representatives and to be followed up by vists of eight lower level teams. This is a clear case where the "entrance theory" was applied in the formation of foreign policy toward the Soviet Union. The Japanese side is apparently trying to use its economic and technological achievement to enhance its bargaining power.

It is, however, an exaggeration to believe that the territorial issue is hampering the restructuring of Soviet exports to Japan.

(2) The Soviet policy in the Asia-Pacific region: In April 1986, the Soviet government issued a statement that the USSR is considering a new policy towards Asia, followed up by Gorbachev's speech in July that year. According to an observer, "while the USSR is calling for new state-to-state relationships in Asia (further rapproachment with China and Japan), they are actually intensifying their campaign against the deepening alliances in the Washington-Tokyo-Seoul triangle."[15]

Against this background, the Soviet Union has decided to enter into official trade relations with South Korea by mutually opening trade offices. This signifies political recognition of Korea by the Soviets and opens up the possibility of enhancing economic ties through resources and energy development in the Soviet Far East and Siberia.

Korea is still in the process of rapid industrial expansion. Although Japanese demand for Soviet raw materials has tapered off reflecting the structural change of the economy, Korea's participation in the picture may actually enhance the prospects for economic cooperation in resource development.

(3) COCOM and high-tech trade: For the business world in the West, political complexity is a real barrier in expanding trade, especially when the market is small to begin with. Added to the difficulty is the uncertainty surrounding exports of manufactured goods. COCOM is seen among Japanese businessmen as somewhat ambiguous in its stipulation and somewhat arbitrary in its implementation. The lack of trans-

parency surrounding COCOM regulation thus represents a real hazard for the Japanese business. Unavailability of official finance in the case of plant exportation may seem a nominal constraint because commercial credit should now be readily available, but in the eyes of commercial banks, denial of official finance signifies some added economic uncertainty, in addition to being a clear political barrier.

Such barriers in trade, although a real one, solely concern Western exports to the East. The trade restriction is practically nonapplicable to Soviet exports to the West including Japan.

(4) Organizational problems: This refers to the fact that the Soviets conduct state trade whereas Japanese trade is left to private firms. The two systems tend to differ in time horizon in dealing with business transactions; they also have different sensitivity to risks and uncertainties. As a result, while the Soviet trade authority is willing to take up long-term development plans which necessitate huge investment, their Japanese partners tend to shy away from such projects. This is one of the reasons why Japanese firms generally expect to be covered by some political umbrella such as extensiion of credit by government-backed financial institutions, official agreement or statement by the two governments, or joint venture with a third country such as the United States.

However, unlike the case of natural resource development, organizational differences do not seem to constitute a major obstacle in import business for such items as machinery because detailed specification and terms of delivery can be agreed upon at the time of concluding contract, thus, minimizing risks and uncertainties. Economic security was one of the concerns in deciding the sources of supply for energy and other natural resources. Here again, given the relatively small percentage in total machinery imports, the transactions will be regarded as purely economic.

Japan is running a trade surplus with the Soviet Union. As we have seen in the preceding sections, the Soviet export structure is not well suited to the changing Japanese demand. Under such circumstances, the Soviet foreign trade policy which requires bilateral balance rather than global equilibrium, and the Soviet inability to promote exports even when it wanted to resort to global balance strategy abandoning traditional policy, poses some constraints in expanding the Soviet-Japanese trade.

Political constraint is a real one, making it difficult for government officials to take initiatives in easing tension because it is certainly more comfortable to continue the status-quo for the bureaucracies in the two countries. Not only that, it would take a lot of persuation in order to turn the public opinion in Japan which is generally not particularly warm to the northern neighbor. It has been relatively easy to take advantage of this situation for political purposes.

Even allowing for such factors, however, we may conclude that the Soviet export performance (not import) is largely determined by economic factors. It is the lack of attractive products which is hampering the expansion of Soviet exports. A most likely development in the Soviet exports to Japan is increased contribution of nonferrous metals. Japanese importation of this item has been on the increase reflecting the shift in the industrial demand. The Soviets apparently have competitiveness for this item in the world market reflecting rich resource endowment.

When it comes to technology-intensive items such as machinery, the Soviets do not seem to enjoy competitive edge, according to our examination of trade statistics between the two countries. What should be the policy prescription if the Soviet machinery export to Japan is to be promoted? In economic relationship with the other parts of the world including NICs and the United States, Japan's direct foreign investment worked as a vehicle not only transferring capital but also technology. Japanese imports from those areas are exploding as a result. Industrial standards and design are also important ingredients in accepting goods produced abroad, and this problem can be solved by direct foreign investment. Some arrangements to locate Japanese-managed production facilities in the Soviet Union may be desirable in this regard. There are problems including lack of experienced labor force in the Soviet Union (especially in the area closer to Japan), and lack of parts producing industry, but experience elsewhere has proven that such problems are not unsurmountable.

Footnotes:

1 See Uno (1983a).

2 This point is explained in Smith (1987). The pertinent projects include the Soviet Far East Forest Resources Development Project (1968), the Wrangel Port Construction Project (1970), the Ship and Pulp Development Project (1971), the South Yakutsk Coal Development Project (1974), the Soviet Far East Forest Resources Development Project—Phase II (1974), the Yakutsk Natural Gas Project (1974), and the Sakhalin Continental Shelf Oil and Gas Project (1975).

3 Here I have in mind the discussion which took place at a conference "The Fall of the Soviet Empire:" Prospects for Transition to a Post-Soviet World, August 1985 in Geneva, Switzerland. Despite prevalence of collapse story among political scientists, Alec Nove, for example, commneted that "It is true also that some Western commentators exaggerate Soviet economic weakness (while simultaneously exaggerating Soviet military strength), which produces various kinds of wishful thinking about the 'fall of the Soviet empire', and policies designed to speed this collapse by speeding up the arms race." Alec Nove, "Is a Within-System Reform Possible," 1985, p.2. Peter Wiles took

a similar line when he observed that "the 'Soviet Empire' is not 'falling': it is stumbling, and stumbling slowly forward." Peter Wiles, "The Second Economy and the Economic Crisis in the USSR," 1985, p.10.

4 "A major additional obstacle is constituted by the military. Even in a report not intended for publication, Zaslavskaya could not even mention the military-industrial complex. Yet in the short run this is a double problem for the reformers. Firstly, the arms industry is evidently a sector which benefits from central planning. And, secondly, the military are beneficiaries of centrally imposed priorities, which are of particularly vital importance when the economy as a whole suffers from chronic shortages. Alec Nove, ibid., pp.,13–14."

5 Peter Wiles, ibid., pp.2–6.

6 In quantitative terms, a slight decrease was recorded; th 1987 figure stood at 29.1 tons as compared to 34.0 tons in 1986. The gold recorded here is not for coinage. See MITI, *International Trade White Paper, 1988*, (detailed description volume), p.717.

7 Uno, [1989a], pp.31–33.

8 The Indexes of Raw Materials Consumption and Inventory is compiled monthly by the Ministry of International Trade and Industry. 262 items for consumption and 204 items for inventory are selected from among the items inquired as raw materials in the *Current Production Statistics Survey* of MITI.

9 *Japan Economic Journal* (Japanese), December 17, 1988.

10 *Japan Economic Journal* (Japanese), August 14, 1989.

11 ibid.

12 The official price of Arabian light reached 32.0 dollers per barrel in November 1980 and further increased to 34.0 dollars in October 1981. The official price was reduced to 28.0 dollars per barrel in February 1985, with actual market price hovering around 15 dollars per barrel. The 1987 official price was posted at 17.52 dollars per barrel, with actual price tending toward 18 dollars.

13 Ito [1988], p.38.

14 *Japan Economic Journal* (Japanese), October 29, 1988.

15 Akino [1987], p.423.

Part 2

Technology

Chapter 4. The impact of research and development

4-1 Introduction

Technology is one of the key factors in understanding today's international economic relations, and economic relations, in turn, portray significant political implications. Such is the case in East-West as well as in North-South context, not to speak of relations among industrialized countries.

"Japanese companies are now investing more in R&D than in plant and equipment. High-tech firms are spending on average 80% more on R&D than plant and equipment. When R&D expenses are greater than capital investment in many companies, we need to rethink what manufacturing companies are. Today's leading Japanese firms have entered the stage where they survive by adapting to the changing environment, based on consistent, dependable R&D. The corporate archetype is, therefore, changing from producing organization to thinking organization." "These ratios, for example, are 2.04 for Hitachi, and 1.30 for NEC. In other words, these companies are spending 104% or 30% more on R&D than on plant and equipment. The average R&D/Capital ratio of the top 50 Japanese manufacturing companies makes 1.29. In other words, on average, the major Japanese manufacturing companies are spending 29% more on R&D than equipment." [Kodama, 1990]

The national total figures for all manufacturing companies are provided by the same author (Table 4-1). Few words on data sources are in order. The R&D expenditure figures are from the Statistical Bureau, Management and Coordination Agency, which carries out *Survey of Research and Development*. This source is based on annual surveys which covers all the firms in manufacturing, transportaion, communication, and public utilities with capital of one billion yen and over, all the firms which conducted research in the previous survey, and samples from all the rest. The number of the sample totals 12,650 firms in the case of the survey conducted in 1989. Capital investment figures are from the Ministry of International Trade and Industry's *Plant and Equipment Investment Plans in Major Industries*, which is based on about 1,500 firms in the case of the 1990 survey. Although the latter has the advantage of providing sectoral details, the figures are considerably smaller than the SNA figures.[1] We should keep in mind that the R&D/capital investment ratio in the table tend to exaggerate reality. However, one can also say that since R&D is carried out by larger firms, R&D figures among the firms comparable to those in the samples of the latter survey may not be much different from the ones obtained from much larger samples.

Table 4-1 R&D expenditures compared with capital investment in the Japanese manufacturing firms

(unit: billion yen, ratio)

Year	R&D Expenditures (¥billion)	Capital Investment (¥billion)		R&D/Capital Ratio	
	(a)	(b)	(c)	(b/a)	(c/a)
1980	2,896	4,651	4,372	0.62	0.66
1981	3,374	5,161	4,784	0.65	0.71
1982	3,756	5,099	4,727	0.74	0.79
1983	4,257	4,762	4,352	0.89	0.98
1984	4,777	5,788	5,285	0.83	0.90
1985	5,544	6,110	5,469	0.91	1.01
1986	5,740	4,896	4,343	1.17	1.32
1987	6,101	4,860	4,151	1.26	1.47

Note: R&D figures are from Management and Coodination Agency, *Report on the Survey of Reserch and Development;* capital investment figures are from MITI, *Plant and Equipment Investment Plans in Major Industries.*
Source: Kodama [1990].

The table provides two series for capital investment, namely columns (b) and (c); the former being total investment in plant and equipment and the latter adjusted to exclude R&D-related investment. It is shown that the Japanese firms spent 6.10 trillion yen for R&D and 4.15 trillion yen for capital investment. The ratio of the two stood at 1.47. In 1980, the ratio was calculated to be 0.66. As long as calculation is based on the two data sources employed here, the reversal occurred in 1985 when the ratio exceeded unity for the first time.

The concept of capital formation traditionally refers to tangible assets. However, there is an increasing recognition of the fact that unless we measure the intangible capital assets together with tangibles, we are indeed committing a serious error in assessing the performance of our economies. For example, Thomas Juster conceptualized the capital stock as including the following five categories.[2]

K1: tangible capital assets (equipment and structure)
K2: intangible capital assets (knowledge)
K3: human capital assets (skills and talents)
K4: physical environmental assets (air, river, ocean, and cities)
K5: socio-political environmental assets (equity, security, privacy, and freedom)

When it comes to actually measuring knowledge per se, however, we encounter a major problem. This is so either in terms of technological level or the effort to improve it. In fact, despite its importance, it is next to impossible to construct a generally acceptable measure of technology pertinent to a specific country or for international comparions. Rather than focusing on a particular aspect of technology, we are looking at the technological aspect of an economy from various viewpoints in this series of work. In this chapter, we examine a country's effort devoted to technology based on proxy variables representing the outcome of such

Table 4-2 R&D expenditures and number of researchers in major countries

Country	F.Y.	R&D expenditures: National currency (million)	R&D expenditures: billion yen	Government funds (%)	Government funds excluding defense R&D (%)	R&D Expenditures as percent of gross national product (%)	R&D Expenditures as percent of national income (%)	Researchers (persons)	Researchers per 1,000 population (persons)	R&D Expenditures per researcher (thousand yen)
Japan	1985	—	8116.4	19.4	18.8	2.53	3.19	381,282	3.1	21290
	1986	—	8415.0	19.6	19.0	2.52	3.18	405,554	3.3	20750
	1987	—	9016.2	19.9	19.3	2.57	3.29	418,337	3.4	21550
	1988	—	9775.2	18.4	17.7	2.62	3.35	441,876	3.6	22120
U.S.A.	1985	107,757	25700.0	47.9	29.4	2.69	3.03	772,700	3.2	33260
	1986	112,497	18955.7	48.3	26.3	2.66	2.94	791,100	3.3	23960
	1987	118,782	17175.9	48.2	26.8	2.62	2.94	806,200	3.3	21300
	1988	126,115	16167.9	48.0	27.3	2.59	2.89	—	—	—
West Germany	1985	51,598	4181.0	38.4	35.2	2.80	3.19	143,627	2.4	29110
	1986	53,516	4153.4	37.5	34.3	2.75	3.13	—	—	—
	1987	56,860	4575.5	37.7	34.4	2.81	—	—	—	—
France	1985	96,198	2819.1	53.7	42.2	2.27	2.60	102,336	1.9	27480
	1986	105,917	2755.6	53.2	41.5	2.29	2.62	104,953	1.9	27460
	1987	120,200	2964.1	52.4	40.1	2.30	2.64	109,359	2.0	26700
	1988	130,500	2807.1	50.9	36.8	—	—	—	—	—
U.K.	1983	6,583.1	(2371.9)	(48.9)	(26.9)	(2.16)	(2.45)	(94,000)	(1.7)	(25230)
	1985	7,919.1	2448.6	42.2	17.9	2.22	2.56	89,974	1.6	27210
	1986	8,777.8	2169.9	38.5	17.2	2.29	2.70	—	—	—
U.S.S.R.	1984	27,600	7711.4	47.2	—	—	4.85	1,463,800	5.3	5270
	1985	28,600	8860.3	47.0	—	—	4.95	1,491,300	5.4	5940
	1986	29,500	7268.8	48.3	—	—	5.02	1,500,500	5.4	4840
	1987	32,800	7881.9	46.8	—	—	5.47	1,517,900	5.4	5190

Source: Science and Technology Agency, *Indicators of Science and Technology*.

Table 4-3 R&D expenditures by sector

(unit: million yen)

Organi-zation / F.Y.	Total	%	Industry	%	Research institutes	%	Universities and colleges	%
1970	1,195,328	100.0	823,265	68.9	154,619	12.9	217,444	18.2
1971	1,345,919	100.0	895,020	66.5	200,466	14.9	250,433	18.6
1972	1,586,708	100.0	1,044,928	65.9	252,885	15.9	288,896	18.2
1973	1,980,896	100.0	1,301,927	65.7	320,740	16.2	358,229	18.1
1974	2,421,367	100.0	1,589,053	65.6	387,073	16.0	445,241	18.4
1975	2,621,827	100.0	1,684,847	64.3	420,699	16.0	516,281	19.7
1976	2,941,373	100.0	1,882,231	64.0	471,489	16.0	587,654	20.0
1977	3,233,543	100.0	2,109,500	65.2	494,345	15.3	629,698	19.5
1978	3,569,953	100.0	2,291,002	64.2	566,333	15.9	712,618	20.0
1979	4,063,627	100.0	2,664,913	65.6	621,032	15.3	777,683	19.1
1980	4,683,768	100.0	3,142,256	67.1	717,612	15.3	823,900	17.6
1981	5,363,986	100.0	3,629,793	67.7	848,834	15.8	885,359	16.5
1982	5,881,539	100.0	4,039,018	68.7	894,310	15.2	948,211	16.1
1983	6,503,737	100.0	4,560,127	70.1	915,254	14.1	1,028,356	15.8
1984	7,176,511	100.0	5,136,634	71.6	976,102	13.6	1,063,775	14.8
1985	8,116,399	100.0	5,939,947	73.2	1,101,041	13.6	1,075,410	13.2
1986	8,414,993	100.0	6,120,163	72.7	1,172,966	13.9	1,121,864	13.3
1987	9,016,186	100.0	6,494,268	72.0	1,312,340	14.6	1,209,579	13.4
1988	9,775,165	100.0	7,129,318	73.9	1,316,296	13.5	1,239,551	12.7

Source: Same as table 4-2.

effort and input which went into it, or the number of patent application and R&D expenditures, respectively.

4-2 R&D and its benefits

Research and development are the main contributing factors to knowledge production. An attempt is made in this section to derive benefit of R&D accrued to individual industrial sector and final demand.

Before we start the task, we refer to a series of tables for summary view of R&D activities. There exist some misconceptions commonly held among many observers outside Japan regarding the organizational structure of the Japanese economy, and R&D is no exception.

First, it is commonly held that Japanese industrial policy, envisaged and implemented by the Ministry of International Trade and Industry (MITI), is the key to Japanese advance. "Targetting" by the public sector may have existed particularly during the capital-scarce high-growth era. It was also required during the high-growth era in order to maintain sectoral balance in a rapidly changing industrial structure and avoid bottle necks from emerging. This ceased to be true in the past two decades. To be exact, government policy and guidance still exist but its effectiveness has been eroded to a considerable extent.[3] One of the main reasons is the shift of the Japanese economy into capital-abundant phase in contrast to capital-scarce phase which characterized most ot the rapid industrialization period. As is widely known, the single most effective means of conveying official message to the private sector was through capital rationing. Depite relative scarcity of capital, interest rate was kept at an artificially low level for the sake of international competitivenes of the industry, which of course gave rise to excess demand of investment fund. This situation provided a leverage on the government side, which was effectively utilized in favor of the strategic sectors. The situation today is fundamentally different.

Contrary to popular belief, 80% of R&D spending in Japan is financed by the private sector. Table 4-2 provides a summary view on R&D activities in major industrial countries in terms of expenditures and researchers. The absolute amount of expenditures are converted to yen terms for comparison based on prevailing rate of exchange. (Note that, for example, U.S. expenditures are increasing constantly in dollar terms but not so after the conversion.) The gist here is the share of government funds, especially nonmilitary portion of it. The table reveals that in Japan, the share of government funds is exceptionally small among major industrial countries, and nearly all of government funding is nonmilitary. This situation somewhat resembles the German case, although the

Table 4-4 R&D expenditures by purpose

F.Y.	Organization / Purpose	Nuclear energy development	Space development	Ocean development	Information processing	Environment protection	Total
1983	Total	314,443	116,146	44,454	289,605	144,103	908,751
	Industry	60,011	27,692	11,032	241,500	104,128	444,363
	Research institutes	230,081	66,410	25,801	37,579	28,757	388,628
	Universities and colleges	24,351	22,044	7,621	10,526	11,218	75,760
1984	Total	317,295	121,285	37,583	388,189	139,480	1,003,832
	Industry	62,689	19,349	9,256	343,641	101,199	536,134
	Research institutes	234,615	82,521	21,152	33,604	28,405	400,297
	Universities and colleges	19,991	19,415	7,175	10,944	9,876	67,401
1985	Total	348,574	151,972	40,627	449,407	149,932	1,140,512
	Industry	62,043	30,308	9,714	401,527	108,446	612,038
	Research institutes	265,727	107,056	23,498	35,144	30,419	461,844
	Universities and colleges	20,804	14,608	7,415	12,746	11,067	66,630
1986	Total	399,852	158,677	50,672	492,795	151,605	1,253,601
	Industry	67,182	42,770	20,210	444,371	107,384	681,917
	Research institutes	310,857	99,988	22,915	31,337	32,777	497,874
	Universities and colleges	21,813	15,919	7,547	17,087	11,444	73,810
1987	Total	421,165	171,042	61,195	604,671	154,520	1,412,593
	Industry	67,456	38,911	17,774	554,455	105,066	783,662
	Research institutes	329,933	113,440	33,173	30,930	36,972	544,448
	Universities and colleges	23,776	18,691	10,248	19,286	12,482	84,483
1988	Total	449,687	177,927	58,395	744,708	170,436	1,601,153
	Industry	73,203	37,508	15,182	697,728	119,834	943,455
	Research institutes	354,291	115,828	30,869	25,468	37,257	563,713
	Universities and colleges	22,193	24,591	12,344	21,512	13,345	93,985

Source: Same as table 4-2.

share of government funding is considerably larger there.

As for spending, 72 to 73% of total expenditures are dispersed by industry (the difference is spent by research institutions or universities under research contracts with industrial sector) (Table 4-3). This figure is exactly the same as in the United States, where the industry disperses 73% of R&D expenditures.[4] The ratio is uniformly higher than in major European countries. If one holds the view that Japanese research efforts is led by the government, it has to be corrected accordingly.

One many say that the government can take initiative in R&D without actually paying for it. The government coodinates various research efforts in Japan, and there have been successful cases. Even in those cases, on should not forget that this achievement was not possible without initial efforts from the private sector. It is not so much due to the unilateral foresight or decision by the public sector. Research consortiums are often formed in Japan to coordinate research efforts and to diffuse economic risks involved. Even then, considerable portion of research fund and staff came from the private sector. In other words, the involvement of the private sector, with their careful scrutiny as to economic feasibility and timing of the research, was one of the key factors in the successful cases.

Second, it is commonly held that in three categories of R&D including basic, applied, and development, Japan is deliberately focusing on the last phase, and that this assured quick commercial success. The implication is that she is free-riding the basic research conducted by someone else and concentrating on the last stage which is more directly related to industrial production. If the argument is aimed at pointing out that imported technology played an important role in Japanese economic development, it is quite right. However, if it is intended to describe the current situation, it is misguided. The share of basic research in total R&D expenditure in Japan stands at around 13 to 14% in the 1980s without a particular time trend. The comparable ratio in the United States stood at 12 to 14%, with some upward trend. As for R&D expenditures by industry, the share of basic research in Japan has increased from around 5.5% in early 1980s to 6.6% recently. The comparable ratio for the United States stood at around 3%, and is consistently lower than in Japan. Thus, the belief that Japan favors commercial research to the neglect of basic research is ill-founded. In conducting survey based on which these data have been derived, it may be difficult to maintain definitional consistency as to what is "basic" and what is "applied" or "developmental". But, there have been attempts to make the definition comparable at least from the Japanese perspective.

Third, let us look at the statistics on R&D expenditures by purpose (Table 4-4). Nuclear energy development, space development, ocean

Table 4-5 R&D expenditures by product field

(unit: billion yen)

Sector Name / Year	Total	Machinery	Household equipment	Communication electronics	Other electric products	Motor vehicles	Precision instrument
1970	466	44	46	71	21	57	7
1971	690	71	65	106	27	74	13
1972	819	78	68	139	37	89	14
1973	954	90	84	166	45	113	17
1974	1,204	126	95	203	58	156	22
1975	1,446	156	110	237	70	187	26
1976	1,519	149	125	231	67	187	25
1977	1,729	189	146	271	75	220	34
1978	1,928	204	133	315	89	276	52
1979	2,122	206	159	361	96	337	54
1980	2,463	240	176	422	131	378	62
1981	2,913	282	216	503	138	428	79
1982	3,372	304	271	604	180	521	88
1983	3,810	355	321	729	208	584	89
1984	4,311	407	326	906	228	652	123
1985	4,880	461	342	1,106	278	726	132
1986	5,635	496	423	1,372	264	853	154
1987	5,843	505	370	1,490	279	902	154
1988	6,194	521	394	1,613	303	890	170

Note: The samples are companies with capital of 100 million yen or more.
Source: Uno, *Fixed Capital Formation and R&D Benefit.* For data in selected years, see Appendix Tables A-1 through A-5. Original data are from Bureau of Statistics, *Report on the Survey of Research and Development.*

development, information processing, and environment protection are distinguished among research purposes. It should be noted that not all expenditures are classified by purpose. For example, in 1988, total R&D expenditure amounted to 9,676 billion yen, but the data in Table 4-4 is limited to the portion for which the purposes have been identified. Of the five purposes listed above, the largest sum is allocated to information processing (46% of the total in 1988), exceeding nuclear energy development (28%) by a large margin. Space development is gaining a considerable share in recent years and has become more or less comparable to environmental protection, which at one time was the third largest item. The spending pattern differs among organizations. For example, research institutions are responsible for nuclear energy development and space development. As for information processing, most of the expenditure (94% in 1988) is borne by industry, and this ratio has been rising. This confirms the importance of information technology for the recent technological change and industrial development.

In order to reveal the distribution of R&D expenditures by product field, we have compiled table 4-5 from the data supplied in a survey by the Bureau of Statistics. Appendix Tables A-1 through A-5 provide data for selected years. Showing spending sectors (business firm basis, defined according to major line of product) and product fields in a matrix form, this data set is valuable in knowing the diversification of research

Table 4-6 R&D benefits received

(unit: billion yen)

	total	general machinery	electrical machinery	precision instrument
(a) Intermediate demand:				
1975	1,131	96	261	15
1980	1,280	122	258	19
1985	1,786	178	457	30
1987	2,171	221	592	39
Ratio '87/'75	1.9	2.3	2.3	2.6
(b) Final demand:				
1975	945	104	375	27
1980	1,033	121	374	45
1985	1,616	157	689	69
1987	2,015	196	893	91
Ratio '87/'75	2.1	1.9	2.4	3.4
(c) Private consumption				
1975	218	0	78	9
1980	206	0	56	11
1985	292	0	79	16
1987	358	0	103	21
Ratio '87/'75	1.6	—	1.3	2.3
(d) Fixed capital formation:				
1975	331	69	161	5
1980	299	67	118	8
1985	484	84	246	14
1987	612	105	319	19
Ratio '87/'75	1.8	1.5	2.0	3.8
(e) Exports:				
1975	306	27	106	10
1980	387	41	132	19
1985	665	60	259	30
1987	823	74	337	39
Ratio '87/'75	2.7	2.7	3.2	3.7

Source: Compiled from Appendices B-1 through B-5.

activities which tends toward cross fertilization.[5] For example, more electronic goods and plastics are used in producing automobiles and ceramic engines are being experimented, and motor vehicle industry is compelled to engage in R&D in different product fields other than their traditional line of product. Put it differently, for a strategically important product like computer and electronic products, sectors such as communication, ceramics, nonferrous metals, iron and steel, precision instrument, chemicals are engaged in research.

Rearranging the data, Table 4-5 lists R&D expenditures for selected product fields which relate to machinery sectors. Particularly marked is

Table 4-7 Patent application of own nationals in major countries

	Japan	France	W. Germany	U.K.	U.S.A.	USSR
Variables	QPATN@J	QPATN@F	QPATN@G	QPATN@UK	QPATN@US	QPATN@R
1970	100,522	14,166	32,772	25,227	76,195	110,574
1971	78,425	14,962	32,874	24,771	71,089	124,034
1972	101,328	14,807	33,381	24,337	65,943	127,435
1973	115,221	13,458	31,909	22,472	66,935	110,846
1974	121,509	12,706	30,534	20,545	64,093	100,763
1975	131,118	12,110	30,198	20,842	64,445	114,455
1976	135,762	11,471	31,065	21,797	65,050	128,582
1977	135,991	11,811	30,247	21,114	62,863	121,907
1978	141,517	11,445	30,310	19,384	61,441	140,205
1979	150,623	11,303	30,879	19,468	60,535	153,799
1980	165,730	11,000	28,683	19,612	62,098	165,459
1981	191,645	10,945	29,841	20,808	62,404	149,500
1982	210,897	10,681	30,668	20,530	63,316	159,958
1983	227,707	11,147	31,658	19,893	59,391	151,970
1984	256,194	11,333	31,984	19,093	61,841	148,320
1985	274,373	12,050	32,243	19,785	63,874	165,648
1986	290,202	12,155	32,224	20,228	65,487	169,472
1987	311,006	12,695	31,663	20,193	68,671	178,082

Source: Compiled from world patent application matrix. See Appendix C for selected years. Data are from World Intellectual Property Organization (WIPO), *Industrial Property Statistics* as reported in Patent Agency, *Annual Report of the Patent Agency*.

the expansion of spending for "communication and electronics" and "precision instrument". The former has grown 22.6 times and the latter 21.4 times during the period 1970 to 1988 as compared to 13.2 times for total (the figures are not adjusted for price change). The data rearranged by product field is amenable to input-output data since the former is now closer to classification based on activities rather than establishments.

Based on data on R&D expenditures by product field, a methodology was suggested for estimating the flow of R&D benefits to individual industrial sectors and final demand items.[6] Obviously, when technological progress takes place in a particular sector owing to R&D, benefit is derived not only for the sector conducting research but also to the ones purchasing the products of this sector either as intermediate inputs or as capital goods (process innovation). The method originally employed by Terlecskyj enables us to estimate R&D expenditure which flowed into purchasing sectors by the use of input-output tables. To recapitulate, (a) due consideration is given to the time lag between R&D activities and actual production and also for imported technology; (b) the benefit received by other sectors through intermediate inputs is estimated by the output ratio to intermediate demand which is obtained from input-output tables; (c) the benefit received by individual final demand items is also estimated by the ratios of output obtainable from input-output tables; and (d) of the final demand items, the flow of R&D benefit received by other sectors through investment goods is distributed to the purchasing sectors by the ratios obtained from fixed capital formation matrix.[7]

Our next task is to employ the above data set and methodology and estimate the R&D benefit accrueing to individual industrial sectors and final demand. Appendix Tables B show some of the results in time series. Table B-1 refers to R&D benefit received through intermediate inputs to each industrial sector and Table B-2 to the benefit going to final demand. The following three tables relate to individual final demand, namely private consumption (Table B-3), fixed capital formation (Table B-4), and exports (Table B-5).

Table 4-6 is a summary of the attempt to estimate R&D benefits accrued to intermediate demand and final demand. Of the latter, further break down is given for private consumption, fixed capital formation, and exports. It is reminded here that the figures in this table are obtained from the indigenous R&D effort and technology imports, each appropriately lagged, and distributed to intermediate sectors and final demand according to the information obtained from input-output tables. Thus, they differ from the figures in Table 4-5 which pertains to annual expenditures in respective years. We note, first of all, rapid increase of benefits after 1980 whereas the period 1975–1980 did not see much

Figure 4-1 Average time required for patents acquisition

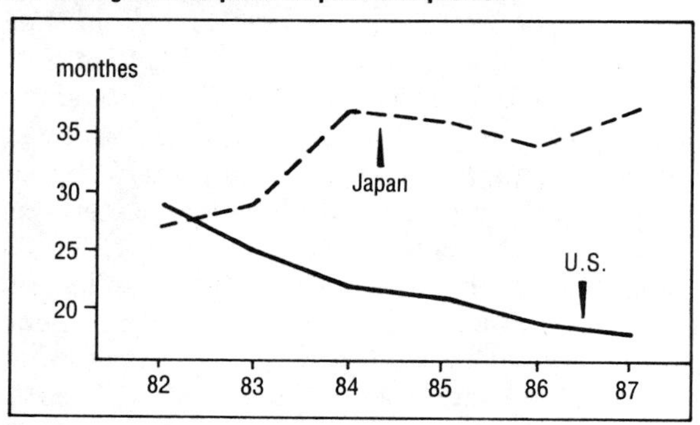

Note: Figures refer to fiscal year for Japan and calendar year for the U.S.
Source: *The Japan Economic Journal* (in Japanese), July 27, 1989.

increase. This is a reflection of rather stagnant R&D activities after the first Oil Crisis and the sluggish economy toward the end of the 1970s due to the second Oil Crisis. Secondly, we note that benefits of R&D accrueing to exports showed the most rapid increase (2.7 times in current prices between 1975 and 1987), followed by fixed capital formation (1.8 times) and private consumption (1.6 times). Benefit accrueing to total final demand increased 2.1 times and to intermediate demand, 1.9 times between 1975 and 1987.[8] Thirdly, of the machinery sectors listed in the table, the benefits accrueing from R&D in precision instrument and electrical machinery gained the most. For example, in the case of exports, it increased 3.7 times and 3.2 times, respectively. These facts point to the importance of technological progress being achieved based on electronics.

4-3 The world patent application matrix

Although it is difficult to measure technology per se, patent statistics serve as a proxy to the amount of technological knowledge produced. This may be even more true when one is interested in knowledge related to manufacturing activities. In this section, we employ a dataset on the international patent application matrix which is compiled by the World Intellectual Property Organization (WIPO). See Appendix C for detailed tabulation for selected years. The data are in a matrix form, indicating the number of patents applied for by selected countries in major foreign countries as well as at home. Thus, the table shows row-wise the number of patent applications originating from a particular country and column-wise the number of patent application received in a particular country with a breakdown by the nationality of the applicants. The dataset provides a bird's eye view regarding the origin and the flow of technological knowledge.

The diagonal entries of the matrix show the applications by one country's nationals in their home country. Table 4-7 provides time-series of such data. The figure for Japan in 1987 stood at 311,006, which is considerably larger than other major industrial countries. For example, the U.S. figure in the same year stood at 68,671 and that of FRG 31,663. Time-series comparisons reveal that, whereas in other countries the number of patent application remained stable over the years, the Japanese figure tended to increase at a steady pace. For example, 1970 figure stood at 100,522 and in 1980, at 165,730.

One can argue, however, that the Japanese superiority is superficial. WIPO also publishes patent registration statistics, and 1987 figure for Japan, U.S., and FRG stood at 54,087, 43,518, and 16,194, respectively. One can easily see that the gap is considerably narrower here. One may suspect that this is a preferred data set since it represents the true addition to the scientific knowledge after scrutiny by patent agencies in respective countries. But, here again, the screening process differs among countries. For example, some countries do not have official screening of application. The U.S. policy is to have the screening but the prior examination as to duplication of existing patents is the responsibility of the applicant. In the Japanese system, it is the responsibility of the Patent Agency to examine the existing ones.

There is a complicating factor in comparing patent application and registration figures, that is, the time required for examination varies over time and among countries. Figure 4-1 reveals this point, showing that such time lag has been shortened in the United States whereas the opposite was true in Japan. In fact, time required before registration in Japan in both 1988 and 1989 stood at 37 months.[9]

Since our purpose in this paper is to examine the relation between R&D effort (which is the input) and the inventiveness (which is the output), such a long and varying lag causes difficulty in the analysis. We intend to bypass the lag problem by using the patent application data.

This procedure, however, is not without its problems. The ratio between the application and the registration may not be stable overtime. In the case of Japan, indications are that the ratio has had some upward trend. It is reported that the registration/application ratio for patents and utility models in Japan has improved from 50% in 1986 to 53% recently.[10] The ratio in the case of the United States stood at 62.3% in 1986, 63.9% in 1987, and 66.4% in 1988. It is therefore too simplistic to employ the application figures as proxy for true inventiveness.

A more fundamental question is the quality of patents. As for the problem of differing degrees of inventiveness imbedded in a patent, we only have to ignore the problem because there is no established way of measuring it based on the available data. There have been attempts to distinguish epoch-making inventions in the history of industrialization, but this case-study approach does not refer to the average quality of patents in individual countries.[11] In Japan at least, there has been policy effort by the Patent Agency to apply for a patent for related inventions collectively rather than making them independent patents.[12] It is safe not to attempt comparisons among countries based on the mere number of patent applications, and limit our examination on the time trend within a particular country where institutional set-up tends to stay stable. Due consideration should be paid where there is information indicating changes in institutions.

It should be added in connection with the quality of patents that in some countries such as Japan, Germany, and Spain, there exists utility models besides patents. In Japan, the utility model applications numbered 201,614 cases in 1987. In West Germany, they numbered 16,091. The distinction between patents and utility models is in its degree of inventiveness, so to speak, and they apply for almost identical spheres of industrial property rights. Although the number of utility model applications is not increasing in Japan (it is on the decline in Germany), in the absence of utility models, some of the application in this category would have gone to patents. In the following discussion, however, we should focus our attention on patents, unless otherwise noted.

According to Appendix C-1 which refers to 1970, of the total of 130,829 cases, there were 100,511 applications made by Japanese nationals and 30,318 (23% of the total) by foreign nationals. Of the latter, 13,805 applications (11% of the total) were attributable to Americans. The Japanese applications numbered 135,118 in 1975, 165,730 in 1980, and 274,373 in 1985. Application by foreign nationals numbered 24,703 (15% of the total) in 1975, 25,290 (13%) in 1980, and 28,622 (9%) in 1985. The latest figure which pertains to 1987 stood at 30,089 which is slightly less than 9% of the total. We should not be too concerned about the absolute numbers because the problem of quality comparison remains unresolved, and we should pay more attention to the trend, instead. Clearly, the growth rate of the Japanese applications exceeded that by foreign nationals.

In the United States, herself a major source of technological knowledge and the world's largest market in which these knowledge can be put into practical use, the number of patent applications remained more or less stable over the period under consideration. In 1970, the application by American nationals in the U.S. stood at 76,195 cases. In 1975, it was 64,445; in 1980, 62,098; and in 1985, 63,874. The 1987 figure stood at

68,671. In contrast, the application by foreign nationals tended to increase over time, rising from 26% in 1970 to about 40% in 1980 and 49% in 1987. The Japanese application in the United States stood at 5% in 1970, 8% in 1975, 12% in 1980, and 18% in 1985. The recent figure is 19%.

During this time period, we have observed a reversal in the number of patent applications between Japan and the United States.[13]

	American application in Japan	Japanese application in the U.S.
1970	13,805	5,295
1975	10,490	8,566
1980	10,391	12,951
1985	12,637	21,431
1987	12,843	25,526

Inspection of annual tables reveals that the reversal occurred in 1979.[14] Although the sheer numbers do not tell us anything about the importance of technological knowledge contained in patents, and hence one can not conclude Japanese superiority based on these figures, one can at least say that the technological strength of Japanese industry has improved in recent years.

Also, if we calculate the Japanese share in the world total, we observe consistent gains. The 1970 figure stood at 35%, which has risen to 46% in 1975 and 51% in 1980. The figure for 1985 stood at 61% and for 1987, 64%. The world total is calculated here as the sum of applications by the countries' own nationals, which are represented as the diagonal elements in the world patent application matrix.[15] The Soviet figures up to 1980 only refer to the patents and does not include inventor's certificates which far outnumber patents.

Here again, we should not be too concerned about the absolute levels because it raises the question regarding the quality of patents. It suffices here to note that the Japanese inventiveness has shown consistent improvement in the last two decades. At any rate, a point can be made that Japan has emerged as a major contributor in the production of scientific knowledge as far as it is reflected in the number of patent applications.

4-4 Techno-rivalry?

It was reported that in the United States, of the top ten business firms in terms of new acquisition of industrial patents, five were Japanese (1988 figure).[16] They included Hitachi, Toshiba, Canon, Fuji Film, and Mitsubishi Electric. If the U.S. subsidiary of Phillips (the Netherlands) is excluded together with two German firms, only two American firms were among the top ten, namely, GE and IBM. Of the top 50, 17 were Japanese. Here we find Honda, NEC, Toyota, Sony, Matsushita, Fujitsu, Nissan, Alps, Olympus, Ricoh, Minolta, and Mazda. The best-ten ranking of patent acquisition in the U.S. in 1988 (together with their ranks in 1987) is as follows.

1988	1987		number of patents
1	2	Hitachi	907
2	3	Toshiba	750
3	1	Canon	723
4	4	General Electric	690
5	11	Fuji Film	589
6	5	Philips	581
7	8	Siemens	562
8	7	IBM	549
9	9	Mitsubishi Electric	543
10	19	Bayer	442

Such "patent acquisition rush" in high-technology fields by the Japanese firms may be perceived as economic challenge. This has direct bearing on the international competitiveness of industry. The importance of civilian technology is increasing even in military applications. There is an increasing number of technology and industrial experts who believe that the spill-over effect from space rockets, fighter planes, and nuclear submarines to industrial application has its limits. There are variety of reasons cited for this, but the main one probably is the mass-production orientation of civilian production, and its effect on cost reduction, quality control, and emergence of wide-spread new application fields. On the other hand, high quality, mass-produced civilian technology is increasingly finding its way into military use. Semiconductors, electronics devices, new materials, and other high-technology products are the case in question. "The relationship between technological supremacy and military spending is changing. In the 1960s it was a safe bet that billions of dollars poured into space programs or new missiles would eventually help American firms in their commercial pursuits. But technology no longer just spins off from military research into the market; often it spins on, in the other direction," *the Economist* wrote.[17] Examples are high-definition television, carbon fibers, among others.[18]

Against this background, it was reported that the U.S. R&D expenditure for 1989 is likely to grow only 1% in real terms, the lowest increase reported since 1975.[19] After adjusting for inflation, annual growth of R&D expenditures stood at 4.5% between 1977 to 1982, which accelerated to 6.9% between 1982 to 1985. This has decelerated to an annual growth of 2 to 3% since 1986.

The ratio of R&D expenditures to GNP will also drop to 2.6% level. This is comparable to the Japanese and West Germany figures, which stood at 2.5% and 2.8% in 1987, respectively. One of the reasons for this drop is the expected decline of Federal expenditures in absolute terms. Negative growth of governemnt R&D is recorded for the first time since 1975, a measure aimed at curbing fiscal deficit. The real expenditure by private firms is estimated to grow 1% in real terms, it was reported.

The Japan Economic Journal article interpreted this as a reflection of hesitance among American managers, except in the case of some excellent companies, to engage in research activities which require long-term perspectives. "The divident ratio (the share of divident in after-tax profit) has jumped in the past ten years from 40% to about 60%, another reflection of the situation where short-term consideration takes precedence in which American business managers find themselves," the article wrote.[20]

On the other hand, it is widely recognized that the U.S. is active in pursuing and maintaining its advantage in intangible intellectual property such as software and logics. This is a departure from the previous way of thinking that only knowledge pertaining to hard goods can be patented.

AT&T's case is a typical one. AT&T Bell Laboratory registered a patent covering the computer integrated manufacturing (CIM) technology.[21] This patent covers product development and process control technology consisting of design, fabrication, and assembly, which makes efficient and centralized scheduling of each production stage through feedback mechanism involving computers. This concept is often referred to as CIM. The application was filed on August 10, 1987 and was granted on February 21, 1989, with its registration number 4,807,108.

The abstract of the patent is as follows: "A method for controlling a process of realizing a product. The method defines activities of the process, their precedence relationships and the flow of information among the interconnected activities required to create the product. Resources are allocated and the defined activities are scheduled to complete the process. The method monitors the allocated resources and outputs of the interconnected activities and controls the process by dynamically reconfiguring the activities in accordance with time-variant criterion and selectively modifying the activities in accordance with monitored outputs of the activities to maintain optimal design, fabrication and assembly of the product."

The claim include the following: "A method for managing a process of realizing a product comprising the steps of: generating directed data flows defining activities interconnected in a precedence relationship to form the product realization process, simulating operation of the generated activity directed data flows, allocating resources to and scheduling the defined activities of each activity, determining status of each activity,

Figure 4-2 Technology balance of payments by sector

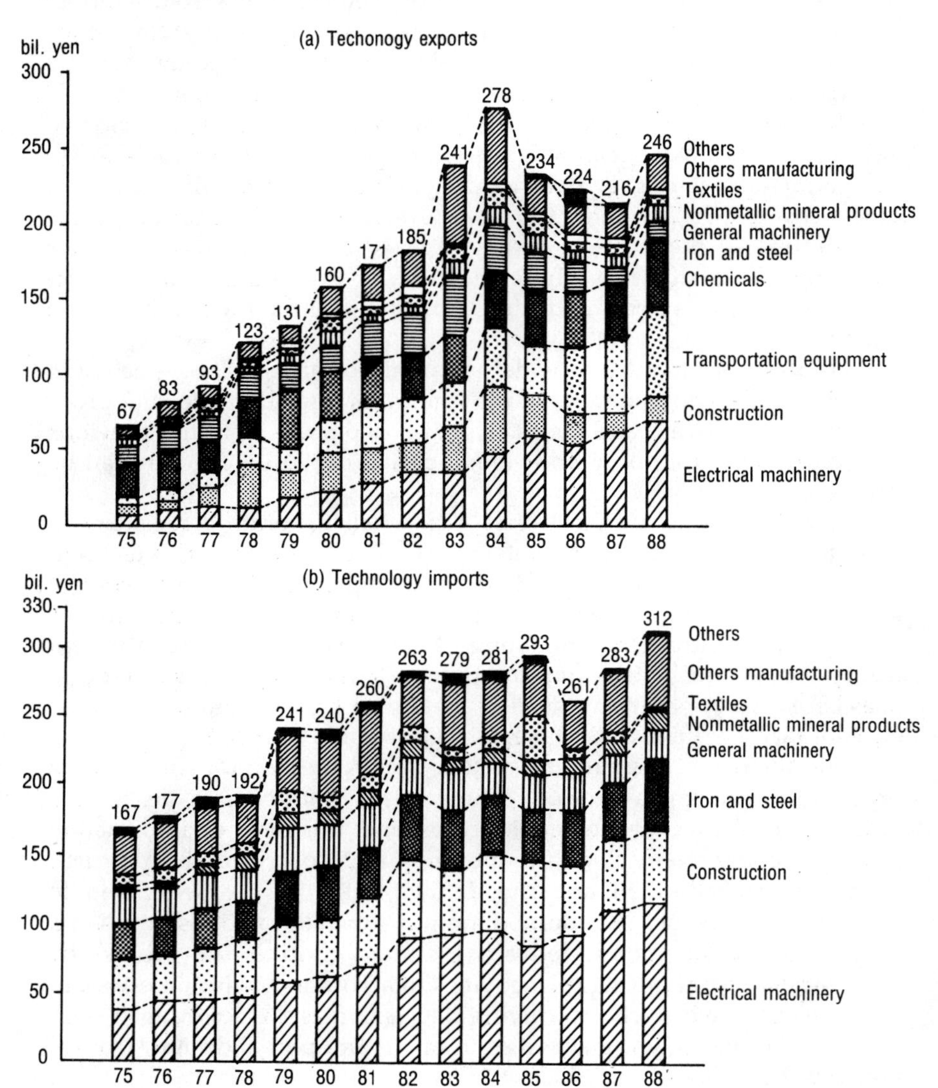

Source: *Indicators of Science and Technology 1990.*

estimating time required to perform each activity, receiving status of an initiation and completion of activities and of the allocation of the resources, deriving solutions in response to operation of the activities for enabling reconfiguration of the product realization process and assigning classification codes to each derived solution identifying resulting design and manufacture changes of the product, selecting ones of the derived solutions in accordance with the assigned classification codes, and modifying ones of the activities in accordance with the selected solutions to maintain optimal design and manufacture of the product."[22]

The patent concerns algorithm. The coverage of the patent is extremely wide, covering virtually all spheres of manufacturing employing C-C-C technology. Whereas comprehensive patent such as this one is actually granted in the United States, in other countries including Japan, patents have to be narrowly and technologically defined. It is said that as a result, Japanese patent system is not fit to something basic and comprehensive, and tend to spur defensive applications around a particular key inventions to protect it against possible by-passes. Japanese firms in general saw the concept of CIM unfit for patents. They will be obliged to find a proper way to cope with the new development. In the meantime, AT&T has reportedly told that any user should obtain license from them. This apparently caught Japanese business firms, which are engaged in production of CIM-related equipment, by surprise.

It appears that such trends on both sides of the Pacific symbolize conflicting interests among trading nations. This may even represent a new form of trade war. However, the truth of the fact is that it merely reflects increased linkages among nations not only in terms of goods and capital but also in scientific knowledge itself. In Japan, it is well known that imported technology played an extremely important role in its economic catch-up. Even in recent years, technology import is still needed to supplement indigenous effort. This point is illustrated in Figure 4-2. For example, technology export of electrical machinery industry is expanding rapidly, but this is preceded by large amount of technology import in this sector. Even in recent years, technology import exceeds export. Similar trend can be observed for the transport equipment sector. Focusing specifically on high-tech, Japanese importation of semiconductor technology has jumped from 41 cases in 1980 to 129 in 1985 and 240 in 1988; that of computer technology from 181 cases in 1980 to 624 in 1985 and 1067 in 1988. In fact, no country can be expected to be self-sufficient in technological development. So is true in the United States whose economy is tending more toward service activities. Obviously, the use of Japanese-born technology in the U.S. industry is indispensable and mutually advantageous.[23]

Footnotes:

1 For capital formation data on disaggregated industry level which are consistent with the SNA figures, see fixed capital formation matrix explained in chapter 6. These data, however, are available only at 5-year intervals.

2 Thomas F. Juster, "On the Measurement of Economic and Social Performance," 50th Annual Report of the National Bureau of Economic Research, September 1970. The measurement of intangibles such as software and scientific knowledge is now seriously considered among academics as well as international economic organizations. The International Association for Research in Income and Wealth takes up the issue in its 1992 general conference. OECD's statistical office is also considering the problem.

3 A brief discussion on industrial policy can be found in Uno [1987].

4 National Science Foundation, *National Patterns of R&D Resources 1989*. Cited here from Science and Technology Agency, *Annual Report of Science and Technology Agency 1990*, p. 30.

5 Uno, [1990c] contains annual compilation of such data on which table 4-5 is based.

6 Uno [1989a], pp.233–239. The methodology suggested is due to Terlecskyj [1980, 1982].

7 For fixed capital formation matrix for selected years, see Appendix E.

8 Most of the gains were realized in the 1980s due to the reasons cited above.

9 Patent Agency, *Annual Report of the Patent Agency*, 1990, p.11.

10 ibid., p.51.

11 See, for example, Bieshaar and Kleinknecht [1984][1986], Kleinknecht [1987], Mensch [1979].

12 Patent Agency, ibid., p.50.

13 Data from Appendix C.

14 See Uno [1990c].

15 Due to unavailability of data, some countries are not included in the total. The cases in question are Italy (1970, 1975, 1985, and 1987) and East Germany (1970).

16 *The Japan Economic Journal* (Japanese), June 2, 1989.

17 *The Economist*, May 20, 1989, p.112.

18 In fact, in the planned joint development of FSX (next generation of ground support fighter planes planned in Japan), General Dynamics is demanding Mitsubishi Heavy Industries, the Japanese main contractor, to transfer them Japanese technology for producing wings using new material.

19 National Science Foundation estimates as reported in *The Japan Economic Journal* (Japanese) on July 1, 1989.

20 The short-sightedness seems to be shared by the American government, too, as can be witnessed in the case of a joint project involving the United States and Japan aimed at developing substitute fuel which was terminated unilaterally by the American side in the face of (short-lived) cheapening of crude oil.

21 *The Japan Economic Journal* (in Japanese), June 1, 1989 and June 2, 1989.

22 The text cited here is from Patents Newsletter Database supplied by DIALOG.

23 See *The Economist*, May 20, 1989, pp.109–112. They report, citing National

Science Foundation, the share of Japanese-invented U.S. patents in respective industry sectors as follows.

SIC category	Share of total patents granted (%)	
	1975	1985
Food	8	11
Textiles	10	17
Chemicals and allied products	10	15
Petroleum	3	6
Rubber	10	18
Ceramics	8	20
Primary metals	13	23
Fabricated metals	5	12
General machinery	7	15
Computing and accounting machines	13	33
Electrical machinery	10	21
Communications equipment and electronic components	13	26
Motor vehicles	7	23
Aircrafts and parts	10	30
Professional and scientific instruments	12	23
All fields	9	19

Chapter 5. Diffusion of C-C-C technology

5-1 Computer-communication-control technology

Microelectronics technology is based on semiconductors and ICs and its application goes far beyond computers. In manufacturing plants, factory automation (FA) is in progress combining NC metalworking machinery and industrial robots aimed at automatic production processes. In offices, office automation (OA) is taking a concrete shape utilizing computers, facsimiles, and word processors, all aimed at quick and accurate execution of business and information processing, and are increasingly linked by a communication network. In fact, database on computer network has drastically gained importance and changed the nature of information processing altogether.

The progress of microelectronics revolution is best illustrated by production statistics concerning semiconductors and integrated circuits, which we cite below.[1]

	Semiconductors		Integrated circuits	
	number (million)	value (billion ¥)	number (million)	value (billion ¥)
1970	3,716	180	136	53
1975	4,574	159	330	118
1980	16,328	294	2,660	570
1985	38,283	568	9,350	1,842
1987	46,906	562	12,015	1,925

The case of mainframe computers needs no elaboration. They became faster and cheaper, finding their way everywhere in our society, including factories, offices, banks, hospitals, governments, universities, research institutions, and in transportation and communication. Fundamental changes occurred in the last decade, however.

First, computers are now linked by data communication network. The emergence of a computer network is one of the key characteristics of the present-day innovation because this completely changed the concept of distance and time. Customers and producers can communicate instantaneously. Producers and their suppliers can adjust their production and delivery schedule instantaneously. The logistics, including transportation, storage, and delivery, are synchronized with producers and customers. Automobile industry is a case in question. Financial transaction is a typical example where we have witnessed an emergence of a global market in the true sense of the word. Airline is another example where enormous number of transactions are carried out daily encompassing the global market. Thus, the relationship between firms and industries are now organized in an altogether different manner because of the collapse of traditional institutional barriers. The coming of a network society, as opposed to a hierarchical one, has its technological foundation from the emergence of data communication network. Various organizations are now linked horizontally with the ones directly linked functionally. As transactions become borderless, the roles of a national government are being altered because their authority is typically confined to within national boundaries. This in turn gave rise to global rules governing various fields of services.

One need to go into some statistical evidence in order to observe the rapid expansion of new technologies. We have the following statistics related to data communication in Japan.[2]

	Digital transmission			Packet switching
	exclusive: standard (circuits)	exclusive: high-speed (circuits)	public (terminals)	(circuits)
1975	n.a.	—	3,570	—
1980	83,933	—	7,786	59
1985	178,653	640	15,369	14,158
1987	203,874	4,407	25,748	53,336

Second, database has emerged. This is particularly an important development because for the first time in history, human beings are dealing with a common stock of knowledge. Since the invention of printing press by Guthenberg, printed information existed for 500 years now but the information contained had to be digested by individual persons. The fact that they are stored on computer memory and can be retrieved in a systematic manner regardless of personal memory makes it crucial in the operation of the economy and society today. Being accessible on-line, they also nullified the geographical distance.

Disregarding the inhouse databases used for internal purposes, we have the following figures for the development of commercial databases in Japan.[3]

	Number of databases[4]	Annual sales (billion yen)
1975	n.a.	14.3
1980	334 ('82)	44.1
1985	1,008	100.8
1988	1,436	(155.0)[5]

Third, there is the increased use of word processors, facsimiles, electronic files, electronic tellers, POS (point-of-sales) systems, and other types of office automation equipment. And they are often integrated into a computer system with access to databases. We list below some statistics concerning facsimiles as a typical equipment for OA.[6] We are even beginning to use electronic translation system.

	Network service subscribers	Facsimile installations	Facsimile production: number	value (bil.¥)
1975	n.a.	2,885	22,163	12
1980	n.a.	14,553	100,356	81
1985	46,271	105,532 ('84)	865,575	313
1987	201,058	n.a.	2,411,221	365

Apparently, not every aspect of new technology can be included in our analysis. In this chapter, we look into a particular segment of new technology, namely computer, communication, and control technology. The triple-C represents typical application of electronic technology in industry. The speed of diffusion of this new technology has been marked and has already had significant impact on production, trade, and employment. We can even say that the differentials in the speed of diffusion among countries can be blamed for various international conflicts. As indicators of the diffusion of triple-C technology which comprise the crux of present-day innovation, we have decided to include numerically controlled (NC) machines, industrial robots, vending machines, and mainframe computers in our model structure. They represent technological change which is taking place on a global scale, and their production (flow) and diffusion rates (stock) can be measured with reasonable confidence based on existing data.

The case of mainframe computers seems obvious. But, in this case too, we have seen fundamental changes due to widespread use of database and communication network. Computers are not simply computing machines. Due to development of database, computers now store information in a systematic manner, making it possible to stock knowledge and to retrieve it whenever required in whatever form regardless of the geographical distance. The communication network now spreads over factories and offices. Not only that, it covers the entire nation and entire world through optical fiber links and via communication satellites. This has given a dramatic impact on banking and securities field due to the emergence of an integrated global market. This has also changed logistics including transportation, warehousing, wholesale and retail trade, tourism, and various services. Uses of work stations and CAD-CAM system are now widespread, and this is only the beginning.

Widespread use of NC metalworking machines and industrial robots is a typical example of application of triple-C technology in manufacturing. This has resulted in improved quality of products and added flexibility in the production process which was unseen under the existing mode of production. Not only that, the new production system, often termed as FMS (a flexible manufacturing system), employing NCs, industrial robots, and electronically controlled logistic system such as transportation and warehousing, has changed the technological characteristics of production. Economies of scope, rather than economies of scale, became the key concept in successful business. Systematic treatment of information has become the decisive factor, changing the nature of required skill. It also made it possible to substitute labor force with capital and the labor augmenting nature of triple-C technology has made industrialized countries less vulnerable to labor shortage and resultant rising wages.

Office automation through application of electronic equipment such as word processors, facsimile, database and data communication, among others, which are used in combination with computer systems, has opened a new possibility for efficiency improvement. Automatic vending machines, which are widespread in Japan, can be seen as an attempt to overcome labor shortages in the service sector. Computer-aided instruction is now becoming a commonplace in schools. The shift toward services in final demand and intermediate demand is observed the world over. However, productivity gains in this sector, which is comprised of business services, personal services, and public services, has been a limited one, and the expansion of production has been achieved mainly by increased inputs of labor and capital. With the emergence of triple-C technology, the developed economies will be able to avoid full employment ceiling.

We may say, therefore, that technological progress along this line changed the comparative advantages among countries in a fundamental way. Because capital is cheaper in developed economies, capital-abundant developed economies are now in a position to retain activities which hitherto were labor-intensive. They can also engage in the production of capital-intensive products. These products are also R&D- and knowledge-intensive. Developed economies tend to have an advantage in both physical and human capital, giving them an edge in a wide range of economic activities. This observation is valid not only in the North-South and East-West context but also among industrialized countries themselves. It is probably too naive to believe that the increased diffusion of triple-C technology would bring about harmonious development of the world community. Thus, we should be prepared for wide repercussions stemming from the diffusion of triple-C technology in international economic relations.

5-2 Diffusion of new technology

The case of NC machines: Metalworking machineries are often termed as the mother machines because they are machines which produce machines. Production of metalworking machinery, and craftmanship that operates these machines, are considered to be indicators of the technological level of an economy. Although the main thrust of the advanced economies has shifted to service activities in a wide sense, these indicators remain to be ture in manufacturing sectors. A major technological innovation in this field is the numerically controlled (NC) machine. Traditionally, metalworking has been a joint work of machinery and human skills. NC machines replace human factor by computer control wherein coded instructions control the operation of the machines. Starting from tape-based control, NC machines are now controlled by microelectronics (computerized numerical control, or CNC).

Compared to conventional machines, NC machines have the following advantages:

(1) Due to reduced human labor, operators can work with several units of machines at the same time, resulting in considerable savings of labor.
(2) Metalworking is conducted through computer commands, which can reduce human errors while making it possible to obtain products of uniform quality.
(3) Designs involving complex curvature can be produced without difficulty.
(4) Flexible adaptation to design alterations and introduction of new models are made extremely easy and costless.
(5) Unlike specialized machines, NC machines are multipurpose. These make them suitable for small quantity production. Production lines can be altered without halting production, for retooling.

With the progress of electronics technology, the price of NC machines has been reduced at a rapid pace. They come to play the central role in flexible manufacturing system (FMS) where several machining centers are linked by automatic transportation system, making computer control of the whole manufacturing process and logistics a reality.

Technological progress in manufacturing takes various forms, but we can assume from the above observation that the diffusion of NC machines serves as an indicator of technological level in the case of machinery sectors.

The Ministry of International Trade and Industry has conducted a series of surveys on the installation of metalworking machines, providing a detailed picture on the diffusion process in Japanese industry for selected years.[7] The survey provides information classified by individual machine type (for example, lathes are classified into seven categories) at 3 to 4-digit industrial classification level, and number of years in use by sector and machinery type, in addition to information by size of the firm,

Table 5-1 Diffusion of NC machines

a. Metal cutting machine tools

(unit: number of units, million yen, %)

	Sector	1967 Survey[a]	1973 Survey[a]	1973 Survey[a*]	1981 Survey[b*]	1987 Survey[b]	
		Number[c]	Number[c]	Number[d]	Number[d]	Number	Value
(1)	Total						
	All industries	683,860	825,774	545,142	531,392	648,289	1,998,684
31	Iron and steel	40,042	42,469	n.a.	n.a.	17,456[e]	44,779[e]
32	Nonferrous metals	18,151	23,926	n.a.	n.a.		
33	Fabricated metals	66,923	80,863	n.a.	n.a	33,859	71,431
34	General machinery	208,652	252,264	222,832	194,934	232,931	702,847
35	Electrical machinery	127,754	139,753	89,093	82,042	90,346	282,396
36	Transport equipment	163,995	214,183	173,077	206,785	227,076	819,732
36M	Transport equipment, motor vehicles			148,252	188,926	210,090	767,973
37	Precision instrument	57,697	70,996	60,140	47,631	39,376	56,971
(2)	of which NC						
	All industries	769	5,402	4,861	19,549	70,465	670,388
31	Iron and steel	47	85	n.a.	n.a.	1,572[e]	15,092[e]
32	Nonferrous metals	11	254	n.a.	n.a		
33	Fabricated metals	74	202	n.a.	n.a.	2,537	24,344
34	General machinery	264	2,765	2,783	9,378	28,195	284,984
35	Electrical machinery	85	832	832	3,185	11,932	101,343
36	Transport equipment	257	948	948	5,404	21,981	213,330
36M	Transport equipment, motor vehicles			604	4,293	20,123	189,853
37	Precision instrument	71	298	298	1,582	3,520	22,850
(3)	Diffusion rate (=B/A),%						
	All industries	0.1	0.7	0.9	3.7	10.9	33.5
31	Iron and steel	0.0	0.2			9.0[e]	33.7[e]
32	Nonferrous metals	0.1	1.1				
33	Fabricated metals	0.1	0.2			7.4	34.1
34	General machinery	0.1	1.1	1.2	4.8	12.1	40.5
35	Electrical machinery	0.1	0.6	0.9	3.9	13.2	35.9
36	Transport equipment	0.2	0.4	0.5	2.6	9.7	26.0
36M	Transport equipment, motor vehicles			0.4	2.3	9.6	24.7
37	Precision instrument	0.1	0.4	0.5	3.3	8.9	40.1

b. Secondary metalworking machinery

(unit: number of units, million yen, %)

	Sector	1967 Survey[a]	1973 Survey[a]	1973 Survey[a]	1981 Survey[b]	1987 Survey[b]	
		Number[c]	Number[c]	Number[d]	Number[d]	Number	Value
(1)	Total						
	All industries	165,172	199,441	118,834	132,680	205,438	706,628
31	Iron and steel	14,729	18,275	n.a.	n.a.	9,432	45,513
32	Nonferrous metals	9,161	10,659	n.a.	n.a.		
33	Fabricated metals	29,316	37,133	n.a.	n.a.	31,967	90,166
34	General machinery	24,704	30,498	28,146	27,741	33,965	89,543
35	Electrical machinery	47,697	50,660	42,549	43,728	50,436	140,363
36	Transport equipment	29,998	41,106	39,278	52,198	68,614	309,916
36M	Transport equipment, motor vehicles			33,662	47,705	63,153	294,384
37	Precision instrument	9,209	10,856	8,861	9,013	7,059	10,997
(2)	of which NC						
	All industries	—	162	115	952	4,329	48,762
31	Iron and steel	—	5	n.a.	n.a.	14	337
32	Nonferrous metals	—	11	n.a.	n.a.		
33	Fabricated metals	—	31	n.a.	n.a.	657	6,083
34	General machinery	—	22	22	280	1,078	12,392
35	Electrical machinery	—	66	66	467	1,308	13,400
36	Transport equipment	—	25	25	186	1,054	12,877
36M	Transport equipment, motor vehicles			12	114	960	11,361
37	Precision instrument	—	2	2	19	89	1,148
(3)	Diffusion rate (=B/A),%						
	All industries	—	0.1	0.1	0.7	2.1	6.9
31	Iron and steel	—	0.0			0.1	0.7
32	Nonferrous metals	—	0.1				
33	Fabricated metals	—	0.1			2.1	6.7
34	General machinery	—	0.1	0.1	1.0	3.2	13.8
35	Electrical machinery	—	0.1	0.2	1.1	2.6	9.5
36	Transport equipment	—	0.1	0.1	0.4	1.5	4.2
36M	Transport equipment, motor vehicles			0.0	0.2	1.5	3.9
37	Precision instrument	—	0.0	0.0	0.2	1.3	10.4

Notes: a. Refers to establishments with more than 100 employees. b. Refers to establishments with more than 50 employees. c. Total includes ordinance and accessories sector. d. Sectors 34, 35, 36, and 37 only. e. Casting and forging only.

Source: Compiled from the Ministry of International Trade and Industry, *Survey on Machine Tools Installation*, various issues.

Table 5-2 Diffusion of industrial robots and FMS

(unit: number of units)

	Sector	1967 Survey	1973 Survey	1981 Survey[b*]	1987 Survey[b]
		Number	Number[c]	Number[d]	Number
a.	Automatic assembly system				
	All industries	n.a.	7,620	22,833	49,736
31	Iron and steel		30	n.a.	48[e]
32	Nonferrous metals		34	n.a.	
33	Fabricated metals		261	n.a.	930
34	General machinery		1,830	2,406	5,181
35	Electrical machinery		2,632	13,270	28,596
36	Transport equipment		1,485	5,477	11,787
36M	Transport equipment, motor vehicles			5,378	
37	Precision instrument		1,348	1,680	3,110
b.	Industrial robots				
	All industries	n.a.	3,058	14,158	47,308
31	Iron and steel		53	n.a.	750[e]
32	Nonferrous metals		150	n.a.	
33	Fabricated metals		120	n.a.	1,372
34	General machinery		205	1,253	5,380
35	Electrical machinery		423	3,859	16,475
36	Transport equipment		1,610	8,383	20,901
36M	Transport equipment, motor vehicles		1,592	8,315	20,229
37	Precision instrument		495	663	2,094
c.	Flexible manufacturing system				
	All industries	n.a	n.a.	n.a.	259
31	Iron and steel				
32	Nonferrous metals				
33	Fabricated metals				
34	General machinery				171
35	Electrical machinery				44
36	Transport equipment				40
36M	Transport equipment, motor vehicles				21
37	Precision instrument				2

Source: Same as table 5-1.

etc. For our purpose, we chose sectoral classification at 2-digit level and aggregated machine types to be consistent with our analysis elsewhere.

Table 5-1 provides an overview on the NC machines diffusion, covering the period from 1967 to 1987. The table has been compiled from a series of surveys, and contains some differences in coverage which have been unavoidable due to changes in survey design regarding firm size, etc. The comparison between 1967 and 1973 has been taken from the 1973 survey report where 1967 results are adjusted to conform to the 1973 survey framework.[8] Panel (a) of the table refers to metal cutting machines such as lathes, drilling machines, milling machines, grinding machines, and gear cutting and finishing machines, whereas panel (b) refers to secondary metal working machinery such as bending machines, presses, shearing machines, and forging machines.

According to panel (a), total number of NC metal cutting machine tools is put at 769 in 1967 and 5402 in 1973. The share of NC machines in total metal cutting machine tools stood at 0.1% and 0.7% in respective years. According to the 1981 survey which again provides figures for 1973, the share of NC is calculated as 0.9% in 1973. This ratio is higher because the total figure reported was lower whereas the 1973 survey reports the results covering iron and steel, nonferrous metals, and fabricated metals, in addition to machinery sectors. Because of this, we have to be content with a pairwise comparison between two consecutive survey years, rather than a truly consistent time series. The number of NC machines are essentially the same in two reportings for 1973, though.

For the diffusion between 1973 and 1981, we should rely on the 1981 Survey.[9] For 1973, the data refer to establishments with more than 100 employees and for 1981, more than 50. The coverage is limited to machinery sectors for both years. Despite the fact that the scope of the 1981 Survey was wider including smaller establishments, actual number of metal cutting machine tools turned out to be smaller, standing at 531 thousand units as compared to 545 thousand units in 1973. The number of NC machines increased considerably, however, from about 4900 units in 1973 to about 19500 units in 1981. This amounts to an annual rate of increase of 19%. Diffusion rate has increased from 0.9% in 1973 (notice some discrepancy from the figure cited in 1967–1973 comparions, which is partly attributable to the exclusion of primary metals and fabricated metals sectors where the diffusion remained relatively low) to 3.7% in 1981.

In 1987 when the latest results were obtained, total number of NC metal cutting machine tools exceeded 70,000 units for all industries (or just over 66,000 units for machinery sectors only which are covered by the 1981 Survey), which is 10.9% of the total. If we calculate the annual growth rate between 1981 and 1987 on comparable basis (i.e., when the calculation is made for the machinery sectors only which include general machinery, electrical machinery, transport equipment, and precision instrument), we obtain about 22.7%.

So far, the diffusion rates were calculated in terms of number of units. One interesting point is the share of NC machines in value terms. In terms of value, the share of NC machines stood at 33.5% of total metal cutting machine tools in 1987. The Survey counted the value based on book value.[10] This would result in giving higher weights to newer units (which include NC machines in larger proportions) as compared to older ones which are depreciated, and the diffusion rate based on value may be biased upward. In contrast, the diffusion rate based on the number of units is downward biased because the Survey counts machinery owned by the establishments, including the ones which are not in use, i.e., being repaired or being stored away.[11] In addition, while conventional units require constant human attendance, NC machines are often operated on 2-shifts or 3-shifts without requiring constant human attend-

Table 5-3 NC machines, industrial robots, and FMS by year of installation

(unit: number of units, percent)

	Number of machines	10 years and older (~1977) (%)	5 to 9 years (1978~1982) (%)	3 to 5 years (1983,1984) (%)	Less than 3 years (1985~1987) (%)
Metal cutting machine tools	648,289 (100.0)	355,195 (54.8)	142,686 (22.0)	68,933 (10.6)	81,475 (12.6)
of which NC	70,465 (100.0)	8,284 (11.8)	19,419 (27.6)	16,408 (23.3)	26,354 (37.4)
Secondary metal working machinery	205,438 (100.0)	104,716 (51.0)	46,850 (22.8)	24,247 (11.8)	29,625 (14.4)
of which NC	4,329 (100.0)	563 (13.0)	1,233 (28.5)	978 (22.6)	1,555 (35.9)
Welding machines and welding and cutting machines	329,223 (100.0)	173,550 (52.7)	75,557 (23.0)	37,614 (11.4)	42,502 (12.9)
Laser machines	1,672 (100.0)	117 (7.0)	369 (22.1)	489 (29.2)	697 (41.7)
Automatic assembly system	49,736 (100.0)	7,621 (15.3)	14,453 (29.1)	12,119 (24.4)	15,543 (31.3)
Industrial robots	47,308 (100.0)	3,264 (6.9)	9,995 (21.1)	11,984 (25.3)	22,065 (46.6)
FMS	259 (100.0)			137 (52.9)	122 (47.1)
cutting	188 (100.0)			90 (47.9)	98 (52.1)
forming	71 (100.0)			47 (66.2)	24 (33.8)
Clean rooms	5,203 (100.0)			3,296 (63.3)	1,907 (36.7)

Note: The figures refer to the number of machines being used at the time of the 1987 Survey which was conducted on September 30, 1987.
Source: Compiled from the Ministry of International Trade and Industry, *Survey of Machine Tools Installation, 1987*.

Table 5-4 NC ratios by type of machinery

(unit: %)

	1981 Survey	1987 Survey	of which machinery installed within 3 years	
			1981 Survey (1969-1981)	1987 Survey (1985-1987)
Metal cutting machine tools	3.6	11.1	12.1	33.0
Lathes	6.6	21.0	27.3	61.7
Drilling machines	1.5	3.8	3.1	17.2
Boring machines	5.8	10.4	14.6	34.6
Milling machines	4.4	9.0	15.5	30.0
Grinding machines	0.6	3.7	2.5	14.5
Gear cutting and gear finishing machines	—	2.6	—	18.9
Special machines	0.7	4.9	1.3	12.7
Electric discharge machines	22.8	57.7	46.1	77.6
Secondary metalworking machinery	0.8	2.2	2.2	5.2
Bending machines	1.9	8.2	5.8	24.1
Hydraulic presses	0.6	2.3	1.4	5.6
Machine presses	0.8	1.9	2.4	4.9
Shearing machines	0.5	4.1	1.7	10.6
Forging machines	—	1.0	—	1.4
Wire forming machines	—	1.8	—	3.4

Note: The figures refer to machinery sectors only including general machinery, electrical machinery, transport equipment, and precision instrument.
Source: Ministry of International Trade and Industry, *Survey on Machine Tools installation, 1987.*

ance. It is also very likely that NC machines are more efficient, in terms of set-up time and processing time, not to speak of precision and higher productivity. Thus, there are reasons to believe that real contribution of NC machines to production may be higher than is suggested by the diffusion rate.

General machinery sector has the largest number of NC machines, followed by transport equipment and electrical machinery sectors. In terms of number of units, the highest diffusion rate is observed for electrical machinery sector (13.2%) followed by general machinery and transport equipment. The rate in motor vehicle sector stands at 9.6%. In terms of value, however, the highest rate is observed for general machinery (40.5%), followed by precision instrument, electrical machinery, and transport equipment. The rate in motor vehicles in this case stands at 24.7%.

Looking at the types of machinery, lathes have a share of 42% of total NC metal cutting machine tools, which is followed by machining centers with a share of 22.2%.[12]

Table 5-1-b refers to secondary metal working machinery. According to the MITI survey, there were no NC machines for this category in 1967. By 1973, there were a total of 162 units in all industries (115 units in machinery sectors). Compared to the total number of 199 thousand (about 119 thousand in machinery sectors), the diffusion rate was negligible at 0.1%. By 1981, the number has increased to 952 in machinery sectors alone, showing an annual rate of growth of about 30%. The latest

Table 5-5 Diffusion rates of NC machines in production

(unit: percent)

Types of machinery	Year	1975	1976	1977	1978	1979	1980	1981	1982	1983	1984	1985	1986	1987
Lathes	Value	25.7	34.2	45.8	52.3	64.0	69.2	70.3	73.2	76.6	79.7	83.1	85.3	87.7
	Unit	7.1	9.7	16.2	21.8	28.5	34.6	36.7	41.7	45.9	52.6	56.9	62.8	72.3
Drilling machines	Value	12.4	20.7	30.1	21.5	11.2	14.7	13.1	12.1	31.4	27.9	29.6	45.5	62.4
	Unit	0.4	0.3	0.7	0.7	0.3	0.6	0.9	0.6	1.7	1.6	1.8	5.1	6.9
Boring machines	Value	12.4	10.9	11.8	15.3	14.7	26.3	36.1	36.7	39.0	44.9	36.5	49.1	56.1
	Unit	2.3	1.7	2.3	2.8	2.5	4.1	4.9	6.1	6.7	12.3	8.2	13.3	19.3
Milling machines	Value	16.6	19.0	17.2	21.6	26.9	31.9	41.1	44.9	51.6	51.5	52.1	54.2	66.8
	Unit	4.6	5.3	5.5	7.2	10.6	14.0	20.2	21.9	25.4	25.9	23.4	27.2	37.3
Grinding machines	Value	0.8	2.8	2.3	1.3	3.2	4.5	4.5	6.7	8.4	11.7	14.2	19.6	24.2
	Unit	0.2	0.3	0.7	0.3	0.1	1.4	2.0	2.6	3.5	5.0	7.3	10.0	11.3
Machining centers	Value	100.0	100.0	100.0	100.0	100.0	100.0	100.0	100.0	100.0	100.0	100.0	100.0	100.0
	Unit	100.0	100.0	100.0	100.0	100.0	100.0	100.0	100.0	100.0	100.0	100.0	100.0	100.0
Electric discharge machines	Value	—	—	—	—	57.4	73.8	79.0	84.4	91.1	93.9	95.1	95.8	95.7
	Unit	—	—	—	—	49.0	65.9	72.4	78.7	87.1	89.8	90.9	92.7	93.7
Others	Value	2.0	5.7	3.7	3.3	8.4	8.2	9.7	10.9	17.5	34.2	30.8	29.1	29.4
	Unit	0.08	0.5	0.2	0.2	0.5	0.4	0.5	0.7	1.7	3.2	3.7	4.3	3.6
Total	Value	17.3	22.4	25.7	29.4	42.4	49.8	51.0	53.9	60.7	66.9	67.0	67.9	70.7
	Unit	2.5	2.8	4.1	5.4	8.7	12.3	15.6	16.5	18.8	22.0	25.7	28.3	28.2

Source: Japan Machine Tools Industry Association, *Statistical Handbook on Machine Tools*. Cited here from Sangyo Kenkyujo [1988b].

survey in 1987 reveals that there exist 4329 units in all industries (3658 units in machinery sectors). The diffusion rate is calculated to be 2.1% for all industries and 2.2% for machinery sectors total.

Here again, the share of NC machines is larger in value terms. Of the total value of secondary metal working machines at 707 billion yen, 49 billion yen (or 6.9%) is attributed to NC machines. The average annual growth rate between 1981 and 1987 is about 25%.

Before turning to other types of machinery related to triple-C technology, let us look at table 5-3 which shows the age structure of metalworking machinery as of 1987. According to the table, total number of metal cutting machine tools which were installed within the last three years stood at about 81 thousand units, of which about 26 thousand units were NCs. Thus, although the diffusion rate stood at 10.9% for total machinery, the share of NC machines was much higher at 32.3% among the units installed between 1985 and 1987. (In the machinery sectors alone, the ratio stood at 33.0%. See table 5-4.)

Likewise, in the case of secondary metalworking machinery, of the total of about 30 thousand units installed in the last three years, 1555 units were NCs. Thus, in contrast to the diffusion rate for the total stock of 2.1%, the NC share within the last 3 years stood at 5.2%.

The trends of diffusion in the future can be gauged by production statistics. Table 5-5 provides annual diffusion figures concerning production of different types of metalworking machinery. The latest total figure stands at 28.2% in terms of number of units. In value terms, the ratio exceeds 70%.

Thus, we may summarize that the diffusion rate of metal cutting machine tools has been as follows in the past 20 years. The calculation is based on the number of units and disregards slight differences in the coverage of the Surveys.

	Metal cutting	Secondary
1967 stock	0.1%	— (table 5-1)
1973 stock	0.9%	0.1% (″)
1981 stock	3.7%	0.7% (″)
1987 stock	10.9%	2.1% (″)
New installation ('85–'87)	32.3%	5.2% (table 5-3)
Production (1987)	28.2%	n.a. (table 5-5)

In value terms, which approximate the real contribution of NC machines, the following observations are obtained.[13]

	Metal cutting	Secondary
1987 stock	33.5%	6.9% (table 5-1)
Production (1987)	70.7%	n.a. (table 5-5)

In assessing the trends in NC diffusion, it should be noted that the

Fiture 5-1 Number of simultaneously controlled axes of NC machines

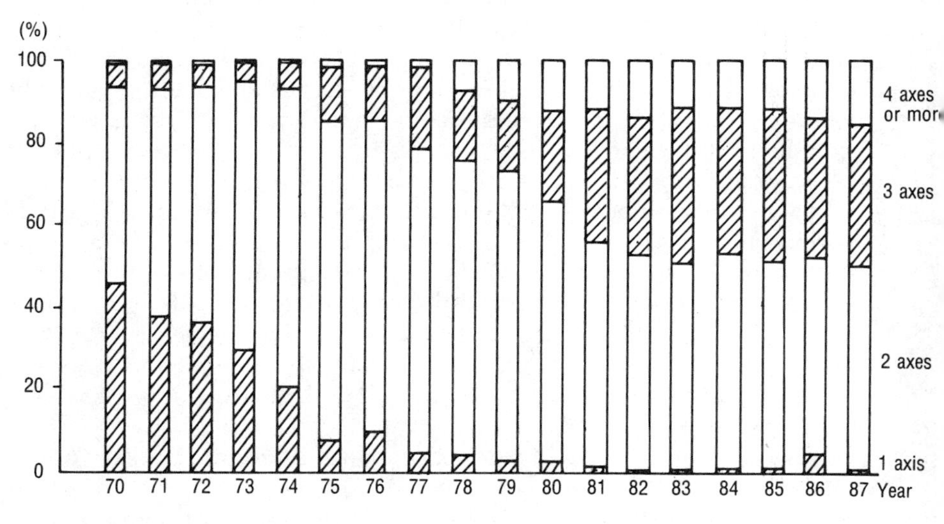

Source: Sangyo Kenkyujo [1988b].

economy has entered a recession in 1985. This is attributed to the rapid appreciation of the yen as a result of the G5 agreement in fall 1985. Subsequently, the economy entered a period of uninterrupted expansion in the fall of 1986 which continued into 1990 and beyond. In our context, we need to keep in mind that the diffusion process preceding the 1987 Survey may reflect temporary slow down of investment. Recent round of economic expansion is very likely not simply a cyclical phenomena judging from the innovation that is taking place in virtually all segments of the economy. We are about to witness a new round of technology-induced economic growth.

Industrial robots: In fact, the introdution of industrial robots seems to have entered a phase of rapid diffusion toward the end of the 1980s. Robot production in Japan is literally exploding in recent years. For example, Kawasaki Heavy Industry anticipated 43% increase in robot production during fiscal 1989 whereas original forecast was 20%. Fujikoshi expanded the floor space of its robot plant from the current 5,500 square meters to 8,000 to 9,000 square meters during fiscal 1989. They expect sales in the next fiscal year to increase by 50 to 60%. Yasukawa Electric revised their sales plan from a 30% increase to 40 to 50% increase during fiscal 1989.

A recent press report cited 'labor shortage' as the largest contributing factor to the recent acceleration of robot diffusion.[14] The automobile industry, which is the largest customer of industrial robots, is particularly eager to introduce robots at a faster pace. Industrial circles say that they have encountered difficulty in recruiting workers, inducing to use industrial robots instead regardless of the cost-benefit calculation. Demand for robots is spreading to electric machinery industry and construction where labor shortage is particularly keen.

Technological progress in robot production is another factor behind increased diffusion. The need for robot introduction is spreading to the assembly processes in electrical machinery and automobile sectors. Unlike welding and painting processes where robots can be easily placed alongside the production line, assembly process requires manipulation of small products with the precision comparable to human skills. This necessitates provision of a comprehensive system composed not only of robots but also software and peripheral equipment. The fact that industrial robots are a direct application of triple-C technology is well illustrated by the fact that 69.0% of them are controlled by electronics. Other modes of control include relay (19.7%), pneumatic devices (4.3%), electrically controlled oil pressure (4.0%), and others (3.9%).[15]

Many robots are now produced with high degree of sophistication to match customers' needs (See figure 5-1). They find their way into such processes in manufacturing:[16]

Assembly	37%
Shipping	14%
Machine tooling	11%
Measurement and testing	10%
Plastic working	7%
Pressing	7%
Welding	5%
Forging	3%
Casting	2%
Material handling	1%
Heating processes	1%
Painting	1%
Cutting	1%

The 1987 Survey reveals that there exist 47,308 industrial robots in Japanese industry (table 5-2). The 1973 Survey reported 3,058 robot population (2,735 for machinery sectors), and the 1981 Survey, 14,158. Average annual growth rate is calculated to be about 21% for both 1973 to 1981 and 1981 to 1987 periods, excluding from the 1987 Survey the robots not belonging to machinery sectors in order to maintain consistency with the 1981 figure. Nearly 80 percent of total industrial robots are operated in transport equipment sector (44.2%, most of them in motor vehicle production) and electrical machinery sector (34.8%).

Flexible manufacturing system (FMS): According to the same MITI survey, Japanese industry possessed 259 flexible manufacturing systems

Table 5-6 Production of flexible manufacturing system (FMS)

(unit: number of unit)

Purchasing sectors year	1979 and before	1980	1981	1982	1983	1984	1985	Total
Primary metals							1	1
Fabricated metals	2		1	4	1	1	4	13
General machinery	8	3	2	4	11	10	10	48
Electrical machinery	1	2	1	2		6	2	14
Transport equipment, motor vehicles			3	3	4	4	9	23
Transport equipment, others	4	1	2	1	6	2	3	10
Precision instrument			1	4	2	1	4	12
Other manufacturing				1		2	2	5
Other sectors				2	1	1		4
Exports				1		1	6	8
Own use of machine tools producers	3	1		5	10	5	7	31
Total	18	7	10	27	35	33	48	178

Source: Sangyo Kenkyujo [1988b].

as of 1987. As is indicated in panel (c) of table 5-2, general machinery sector posessed 171 units, followed by electrical machinery which had 44 units and transport equipment 40 (of which 21 were in motor vehicle industry).

The diffusion process of FMS is provided in table 5-3. According to this table, nearly one half of the systems are less than 3 years old. When one classifies the FMS by purpose into cutting and forming, the former type is of more recent vintage.

It is reported that the member companies of the Japan Machine Tools Industry Association have produced 178 FMS (table 5-6) by 1985 of which 8 systems were for exports. This leaves 170 systems produced for domestic use. The discrepancy between the figure cited in the Survey can be explained by the fact that the production statistics are nearly two years older than the survey and that FMS are being assembled by the users themselves. This can be easily done in the case of more sophisticated users who purchase machining centers and other necessary components in the market and build the system according to their own designs. Otaka [1988] cites 300 to 400 as the number of FMS being operated in Japan. Allowing time to elapse after the MITI Survey in 1987, which gives 259 as the total number, one can vaguely grasp the diffusion process of FMS.

Other manufacturing equipment: Table 5-3 provides information on the diffusion of clean rooms and laser machines. Clean rooms are indispensable for the production of electronic products such as IC and LSI which require strict control of the production environment in order to ensure precision and quality. Japanese industry possessed 5203 clean rooms in 1987. In addition, the Survey reports that there existed 21,768 units of clean bench and 28,298 units of vacuum apparatus in that year. The semiconductor industry entered a recession after considerable expansion in terms of capacity in 1984, and the diffusion process is apparently affected by the prevailing business condition. This explains the relatively small percentage of the system being introduced in the immediate past.

As for automatic assembly systems, there existed 49,736 units as of 1987 (table 5-3), of which majority (28,596 units, or 57.4%) belonged to the electrical machinery sector. Transport equipment sector had 11,787 units, or 23.7% of total. These two sectors are typical assembly industries. In 1973 when the statistics were first collected, there were 7,620 systems in total industry (7,295 for machinery sectors). By 1981, the number rose to 22,833; by 1987, the number had more than doubled to 49,736 (48,758 for machinery sectors).

The diffusion of triple-C technology is of course a fairly universal phenomenon. Tani [1989b], based on various country sources, gives the following figures as the number of NC machines.

U.S.A.	1983	103,308 units
Japan	1987	70,255
F.R.G.	1985	50,000
France	1985	35,000

As for stock of industrial robots, Tani [1989a] provides the following data based on various sources. (The figure cited for Japan is larger than the one from the MITI survey in table 5-2.)

U.S.A.	1985	20,000
Japan	1985	93,000
F.R.G.	1985	8,800
France	1984	2,750
U.K.	1985	3,017
Italy	1984	2,585

Regarding FMS, Tchijov and Sheinin [1989] says that, of the 394 cases of FMS entered in their database, the U.S.A. had 20.6%, Japan 18.5%, FRG 6.3%, France 12.2%, and the U.K. 17.0%. (Their figure for Japan seems to be underrepresented judging from the data on FMS in table 5-2, although similar situation may prevail for other countries.)

Automatic vending machines: This is a case relating to the application of C-C-C technology in services. Automatic vending machines are widely used in retail outlets, but they are also prevalent in transportation (train and subway tickets, toll gates) and finance (automatic tellers, cash transfer machines) as well as in communication (pre-paid telephone cards).

"In Japan, one is never far from a vending machine. Over five million of these steel-suited servitors sell everything from stamps to underwear. ... Today, these mighty machines do a huge business: last year's annual sales were just under ¥5 trillion (about 40 billion dollars). This impressive figure breaks down to 40.4% of the total going for beverages, 24.9% being spent on tickets, 24.8% on cigarettes, 5.9% on miscellaneous items, 2.5% on foodstuffs, and 1.5% going into such equipment as pay TVs, coin lockers, and parking meters." "Although alcohol and cigarettes are banned for those under 20, these items are readily available from vending machines. In the case of alcoholic beverages, the machines are shut down from 11 p.m. to 5 a.m. to restrict the possibilities of drunk driving and young people having access to the array of beers or spirits displayed inside. Japan's self-regulating society appears to ensure that unauthorized access will not become a problem. By the same token, vending machines are usually located out of doors, often in quite isolated locations in the countryside, safe in the knowledge that they won't be broken into or vandalized." "Not exactly service with a smile, but then some of Japan's vending machines can speak—thanking their customers for their patronage in their IC voices—and certainly all of them do make life more convenient for their contended users." The above is an excerpt from a journal article on the advent of vending machine age.[17] Vending machines are not unique in Japan, but its wide diffusion certainly is peculiar. The article clarifies economic impact as well as social conditions and technological trend.

Wide use of automatic vending machines is attributable to labor shortage in services. The demand for private services tend to fluctuate according to time of the day, days of the week, and seasons of the year. On the other hand, production of private services usually takes human attendance. In an urban environment, people work round the clock. In an economy where labor is getting scarce, a rapid increase in service prices or long queues at the peak of demand may result. It is for the benefit of both suppliers and customers to deploy machines where quick, uninterrupted service is an important ingredient of services. Where human attendance is appreciated, services are provided with courtesy but at high prices.

5-3 Explaining the diffusion process

Electronics technology is already having a tremendous impact on our society, and yet full impact is yet to unfold toward the 21st century and beyond. As an indicator of such development, one can look at production statistics of semiconductors, the progress of digital communication, or the development of database technology. They all represent electronics revolution. In this section, we examine the diffusion process of mainframe computers, NC metalworking machines, industrial robots, and automatic vending machines as representing C-C-C technology. Figure 5-2 represents the result of simulation of C-C-C diffusion based on a multisectoral industry model COMPASS (solid lines show actual figures and dotted lines, calculated values). Represented on the vertical axis is the share of C-C-C related machinery and equipment in total capital stock in respective industrial sectors.

Contributing factors behind the C-C-C diffusion are as follows:

(a) Relative price of labor and capital: As labor becomes scarce compared to capital, producers are tempted to replace labor by capital. The relative price is determined by wage rate per hour and the price of investment goods.

(b) Investment in plant and equipment: Capital formation is motivated by such factors as labor saving, research, and energy conservation, in addition to capacity expansion and cost considerations arising from rate of interest.

The latter in turn is determined in the market based on saving-investment balance in a macroeconomic sense. The stimulation of investment due to innovation, therefore, help narrow the macroeconomic imbalance due to excess saving in the Japanese context. The Japanese economy has continued to expand in the 1980s along the high-tech path, compared to general stagnation in the 1970s when it suffered from resource constraints. Growth has been strong since 1985 mainly due to active domestic investment among generally favorable expansion of other final demand items including housing investment, private consumption, and exports, in addition to half-hearted resumption of fiscal policy which is aimed at promoting domestic demand after a decade of austerity. It is generally agreed that the contributing factors behind active business investment lie in the diffusion of triple-C technology. This includes expansion of productive capacity in this field and the need to construct office building which actually is a new form of factory in the age of electronics.

A few words on statistical data are in order. In a previous work, we have already developed time series data on the stock of mainframe computers, industrial robots, and automatic vending machines. The value of mainframe computers being used in industrial sectors are compiled in Japan. We use the published data without adjusting for the quality change. As for industrial robots and vending machines, only production statistics are available. The MITI survey in this case gives only the number of industrial robots and not the values. Thus, we were obliged to estimate the stock of industrial robots assuming an expected life expectancy of such machinery. The same procedure was adopted for automatic vending machines.[18]

As for NC machines, for which time series data were developed here

Figure 5-2 Diffusion of high-tech, simulation results

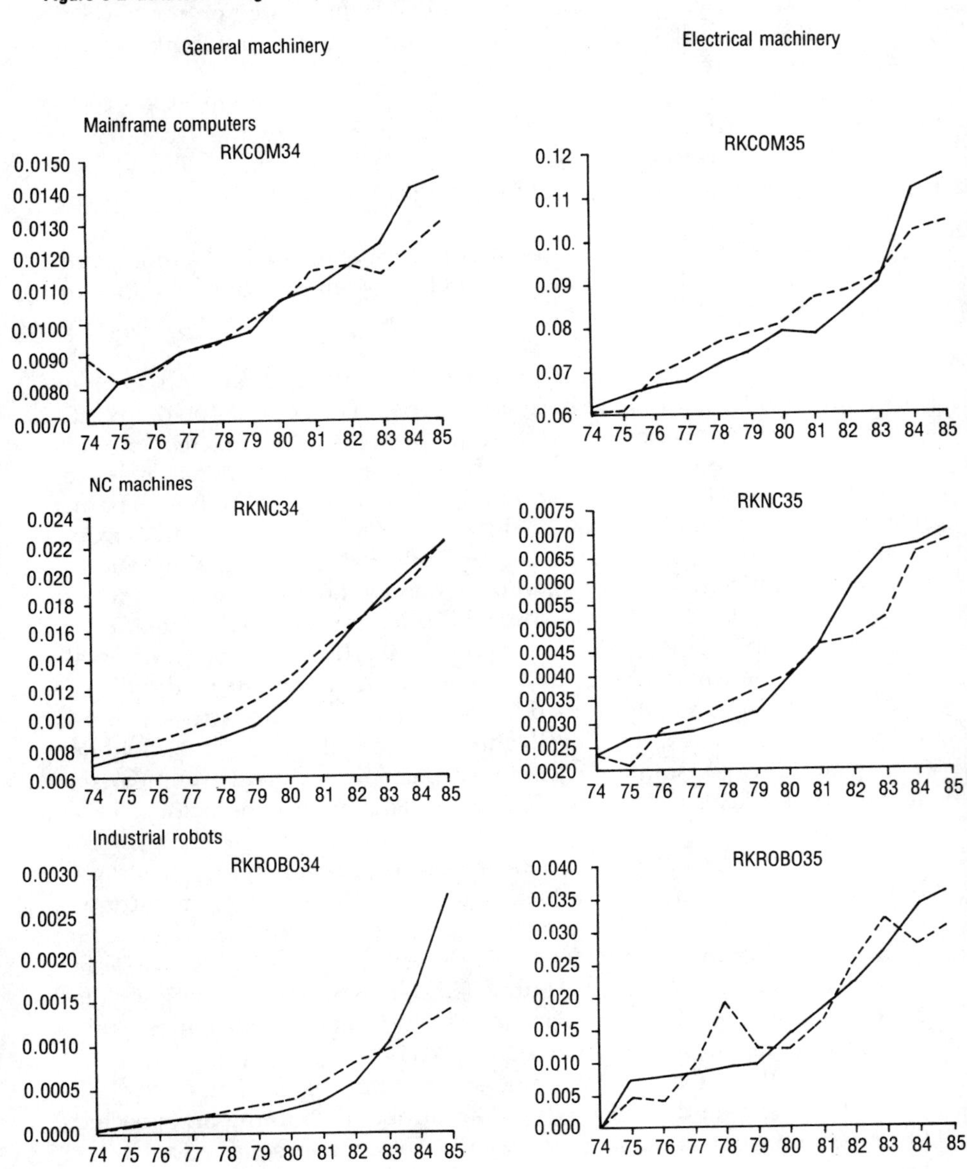

Source: COMPASS simulation results.

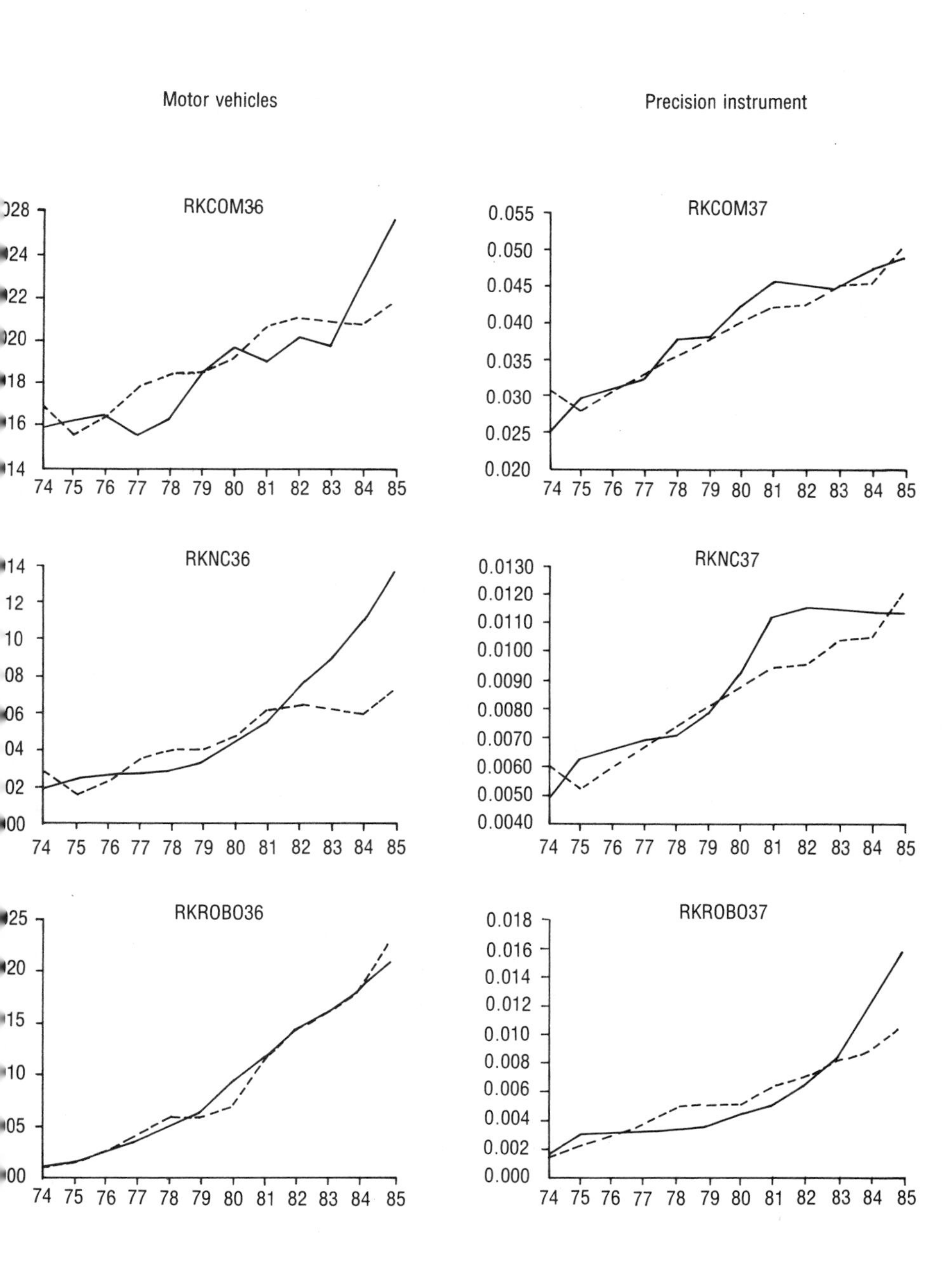
Motor vehicles
Precision instrument
RKCOM36
RKCOM37
RKNC36
RKNC37
RKROBO36
RKROBO37
0.055
0.050
0.045
0.040
0.035
0.030
0.025
0.020
0.0130
0.0120
0.0110
0.0100
0.0090
0.0080
0.0070
0.0060
0.0050
0.0040
0.018
0.016
0.014
0.012
0.010
0.008
0.006
0.004
0.002
0.000
74 75 76 77 78 79 80 81 82 83 84 85

Table 5-7 Estimated series on NC machines in use by industry

(unit: billion yen)

Modified JSIC Code	Industrial sector	1970	1975	1980	1981	1982	1983	1984	1985	1986	1987
34	General machinery	8.662	38.105	71.438	94.789	120.693	145.855	171.303	206.508	248.503	284.984
35	Electrical machinery	2.242	9.869	19.970	27.051	27.169	46.997	56.937	70.688	87.091	101.343
36M	Transport equipment, motor vehicle	4.784	14.208	36.692	52.446	74.358	95.642	117.168	146.947	182.470	213.330
36S	Transport equipment, others	2.981	9.311	27.645	40.502	60.843	80.602	100.585	128.229	161.205	189.853
37	Precision instrument	0.941	2.934	7.245	10.269	11.982	13.646	151.329	17.657	20.434	22.850
34&	Machinery sectors total	17.234	65.297	135.941	185.420	244.951	302.777	361.259	442.163	538.671	622.507

Note: Estimated by author. See text for the estimation procedure.
Source: Tables 5-1 and 5-5.

for the first time, we have figures on the value of existing stock (evaluated at book value) as well as the number as of 1987 in the MITI's *Survey on Machine Tools Installation, 1987*. The same publication in earlier years provided only the number of industrial robots for 1967, 1973, and 1981. The data are tabulated in table 5-2 above. We also provided series on the production of NC machines in table 5-5 above. An obvious choice is to come up with an estimated series on NC machine stock in value based on these data. More precisely, we followed the following steps.

(1) For machinery sectors total, general machinery, electrical machinery, transportation equipment, automobiles, and precision instrument sectors for which data are provided in table 5-2, we adopt the stock figures for the survey years.

(2) For interim years, we first calculate the increments between surveys. The increment in number of robots has been proportioned annually based on the production figures during the period in question. One problem here is that the production series do not provide data on purchasing sectors. We had to assume, therefore, that identical time pattern had prevailed among machinery sectors. This procedure preserves the time pattern of economic boom and recession which characterized the diffusion process of metalworking machinery, of which industrial robot is one.

(3) Based on the time series data on the estimated stock of industrial robots in terms of number of units, we obtained estimated series in terms of value using the 1987 book values.

Thus, we have time series data on mainframe computers, NC machines, industrial robots, and automatic vending machines, although the basis of estimation is not entirely consistent. We believe that the data are reasonably good proxy for the existing stock of C-C-C related equipment, pending availability of more direct statistics. Two points need to be mentioned here. First, they are basically evaluated at different prices at different points in time. They are not quality-adjusted. Second, they do not include values of peripheral equipment. For example, in the case of industrial robot introduction, it is reported that, taking the price of robot itself as 1, cost of peripheral equipment amounts to an additional 1.13. Adding other cost (training, engineering, etc.) which is an additional 0.27, total cost becomes 2.4.[19] A situation like this may be true for other equipment, but this is not reflected in our calculation of the share of C-C-C diffusion in total capital stock which we use below.

With estimated statistical data in hand, our strategy is to use economic variables which are endogenously generated in the model framework in explaining the diffusion process. We believe it important to explain the process in an interdependent model framework rather than an isolated process because of complex feedback process. As a working hypothesis, we may assume based on various surveys that labor saving is one of the dominant objectives in introducing industrial robots. We may also assume that the same is true for the introduction of automatic vending machines. Industry wants to replace labor with capital whenever wage rate becomes relatively expensive. Whether the relative price is significant or not is the test whether new technology is of labor saving nature or not. But labor substitution can only be achieved when business condition is good and warrants investment. When the demand for a particular industry is stagnant, industry would not carry out investment even if relative price of labor is undesirably high. In specifying the equation which describes the diffusion, we have examined the possiblity of assuming some asymptotic level at which the process comes to a saturation point. Our tentative conclusion is that it is too early in the diffusion process to contemplate saturation. Even when a particular type of equipment comes to a saturation point after which new installation comes to a halt, there emerge new types of equipment in related fields. However, our empirical examination suggests that the function which incorporates saturation level and uses logarithmic, reciprocal transformation generally performs better.[20]

In the model, diffusion rates (RK—i) in respective sectors are explained by the relative price of labor and capital (WHRi) and the real capital formation (IPi). In the following RKROBOi, RKNCi, RKCOMi, and RKVENDi refer to diffusion rates (i.e., shares in capital stock) of industrial robots, NC metalwarking machines, mainframe computers, and automatic vending machines, respectively.

$$\left.\begin{array}{l} \text{RKROBOi} \\ \text{RKNCi} \\ \text{RKCOMi} \\ \text{RKVENDi} \end{array}\right\} = \text{f (WHRi, IPi)}$$

The reasoning behind the specification is that the diffusion of new technology would be accelerated as the relative price of capital becomes lower, either due to appreciation of wage level or cheapening of capital equipment prices. Capital formation exhibits fluctuations reflecting the changes in demand-supply gap and/or the levels of interest rate. It can be assumed that the introduction of new technology would be easier when investment is being carried out in order to cope with rising demand. Empirical examination of the function gave fairly good results, as we list below.

[Diffusion of industrial robots]
Manufacturing total (sample 1974–1985):

$$\ln RKROBO0M = \underset{(23.96)}{7.6430} \ln WHR0M + \underset{(2.53)}{0.4853} \ln IP0M \underset{(-37.53)}{-101.6350}$$

S.E.=0.1031 ADJ R-SQ=0.9934 D.W.=1.1136

General machinery (sample 1974–1985):

$$\ln RKROBO34 = \underset{(11.73)}{7.3604} \ln WHR34 - \underset{(-12.51)}{96.5137}$$

S.E.=0.3216 ADJ R-SQ=0.9254 D.W.=0.4950

Electrical machinery (sample 1974–1985):

$$\ln RKROBO35 = \underset{(6.42)}{7.1979} \ln WHR35 \underset{(-6.76)}{-89.532}$$

S.E.=0.5922 ADJ R-SQ=0.7856 D.W.=1.6877

Transportation equipment, motor vehicles (1974–1985):

$$\ln RKROBO36M = \underset{(10.91)}{5.3634} \ln WHR36 + \underset{(2.40)}{0.3884} \ln IP36M - \underset{(-14.08)}{72.1051}$$

S.E.=0.1584 ADJ R-SQ=0.9754 D.W.=1.0075

Precision instrument (sample 1974–1985):

$$\ln RKROBO37 = \underset{(8.86)}{3.9612} \ln WHR37 \underset{(-9.86)}{-52.1722}$$

S.E.=0.2272 ADJ R-SQ=0.8757 D.W.=0.6492

[Diffusion of NC metalworking machines]

General machinery (sample 1968–1985):

$$\ln RKNC34 = \underset{(1.10)}{0.3093} \ln WHR34 + \underset{(2.53)}{0.1940} \ln IP34 + \underset{(5.31)}{0.7564} \ln RKNC34(-1) - \underset{(-1.41)}{5.9898}$$

S.E.=0.6403 ADJ R-SQ=0.9923 D.W.=1.4213

Electrical machinery (sample 1967–1985):

$$\ln RKNC35 = \underset{(18.31)}{1.7460} \ln WHR35 + \underset{(2.96)}{0.2028} \ln IP35 - \underset{(-33.23)}{27.4931}$$

S.E.=0.1151 ADJ R-SQ=0.9813 D.W.=0.7304

Transportation equipment, motor vehicles (sample 1967–1985):

$$\ln RKNC36M = \underset{(5.66)}{1.4639} \ln WHR36 + \underset{(2.21)}{0.5332} \ln IP36M - \underset{(-11.31)}{26.5099}$$

S.E.=0.3384 ADJ R-SQ=0.8356 D.W.=0.5584

Precision instrument (sample 1967–1985):

$$\ln RKNC37 = \underset{(7.32)}{1.0278} \ln WHR37 + \underset{(2.00)}{0.1857} \ln IP37 - \underset{(-13.82)}{17.8616}$$

S.E.=0.1330 ADJ R-SQ=0.9353 D.W.=0.7359

[Diffusion of mainframe computers](the results for nonmanufacturing sectors are omitted here)

All industries (sample 1967–1985):

$$\ln RKCOM00 = \underset{(12.15)}{0.8586} \ln WHR00 + \underset{(4.68)}{0.4347} \ln IP00 - \underset{(-54.13)}{18.5266}$$

S.E.=0.0486 ADJ R-SQ=0.9906 D.W.=1.7715

General machinery (sample 1967–1985):

$$\ln RKCOM34 = \underset{(10.76)}{0.7177} \ln WHR34 + \underset{(3.26)}{0.2850} \ln IP34 - \underset{(-26.05)}{15.0692}$$

S.E.=0.0876 ADJ R-SQ=0.9466 D.W.=1.2721

Electrical machinery (sample 1967–1985):

$$\ln RKCOM35 = \underset{(10.03)}{1.0294} \ln WHR36 + \underset{(0.91)}{0.0674} \ln IP35 - \underset{(-16.99)}{15.12}$$

S.E.=0.1238 ADJ R-SQ=0.9341 D.W.=0.5324

Transport equipment (sample 1967–1985):

$$\ln RKCOM36 = \underset{(5.69)}{0.4910} \ln WHR36 + \underset{(1.91)}{0.1841} \ln (IP36M+IP36S) - \underset{(-15.37)}{11.1047}$$

S.E.=0.1063 ADJ R-SQ=0.8422 D.W.=0.8962

Precision instrument (sample 1967–1985):

$$\ln RKCOM37 = \underset{(4.67)}{0.5975} \ln WHR37 + \underset{(2.23)}{0.1886} \ln IP37 - \underset{(-9.55)}{11.2544}$$

S.E.=0.1212 ADJ R-SQ=0.8837 D.W.=1.5763

[Diffusion of automatic vending machines]

Wholesale and retail (sample 1965–1985):

$$\ln RKVEND = \underset{(4.19)}{1.6106} \ln WHR40 + \underset{(2.85)}{0.9284} \ln IP40 - \underset{(-13.47)}{29.7386}$$

S.E.=0.1979 ADJ R-SQ=0.9782 D.W.=0.8486

5-4 Further remarks

It is generally believed that the introduction of C-C-C technology aims at labor saving in the face of changing relative prices of labor and capital. However, the purpose of factory automation (FA) and office automation (OA) is not totally attributable to this factor. According to a survey conducted in 1985 by the Japan Society for the Promotion of Machine Industry cited in Mori [1989], the main purpose of FA in 213 Japanese factories were are the following. The survey covers machinery sectors.

Quality of products	54.5%
Lead time reduction	38.5%
Labor saving	80.3%
Production capacity expansion	39.4%
Flexibility	33.3%
Cost stabilization	8.9%
Safety of workers	12.7%
Others	2.8%

Although the most often cited objective of factory automation is labor saving, we may interpret the survey result that quality improvement and lead time reductions, together with increased flexibility are among the important objectives pursued by industry.

Similar points can observed from the survey conducted by Kokichi Omi and cited in Otaka [1988]. Omi reports on the after-the-introduction evaluation of FMS in 11 Japanese factories. As for labor inputs, the responding firms say that saving from 1/3 to 20/1 has been achieved, with the mode ranging around 1/5 to 1/8. They all report increased capital investment while at the same time reporting increased operating time. Most of them report an increase from one shift (8 hours) to 3 shifts (21 to 24 hours). The rate of capacity utilization is reported to have increased from 20% to 70%, 55% to 75%, or 67% to 93%, depending on the cases. As a result, cost reduction of 30% to 90% has been reportedly achieved. Production time has been reduced by as much as 1/3 to 1/4 than previously was the cae.

By adopting new technology, therefore, quality improvement and cost reductions are being achieved hand-in-hand. In a sense, they are inseparable objectives of the innovation process.

One may suspect that the labor saving nature of new technology may invite opposition from labor. A survey by the MITI takes issues at this point. Direct impact of the introduction of C-C-C technology is the displacement of workers.[21] Of the sections where FA and OA have been introduced, 62.0% experienced reduction of staff, and 23.4% of sections related to the ones with increased automation also experienced reduction.

Despite reduction of workers, however, no business firms responded that labor union problem was involved in the introduction of FA. There was a 1987 survey by the Japan Society for the Promotion of Machine Industry with 147 responding factories. The following factors are cited as the obstacles in CIM penetration according to the Japanese industry (machinery sectors including general machinery, electrical machinery, transport equipment, and precision instrument)(in number of cases, multiple answers).[22]

Huge investment	64
Price of microelectronics equipment	35
Insufficient facility	20
Insufficient preparation	29
Management problem	49
Standardization of products required	50
Standardization of microelectronics insufficient	13
Economic difficulties	7
Labor union problems	0
Anxiety to secure demand	9
Support of top management	6
Others, unknown	10

Behind this may lie the fact that most establishments are experiencing severe shortage of skilled workers. With increased automation, physical skills which require long period of on-the-job training can be replaced by young but technically-trained personnel. We may assume that the inevitability of substitution of workers by machinery is in this sense well understood by the unions. Second factor which alleviates labor union opposition is that redundant workers are being assigned new jobs by the firms, without causing loss of employment opportunity. The survey by MITI cited above reports that in the case of large firms (more than 3,000 employees), 80.0% cope with the labor redundancy by job reassignment, 20.0% by assigning outside jobs, and 24.0% through other measures. There were none which responded that early retirement was the solution. In the case of smaller firms (less than 499 workers), the response was 93.5%, 3.3%, and 7.6%, respectively. In addition, 4.3% said that they recommend early retirement. Of those who undergo job reassignment, 92.0% were within the same establishment and 6.2% were for other establishments of the firm. (Remaining 1.8% of the cases were 'unknown.') This means that the majority of workers found new jobs without having to change their place of work.

That is, reduction of workers directly involved in production is compensated to a large degree by creation of new jobs within the same establishment or within the same firm.[23] Introduction of C-C-C technology requires increased number of programmers, maintenance workers, etc., often implying the necessity of upgrading required skill levels. The above survey points out considerable decrease in the demand for skilled workers, and practically no change for unskilled category, female workers, and part-time workers. At the same time it reports considerable increase of maintenance workers, production engineers, and information processing engineers. The roles of the workers are also changing. In the case of production workers, increased functions include participation in maintenance (58.9%), programming (63.1%), and operation of multiple units (84.7%). As for maintenance workers, increased roles include jobs requiring knowledge on electricity and electronics (97.7%), technical consultation with workers (71.2%), participation in the preparation of operation of equipment (37.8%), and programming (58.3%).

All this points to the importance of flexible employment practices, retraining of workers, and basic scientific knowledge on the part of the working force.

Footnotes:

1 The data are from the Ministry of International Trade and Industry, *Current Production Statistics Survey*.

2 Data are compiled by the Ministry of Posts and Telecommunications. Cited here from *Japan Statistical Yearbook*, 1989, p.317.

3 Kase [1989], pp.4–7. For detailed description of database in Japan, see Database Promotion Center, *Database White Paper*.

4 The number of databases are in net terms. Identical database is sometimes available from more than one database vender. The gross number in 1988 stood at 2040. Of the total number of 1,436, 26.9% is reported to be produced by Japanese firms and the rest are produced abroad.

5 The data are from the Ministry of International Trade and Industry, *Report on the Survey on Selected Service Industries*. The sales of database industry is entered under "information providing service" up to 1986. After 1987, this item was abolished and succeeded by "database service." The 1988 figure based on quick report is 106.3 billion yen. Kase [1989] says that the figure is underestimated reflecting changes in reporting practice. The 1988 figure cited here is an estimate by Kase.

6 The data for facsimile network subscribers are from the Ministry of Posts and Telecommunications; cited here from *Japan Statistical Yearbook, 1989*, p.317. The production statistics is from the Ministry of International Trade and Industry, *Current Production Statistics Survey*. Production figures include exports.

7 MITI, *Survey on Machine Tools Installation*. The survey, designated statistics No.47, was first carried out in 1952. Recent ones which contain information on NC machines include the 1973 Survey (the 5th), 1981 Survey (the 6th), and 1987 Survey (the 7th). The surveys were undertaken as of September 30. The 1973 survey covered establishments with more than 100 employees, whereas the surveys in 1981 and 1987 covered those with more than 50 employees. For detailed comparisons of coverage, etc. of the surveys, see *Survey on Machine Tools Installation, 1987*, p.6.
8 *Survey on Machine Tools Installation, 1973*, pp.26–27.
9 *Survey on Machine Tools Installation, 1981*, pp.26–27.
10 *Survey on Machine Tools Installation, 1987*, p.10. The value of rented units, however, has been assessed based on the market value.
11 ibid., p.10.
12 ibid., p.18.
13 Here again, we neglect small differences in diffusion rates for all industries and for machinery sectors.
14 *Japan Economic Journal* (Japanese), Aug. 8, 1989.
15 The Japan Industrial Robot Association [1989], p.6.
16 Ibid., p.11.
17 *Sumitomo Corporation News*, No.77, November 1989, p.7.
18 See Uno [1989a], pp.149–152. We assumed that industrial robots and automatic vending machines will remain in service for 5 years.
19 Mori [1987], p.8.
20 For this and other types of linear transformation, see, for example, Jhonston [1963], pp.44–45.
21 Ministry of International Trade and Industry, *Report on a Survey on Employment under Service — and information — Orientation of the Economy* (Sabisu Joho Deizaika Koyo chosa Kenkyu Hokohusho)*, cited in MITI [1985].
22 Cited here from Mori [1989].
23 Similar observations have been dominant in Japan. See, for example, Ministry of Labor, *Labor White Paper, 1983*, p.121; *Labor White Paper, 1985*, p.6; Matsugu "The Diffusion of Microelectronics and Its Impact on Employment, A Comparison of Japan and West Germany* (Maikroerekutoronikusuno Donyu Jokyoto Koyoeno Eikyo—HihontoNishikoitsuno Hikaku Kenkyu)" in Mizuno, et al. [1986].

Part 3

Investment

Chapter 6. Innovation and finance

6-1 Investment reversal

In the latter half of the 1980s, there have been two developments in investment trends which symbolizes the emergence of Japan as a major capital contributor. One is that Japan's investment in plant and equipment surpassed that of the United States in 1988. The other is that Japan has become the single largest capital exporter in the world. Japan's saving-investment balance and its implication on capital formation trends and foreign economic relations is examined empirically in this chapter.

Investment in plant and equipment is the vehicle by which new technology is implemented in production processes. It is noteworthy in this sense that in 1988, Japan's private investment in productive facilities exceeded that of the United States. National economic accounts for 1988 reveals that investment in plant and equipment in Japan amounted to 498 billion dollars (converted at one U.S.$ = ¥128.15), exceeding the U.S. figure of 488.4 billion dollars by 9.6 billion dollars (Table 6-1).

The reversal in the country-ranking occurred first in 1988. In 1987, Japan's private investment in plant and equipment was 388.4 billion dollars in current value (converted at one U.S.$ = ¥144.62). Compared to the U.S. value of 446.8 billion dollars, this was 58.4 billion dollars short. In 1988, Japan's investment has grown 28.2% over the previous year in dollar terms as opposed to 9.3% growth in the United States. The U.S. investment growth was particularly high in 1988 reflecting economic boom. In this sense, the alleged fault of American business, which can be traced to M&A's (mergers and acquisitions) and short-term improvement in balance sheet rather than long-term improvement in productive efficiency through investment in plant and equipment, was at least partly corrected during that year. However, Japanese business proved to be more active in real investment.

One of the reasons for Japan's emergence as the major source of capital is the appreciation of the yen currency. It is true, therefore, that the Japanese trend is exaggerated, representing nominal expansion rather than real. In fact, in terms of the yen currency, the growth of Japan's investment in plant and equipment is recorded at 14.0% in 1988, which is only one half of the figure in dollar terms.

However, even in terms of the yen currency, Japan's investment in plant and equipment has shown a rapid growth in the recent past (Table 6-3). The trend is expected to continue in 1989 and beyond. This is particularly true in high-technology field such as semiconductors where

Table 6-1 Private investment in plant and equipment in selected countries, 1988
(unit: billion dollars, %)

	Japan	U.S.	F.R.Germany	U.K.	France
GNP (growth over previous year, %)	2,863.3 (19.3)	4,864.3 (7.5)	1,208.0 (7.5)	817.0 (20.1)	949.2 (7.6)
Plant and equipment investment (growth over previous year, %)	498.0 (28.2)	488.4 (9.3)	147.7 (11.1)	n.a.	105.8 (13.5)
Share in GNP (%)	17.4	10.0	12.2	n.a.	11.1

Source: *Japan Economic Journal* (J), May 19, 1989.

production facilities for 1M-DRAM (one mega dynamic random access memory) and even for 4M-DRAM are being built at a rapid pace. Investment in information and communication field, such as digital communication network and communication satellites, is also expected to nearly double within a year. As a consequence of sound expansion of the economy, basic material industries such as iron and steel, petrochemicals, and paper and pulp are also expanding their productive capacities, a phenomena not experienced in the recent past.

Owning to the new production facilities which take advantage of the latest R&D, Japanese business will be able to produce new products, high-quality products, and price-competitive products. Unless this trend is countered by the American business, international competition on a global scale will end up in Japan's favor.

The U.S. government officials are reportedly concerned with active Japanese investment in plant and equipment. In the U.S.-Japan structural negotiations, the American side expounded on the following points: (1) increased investment in plant and equipment would accelerate Japan's exports and (2) public investment should be activated rather than spending for private investment.[1] They mentioned that increased investment in industrial sectors where surplus capacity exists would lead to expansion of exports and that they urged Japanese business and the government to take account of the U.S. concern. They pointed out automobiles, iron and steel, electronics, and shipbuilding as the sectors where surplus capacity was observed. The indications are that they expect Japan to voluntarily restrain investment in these sectors, although they have carefully told that their comment should not be interpreted as U.S. demand to curtail private investment in Japan. They pointed out that if Japan continues to expand productive capacity in sectors where there is already an excess capacity world-wide, Japan's business profit will have to be squeezed, too. The U.S. is concerned because Japanese busineses tend to act in a concerted manner in order to compete with each other.

As to the U.S. demand to expand public investment, the Japanese finance minister reportedly responded that Japanese fiscal policy is to be decided by the Japanese themselves; likewise, the Japanese have not intervened in the budgetary process in the U.S.[2] He said that (1) there is no change in the stated policy of nullifying deficit financing in 1990 and that (2) judging from the state of the domestic economy, there is no need for activating fiscal policy in order to promote business conditions. Finance Ministry officials also did not hide irritation over U.S. demand to activate investment in airports and expressways saying that they "did not expect the U.S. to intervene to such a degree." They interpret the American demand as intervention in the budgetary process. They are doubly sensitive because of the timing of the demand which just preceded a general election.[3]

Business circles also responded strongly. Evidently, in such sectors as steel, auto, shipbuilding, and electronics, insufficient investment in the U.S. resulted in insufficient gains in productivity and insufficient cost reductions, and created lags in technological innovation. However, the Japanese business reiterated that the U.S. accusation of Japanese practice of reinvesting the profit based on long term business strategy is ill-founded. For example, in semiconductor industry, mass production of 4MDRAM is just beginning, with planned investment of 95 billion yen for Toshiba and Hitachi, and 90 billion yen for NEC, whereas the production of 1MDRAM, which is currently in the main stream and its price tending to decline, is being tapered off. "Investment is an absolute must in order to prepare for the production of next generation products. It is not simply intended to expand production capacity." (Toshiba) "Production level of semiconductors are constantly being adjusted judged from the trends in demand and the market conditions. Investment in plant and equipment does not directly lead to excess supply." (Hitachi) In automobiles, Japanese direct investment in the North America alone will be enough to produce 2.4 million cars a year in the early 1990s, and car producers cannot afford excess capacity in the domestic market. "In the coming years, we prefer local production, at the cost of voluntarily restraining exports. Investment in Japan will not result in increased car exports." (Nissan) "We need some excess capacity in order to shift to new product line." (Toyota) In steel industry, active investment is intended for high-value added, high-technology products. The industry is to continue scrapping and consolidating existing plants. "Investment in plant and equipment is the vital issue to management. It is an inevitable strategy for survival along the expansion of the market." (Kawasaki Steel) In shipbuilding, the planned capacity lies well within the agreed-upon regulation. Some idle shipbuilding capacity will also be put into operation, but "We have drastically curtailed the production capacity only recently. New investment is intended for replacing old facilities and to cope with labor shortage, and is not intended to expand

Table 6-2 Capital account balance in selected countries

(unit: billion dollars)

	Japan	U.S.	F.R.Germany	U.K.	France	EC
Capital account balance						
1965	(−) 0.5	(−) 6.6	0.5	(−) 0.4	(−) 0.2	
1970	(−) 0.6	(−) 5.2	0.7	(−) 0.4	1.4	
1975	0.4	(−) 23.6	(−) 4.0	1.3	(−) 1.5	
1980	14.5	(−) 26.1	1.4	(−) 5.2	6.1	
1981	(−) 16.6	(−) 22.9	5.1	(−) 11.4	1.8	
1982	(−) 14.7	(−) 20.8	0.1	1.5	8.6	
1983	(−) 20.1	24.0	(−) 5.7	(−) 8.0	8.0	
1984	(−) 35.9	75.0	(−) 13.2	(−) 21.6	3.0	—
1985	(−) 53.0	103.1	(−) 19.3	(−) 14.9	2.3	—
1986	(−) 72.6	88.9	(−) 38.6	(−) 16.8	(−) 1.9	—
1987	(−) 43.9	86.1	(−) 26.1	(−) 22.2	(−) 4.6	—
1988	(−) 66.2	100.5	(−) 68.0	0	2.5	—
Long-term capital						
1965	—	—	—	—		
1970	—	—	—	—	—	
1975	(−) 0.1	(−) 16.2	(−) 5.6	0.9	(−) 0.9	
1980	1.8	(−) 5.1	2.3	(−) 7.6	(−) 6.5	
1981	(−) 5.6	(−) 0.6	3.0	(−) 15.4	(−) 7.7	
1982	(−) 14.6	(−) 4.5	(−) 5.4	(−) 14.2	1.2	
1983	(−) 17.6	(−) 6.3	(−) 2.9	(−) 12.9	8.8	
1984	(−) 49.0	31.8	(−) 6.9	(−) 21.9	5.2	(−) 20.1
1985	(−) 64.5	73.3	(−) 4.7	(−) 21.5	3.8	(−) 21.5
1986	(−) 131.5	72.0	15.0	(−) 31.9	(−) 7.1	(−) 35.9
1987	(−) 136.5	33.6	(−) 12.8	0.4	2.0	8.3
1988	(−) 130.9	92.2	(−) 48.4	(−) 22.1	0.2	(−) 47.5
of which direct investment						
1965	(−) 0.0	(−) 4.6	0.6	(−) 0.3	0.1	
1970	(−) 0.3	(−) 5.9	(−) 0.3	(−) 0.4	0.2	
1975	(−) 1.3	(−) 9.6	(−) 0.6	(−) 1.0	0.0	
1980	(−) 1.6	(−) 0.4	(−) 2.8	(−) 1.3	0.1	
1981	(−) 4.0	13.5	(−) 3.0	(−) 7.1	(−) 1.8	
1982	(−) 3.7	16.7	(−) 1.5	(−) 2.3	1.1	
1983	(−) 3.0	6.1	(−) 1.5	(−) 1.9	0.0	
1984	(−) 5.8	17.5	(−) 3.8	(−) 8.2	0.3	—
1985	(−) 5.8	2.2	(−) 4.3	(−) 5.7	0.4	—
1986	(−) 14.3	5.4	(−) 8.6	(−) 9.1	(−) 2.1	—
1987	(−) 18.4	2.8	(−) 7.0	(−) 17.4	(−) 4.0	—
1988	(−) 34.7	40.9	(−) 8.7	(−) 13.1	(−) 6.0	—

Note: (−) indicates payments.
IMF data in terms of SDR have been converted to US$ by the annual average of exchange rate.
Source: IMF, *Balance of Payments Yearbook* and other country data. Cited here from The Bank of Japan, *Comparative Economic and Financial Statitics, Japan and Other Major Countries.*

the capacity." (Japan Shipbuilding Industry Association)

The U.S. demand to curtail investment is an interesting one from a policy point of view. First, it is contradictory to the policy coordination plans among leading nations that countries running balance of payments surplus should stimulate domestic demand. Active investment in plant and equipment has been a factor contributing to the expansion of domestic demand. This was an American demand, and actually, U.S. exports of capital goods such as machinery are expanding, thanks to stimulated investment in Japan. The curtailment of investment may invite deceleration of the growth of domestic demand, resulting in slower growth of imports.

Second, investment in plant and equipment is a decision by the private businesses based on the free will. The curtailment is only possible through direct government persuasion by the MITI and other ministries, and the United States has been critical of such practice. Actually, Mazda recently had to change their investment plan of their Second Bofu Factory from 240,000 cars to 150,000 cars in response to guidance given by the MITI. It is an irony that the U.S., accusing government intervention as a factor which is creating closedness of the Japanese market in various occasions including the U.S.-Japan structural negotiation, should rely on administrative guidance themselves.

Third, since the American side should be also aware of contradictory implication of their demand, one has to try to interpret the statement in a new context. That is, the U.S. is quietly shifting the policy from free trade to administered (or controlled) trade. Their argument would be to restrain Japanese investment in order to safeguard the free trade regime itself. Prevention of flooding of the market by Japanese products is the only way to preempt protectionist sentiment in the U.S., it may be alleged. Otherwise, the U.S. industry will be damaged by the superior supply capacity of the Japanese. On the Japanese side, slack in demand can be filled by increased public investment, and macroeconomic balance will be maintained. The wisdom of resorting to government intervention, with its rigidities and almost inevitable creation of rent-seeking activities by all the parties concerned, must be questioned at a time when macroeconomic policy of stimulating domestic demand is going on smoothly and the exchange rate adjustment is having its effect through reduced exports, increased imports, and active foreign direct investment.

Today, Japan is the largest money-saver in the world community, a factor which enabled her to become the largest source of overseas investment fund in the world. Direct investment increased dramatically as well as portfolio investment (Table 6-2). It is noted that the negative signs in the table reflect outflow of capital (or positive investment) from a particular country. Continued appreciation of the yen has made it economically desirable to locate production facilities overseas. Increased protectionism in her main trading partners was another factor which obliged direct foreign investment. This trend also necessitates investment in services such as finance, insurance, and sales outlet. The table reveals that Japan has merged as the largest source of capital in the world community. While the U.S. ceased to be the largest supplier of capital in the early 1980s and turns into a major importer of capital, Japan managed to replace the American role. The point is summarized in Table 6-2 which

Table 6-3 Supply of industrial funds in major countries

	Year	Japan (¥100 mil)	U.S. (US$100 mil)	U.K. (Stg £mil)	F.R.Germany (DM 100 mil)	France (FFr 100 mil)
Internal funds	1984	369,835 (59.3)	3,363 (77.8)	31,488 (91.5)	1,736.2 (77.4)	2,987.1 (40.7)
	1985	418,450 (58.4)	3,523 (87.4)	32,490 (82.3)	1,797.8 (76.0)	3,373.4 (58.0)
	1986	465,376 (58.2)	3,449 (73.7)	33,839 (69.4)	2,075.7 (73.2)	4,352.8 (59.8)
	1987	479,939 (52.9)	3,526 (83.6)	39,923 (55.3)	2,305.3 (83.3)	4,621.9 (41.8)
	1988	506,250 (48.3)	3,725 (84.8)	43,235 (56.2)	2,489.8 (80.6)	4,981.1 (47.8)
Funds raised in markets	1984	254.117 (40.7)	958 (22.2)	2,911 (8.5)	507.2 (22.6)	4,344.1 (59.3)
	1985	297.729 (41.6)	509 (12.6)	6,984 (17.7)	566.8 (24.0)	2,447.6 (42.0)
	1986	334.151 (41.8)	1,230 (26.3)	14,886 (30.6)	528.9 (18.7)	2,925.9 (40.2)
	1987	426,753 (47.1)	689 (16.4)	32,289 (44.7)	463.8 (16.7)	6,422.6 (58.2)
	1988	541,930 (51.7)	670 (15.2)	33,633 (43.8)	600.1 (19.4)	5,439.3 (52.2)
Borrowings	1984	212,836 (34.1)	906 (21.0)	4,278 (12.4)	453.0 (20.2)	3,337.3 (45.5)
	1985	239,880 (33.5)	346 (8.6)	6,319 (16.0)	446.1 (18.9)	1,268.1 (21.8)
	1986	269,394 (33.6)	813 (17.4)	8,782 (18.0)	337.7 (11.9)	476.8 (6.6)
	1987	277,280 (30.6)	446 (10.6)	15,516 (21.5)	271.8 (9.8)	4,194.3 (38.0)
	1988	339,760 (32.4)	725 (16.5)	31,379 (40.8)	522.6 (16.9)	3,279.3 (31.5)
Securities	1984	45.077 (7.2)	− 79 (−1.8)	−1,367 (−4.0)	54.2 (2.4)	1,006.8 (13.7)
	1985	50,459 (7.0)	149 (3.7)	665 (1.7)	120.7 (5.1)	1,179.5 (20.3)
	1986	63,728 (8.9)	306 (6.5)	6,104 (12.5)	191.2 (6.7)	2,449.1 (33.6)
	1987	102,497 (11.3)	225 (5.3)	16,773 (23.2)	192.0 (6.9)	2,228.3 (20.2)
	1988	111,154 (10.6)	−163 (−3.7)	2,254 (2.9)	77.5 (2.5)	2,160.1 (20.7)
Total	1984	623,952 (100.0)	4,321 (100.0)	34,399 (100.0)	2,243.4 (100.0)	7,331.2 (100.0)
	1985	716,179 (100.0)	4,032 (100.0)	39,474 (100.0)	2,364.6 (100.0)	5,820.9 (100.0)
	1986	799,527 (100.0)	4,679 (100.0)	48,725 (100.0)	2,834.2 (100.0)	7,208.7 (100.0)
	1987	906,692 (100.0)	4,216 (100.0)	72,212 (100.0)	2,769.1 (100.0)	11,044.5 (100.0)
	1988	1,048,180 (100.0)	4,395 (100.0)	76,868 (100.0)	3,089.9 (100.0)	10,420.4 (100.0)

Notes: 1. Figures in parenthesis show the composition ratios of fund sources.
2. The data refer to nonfinancial corporate sector, and do not include interfirm credits.
3. Japanese data on internal funds are based on national Accounts compiled by the Economic planning Agency. Of the funds raised in the market, the table does not list borrowing from the rest of the world.
4. The data for Germany and France include personal business and public corporations.

Source: The Bank of Japan, *Comparative Economic and Financial Statistics, Japan and Other Major Countries.*

depicts the capital accounts of selected countries. The figures here refer to the total of long-term and short-term international transactions in respective countries. Up to 1982, the United States continued to be the largest supplier of capital to the world market. Since 1983, however, she has turned to be a net recipient of capital and Japan emerged as a net supplier. In fact, in 1986, Japan recorded capital outflow amounting to 72.6 billion dollars, and in 1987, it was 43.9 billion dollars. In contrast, the United States recorded 78.6 billion dollars worth net inflow in 1986.

This chapter discusses new development in Japan's investment trend and its implication to the domestic economy as well as to international economic relations.

6-2 The flow of funds

Investment has to be financed. Japanese business is known to rely heavily on borrowing. Such practice is inevitable when business is growing rapidly because internal funds may not be large enough to cover the investment requirement. According to statistics on the supply of industrial funds, we notice that the portion financed by internal fund such as depreciation and retained profits tend to shrink at a time of active investment and vice versa. Thus, following the first Oil Crisis, the share of internal funds in total supply of industrial funds reached 60%.[4] Throughout the late 1970s and early 1980s when the economy stagnated, the ratio remained around 55 to 58%. There is an evidence that the ratio of internal funds is declining in the latter half of the 1980s. This can be seen in Table 6-3. In 1987 when the most recent figures were available, 53.2% was financed internally and 46.8% externally. Although this ratio is lower than in the high growth era when it recorded about 40%, increasing dependence on external funds clearly indicates rising business investment. And large portion of external funds is due to borrowing. The share of funds raised by securities is rising but, in 1987, it remained about 1/4 of total external funds, or 10,250 billion yen out of 42,675 billion yen.

In other major industrial countries such as the United States and Germany, the ratio of internal funds is much higher at around 80% (Table 6-3).

The fact that Japanese business has been able to raise industrial funds fairly easily when needed seems to indicate that financing has never been a constraint to growth. This is attributable to ample supply of savings and the existence of financial mechanism through which financial resources can be channeled into industrial use.

As for the supply of savings, let us look at Table 6-4 which shows the

Table 6-4 Financial surplus or deficit by economic sector in major countries

	Year	Public	Business	Personal	Overseas
Japan (¥ 100 mil)	1984	(−)172,742	(−) 51,303	292,957	(−) 83,504
	1985	(−)131.741	(−) 59,460	310,990	(−)115,176
	1986	(−)137,580	(−) 43,349	337,757	(−)141,787
	1987	(−) 48,143	(−) 77,207	273,864	(−)125,413
	1988	21,757	(−) 169,332	277,428	(−)101,923
	1989	23,269	(−) 268,634	363,905	(−) 78,532
U.S. (US$ 100 mil)	1984	(−) 1,739	(−) 242	1,746	718
	1985	(−) 2,004	(−) 220	1,287	1,042
	1986	(−) 2,233	(−) 465	1,665	1,326
	1987	(−) 1,934	(−) 280	1,230	1,503
	1988	(−) 1,995	(−) 329	1,276	1,362
	1989	(−) 2,049	(−) 521	1,985	688
U.K. (Stg £ mil)	1984	(−) 14,016	7,752	12,166	(−) 879
	1985	(−) 10,015	6,589	10,913	(−) 3,450
	1986	(−) 7,979	5,417	212	199
	1987	(−) 4,036	1,877	(−) 6,506	3,822
	1988	6,003	(−) 6,236	(−) 14,495	14,672
F.R. Germany (DM 100mil)	1984	(−) 337.2	(−) 279.3	1,109.3	(−) 157.9
	1985	(−) 197.0	(−) 337.3	1,138.6	(−) 380.5
	1986	(−) 238.7	(−) 371.0	1,265.3	(−) 786.8
	1987	(−) 359.2	(−) 295.9	1,288.7	(−) 773.2
	1988	(−) 452.0	(−) 345.1	1,430.7	(−) 842.0
	1989	38.4	(−) 705.5	1,486.7	(−) 975.9
France (FFR 100 mil)	1984	(−) 1,201.6	(−) 868.9	1,564.0	(−) 39.7
	1985	(−) 1,346.7	(−) 767.8	1,621.6	(−) 106.7
	1986	(−) 1,385.6	(−) 492.9	1,356.4	(−) 271.7
	1987	(−) 1,037.1	(−) 814.0	1,749.2	234.1
	1988	(−) 772.5	(−) 1,033.4	962.3	221.2

Note: Public sector includes public corporations in addition to central and local governments.
Source: Same as table 6-3.

Table 6-5 Financial surplus or deficit by economic sector

Year	Household	Corporate	Corporate: Non-financial	Corporate: Financial	General Government	Overseas
1965	2,517.6	(−) 1,261.9	(−) 1,429.7	167.8	(−) 920.5	(−) 335.2
1966	3,318.8	(−) 1,399.2	(−) 1,737.1	337.9	(−) 1,469.2	(−) 450.4
1967	4,115.4	(−) 2,819.4	(−) 3,177.2	357.8	(−) 1,364.8	68.8
1968	4,679.2	(−) 2,906.1	(−) 3,439.7	533.6	(−) 1,395.8	(−) 377.3
1969	5,197.0	(−) 3,453.9	(−) 4,107.0	653.1	(−) 980.3	(−) 762.8
1970	5,775.4	(−) 4,402.8	(−) 5,058.7	655.9	(−) 663.3	(−) 709.2
1971	7,572.5	(−) 4,037.4	(−) 5,014.8	977.4	(−) 1,533.5	(−) 2,001.6
1972	10,661.8	(−) 6,146.4	(−) 7,364.8	1,218.4	(−) 2,475.2	(−) 2,040.2
1973	9,997.7	(−) 6,782.3	(−) 8,575.2	1,792.9	(−) 3,247.2	31.8
1974	13,845.0	(−) 10,172.0	(−) 11,516.3	1,344.3	(−) 5,002.2	1,329.2
1975	15,663.9	(−) 4,963.6	(−) 6,136.9	1,173.3	(−) 10,900.9	200.6
1976	19,007.7	(−) 5,526.9	(−) 6,583.9	1,057.0	(−) 12,403.1	(−) 1,077.7
1977	20,567.7	(−) 4,286.5	(−) 4,786.5	500.0	(−) 13,438.2	(−) 2,483.0
1978	22,582.2	(−) 586.4	(−) 2,067.3	1,480.9	(−) 18,511.3	(−) 3,484.5
1979	20,133.5	(−) 4,649.3	(−) 6,711.4	20,621	(−) 17,453.6	1,969.4
1980	19,598.7	(−) 6,083.5	(−) 8,310.8	2,227.3	(−) 16,092.3	2,577.1
1981	28,131.8	(−) 8,272.1	(−) 7,801.8	(−) 470.3	(−) 18,712.7	(−) 1,147.0
1982	29,034.5	(−) 8,599.6	(−) 10,264.5	1,664.9	(−) 18,660.1	(−) 1,774.8
1983	29,103.5	(−) 5,148.0	(−) 10,312.2	5,164.2	(−) 18,995.1	(−) 4,960.4
1984	27,817.1	(−) 2,192.5	(−) 6,198.9	4,006.4	(−) 17,274.2	(−) 8,350.4
1985	30,003.0	(−) 5,311.3	(−) 7,703.8	2,392.5	(−) 13,174.1	(−) 11,517.6

Note: Figures are in terms of calendar year.
Source: Bank of Japan, *Flow of Funds*.

Table 6-6 Interest rate differentials between Japan and the United States

(unit: percent per annum)

	Japan			United States		
	Discount rate	Lending rate	Government bond yield	Discount rate	Lending rate (prime rate)	Government bond yield, long-term
1965	5.48	7.80	—	4.50		4.27
1966	5.48	7.48	6.86	4.50		4.77
1967	5.84	7.32	6.91	5.50		5.01
1968	5.84	7.46	7.03	6.00		5.46
1969	6.26	7.41	7.09	5.50		6.33
1970	6.00	7.66	7.19	4.50		6.86
1971	4.75	7.59	7.28	4.50		6.12
1972	4.25	7.05	6.70	7.50		6.01
1973	9.00	7.19	7.26	7.75		7.12
1974	9.00	9.11	9.26	6.00		8.06
1975	6.50	9.10	9.20	5.25		8.19
1976	6.50	8.26	8.72	6.00		7.87
1977	4.25	7.56	7.33	9.50		7.67
1978	3.50	6.31	6.09	12.00		8.49
1979	6.25	6.29	7.69	12.00		9.33
1980	7.25	8.32	9.22	13.00		11.39
1981	5.50	7.56	8.66	12.00	18.87	13.91
1982	5.50	7.15	8.06	8.50	14.86	13.00
1983	5.00	6.81	7.42	8.50	10.79	11.00
1984	5.00	6.54	6.81	8.00	12.04	12.52
1985	5.00	6.47	6.34	7.50	9.93	10.62
1986	3.00	5.59	4.94	5.50	8.35	7.68
1987	2.50	4.94	4.21	6.00	8.21	8.38
1988	2.50	4.93	4.28	6.50	9.32	8.85

Source: *International Financial Statistics*, Lending rate for Japan is the average contracted interest rates on loans and discounts of all banks, end of year, from the Bank of Japan, *Economic Statistics Annual*.

financial surplus or deficit by economic sector.

In the United States, household surplus of 141.5 billion dollars in 1988) was not enough to meet deficit of the government (194.6 billion dollars) and the business sector (62.6 billion dollars) and the gap has to be financed from abroad (119.8 billion dollars).

As for Japan, we realize first of all that the deficit in the business sector has expanded from 4,335 billion yen in 1986 to 7,721 billion yen in 1987 and 16,930 billion yen in 1988. In the case of Japan, extremely rapid expansion of financial deficit of the business sector (i.e., investment exceeding saving of the sector) in the recent past has been easily financed by the surplus in the household sector. In 1988, the government recorded surplus for the first time in many years, but even when this sector recorded deficit in the past, the household saving surplus was large enough to finance deficit in the government sector. A considerable portion of household surplus is going into overseas and helping finance saving shortage abroad, but the absolute amount seems to have levelled off since 1986. In fact, as can be observed in table 6-5 which gives the long-term perspectives of financial surplus or deficit by sector, household surplus was absorbed by the business sector. After the oil crisis and the resultant slower growth of the economy, business sector failed to do so, and this created a need for the government to run considerable amount of deficit. Overseas sector also absorbed the surplus. Such sectoral imbalance is being corrected by the recent surge of business investment.

6-3 Interest rate differentials

Heavy dependence on external funds used to mean heavy burden of interest payments, and, in fact, it was often cited as a factor which hindered Japanese business from becoming internationally competitive. According to table 6-6 which provides time series data on various interest rates in Japan and the United States, Japanese interest rates were uniformly higher till around 1976. If we compare lending rate in Japan with long-term government bond yield in the United States, in 1965 the former stood at 7.80% per annum and the latter at 4.27%; in 1975, the former stood at 9.10% and the latter 8.19%. (The lending rate in Japan was judged here as representative of Japanese interest rate; comparable figures for the U.S. is not available and was substituted by the government bond yield.) Similar trend is observed for the discount rate. In 1977, a reversal in the interest rate differentials between the two countries was experienced. Japanese discount rate was reduced to 4.25% from the previous level of 6.50%; in the United States, it was raised to 9.50% from 6.00%. The condition of the financial market was reflected in the lending rate in Japan and it became lower than the American rate for the first time.

Toward the end of the 1970s and the early 1980s, the U.S. interest rate had to be raised. In 1981, for example, the U.S. discount rate stood at 12.0% and the lending rate 18.87%. The U.S. monetary authority was fighting a two-digit inflation at that time. In the same year, the comparable figures for Japan stood at 5.50% and 7.56%, respectively.

More recently, Japanese interest rate stands at about 1/2 of the U.S. This differential is needed for the U.S. to attract foreign funds in order to supplement domestic financial resources. Financial balance can thus be obtained, but high interest rate is a heavy burden for real investment. This is so because the interest rate has to be paid out of profit. Also, the American producers are faced with keen competition from abroad (Japan is not the only one) and are not sure enough to commit themselves to investment projects which require long-term exposure. New technologies are themselves risky. Even if it becomes a technological success, one may be faced with competition from abroad and may turn out to be

Table 6-7 New loans for investment in plant and equipment

(unit: current prices, billion yen)

Sector	Modified JSIC Code		1980	1981	1982	1983	1984	1985	1986	1987	1988
(1)	01&	Agriculture, forestry, and fisheries	802	801	792	787	752	738	704	858	820
(2)	10&	Mining	82	121	151	125	103	90	74	124	108
(3)	18	Food processing	386	410	385	389	415	450	466	616	638
(4)	20&	Textiles	405	464	419	369	392	417	422	497	516
(5)	22	Lumber and wood products									
(6)	23	Furniture and fixtures									
(7)	24	Pulp, paper, and paper products									
(8)	25	Printing and publishing									
(9)	29	Leather and leather products									
(10)	28	Rubber products									
(11)	26	Chemicals	712	788	698	589	552	557	477	636	522
(12)	27	Petroleum (refining)	291	225	171	146	170	175	255	246	
(13)	30	Nonmetallic mineral products	355	379	302	267	254	288	232	294	323
(14)	31A	Iron and steel materials }	560	698	714	628	562	615	560	752	403
(15)	31B	Basic iron and steel products									
(16)	32	Basic nonferrous metal products									
(17)	33	Fabricated metals									
(18)	34	General machinery									
(19)	35	Electrical machinery									
(20)	36M	Transport equipment, motor vehicles }	984	1,309	1,156	1,131	1,348	1,633	1,376	1,431	1,537
(21)	36S	Transport equipment, others									
(22)	37	Precision instrument									
(23)	38&	Other manufacturing									
(24)	15	Construction	785	840	848	923	1,077	1,181	1,365	1,898	2,229
(25)	70	Electric power, gas, and water	1,942	2,350	2,294	2,402	2,426	2,243	1,973	2,463	2,160
(26)	40	Wholesale and retail trade	3,314	3,527	3,464	3,507	3,941	4,242	5,027	6,160	6,532
(27)	50&	Real estate	1,490	1,959	2,179	2,596	3,355	4,482	6,065	9,202	9,623
(28)	56R	Real estate rent									
(29)	60T	Transportation }	1,518	1,895	1,890	1,948	2,191	2,307	2,232	2,989	3,009
(30)	60C	Communication									
(31)	97	Public administration									
(32)	75P	Public services									
(33)	75M	Business and personal services	3,690	4,296	4,831	5,255	5,895	6,583	7,005	9,010	9,567
		Total	18,705	21,689	21,817	22,511	25,030	27,917	30,047	39,471	40,760
		Manufacturing total	5,082	5,900	5,367	4,968	5,283	6,044	5,597	6,671	6,704
		Capital formation (IP)			40,804	41,493	45,992	51,583	53,289	55,981	63,796

Note: Beginning 1970, stocks are excluded. Beginning 1975, industrial bonds are excluded.
Source: The Bank of Japan, *Economic Statistics Annual*.

Table 6-8 Private investment in plant and equipment by industry

(unit: billion yen 1980 prices)

Sector	Modified JSIC Code		1980	1981	1982	1983	1984	1985	1986	1987	1988
(1)	01&	Agriculture, forestry, and fisheries	5,405.3	5,049.3	5,032.5	4,919.8	5,132.8	5,230.6	5,311.6	5,463.1	5,587.6
(2)	10&	Mining	188.4	229.1	192.3	198.3	206.7	193.7	186.6	176.0	179.3
(3)	18	Food processing	849.5	897.0	1,005.3	908.6	946.5	1,163.5	1,275.9	1,510.9	
(4)	20&	Textiles	326.0	357.5	426.7	432.1	591.4	529.2	585.9	633.7	
(5)	22	Lumber and wood products									
(6)	23	Furniture and fixtures									
(7)	24	Pulp, paper, and paper products	560.7	388.5	409.5	518.3	579.1	728.5	787.9	889.9	
(8)	25	Printing and publishing	451.9	462.4	375.2	376.1	504.1	664.2	697.1	812.1	
(9)	29	Leather and leather products									
(10)	28	Rubber products									
(11)	26	Chemicals	1,316.5	1,347.6	1,454.1	1,521.0	1,613.8	2,001.9	1,908.4	2,095.6	
(12)	27	Petroleum and coal products	379.7	418.8	331.8	299.8	339.9	377.6	444.9	439.8	
(13)	30	Nonmetallic mineral products	670.5	688.0	624.9	565.9	656.3	757.2	701.7	739.3	
(14)	31A	Iron and steel materials									22,661.1
(15)	31B	Basic iron and steel products	1,039.2	1,254.8	1,633.7	1,507.9	1,298.2	1,161.9	1,321.8	1,028.3	
(16)	32	Basic nonferrous metal products	383.6	432.1	476.0	511.9	505.9	523.6	501.3	505.8	
(17)	33	Fabricated metals	876.2	822.6	772.4	893.7	1,150.6	1,075.8	1,170.6	1,175.2	
(18)	34	General machinery	1,355.7	1,633.4	1,615.2	1,442.1	1,701.5	2,034.1	1,714.2	1,575.3	
(19)	35	Electrical machinery	1,494.6	1,928.1	1,865.2	2,134.6	3,597.2	3,816.9	2,960.4	2,709.1	
(20)	36M	Transport equipment, motor vehicles	1,708.1	1,868.0	1,902.6	1,794.1	1,763.6	2,590.6	2,718.8	2,343.9	
(21)	36S	Transport equipment, others									
(22)	37	Precision instrument	312.5	355.0	354.4	430.4	430.2	608.0	595.1	679.7	
(23)	38&	Other manufacturing	985.0	904.5	944.6	1,010.3	1,137.9	1,182.5	1,337.3	1,543.4	
(24)	15	Construction	2,124.4	2,166.4	2,168.9	2,179.5	2,264.1	1,866.2	2,085.5	2,527.4	3,154.4
(25)	70	Electric power, gas, and water	3,526.6	4,082.9	3,914.5	4,077.9	3,869.1	4,048.0	4,294.7	4,937.8	4,557.2
(26)	40	Wholesale and retail trade	4,392.0	4,222.6	4,180.6	4,078.3	4,264.7	4,287.2	5,106.4	6,043.7	7,344.1
(27)	50&	Finance, insurance	923.9	941.0	952.1	1,055.8	1,167.7	1,206.8	1,379.9	1,695.6	2,035.8
(28)	50R	Real estate	739.1	729.9	879.4	884.0	1,103.7	1,433.7	1,557.5	2,106.8	2,838.8
(29)	60T	Transportation	2,774.4	2,843.4	3,019.0	2,841.2	2,917.1	4,501.1	5,553.9	6,682.2	7,829
(30)	60C	Communication									
(31)	97	Public administration									
(32)	75P	Public services									
(33)	75M	Business and personal services	3,387.5	4,124.0	4,505.0	5,275.8	6,730.1	8,293.7	9,067.5	8,972.4	11,072.3
		Total	36,171.4	38,147.1	39,035.6	39,857.2	44,472.2	50,286.6	53,265.1	57,287.0	66,613.5
		Manufacturing	12,709.8	13,758.4	14,191.4	14,346.7	16,816.3	19,235.5	18,721.5	18,682.0	22,661.1
		Capital formation (IP) total	37,616	39,778	40,804	41,493	45,972	51,583	53,289	55,981	63,796

Source: Economic Planning Agency, *Capital Stock of Private Enterprises*, December 1988; the data for 1988 are from Economic Planning Agency, *Capital Stock of Private Enterprises*, Quarterly Report, June 1989.

Table 6-9 Supplying sectors for private fixed capital formation, summary table

(unit: ratio of total)

Code	Sector names	1975	1980	1981	1982	1983	1984	1985
34	General machinery	0.1394	0.1230	0.1328	0.1297	0.1321	0.1378	0.1665
35	Electrical machinery	0.0806	0.0872	0.1217	0.1070	0.1252	0.1417	0.1317
36M	Motor vehicles	0.0518	0.0535	0.0540	0.0576	0.0581	0.0581	0.0487
36S	Other Transport equipment	0.0116	0.0177	0.0112	0.0187	0.0177	0.0166	0.0237
37	Precision instrument	0.0067	0.0094	0.0090	0.0098	0.0102	0.0110	0.0132
	Machinery sectors total	0.2899	0.2872	0.3286	0.3223	0.3429	0.3650	0.3835
15	Construction	0.6054	0.6097	0.5562	0.5655	0.5532	0.5295	0.4947
	Total	1.0000	1.0000	1.0000	1.0000	1.0000	1.0000	1.0000

Note: Total includes other sectors such as furniture and fixture, fabricated metals, and wholesale and retail trade.
Source: Kimio Uno, *Annual Input-Output Tables in Japan, 1975-1985*, 1990.

an economic failure. This is particularly so when the interest rate is high. Spending a lot of money on R&D may not be a wise choice when the fund is scarce and shareholders are short-sighted. Thus, rather than risk new technologies, businesses are tempted into mergers and acquisitions where less time-factor is involved and immediate gains are guaranteed. Such M&A's are a form of financial investment rather than real, because there would be no gains in the real economic sense (gains in productivity, improved quality, new products, and increased employment). It is true that in the United States new investment is active in business services, but it affects international competitiveness and trade balance in a rather round about way. Thus, it seems that the interest rate differentials, which emerged in the late 1970s and now firmly established, seem to have created a skewed business behavior in the United States.

6-4 Capital formation and the new technology

Table 6-7 looks at the investment in plant and equipment from the financial side. The figures refer to the new supply of industrial equipment funds (in current prices) surveyed by the Bank of Japan.[5] New loans for the manufacturing sector as a whole are compared with that for the total industry at the bottom of the table. It is revealed that the share of loans for the manufacturing sector used to amount to nearly 45% of total in 1965 and 1970. The share has declined to about 27% in 1980 and 22% in 1985. The latest figure stood at around 16%. In fact, in the 1980s, rapid increase in new loans has been recorded for real estate (6.46 fold), construction (2.83 fold), transportation (1.98 fold), wholesale and retail trade (1.97 fold), and business and personal services (1.88). Such trend is a clear indication of service orientation of the economy and investment need which accompany the structural change. Investment in manufacturing industry as a whole has increased only 1.32 fold during the same period. One important exception among manufacturing sectors is the machinery sector where new loans increased 1.56 fold.

Table 6-8 looks at investment in plant and equipment from the real side. The figures refer to capital formation series (in 1980 prices) compiled by the Economic Planning Agency and are the basis of our analysis in the next chapter on sources of growth. It is revealed that, here again, real estate sector recorded the most rapid expansion in investment (3.84 fold during 1980–1988 period), followed by business and personal services (3.27 fold), transportation and communication (2.59 fold), finance and insurance (2.20 fold), wholesale and retail trade (1.67 fold), and construction (1.48 fold).[6] Among the manufacturing sectors, electrical machinery where investment increased 1.81 (up to 1987) is particularly marked. The increase in transport equipment sector is recorded at 1.37 fold during the 1980–1987 period.

In absolute terms, machinery sectors combined (including general machinery, electrical machinery, motor vehicles, other transport equipment, and precision instrument) dominate the manufacturing sector amounting to 7308 billion yen and shares 39% of total manufacturing investment in 1987.

From the above observation, we may say that the Japanese economy is tending toward services in a wide sense including business and personal services; finance, insurance, and real estate; wholesale and retail trade, and transportation and communication. The construction sector is also extremely active.

The source of this structural change is the machinery sectors, in particular electric machinery. It seems safe to assume that electronics revolution represented by computer-communication-control (C-C-C) technology is the driving force of this sector. It is also very likely that other sectors are also being influenced by this technological change. The question then is the methodology to measure the magnitude of the diffusion of this new technology. For this purpose input-output framework is most suitable in that it provides most general description of economic structure and enables us to look into interindustry repercussion. Thus, we examined private fixed capital formation based on (a) annual input-output tables covering the 1975–1985 period and (b) fixed capital formation matrices covering the same period at five year intervals.[7]

The former enables us to examine the changes in sectoral composition of the supplying sector for private fixed capital formation.[8] The basis of our analysis is annual input-output tables for the Japanese economy in the past 10 years. The sectoral ratio of supplying sector for final demand is sometimes called converters. Table 6-9 shows converters for private fixed capital formation, focusing on machinery sectors including general machinery, electrical machinery, motor vehicles, other transport equipment, and precison instrument. Construction sector is also listed for comparison. Needless to say, the table shows the share of each sector, total being unity.

The table reveals that the share of machinery sectors total has steadily increased during the 1980–1985 period. The figures for 1975 and 1980 are not particularly different, and closer examination of annual figures confirms this point. We may say that the structural change of private fixed capital formation started around 1980 in Japan. What characterizes the new trend is the rising share of machinery sectors, especially electrical machinery and general machinery. The share of precision instrument has also risen steadily. Thus, during 1980 and 1985, the share of machnery sectors total has risen nearly ten percentage points, from 28.7% to 38.3%. During the same period, electrical machinery has gained most, expanding its share from 8.7% to 13.2%. General machinery sector increased the share from 12.3% to 16.7%. The share of precision instrument is inherently smaller than these sectors, but it has also increased the share from 0.9% to 1.3%. In constrast, the construction sector dropped its share from around 60% in 1975 and 1980 to less than 50% in 1985. This is a firm evidence of the nature of technological change that is taking place in our economies.[9]

The above data pertain to total economy. It is of interest for us to examine the supplying sectors for fixed capital formation in particular sectors. In other words, we are able to know that fixed capital formation in a particular year included so much of electrical machinery, so much of steel, so much of construction, etc. This kind of information reveals the diffusion of triple-C technology in individual sectors, which is represented by the rising shares of machinery sectors. For this purpose, we have compiled Tables 6-10 a through h. Table 6-10-a was compiled from time series input-output tables which give fixed capital formation in the private sector as a whole and its breakdown by the supplying sector. According to the table, it is revealed that the share of electrical machinery has jumped from 8.4% in 1980 to 15.1% in 1985. This is a firm indication that this sector is actually the key in understanding the diffusion of new technology.

In order to obtain similar information on individual sectors, we have compiled fixed capital formation matrices for 1970, 1975, 1980, and 1985. (See Appendix E.) Needless to say, a fixed capital formation matrix provides information on the supplying sectors and purchasing sectors regarding fixed capital formation. In the usual input-output tables, final demand includes information on the supplying sector (i.e., in a column) for each demand item including fixed capital formation. With the help of fixed capital formation matrix, we are able to obtain information as to the structure of investment in each sector. Focusing on the service orientation of the economy as well as the diffusion of C-C-C technology, we have chosen the following sectors for our analysis: machinery sectors (general machinery, electrical machinery, transport equipment, and precision instrument); wholesale and retail trade; finance, insurance, and real estate; and services.

The results, which are reported in Tables 6-10-b through h, may be summarized as follows. Figures indicate the percentage share of electrical machinery sector in the fixed capital formation in individual sectors.

	1980	1985
General machinery:	12.9%	34.6%
Electrical machinery:	11.2%	44.6%
Transport equipment:	56.0%	(59.4%)
Precision instrument:	12.2%	24.3%
Wholesale and retail trade:	6.6%	17.3%
Finance, insurance, and real estate:	1.8%	7.2%
Services:	12.1%	21.4%

Some additional observations are in order. First, in the case of transport equipment, the figure for 1985 refers to motor vehicles only. Second, there are sectors where an increased share was observed for general machinery sector, in addition to electrical machinery. This presumably reflects increased automation of the production process in these sectors. The cases in question include electrical machinery (where an increase from 15.5% to 18.2% was recorded during the 1980–1985 period), precision instrument (from 20.3% in 1980 to 27.6% in 1985), wholesale and retail trade (from 10.3% in 1975 to 14.6% in 1980 and 15.4% in 1985), and services (from 1.5% in 1980 to 9.8% in 1985).

We may conclude from our observation above, together with the information on the diffusion of new technologies concerning triple-Cs involving computer, communication and control which was taken up in the preceding chapter, that we have seen a rapid diffusion of new technologies in the productive facility. This justifies the use of average age of capital as a proxy for the quality of capital. Capital stock vintage approach which we have adopted in explaining the technological change is based on this supposition.

Footnotes:

1 *Japan Economic Journal* (J), November 11, 1989.
2 ibid.
3 *Japan Economic Journal* (J), November 8, 1989.
4 For investment financing, see Kimio Uno [1987], pp.59–67.
5 The table aims at clarifying the amount of funds supplied to industries, and, in this connection, excludes the supply of funds to financial institutions, local public bodies, and personal funds (funds for non-business purposes), yen credits overseas, loans by domestic foreign exchange banks to companies overseas. Further, loans made from the special accounts for public investment and loans are limited to special companies (*tokushu gaisha*, such as the Electric Power Development Co., ltd.) and *jigyodan* (the Small Business Promotion Corporation and similar corporations), and loans to public cooperations (*kosha* and *kodan*) are excluded.

Table 6-10 Industry origin of fixed capital formation

a. Total industry

(unit: current prices billion yen, %)

Sector Number	Modified JSIC Code		1970		1975		1980		1985	
(1)	01&	Agriculture, forestry, and fisheries	94.0	(0.5)	89.1	(0.3)	183.0	(0.3)	158.1	(0.2)
(2)	10&	Mining								
(3)	18	Food processing								
(4)	20&	Textiles	37.9	(0.2)	62.2	(0.2)	83.5	(0.2)	79.0	(0.1)
(5)	22	Lumber and wood products	11.4	(0.1)	22.1	(0.1)	26.4	(0.1)	26.1	(0.0)
(6)	23	Furniture and fixtures	186.8	(1.0)	316.8	(0.9)	459.4	(0.9)	398.3	(0.6)
(7)	24	Pulp, paper, and paper products								
(8)	25	Printing and publishing								
(9)	29	Leather and leather products								
(10)	28	Rubber products								
(11)	26	Chemicals								
(12)	27	Petroleum and coal products								
(13)	30	Nonmetallic mineral products								
(14)	31A	Iron and steel materials	(−) 42.8	(−0.2)	(−) 70.0	(−0.2)	(−)109.1	(−0.2)	(−) 97.6	(−0.2)
(15)	31B	Basic iron and steel products								
(16)	32	Basic nonferrous metal products	(−) 94.6	(−0.5)	(−)125.1	(−0.4)	(−) 59.6	(−0.1)	163.3	(0.3)
(17)	33	Fabricated metals	163.9	(0.9)	332.8	(1.0)	451.5	(0.9)	520.8	(0.8)
(18)	34	General machinery	3,444.3	(18.0)	4,821.1	(13.9)	6,479.7	(12.3)	8,371.8	(13.2)
(19)	35	Electrical machinery	1,697.7	(8.9)	2,786.6	(8.1)	4,409.2	(8.4)	9,567.7	(15.1)
(20)	36M	Transport equipment, motor vehicles	1,564.3	(8.2)	1,789.8	(6.2)	2,817.4	(5.3)	3,464.2	(5.4)
(21)	36S	Transport equipment, others	496.9	(2.6)	401.2	(1.2)	932.9	(1.8)	1,012.4	(1.6)
(22)	37	Precision instrument	101.8	(0.5)	233.0	(0.7)	497.4	(0.9)	687.5	(1.0)
(23)	38&	Other manufacturing	76.8	(0.4)	224.7	(0.6)	351.9	(0.7)	475.1	(0.7)
(24)	15	Construction	9,979.1	(52.1)	20.930.8	(60.5)	32,113.0	(61.0)	33,168.8	(52.3)
(25)	70	Electric power, gas, and water								
(26)	40	Wholesale and retail trade	1,383.5	(7.2)	2,331.2	(6.7)	3,795.2	(7.2)	5,062.3	(8.0)
(27)	50&	Finance, insurance, and real estate								
(28)	50R	Real estate rent								
(29)	60T	Transportation	90.5	(0.5)	225.9	(0.7)	234.6	(0.4)	398.4	(0.6)
		Total	19,171.9	(100.0)	34,575.2	(100.0)	52,666.4	(100.0)	63,456.1	(100.0)

Note: Figures refer to private fixed capital formation including plant and equipment.
Source: Kimio Uno, *Input Output Tables in Japan 1951–1985*.

b. General machinery

(unit: current prices billion yen, %)

Sector Number	Modified JSIC Code		1970	1975	1980	1985
(1)	01&	Agriculture, forestry, and fisheries	0	0 (0)	0 (0)	0 (0)
(2)	10&	Mining				
(3)	18	Food processing				
(4)	20&	Textiles	0.4	0.9 (0.2)	0 (0)	2.4 (0.1)
(5)	22	Lumber and wood products	0	0 (0)	0 (0)	0 (0)
(6)	23	Furniture and fixtures	5.3	4.7 (0.9)	14.7 (1.3)	8.0 (0.4)
(7)	24	Pulp, paper, and paper products				
(8)	25	Printing and publishing				
(9)	29	Leather and leather products				
(10)	28	Rubber products				
(11)	26	Chemicals				
(12)	27	Petroleum and coal products				
(13)	30	Nonmetallic mineral products				
(14)	31A	Iron and steel materials				
(15)	31B	Basic iron and steel products				
(16)	32	Basic nonferrous metal products			0 (0)	0 (0)
(17)	33	Fabricated metals	0.1	0 (0)	0 (0)	0 (0)
(18)	34	General machinery	173.8	224.2 (40.7)	635.2 (56.2)	617.3 (32.8)
(19)	35	Electrical machinery	39.1	870 (15.8)	145.6 (12.9)	651.8 (34.6)
(20)	36M	Transport equipment, motor vehicles	26.8	12.0 (2.2)	18.2 (1.6)	19.3 (1.0)
(21)	36S	Transport equipment, others	0.3	0 (0)	1.1 (0.1)	13.4 (0.7)
(22)	37	Precision instrument	5.0	3.0 (0.5)	17.7 (1.6)	25.5 (1.4)
(23)	38&	Other manufacturing	0	0 (0)	0 (0)	0 (0)
(24)	15	Construction	162.9	149.8 (27.2)	122.8 (10.9)	285.8 (15.2)
(25)	70	Electric power, gas, and water				
(26)	40	Wholesale and retail trade	n.a.	62.9 (11.4)	165.3 (14.6)	241.6 (12.8)
(27)	50&	Finance, insurance and real estate				
(28)	50R	Real estate rent				
(29)	60T	Transportation	n.a.	5.6 (1.0)	10.0 (0.9)	14.5 (0.8)
(30)	60C	Communication				
		Total	413.5	550.2 (100.0)	1,130.8 (100.0)	1,883.4 (100.0)

Source: Appendix table E-1 to E-4.

c. Electrical machinery

(unit: curvent prices, billion yen, %)

Sector Number	Modified JSIC Code		1970	1975		1980		1985	
(1)	01&	Agriculture, forestry, and fisheries	0	0	(0)	0	(0)	0	(0)
(2)	10&	Mining							
(3)	18	Food processing							
(4)	20&	Textiles	0.4	0.9	(0.2)	0	(0)	1.6	(0.1)
(5)	22	Lumber and wood products	11.4	0	(0)	0	(0)	0	(0)
(6)	23	Furniture and fixtures	5.8	10.6	(2.7)	4.6	(0.5)	16.6	(0.6)
(7)	24	Pulp, paper, and paper products							
(8)	25	Printing and publishing							
(9)	29	Leather and leather products							
(10)	28	Rubber products							
(11)	26	Chemicals							
(12)	27	Petroleum and coal products							
(13)	30	Nonmetallic mineral products							
(14)	31A	Iron and steel materials							
(15)	31B	Basic iron and steel products							
(16)	32	Basic nonferrous metal products				0	(0)	0	(0)
(17)	33	Fabricated metals	6.8	13.6	(3.4)	0	(0)	2.8	(0.9)
(18)	34	General machinery	133.4	54.8	(13.7)	157.1	(15.5)	547.8	(18.2)
(19)	35	Electrical machinery	129.5	86.9	(21.7)	113.4	(11.2)	1,343.2	(44.6)
(20)	36M	Transport equipment, motor vehicles	15.0	9.0	(2.3)	14.4	(1.4)	12.8	(0.4)
(21)	36S	Transport equipment, others	0	0	(0)	0	(0)	0	(0)
(22)	37	Precision instrument	3.6	3.0	(0.8)	33.3	(3.3)	45.8	(1.5)
(23)	38&	Other manufacturing		0	(0)	0	(0)	0	(0)
(24)	15	Construction	148.5	185.9	(46.5)	623.2	(61.7)	680.1	(22.6)
(25)	70	Electric power, gas, and water							
(26)	40	Wholesale and retail trade	n.a.	31.5	(7.9)	60.5	(6.0)	323.2	(10.7)
(27)	50&	Finance, insurance, and real estate							
(28)	50R	Real estate rent							
(29)	60T	Transportation	n.a.	3.7	(0.9)	4.0	(0.4)	20.7	(0.7)
		Total	454.3	399.9	(100.0)	1,010.5	(100.0)	3,014.6	(100.0)

Source: Same as Table 6-10-b.

d. Transport equipment

(unit: current prices, billion yen, %)

Sector Number	Modified JSIC Code		1970	1975	1980	1985 Motor vehicles	1985 Other
(1)	01&	Agriculture, forestry, and fisheries	0	0 (0)	0 (0)	0 (0)	0 (0)
(2)	10&	Mining					
(3)	18	Food processing					
(4)	20&	Textiles	0.3	0.7 (0.1)	0 (0)	0.5 (0)	1.0 (0.2)
(5)	22	Lumber and wood products	0	0 (0)	0 (0)	0 (0)	0 (0)
(6)	23	Furniture and fixtures	4.2	7.8 (0.8)	9.4 (0.7)	7.1 (0.4)	2.7 (0.5)
(7)	24	Pulp, paper, and paper products					
(8)	25	Printing and publishing					
(9)	29	Leather and leather products					
(10)	28	Rubber products					
(11)	26	Chemicals					
(12)	27	Petroleum and coal products					
(13)	30	Nonmetallic mineral products					
(14)	31A	Iron and steel materials					
(15)	31B	Basic iron and steel products					
(16)	32	Basic nonferrous metal products			0 (0)	0 (0)	0 (0)
(17)	33	Fabricated metals	0.6	0.4 (0)	0.2 (0)	1.1 (0.1)	1.6 (0.3)
(18)	34	General machinery	207.3	406.6 (43.1)	749.7 (56.0)	1,179.7 (59.4)	308.3 (51.5)
(19)	35	Electrical machinery	91.8	58.1 (6.2)	92.3 (6.9)	146.5 (7.4)	85.1 (14.2)
(20)	36M	Transport equipment, motor vehicles	7.5	4.2 (0.4)	5.9 (0.4)	2.0 (0.1)	3.5 (0.6)
(21)	36S	Transport equipment, others	6.4	6.6 (7.0)	20.2 (1.5)	18.6 (0.9)	10.5 (1.8)
(22)	37	Precision instrument	9.8	5.4 (0.6)	23.3 (1.7)	29.2 (1.5)	4.9 (0.8)
(23)	38&	Other manufacturing	0.3	1.1 (0.1)	2.2 (0.2)	0 (0)	0 (0)
(24)	15	Construction	197.4	334.5 (35.5)	246.3 (18.4)	316.0 (15.9)	121.0 (20.2)
(25)	70	Electric power, gas, and water					
(26)	40	Wholesale and retail trade	n.a.	999 (10.6)	178.1 (13.3)	268.0 (13.5)	56.0 (9.3)
(27)	50&	Finance, insurance, and real estate					
(28)	50R	Real estate rent					
(29)	60T	Transportation	n.a.	7.9 (0.8)	10.7 (0.8)	16.3 (0.8)	4.4 (0.7)
		Total	525.6	943.2 (100.0)	1,338.4 (100.0)	1,985.1 (100.0)	599.0 (100.0)

Source: Same as Table 6-10-b.

e. Precision Instrument

(unit: current prices, billion yen, %)

Sector Number	Modified JSIC Code		1970	1975	1980	1985
(1)	01&	Agriculture, forestry, and fisheries	0	0 (0)	0 (0)	0 (0)
(2)	10&	Mining				
(3)	18	Food processing				
(4)	20&	Textiles	0	0.2 (0.3)	0 (0)	0.5 (0.1)
(5)	22	Lumber and wood products	0	0 (0)	0 (0)	0 (0)
(6)	23	Furniture and fixtures	1.0	0.6 (0.9)	0.8 (0.3)	0.9 (0.3)
(7)	24	Pulp, paper, and paper products				
(8)	25	Printing and publishing				
(9)	29	Leather and leather products				
(10)	28	Rubber products				
(11)	26	Chemicals				
(12)	27	Petroleum and coal products				
(13)	30	Nonmetallic mineral products				
(14)	31A	Iron and steel materials				
(15)	31B	Basic iron and steel products				
(16)	32	Basic nonferrous metal products			0 (0)	0 (0)
(17)	33	Fabricated metals	0	0 (0)	0 (0)	0.7 (0.2)
(18)	34	General machinery	15.8	10.5 (16.4)	50.2 (20.3)	94.5 (27.6)
(19)	35	Electrical machinery	7.1	4.1 (6.4)	30.3 (12.2)	83.1 (24.3)
(20)	36M	Transport equipment, motor vehicles	4.6	4.8 (7.5)	7.0 (2.8)	8.0 (2.3)
(21)	36S	Transport equipment, others	0	0 (0)	0 (0)	0 (0)
(22)	37	Precision instrument	1.1	22.7 (35.5)	9.2 (3.7)	67.5 (19.7)
(23)	38&	Other manufacturing	0	0 (0)	0 (0)	0 (0)
(24)	15	Construction	25.1	11.2 (17.5)	130.2 (52.5)	31.1 (9.1)
(25)	70	Electric power, gas, and water				
(26)	40	Wholesale and retail trade	n.a.	8.8 (13.8)	19.0 (7.7)	45.8 (13.4)
(27)	50&	Finance, insurance, and real estate				
(28)	50R	Real estate rent				
(29)	60T	Transportation	n.a.	0.9 (1.4)	1.1 (0.4)	3.1 (0.9)
		Total	54.9	63.9 (100.0)	247.8 (100.0)	342.2 (100.0)

Source: Same as Table 6-10-b.

f. Wholesale and retail trade

(unit: current prices, billion yen, %)

Sector Number	Modified JSIC Code		1970	1975		1980		1985	
(1)	01&	Agriculture, forestry, and fisheries	0	0	(0)	0	(0)	0	(0)
(2)	10&	Mining							
(3)	18	Food processing							
(4)	20&	Textiles	3.0	6.4	(0.3)	0	(0)	31.4	(0.7)
(5)	22	Lumber and wood products	0	0	(0)	0	(0)	0	(0)
(6)	23	Furniture and fixtures	63.8	39.1	(1.6)	33.5	(7.8)	146.0	(3.2)
(7)	24	Pulp, paper, and paper products							
(8)	25	Printing and publishing							
(9)	29	Leather and leather products							
(10)	28	Rubber products							
(11)	26	Chemicals							
(12)	27	Petroleum and coal products							
(13)	30	Nonmetallic mineral products							
(14)	31A	Iron and steel materials							
(15)	31B	Basic iron and steel products							
(16)	32	Basic nonferrous metal products				0	(0)	0	(0)
(17)	33	Fabricated metals	0	0	(0)	0	(0)	95.2	(2.1)
(18)	34	General machinery	146.9	250.4	(10.3)	631.2	(14.6)	706.2	(2.1)
(19)	35	Electrical machinery	41.9	124.5	(5.1)	285.2	(6.6)	793.2	(17.3)
(20)	36M	Transport equipment, motor vehicles	416.8	369.7	(15.2)	550.0	(12.8)	345.2	(7.5)
(21)	36S	Transport equipment, others	44.1	52.0	(2.1)	81.9	(1.9)	16.5	(0.4)
(22)	37	Precision instrument	0	3.4	(0.1)	1.0	(0)	79.9	(1.7)
(23)	38&	Other manufacturing	17.8	47.9	(2.0)	88.6	(2.1)	6.0	(0.1)
(24)	15	Construction	746.4	1,311.9	(53.8)	2,216.2	(51.4)	1,914.8	(41.8)
(25)	70	Electric power, gas, and water							
(26)	40	Wholesale and retail trade	n.a.	210.3	(8.6)	394.1	(9.1)	417.0	(9.1)
(27)	50&	Finance, insurance, and real estate							
(28)	50R	Real estate rent							
(29)	60T	Transportation	n.a.	22.0	(0.9)	31.6	(0.7)	29.3	(0.6)
		Total	1,480.7	2,437.6	(100.0)	4,313.2	(100.0)	4,580.6	(100.0)

Source: Same as Table 6-10-b.

g. Finance, insurance, and real estate

(unit: current prices, billion yen, %)

Sector Number	Modified JSIC Code		1970	1975	1980	1985
(1)	01&	Agriculture, forestry, and fisheries	0	0 (0)	0 (0)	0 (0)
(2)	10&	Mining				
(3)	18	Food processing				
(4)	20&	Textiles	1.9	3.5 (0.3)	0 (0)	2.5 (0)
(5)	22	Lumber and wood products	0	0 (0)	0 (0)	0 (0)
(6)	23	Furniture and fixtures	24.7	22.4 (1.7)	23.2 (0.6)	139.2 (2.1)
(7)	24	Pulp, paper, and paper products				
(8)	25	Printing and publishing				
(9)	29	Leather and leather products				
(10)	28	Rubber products				
(11)	26	Chemicals				
(12)	27	Petroleum and coal products				
(13)	30	Nonmetallic mineral products				
(14)	31A	Iron and steel materials				
(15)	31B	Basic iron and steel products				
(16)	32	Basic nonferrous metal products			0 (0)	0 (0)
(17)	33	Fabricated metals	0	0 (0)	0 (0)	25.1 (0.4)
(18)	34	General machinery	20.1	153.6 (11.4)	98.2 (2.4)	124.4 (1.9)
(19)	35	Electrical machinery	70.3	74.5 (5.5)	74.1 (1.8)	476.5 (7.2)
(20)	36M	Transport equipment, motor vehicles	31.0	54.8 (4.1)	29.6 (0.7)	29.4 (0.4)
(21)	36S	Transport equipment, others	0	12.9 (1.0)	19.8 (0.5)	0.1 (0)
(22)	37	Precision instrument	0	0.1 (0)	10.3 (0.3)	1.0 (0)
(23)	38&	Other manufacturing	0	0 (0)	0 (0)	0 (0)
(24)	15	Construction	1,319.7	953.7 (70.6)	3,783.5 (92.4)	5,608,4 (85.5)
(25)	70	Electric power, gas, and water				
(26)	40	Wholesale and retail trade	n.a.	67.5 (5.0)	53.3 (1.3)	142.0 (2.2)
(27)	50&	Finance, insurance, and real estate				
(28)	50R	Real estate rent				
(29)	60T	Transportation	n.a.	7.3 (0.5)	3.1 (0.1)	8.3 (0.1)
		Total	1,467.7	1,350.5 (100.0)	4,095.2 (100.0)	6,557.2 (100.0)

Source: Same as Table 6-10-b.

h. Services

(unit: current prices, billion yen, %)

Sector Number	Modified JSIC Code		1970*	1975*		1980*		1985			
								Public services		Business & personal services	
(1)	01&	Agriculture, forestry, and fisheries	14.0	25.1	(0.5)	38.9	(0.4)	0	(0)	46.5	(0.6)
(2)	10&	Mining									
(3)	18	Food processing									
(4)	20&	Textiles	4.2	9.1	(0.2)	0	(0)	4.2	(0.1)	116.1	(1.4)
(5)	22	Lumber and wood products	0	8.9	(0.2)	8.7	(0.1)	0	(0)	0	(0)
(6)	23	Furniture and fixtures	33.5	139.4	(2.7)	208.5	(2.3)	174.1	(5.0)	216.0	(2.7)
(7)	24	Pulp, paper, and paper products									
(8)	25	Printing and publishing									
(9)	29	Leather and leather products									
(10)	28	Rubber products									
(11)	26	Chemicals									
(12)	27	Petroleum and coal products									
(13)	30	Nonmetallic mineral products									
(14)	31A	Iron and steel materials									
(15)	31B	Basic iron and steel products									
(16)	32	Basic nonferrous metal products				0	(0)	0	(0)	0	(0)
(17)	33	Fabricated metals	70.7	128.0	(2.5)	103.2	(1.2)	0.7	(0)	92.1	(1.1)
(18)	34	General machinery	160.5	313.8	(6.1)	324.5	(3.7)	53.1	(1.5)	792.2	(9.8)
(19)	35	Electrical machinery	612.4	1,161.0	(22.6)	2,109.8	(23.7)	419.0	(12.1)	1,728.9	(21.4)
(20)	36M	Transport equipment, motor vehicles	175.5	478.9	(9.3)	913.2	(10.3)	235.9	(6.8)	936.6	(11.6)
(21)	36S	Transport equipment, others	26.2	51.3	(1.0)	59.9	(0.7)	2.7	(0.1)	120.7	(1.5)
(22)	37	Precision instrument	46.6	130.8	(2.5)	219.7	(2.5)	305.4	(8.8)	69.0	(0.9)
(23)	38&	Other manufacturing	44.8	114.5	(2.2)	170.1	(1.9)	218.4	(6.3)	103.0	(1.3)
(24)	15	Construction	797.2	1,913.9	(37.2)	3,606.7	(40.6)	1,736.6	(50.0)	2,913.6	(36.0)
(25)	70	Electric power, gas, and water									
(26)	40	Wholesale and retail trade	—	609.5	(11.9)	1,053.4	(11.9)	306.7	(8.8)	885.4	(11.0)
(27)	50&	Finance, insurance, and real estate									
(28)	50R	Real estate rent									
(29)	60T	Transportation	—	58.5	(1.1)	68.3	(0.8)	19.4	(0.6)	58.5	(0.7)
		Total	1,985.7	5,142.8	(100.0)	8,885.0	(100.0)	3,476.2	(100.0)	8,078.8	(100.0)

Source: Same as Table 6-10-b.

6 Due to privatization of former public corporations, Nippon Telephone and Telegraph (transportation and communication sector), and Japan Tobacco (manufacturing) is included in the statistics since April–June quarter in 1985 Electric Power Development Co. (electricity, gas, and water sector) from October–December quarter in 1986, and Japan Rail (transportation and communication sector) from April–June quarter in 1987.
7 See Uno [1990b] and [1990c].
8 It should be noted that this demand category includes private housing construction in addition to private investment in plant and equipment. Since the former includes more construction element, the ratios presented in the table understates the increasing importance of machinery sectors in private fixed capital formation.
9 This observation is based on current prices. It is important to note that the price of C-C-C related products has exhibited secular decline during this period. Current price figures provide a picture which is a mixture of rapid diffusion of C-C-C technology and declining prices. What is lacking is an appropriate measure of quality improvement. There are sporatic attempts to estimate quality-adjusted price indexes in this field. According to their results, the price of mainframe computers has dropped from the base year level of 100 in 1970 to 21 in 1980 and 7 in 1987; in the case of industrial robots, it has dropped from 100 in 1970 to about 40 in 1985. The deflator for electric machinery on SNA basis showed a deline of about seven percentage points, whereas that for general machinery has risen by about 60% during the 1970–1985 period. Therefore, we can say that the importance of C-C-C related sectors such as electric machinery and precision instrument must have risen at a much faster rate than is suggested by the current price figures. See Cartwright [1986] for quality adjusted deflator for mainframe computers and Mori [1987] for industrial robots. Sectoral deflators are from Economic Planning Agency, *Annual Report on National Accounts*.

Chapter 7. Capital stock vintage and potential growth

7-1 Structural adjustment and potential growth

This chapter is aimed at reexamining the concept of potential growth which has been in use for some time now.[1] In view of the renewed interest in this concept, it has been deemed necessary to rectify the analytical basis in order to cope with some new factors which have come into existence during recent years. An attempt is made to search for possible improvement. A case study is provided based on empirical data from Japan.

The economic growth potential is once again a focal point in the economic policy debate of many countries. The reasons for this renewed interest may be enumerated as follows:

(1) Energy and other resource constraints have been largely removed. We have left behind the years when recurring oil crises and continued inflation made necessary the resorting to aggregate demand constraints. The focal point has shifted from restraining demand to production possibilities.

(2) The environmental pollution problem which plagued continued growth during the 1960s and 1970s has also been contained. Although there are new environmental concerns such as hazards created by global warming, ozone holes, acid rain, and the destruction of tropical rain forests, pollution is not considered a serious threat to society, at least not in Japan.[2] As a result, anti-growth sentiment has faded away.

(3) In the 1980s, the world has entered into a new stage in which almost all industrialized countries in the West are on a rather strong growth path. The new stage of economic growth has been set by high-technology sectors and services.

(4) At the same time, organizational rigidities which evolved in the public sector and nationalized industries have more or less been torn down by administrative reforms.

(5) Output growth and price stability are considered to be the economic fundamentals which determine foreign trade performance and the exchange rates.

The question is, what are the growth potentials in the new economic environment. More specifically, one may wish to know:

- Whether the growth trend is accelerating due to new factors such as high-tech diffusion and service orientation, or should we be prepared for slower growth?
- Have we observed accelerated factor productivity in the 1980s, as compared with the 1960s and 1970s? A method which allows us to

trace the annual shift in productivity is necessary.
— Which industries are likely to be affected favorably by the diffusion of high-technology? What is the industrial structure going to be?

In addition, there are short-term considerations. After experiencing continued growth in the 1980s, concerned voices are heard concerning about further economic growth for fear of hitting the ceiling of supply capacity and inviting inflation. Such was the case in the United States, where monetary policy came under sharp political debate. This was also the case in Japan when the Bank of Japan became alarmed by the slight depreciation of the yen in 1988–1989 and again in mid 1989 for fear of triggering inflation at a time when the economy was already near full-employment. However, in either case, there are those who are rather optimistic about growth potentials on the grounds that this round of economic growth is not simply a cyclical phenomena but is one boosted by an economic upswing due to fundamental technological change. The demand will continue to be strong, especially investment in plants and equipment in order to implement new technologies, though other demand items will also continue to be strong. On the production side, the supply capacity of electronics which is the crux of new technologies can be easily expanded according to the demand expansion and, unlike growth in the past, there will be no resource constraints. At this point, the short-term consideration of growth potentials is already being discussed in terms of medium-term implications.

7-2 The framework of analysis

Potential output is commonly measured on the assumption that:
(1) unemployment is maintained at some 'natural' level;
(2) the rate of capacity utilization of capital and the working hours are at the rate which would be associated with the 'natural' rate of unemployment; and
(3) other conditions have been at the level which actually prevailed.[3]

It is questionable, however, whether a straightforward application of this methodology would enable us to answer the questions we set out to solve.

It order to obtain relevant insights into the potential output in a changing economic environment, it seems necessary to incorporate the following factors. First, the technology factor needs to be included explicitly in view of the importance of technological changes in recent industrial growth. The conventional treatment of potential output assumes away the problems associated with technological change, and deals only with cyclical fluctuations. Second, the analysis needs to be disaggregated. Today's economy is characterized by rapid structural change which is attributable to differing patterns of technological change, differing responses to changes in raw material prices such as energy, increasing international division of labor both vertically and horizontally, and shifts in final demand from hardware to services.[4] Measurement of potential growth typically has been carried out on aggregate level. Third, the analytical framework should be incorporated within an econometric model. This is because such variables as capital formation, rate of capacity utilization, labor force participation, and working hours are determined interdependently. Investment in plant and equipment is the key vehicle through which new technology is implemented in practice, a factor which is related to the first point above. Coupled with the second point, this amounts of the necessity of a multisector industrial model.

In addition, the demand side should be considered. Demand levels for individual sectors must be derived. This in turn will enable us to derive a demand-supply gap for each sector. Tightness of the market as represented by the demand-supply gap determines the utilization rates of the factors of production. From a policy point of view, this enables us to look into the changing patterns of economic growth in Japan, for example, from export-led growth to the one led by domestic demand, when individual final demand items are estimated as the basis for aggregate final demand.

In order to achieve our purpose, we have based our analysis on a multisector industry model of Japan named the Comprehensive Model for Policy Assessment (COMPASS) version III. The model has 25 sectors.[5] The classification scheme is designed to be identical to the 36 sector standardized input-output tables, except for some minor manufacturing sectors (lumber and wood, furniture and fixtures, printing and publishing, rubber products, and leather and leather products) which are lumped together under 'other manufacturing' and excluding the dummy sectors in the input-output tables (real estate rent, office supplies, and packing materials).[6]

The model framework is particularly suitable for structural analysis. The aspects which are relevant to our purpose of measuring the potential output of an economy include the following:

(1) Detailed sectoral disaggregation is provided. The industrial classification adopted here is close to the maximum allowable within the availability of consistent statistical data.

(2) Technological factors of the economy are integrated in the model, including the rate and level of technological progress, the average age of capital stock, and the effect of changing vintage on productivity gains.

(3) The sources-of-growth accounts are provided for individual sectors.

The sources of growth consist of six components which include capital input, rate of capacity utilization, labor input, working hours, technological progress embodied in capital, and the capital stock vintage.
(4) Potential output is calculated endogenously. This is made possible by inclusion of the rate of capacity utilization and working hours in the sources-of-growth accounts in the framework of analysis. The working hours equations include capacity utilization rates among explanatory variables. By inserting the maximum rate of capacity utilization, which is unity, and hypothetical working hours which would be provided under full capacity utilization, potential output can be obtained.
(5) Sectoral demand is derived based on final demand in addition to sectoral supply. This enables us to calculate the gap between potential output and actual demand. In the model framework, the demand-supply gap determines the capacity utilization ratio, which in turn is employed in determining the capital formation and working hours in each sector.

As is well known, Robert Solow [1957] has used the Cobb-Douglas model of production in measuring technological change as the residual. The rate of output growth is expressed as:

$$\Delta V/V = \Delta A/A + \beta(\Delta L/L) + (1-\beta)(\Delta K/K) \qquad (1)$$

where $\Delta V/V$: rate of growth of output
$\Delta L/L$: rate of growth of labor input
$\Delta K/K$: rate of growth of capital input
$\Delta A/A$: rate of growth of total factor productivity
β: elasticity of output with respect to labor.

Richard Nelson [1964] has shown that, under the embodiment hypothesis where technological improvements need to take the form of new capital equipment, the rate of output growth can be approximated by the following:[7]

$$\Delta V/V = \Delta A'/A' + (1-\beta)\lambda k - (1-\beta)\lambda k\, \Delta a + \beta \Delta L/L + (1-\beta)\Delta K/K \qquad (2)$$

where $\Delta A'/A'$: rate of growth of total factor productivity excluding the embodiment effect of new technology
λk: rate of quality improvement of new capital
Δa: change in the average age of capital.

On the assumption that all the total factor productivity growth must be embodied in capital, the first term on the righthand side of the equation (2) vanishes. Thus, we are left with an equation expressing the

output growth in terms of four components. Since the growth of labor and capital inputs are further decomposed by taking into account working hours and the rate of capacity utilization, respectively, we have six terms which explain the output growth, i.e.,
(1) labor,
(2) working hours,
(3) capital stock,
(4) the rate of capacity utilization,
(5) technological progress embodied in capital, and
(6) the changes in capital stock vintage.

We take Nelson's formulation to be the theoretical basis of our analysis. His approach allows us to decompose the residual in Solow's method into the effect of the embodied technological change and the portion attributable to changes in the vintage of the capital stock. In view of the importance of new technology in promoting economic growth in recent years, the formulation above appears to be viable.

Needless to say, by explicitly considering the rate of capacity utilization and working hours, technology term in the above formulation is net of cyclical fluctuations. Any change in total factor productivity due to short-term cyclical movement will be prevented from confusing the long-term trends in efficiency change.

7-3 Empirical measurement

The analysis attempted here covers the Japanese experience between 1955 and 1988.[8] A few words on the data sources are in order. The output data are the gross value of production in terms of the SNA definition available from the Economic Planning Agency [1988b] and *National Account* which is deflated by deflators on outputs available from the same source. The base year has been shifted from 1980 in the original source to 1970 in order to maintain consistency with other industrial analyses by the present writer. For the most recent years (1987 and 1988), the data were estimated based on production indexes for mining and manufacturing and for tertiary industry, both from the Ministry of International Trade and Industry. (Unit: 1970 prices, billion yen)

Labor's share has been calculated from the Economic Planning Agency [1988b] and *National Account*. (Unit: ratio)

Capital formation data and capital stock data are from the Economic Planning Agency [1988a]. The base year has been shifted to 1970 for the same reason as above. Capital formation in the most recent years has been supplemented by the *Business and Investment Survey of Incorporated Enterprises* by the MITI. (Unit: 1970 prices, billion yen)

Table 7-1 Capital stock vintage in selected industries

(unit: years)

	All industries	Manufac-turing	Iron & steel	Electrical machinery	Motor vehicle	Wholesale & retail	Private services
1955	15.33	14.07	17.21	18.11	9.30	11.55	20.78
1956	15.00	13.61	17.20	15.79	8.95	12.02	20.50
1957	14.53	12.86	15.98	12.82	8.78	12.51	20.04
1958	14.24	12.47	14.82	11.08	9.07	13.10	20.84
1959	13.85	11.83	13.19	9.54	9.01	13.62	20.35
1960	13.15	10.72	11.08	7.75	8.35	14.02	19.78
1961	12.22	9.51	9.28	6.19	8.15	14.27	18.89
1962	11.54	8.86	8.52	5.54	8.14	14.36	18.13
1963	11.00	8.44	8.20	5.43	8.06	14.29	17.26
1964	10.44	8.04	7.97	5.52	8.05	14.01	15.68
1965	10.16	7.98	7.95	5.86	8.43	13.90	14.66
1966	9.87	7.94	8.07	6.08	8.82	13.64	13.49
1967	9.46	7.65	7.69	6.02	8.83	13.35	12.37
1968	8.95	7.22	7.27	5.83	8.35	12.86	11.64
1969	8.41	6.84	7.02	5.25	8.00	12.10	10.61
1970	7.96	6.53	6.83	5.00	7.93	11.37	9.56
1971	7.69	6.47	6.74	5.16	8.19	10.82	8.76
1972	7.54	6.56	6.88	5.37	8.33	10.16	8.02
1973	7.31	6.56	7.10	5.22	8.15	9.31	7.33
1974	7.33	6.66	7.23	5.33	8.25	8.95	7.08
1975	7.54	7.03	7.47	5.87	8.69	8.80	6.98
1976	7.67	7.32	7.59	5.97	9.23	8.73	6.91
1977	7.75	7.62	7.90	6.14	10.07	8.62	6.82
1978	7.94	7.97	8.39	6.28	10.75	8.61	6.74
1979	8.00	8.18	8.80	6.26	11.24	8.53	6.56
1980	8.05	8.29	9.19	6.10	11.72	8.50	6.43
1981	8.11	8.38	9.42	5.85	12.09	8.58	6.28
1982	8.20	8.47	9.44	5.81	12.34	8.71	6.18
1983	8.31	8.60	9.56	5.74	12.76	8.90	6.07
1984	8.38	8.63	9.82	5.30	13.13	9.08	5.91
1985	8.51	8.61	10.15	5.09	13.51	9.28	5.70
1986	8.61	8.72	10.51	5.11	13.86	9.40	5.60
1987	8.65	8.81	10.97	5.17	14.20	9.55	5.60
1988	8.65	8.85	11.46	5.04	14.53	9.67	5.55

Source: COMPASS simulation results.

The average age of capital stock for each sector was generated by the model COMPASS endogenously based on annual investment data. The base year figures (which in this case is 1960) was estimated based on the itemized capital acquisition data from 1950 to 1960, converting them into a constant price series, and attaching weights according to the number of years after the acquisition.[9] (Unit: years)

The rate of capacity utilization is from the *Indexes of Mining and Manufacturing* by the MITI. The indexes with different base years were linked, taking 1970 as the base year. (Unit: ratio)

Employment figures are from the *Labour Force Survey* by the Ministry of Labor. This source does not provide employment within the manufacturing sector at a disaggregated level. We have used the employment index in *Monthly Labour Statistical Survey* for individual sectors of the same ministry. The latter covers the establishments with 30 or more regular workers, but the bias caused by the difference in the coverage was deemed minimal. The index was converted to number of workers based on the *1970 Population Census* data which provide sectoral employment figures.[10] (Unit: thousand persons)

The data on working hours are also available in the *Monthly Labour Statistical Survey* by the Ministry of Labor for the entire period. Since this source gives figures in actual number of hours, we have converted the series into indexes with 1970 as the base year. (Unit: 1970=1.00)

The results of the sources-of-growth calculations for selected sectors for the 1955–1988 period are provided in Appendix F. The sectors represented are total industry, manufacturing sector total, iron and steel, general machinery, electric machinery, motor vehicles, precision instrument, wholesale and retail, and business and personal services.[11]

The first column of panel b of the tables shows the annual growth of output in a particular sector. The next three columns concern labor input. The second column indicates the labor input as a whole, whereas the third and fourth show the number of workers and working hours, respectively. The fifth through seventh columns concern the capital input. The fifth column refers to the input of capital as a whole, which is decomposed into the capital stock and its utilization rate in the subsequent two columns. The eighth column indicates the residual, or the rate of technological progress according to Solow's method. According to the full embodiment hypothesis, the effects of embodied technological progress are shown in the ninth column. The effect of changing average age of capital stock is entered in the last column.[12]

For industry as a whole, which is shown in Appendix table F-1, we realize a dramatic decline in the growth rate. The production of the economy grew at an annual rate of around 10% until 1973. After experiencing negative growth in 1974 and a virtual standstill in 1975, the

Table 7-2 Technical levels in selected industries

(unit: index, 1955=1.00)

	All industries	Manufac-turing	Iron & steel	Electrical machinery	Motor vehicle	Wholesale & retail	Private services
1955	1.0000	1.0000	1.0000	1.0000	1.0000	1.0000	1.0000
1956	.9985	1.0498	1.1010	1.1423	1.2284	1.0469	1.0410
1957	1.0385	1.1003	1.1669	1.2083	1.5088	1.1620	1.1071
1958	1.1127	1.1087	1.3240	1.1419	1.7727	1.1865	1.1905
1959	1.1167	1.1635	1.1725	1.2048	1.3246	1.3277	1.2395
1960	1.1572	1.2323	1.1844	1.2659	1.2024	1.4086	1.3570
1961	1.2179	1.2785	1.1815	1.2549	1.4040	1.6332	1.3725
1962	1.2956	1.3001	1.1764	1.1997	1.4691	1.7777	1.4005
1963	1.3325	1.3425	1.2004	1.1183	1.5793	1.9094	1.3773
1964	1.3597	1.3670	1.2253	1.2152	1.7378	2.1374	1.3282
1965	1.4040	1.4157	1.2543	1.2349	2.0108	2.1681	1.2609
1966	1.4233	1.4577	1.2654	1.2539	2.0722	2.3939	1.2788
1967	1.4397	1.4869	1.3576	1.3962	2.2454	2.5286	1.3340
1968	1.4727	1.5038	1.3655	1.5104	2.2438	2.7850	1.4204
1969	1.5542	1.6025	1.4027	1.7362	2.4519	2.9667	1.4439
1970	1.6093	1.6842	1.4415	1.8569	2.7789	3.1006	1.3348
1971	1.6418	1.7030	1.4707	1.9278	2.9688	3.0808	1.2668
1972	1.6849	1.7456	1.4980	2.0841	3.0551	3.2249	1.2512
1973	1.6507	1.7344	1.5367	2.2599	2.9440	3.0968	1.1849
1974	1.6359	1.7308	1.5032	2.3108	3.1536	2.9179	1.0704
1975	1.7208	1.8089	1.5614	2.1608	3.5479	2.7568	1.0186
1976	1.6775	1.8156	1.6112	2.4521	3.4771	2.7400	.9671
1977	1.7385	1.8755	1.6495	2.6637	3.5796	2.7005	.9599
1978	1.7086	1.9161	1.6568	2.8056	3.6419	2.7042	.9507
1979	1.6757	1.9158	1.6572	2.9372	3.6714	2.6807	.9355
1980	1.7138	1.9842	1.6281	3.2950	4.0476	2.5953	.8934
1981	1.7776	2.0615	1.6757	3.7355	3.4584	3.1472	.8635
1982	1.7823	2.0800	1.6962	3.8730	3.3966	3.1128	.8549
1983	1.7760	2.0890	1.6737	4.3881	3.3952	3.1319	.8305
1984	1.7553	2.0989	1.6732	4.8100	3.6357	3.0892	.7995
1985	1.7122	2.1094	1.6307	4.4672	3.8989	3.0654	.7769
1986	1.7535	2.1524	1.6516	4.9789	4.0627	3.1279	.7591
1987	1.7660	2.1365	1.6470	5.2788	3.7116	2.8072	.7207
1988	1.7568	2.1813	1.6703	5.8902	3.8315	2.9415	.7142

Source: COMPASS simulation results.

economy regained some growth momentum but the growth rate remained around 5%. In the process of economic adjustment to energy shortages and, more importantly, to energy price hikes, Japanese industry has succeeded in shifting its leading sector from heavy industry to electronics, information, and services.[13]

Among the sources of growth, working hours declined over time and were consistently a negative factor throughout the period except for the periods of economic recovery: examples are the late 1950s, 1966, the late 1970s, and 1984.[14] More recently, 1987 also exhibited a similar phenomena. On the whole, however, the working hours index (1970 as the base year) shortened from 1.086 in 1960 to 0.943 in 1987–1988. In actual numbers, this amounts to a reduction from 202.7 hours per month to 175.9 hours per month. The number of workers, on the other hand, continued to contribute to the output growth except for the 1974–1975 period.

Capital inputs have played an increasingly important role. Cyclical fluctuation is clearly reflected in the movement of the capacity utilization rate. The dips in this variable clearly correspond to the dips in working hours except that the former do not exhibit a secular trend as in the case of the latter. The scars attributable to the first and second oil crises are reflected in the rather sizable negative contribution of the capacity utilization of capital during the 1974–1975 period and again during the 1980–1982 period. Contrary to experiences of the 1970s, the situation in the 1980s in general has been favorable as far as cycles are concerned. The contribution of capital stock per se explains the considerable portion of output growth, especially in recent years.

The residual term had been consistently positive in the 1950s and the 1960s. After experiencing a kink in output growth in the early 1970s, this variable often exhibited negative contribution. In earlier years, both the embodied technological changes and the capital vintage effect have been positive, the former typically contributing 2 to 5 percent of the total output growth of around 10 percent. This has been no more so over the last decade.

As we see in table 7-1, the average age of capital stock for the economy as a whole is estimated to be 15.3 years in 1955; throughout the high-growth era, this has shortened considerably and reached 10.2 years in 1965 and 7.3 years in 1973.[15] Since then, however, the trend has been reversed and the most recent figure is estimated at 8.7 years. Together with declines in the embodied rate of technological change, the contribution of efficiency gains for the last decade has been rather minimal, a fact which is observed of the technological level in table 7-2. This variable was obtained by taking an arbitrary year as the base (which in our case is 1955) and calculating the relative levels consecutively considering the

Table 7-3 Demand-supply gap in selected industries

(unit: ratio)

	All industries	Manufac-turing	Iron & steel	Electrical machinery	Motor vehicle	Wholesale & retail	Private services
1956	1.0502	—	—	—	—	—	1.0131
1957	.9962	.9948	1.0263	1.0272	1.0694	1.0003	.9981
1958	.9314	.9306	.8274	.9220	.9146	1.0189	.9987
1959	1.0880	1.0897	1.3901	1.1986	1.1443	.9898	1.0079
1960	1.0476	1.0486	1.0809	1.0327	1.0115	.9941	1.0084
1961	1.0021	1.0018	1.0352	.9972	.9600	.9985	.9972
1962	.9584	.9560	.8848	.9707	1.0286	.9964	.9970
1963	1.0059	1.0082	1.0176	.9833	.9977	1.0051	1.0017
1964	1.0370	1.0385	1.0911	1.0109	1.0350	1.0041	1.0007
1965	.9622	.9590	.9408	.9333	.9426	.4135	.9923
1966	1.0451	1.0490	1.0446	1.0907	1.0902	2.4282	1.0062
1967	1.0526	1.0560	1.0761	1.0665	1.0639	1.0055	1.0048
1968	1.0203	1.0190	.9941	1.0489	1.0458	1.0104	1.0038
1969	1.0052	1.0075	1.0412	.9964	.9761	.9972	.9996
1970	.9861	.9889	.9988	.9680	.9729	.9994	.9895
1971	.9671	.9603	.9051	.9630	.9707	.9939	1.0077
1972	1.0044	1.0063	1.0189	1.0241	1.0156	1.0114	.9995
1973	1.0424	1.0481	1.0975	1.0434	1.0307	.9979	1.0095
1974	.9394	.9352	.9447	.9294	.9496	1.0018	.9828
1975	.9221	.9146	.8868	.9158	.9125	1.0027	.9893
1976	1.0449	1.0501	1.0085	1.0808	1.0693	.9973	1.0053
1977	.9925	.9865	.9559	.9842	1.0060	.9989	.9971
1978	1.0168	1.0175	.9758	1.0299	1.0179	1.0002	1.0009
1979	1.0408	1.0414	1.0735	1.0522	1.0562	1.0212	1.0046
1980	.9708	.9716	.9997	1.0230	1.0329	1.0020	.9975
1981	.9776	.9747	.9320	.9910	.9795	1.0015	.9983
1982	.9856	.9850	.9663	.9924	.9621	1.0007	.9984
1983	1.0095	1.0123	1.0011	1.0511	1.0086	.9996	.9998
1984	1.0408	1.0429	1.0867	1.0568	1.0203	1.0052	1.0082
1985	1.0029	1.0006	1.0164	1.0475	1.0230	.9953	.9937

Note: The data refer to the ratio (actual demand/potential supply).
Source: COMPASS simiulation results.

annual gains in efficiency (or the residual) which are taken from the 8th column in Appendix table F-1b. The recent figure stands at around 1.7 or 1.8, which is not different from the figures a decade ago.

We may say, therefore, that for the economy as a whole, we can produce 1.7 times more output from the same input in the base year but that efficiency gains ceased to be a contributor to growth.

Appendix table F-2, which shows the sources of growth calculation for the manufacturing sector, generally exhibit similar trends as for the whole economy. In other words, the trends for the whole economy more or less reflect the situation in the manufacturing sector. The differences are that fluctuations in output and input tend to be more marked in the case of the manufacturing sector. The aggregate picture, however, hides the sectoral characteristics, to which we turn next.

It would be wrong to assume from the above observation that the efficiency gains ceased to be a major contributor to growth and hence the economy has become stagnant. There are important structural changes taking place within the manufacturing and service sectors.

Among the manufacturing sectors, we have electrical machinery as the leading sector (Appendix table F-5). The growth of output is particularly high in this sector. Labor input and capital input have been strong. More importantly, we have observed considerable gains in embodied technological progress and a shift to younger capital vintage. Unlike most other manufacturing sectors, the average age of capital in the electrical machinery sector is actually becoming younger. Starting from about 18.1 years in 1955, it quickly reached 5.0 years in 1970. In subsequent years it tended to become older as a result of rather careful investment behavior. In the late 1970s, the average age of capital was estimated to be about 6.3 years. As we entered the 1980s, electronic innovation triggered explosive growth in this sector. Extremely active capital formation contributed to the shortening of the average age of capital to about 5 years. Coupled with the high rate of embodied technological progress, efficiency gains have been particularly remarkable. In the past ten years, it is estimated that the technological level has more than doubled, as is shown in table 7-2. The precision instrument sector also belongs to this category where capital stock vintage has been kept rather young. Efficiency gains, however, have been less remarkable.

The automobile industry is often regarded as the leading sector of Japan's economic growth (Appendix table F-6). Actually, this sector has shown remarkable growth in output. This was more so in earlier years and the growth rate in the recent past has been more modest. Efficiency gains were faster than in the electrical machinery sector, but have tapered off in the last decade, too. In early 1970s, total factor productivity in this sector stood at around 3 (1955 as the base year) compared to around 2 in electrical machinery. The 1988 level is estimated to be 3.8 as compared to 5.9 in the latter.

Iron and steel is another case of interest (Appendix table F-3). This sector was undoubtedly the leading industry during the high growth era of the 1950s and 1960s, although it suffered from cyclical flctuations more than any other sectors. We have observed increasing employment as well as very strong investment. Embodied technological progress and the vintage effect have been strong. We have an entirely different picture in the latter half of our observation period. Employment has been reduced considerably, as can be seen in the consistently negative contribution of employment to growth. Capital formation has also been weakened considerably, and the growth contribution of this factor has rarely exceeded 2 percent in recent years. This can be compared to contributions often exceeding 10 percent in the earlier period. Capital stock vintage in recent years has exceeded 10 years, compared to less than 7 years in 1970. The technological level is not particularly high compared with the level a decade ago.

Petroleum and coal, chemicals, nonmetallic mineral products, nonferrous metals, fabricated metals, and transportation equipment other than motor vehicles also exhibited similar trends regarding factor input and productive efficiency. Pulp, paper, and paper products were regarded as belonging to this category until quite recently, but in the last few years, we have witnessed rather strong gains in output, which is attributable to increased employment and investment, as well as the cyclical factor. Capital stock vintage in this sector is becoming younger. According to industrial observers, the performance of this sector is associated with the progress of information technology which invited increased demand in this sector.

Among tertiary sectors, we have shown wholesale and retail trade and private services in Appendix F-8 and F-9, respectively. They represent the service sectors in a wide sense which have become leading sectors in the 'post-industrial' society.[16] Reflecting a secular increase in demand, the output of both sectors has increased steadily. The sources of growth, however, differed somewhat in the two sectors. Employment has increased in both sectors, and so did capital input. When it comes to efficiency change, however, wholesale and retail trade has exhibited a slight increase from about 2.7 in the mid 1970s (which is lower than the level reached before the oil crisis) to about 2.8 to 3.1 in the recent period, whereas in private services we have witnessed a decline from about unity in the mid 1970s to 0.7 recently.

The private service sector includes various personal services as well as business services, and its input into production is gaining importance. Our analysis reveals that increased output is made possible by an even larger increase in factor inputs in order to offset decreasing efficiency. The efficiency gains in this sector have been consistently negative since 1970. Despite a shift to younger capital vintage (from more than 8 years in the early 1970s to about 5.6 years recently), overall gains have been negative reflecting the rate of embodied technological progress which is estimated to be negative. It should be noted here that we are dealing with sources of growth in real terms. Needless to say, economic transactions and business accounting are conducted in terms of current prices, and relative prices of service sectors have been rising throughout the period under consideration.

Finally, table 7-3 shows the demand-supply gap which is the ratio of actual demand to potential output. Thus, when the ratio exceeds unity, the demand level exceeds the supply capacity, and vice versa. As we have discussed earlier, potential output is obtained based on the sources of growth account by assuming full capacity utilization of capital and substituting hypothetical working hours which would prevail under such circumstances. This is done based on empirically estimated working hours equations for each sector which incorporate the rate of capacity utilization among the explanatory variables. In the model framework, demand is derived for each sector based on actual final demand. Sectoral multipliers, which are obtained based on input-output tables, are utilized in calculating the effect of changing final demand on each industrial sector.[17]

The results reveal that demand fell short of supply capacity in 1958, 1962, 1965, 1970–1971, 1974–1975, and 1980–1982. On the other hand, excess demand is observed in 1956, 1959–1960, 1964, 1966–1967, 1973, 1976, 1979, and 1984. This is exactly what we would expect based on other sources of information such as the diffusion index, and justifies the legitimacy of the methodology used here.

On a sectoral basis, we notice a consistently high demand-supply gap in the electrical machinery sector. This is clearly an indication of the shift of demand to electronics related products. It is generally accepted that this shift in demand is induced by a new round of technological change in triple-Cs related fields.

7-4 Remaining problems

We may conclude that, based on our empirical analysis, a measurement of potential output is possible on the disaggregated sectoral level as well as for the economy as a whole. The sources of growth approach to the potential growth analysis proved useful in obtaining information concerning the factor inputs and efficiency improvements.

Comparison of potential output with demand, either for total industry or for individual sectors, can be made. Such information is valuable in assessing the need for capital formation and the threat of demand-induced price rises. The importance of a disaggregated analysis is confirmed in view of the considerable difference in performance among industrial sectors. The usefulness of the econometric model building incorporating both the demand and supply aspects must be emphasized in order to capture the interrelationship among various economic variables such as sources of growth, potential output, demand-supply gap, capital formation, prices, employment, the rate of capacity utilization, and working hours.

Compared to the list of questions concerning the growth potentials which we set out to answer, however, we realize that we have only partially succeeded. There still remain questions to be answered.

On the production side, we believe the following questions are particularly important.

(1) The feedback effect of R&D expenditures: In our framework, the rate of embodied technological progress remains unexplained. The residual, which is sometimes referred to as "the measure of our ignorance", is broken down into embodied technological progress and the vintage effect. The latter has been endogenized, and the average age of capital is derived based on existing stock of capital and new investment. This is one step forward. When sectoral analysis is provided, it is another step forward because macroeconomic performance is then broken down to the differing sectoral performance. In the real world, we observe increasing R&D expenditures which are clearly aimed at improving economic efficiency by obtaining new knowledge and making new products and new production processes possible. There still exists a huge blackbox between R&D expenditures on the one hand and efficiency gains on the other.

One promising way out is indicated by Terlecskyj who tried to trace the flow of benefit from R&D expenditures employing input-output tables.[18] Starting from R&D spending in individual sectors, and assuming that the benefit would accrue to the purchasing sectors including the sector in question itself, he distributed the R&D expenditures to intermediate demand and final demand. Private consumption and exports are among the final demand. As for capital formation, R&D benefit is incorporated in the capital goods and accrues to the purchasing sectors. Employing a fixed capital formation matrix which shows the purchasing sectors, he was able to distribute the benefits which accompany capital formation.

This framework was tested in the Japanese context by Goto et al. and myself employing pooled cross section data from 1980.[19] In both cases it was shown that indirect benefit accrueing through intermediate goods and capital goods explains the productivity gains. Our framework of analysis in this paper removes the vintage effect from the residual. Thus, the remaining task seems to be testing the links between R&D benefit and embodied technological progress.

(2) Diffusion of new technology and quality change: An important aspect in the renewed surge in economic growth is the wide diffusion of new technology incorporating electronics. This is sometimes referred to as the triple-Cs, including computers, communication, and control. We need not point out the wide spread use of mainframe computers and work stations, and the formation of communication networks. Computers are not just computing machines, but they are instrumental in accumulating knowledge in a systematic way (in contrast to a personal way) which enables us to talk about the stock of knowledge for the first time. The cases in question include databases of various sorts. As for electronic technology for control, we only have to mention industrial robots.

The rapid improvement in quality of equipment related to the triple-C technology has posed a major problem for the measurement of production and capital formation. A major breakthrough in the quality-adjusted price index for mainframe computers came in 1986 when a group of economists from IBM published time series statistics employing hedonic methods. Unlike the traditional "matched model" method where prices of identical models are compared over time, the hedonic function employs regression analysis in relating the quality change to price change. According to their results, the matched-model price indexes decline much less than the hedonic indexes.[20] This undoubtedly results in an underestimation of production, capital formation, etc. in triple-C related fields. The group worked closely with BEA and the results were used in the improvement of computer-related statistics in the U.S. national income statistics. Similar attempts have to be made in Japan.

(3) Demographic factors and technological factor in labor supply: In a period of continued expansion, an economy will hit the full employment ceiling sooner or later and cost push inflation will ensue. This is one of the reasons for policy intervention in view of smoothing out the cyclical fluctuations. In the long term, however, many industralized countries today face aging populations, and Japan is no exception. Perhaps the problem is compounded in Japan because the process is occurring at a faster pace due to a longer life expectancy and declining child births. If we assume a normal retirement age, it would mean that a smaller

segment of the working population has to support the entire population. This poses a serious limitation to growth mainly through labor supply constraints. We have seen in our analysis that the room for efficiency improvement in services is rather limited, as far as past records are concerned, and the demand is shifting toward more services.

In order to obtain a more realistic picture of labor supply, we have to approach the problem from two sides. One is demographic changes per se. One important parameter is the retirement age. If this is an economic variable and people decide to stay in the labor force beyond the current retirement age, the problem will become less serious. There remains a problem of a mismatch in skills, but this is probably more manageable than an absolute shortage. The second factor is the labor force participation of the female population. The female labor force participation ratio in Japan is not particularly low today and it tends to rise further, and there are various factors at work in this regard. In the younger age bracket, increased attendance at institutions of higher education tend to lower the participation rate. After finishing schooling, more women choose to work formally even after their marriages. Due to fewer child births, however, the labor force participation during the child bearing age has been rising. Not much change has occured in the old age bracket. The expansion of labor demand in service sectors tend to facilitate the labor force participation of women.[21]

Another factor is the spread of new technology represented by triple-Cs. There are indications that computers, industrial robots, and automated vending machines have a labor saving effect.[22] In a work based on Japanese data, Mori [1987] has shown that industrial robots can actually replace labor, and in this sense are labor augmenting. If this is actually the case, we may say that substitution possibilities between capital and labor are high and that, in the long-run, we may be able to remove the full-employment ceiling.

Footnotes:

1 The application of the concept of potential GNP can be traced back to the *Annual Report of the Council of Economic Advisers, 1962.*

2 For a detailed account, see Uno [1987] pp.217–310, Uno [1989a] pp.75–83, and Kimio Uno, "Economic Growth and Environmental Change in Japan: Net National Welfare and Beyond." Franco Archibugi and Peter Nijkamp, eds. *Economy and Ecology: Towards Sustainable Growth?"* Dordrecht, the Netherlands: Kluwer Academic Publishers, 1989.

3 The concept of potential output developed by Arthur Okun [1962] refers to the level of real national product under full employment. In the U.S. in the 1960s, full employment actually accompanied unemployment of 4 to 4.5%. Thus, potential output was measured assuming unemployment of about 4%. This

convention was followed, for example, by Denison [1979], p.12.

4 The problem of structural change is analyzed in Uno [1989a] in terms of both production and employment.

5 See chapter 10 for details. One of the major improvements in this version of COMPASS is that the output series have been shifted completely to the revised SNA basis. At the time of the shift from the old SNA to the new SNA in Japan which took place in 1978, a major portion of the system has been published recursively since 1965 but the disaggregated production figures and relevant sectoral deflators have been made available only since 1970. This has caused some inconvenience for long-term analysis, necessitating the use of production figures from the old SNA and the substitution of deflators by sectoral wholesale price indexes. In 1988, however, a historical series of revised SNA were made available. This considerably facilitates long-term sectoral analysis by removing discontinuity in the data around 1970. Our analysis in this paper is one of the first to employ this new data set.

6 For details of the model specification, see chapter 10 below and Uno [1987]. The latter refers to version I, covering the period from 1955 to 1980. The observation period was extended to 1985 in version II. A series of input-output analyses covering the 1951–1985 period are provided in Uno [1989a].

7 For details of the methodology, refer to Nelson [1964]. See also Uno [1987], pp.159–163.

8 Some of the data series for 1987 and 1988 are provisional.

9 The estimation procedure as well as basic data such as durable years by asset are provided in Uno [1987], pp.100–103. Capital stock vintage, or the average age of capital stock, is estimated folowing Nelson as below:

$$at = \frac{(1-r)}{(1+\Delta K/K)} (at-1 + 1)$$

where at: average of capital stock at time t

$\Delta K/K$: rate of growth of capital stock

r: rate of depreciation.

10 A detailed explanation is provided in Uno [1987], pp.126–127.

11 The results for all 25 sectors are available upon request.

12 When the data on the rate of capacity utilization or the working hours is not available, its effects are shown by null values in the tables.

13 For a full exposition of the structural change, see Uno [1989a].

14 For a detailed exposition of business cycles in Japan, see Uno [1987], pp.107–119.

15 For an alternative estimate of the average age of capital stock (as of 1970) for individual sectors, see Economic Council, ed., *Multisectoral Models for Economic Planning—The 5th Report of the Econometric Committee—** (Keizai Keikakuno Tameno Tabumon Keiryo Moderu), Tokyo: Ministry of Finance Printing Bureau. 1977.

16 See Uno [1989a].

17 For details, see Uno [1987]. pp.201–211.

18 Terlecskyj [1980][1982].

19 See Goto et al. [1986]. The result of my experiment is reported in Uno [1989],

pp.233–242.

20 See Cole, et al. [1986]; Cartwright [1986][1988].

21 The labor supply is analyzed in a demographic model developed by the present author. The model explains labor force participation and other usual demographic variables such as births and deaths for each age bracket, for male and female.

22 Uno [1989a], pp.145–164.

Part 4

International trade

Chapter 8. New trends in the world trade

8-1 Introduction

There have been major changes in the international economic relations in the 1980s. Trade in machinery is the main thrust of expansion in international transactions. Not only that, there has been a major shift among the major participants in the world trade. A typical case is the rise of newly industrializing economies (NIEs) in Asia. Coupled with continued surge of Japan especially in machinery export including general machinery, electrical machinery, automobiles, and office equipment, the Pacific rim has emerged as the bright spot in the world trade scene. Across the Pacific, the United States and Canada have entered into free trade agreement. European integration is expected in 1992. In contrast, economic stalemate in Eastern Europe and China became all too apparent. Many of the less developed countries (LDCs) are suffering from inability to export. Unlike in the 1960s and the 1970s, world trade in natural resources is stagnant. World demand for raw materials and energy has become rather stable, and their prices have receded. Because of the erosion of world resources market, resource exporting countries have encountered considerable economic difficulty. The case in question include Mideast countries and some of the Latin American and African countries. Even the Soviet Union was not immune from the trend. Thus, world trade scene in the 1980s is characterized by increased imbalance in various respects.

As we enter the 1990s, the contrasting situation seems to be aggravating, as witnessed by trade frictions among exporting countries, widening gaps in economic and trade performance between the North and the South and the West and the East.

One may suspect that technological change is the major factor which lies behind the imbalance. Major industrialized countries are expanding production along new product lines based on high-tech. Static concept of comparative advantage based on inherent factor endowment has little power in explaining a world trade structure in a rapid technological change. Research and development (R&D), new investment, and technological capability of the population seem to be the key elements for successful economic performance. Cheap labor alone ceased to attract investment from abroad. This leads us to believe that the first and the most important change that is taking place is the technological innovation related to the diffusion of electronics technology. Computers have been with us more than three decades now, but widespread use of electronics in computer-communication-control (triple-Cs) technology is a distinct phenomenon of the 1980s and the trend is expected to continue to the year 2000 and beyond, with its profound implication for production, employment, capital formation, and foreign trade.

The second factor is financial resources. Capital formation is carried out to cope with the changing relative prices and new technology, and it has to be financed through savings, domestic or foreign. R&D effort is becoming the most crucial economic activity for the industry and this ever-mounting, risky expenditure also has to be financed. A country with strong saving basis is in a better position to accomodate these financial needs, whereas those with less favorable economic fundamentals need to attract foreign fund by paying higher rate of interest. In the 1980s, we saw a widening gap in the countries' ability to finance investment and technology.

Third, we saw continued liberalization of trade. The multilateral framework of the GATT is poised in the 1980s to achieve agreement on rules in service trade after accomplishing major tariff reductions in the earlier years. Instead, trade negotiations in the 1980s and beyond seem to assume bilateral character. Through a series of negotiations with the United States, Japanese market is becoming more transparent and open whereas the U.S. is in effect enforcing voluntary export restrictions of major items upon her trading partners through bilateral negotiations. Here we are not talking about tariffs because in Japan they are already among the lowest in the major trading countries. What matters is the government procurement, government monopolies (such as tobacco), quantitative restrictions, industrial standards, testing and certification, among others. There are additional issues concerning trade in services where free business activities by foreign firms are hampered by various institutional barriers. The United States also negotiated a free trade agreement with Canada. We should expect measures aimed at liberalization of trade when the European Community becomes tightly integrated in 1992. Thus, we can distinguish a trend toward a borderless world economy.

Fourth factor is the major exchange rate adjustment which took place in 1985. In order to cope with mounting imbalance in trade, major industrial countries have resorted to exchange rate realignment. There are short-term and long-term effects involved; the former refers to a shift in relative prices which directly reflects the changes in the exchange rates. The latter refers to changes in the investment pattern both at home and abroad, with its second round effect on the patterns of trade among countries. The resurgence of economic growth in the 1980s has not automatically restored world economic balance. Many countries are suffering from trade imbalance (some from deficit and some from surplus), and this happened despite repeated exchange rate realignment.

However, exchange rate adjustment is only one aspect of increased international policy coordination. Macroeconomic performance also has to be adjusted through monetary and fiscal policies. Major industrial powers continually exchange views through G7, G5, or G2 (the United States and Japan) meetings.

In section 2 which follows, we should look at the world trade matrices in order to grasp the magnitude of the structural change. In section 3, we shall review existing empirical study on trade structure and international economic linkages through trade. In sections 4 and 5, we look into policy debate between the United States and Japan regarding foreign trade and direct foreign investment because it has global implications. In section 6, we try to assess the technological factor in international trade. We examine in particular the effect of diffusion of triple-C technology on exports of machinery sectors.

8-2 Changing structure of world trade

The flow of goods among countries are represented in a form of trade matrix which provides an overview of the economic ties on a global scale. The data are provided in this section for overall trade as well as for major product categories. First, let us look at table 8-1 in order to gain a bird's eye view of the structure of world trade. Panel (a) shows the origin of exports and (b) the destination. The data are summarized from full matrices. Detailed table is provided for machinery and tranport equipment in Appendix G.[1] Commodities are classified according to the SITC. One of the focal points in the last two decades was "mineral fuels" (SITC 3). It is shown that the international transaction in this category has not kept pace with the growth of world trade, as indicated by its shrinking share. In contrast, the focal point in recent years is the "machinery and transport equipment" (SITC 7). As we have seen in preceding chapters, this category of products is directly linked to recent technological progress. Even within a short span of the recent five years, we note rapid emergence of Japan and Other Asia (i.e., Asia other than Mid East). The former gained nearly 5 percentage points between 1980 and 1985 to reach nearly 20% of the world total. During the same period, the latter expanded the share from 3.9% to 6.6%. The share of Europe tended to decline whereas that of the United States more or less remained stable. This picture is reflected in the total exports.

As for destination of machinery and transport equipment exports, which is shown in panel (b), what is remarkable is the rapid expansion of U.S. share. Starting from 12.2% in as recent as 1980, it nearly doubled to reach 22.4% in 1985. It should be added that a similar situation prevails

Table 8-1 World trade structure

a. Origin of exports

Origin or destination →	World	Market economies			Centrally planned economies	Developed market	
		Deve-loped	Developing			Europe	
Year			Total	OPEC		Total	EEC
	0-9 Total all commodities						
1980	100.0	62.9	28.3	15.3	8.8	40.1	33.2
1982	100.0	63.2	26.7	12.1	10.1	38.5	31.7
1983	100.0	63.6	25.4	10.0	11.0	38.4	31.6
1984	100.0	64.3	25.1	8.9	10.6	37.4	30.4
1985	100.0	65.5	23.9	8.0	10.5	39.0	31.8
	0&1 Food live animals and beverages tabacco						
1980	100.0	64.3	28.6	1.9	7.1	38.4	34.2
1982	100.0	63.4	29.8	1.6	6.8	37.7	33.5
1983	100.0	62.1	30.7	1.6	7.2	36.9	32.7
1984	100.0	62.1	31.3	1.7	6.7	36.5	32.2
1985	100.0	61.9	30.7	1.8	7.4	39.2	34.6
	2&4 Crude materials oils and fats (Fuels excluded)						
1980	100.0	61.5	29.1	3.7	9.4	24.5	16.4
1982	100.0	62.2	27.6	2.4	10.2	23.6	16.3
1983	100.0	61.9	27.7	2.2	10.4	24.3	16.9
1984	100.0	61.7	28.4	2.2	9.9	24.4	16.9
1985	100.0	60.2	29.2	2.2	10.6	25.4	18.1
	3 Mineral fuels and lubricants related material						
1980	100.0	18.3	72.3	60.4	9.4	13.9	11.3
1982	100.0	22.8	64.1	49.0	13.1	16.2	13.2
1983	100.0	24.7	59.2	43.6	16.2	17.9	14.1
1984	100.0	25.8	57.3	41.3	16.8	18.4	14.3
1985	100.0	27.8	55.3	39.0	16.9	19.5	15.3
	5 Chemicals						
1980	100.0	86.9	6.8	1.0	6.3	63.3	54.4
1982	100.0	84.0	8.2	1.3	7.8	60.0	51.1
1983	100.0	83.7	8.3	1.3	8.0	60.2	51.2
1984	100.0	83.9	8.4	0.8	7.8	59.1	50.2
1985	100.0	83.3	8.4	0.9	8.3	60.3	51.3
	7 Machinery and equipment transport						
1980	100.0	85.0	5.9	0.3	9.1	50.0	42.7
1982	100.0	83.9	7.0	0.4	9.1	45.6	38.4
1983	100.0	82.1	8.2	0.3	9.7	42.9	36.1
1984	100.0	81.8	9.3	0.3	8.9	39.8	33.2
1985	100.0	82.3	9.2	0.3	8.5	40.7	34.0
	6&8 Other manufactured goods						
1980	100.0	77.1	16.0	0.8	7.0	54.9	43.6
1982	100.0	73.7	18.5	0.8	7.7	51.0	40.0
1983	100.0	72.0	20.0	1.0	8.0	49.9	39.2
1984	100.0	70.7	21.6	1.0	7.7	48.6	37.7
1985	100.0	71.4	21.2	0.9	7.4	50.1	39.0

Source: United Nations, *Yearbook of International Trade Statistics*.

(unit: percent)

economies			Developing market economies				Centrally planned economies	
U.S.A.	Japan	Australia, New Zealand	Africa	America	Asia		Asia	USSR
					Mid. East	Other		
10.8	6.5	1.3	4.7	5.4	10.5	7.1	1.0	3.8
11.2	7.5	1.4	3.6	5.8	8.4	8.1	1.2	4.7
10.8	8.1	1.4	3.4	5.8	6.8	8.8	1.4	5.0
11.1	8.9	1.5	3.3	5.9	5.7	9.5	1.4	4.8
10.7	9.1	1.4	3.1	5.5	5.4	9.3	1.6	4.5
15.1	0.8	4.8	4.7	14.4	1.4	7.3	2.4	0.6
14.3	0.7	4.8	4.2	15.0	1.8	7.9	1.8	0.7
14.6	0.8	4.0	4.7	15.6	1.6	7.9	2.2	0.7
14.6	0.8	4.7	4.2	15.8	1.7	8.7	2.0	0.7
12.5	0.7	4.5	4.3	15.7	1.6	8.3	2.5	0.7
18.6	1.1	5.6	5.0	8.3	1.1	13.6	1.8	5.1
18.6	1.2	7.0	4.6	8.9	1.2	11.7	1.8	5.3
17.8	1.3	6.4	4.7	8.0	1.2	12.8	2.2	5.1
17.8	1.2	6.0	4.5	8.8	1.2	12.7	2.6	4.7
15.2	1.2	6.4	4.1	9.8	1.3	13.0	2.9	4.8
1.7	0.1	0.5	14.9	9.7	41.4	6.3	0.6	7.5
3.0	0.1	0.9	11.3	11.4	33.1	8.2	1.0	10.6
2.5	0.1	1.2	10.7	11.2	28.7	8.5	1.4	12.8
2.5	0.1	1.4	11.6	11.5	25.2	8.9	1.5	13.3
2.8	0.2	1.6	11.4	10.3	24.8	8.7	2.0	12.8
14.7	4.7	0.5	0.6	2.2	1.0	2.3	0.8	1.2
15.1	4.7	0.5	0.8	2.5	1.4	2.7	0.9	1.7
14.4	5.0	0.5	0.8	2.7	1.4	2.7	1.0	1.8
15.3	5.1	0.4	0.9	3.0	0.7	3.1	1.0	1.9
14.0	5.0	0.4	0.7	2.7	0.9	3.3	1.0	1.8
16.5	14.8	0.3	0.1	1.0	0.3	3.9	0.1	2.4
17.0	16.6	0.2	0.1	1.0	0.4	4.8	0.2	2.2
15.9	18.0	0.2	0.1	1.3	0.4	5.8	0.3	2.2
15.9	20.0	0.2	0.1	1.4	0.4	6.9	0.3	2.0
15.7	19.8	0.2	0.1	1.5	0.4	6.6	0.2	2.0
8.1	8.7	0.8	1.0	2.6	0.8	10.7	1.7	1.0
7.7	10.0	0.8	0.9	2.4	1.2	12.9	2.3	1.2
7.1	9.7	0.8	1.0	2.9	1.2	13.9	2.3	1.2
6.8	9.7	0.8	0.8	3.2	1.4	15.1	2.2	1.3
6.4	9.4	0.8	0.8	3.1	1.4	14.9	2.0	1.1

b. Destination of exports

Origin or destination →	World	Market economies			Centrally planned economies	Developed market	
		Deve-loped	Developing			Europe	
Year			Total	OPEC		Total	EEC
	0-9 Total all commodities						
1980	100.0	66.8	23.7	6.4	8.3	43.8	35.1
1982	100.0	63.5	25.9	7.9	9.0	39.9	32.0
1983	100.0	64.8	24.0	6.9	9.5	39.3	31.5
1984	100.0	66.0	23.0	5.8	9.3	37.8	30.6
1985	100.0	65.5	23.9	8.0	10.5	39.0	31.8
	0&1 Food live aminals and beverages tabacco						
1980	100.0	61.4	24.8	8.0	12.6	43.8	38.1
1982	100.0	59.8	25.0	8.9	14.6	41.3	35.8
1983	100.0	61.0	25.1	8.4	13.3	41.2	35.6
1984	100.0	61.5	25.0	8.5	12.8	39.7	34.6
1985	100.0	63.9	23.4	7.5	12.0	41.8	36.4
	2&4 Crude materials. oils and fats. (Fuels excluded)						
1980	100.0	69.1	18.5	3.0	10.0	44.5	36.9
1982	100.0	67.0	19.9	3.8	10.7	42.3	34.5
1983	100.0	67.0	20.2	3.8	10.4	41.7	34.2
1984	100.0	66.1	21.8	3.6	9.5	40.7	33.5
1985	100.0	65.3	21.9	3.3	10.3	40.9	33.4
	3 Mineral fuels and lubricants related material						
1980	100.0	75.5	18.5	1.1	4.0	41.7	34.0
1982	100.0	70.1	21.8	1.3	5.8	39.9	32.7
1983	100.0	70.1	19.7	1.3	7.4	39.3	31.7
1984	100.0	70.3	20.1	1.2	7.7	40.0	32.4
1985	100.0	67.1	22.8	1.4	8.3	38.3	31.1
	5 Chemicals						
1980	100.0	63.9	26.8	6.4	8.9	49.6	39.5
1981	100.0	64.2	26.0	6.8	9.1	47.7	38.3
1983	100.0	64.9	25.9	6.5	8.6	47.2	37.8
1984	100.0	64.8	25.6	5.9	8.9	45.9	37.2
1985	100.0	65.4	24.8	5.4	9.2	47.2	38.1
	7 Machinery and equipment transport						
1980	100.0	59.5	30.0	10.1	10.0	38.1	29.8
1982	100.0	58.3	31.3	12.2	9.4	34.5	26.9
1983	100.0	61.6	27.5	9.8	10.1	34.0	26.5
1984	100.0	64.4	25.3	7.6	9.7	31.8	25.1
1985	100.0	65.6	22.7	6.1	11.0	32.6	25.5
	6&8 Other manufactured goods						
1980	100.0	69.1	22.8	8.1	7.6	50.8	39.7
1982	100.0	65.6	26.0	10.2	7.8	43.9	34.7
1983	100.0	67.1	23.9	8.9	8.2	43.1	34.2
1984	100.0	69.2	21.8	7.1	8.1	41.1	32.7
1985	100.0	69.8	20.6	6.2	9.0	42.1	33.4

Source: Same as table 8-1-a.

(unit: percent)

economies			Developing market economies				Centrally planned economies	
					Asia			
U.S.A.	Japan	Australia, New Zealand	Africa	America	Mid. East	Other	Asia	USSR
12.0	6.2	1.2	4.2	6.3	4.8	7.5	1.1	3.1
12.3	6.2	1.5	4.2	6.1	6.3	8.6	1.1	3.7
14.1	6.2	1.3	3.7	4.7	6.1	8.8	1.3	3.8
16.4	6.0	1.5	3.4	5.1	5.1	8.7	1.5	3.6
10.7	5.8	1.4	3.3	5.0	4.6	8.6	2.2	3.6
8.6	6.3	0.6	6.0	5.9	5.8	6.4	1.7	7.1
8.6	6.7	0.7	6.2	5.0	6.7	6.6	2.0	9.5
9.5	7.2	0.7	5.8	5.1	6.8	7.1	1.7	8.8
11.0	7.5	0.8	5.9	4.7	7.3	6.6	1.4	8.7
11.4	7.6	0.7	6.0	4.4	6.2	6.3	1.1	8.6
7.3	14.0	0.8	2.6	3.6	2.1	9.2	2.7	2.4
7.7	13.7	0.8	2.9	3.7	2.6	9.6	2.4	3.0
8.4	13.4	0.8	2.8	3.5	2.8	10.2	2.2	3.2
8.9	12.8	0.8	2.8	4.3	2.6	11.1	2.2	2.9
8.6	12.4	0.8	3.0	4.0	2.4	11.2	2.6	3.0
17.8	13.5	0.9	1.6	6.8	2.6	2.0	0.1	0.3
14.0	13.8	1.0	1.7	7.5	2.6	9.2	0.2	0.3
14.5	14.2	0.7	1.7	5.8	2.4	9.0	0.3	0.3
14.2	13.9	0.8	1.6	7.1	2.3	8.1	0.3	0.3
13.4	13.6	0.6	1.6	6.9	2.7	10.3	0.4	0.4
5.7	3.8	1.5	4.7	8.0	4.2	8.7	1.5	3.5
6.8	4.7	1.7	4.0	7.1	4.7	9.2	1.8	3.6
7.8	4.7	1.6	3.7	6.2	5.0	10.0	1.9	3.1
8.9	4.5	1.8	3.4	6.5	4.5	10.2	2.4	3.1
8.9	4.4	1.5	3.6	6.5	4.1	9.5	2.5	3.2
12.2	1.4	1.7	6.2	7.8	6.9	8.1	1.3	4.1
14.1	1.4	2.1	5.9	7.0	8.8	9.0	0.9	4.8
17.6	1.6	1.8	4.8	4.9	8.0	9.1	1.1	5.2
21.6	1.7	2.0	4.2	5.3	6.1	9.1	1.6	4.7
22.4	1.7	2.1	3.7	3.7	3.4	5.1	0.1	4.6
10.9	2.7	1.4	4.3	4.9	6.0	6.8	1.2	3.3
13.3	3.1	1.8	4.3	4.5	8.2	8.3	1.2	3.8
15.6	3.1	1.6	3.6	3.2	8.0	8.5	1.7	3.7
18.8	3.5	1.8	3.1	3.3	6.3	8.5	2.1	3.3
18.9	3.3	1.7	3.0	3.3	5.9	7.6	2.9	3.4

Table 8-2 Commodity composition of trade of selected countries

a. Exports

Origin or destination →		Market economies			Centrally planned economies	Developed market	
	World	Deve-loped	Developing			Europe	
Year			Total	OPEC		Total	EEC
0-9 Total all commodities							
1980	100.0	100.0	100.0	100.0	100.0	100.0	100.0
1982	100.0	100.0	100.0	100.0	100.0	100.0	100.0
1983	100.0	100.0	100.0	100.0	100.0	100.0	100.0
1984	100.0	100.0	100.0	100.0	100.0	100.0	100.0
1985	100.0	100.0	100.0	100.0	100.0	100.0	100.0
0&1 Food live animals and beverages tabacco							
1980	10.0	10.2	10.1	1.2	8.1	9.6	10.3
1982	10.2	10.2	11.4	1.3	8.9	10.0	10.8
1983	10.2	9.9	12.3	1.6	6.6	9.7	10.5
1984	9.8	9.4	12.2	1.9	6.1	9.5	10.3
1985	9.2	8.7	11.8	2.1	6.4	9.2	10.0
2&4 Crude materials oils and fats (Fuels excluded)							
1980	6.9	6.8	7.1	1.7	7.4	4.2	3.4
1982	6.1	6.0	6.3	1.2	6.1	3.7	3.1
1983	6.2	6.0	6.8	1.4	5.9	3.9	3.3
1984	6.5	6.3	7.4	1.6	6.1	4.3	3.6
1985	6.2	5.7	7.6	1.7	6.2	4.0	3.5
3 Mineral fuels and lubricants related material							
1980	24.1	7.0	61.4	94.8	25.8	8.3	8.2
1982	23.2	8.4	55.8	94.1	30.0	9.8	9.6
1983	21.0	8.2	49.3	92.5	31.0	9.8	9.5
1984	19.7	7.9	45.1	91.7	31.3	9.7	9.3
1985	18.7	8.0	43.3	91.1	29.9	9.4	9.0
5 Chemicals							
1980	7.0	9.7	1.7	0.5	5.0	11.1	11.5
1982	7.2	9.5	2.2	0.7	5.5	11.2	11.5
1983	7.6	10.0	2.5	1.0	5.5	11.8	12.3
1984	7.7	10.0	2.6	0.7	5.6	12.1	12.7
1985	7.9	10.0	2.8	0.9	6.2	12.2	12.7
7 Machinery and equipment transport							
1980	25.6	34.7	5.3	0.5	26.5	32.0	33.0
1982	27.7	36.8	7.3	0.8	25.0	32.8	33.6
1983	28.7	37.0	9.3	0.9	25.3	32.0	32.8
1984	29.7	37.8	11.0	1.1	24.7	31.5	32.4
1985	31.1	39.1	11.9	1.2	25.1	32.5	33.3
6&8 Other manufactured goods							
1980	24.0	29.4	13.5	1.2	19.1	32.9	31.8
1982	23.1	27.0	16.1	1.6	17.6	30.6	29.2
1983	23.6	26.8	18.7	2.3	17.1	30.7	29.4
1984	23.9	26.3	20.6	2.7	17.4	31.0	29.6
1985	24.2	26.4	21.4	2.8	17.0	31.1	29.7

Source: Same as table 8-1-a.

(unit: percent)

economies			Developing market economies				Centrally planned economies	
U.S.A.	Japan	Australia, New Zealand	Africa	America	Asia		Asia	USSR
					Mid. East	Other		
100.0	100.0	100.0	100.0	100.0	100.0	100.0	100.0	100.0
100.0	100.0	100.0	100.0	100.0	100.0	100.0	100.0	100.0
100.0	100.0	100.0	100.0	100.0	100.0	100.0	100.0	100.0
100.0	100.0	100.0	100.0	100.0	100.0	100.0	100.0	100.0
100.0	100.0	100.0	100.0	100.0	100.0	100.0	100.0	100.0
14.0	1.2	36.3	9.9	26.5	1.3	10.3	23.8	1.7
13.0	1.0	34.5	11.7	26.5	2.2	9.9	15.9	1.4
13.7	0.9	29.9	14.3	27.3	2.4	9.1	16.8	1.4
12.8	0.8	31.3	12.4	26.4	2.8	8.9	13.6	1.4
10.7	0.7	28.5	12.8	26.3	2.7	8.1	14.9	1.4
11.9	1.2	28.9	7.3	10.5	0.7	13.2	12.2	9.2
10.0	1.0	29.6	7.7	9.3	0.9	8.7	9.4	6.8
10.2	1.0	29.1	8.7	8.5	1.1	9.1	10.2	6.3
10.5	0.9	26.8	8.9	9.8	1.4	8.7	11.5	6.3
8.8	0.8	27.4	8.3	11.1	1.5	8.7	11.5	6.6
3.7	0.4	9.1	75.6	42.8	94.6	21.3	14.8	47.0
6.2	0.3	14.6	72.4	45.8	91.0	23.4	19.5	52.3
4.9	0.3	18.1	67.6	41.0	88.7	20.5	21.1	53.8
4.4	0.3	19.4	69.6	38.6	86.7	18.4	21.1	54.5
4.8	0.3	21.4	69.3	35.4	85.6	17.6	23.8	53.0
9.6	5.1	2.5	0.8	2.9	0.7	2.3	5.5	2.2
9.6	4.5	2.4	1.5	3.1	1.2	2.4	5.3	2.6
10.1	4.6	2.5	1.8	3.6	1.6	2.3	5.4	2.6
10.6	4.4	2.3	2.0	3.9	1.0	2.5	5.1	3.0
10.3	4.3	2.3	1.9	3.8	1.3	2.8	4.9	3.2
39.0	58.4	5.0	0.4	4.7	0.8	14.3	2.8	16.0
42.0	61.3	3.7	0.5	4.9	1.3	16.5	4.2	13.1
42.1	63.8	3.9	0.5	6.6	1.6	19.1	5.6	12.7
42.4	66.6	3.7	0.5	6.9	2.0	21.5	5.7	12.6
45.7	67.8	3.5	0.8	8.4	2.3	22.1	3.0	13.5
17.9	32.4	13.9	5.2	11.5	1.8	36.5	40.4	6.5
15.9	30.8	12.4	5.7	9.7	3.3	36.8	44.1	5.8
15.5	28.3	14.1	6.8	11.9	4.3	37.6	39.3	5.6
14.7	26.0	13.3	6.2	13.1	5.9	37.9	36.9	6.5
14.4	25.0	12.9	6.4	13.7	6.4	38.7	30.4	5.8

b. Destination of exports

Origin or destination →	World	Market economies			Centrally planned economies	Developed market	
		Deve-loped	Developing			Europe	
Year			Total	OPEC		Total	EEC
0-9 Total all commodities							
1980	100.0	100.0	100.0	100.0	100.0	100.0	100.0
1982	100.0	100.0	100.0	100.0	100.0	100.0	100.0
1983	100.0	100.0	100.0	100.0	100.0	100.0	100.0
1984	100.0	100.0	100.0	100.0	100.0	100.0	100.0
1985	100.0	100.0	100.0	100.0	100.0	100.0	100.0
0&1 Food live aminals and beverages tabacco							
1980	10.0	9.2	10.4	12.6	15.1	10.0	10.8
1982	10.2	9.6	9.8	11.5	16.6	10.6	11.4
1983	10.2	9.6	10.6	12.3	14.3	10.7	11.5
1984	9.8	9.1	10.6	14.3	13.4	10.2	11.1
1985	9.2	8.8	9.5	13.6	10.9	10.0	10.9
2&4 Crude materials. oils and fats. (Fuels excluded)							
1980	6.9	7.1	5.4	3.2	8.3	7.0	7.2
1982	6.1	6.4	4.6	2.9	7.2	6.4	6.5
1983	6.2	6.4	5.2	3.4	6.8	6.6	6.7
1984	6.5	6.5	6.2	4.1	6.7	7.0	7.2
1985	6.2	6.1	6.0	4.0	6.3	6.6	6.7
3 Mineral fuels and lubricants related material							
1980	24.1	27.2	18.7	4.2	11.7	22.9	23.3
1982	23.2	25.6	19.5	3.9	15.1	23.2	23.6
1983	21.1	22.9	17.3	4.0	16.4	21.2	21.3
1984	19.7	21.0	17.2	4.1	16.2	20.9	20.9
1985	18.7	19.0	19.1	5.3	15.4	18.8	19.0
5 Chemicals							
1980	7.0	6.7	7.9	7.1	7.5	8.0	7.9
1982	7.2	7.2	7.2	6.2	7.3	8.6	8.6
1983	7.6	7.6	8.2	7.1	6.8	9.1	9.1
1984	7.7	7.5	8.5	7.8	7.3	9.3	9.4
1985	7.9	7.8	8.7	8.3	7.2	9.7	9.8
7 Machinery and equipment transport							
1980	25.6	22.8	32.4	40.6	30.7	22.3	21.7
1982	27.7	25.5	33.6	43.1	29.1	24.0	23.2
1983	28.7	27.3	32.8	40.7	30.4	24.8	24.1
1984	29.7	28.9	32.6	38.7	30.7	24.9	24.3
1985	31.1	30.8	31.5	37.2	33.9	26.5	25.8
6&8 Other manufactured goods							
1980	24.0	24.8	23.1	30.3	21.9	27.8	27.1
1982	23.1	23.9	23.2	30.0	20.1	25.5	25.1
1983	23.6	24.5	23.6	30.4	20.5	25.9	25.7
1984	23.9	25.1	22.6	29.2	20.7	26.0	25.6
1985	24.2	25.5	22.2	29.8	21.7	26.7	26.3

Source: Same as table 8-1-a.

(unit: percent)

economies			Developing market economies				Centrally planned economies	
U.S.A.	Japan	Australia, New Zealand	Africa	America	Asia		Asia	USSR
					Mid. East	Other		
100.0	100.0	100.0	100.0	100.0	100.0	100.0	100.0	100.0
100.0	100.0	100.0	100.0	100.0	100.0	100.0	100.0	100.0
100.0	100.0	100.0	100.0	100.0	100.0	100.0	100.0	100.0
100.0	100.0	100.0	100.0	100.0	100.0	100.0	100.0	100.0
100.0	100.0	100.0	100.0	100.0	100.0	100.0	100.0	100.0
7.2	10.1	4.7	14.3	9.4	12.0	8.5	15.1	23.0
7.4	11.0	4.5	15.1	8.4	10.8	7.8	18.8	26.1
6.9	11.9	5.3	16.1	10.9	11.0	8.2	13.5	23.3
6.6	12.1	5.1	17.0	8.9	14.0	7.4	8.7	23.7
6.3	12.1	4.7	16.9	8.0	12.2	6.7	4.4	21.8
4.2	15.6	4.4	4.3	3.9	3.0	8.4	16.2	5.4
3.8	13.3	3.3	4.3	3.7	2.5	6.8	13.2	4.9
3.7	13.5	3.8	4.6	4.6	2.8	7.2	10.9	5.2
3.6	13.8	3.7	5.4	5.5	3.3	8.4	9.2	5.2
3.2	13.3	3.2	5.7	5.0	3.2	8.0	7.2	5.2
35.7	52.4	17.0	9.3	25.8	10.1	23.6	2.8	2.3
26.3	51.5	15.5	9.3	28.7	9.6	24.9	4.3	1.7
21.7	48.6	11.9	9.7	25.8	8.5	21.6	5.1	1.8
17.1	45.4	10.2	9.3	27.2	9.0	18.5	4.4	1.8
15.1	44.0	7.5	9.3	25.7	10.9	22.4	3.3	2.2
3.4	4.3	8.8	7.9	8.9	6.2	8.2	9.5	7.9
3.9	5.4	8.1	6.8	8.4	5.3	7.7	11.5	6.9
4.2	5.7	9.1	7.6	9.9	6.2	8.6	11.1	6.1
4.2	5.8	9.3	7.6	9.8	6.8	9.0	11.9	6.7
15.1	6.0	8.7	8.6	10.2	7.0	8.6	8.8	7.0
26.0	5.9	35.6	37.5	31.6	36.5	27.7	29.5	34.0
31.8	6.4	39.3	39.0	31.8	38.7	29.0	23.6	35.4
35.7	7.4	40.0	37.4	29.8	37.9	29.7	25.0	39.3
39.4	8.2	40.5	36.9	30.7	35.2	31.2	30.9	39.1
41.9	9.1	46.0	34.9	32.2	33.9	29.1	41.5	40.0
21.8	10.6	27.8	24.7	18.6	29.9	21.8	24.5	25.8
25.1	11.6	27.7	23.8	17.3	30.1	22.3	25.8	23.7
26.1	12.0	28.3	22.9	16.1	31.0	23.0	31.7	22.7
27.4	13.7	29.4	21.9	15.3	29.5	23.4	32.6	22.0
27.5	14.0	27.9	22.4	16.0	31.0	21.2	31.6	22.7

for "other manufactured goods" (SITC 6 and 8) where the U.S. share jumped from 10.9% in 1980 to 18.9% in 1985. We may say that the United States has emerged in the 1980s as a major importer of manufactured goods.

Second, the commodity structure of exports and imports for each country/region is shown in table 8-2. As for exports, which is shown in panel (a), the share of machinery and transport equipment is the highest for Japan (67.8% in 1985), followed by the U.S. (45.7%) and Europe (32.5). It can also be observed that Japan's exports almost solely consist of manufactured goods and that, among them, the share of "machinery and transport equpment" is rising rapidly at the expense of "other manufactured goods." Similar situation prevails in the United States whereas in Europe, export share of machinery and transport equipment is more or less stable.

As for the commodity structure of imports, which is shown in panel (b), Japan's imports almost solely consist of mineral fuels (44.0% in 1985), food (12.1%), and crude materials (12.1%). Many of these items are not available domestically in Japan. This is a good example where the direction of trade is explained by availability theory. On the export side, too, one can theorize that the key factor explaining Japan's apparent competitiveness in machinery and transport equipment is availability due to technological factor. That is, embodiment of new technology in these products makes them unique to the purchasers' eyes. We shall turn to this point later in this chapter when we discuss the relation between the high-tech diffusion and export trends.

The share of machinery and transport equipment in total imports is the lowest in Japan (9.1% in 1985), compared to the U.S. (41.9%) and Europe (26.5%). This is not a good indicator of closedness of the economy to international trade, since endowment of natural resources has a great deal to do with the import structure.

Third, we turn to the examination of individual items within machinery. Table 8-3 includes trade matrices for selected items such as metalworking machine-tools (SITC 736), office machines (SITC 751), automatic data processing equipment (SITC 752), television receivers (SITC 761), sound recorders and phonographs (SITC 763), telecommunication equipment, parts, accessories (SITC 764), transistors, valves, etc. (SITC 776), and passenger motor vehicles excluding buses (SITC 781). These are not intended to provide an exhaustive list; rather, they have been selected to represent the major trend.

The construction of the table needs to be explained here. The commodity matrix tables, adopted from the U.N. trade statistics, list major exporting countries in horizontal direction, ranked by value for each commodity. Immediately below the exporting country names are

Table 8-3 Major exporters and importers for selected products

a. Metal working machine-tools (SITC736)

	Exporters: Germany	Japan	Switzerland	Italy	USA	UK
Percent Cum. % Exp. value	26.50 26.50 4124660	21.20 47.70 3299228	11.47 59.17 1785159	8.69 67.85 1351737	8.28 76.14 1289222	4.71 80.84 732671
Importers: USA 18.11	17533 464082 449161	127125 1196603 1245179	4172 168058 145391	8057 102056 94144		11691 147229 133670
Germany 29.15		11330 222581 202137	19184 519442 497146	14221 205047 189743	3887 87688 67473	6268 87098 77136
France 36.17	16707 327100 334141	2759 43672 96336	4293 144483 136893	12986 197033 194614	1487 22348 31567	6532 52704 50156
UK 41.37	10708 235276 255822	10902 130052 119013	1488 53542 52386	3029 51635 39805	5410 84826 72331	
Italy 46.40	15842 322090 287141	2314 40382 57275	4453 118682 120430		2432 38099 24425	3288 32675 36191

Note: Tables 8-3 a through h show the trade matrices of selected commodities at the group (3-digit) level of the SITC Revision 2. Major exporting countries and major importing countries are ranked by value for each commodity. "Percent" refers to exporter's percentage of market economy total export value, "cum. %" cumulative percentage of total export value, and "exp. value" total exports reported by the exporter (value in U.S. dollars). Data refer to 1985.

Source: United Nations, *Yearbook of International Trade Statistics*.

b. Office machines (SITC751)

	Exporters: Japan	Germany	Netherlands	UK	USA	Hong Kong
Percent Cum. % Exp. value	44.72 44.72 3817304	12.32 57.04 1052030	7.53 64.57 642756	7.21 71.79 615626	6.81 78.60 581278	5.30 83.89 452212
Importers: USA 28.40	1782154 1701016	3404 97207 87683	5269 122693 94943	3121 63777 45269		122111 87315
Germany 37.40	386793 357416		2804 86356 65567	3221 96336 91718	744 29697 61763	50510 38388
France 45.60	125011 249177	5641 193414 117491	3467 103310 82809	3548 104664 72009	1326 16654 34108	21635 25673
UK 53.25	168812 172914	4938 171585 164866	3157 90666 78548		982 38157 72869	17032 16106
Italy 59.37	97117 143975	3107 112008 108852	1761 50712 78809	1529 43860 38715	388 13754 14184	25233 21388

Source: Same as table 8-3-a.

c. Automatic data processing unit (SITC752)

	Exporters: USA	Japan	Germany	UK	France	Singapore
Percent	22.82	21.47	9.67	6.81	5.50	5.41
Cum. %	22.82	44.29	53.97	60.78	66.28	71.69
Exp. value	9965266	9374521	4223722	2973958	2403213	2362727
Importers:						
USA		120846	3937	3213	791	
		4735091	278143	444246	83698	1503722
16.38		3599867	232192	164057	56456	375926
UK	12037	14799	5781		2141	
	1345583	649811	639108		348285	130969
28.34	1508619	667675	586638		355577	122133
Germany	9229	20592		3833	3300	
	979363	1118855	479235	503372	134632	
39.93	1193958	1049283		666922	465241	123323
France	5557	4871	6276	4379		
	587810	261793	621494	451211		38884
49.22	1464437	587540	468702	405589		80257
Canada	37558	3812	93	101	49	
	1621304	121511	10825	9591	5977	19199
55.34	2312951	136027	9204	18223	6485	27114

Source: Same as table 8-3-a.

d. Television receivers (SITC761)

	Exporters: Japan	Korea	Germany	Singapore	Belg. Lux.	Hong Kong
Percent	19.69	14.42	11.50	7.43	6.34	6.03
Cum. %	19.69	34.11	45.61	53.04	59.38	65.43
Exp. value	1638546	1200407	956815	618592	527691	503285
Importers:						
USA		47503	248		89	
	414208	425787	11202	206745	6987	92085
21.15	323940	379299	3849	90891	501	50567
Germany	10192			6814		
	74694	98550		65970	105661	41478
31.30	82116	99006		53185	107927	15852
Italy		1746	17663		4884	
	5437	19383	286408	22343	82700	8347
39.37	3658	18988	293014	22317	92390	1203
France		693	6836		5835	
	29307	7845	116376	52248	105213	26996
46.40	44022	13297	113993	44988	97023	33585
UK		3484	3019		1028	
	42626	32415	45483	41894	18276	51420
51.64	63272	40752	46287	36369	23999	53408

Source: Same as table 8-3-a.

e. Sound recorders (SITC763)

	Exporters: Japan	Korea	Germany	Hong Kong	UK	USA
Percent	61.95	8.71	8.23	4.16	3.38	2.73
Cum. %	61.95	70.66	78.89	83.05	86.44	89.17
Exp. value	8593041	1207850	1141379	577381	469399	379347
Importers: USA		25533	1106			126
	4037729	491537	46814	103949		11176
38.33	4130363	593689	35070	101525		17475
Germany		4935			150	1948
	659506	119387		83275	10169	88175
47.42	894677	102870		21763	7932	78478
UK		4013	4128		380	
	381143	95090	190391	121530	33972	
54.60	428365	89703	198877	82444	22835	
France		1772	5549		54	1111
	202593	37040	287106	25859	7389	55277
60.16	407706	40285	209376	11260	5472	53185
Italy		1437	3670		116	611
	116884	35550	189584	14513	11150	23072
64.70	206063	35207	198448	5468	10609	31209

Source: Same as table 8-3-a.

f. Telecommunication equipment (SITC764)

	Exporters: Japan	USA	Germany	Hong Kong	France	UK
Percent	31.95	12.84	9.37	5.96	5.29	4.41
Cum. %	31.95	44.78	54.16	60.12	65.40	69.81
Exp. value	12,461,394	5,008,247	3,655,962	2,324,534	2,062,718	1,719,335
Importers: USA			1,385		703	3,361
	4,623,153		123,138	469,561	106,445	149,764
26.31	4,196,662		93,877	403,751	88,256	138,658
Germany		2,088			3,915	3,412
	1,054,983	173,716		22,240	241,027	173,752
33.42	1,086,093	178,216		18,305	266,562	160,550
UK		3,668	3,372		1,043	
	788,873	382,994	191,514	48,640	82,127	
39.88	758,060	345,905	185,792	63,015	79,806	
Hong Kong		2,949	99		335	723
	431,670	101,730	4,965		4,090	36,394
43.49	526,957	114,489	7,471		3,254	44,801
Canada		29,361	107		35	902
	301,602	556,516	6,236	20,710	4,171	43,761
47.10	328,934	710,795	12,281	22,507	6,417	37,295

Source: Same as table 8-3-a.

g. Transistors, etc. (SITC776)

	Exporters: USA	Japan	Hong Kong	Malaysia	Korea	Singapore
Percent	22.38	21.23	6.88	6.31	6.12	6.04
Cum. %	22.38	43.61	50.48	56.80	62.92	68.96
Exp. value	8,765,994	8,312,260	2,692,448	2,472,359	2,396,014	2,366,840
Importers:						
USA					4,938	
		2,135,700	372,438		977,136	839,748
22.03		2,212,502	124,481	1,290,450	822,003	824,896
Germany	1,341				1,884	
	439,107	496,799	33,096		67,078	92,873
29.89	366,631	521,723	49,286	89,571	60,610	92,529
Singapore	1,130				7,654	
	639,241	684,908	242,686		147,494	
37.32	909,531	724,347	46,161	411,534	88,077	
Malaysia	1,102				454	
	1,231,917	347,727	50,035		124,967	534,482
44.19						
Korea	1,756					
	625,141	1,146,089	356,870			50,038
50.94	735,905	1,251,505	146,216	63,318		100,713

Source: Same as table 8-3-a.

h. Passenger motor vehicles (SITC781)

	Exporters: Japan	Germany	Canada	Belg. Lux.	France	USA
Percent	28.07	26.14	8.46	7.54	6.68	5.94
Cum. %	28.07	54.21	62.67	70.21	76.89	82.84
Exp. value	35,693,230	33,243,524	10,763,155	9,586,555	8,498,979	7,555,779
Importers:						
USA		484,043		35,157	32,734	
	21,421,933	9,306,943	10,677,881	339,383	296,245	
39.93	22,752,749	9,141,098	10,256,938	274,885	266,999	
Germany				420,897	158,571	15,791
	2,793,002		15,612	3,559,013	1,224,055	150,193
47.82	3,215,196		7,076	3,277,018	1,406,956	71,406
Canada		36,801		204	11,696	583,639
	1,806,970	524,198		1841	110,412	6,089,363
55.38	1,851,132	466,590		240	22,250	6,626,212
UK		329,115		98,015	96,582	2,753
	1,169,055	3,559,311	534	833,995	757,622	61,611
61.98	1,201,055	3,830,056	1322	394,778	1,141,553	31,560
France		216,212		224,617		12,263
	391,731	2,247,776	783	1,614,575		132,540
67.99	455,785	2,684,938	227	1,010,384		13,112

Source: Same as table 8-3-a.

listed exporter's percentage of market economy total. Cumulative percentage is then shown. The third figure below the name of exporting country is the total value of exports reported by the exporter. Importing countries are listed in vertical direction. For each country, importer's percentage of market economy total import value is shown, followed by cumulative percentage. In individual cells of the matrix, total exports reported by the exporter (above) and total imports reported by importer (below) are shown.[2]

Look at panel (a) of table 8-3 where trade matrix of metalworking machine-tools is shown. Pertinent year is 1985. FRG is the largest exporter here, but her exports go to European countries besides the United States. In the case of Japan who is the second largest exporter of machine-tools, large percentage goes to the United States. Thus, in the U.S. machine-tools market which is the world's largest, Japan supplies nearly one half of the total. Other major suppliers of this item include Switzerland, Italy, U.S., and U.K.

In the case of office machines (panel b), Japan alone supplies 44.7% of world's exports. About 45% of Japan's exports goes to the American market. This amounts to about 69% of the U.S. imports of office machines. Other major suppliers include FRG, Netherlands, U.K., and U.S.A. Hong Kong is ranked sixth and Singapore (not shown here) the ninth, underlining the emergence of Asian NIEs.

Panel (c) refers to automatic data processing equipment. The United States is the leading exporter in this category supplying 22.8% of the world exports, followed by Japan which supplied 21.5% in 1985. The United States is the largest importer while being a leading supplier, whereas Japan's position as an importer is ranked ninth between Switzerland and Spain. Many European countries are engaged in both exports and imports. Singapore is listed as the sixth largest exporter of this item.

The emergence of Asian NIEs is evident in the case of television receivers (panel d) and sound recorders (panel e), where Japan, Korea, Singapore, and Hong Kong are listed among the major exporters.

Panel (f) shows the situation for telecommunication equipment. Here again, Japan is the leading exporter supplying 32% of the world total, followed by U.S. and FRG. Japan's share in the U.S. stands around 44% in 1985. In other major markets, Japan is supplying around 30%.

The United States is the leading supplier of transistors etc. (panel g), but other exporters are all Asian, including Japan, Hong Kong, Malaysia, Korea, and Singapore. In many cases, it should be noted, these countries are hosts to U.S. direct foreign investment.

Major exporters of passenger motor vehicles include Japan, FRG, Canada, Belgium and Luxemburg, France, and U.S. (panel h). In the case

Table 8-4 Summary table of Asia-Pacific linked input-output table, 1975

(unit: million dollars)

To / From	Intermediate demand								
	① IDN	② MYS	③ PHL	④ SGP	⑤ THA	⑥ JPN	⑦ KOR	⑧ USA	Total
① Indonesia	15,258	7	57	486	2	3,251	176	1,777	21,014
② Malaysia	11	4,913	3	195	10	208	87	454	5,881
③ Philippines	8	1	11,129	7	5	919	24	342	12,435
④ Singapore	337	136	4	4,196	21	377	8	343	5,422
⑤ Thailand	18	45	11	43	11,242	597	43	148	12,147
⑥ Japan	1,150	263	417	553	546	582,576	1,608	7,544	594,657
⑦ Korea	31	7	6	25	18	903	19,942	761	21,693
⑧ U.S.A.	361	108	336	378	109	9,429	1,441	1,314,110	1,326,272
FI+ID[a]	791	159	576	138	318	2,462	414	4,838	9,696
R.O.W.	1,142	891	1,133	2,580	1,218	42,248	2,249	71,307	122,798
Intermediate inputs total	19,107	6,530	13,672	8,601	13,489	642,970	26,022	1,401,624	2,132,015
Value added	32,770	8,125	15,803	5,114	17,063	499,373	20,106	1,512,406	2,110,760
Total input	51,877	14,655	29,475	13,715	30,552	1,142,343	46,128	2,914,030	4,242,775

	Final demand									R.O.W. +C1[b]	Total demand
	① IDN	② MYS	③ PHL	④ SGP	⑤ THA	⑥ JPN	⑦ KOR	⑧ USA	Total		
①	28,535	14	0	23	4	46	17	494	29,133	1,728	51,875
②	5	6,911	1	66	17	38	−2	221	7,257	1,517	14,655
③	2	21	15,491	9	5	32	0	194	15,735	1,305	29,475
④	140	85	7	4,550	43	89	3	252	5,169	3,123	13,714
⑤	7	50	24	51	16,667	73	2	56	16,930	1,477	30,554
⑥	566	236	474	269	440	492,256	783	5,186	500,210	47,477	1,142,344
⑦	5	6	3	11	12	614	20,483	672	21,806	2,630	46,129
⑧	354	155	404	,406	83	2,161	435	1,473,308	1,477,306	110,451	2,914,029
	410	201	660	117	893	1,047	160	3,317	6,805	0	16,501
	912	748	556	837	274	4,934	490	43,770	52,521	0	175,319
	30,936	8,408	17,620	6,339	18,438	501,290	22,371	1,527,471	2,132,873	169,708	4,434,596

Notes: [a] International freight and insurance + Import duties.
[b] Rest of the world + Changes in in-transit inventory.

Source: Institute of Developing Economies, *International Input-Output Table for ASEAN Countries.*

of Canada and the United States, trade flows almost exclusively between themselves. Other exporters are Italy, Spain, U.K., Sweden, and Korea. The United States is by far the largest importer of passenger motor vehicles, followed by FRG, Canada, U.K., France, and Italy. In 1985, Japan was ranked 12th among importers and barely matched Spain and Austria.

We may summarize the above observation that, in the case of sophisticated equipment such as metalworking machine-tools, automatic data processing equipment, telecommunication equipment, and passenger motor vehicles, industrialized countries still dominate the world export market. This is also true of office machines, although Asian NIEs are joining in. When it comes to consumer electronic goods such as television receivers and sound recorders, Asian NIEs in 1985 already captured considerable portion of the world market. In the case of transistors, the United States is both selling to and buying from Asian NIEs, reflecting outsourcing of U.S. industry. Japan is supplying a large percentage of consumer electronics as well as equipment for industrial use in the United States.

8-3 International linkages through trade

We summarize in this section major findings from the existing literature concerning economic linkages among countries which are based on trade matrices in one way or the other. We have already conducted simulation experiments regarding the effects of 1985 exchange rate adjustment. See Uno [1988]. However, our model COMPASS focuses on the Japanese industry and is not suitable to trace international linkages, and the analyses introduced here are intended to provide supplementary information on this particular point.

(1) *Industrial structure and trade in Asia in 1975*: In an effort to shed light on the economic interdependence among Asian NICs and ASEAN countries with Japan and the United States, Yamazawa and Tanaka [1985] employed a linked international input-output table prepared by the Institute of Developing Economies.[3]

Table 8-4 shows the internationally linked input-output table in a very concise manner. Whereas in the original form each country consists of a matrix with 56 sectors, in the summary table each country is represented as consisting of only a single sector. The intermediate demand is contained in rows 1 to 9 and columns 1 to 9; the final demand is contained in columns 10 to 18. The diagonal entries represent the transaction within each country, whereas off-diagonal entries represent

Table 8-5 Trade matrix for Asia-Pacific region, 1975

(unit: million dollars)

From \ To	① IDN	② MYS	③ PHL	④ SGP	⑤ THA	⑥ JPN	⑦ KOR	⑧ USA	R.O.W.	Total
① Indonesia	0	21	58	510	6	3,297	193	2,272	1,829	8,184
② Malaysia	16	0	4	261	28	246	85	675	1,778	3,092
③ Philippines	10	3	0	17	10	951	24	535	691	2,241
④ Singapore	477	221	11	0	64	466	11	595	1,626	3,472
⑤ Thailand	25	95	34	94	0	670	45	203	1,370	2,536
⑥ Japan	1,715	499	891	822	986	0	2,392	12,730	47,960	67,995
⑦ Korea	36	13	8	36	30	1,517	0	1,433	2,098	5,171
⑧ U.S.A.	715	263	740	784	192	11,591	1,876	0	110,393	126,553
R.O.W.	2,054	1,639	1,689	3,417	1,492	47,182	2,769	117,846		
Fr. & ins.	1,201	360	1,236	146	1,211	3,509	574	8,155		
Total	6,249	3,114	4,671	6,087	4,019	69,429	7,949	144,444		

Note: "Fr. and ins." in the table refers to freight and insurance.
Source: Shinohara, ed., *Future Scenario for the Asia-Pacific Region.*

Table 8-6 Production inducement coefficients for Asia-Pacific region,1975

(unit: ratio)

From \ To	① IDN	② MYS	③ PHL	④ SGP	⑤ THA	⑥ JPN	⑦ KOR	⑧ USA
① Indonesia	1.3825	0.0053	0.0297	0.0035	0.0011	0.0086	0.0064	0.0017
② Malaysia	0.0010	1.2017	0.0425	0.0005	0.0021	0.0033	0.0007	0.0007
③ Philippines	0.0180	0.0306	1.0942	0.0010	0.0047	0.0008	0.0010	0.0006
④ Singapore	0.0007	0.0008	0.0037	1.4663	0.0009	0.0013	0.0026	0.0006
⑤ Thailand	0.0015	0.0161	0.0198	0.0034	1.3683	0.0026	0.0020	0.0002
⑥ Japan	0.0023	0.0029	0.0081	0.0011	0.0029	1.5965	0.0048	0.0016
⑦ Korea	0.1362	0.1270	0.2341	0.1223	0.1197	0.1833	1.9652	0.0197
⑧ U.S.A.	0.0453	0.0549	0.1884	0.0832	0.0213	0.1405	0.0420	1.7448
Total	1.5876	1.4393	1.6204	1.6812	1.5209	1.9368	2.0248	1.7700
R.O.W.	0.2051	0.2376	0.5264	0.2149	0.1526	0.3403	0.0596	0.0252

Source: Same as table 8-5.

transaction with trading partners. Table 8-5 shows a trade matrix derived from table 8-4 by extracting only the transactions with other countries which are contained in either intermediate or final demand. For example, Indonesia imports $11 million from Malaysia to meet intermediate demand and $5 million to meet final demand (Table 8-4); thus, total imports from Malaysia become $16 million (Table 8-5). We observe that trade among Asian countries tends to be small compared to their trade with Japan and the United States. For example, in the case of Indonesia, of the total export of 8 billion dollars, about 3 billion dollars goes to Japan and 2 billion dollars to the United States. In the case of Korea, of the total exports in 1975 valued at 5 billion dollars, 1.4 billion dollars worth of exports were recorded with Japan and 2 billion dollars with the United States. Similar pictures emerge as for the import structure.

The division of labor among the eight countries represented in the table can be analyzed by giving the amount of final demand and evaluate the value of production (or value added) or foreign trade derived in each country. Table 8-6 lists the coefficients of production inducement. For example, one unit increase of final demand in Indonesia will induce 1.3825 unit of production within the country, while inducing 0.0010 unit of production in Malaysia, 0.0180 in Singapore, and so on. Total production induced will amount to 1.5876 unit, of which 0.2051 in foreign countries. The table reveals that the total production inducement coefficients are larger in Japan, Korea, and the United States than in ASEAN countries.

The bottom row of the table provides information as to how much production is induced in the trading partners. Evidently, we have small coefficients for the United States and Japan, amounting only to less than 0.03 and about 0.06, respectively. This signifies the fact that much of the production inducement would occur within respective economies. In contrast, ASEAN countries in general have coefficients ranging between 0.15 and 0.24. The Korean figure is larger at 0.34. It is also revealed that much of the inducement occurs in Japan, followed by the United States.

The situation such as this can be explained by the fact that, owing to underdeveloped heavy industry and chemical industry within their own economies, at least in 1975 to which the data refer to, any deficiency in supply has to be met by foreign suppliers.

Given this structure, Yamazawa and Tanaka contend, unless the regional production and trading patterns are changed, disproportionate growth of production and trade would be unavoidable among the United States and Japan on the one hand and Korea and ASEAN countries on the other.[4]

(2) *The U.S.-Japan linkages in trade and industry*: A research team led by

Gerald Adams of University of Pennsylvania and Shuntaro Shishido of International University of Japan conducted a series of simulation experiments employing linked U.S.-Japan models.[5] On the U.S. side, the Wharton Econometric Annual Industry Model was used with extensions to deal with the international trade question. For this purpose, trade equations were added to measure the responsiveness of U.S. imports of specific categories of manufactures to income and relative prices in the U.S. and abroad.[6] "This trade disaggregation involved two stages; first the overall sector imports of the U.S. from all sources and, secondly, the determination of the Japanese share of total U.S. imports." The Japanese model is basically a Leontief type input-output system combined with Keynesian type demand-oriented equations. The U.S. model has 56 sectors and the Japanese model 64, and the major difference is that the latter has detailed disaggregation for agriculture, food, textiles, etc., which are not the focal point in the analysis. Thus, we may say that the two models are comparable in their sectoral disaggregation.[7]

They report the results of linked multiplier simulations as follows. First, as for the US stimulation on Japan, a one percent stimulus to demand in the United States increases the real Japanese exports substantially, ranging from 1 to 2 percent. This will in turn increase the GNE about 0.1 percent.[8] The impact on Japanese imports is small. On industry level, whereas many industries are not greatly affected, sectors like instruments, miscellaneous manufacturing, automobiles, rubber goods, and aluminum are highly responsive to an expansion of the US economy.

Second, as for the impact of stimulus to the Japanese economy on the United States, it is described as "small, if not imperceptible."[9] They interpret this result as a reflection of the lack of sensitivity of Japanese imports from the United States to economic activity in Japan, rather than the problems of the model simulations. "This does not appear to be a result of the model's idiosyncracy so much as a real phenomenon."[10] It should be added that Japanese imports themselves are relatively insensitive to economic stimulus.

Thus, the implication of their experiment is that Japanese macroeconomic policy stimulus would have 'imperceptible impact' on United States exports and economic activity.[11]

They have carried out a series of scenario simulations, of which exchange rate simulations are deemed relevant in our context. The assumption is a 10 percent devaluation of the U.S. dollar with respect to all currencies. In reality, total effects of exchange rate adjustment have not been passed through to the US price of Japanese goods. Therefore, this experiment should be viewed as assuming a full pass through (or that a dollar devaluation of a greater magnitude with less than full pass through, the net effect being 10 percent). The assumption implies a 10 percent rise in US import prices and a 10 percent decline in US export prices in foreign markets. A significant increase in real exports will result amounting to approximately 5 percent over the base case and a decline in real imports amounting to 5 percent below the base case. In current prices, however, due to the J-curve effect, increase in exports, while considerable, is substantially offset by an increase in imports for the first three years. Ultimately, there is a significant improvement in the US trade balance. The GNP level shows gradual expansion in real terms amounting to 2.7 percent over the standard case. The feedback from the Japanese economy to the United States is relatively small, amounting to 0.5 percent for exports and 0.2 percent for GNP.[12]

(3) *Robotization in an international context*: The papers by Kinoshita and Yamada [1988, 1989] look into the international repercussion of diffusion of industrial robots. The analysis is based on their multicountry model. The model has regional breakdown which include Japan, the United States, Korea, EC (France, Germany, Italy, and the United Kingdom), Asian NIES (Taiwan, and Hong Kong), ASEAN (Indonesia, Malaysia, the Philippines, Singapore, and Thailand), other developed countries (OECD countries excluding Japan, the United States, and EC four), and the rest of the world. The model is composed of four parts which include (1) the countries with input-output information (Japan, the United States, and Korea), (2) developed countries only with macroeconomic variables (EC countries), (3) developing countries only with trade variables, and (4) international trade flow.[13]

Their observation seems to be compatible to what one would expect from the linked international input-output tables for 1975 which we discussed above. Assuming a 10 percent decline in Japan's export price, they estimate an increase of her export volume by 4.1 percent in the first year and 7.7 percent in the fifth year. The impact on exports of her trading partners are all negative, amounting to –10.4 percent for ASEAN and –4.2 percent for Korea in the fifth year. The main focus of the simulation experiment is placed on the effects of robotization, so far as it manifests itself in price reduction.

As for the impact of robotization, they envisage price reduction of the outputs due to labor displacement (or, the same thing, increased labor productivity), and inducement to investment via increased profitability. Investment will also be enhanced reflecting increased production in the robot industry.[14]

Their model, however, is not designed to trace the chain of events endogenously. Instead, the model simply assumes an exogenous downward shift of labor demand function and an upward shift in investment function. These assumptions are aimed at describing the changes which

Table 8-7 Summary table of Japan-U.S. linked input-output table, 1985

(unit: billion dollars)

		Intermediate Demand			Domestic final demand			Exports to the R.O.W.	Total Final Demand	Output
		Japan	U.S.	Total	Japan	U.S.	Total			
Inter-mediate input	Japan	1,084	20	1,104	1,261	45	1,306	135	1,441	2,545
	U.S.	17	2,683	2,700	5	3,881	3,887	253	4,139	6,840
	Imports from the R.O.W.	109	179	288	18	163	181	—	—	
	Custom duties, freight	7	7	14	2	13	15	—	—	
	Total	1,217	2,889	4,106	1,286	4,102	5,388	387	5,580	
Value added		1,328	3,951	5,278						
Output		2,545	6,840	9,384						

Note: Foreign trade with the ROW (Rest of the World) include non-ordinary trade between Japan and the U.S., and adjustment item. Conversion to the dollar is based on the annual average exchange rate for 1985 (238.54 yen to a dollar).
Source: Ministry of International Trade and Industry, *Preliminary Report on the 1985 Japan-U.S. Input-Output Table.*

are induced by the increased diffusion of industrial robots, and are based on separate analysis conducted outside the model structure itself. Regarding the labor displacement effect of robot use, the assumption is that the effect amounts to 10,000 per year for each of three machinery producing sectors (general machinery, electrical machinery, and transport equipment) and 5,000 for precision instrument sector. These figures are based on the estimates by JIRA and by Saito.[15] The same magnitude of direct labor displacement is introduced in the United States and one-fourth of the effect in Korea.

As for an upward shift of the investment function, it is assumed that the robot investment in order to displace 10,000 workers will amount to 65 billion yen (1980 prices). Additional investment is made amounting to 10 percent of initial investment from the second year onwards.[16]

The main findings for the case of increased diffusion of robots in Japan is that it will result in GNP increase amounting to about 0.35 percent in the fifth year compared to the control solutions. This is due to increased exports and domestic investments. This, in turn, will have small but negative impact on the US economy through decreased net exports and invertment, which exceed the positive effects on private consumption and housing investment. For Korea, total effect is estimated to be negligible, where export decline is more or less cancelled by induced investment. In the case of Korea, since she is heavily dependent on Japan for the supply of capital goods, cheaper imports from Japan will contribute to lowering capital goods price.

The impact on employment will amount to 63.3 thousand lost jobs in the fifth year disregarding the demand side effect of robot investment. If the latter is taken into account, the labor displacement effect will be reduced by about 10 thousand initially.

Their experiments show that the introduction of robots in the US will have negative effects on the US economy. This is attributable to relatively small price decrease from robotization, weak response in her exports due to price decline, less sensitivity of investment demand to increased profits, and the wage rate which is less sensitive to changing labor market condition.

In the case of Korea, they analyze that the positive effect of increased introduction of industrial robots tends to spill over to her trading partners, Japan being a major one.[17]

Saito's estimates on labor displacement by industry sector, which are the bases for Kinoshita-Yamada's assumption, are based on production functions which include technological progress term of labor augmenting type. Labor displacement is represented by the ratio of workers that are vulnerable to the diffusion of robots in each sector.[18]

Figure 8-1 Production inducement in the partner country in response to demand increase
(unit: million dollars)

a. Inducement of the U.S. production by Japanese industry

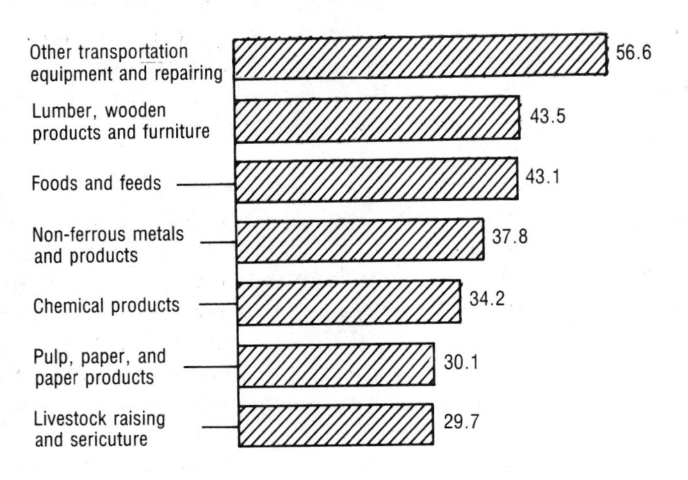

b. Inducement of the Japanese production by U.S. industry

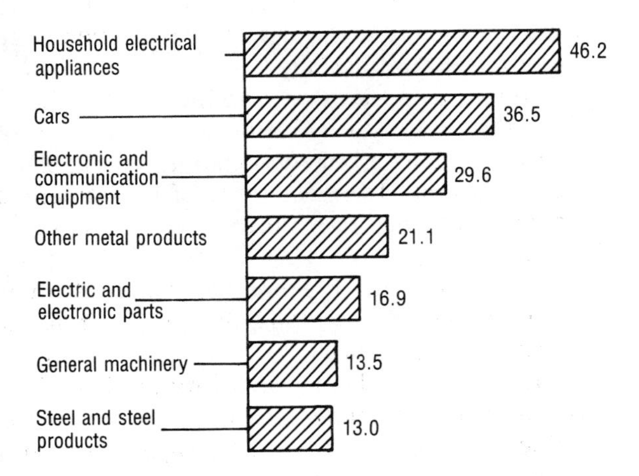

Note: Imports induced by 1 billion production activities of each country.
Source: Same as table 8-7.

(4) *U.S.-Japan linked input-output table for 1985*: The Ministry of International Trade and Industry published an international input-output table linking the U.S. economy with that of Japan. In 1986, the MITI has embarked on a 6-year project to compile an international input-output table and the U.S.-Japan table is the first portion which was completed. The table, when completed, will supersede the 1975 table reported above. The purpose of such an attempt is contained in following words. "Since autumn in 1985, changes have been taking place in the economy as a result of sudden fluctuations of the exchange rate. Especially, changes in terms of foreign trade have stimulated adjustment in international industrial structure, accompanied by increased economic interdependence among countries. ... However, useful analytical tool has not been established up to now which can make clear economic interdependence among countries, and analyze quantitatively how one country's economy and changes there influence other countries. The international input-output table serves as a powerful, indispensable tool for quantitative analysis of the international industrial structure."[19] Prices are evaluated at producers' price in each country. The table is in dollar terms and the conversion of yen into dollar is based on the annual average exchange rate for 1985 (238.54 yen). Table 8-7 presents a summary where each country is reduced to an aggregated one sector.

The linked international input-output table introduced in (1) above refers to the year 1975. Comparisons with the 1985 table, now partly available for the U.S.-Japan portion, will reveal structural change of the economies concerned and foreign trade. However, its validity has to be limited by the fact that radical structural adjustment has been triggered by the 1985 exchange rate realignment and not before. The 1985 economic structure does not reflect such changes. In this sense, the 1985 table introduced here only presents the starting point.

Based on the linked U.S.-Japan table, an assessment can be made on the repercussion effects which one economy exerts on the other. One can ask a question "when one million dollar demand occurs in one country's industry, how much production is induced in the partner country?" The report provides a case where one million dollar demand is created in each industry in the two countries. The results are shown in figure 8-1. Intermediate products in Japan have a relatively large effect on the U.S. production activity, as can be observed in panel (a). Examples are forest products such as lumber, pulp and paper, foods and feeds, non-ferrous metals, and livestock. "Other transportation equipment" including aircraft is an exception. On the other hand, demand for machinery and metal product sectors in the United States have a relatively large effect on Japan. As is shown in panel (b), the cases in question include household electrical appliances, motor vehicles, electronic and communication

Figure 8-2 Production inducement by domestic demand, partner's demand, and the R.O.W. demand
(unit: billion dollars)

a. Japanese industry: Domestic production in Japan induced by U.S. production activities

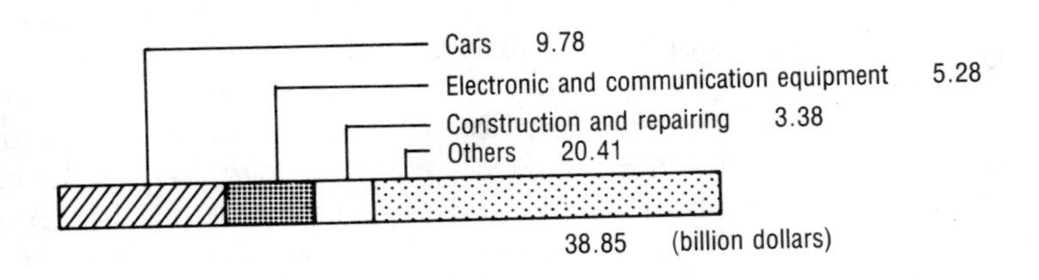

b. U.S. industry: Domestic production in U.S. induced by Japanese production activities

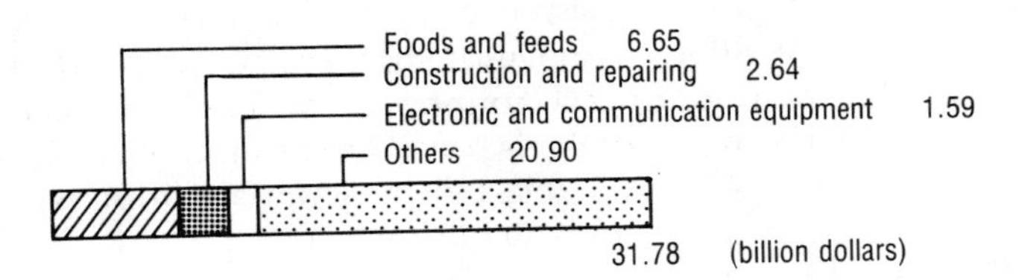

Source: Same as table 8-7.

equipment and parts thereof, metal products, and general machinery.

In 1985, production activities in the U.S. induced 38.9 billion dollars of production in Japan (Figure 8-2). Major items include automobiles and electronic and communication equipment. In the same vain, Japanese production activities induced 31.8 billion dollars worth of production in the United States, major items being food and feeds, construction, and electronic and communication equipment. One notices the fact that the two countries are contributing to each other's production by nearly the same amount. However, considering that the U.S. economy is 2.7 times larger than that of Japan, a unit production in Japan induces about 2.2 times larger production for the trade partner than the U.S. industry does.

A more meaningful figure which reveals the interrelations between the two economies is the production inducement coefficient. The coefficient is derived as the ratio of total demand induced and the final demand. For the Japanese economy total, the coefficient is calculated to be 1.729, of which 1.701 is derived within Japan and 0.028 in the United States. Needless to say, this means that, given a unit increase in final demand, domestic industrial production would go up 1.701 times the initial increase in final demand and U.S. production 0.028 times. For the

U.S. economy, the coefficient is calculated to be 1.591, of which 1.562 is induced within the country and 0.029 in Japan.[20] Judging from the coefficients in the two countries (0.028 vs. 0.029), we may say that a unit increase in final demand tend to induce nearly the same amount of production in the partner economy.

Direct comparisons with the 1975 figures reported earlier can not be made because of lack of linkages with the other countries. Being a bilateral U.S.-Japan table, the 1985 table is not capable of capturing the feedback effect via the third countries. Focusing on the bilateral relations between the two countries, it is interesting to see that in 1975 the production inducement coefficient for Japan stood at 1.965 for domestic production and 0.042 for U.S. production. Comparable figures for the United States stood at 1.745 and 0.020, respectively (see table 8-6). Crude observation reveals that the Japanese final demand (i.e., per unit) exerts less influence on the U.S. industry today than 10 years ago whereas the U.S. final demand has become more dependent on Japanese industry.

The 1985 U.S.-Japan linked input-output table has 163 industrial sectors for both countries, from which general machinery (sector code 14 which corresponds to our sector 34), electrical machinery (sector code 15 which corresponds to our sector 35), transport equipment (sector code 16 which corresponds to our sector 36), and other machinery (sector code 17 which corresponds to our sector 37 named precision instrument) are extracted together with total figures in table 8-8. This table is directly comparable to table 8-7 in its construction and data. Even before the full effect of the 1985 exchange rate realignment was felt, industries in two countries were inseparably integrated as can be witnessed by input and output relations.

8-4 Impediments to trade

We have seen that Japan's role as an importer is rather meager as of mid-1980s at least, in contrast to her dominant role as an exporter. This leads us to exame of the trade and investment policies. Although income and relative prices are the factors determining the direction and the magnitude of international trade, it is affected by many other factors. Trade barriers are installed, either intentionally or unintentionally, giving rise to various distortions in the pattern of international trade. As for foreign trade barriers in America's trading partners, the Office of the U.S. Trade Representatives (USTR) publishes annual surveys.[21] In the following, we summarize what the USTR considers as trade barriers (including services) in Japan in order to evaluate the impediment effects. We cite heavily from the document for the purpose of conveying the overall

Table 8-8 Economic linkages between Japan and the United States, selected sectors

(unit: 100,000 dollars)

Input sectors \ Output sectors	Intermediate demand — Japan: Total	General Machinery	Electrical Machinery
	01 — 26	14	15
01 Agriculture	400,281	146	359
02 Forestry	51102	0	0
03 Fishing	85,222	94	192
04 Mining	81,884	22	23
05 Food processing	461,996	1,235	2,498
06 Textile products	206,626	965	2,342
07 Pulp, paper, and wood products	523,525	2,708	15,945
08 Chemical products	571,951	4,649	28,811
09 Petroleum products	475,755	3,670	7,801
10 Ceramic, stone and clay products	309,013	6,627	18,863
11 Steel and steel products	427,589	89,259	27,863
12 Non-ferrous metals and products	200,078	17,219	53,069
13 Other metal products	469,730	46,187	41,429
14 General machinery	142,948	25,403	16,504
15 Electrical machinery	415,932	26,261	225,300
16 Transport equipment	108,461	3,073	0
17 Other machines and instrument	33,449	4,093	1,535
18 Other manufactured products	618,878	17,958	63,347
19 Construction	207,831	802	2,596
20 Electricry, gas water, and energy	526,835	19,971	31,011
21 Commerce	869,742	33,032	67,286
22 Finance, insurance, and real estate	963,730	29,102	46,054
23 Transport	571,843	22,455	27,520
24 Governmene services	0	0	0
25 Services	1,861,621	54,142	109,778
26 Unclassified	252,995	16,562	23,977
Japan Total	10,839,017	425,635	814,103
01 Agriculture	23,646	0	0
02 Forestry	7,703	0	0
03 Fishing	471	0	0
04 Mining	6,482	6	0
05 Food processing	14,402	0	0
06 Textile products	685	1	1
07 Pump, paper, and wood products	8,222	0	53
08 Chemical products	24,997	27	249
09 Petroleum products	6,478	21	134
10 Ceramic stone and clay products	1,292	55	141
11 Steel and steel products	248	79	7
12 Non-ferrous metals and products	5,575	95	979
13 Other metal products	1,502	205	222
14 General machinery	3,598	2,155	412
15 Electrical machinery	15,284	344	12,040
16 Transport equipment	8,932	0	0
17 Other machines and instrument	4,844	15	3
18 Other manufactured products	3,281	71	254
19 Construction	0	0	0
20 Electricry, gas water and energy	0	0	0
21 Commerce	22,420	589	2,128
22 Finance, insurance, and real estate	0	0	0
23 Transport	11,625	176	333
24 Governmene services	0	0	0
25 Services	0	0	0
26 Unclassified	98	0	1
U.S. Total	171,785	3,839	16,957
Japan, U.S. Total	11,010,802	429,474	831,060
01 Tariffs	5,104	95	442
02 Freight and insurance	25,685	209	634
R.O.W. total	1,087,216	8,414	26,343
27 Tariffs	37,589	113	350
Import tax, freight, etc.	68,378	417	1,426
Total endogenous (excl. Japan)	1,327,379	12,670	44,726
Total endogenous (excl. U.S.)	11,994,611	434,466	841,872
Total endogenous	12,166,396	438,305	858,829
29 Labor income	7,187,346	200,034	271,745
30 Property income	5,101,977	139,694	215,016
31 Indirect tax	989,159	15,289	40,030
Value added total	13,278,482	355,017	526,791
32 Domestic production	25,444,878	793,322	1,385,620

Source: Same as Table 8-7

		U.S.				
Transport equipment	Other machines and instrument	Total	General Machinery	Electrical Machinery	Transport equipment	Other machines and instrument
16	17	01 — 26	14	15	16	17
197	50	51	0	0	0	0
4	0	62	0	0	0	0
61	19	2,561	0	0	0	0
21	4	33	5	0	0	0
824	239	966	0	0	0	0
2,567	356	5,333	6	0	58	13
3,777	3,985	1,831	12	25	17	17
16,381	7,311	9,651	74	123	55	77
5,429	1,224	526	0	0	0	0
8,098	3,014	4,364	68	439	380	65
59,514	4,750	31,175	4,419	1,327	2,697	71
26,422	6,863	5,122	519	401	312	76
28,888	4,836	12,295	659	508	6,314	146
22,612	2,377	17,871	7,208	335	3,504	22
61,566	18,683	52,747	1,931	35,371	8,215	1,223
13,145	0	27,720	0	0	22,899	0
792	101	7,295	43	57	267	1,151
63,768	16,351	7,007	186	318	1,712	98
3,399	492	0	0	0	0	0
20,552	4,301	0	0	0	0	0
57,319	13,725	12,980	703	3,188	3,493	269
23,377	9,109	0	0	0	0	0
20,985	4,765	1,691	86	186	353	19
0	0	0	0	0	0	0
54,345	17,463	0	0	0	0	0
6,350	3,421	238	0	0	3	1
500,393	123,439	201,519	15,919	42,278	50,279	3,248
0	0	1,245,187	0	0	0	0
0	0	149,089	0	0	0	0
0	0	19,052	0	0	0	0
1	0	1,683,633	650	297	893	81
0	0	809,984	0	0	0	0
15	1	364,568	1,529	1,192	45,012	5,578
1	3	1,160,025	11,406	23,751	20,377	11,193
609	233	1,117,019	9773	21,933	27,610	15,322
34	10	971,448	8,339	7,299	10,557	2,490
26	88	459,791	8,596	16,565	24,284	4,217
11	1	505,493	115,731	23,962	99,379	2,191
184	78	369,205	43,622	62,040	51,858	8,991
75	38	974,280	47,252	73,765	183,025	16,641
243	55	693,733	64,927	29,402	122,027	4,839
168	1,522	697,169	44,703	227,240	90,134	38,124
8,929	0	171,816	4,514	1,074	3,636	0
24	2,503	123,340	1,603	3,453	7,533	217
312	60	1,284,404	18,989	66,359	86,059	29,613
0	0	605,760	9,738	10,134	9,149	1,902
0	0	1,378,353	22,843	28,020	24,592	5,244
877	799	2,256,938	97,756	133,624	135,981	26,288
0	0	2,133,480	20,138	59,187	29,677	8,954
232	68	1,134,424	21,291	30,740	35,609	7,330
0	0	−1	0	0	0	0
0	0	6,047,446	93,803	168,092	166,285	492,519
2	2	415,040	23,429	11,243	7,384	7,358
11,743	5,461	25,830,677	570,532	999,372	1,182,061	246,092
512,136	128,900	27,032,196	586,551	1,041,650	1,232,340	249,340
65	133	10,828	684	2,153	2,681	169
384	208	7,729	85	2,478	2,109	262
10,980	3,187	1,790,932	59,301	102,984	158,713	22,362
378	145	47,769	2,254	4,980	4,794	948
827	486	66,326	3,023	9,611	9,584	1,379
23,550	9,134	28,687,935	732,956	1,111,967	1,350,358	269,833
512,200	127,112	2,058,777	78,243	154,873	218,576	26,989
523,943	132,573	28,889,454	748,875	1,154,245	1,400,637	273,081
188,004	57,866	23,684,829	622,338	762,565	793,876	185,645
124,953	49,470	12,653,332	164,951	200,375	132,564	112,107
49,533	7,170	3,167,823	23,206	17,488	35,445	4,654
362,490	114,506	39,505,984	810,495	980,428	961,885	302,406
886,433	247,079	68,395,438	1,559,370	2,134,673	2,362,522	575,487

Final demand						
Japan					U.S.	
Total	Private consumption	Private investment	Gov't expenditures	Increase in stock	Total	Private consumption
30 — 33	30	31	32	33	30 — 33	30
140,222	120,636	9,880	1,165	8,541	65	64
583	0	0	0	583	12	12
28,279	27,826	0	318	135	124	119
−1,870	−502	0	106	−1,474	23	26
1,045,399	1,034,465	0	5,302	5,632	1,914	1,943
265,093	249,187	10,021	3,334	2,551	4,033	3,962
79,090	31,508	36,305	11,329	−52	1,753	730
123,851	84,061	11,722	26,747	1,321	1,812	1,350
126,398	116,202	0	15,297	−5,101	197	30
16,429	13,008	0	1,362	2,059	3,446	3,432
4,014	382	0	35	3,597	−133	2
4,421	4,040	0	465	−84	12	0
38,151	18,358	17,480	2,238	75	2,596	983
457,819	170	422,113	17,582	17,954	41,150	1,370
564,139	136,642	335,105	72,489	19,903	117,961	69,297
300,885	112,947	158,021	26,734	3,183	179,746	105,754
98,956	29,107	55,288	9,131	5,430	34,380	7,385
229,375	166,523	21,139	39,922	1,791	15,181	13,609
2,140,332	0	1,319,604	820,728	0	0	0
288,020	233,913	0	54,107	0	0	0
1,546,336	1,279,350	215,353	41,289	10,344	37,239	21,206
1,488,470	1,459,892	0	28,578	0	0	0
380,827	340,423	15,259	22,790	2,355	3,106	1,799
982,562	0	0	982,562	0	0	0
2,272,507	2,158,560	0	113,947	0	0	0
−6,278	−1,896	−16,589	11,757	0	557	546
12,613,560	7,614,802	2,610,701	2,309,314	78,743	445,174	233,619
699	1,066	6	2	−375	268,010	175,754
0	0	0	0	0	−1,275	8,689
127	126	0	1	0	3,470	3,324
9	19	0	2	−12	7,740	3,583
4,384	4,284	0	6	94	2,028,016	1,961,603
480	450	26	10	−6	559,391	528,695
63	23	37	10	−7	448,511	268,717
1,404	809	70	516	9	431,770	349,762
163	144	0	65	−46	780,623	674,792
95	88	0	7	0	24,879	18,232
1	0	0	0	1	−1,582	108
264	225	0	12	27	−772	789
370	275	71	21	3	76,304	42,099
5,660	1	5,270	316	73	656,243	19,206
13,044	919	9,892	2,188	45	1,092,697	224,907
12,383	176	9,439	2,768	0	1,803,675	719,517
3,153	683	2,018	418	34	374,152	62,463
2,805	1,594	228	988	−5	805,236	495,993
0	0	0	0	0	4,041,649	0
0	0	0	0	0	1,103,000	961,689
5,815	2,085	2,825	861	44	4,998,101	4,371,708
0	0	0	0	0	5,747,964	5,451,662
908	491	241	171	5	915,714	731,547
0	0	0	0	0	4,188,091	0
0	0	0	0	0	8,388,219	7,598,377
10	11	0	−1	0	73,867	262,545
51,837	13,459	30,123	8,361	−116	38,813,693	24,935,761
12,665,397	7,628,271	2,540,824	2,317,675	78,627	39,258,867	25,169,380
2,152	1,219	734	181	18	25,261	13,805
2,794	1,309	1,165	283	37	26,801	11,578
180,343	140,712	23,612	10,456	5,563	1,628,073	11,141,165
11,670	10,207	1,007	215	241	76,998	61,322
16,616	12,735	2,906	679	296	129,060	86,705
248,796	166,916	56,641	19,496	5,743	40,570,826	26,136,631
12,810,519	7,768,249	2,637,219	2,320,449	84,602	2,202,307	1,434,489
12,862,356	7,781,718	2,667,342	2,328,810	84,486	41,016,000	26,370,250
0	0	0	0	0	0	0
0	0	0	0	0	0	0
0	0	0	0	0	0	0
0	0	0	0	0	0	0
0	0	0	0	0	0	0

			Total			
Private investment	Gov't expenditures	Increase in stock	Exports	Adjustment	Final demand total	Domestic production
31	32	33	34	36	30 — 36	990
0	1	0	1,499	82	141,868	542,200
0	0	0	62	−75	582	51,746
0	0	5	913	−2,018	27,298	115,081
1	−4	0	511	30	−1,306	80,611
0	41	−70	8,906	463	1,056,682	1,519,644
18	61	−8	36,923	−198	305,851	517,810
975	47	1	10,214	−1,186	89,871	615,227
38	441	−17	63,783	−329	189,117	770,719
0	167	0	14,438	186	141,219	617,500
0	40	−26	15,568	−173	35,270	348,547
0	22	−157	103,937	−4,553	103,265	562,029
4	3	5	16,538	603	21,574	226,774
566	1,040	7	20,941	−1,175	60,513	542,538
36,488	3,309	−17	140,061	−6,527	632,503	793,322
39,394	9,462	−192	241,159	−6,318	916,941	1,385,620
63,170	10,822	0	248,698	20,923	750,252	886,433
21,996	4,995	4	67,574	5,425	206,335	247,079
421	1,191	−40	39,348	−643	283,261	909,146
0	0	0	0	5	2,140,337	2,348,168
0	0	0	910	−14	288,916	815,751
13,433	2,588	12	5,328	68,920	1,657,823	2,540,545
0	0	0	11,512	−1	1,499,981	2,463,711
1,093	214	0	148,313	10,416	542,662	1,116,196
0	0	0	0	0	982,562	982,562
0	0	0	24,890	−15	2,297,382	4,159,003
0	11	0	34,875	4,879	33,583	286,816
177,597	34,451	−493	1,256,901	88,707	14,404,342	25,444,878
0	16,512	75,744	112,210	2,363	383,282	1,652,115
0	−9,310	−654	7,294	−1,431	4,588	161,380
0	146	0	−21	−526	3,050	22,573
4,147	4,856	−4,846	41,295	3,699	52,743	1,742,858
0	67,945	−1,532	112,173	2,222	2,146,795	2,971,181
16,170	18,987	−4,461	32,878	709	593,458	958,711
117,259	62,553	−28	49,232	556	498,362	1,666,610
7,029	76,897	−1,918	175,535	−694	608,015	1,810,031
0	105,976	−145	56,055	356	837,197	1,815,123
0	8,000	−1,353	17,629	−166	42,437	503,520
0	3,269	−4,959	11,293	7	9,719	515,460
1,441	2,510	−5,512	25,419	−913	23,998	398,778
13,223	20,837	145	38,952	−734	114,892	1,090,674
575,084	64,884	−2,931	198,910	1,226	862,039	1,559,370
579,750	288,948	−908	316,611	−132	1,422,220	2,134,673
578,755	466,013	39,390	368,940	−3,224	2,181,774	2,362,522
237,119	73,335	1,235	70,215	−217	447,303	575,487
23,050	265,964	20,229	81,782	−1,438	888,351	2,176,070
3,130,414	911,235	0	548	0	4,042,197	4,647,957
0	141,311	0	6,853	0	1,109,853	2,488,206
491,626	134,767	0	196,822	−4,058	5,196,680	7,476,038
176,632	119,670	0	183,919	0	5,931,883	8,065,363
39,002	145,165	0	186,611	97,424	1,200,657	2,346,706
0	4,188,091	0	0	0	4,188,091	4,188,090
73,927	715,915	0	109,858	436	8,498,513	14,545,977
−197,711	9,033	0	36,210	−5,242	104,845	519,965
5,866,917	7,903,519	107,496	2,437,223	90,223	41,392,976	68,395,438
6,044,514	7,937,970	107,003	3,694,124	178,930	55,797,318	93,840,316
9,521	1,926	9	0	0	27,413	43,345
12,429	2,781	13	0	0	29,595	63,009
278,219	224,675	11,014	0	0	1,808,416	4,686,564
10,059	4,949	668	0	0	88,668	174,026
32,009	9,656	690	0	0	145,676	280,380
6,177,145	8,137,850	119,200	2,437,223	90,223	43,347,068	73,362,382
487,825	268,782	11,211	1,256,901	88,707	16,358,434	30,411,822
6,354,742	8,172,301	118,707	3,694,124	178,930	57,751,410	98,807,260
0	0	0	0	0	0	0
0	0	0	0	0	0	0
0	0	0	0	0	0	0
0	0	0	0	0	0	0
0	0	0	0	0	0	0

picture and nuance in the original text. Although the document is bilateral in nature, the description is relevant to other trading partners.

(1) *Import policies*:

Tariffs "Japan's average tariff rates on industrial products are among the world's lowest at two percent. However, high tariffs remain on certain manufactured and agricultural products of U.S. interest," the report writes.

Cigarettes and tobacco products: "Inefficiencies in Japan's local tobacco tax reporting and collection system continue to inhibit the distribution of imported U.S. tobacco products."

Leather and leather footwear: "Discuss possible improvements in administering the tariff quota system to ensure all quotas can be used."

Wood and paper products: "Japan's tariffs ... as well as its building codes and product standards that favor other nonwood construction materials continue to dampen the demand for wood in general. ...unnecessarily restrictive building and fire codes inhibit U.S. exports..."[22]

Aluminum: "Japan lowered its tariffs on aluminum ingot and semi-finished aluminum. ... high tariffs ranging from 9.2 to 10.2 percent remain on aluminum bar, wire, rod and foil."

Quantitative restrictions

Agricultural products: "In 1988 Japan agreed to eliminate a substantial number of quota categories on ... beef, prepared and preserved beef, oranges, orange juice and other processed foods. Japan continues to maintain quotas on ... wheat, wheat flour, barley and rice."

Feedgrains: "The Japanese mixed feed sector is restricted by law and policies that limit competition."

Rice: "Japan maintains a strict prohibition on rice imports."

Fish products: "Japan maintains import quotas on several products of U.S. interest including pollock, herring, cod, mackerel, squid and other."

(2) *Standards, testing, labeling, certification*:

"Telecommunication terminals, radio equipment and systems: During the MOSS telecommunications negotiations the United States and Japan resolved many technical standards issues. As a result, the Japanese Ministry of Posts and Telecommunications (MPT) has established an impartial system for approving telecommunications terminal equipment under the Japan Approvals Institute for Terminal Equipment (JATE) and other radio equipment under the Radio Equipment Approval Agency, the MKKK. ... Both systems are based upon accepting manufacturer-generated test data to certify that equipment meets Japanese standards."

"Implementation of MOSS measures has generally been good. However, problems in several key areas including cellular and radio communication and competition in international services indicate a continued Japanese policy of substituting government control for outcomes that should be based on market forces."

Pharmeceuticals, medical devices: "One major issue concerns Japan's nonacceptance of U.S.-generated quality control data."

Food additives: "Ministry of Health and Welfare (MHW) continues to maintain a restrictive policy on approving new food additives and new uses for already-approved additives."

(3) *Government procurement*:

Supercomputers: "Despite an 80 percent share of the world supercomputer market, ... U.S. firms supply only six percent of Japan's government and publicly funded university market. ... Approximately 40 percent of the Japanese supercomputer market is publicly funded." "In August 1987 U.S.-Japanese negotiations produced a procurement agreement. The agreement called for a transparent, nondiscriminatory procurement process effective August 7, 1987. ... Unfair exclusion from the market, deep price discounting, and aggressive marketing by Japanese companies were cited as the impediment for market entry by the U.S. firms."

Satellites: "In 1983 Japan's 'long-range vision on space development' articulated a policy of autonomously developing a satellite and associated launch service industry. The policy included a prohibition against procuring foreign satellites. In response to U.S. concerns, Japan has clarified its policy. Private Japanese companies may buy imported telecommunications satellites. ... Although U.S. firms have supplied a large proportion of the components used in Japan's telecommunications, broadcast and weather satellites, they would prefer to sell whole satellites."

Government procurement code implementation: Under the GATT Government Procurement Code's 1987 revisions, code signatories were ... required to reduce the descriminatory effects of qualification and delivery time requirements. Japan has increased its bid deadlines from 30 to 40 days, comparable to the U.S. period."

(4) *Barriers to intellectual property protection*:

Patents: "There are only a few exclusions under Japan's patent laws. However, U.S. firms have complained about the slow applications process. It can take up to six years for a patent to be issued." "Some U.S. companies have complained about Japanese rules on making patent applications public after 18 months. Industrial processes are especially vulnerable to duplication because Japanese courts tend to consider issues one at a time and at separate hearings." "Some U.S. interests have recently complained about 'patent flooding.' This practice is on the narrow scope of claims generally contained in Japanese patents."

Trademarks: "... very slow."

Copyrights: "Protection for sound recording is inadequate. ... Sound recordings produced before 1978 when Japan adhered to the Geneve Phonograms Conventin are unprotected."

(5) *Services barriers*:

Construction, architectural and engineering services: "Japan's closed, nontransparent, noncompetitive bid and tender system has made it difficult for U.S. firms to obtain construction licenses and participate in major construction projects. ... As required by section 1305 of the Omnibus Trade Act of 1988, on November 21, 1988 the United States initiated an investigation of Japanese policies and practices ... "

Legal services: "As a result of bilateral negotiations, the Foreign Lawyers Law was enacted in 1987. ... The United States has objected to certain provisions of the law which inhibit U.S. lawyers ability to practice in Japan."

Insurance: "Japanese regulatory authorities show signs of steadily opening the domestic market to U.S. insurers."

High cube containers: "Until the mid-1980s Japan forbade the transport of high cube containers used by major U.S. shipping lines on its roadways. ... By mid-1987 several routes were approved for use and U.S. carriers began using high cube containers."

(6) *Investment barriers* (see section 8-5 below)

(7) *Other barriers*

Semiconductors: "When the United States entered into the U.S.-Japan Arrangement on Semiconductors on September 2, 1986, the United States agreed to suspend: antidumping cases against Japanese manufacturers of RPROMs and 256K and above DRAMs; and a section 301 case filed on restricted Japanese market access for U.S. semiconductors. On their part the Japanese agreed to end semiconductor dumping in the U.S. market, end all dumping in third country markets and provide increased market access for foreign semiconductors in the Japanese market." "Japan's noncompliance ... caused President Reagan to impose sanctions on certain Japanese imports into the United States valued at $300 million." "The United States is emphasizing the need to increase the use of foreign semiconductors in companies outside the 11 largest Japanese semiconductor users (particularly in the automobile and consumer electronics sectors)."

TRON: "The United States is concerned about the Japanese government's marketplace intervention to support the newly developed TRON operating system (The Real-Time Operating System Nucleus). ... Some U.S. companies are members of the TRON association. ... If this specification is completed ... U.S. operating systems and computers which run only operating systems other than TRON (e.g. Microsoft's MS-DOS and OS/2 and AT&T's UNIX, the accepted world leaders) will be effectively excluded. ... The long-term implication of a general Japanese preference for TRON-based computer systems would ultimately influence purchasing decisions throughout the entire Japanese electronics market."

Optical fibers: "NTT, Japan's dominant telecommunications carrier, has confined most of its optical fiber purchases to three major Japanese suppliers."

Aerospace: "The effects of Japan's targeting efforts have not yet hindered U.S. industry. ... A coherent Japanese government plan is in effect. ... Financial incentives include MITI loans for the development and research stages of aircraft and engines that are repaid only when the commercial venture is a success. ... The Japanese government plans to make aircraft production one of Japan's major industries within 20 years. Japanese competition could come earlier in the rotocraft and aircraft components industries." "Japan is still a leading importer of U.S. aircraft."

Auto parts: "A prerequisite for selling most functional auto parts to Japanese vehicle makers is to become a part of their supplier 'family.' 'Nonfamily' suppliers are precluded from both the original equipment and replacement (aftermarket) auto parts markets for Japanese vehicles." "MOSS talks on auto parts began in May 1986 and concluded August 18, 1987. Among the major accomplishments were agreements for monitoring purchasing levels, Japanese government cooperation in trade promotion events and Japanese government promotional campaigns to help U.S. firms overcome Japanese aftermarket barriers and identify contact points within Japanese firms."

Soda ash: "... U.S. industry continues to assert Japanese producers' anticompetitive practices impede further U.S. market penetration."

Distribution system: "The complexity and rigidity of Japan's distribution system reduces access for U.S. exports. Some generic problems with the distribution system include legal and administrative, and operational or institutional problems." "Examples of legal and administrative problems include regulation of premiums and promotions of large retail stores, and of difficulties in licensing and distributing various products such as alcoholic beverages. Operational problems include the systems's complexity and vertical linkages that affect competition at the final sales point."

Marketing practice restrictions: "The Japan Fair Trade Commission (JFTC) regulations significantly restrict the use of premiums and other sales incentives offered to consumers, distributors and retailers."

Law on large retail stores: "MITI's administration of Japan's Large Retail Store Law (1974, 1978) since 1982 has turned a 'notification' process into an approval system for large store openings. Potential store owners must reach a consensus with local commercial interests before MITI will accept store applications." "Local advisory councils involved in the 'approval' process mainly represent shopowners with an interest in limiting the number of large-sized stores. There is little or no input from consumers or other parties as the law intended." "Since larger retailers are usually more willing to risk introducing new products or agressively promote imported product lines, limits on retail expansion effectively hinder the import of U.S. goods."

We do not go into the examination of U.S. trade barriers to Japanese exports.[23]

The reason why we have closely examined the complaints of the U.S. exporters against alleged trade barriers is to understand the exact nature of trade conflict in recent years. It is not high tariffs that prevent international flow of goods and services: tariffs are nonexistent or the levels have become so slow as to pose no real impediment to trade. Instead, it is the industrial standards, inspection system, procurement practices, distribution channels, and noncompetitive conducts in business which quite often involve the national government.

They may be summarized as institutional factors. What makes the matter rather complex is the fact that the institutional arrangements have been introduced for technological reasons. Industrial standards and inspection systems are originally intended to improve quality of products and technological compatibility among different producers including foreign firms. Long-term procurement practices are honored and prevalent. They serve to facilitate technological improvement which involves long research and gestation period. They are also conducive to "economies of scope" as well as "economies of scale." They are more important than the short-term price advantages because price advantages at one point in time are no guarantee of continued technological advantages. For example, technologically outmoded parts will make the whole product irrelevant and unacceptable to the customers. The cases of noncompetitive conducts are diversified and more difficult to generalize, but, here too, some of the cases are intended to create quasi-market where competitive market would not be conducive for proper supply. Research consortium is a typical case. It is not appropriate to categorically label these cases as anticompetitive and hence undesirable if they reflect technological characteristics of being risky, in need of R&D involving both producers and customers, or requiring large initial investment. Such arrangement is even disirable. Competitive environment can be maintained by having two or more of these groups.

Most countries outside the U.S. measures things in metric system, and this includes Japan. People in Japan drive on the left-hand side of the road, and they tend to speak Japanese language. When they buy American-made products, they are likely to be confronted with English manuals, units being inches and pounds. When they buy American cars, they will find a steering wheel on the wrong side, and will find themselves in an awkward situation each time they go through a tollgate. In addition, in the past at least, American products did not enjoy good maintenance record.

In many cases, therefore, the matter boils down to simply economics such as price, quality, industrial standards, maintenance, durability, and quick delivery. But there remain other factors which work to impede (or facilitate) trade, of which direct foreign investment deserves particular attention. We turn to this topic next.

8-5 Foreign investment barriers

The rapid expansion of direct investment into the United States in recent years, as compared to a relatively minor role played by Japan as a host country, raises a question as to the openness of the investment market in the latter. This leads us to an examination of impediments to direct foreign investment.

According to the OECD Code of Liberalization of Capital Movements, direct investment is defined as "investment for the purpose of establishing lasting economic relations with an undertaking such as, in particular, investments which give the possibility of exercising an effective influence on the management thereof."[24] Country practice may deviate from the definition here. For example, in the United States, the foreign direct investment statistics compiled by the Bureau of Economic Analysis refer to "the ownership or control, direct or indirect, by a single direct investor (including an associated group of persons) of at least 10 percent of the voting stock of an incorporated business enterprise or an equivalent interest in an unincorporated enterprise."[25] In the case of Japan, foreign direct investment statistics are available from two sources, and the figures may differ considerably among them. The Bank of Japan provides data according to the balance-of-payments definition. The Ministry of Finance figure are "based on investment approvals prior to 1980 and on notification by investors to the Ministry since 1980. ... While there is no acknowledged minimum percentage interest characterizing an inward direct investor, outward direct investors must hold at least 10 percent or the equity of a foreign enterprise in order to be classified as such."[26]

We have examined the evolution of Japanese investment policy in a previous work. Our conclusion there was that, as it stands now, the impediments to inward direct investment has been removed as well as the ones concerning outward investment.[27] In this section, we should look at a recent survey undertaken by the OECD concerning the extent of the liberalization of capital movements.[28]

A long-term international comparison of outward direct investment flows is provided by OECD [1987d]. The data end in 1983, unfortunately, due to difficulty involved in collecting direct investment data. Compared to production figures or commodity trade, for instance, compilation of direct investment data tend to be sporadic and unsystematic on individual country level. The data in this source are probably the most comprehensive, being reported directly by the OECD member countries in response to questionnaires on international direct investment statistics and methodology.[29]

The OECD report [1987d] observes that during the period under consideration, the United States has had a growing role as a host country, reflecting significant increases in inward direct investment and decreases in outward investment. Japan continued to grow as a major home country for international direct investment. Nevertheless, among the OECD countries, inward and outward flows tended to become more balanced, it is reported. This is in part a result of expanded role of countries such as France, Italy, Germany, and Japan as home countries for international investment.

We have a slightly different picture if we include the role of reinvested earnings. Among the countries for which information is available, reinvestment played an important role in the United States and the United Kingdom. For the United States, the ratio of reinvested earnings had been 50 to 70 percent in the 1970s, which in the 1980s has come to exceed 100 percent, meaning that this factor has worked to offset negative outward investment excluding reinvested earnings.

In compiling the table, the statistics in local currency have been converted into current US dollars.[30] It is pointed out that the underlying growth of international direct investment might be best judged if outflows were valued in local currencies. On this point, the OECD report responds that "variation in dollar exchange rates do express to a considerable extent real rather than artificial changes in the valuation of assets, and they thus influence international direct investment decisions."[31]

We should note, nevertheless, that the strengthened dollar in the first half of the 1980s, coupled with the decline of US outward investment, leads to some understatement of total outflow of capital worldwide. On the other hand, the weakened dollar in the latter half of the 1980s leads to overestimation of the growth of outward flows from home countries other than the United States. This is certainly the case for Japan.

Regarding inward direct investment flows within the OECD area, the same report notes that the position of the United States has expanded considerably as a recipient country. For the 1980-83 period, it received 52.5 percent of total OECD inflows (excluding reinvested earnings), nearly doubling its share in the 1970s. In contrast, we have witnessed a major reduction in the European share in inward investment from about 50 percent for the latter half of the 1970s to 40 percent in 1980–83. The Japanese share in total OECD inward investment remained relatively small, recording 2.0 percent in the 1975–79 period and 2.5 percent in the 1980–83 period.

The upsurge of direct investment into the United States is attributable to several factors.

- Strong economic growth of the United States economy since 1982;
- Large, stable, and homegeneous nature of the market;
- Fears of protectionist measures;
- Inflows from the United States overseas affiliates due to disinvestment and borrowing in foreign capital markets;
- Appreciation of the dollar which began around 1980 and continued through 1984, during which period it appreciated by 44 percent relative to other major currencies;
- Major growth of Japanese investment.

In this regard, OECD's survey [1987e] on the controls and impediments on inward direct investment provides an across the board picture among its member countries. The survey was undertaken as of August 1986. Until 1984, the liberalization obligation of the OECD's Code of Liberalization of Capital Movements required to authorize automatically transactions and transfers involving international direct investment to or from OECD countries, and it was unclear to what extent this obligation included the capacity of the investor to put the undertaking into operation. In order to allow effective access for the operation of the enterprise in the host country, a new remark was added to the Code which reads that:

"The authorities of Members shall not maintain or introduce: Regulations or practices applying to the granting of licenses, concessions, or similar authorisations, including conditions or requirements attaching to such authorisations and affecting the operations of enterprises, that raise special barriers or limitations with respect to non-resident (as compared to resident) investors, and that have the intent or the effect of

Table 8-9 Position of OECD countries regarding sectral controls and impediments to inward direct investment

Countries \ Sector	1	2	3	4	5	6	7	8	9	10	11	12	13	14	15	16
(1) Australia	RI	R			RI	R	M				MR	MR	R	R	R	R
(2) Austria	RI	I	R	I		M	M			M	R	R	R		R	R
(3) Belgium				I		M	M				M	M	MR			
(4) Canada	RI	R		MR	R	R	M					R			R	R
(5) Denmark				RI												
(6) Finland	RI	RI		MR		MR	MR		M	M	MR	R	R		R	R
(7) France	RI	RI	R	RI	I	MR	M	RI	R		MRI	MR	R			MRI
(8) Germany	I					M	M				M	MRI	R			
(9) Greece	RI			I		M	M				M	M	MI		I	I
(10) Ireland	RI	I		RI		M	M				M	R	RI	R		
(11) Italy	RI			RI		MR	M				M	R	R			I
(12) Japan	I	I				I	MI					I	I	R		R
(13) Luxembourg.				MI		M	M									
(14) Netherlands	RI	I				M	M				M	R	R			
(15) New Zealand				MR			R	M			M	M	R		R	R
(16) Norway	RI	R		RI		M	M				M	R	R	MR	R	R
(17) Portugal	R			RI			M	R			M	M	MR			
(18) Spain		I		MI		MR	M				M	R				
(19) Sweden	R	R		I		M	M			M	M	R	R		R	
(20) Switzerland	RI	I				M	M	R			M	MI	MI		R	
(21) Turkey	RI	I		RI		M	M			R	M	M			R	R
(22) United kingdom	I	I		I		MR	M				M	R	R			
(23) United States	I			I		MR	MR				R	R	R	R	R	R

	17	18	19	20	21	22	23	24	25	26	27	28	29	30	31	32	33	34	35
(1)	R	R	R		M	M				MR									
(2)	R					R				M	R				M	M			
(3)						M													
(4)	R				M									R					
(5)							I												
(6)		R	R			R	R	R	R	M				MR					
(7)	MRI	RI		MRI	RI	M	M		RI	R	R	R	I		M				M
(8)										M									
(9)	M					M				M									
(10)		R																	
(11)	R			M	M	M				M									
(12)	R	R	R												M	M			
(13)						M													
(14)						M	I												
(15)						M													
(16)		M			R	M			R	M				M			M		
(17)	M					M	M		R									M	I
(18)	M			M	I					R					M				
(19)							I			M				M			M		
(20)	M			I	I	I	M							M					
(21)	R					M	M			M				M	M				
(22)						M													
(23)	R			R	R														

Note: Sector codes are as follows.

Sector code

1 Banking
2 Other financial services (including stockbroking)
3 Auditing
4 Insurance
5 Press, publishing, printing
6 Broadcasting (radio, television, cable)
7 Post, telephone, telecommunications
8 Audiovisual works, film distribution
9 Health and social security
10 Employment agencies and services
11 Land transport (includes railways, buses, road construction and maintenance)
12 Air transport (includes airport construction and operation in some cases)
13 Maritime transportation (includes shipping, ship brokerage, forwarding, inland waterways, operation of seaports, cabotage, offshore supply, salvaging and dredging, ownership of fishing vessels)
14 Fishing
15 Real estate
16 Mining, minerals

Sector code

17 Petroleum
18 Agriculture, agricultural products
19 Forestry
20 Nuclear industries
21 Exploitation of water resources, water power
22 Overall energy production and public utilities (including water, gas, electricity)
23 Armaments, exlposives, gunpowder
24 Security guard and private detective services
25 Tourism, travel services
26 Gaming, casinos, lottos, lotteries, etc.
27 Jurisprudence, legal profession
28 Teaching, education
29 Merchants and craftsmen
30 Import, export and distribution of alcoholic beverages
31 Tabacco, matches
32 Salt
33 Pharmaceuticals, medicines, narcotics
34 Steel
35 Public works and services

R = Sectors in which some or all activities are subject to controls or impediments to inward direct investment that are regarded as restrictions in the sense of the Code of Liberalisation of Capital Movements.
I = Sectors in which some or all activities are restricted by other impediments.
M = Sectors in which some or all activities are closed to investment due to public, private or mixed monopolies.

This table shows on a country-by-country basis those sectors which, to a greater or lesser degree, are restricted to foreign investment either because of *obstacles* which apply specifically or more severely to non-resident investors, or because of the presence of public, private or mixed *monopolies*. Where obstacles are considered as restrictions in the sense of the Code they are marked with an R. In other cases, an I (for impediments) is used. Monopolies are indicated with an M. As a result of space limitations, some sectors include a number of specific activities (see for example maritime transportation); the presence of an obstacle or monopoly in any activity of that sector results, as far as this table is concerned, in a mark being entered against the entire sector. In some instances, an activity of a specific sector may be restricted in the sense of the Code and an R appears in the column, while in another activity of the same subject a monopoly may exist, which is reflected by an M. Thus, for the same sector, two letters may appear. Detailed information is not available for Iceland which maintains a general derogation from the obligatins of the Code of Liberalisation of Capital Movements.

Source: OECD, *Controls and Impediments Affecting Inward Direct Investment in OECD Member Countries*.

preventing or significantly impeding inward direct investments by non-residents."[32]

These modifications took effect in July 1986 and the survey is intended to reflect the situation at that point in time. As is evident from the wording of the above modifications, the survey excludes concession or license requirements and regulations which use the *same* standards for or apply equally to resident and non-resident investors.

Regarding the authorization procedure of a general nature, the report says, "In a first group of countries: (Belgium, Denmark, Germany, Greece, Italy, Japan, Luxemburg, the Netherlands, Switzerland, the United Kingdom and the United States), prior authorisation is required in a limited number of instances, mainly in those sectors which are subject to special conditions. In a second group of countries (Australia, Austria, Canada, France, and Spain), prior authorisation is more prevalent..."[33] As for investment by established foreign-controlled (EFC) enterprises, prior authorization is required only in sectors subject to special conditions for countries such as Austria, Denmark, Germany, Greece, Ireland, Italy, Japan, Switzerland, the United Kingdom, and the United States. New Zealand and Turkey required prior authorization for all investment by EFC enterprises, whereas in all other countries (Australia, Belgium, Canada, Finland, Luxemburg, the Netherlands, Norway, Portugal, Spain, and Sweden) the same authorization procedure applies to foreign investment and investment by EFC enterprises.

More specifically, the report describes the Japanese procedures as follows. "Under the Foreign Exchange and Foreign Trade Control Law, prior notification is required before any foreign investment is made. Foreign investment and investment by EFC enterprises are, in most cases, automatically accepted except for i) in primary industry related to agriculture and fisheries, mining, oil,leather and leather products manufacturing; ii) in other sectors falling under the safeguard clauses of the above law, where the Ministry of Finance and other competent ministers consider that Japanese interests might be adversely affected."[34] This is compared to the situtation in Germany which is described in the survey as "There are no authorisation requirements for foreign investment nor for investment by EFC enterprises except for some sectors subject to special condition," or in the United States which is essentially the same as Germany with some additions to the effect that "... some States prohibit or limit investment in some sectors by non-resident foreigners or foreign corporations."

As for sector-specific controls and impediments, the OECD report writes that restrictions are very prevalent in service sectors. Typical examples where activities are largely closed to foreign investment are domestic air transport and maritime transport. Banking, insurance, broadcasting, communication services, and natural resources and energy sectors frequently involve controls and impediments to inward direct investment. There are many measures concerning reciprocity and/or involving discrimination among investors originating in various OECD member countries and measures intended for public order and security considerations.

Japan is reported to have the following controls and obstacles to inward direct investment.

Sectors where restrictive measures apply:
Mining: metal mining, non-metal mineral mining, coal and lignite mining, etc.
Oil industry: oil and natural gas drilling, oil refining, oil retailing, etc.
Agriculture, forestry, and fisheries
Leather and leather products manufacturing
Maritime transport
Air transport
Broadcasting
Telecommunication
Banking and securities business
Insurance

Sectors closed to investment due to public monopolies:
Postal services
Tobacco manufacturing
Salt

The list is more or less comparable to the situation prevalent in other OECD countries. It should be added that considerable liberalization measures have been taken in recent years regarding banking, securities, and insurance. Telecommunication has been privatized as well as tobacco and salt manufacturing.

The United States Trade Representative (USTR) also reports on impediments to direct investment in Japan.[35] The description in their 1989 report is summarized below.

"Formal Japanese legal barriers which controlled foreign direct investment before 1980 have been largely dismantled. However, some limitations or prohibitions on foreign equity ownership remain in the areas of agriculture, fishing and forestry, oil and gas, mining and leather and leather product manufacturing. Investment in tobacco manufacturing is also prohibited. Foreign investment in the banking and securities industries is subject to a reciprocity requirement."

"Foreign direct investment flow remain small partly due to the difficulties foreigners have in breaking into certain areas of the Japanese market. Ties between government and industry, Japanese firms' reluctance to break long-term employee and supplier relationships, distribution system complexities, cross-shareholding among allied companies and the low percentage of common stock within total capital tend to inhibit direct foreign investment in Japan."

Although the USTR's assessment on impediment to direct investment has a rather pessimistic tone about the Japanese situation, the dismantling of formal limitations is nevertheless pointed out. Some sectors such as banking and securities, not to speak of agriculture and mining, are under government control of one kind or another in other countries. In the context of liberalization of trade in services, regulations peculiar to Japan will be removed in the near future where they still remain.

What remains among the USTR's complaints is the close ties among Japanese firms and their relationships with employees and suppliers. This can be described as institutional characteristics of the Japanese industry. One important point is, however, that it is not simply that the Japanese system is exotic. As can be witnessed by the fact that these peculiarities have been strenghtened in recent years, at least the Japanese find some rational in their system. Very likely it is a system designed to strengthen long-term performance by promoting R&D and investment plans with long-gestation period. The reluctance of Japanese owners to sell their business even to fellow Japanese can be explained by their commitment to the endeavor. Even in the case of bankruptcy, Japanese corporate executives are expected to reconstruct a failed business with the help of main banks, customers, suppliers, and trading firms in order to avoid harming the employees and long-established ties among business firms. Although this is merely the expectations which are not always kept in practice, it is true that some of the operating principles of the Japanese firms are different from the ones among the U.S. firms. This should be correctly recognized as the difference, and not impediment to business.

This point is confirmed by a survey by the Group of Thirty cited in OECD [1987d] concerning the investment climate in various regions of the world.[36] The question posed was, "In which geographical area has the climate for foreign direct investment either improved or deteriorated in the past five or ten years? Please list ... the main reasons for the improvement for deterioration." Among the areas in which the climate has improved included Far East/Japan, South East Asia, European NICs/ Spain, Oil exporting countries/Saudi Arabia, and the United States. The areas in which it has deteriorated included Europe, Latin America, Canada, and Africa/Nigeria.

The reasons cited for Japan include:

- government liberalization of rules and regulations of foreign direct investment;

— stable and fast growing markets;
— growing market for financial services; and
— increased product competitiveness.

The reasons for the improvement in the United States are:
— relaxing government attitudes toward anti-trust enforcement;
— relative deterioration in the rest of the world;
— renewed strength of oil and gas exploration;
— improved social climate, resurgence of work ethic; and
— liberalization of banking regulations.

South East Asia is judged to have improved as regard to open door policies by area governments, infrastructure, and emergence of more sophisticated politicians.

The reasons for a deteriorated climate in Europe include market saturation, increasing labor costs, EEC and governmental regulations, non-tariff trade barriers, among others. Canadian climate has deteriorated due to increased government control and Canadianisation, according to the survey.[37]

We may conclude from the observation above that inward direct investment in the Japanese market is not particularly restrictive as compared to practices in other countries. The implication, therefore, is that the imbalanced outflows and inflows of direct investment in Japan can not be attributed to restrictive practices at home. Rather, it should be interpreted as representing the underlying macroeconomic structure concerning saving-investment balance within the economy which is reflected in abundant financial resources and low interest rate. Likewise, the net inflow of direct investment into the United States should be viewed as representing the shortage of investment fund and resultant higher interest rate, in addition to inherent advantages of the American market which we have touched upon earlier.

8-6 High-tech diffusion and export performance

We have started our discussion by looking at the structure of international trade where we observed a rapid shift toward machinery products. Then we looked at institutional barriers to foreign trade and investment where our observation was that they are not particularly restrictive in Japan, and wherever barriers exist, they are being dismantled quickly. Those who claim that they still believe barriers are peculiar to Japan are probably influenced by the memories of the 1960s and 1970s. They typically fail to recognize changing environment in the last decade. Although there remain administrative rigidities in the government control areas, trade and investment in manufacturing sectors can not be explained in terms of government restriction of inward flows and/or government promotion of outward flows. If the Japanese performance in trade in machinery and transport equipment is not attributable to open market abroad as opposed to a closed one at home, a question then arises as to what explains the trend.

In this section, we shall examine the technological factor in international trade. We continue to focus on machinery sectors including general machinery, electrical machinery, transportation equipment (particularly motor vehicles), and precision instrument because these are the sectors where we have seen diffusion of C-C-C technology in the production processes.

For this purpose, we examine the validity of variables representing technological factor in explaining the export performance. Our model differs in its scope from the related works reported in section 3 above. The framework of COMPASS does no include economies of foreign countries. On the other hand, it is far more detailed in domestic portion in sectoral disaggregation and the treatment of technological factors. The repercussion on foreign trade and the balance of payments can also be assessed in detail.

We have derived indicators representing technological factors in previous chapters which can be employed here. The candidate variables include the following:

(1) The diffusion of C-C-C technology, which can be represented by the ratio of computers, industrial robots, and NC metalworking machines to fixed capital stock;
(2) The level of technology by industry;
(3) Capital stock vintage;
(4) The relative level of capital stock vintage vis-a-vis major competitor, such as the United States;
(5) The benefit of R&D or its relative level vis-a-vis major competitor;
(7) The relative level of new scientific knowledge produced or stock thereof, based on patents data, etc.

In our examination, we chose the first of these candidates, which is the diffusion rate of C-C-C technology in four machinery and transport equipment sectors. These variables are added to a standard export function.[38] This specification enables us to establish a direct link between technology diffusion and export performance. Alternative variables are of considerable interest, but the implied causal relationship seems indirect.

The export functions including C-C-C variables are estimated and the results are reported below. The model explains exports (in real terms) in each industry (ERi) by the world industrial production (YWORLD), relative prices which is the ratio of export prices adjusted for the exchange rate fluctuation (REX*PEi) and the world price (PUNi), and proxy variables describing the diffusion of mainframe computers, NC machines, and industrial robots (RKCOMi+RKNCi+RKROBOi). Exchange rate in this specification is represented by dollar per yen.[39]

ERi = f (YWORLD, REX*PEi/PUNi, RKCOMi+RKNCi+RKROBOi)

Pertinent variables are as follows:

ERi — Exports 1970 prices, million yen (Ministry of Finance, *Foreign Trade Statistics*)
PEi — Export prices, yen terms, 1970=1.00 (The Bank of Japan, *Price Indexes Annual*)
PUN7 — World prices, machinery (SITC 7)(United Nations, *Yearbook of International Trade Statistics*)
REX — Exchange rate, dollar per yen (i.e., when $1=¥200, REX is 1/200)(International Monetary Fund, *International Financial Statistics*)
RKCOMi — Share of computers in capital stock (for sources of data and derivation, see chapter 1)
RKNCi — Share of NC metalworking machines in capital stock (for sources of data and derivation, see chapter 1)
RKROBOi — Share of industrial robots in capital stock (for sources of data and derivation, see chapter 1)
YWORLD — World industrial production index, 1970=100 (United Nations, Statistical Yearbook)

Industrial sectors are represented by a subscript (i) where
Sector 34: general machinery
Sector 35: electrical machinery
Sector 36M: transport equipment, motor vehicles
Sector 37: precision instrument

The function was tested for general machinery, electrical machinery, motor vehicles, and precision instrument, as we see below.

General machinery (sample 1974–1985):

$$\ln ER34 = \underset{(3.05)}{1.7278} \ln YWORLD - \underset{(-1.63)}{0.6213} \ln (REX^*PE34/PUN7) + \underset{(3.11)}{0.5640} \ln (RKCOM34+RKROBO34+RKNC34) + \underset{(1.25)}{4.5614}$$

S.E.= 0.0659 ADJ R-SQ=0.9787 D.W.=2.0677

Electrical machinery (sample 1974–1985):

$$\ln ER35 = \underset{(2.26)}{2.4167} \ln YWORLD - \underset{(-1.75)}{0.7936} \ln (REX^*PE35/PUN7)$$

$$+ 0.6342 \ln (RKCOM35+RKROBO35+RKNC35) - 0.3412$$
$$(1.75) \qquad (-0.06)$$
S.E.=0.1111 ADJ R-SQ=0.9696 D.W.=1.8106

Transportation equipment, motor vehicles (sample 1974 – 1985):

$$\ln ER36M = 1.2336 \ln YWORLD + 0.4710 \ln ER36 (-1)$$
$$(1.05) \qquad (0.53)$$
$$+ 0.2920 \ln (RKCOM36+RKROBO36M+RKNC36M) + 2.4186$$
$$(1.13)$$
S.E.=0.1074 ADJ R-SQ=0.9434 D.W.=1.5945

Precision instrument (sample 1974–1985):

$$\ln ER37 = 2.4003 \ln YWORLD - 0.3546 \ln (REX*PE37/PUN7)$$
$$(3.74) \qquad (-2.21)$$
$$+ 0.7934 \ln (RKCOM37+RKROBO37+RKNC37) + 1.9460$$
$$(2.45) \qquad (0.44)$$
S.E.=0.0762 ADJ R-SQ=0.9811 D.W.=1.78

The fit is generally good and the variables representing the diffusion of high-tech have reasonable t-values. Compared to standard equation with comparable observation period, our equations here have higher R-squares (adjusted for degrees of freedom). For example, in the case of general machinery, it improved from 0.9581 to 0.9787.[40]

We may conclude, based on our experiment, that the diffusion of technology is indeed a factor behind the export performance of the machinery sectors. Although world income and relative price terms explain export trade, explicit inclusion of C-C-C diffusion as a ratio to total capital stock turned out to provide significant results in each of the four machinery sectors. The price trends already reflects efficiency gains achieved through structural change because our price equations are specified in such a form as to reflect changes in the input coefficients in a particular sector. However, we can now say that the feedback channel from technological progress to economic performance is not limited to price changes. Our contention is that Japanese gains in international trade, especially in machinery sectors, is due to technological superiority as represented by computers, NC metalworking machines, and industrial robots.

8-7 Concluding remarks

The above analyses do confirm that the international competitiveness of an economy is positively affected by its R&D efforts and high-tech investment. Thus, it seems safe to assume that actual trade pattern is closely linked to technological characteristics of product mix which a country is capable of offering for the world market. This is especially true in sectors closely related to triple-C technology. It is revealed through our observation in this chapter that technological superiority is something being achieved through business activities in a competitive market rather than something artificially created by government intervention. In the case of raw materials and mineral fuels, the trade pattern is predominantly determined by the endowment of such resources. Here again, however, technological change, which is reflected in conservation per unit output in individual sectors, and structural change, which is the relative share of individual sectors within an economy, do take place.[41]

We have seen increased policy interventions in the direction and magnitude of international trade which, in theory at least, can be left to the working of the market mechanism. The reason for policy intervention is in general interpreted as political as well as economic. Political acceptability has emerged as a factor which has to be taken into account in discussing trade relations. However, it may be wrong to assume, judged from empirical evidence, that political intervention would enable us to manipulate the economic mechanism at will. There are increasing numbers of evidences which indicate that the contrary is true.

At the same time, it is important to realize the existence of technological factor which makes market solution unacceptable, because, for instance, a whole segment of the economy would be wiped out due to competition from abroad unless it is allowed adjustment time to shift to a new technology. Governments often try to achieve politically acceptable results through direct intervention (import restriction, imposition of voluntary restriction upon trading partners, etc.), and they are often successful. The important point is that, even if they can be successful in the short-run, economic realities reflecting R&D and technological progress do seem to prevail in the long-run. A case can then be made for technology transfer through direct investment which enables both parties to benefit.

Footnotes:

1 Trade matrices are available in the United Nations, *Yearbook of International Trade Statistics*.

2 Discrepancies may arise, for example, if one country report the country of last consignment and the other the country of production.

3 For detailed exposition of the international input-output table, see Institute of Developing Economies [1982]; Furukuwa [1986]. The table refers to the year

1975 and includes eight countries, namely, ASEAN five (Indonesia, Malaysia, the Philippines, Thailand, and Singapore) Korea, Japan, and the United States. The industrial classification consists of 56 sectors. All transactions are expressed in terms of the U.S. dollar based on official exchange rates.)

4 We discuss a proposal for such structural adjustment in chapter 2.

5 Adams and Shishido [1988].

6 ibid., pp.9–10.

7 ibid., p.43.

8 ibid., p.101.

9 ibid., p.101.

10 ibid., 110.

11 This strengthens our argument for structural adjustment in chapter 2 above. If similar products are produced on both sides of the Pacific through direct investment by Japanese firms, in terms of industrial standards and quality, while sales channels become increasingly open, we should expect the Japanese economy to become more sensitive to price differentials and demand stimulus.

12 They observe that the results are consistent with an earlier calculation. Adams and Gangnes [1987].

13 For a brief introduction of the Kinoshita model, see Uno [1988a], p.330 and p.332, where its structure is compared with other multicountry models.

14 Kinoshita and Yamada [1989], pp.594–596.

15 Saito [1988], pp.80–83.

16 Kinoshita and Yamada [1989], p.598.

17 ibid., pp.599–604.

18 Saito, ibid., pp.80–83.

19 MITI [1989a], p.1. There are 163 common I-O sectors in the table for U.S. and Japan. The analysis here is based on a 26-sector summary table. The U.S.-Japan table itself does not provide the repercussion vis-a-vis the rest-of-the-world. But supporting tables which comprise vectors of exports and imports of the 17 countries/regions devised from the R.O.W. and consistent with the U.S.-Japan table, are available, making it possible to analyze the influence on trade by 17 countries/regions (i.e., except for repercussions).

20 MITI [1989b], p.32.

21 Office of the United States Trade Representative, *National Trade Estimate Report on Foreign Trade Barriers*, various issues. The nature of the report is described as follows: "Section 303 of the Trade and Tariff Act of 1984 directs the Office of the U.S. Trade Representatives (USTR) to submit to the Senate Finance Committee and the House Ways and Means Committee this annual report on significant foreign barriers to and distortions of trade. The statute calls for including significant barriers affecting goods, services, investment and intellectual property rights."

22 The Japanese stipulation came about in order to avoid disasters by fire caused by earthquakes.

23 Almost all trade conflicts between the United States and Japan have ended up with Japan implementing voluntary export restrictions. This is Japan's unilateral action only in letters. In reality, this constitutes erection of trade barriers

which tend to distort resource allocation more than, for example, tariffs. The cases in question include textiles, steel, color television, metalworking machines, and semiconductors.

24 OECD [1987e], p.7.

25 OECD [1987d], p.169. More detailed description is also given there.

26 OECD [1987e], p.128. More detailed description is also given there.

27 Uno [1987]. Komiya [1988] observes that the post-war Japanese market permitted considerable amount of new entries, including foreign-affiliated firms, and that the recent gaps between Japan's outward direct investment and inward direct investment should not be market, but rather as a manifestation of different macroeconomic conditions amoung countries.

28 OECD [1987e], p.9. In 1982, OECD published survey results with the same intention as the 1987 report. But the differing stipulations in the liberalization code do not permit direct comparisons of the results in the two surveys.

29 "Despite the common framework provided by the OECD benchmark definition on foreign direct investment, the statistics ... are still based on different definitions of direct investment and methods of collecting data. Nevertheless, they are on a quite comparable basis." OECD [1987d], p.57.

30 The conversion rate is a yearly average of spot exchange rates for the investment flows and earnings, and an end-of-year rate for the stocks of net assets. See ibid., p.57.

31 ibid., p.10.

32 OECD [1987e], p.8.

33 ibid., p.11.

34 ibid., p.22.

35 Office of the United States Trade Representative, ibid., 1989, pp.107–108.

36 Group of Thirty, *Foreign Direct Investment, 1973–1987* cited in OECD [1987d], p.209.

37 The policy has been reversed in recent years as symbolized by the abolition of FIRA, but fluctuation of policy itself is not particularly welcome for business firms.

38 The specification and empirical result of export functions are discussed in detail in Uno [1987], pp.341–370.

39 An alternative viewpoint is to look at the share of Japan's exports in total imports of her trading partners. If Japan's share tends to increase, and if this trend can be explained by relative technological levels, then we have a clue as to the reason for its rising share. This experiment can be carried out in high-tech related sectors. The dependent variable is as stated above, and can be obtained from trade matrix on machinery and transportation equipment (SITC 7). The major explanatory variable is the relative level of patent application or the stock of knowledge appropriately defined. This is supplemented by relative prices, etc.

40 In the case of motor vehicles, relative price term had to be dropped from the equation, but this was also the case for the standard specification for the same observation period. This is interpreted to reflect imposition of voluntary export restrictions in this sector.

41 For Japanese experience in energy conservation, a multi-sectoral econometric

analysis is provided in Uno [1987], pp.257–270. Related analysis in an input-output framework is given in Uno [1989a], pp.75–83.

Chapter 9. The balance of payments—Japan's changing international economic relations

9-1 The emerging trends

The balance of payments statistics provides an overview of the international economic relations, including trade in goods and services, and capital transactions. In this chapter we look at the balance of payments statistics for Japan for the purpose of providing a summary picture of the structural change in her relationship with the world economy, encompassing technology, investment, and trade,.

After briefly looking at the new trends which characterize Japan's international economic relations as reflected in the balance of payments, we shall focus our attention on the trade in goods. Since we have already discussed export and import trends at the disaggregated level in chapter 8, we simply look at the trade balance in section 2 below. In section 3, we turn to trade in services. Trade in services is the focal point in the Uruguay Round of GATT negotiations which is currently underway and is expected to go beyond 1990. This category includes payments for intellectual property, returns on foreign investment, travel, transportation, and insurance, among others, and has gained importance in recent years. In our context, particularly important are the revenues from foreign investment and patent royalties. In section 4, We examine technology balance of payments. In section 5, transactions in capital is analyzed, with emphasis on long-term capital flows. Based on the external assets and liabilities data, emergence of Japan as a major creditor and its world-wide implication is discussed in section 6. Section 7 then examines foreign economic cooperation. Section 8 analyzes determination of the exchange rate. Explanatory variables are chosen from among the items which are discussed in this chapter.

The balance of payments has always dominated front pages of newspapers in Japan, but the reasons differed from period to period. In earlier years of industrialization, balance of payments constituted a major constraint to economic growth because payments for raw material imports tended to exceed what Japan was able to sell overseas. Thus, economic expansion in this period was always cut short due to emerging trade deficits by means of aggregate demand restriction through fiscal and monetary policy.

Japan was able to overcome these constraints through relative cheapening of the yen in the world market which occurred as a result of continued productivity gains under the fixed exchange regime towards the end of the 1960s. However, the appreciation of the yen triggerred by what the Japanese termed the "Nixon shock" in 1970, was actually an adjustment process long overdue but was delayed by the indecisiveness of the Japanese policy authority. By this time, Japan was enjoying continued trade surplus. For the fear of losing competitiveness in the world market and of stalling the domestic economy, the government initiated a series of policy measures to stimulate the economy (which actually resulted in a hyperinflation). In other words, the Japanese producers did not suffer from appreciation of the yen as can be seen in the continued surplus in trade balance.

The 1973 Oil Crisis included both quantitative restriction on oil sales by the OPEC and quadrupling of oil prices. In retrospect, the former was short-lived and the restriction was lifted within three months or so after some diplomatic efforts. The price hike, however, was a lasting one. Given the fact that nearly 16% of imports at that time constituted of crude petroleum (22% including all mineral fuels including coal and petroleum products), coupled with the fact that prices of other industrial raw materials also continued to rise, it is no wonder that the situation actually constituted a major crisis. The Oil Crisis left its scars in the Japanese balance of payment statistics. The situation was stabilized after several years partly due to rising export prices which reflected shifting price structure within the Japanese industry.[1] The second Oil Crisis in the 1979–1980 period enforced a similar kind of adjustment.

The export performance of the Japanese industry was improved in the 1980s partly helped by the appreciation of the dollar under the Reagan administration. Whether the U.S. administration considered the strong dollar as a part of strong America is debatable. The administration was fighting inflation at that time and high interest rate must have been a powerful tool in bringing down aggregate demand. But there were certain elements on why the administration and the American public in general favored a strong dollar. Whatever the cause of the strong dollar may be, one of the results was chronic trade surplus for Japan. In 1985, major industrial countries were able to agree on the currency realignment, and the Japanese currency was suddenly appreciated from 250 yen to a dollar to about 120 yen to a dollar. The government and the people alike kept watchful eyes on the balance of payments statistics. Nothing happened for some time. Japan kept recording trade surplus just as before. Actually, the growth of export was arrested, but Japanese import of raw materials has been kept at a constant level despite continued industrial expansion, a fact which reflected conservation effort within each sector and the structural shift of the economy as a whole where the economy has shifted toward high-tech sectors and services. Another factor which contributed to the delayed response was the J curve effect where, despite the exchange rate adjustment which in theory should

Figure 9-1 Trends in current balance and long-term capital balance

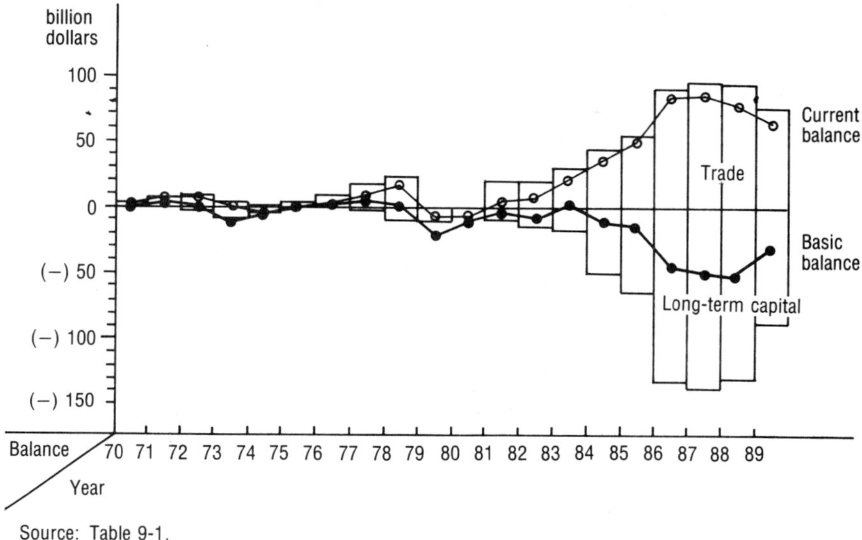

Source: Table 9-1.

reduce a country's export and promote imports, expected trends toward equilibrium is felt with some time lags reflecting transportation and contractual and other inertia.

The emerging trends in Japanese balance of payments may be summarized as presented in table 9-1 for empirical data covering trade in goods, trade in services, transfer payments, long-term capital transactions, and short-term capital transactions, together with current balance (i.e., balance of trade in goods and services plus transfers), basic balance (including long-term capital in addition to current items), and overall balance (including short-term capital transactions and errors and omissions in addition to items included in the basic balance).

We immediately recognize that the trade in services has gained importance in recent years. In 1988, for example, service exports amounted to 111.8 billion dollars as compared to commodity exports of 259.8 billion dollars, and service imports recorded 123.0 billion dollars which is approaching the level of commodity imports that stood at 164.8 billion dollars. Long-term capital outflow from Japan have reached 149.9 billion dollars. This far exceeds the trade surplus. Unrequited transfers which reflect, but not limited to, foreign economic assitance are also increasing rapidly. Thus, the basic balance, which is defined as the sum of current balance (trade balance + service balance + unrequited transfers) and long-term capital balance turned negative and the margin has increased rapidly (see figure 9-1).

Table 9-1 Balance of payments, summary table

(unit: million dollars)

Year	Merchandise trade[1]			Services[2]			Unrequited transfers		
	Balance	Exports	Imports	Balance	Credits	Debits	Balance	Credits	Debits
Variables	BPT$	ESUM$	MSUM$	BPSERVICE$	ESERVICE$	MSERVICE$	BPTRANSFER$		
1970	3,963	18,969	15,006	(−) 1,785	4,009	5,794	(−) 208	98	306
1971	7,787	23,566	15,779	(−) 1,738	4,840	6,758	(−) 252	127	379
1972	8,971	28,032	19,061	(−) 1,883	6,238	8,121	(−) 464	138	602
1973	3,688	36,264	32,576	(−) 3,510	8,493	12,003	(−) 314	149	463
1974	1,436	54,480	53,044	(−) 5,842	12,031	17,873	(−) 287	189	476
1975	5,028	54,734	49,706	(−) 5,324	13,498	18,852	(−) 356	197	553
1976	9,887	66,026	56,139	(−) 5,867	14,459	20,326	(−) 340	228	568
1977	17,311	79,333	62,022	(−) 6,004	16,277	22,281	(−) 389	263	652
1978	24,596	95,634	71,038	(−) 7,387	19,619	27,006	(−) 675	298	973
1979	1,845	101,322	99,387	(−) 9,472	25,596	35,068	(−)1,127	365	1,492
1980	2,125	126,736	124,611	(−)11,343	31,499	42,842	(−)1,528	387	1,915
1981	19,967	149,522	129,555	(−)13,573	39,783	53,356	(−)1,624	441	2,065
1982	18,079	137,663	119,584	(−) 9,848	41,085	50,933	(−)1,381	465	1,846
1983	31,454	145,468	114,014	(−) 9,106	37,587	46,693	(−)1,549	480	2,029
1984	44,257	168,290	124,033	(−) 7,747	42,154	49,901	(−)1,507	565	2,072
1985	55,986	174,015	118,029	(−) 5,165	45,511	50,676	(−)1,652	424	2076
1986	92,827	205,591	112,764	(−) 4,932	53,700	58,632	(−)2,050	419	2,469
1987	96,386	224,605	128,219	(−) 5,702	79,640	85,342	(−)3,669	633	4,302
1988	95,012	259,765	164,753	(−)11,263	111,754	123,017	(−)4,118	1,097	5,215
1989	76,917	269,570	192,653	(−)15,526	143,854	159,380	(−)4,234	1,025	5,259

(continued)

Year	Long-term capital[2,3]			Short-term capital balance[4,5]	Errors and omissioons[6]	Current balance[7]	Basic balance[8]	Overall balance[9]
	Balance	Assets (outflow)	Liabilities (inflow)					
Variables	BPKLONG$	EKLONG$	MKLONG$	BPKSHORT$	BPERROR$	BPCURRENT$	BPBASIC$	BPSUM$
1970	(−) 1,591	(−) 2,031	440	724	271	1,970	379	1,374
1971	(−) 1,082	(−) 2,231	1,149	2,435	527	5,797	4,715	7,677
1972	(−) 4,487	(−) 5,020	533	1,966	638	6,624	2,137	4,741
1973	(−) 9,750	(−) 8,468	(−) 1,282	2,407	(−) 2,595	(−) 136	(−) 9,886	(−)10,074
1974	(−) 3,881	(−) 4,063	182	1,778	(−) 43	(−) 4,693	(−) 8,574	(−) 6,839
1975	(−) 272	(−) 3,392	3,120	(−) 1,138	(−) 584	(−) 682	(−) 954	(−) 2,676
1976	(−) 984	(−) 4,559	3,575	111	117	3,680	2,696	2,924
1977	(−) 3,184	(−) 5,247	2,063	(−) 648	657	10,918	7,734	7,743
1978	(−) 12,389	(−) 14,872	2,483	1,538	267	16,534	4,145	5,950
1979	(−) 12,976	(−) 16,294	3,318	2,735	2,333	(−) 8,754	(−)21,730	(−)16,662
1980	2,324	(−) 10,817	13,141	3,141	(−) 3,115	(−)10,746	(−) 8,422	(−) 8,396
1981	(−) 9,672	(−) 22,807	13,137	2,265	4,93	4,770	(−) 4,902	(−) 2,144
1982	(−) 14,969	(−) 27,418	12,449	(−) 1,579	4,727	6,850	(−) 8,119	(−) 4,971
1983	(−) 17,700	(−) 32,459	14,759	23	2,055	20,799	3,099	5,177
1984	(−) 49,651	(−) 56,775	7,124	(−) 4,295	3,743	35,003	(−)14,648	(−)15,200
1985	(−) 64,542	(−) 81,815	17,273	(−) 936	3,991	49,169	(−)15,373	(−)12,318
1986	(−)131,461	(−)132,095	634	(−) 1,609	2,458	85,845	(−)45,616	(−)44,767
1987	(−)136,532	(−)132,830	(−) 3,702	23,865	(−) 3,893	87,015	(−)49,517	(−)29,545
1988	(−)130,930	(−)149,883	18,953	19,521	2,796	79,631	(−)51,299	(−)28,982
1989	(−) 89,246	(−)192,118	102,872	20,811	(−)22,008	57,157	(−)32,089	(−)33,286

Notes: 1. Excluding processing fees and net receipts on merchanting transactions from July 1979.
2. Including processing fees and net receipts on merchanting transactions from July 1979.
3. Excluding bond transactions with repurchase agreement ("gensaki") from January 1979.
4. Including "gensaki" transactions from January 1979.
5. Excluding transactions which belong to monetary movement.
6. Excluding valuation changes in gold and foreign exchange reserves from July 1979.
7. Sum of balance of trade in goods, services, and unrequitred transfers.
8. Sum of current balance and long-term capital balance, and errors and omissions.
9. Sum of basic balance, short-term capital balance, and errors and omissions.

Source: The Bank of Japan, *Economic Statistics Annual.*

In the following, we examine the balance of payments statistics in more detail as a means of understanding the Japanese foreign economic relations.

9-2 Merchandise trade balance[2]

Today, the balance of trade serves as an economic indicator of considerable policy significance. First, the trade balance is expected to show the effectiveness of the exchange rate realignment. On the export side, the competitiveness of the Japanese products is not simply a matter of relative prices but of technological advantage. Under the umbrella of technological advantage, we include such factors as product innovation which made Japan the sole producer in the world (such as facsimile and video equipment), process innovation which made Japanese products reliable while maintaining price competitiveness (such as semiconductors and automobiles), and considerable supply flexibility in response to changes in the world demand levels (such as steel, chemicals, industrial plants in addition to the items cited above). On the import side, however, the bulk consists of raw materials and foods which are not very price sensitive. Although it is true that the imports of finished goods are expanding quite rapidly in the recent years, adjustment of trade surplus directly through exchange rate realignment is limited by trade structure itself. This is the reason why we need to assess the adjustment effect through Japanese direct foreign investment abroad.

It may be only a matter of time before the adjustment effect is felt in trade statistics, or it may be that the structural change of the Japanese trade has made it sort of immune to exchange rate adjustment. The matter should be largely assessed in an empirical context.

The 1988 balance of payments statistics indicated that the surplus in merchandise trade showed a decline for the first time in six years since 1982.[3] The 1988 trade surplus is recorded at 95.0 billion dollars, or a decrease of 1.4% over 1987. The exports recorded highest growth in 1988 and increased 15.7% over the previous year. Contributing factor is the strong world economy, which prompted exports of such items as semiconductors (an increase of 48.2%), personal computers and other office equipment (27.8%), facsimiles, and video decks. On the other hand, automobile exports were arrested reflecting increased overseas production. Imports also reached their highest level in history in 1988, increasing by 28.5% over the previous year. Particularly noteworthy was the expansion of imports of finished goods. The share of finished goods in total imports now reached 49.0%. This is a rather impressive figure when compared against 31.0% in 1985 when the G5 agreement was reached.

Excluding the crude oil imports from the total, the ratio of finished goods imports has increased from 42.3% in 1985 to 54.5% in 1988.[4]

Thus, we may observe that the exchange rate realignment in 1985 has had its intended effect of balancing exports and imports. Will the trend continue into the future? There seem to be two factors at work here. One is that the yen exchange rate against the dollar tended to cheapen after 1988. This in turn is a result of economic factors such as wide margin in the interest rates and political factors such as instability in the Philippines, Panama, and the Eastern bloc countries. The other is Japan's direct investment overseas which is entering the production phase. There are growing cases where products overseas are exported to the home market.

9-3 Trade in services

Second, turning now to trade in services, table 9-2 provides the details. Trade in services reflects international transactions concerning transportation (freight and passenger), travel, investment income, patent royalties, office expenses and various fees, and insurance. Some of the transactions in services occur accompanying trade in goods. Freight and insurance on shipment are typical examples. As the economy shifts towards services, and away from manufacturing activities, at least in a relative sense, international transactions in services gained importance. This is the case, for example, in finance, non-merchandise insurance, and various fees and expenses. After the appreciation of the yen in 1985, overseas travel became atrractive to Japanese tourists and this is reflected in the balance of payments statistics as the increase in related items. Foreign direct investment and portfolio investment have become vital economic ties among countries, especially after the liberalization of capital movement which took place in the 1980s and income from such investment is increasing rapidly.[5]

More advanced countries such as the United States has competitive edge in trade in services. Despite deficit in merchandise trade, the American position in transportation (especially air transportation), foreign investment, insurance, and technology has been undisputable. In the Uruguay Round of the GATT negotiation, therefore, the United States wants to establish international agreement on this account. The U.S.-Canada Free Trade Agreement which was concluded in 1987 incorportates stipulations regarding trade in services and is regarded by some as a prototype of international agreement.[6] The European Community in its effort to strengthen economic integration by 1992 also attempts to implement various policy measures aimed at liberalizing trade in services within the community. Some of the less developed countries are

Table 9-2 Trade in services

a. exports

(unit: million dollars)

Year	Total[1]	Transportation				Travel	Investment income			
			Freight	Insurance on shipment[2]	Passenger fares			Direct investment income	Interest on loans	Interest on trade credit
Variables	ESERVICE$	ETRANSPORT$	EFREIGHT$	EINSCARGO$	EPASSFARE$	ETRALEL$	EYSUM$	EYIF$	EYOAN$	EYCREDIT$
1970	4,009	1,687	1,473	52	139	232	710	87	62	195
1971	4,840	2,210	1,987	68	126	172	980	115	93	228
1972	6,238	2,654	2,368	82	158	201	1,622	169	143	290
1973	8,493	3,523	3,205	86	168	209	2,655	223	194	296
1974	12,031	5,678	5,266	130	210	235	3,562	349	234	330
1975	13,498	6,429	5,976	135	231	252	3,616	506	263	357
1976	14,459	7,181	6,585	170	296	313	3,460	630	332	418
1977	16,277	7,680	6,967	191	352	425	3,738	841	451	495
1978	19,619	8,328	7,456	217	430	470	5,278	782	758	566
1979	25,596	9,876	8,808	294	514	554	8,965	931	1,006	766
1980	31,499	12,991	11,952	255	524	644	11,115	1,340	815	867
1981	39,783	15,356	14,215	259	548	735	15,761	1,440	976	973
1982	41,085	13,308	12,164	219	555	754	18,320	1,589	1,268	1,208
1983	37,587	12,221	11,071	239	551	825	15,601	2,040	1,386	1,291
1984	42,154	12,886	11,779	290	536	970	18,768	2,201	1,614	1,612
1985	45,511	12,444	11,440	261	570	1,137	22,107	2,538	1,536	1,821
1986	53,700	11,316	10,284	239	666	1,463	29,086	2,670	2,294	2,180
1987	79,640	17,954	11,584	309	878	2,097	49,245	3,548	3,133	2,611
1988	111,754	15,524	13,491	446	1,138	2,893	74,837	3,750	3,747	2,999
1989	143,854	18,090	15,552	428	1,469	3,143	101,785	4,577	4,596	3,641

(continued)

Year	Others[1]						
		Official transactions	Private transactions[1]				
				Office expences	Patent royalties	Fees	Non-merchandise insurance[3]
Variables	ESERVICEMIS$	EGOVT$		EOFFICE$	EPATENT$	EFEES$	EINSOTHER$
1970	1,380	692	688	112	55	207	184
1971	1,478	645	833	172	61	244	222
1972	1,761	736	1,025	171	70	285	299
1973	2,106	765	1,341	185	85	410	362
1974	2,556	732	1,824	202	111	627	472
1975	3,201	810	2391	250	142	714	649
1976	3,505	876	2,629	312	175	762	781
1977	4,434	923	3,511	343	204	963	925
1978	5,543	1,162	4,381	472	281	1,258	1,072
1979	6,201	1,233	4,968	567	321	1,687	715
1980	6,749	1,475	5,274	573	354	2,020	57
1981	7,931	1,968	5,963	730	482	2,001	38
1982	8,703	2,339	6,364	854	559	1,913	(−) 28
1983	8,940	2,250	6,690	886	569	1,814	(−) 235
1984	9,530	2,461	7,069	1,107	695	2,027	(−) 196
1985	9,823	2,667	7,156	1,150	723	2,073	(−) 248
1986	11,835	3,005	8,830	1,507	906	2,354	(−) 77
1987	15,344	2,727	12,617	2,289	1,293	3,271	(−) 21
1988	18,500	2,772	15,728	2,915	1,637	4,265	(−) 199
1989	20,836	2,672	18,164	3,198	2,016	5,920	(−) 223

Notes: 1. Including processing fees and net receipts on merchanting transactions from 1980.
2. Net earnings (premiums received-insurance money paid) of Japanese insurance companies.
3. Net payments (premiums-insurance money).
Source: Same as Table 9-1.

b. imports

(unit: million dollars)

Year	Total[1.]	Transportation				Travel	Investment income			
			Freight etc.	Insurance on shipment[2]	Passenger fares			Direct investment income	Interest on loans	Interest on external bonds
Variables	MSERVICE$	MTRANSPORT$	MFREIGHT$	MINSCARGO$	MPASSFARE$	MTRAVEL$	MYSUM$	MYIF$	MYLOAN$	MYBOND$
1970	5,794	2,887	2,614	89	174	315	919	110	153	62
1971	6,578	3,109	2,794	103	200	509	1,027	139	164	68
1972	8,121	3,660	3,231	125	278	774	1,255	172	166	68
1973	12,003	5,293	4,618	160	482	1,252	2,165	295	181	61
1974	17,873	8,326	7,500	239	550	1,358	4,013	290	232	60
1975	18,852	8,527	7,595	252	637	1,367	3,889	298	292	67
1976	20,326	9,572	8,484	256	772	1,664	3,664	324	319	185
1977	22,281	10,081	8,842	294	860	2,152	3,623	377	297	287
1978	27,006	10,837	9,339	316	1,043	3,717	4,378	406	340	375
1979	35,068	14,207	12,102	406	1,511	4,810	6,954	586	294	486
1980	42,842	17,334	15,118	446	1,488	4,593	10,261	531	214	500
1981	53,356	18,516	16,024	442	1,713	4,616	16,524	624	304	592
1982	50,933	16,729	14,328	408	1,711	4,116	16,602	597	269	668
1983	46,693	15,499	13,160	360	1,704	4,428	12,519	686	135	816
1984	49,901	15,917	13,516	385	1,851	4,607	14,537	773	104	1,052
1985	50,676	15,093	12,676	364	1,874	4,814	15,267	827	102	1,196
1986	58,632	13,853	10,881	446	2,316	7,229	19,613	1,258	131	1,840
1987	85,342	19,060	14,450	786	3,571	10,760	32,575	1,544	714	3,099
1988	123,017	22,960	16,811	889	4,817	18,682	53,805	2,001	2,357	4,346
1989	159,380	25,845	17,803	919	6,538	22,490	78,343	2,278	3,336	5,511

(continued)

	Others								
		Official transactions	Private transactions						
				Office expences	Patent royalties	Fees	Non-merchandise insurance	Advertising	Film rentals
Variables	MSERVICEMIS$	MGOVT$		MOFFICE$	MPATENT$	MFEES$	MINSOTHER$		
1970	1,673	80	1,593	238	413	462	203	62	19
1971	1,933	58	1,875	267	469	556	242	69	24
1972	2,432	72	2,360	326	546	703	301	83	29
1973	3,293	73	3,220	417	681	1,066	360	128	39
1974	4,176	78	4,098	478	737	1,532	491	123	34
1975	5,069	76	4,993	557	697	1,913	687	143	51
1976	5,426	113	5,313	640	800	1,978	780	168	75
1977	6,425	138	6,289	771	986	2,189	958	213	63
1978	8,074	188	7,886	901	1,169	2,677	1,149	276	100
1979	9,097	252	8,845	968	1,274	3,146	819	386	115
1980	10,654	264	10,390	1,190	1,328	4,147	309	504	105
1981	13,700	305	13,395	1,487	1,712	5,405	280	491	79
1982	13,486	306	13,180	1,708	1,754	4,991	179	536	76
1983	14,247	317	13,930	1,793	1,982	4,444	183	553	145
1984	14,840	331	14,509	1,858	2,274	4,701	277	629	105
1985	15,502	392	15,110	2,065	2,361	4,596	178	759	109
1986	17,937	453	17,484	2,334	3,237	4,861	400	954	120
1987	22,947	441	22,506	3,413	3,814	6,589	406	1,091	243
1988	27,570	523	27,047	3,952	5,015	8,003	452	1,496	276
1989	32,702	550	32,152	4,519	5,324	10,934	390	1,748	513

Notes: 1. Including processing fees from 1980.
2. Excluding Japanese insurance companies payments of insurance money and including their receipts of premiums on imports.
Source: Same as Table 9-1.

opposed to discuss the trade in services on GATT negotiation table for fear of being integrated in the competitive global market prematurely.

In this context, trade in services promises to become the focal point of international negotiations in the years to come.

For Japan, too, this aspect of economic activity deserves careful scrutiny because her economy is shifting toward services at a rapid pace.[7] As can be seen in table 9-1, the balance of trade in services has been Japan's deficit, the magnitude of which amounting to about 5 to 7 million dollars in the late 1970s. In 1980–1981, the deficit reached 11 to 14 million dollars. The 1988 figure stood at minus 11.3 billion dollars.

(1) Transportation: As for transportation, which is composed of freight, insurance on shipment, and passenger fares, we observe moderate but continued growth up to 1980–1981 in both payments and receipts. Japan has been a net importer of transportation services. In the 1980s, we observe tapering off in the absolute amount. This item needless to say is closely tied to international trade, or the bulkiness of the cargo involved to be more precise. Thus, the lack of growth of transportation item is largely attributable to general decline in foreign trade in physical quantity, a phenomenon related to the declining imports of natural resources and shift to high-value added exports. One thing noteworthy in this regard is the rapid increase of passenger fares on the import side, which is due to the rapid increase of Japanese tourists to which we turn next.

(2) Travel: Under 'travel' are recorded payments of Japanese tourists on the debit side and the spending of foreign tourists on credit side. As a reflection of booming tourism, imports amounted to 18.7 billion dollars in 1988 as compared to 2.9 billion dollars worth of exports.

It should be added that this was not totally unrelated to the official policy of promoting overseas tours, in addition to being the outcome of rising income and relative cheapening of overseas tourism due to appreciation of the yen currency. The Ministry of Transportation launched a plan named "Ten Million Plan" which aimed at sending out ten million Japanese tourists annually by 1991, thereby reducing the current account surplus by 20 billion dollars per year.

According to the balance of payments statistics for 1988, the net payments related to overseas travel (i.e., travel and passenger fares) amounted to 19.5 billion dollars. This is 1.7 times larger than the figure for the previous year when the net payments stood at 11.4 billion dollars. According to the Ministry of Transportation, overseas travelers totalled 8.409 million persons in 1988, exceeding the 1987 figure by 1.580 million persons. The number of travelers is rapidly approaching the target of ten million set for 1991. Total payments for shopping, hotel stays, and restaurant bills, which are included under the item "travel" in the statistics, amounted to 18.7 billion dollars (15.8 billion dollars in net terms which subtracts the spending by foreign visitors in Japan). Total payments of passenger fares amounted to 4.8 billion dollars (3.7 billion dollars in net terms). The contributing factors include the increased number of travelers abroad reflecting both appreciation of the yen, the favorable economic conditions in Japan, and the increased spending per person (an average Japanese traveler spent 1576 dollars in 1987, which increased in 1988 to 2218 dollars).

(3) Investment income: This item, which includes income from both direct investment and portfolio investment, has shown remarkable growth in both receipts and payments. Such trend was accelerated by the abolishment of 'real-demand principle' in transactions involving foreign exchange in April 1984 and opening of offshore market in Tokyo (JOM) in December 1986. In addition, the Ministry of Finance published "Prospects Concerning the Liberalization and Internationalization of Money and Capital Market" in June 1987, which served as the guiding principle for further liberalization of the capital market.[8]

The Japan's receipts stood at 11.1 billion dollars in 1980, which jumped to 49.2 billion dollars in 1987 and 74.8 billion dollars in 1988 (table 9-2-a); Japan's payments stood at 10.3 billion dollars in 1980, which jumped to 32.6 billion dollars in 1987 and 53.8 billion dollars in 1988. Such rapid increase has been the trend since the previous decade, but now the amount reached a magnitude which cannot be neglected in the world economy. What is to be noted in addition is the fact that the balance has turned to Japan's favor. We may say that foreign investment has been promoted in both outward and inward directions but that the net investment income tend to be positive for Japan. As for the foreseeable future, we should expect the trend to continue because, as we shall see below, Japan's foreign investment is being expanded quite rapidly.

(4) Others: This item includes office expenses, patent royalties, various fees including agents' fees, nonmerchandise insurance, advertising, film rentals, etc. The items under this category tend to increase reflecting increased activities of foreign firms and governments within Japan, and vice versa. The net balance has been Japan's deficit consistently. Among the items included, patent royalties deserve particular attention, to which we turn next.

9-4 Technology balance of payments

Japan has been a technology importer throughout the catching-up phase and it is clearly reflected in the increasing trends in the payment of patent royalties. Technology export, on the other hand, was rather meager in earlier years. The figure in 1970 stood at a mere 55 million

Table 9-3 Technology balance of payments from alternative sources

Item / F.Y.	Statistics of Bank of Japan			Bureau of Statistics		
	Receipts (A)	Payments (B)	Ratio (A)/(B)	Receipts (C)	Payments (D)	Ratio (C)/(D)
	million dollar	(billion yen)		billion yen		
1970	59 (21)	433 (155)	0.136	— (—)	— (—)	— (—)
1971	60 (20)	488 (170)	0.123	27 (11)	134 (15)	0.202 (0.710)
1972	74 (22)	572 (173)	0.129	42 (18)	173 (14)	0.242 (1.259)
1973	88 (23)	715 (194)	0.123	50 (24)	173 (19)	0.293 (1.266)
1974	113 (33)	718 (209)	0.157	57 (20)	159 (14)	0.357 (1.373)
1975	161 (47)	712 (173)	0.129	66 (18)	169 (13)	0.394 (1.419)
1976	173 (51)	846 (250)	0.204	83 (27)	177 (17)	0.470 (1.513)
1977	233 (62)	1,027 (275)	0.227	93 (36)	190 (16)	0.491 (2,149)
1978	274 (57)	1,241 (261)	0.221	122 (47)	192 (38)	0.635 (1.234)
1979	342 (74)	1,260 (276)	0,271	133 (52)	240 (26)	0.553 (1.943)
1980	378 (85)	1,439 (326)	0,263	159 (74)	239 (27)	0.666 (2.683)
1981	537 (118)	1,711 (377)	0.314	175 (70)	259 (24)	0.674 (2.841)
1982	527 (131)	1,796 (447)	0,293	184 (63)	282 (44)	0.654 (1.425)
1983	624 (148)	2,079 (493)	0.300	240 (74)	279 (42)	0.863 (1.765)
1984	693 (164)	2,317 (550)	0.299	277 (90)	281 (31)	0.986 (2.855)
1985	746 (177)	2,522 (601)	0,296	234 (73)	293 (33)	0.799 (2.198)
1986	1,009 (170)	3,375 (568)	0.299	224 (51)	260 (33)	0.860 (0.514)
1987	1,385 (200)	4,177 (603)	0.332	215 (44)	283 (56)	0.761 (0.797)
1988	1,681 (215)	5,076 (650)	0.331	246 (47)	312 (54)	0.789 (0.868)

Note: The ratio based on the Bureau of Statistics figures in parenthesis refers to new contracts only.
Source: Bank of Japan, *Balance of International Payments;* Statistical Bureau, Management and Coordination Agency, *Report on the Survey of Research and Development.*

dollars as opposed to imports which stood at 413 million dollars in the same year (tables 9-2-a and b). In recent years, especially in the 1980s, Japanese technology exports began to rise steadily. On net basis, however, Japan records a deficit in this item because royalty payments tend to increase with the expansion of industrial production and increased finished goods imports. For instance, net payment of patent royalties in 1988 reached 5.0 billion dollars, or an increase of 31.5% over the previous year, largely due to an upswing of the economy. The recent trend does not represent lack of research and development efforts in Japan but is a reflection of past trend when Japan was a technology importer.

The overall technology balance of payments is shown in table 9-3 which draws on two alternative sources.[9] Japan still relies heavily on imported technology, while the export/import ratio has consistently improved. The Bank of Japan statistics show the ratio, which stood at 0.136 in 1970 has increased to 0.263 in 1980 and 0.331 in 1988; the Bureau of Statistics figures show an improvement from 0.202 in 1970 to 0.666 in 1980 and 0.789 in 1988 (the ratio pertinent of new contracts only are much higher, as indicated in the last column of the table).

9-5 Long-term capital transactions

One of the drastic changes in Japan's balance of payments can be observed in the capital transaction sphere. The empirical figures are provided in tables 9-4-a and b. On the asset side, which represents Japan's capital export, we observe that annual outflow stood at a mere 2.0 billion dollars in 1970. The 1980 figure was 10.8 billion dollars, a sizeable increase in a decade. More recently however, the annual outflow exceeded 132 billion dollars in 1987 and 149 billion dollars in 1988.

Long-term capital transactions include direct investment, trade credits, loans, securities, and subscription to international institutions.

Direct investment increased rapidly and reached 19.5 billion dollars in 1987 and 34.2 billion dollars in 1988 as compared to 2.4 billion dollars in 1980. This trend is attributable mainly to two factors. One is the local production in the manufacturing sector. Japanese producers are increasing foreign investment in oder to cope with the appreciation of the yen and worsening trade conflicts. Second is the investment in foreign financial institutions. This reflects the liberalization of financial markets in Japan and in recipient countries.

Loans are extended by the Japan Export-Import Bank and the Overseas Economic Cooperation Fund, as well as long-term lendings by banks and other private firms. Repayments increased rapidly since 1985, but drawings also increased reflecting yen-credit by the Japanese gov-

Table 9-4 Long term capital transactions

a. assets[1]

(unit: million dollars)

Year	Total	Direct investment	Trade credit extended	Loans extended			Securities				Others	
					Drawings	Repayments		Stocks	Bonds	Yen bonds[2]		Subscription to Int'l institutions
Variables	EKLONG$	EKIF$	EKCREDITS$	EKLOAN$			EKSEC$				EKOTHER$	
1970	2,031	355	787	628	675	47	62				199	74
1971	2,231	360	863	594	652	58	195				219	60
1972	5,020	723	324	1,684	1,761	77	1,188				1,101	104
1973	8,468	1,904	1,048	3,038	3,424	386	1,787				691	179
1974	4,063	2,012	672	1,136	2,016	880	141				102	206
1975	3,392	1,763	29	1,295	1,947	652	24				281	234
1976	4,559	1,991	571	1,525	2,287	762	146				326	272
1977	5,247	1,645	1,388	472	2,469	1,997	1,718	7	735	976	24	377
1978	14,872	2,371	142	6,299	7,421	1,122	5,300	124	1,897	3,279	760	470
1979	16,294	2,898	(−)1,288	8,102	10,666	2,564	5,865	575	3,385	1,905	717	655
1980	10,817	2,385	717	2,553	4,878	2,325	3,753	(−) 213	2,996	970	1,409	1,034
1981	22,809	4,894	2,731	5,083	7,647	2,564	8,777	240	5,810	2,727	1,324	683
1982	27,418	4,540	3,239	7,902	10,966	3,064	9,743	151	6,076	3,516	1,994	431
1983	32,459	3,612	2,589	8,425	11,815	3,390	16,024	661	12,505	2,858	1,809	953
1984	56,775	5,965	4,937	11,922	16,964	5,042	30,795	51	26,773	3,971	3,156	1,648
1985	81,815	6,452	2,817	10,427	17,387	6,960	59,773	995	53,479	5,299	2,346	872
1986	132,095	14,480	1,836	9,281	19,958	10,677	101,977	7,048	93,024	1,905	4,521	1,157
1987	132,830	19,519	535	16,190	35,656	19,466	87,757	16,874	72,885	(−)2,002	8,829	1,771
1988	149,883	34,210	6,939	15,211	42,395	27,184	86,949	2,993	85,812	(−)1,850	6,574	2,045
1989	192,118	44,130	4,002	22,495	55,281	32,786	113,178	17,887	94,083	1,208	8,313	1,426

Notes: 1. Minus sign indicates a decrease in assets (capital inflow).
2. Through 1984, including issues and redemptions of foreign currency-denominated bonds by nonresidents in the domestic markets.

Source: Same as Table 9-1.

b. liabilities[1]

(unit: million dollars)

Year	Total[2]	Direct investment	Trade Credit received	Loans received			Securities[2]				Others
					Drawings	Repayments		Stocks	Bonds	Foreign currency bonds	
Variable	MKLONG$	MKIF$	MKCREDITS$	MKLOAN$			MKSEC$				MKOTHER$
1970	440	94	7	80	537	457	2,963			44	(−) 37
1971	1,149	210	8	20	558	538	948			8	(−) 37
1972	533	169	11	(−) 197	409	606	591			(−) 105	(−) 41
1973	(−) 1,282	(−) 42	(−) 12	(−) 313	327	640	(−) 789			198	(−) 126
1974	182	202	(−) 6	(−) 232	263	495	(−) 785			80	1,003
1975	3,120	226	(−) 26	166	554	388	2,753			1,235	1
1976	3,575	113	(−) 5	326	633	307	3,104			1,509	37
1977	2,063	21	(−) 13	(−) 324	287	611	2,355	(−) 778	2,034	1,099	24
1978	2,483	8	(−) 22	(−) 7	414	421	2,487	(−) 807	2,461	833	17
1979	3,318	239	(−) 33	(−) 169	277	446	4,282	329	1,743	2,210	(−)1,001
1980	13,141	278	(−) 16	(−) 231	265	496	13,113	6,546	5,331	1,236	(−) 3
1981	13,137	189	(−) 15	(−) 186	253	439	13,220	5,916	5,936	1,368	(−) 71
1982	12,449	439	(−) 6	(−) 181	66	247	11,860	2,549	5,030	4,281	337
1983	14,759	416	8	(−) 37	242	279	14,148	6,126	2,359	5,663	224
1984	7,124	(−) 10	3	(−) 77	198	275	7,194	(−) 3,610	3,454	7,350	14
1985	17,273	642	29	(−) 75	158	233	16,741	(−) 673	4,524	12,890	(−) 64
1986	634	226	(−) 40	(−) 34	183	217	545	(−)15,758	(−) 2,109	18,412	(−) 63
1987	(−) 3,702	1,165	(−) 1	(−) 119	229	348	(−) 6,081	(−)42,835	6,675	30,079	1,334
1988	18,953	(−) 485	(−) 18	(−) 82	29	111	20,298	6,810	(−)21,628	35,116	(−) 760
1989	102,872	(−)1,054	(−) 9	17,813	18,057	244	85,144	6,998	2,400	75,746	978

Notes: 1. Minus sign indicates a decrease in liabilities (capital outflow).
2. Excluding bond transactions with repurchase agreement ("gensaki").
3. Retroactive figure due to change in tabulation items.

Source: Same as Table 9-1.

Table 9-5 External assets and liabilities

a. assets

(unit: million dollars)

Year	Long-term assets									Short-term assets	Total external assets
		Direct investments	Trade credits externded		Loans extended		Securities	Others			
				Private		Private			Private		
Variables	KOUTLONG$	KOUTIF$	KOUTCREDIT$		KOUTLOAN$		KOUTSEC$	KOUTOTHER$			KOOUTSUM$
1970	9,183	1,560	4,353		2,734		766	589			
1971	11,414	1,920	5,216		3,328		961	808			
1972	16,434	2,643	5,540		5,012		2,149	1,909			
1973	24,902	4,547	6,588		8,050		3,936	2,600			
1974	28,965	6,559	7,260		9,186		4,077	2,702			
1975	32,357	8,322	7,162	6,832	10,481	4,984	4,104	2,288	280	25,977	58,334
1976	36,899	10,313	7,733	7,403	11,952	5,384	4,158	2,743	528	31,091	67,990
1977	42,085	11,958	9,121	8,791	12,344	4,322	5,595	3,067	511	37,925	80,060
1978	63,299	14,329	11,182	10,753	21,679	8,785	12,204	3,905	396	55,426	118,725
1979	83,663	17,227	11,043	10,468	31,512	14,938	19,003	4,878	505	51,702	135,365
1980	87,881	19,612	10,462	9,773	30,346	14,839	21,439	6,022	841	71,699	159,580
1981	117,090	24,506	14,373	13,225	38,880	18,944	31,538	7,793	1,056	92,167	209,257
1982	139,451	28,969	17,027	15,905	43,664	23,228	40,070	9,719	1,853	88,237	227,688
1983	170,905	32,178	19,275	18,110	51,739	29,266	56,115	11,598	2,382	101,051	271,956
1984	229,184	37,921	24,013	22,824	65,092	40,601	87,578	14,580	3,022	112,024	341,208
1985	301,297	43,974	24,665	23,603	70,163	46,870	145,748	16,747	4,263	136,404	437,701
1986	476,136	58,071	33,415	31,992	102,769	69,211	257,933	23,948	7,497	251,170	727,306
1987	646,181	77,022	38,853	37,189	140,614	97,469	339,677	50,015	13,743	425,450	1071,631
1988	832,669	110,780	50,676	48,791	179,233	123,663	427,218	64,762	17,716	636,678	1469,347

b. liabilities[1]

(unit: million dollars)

Year	Total[2]	Direct investment	Trade Credit received	Loans received			Securities[3]				Others
					Drawings	Repayments		Stocks	Bonds	Foreign currency bonds	
Variable	MKLONG$	MKIF$	MKCREDITS$	MKLOAN$			MKSEC$				MKOTHER$
1970	440	94	7	80	537	457	2,963			44	(−) 37
1971	1,149	210	8	20	558	538	948			8	(−) 37
1972	533	169	11	(−) 197	409	606	591			(−) 105	(−) 41
1973	(−) 1,282	(−) 42	(−) 12	(−) 313	327	640	(−) 789			198	(−) 126
1974	182	202	(−) 6	(−) 232	263	495	(−) 785			80	1,003
1975	3,120	226	(−) 26	166	554	388	2,753			1,235	1
1976	3,575	113	(−) 5	326	633	307	3,104			1,509	37
1977	2,063	21	(−) 13	(−) 324	287	611	2,355	(−) 778	2,034	1,099	24
1978	2,483	8	(−) 22	(−) 7	414	421	2,487	(−) 807	2,461	833	17
1979	3,318	239	(−) 33	(−) 169	277	446	4,282	329	1,743	2,210	(−)1,001
1980	13,141	278	(−) 16	(−) 231	265	496	13,113	6,546	5,331	1,236	(−) 3
1981	13,137	189	(−) 15	(−) 186	253	439	13,220	5,916	5,936	1,368	(−) 71
1982	12,449	439	(−) 6	(−) 181	66	247	11,860	2,549	5,030	4,281	337
1983	14,759	416	8	(−) 37	242	279	14,148	6,126	2,359	5,663	224
1984	7,124	(−) 10	3	(−) 77	198	275	7,194	(−) 3,610	3,454	7,350	14
1985	17,273	642	29	(−) 75	158	233	16,741	(−) 673	4,524	12,890	(−) 64
1986	634	226	(−) 40	(−) 34	183	217	545	(−)15,758	(−) 2,109	18,412	(−) 63
1987	(−) 3,702	1,165	(−) 1	(−) 119	229	348	(−) 6,081	(−)42,835	6,675	30,079	1,334
1988	18,953	(−) 485	(−) 18	(−) 82	29	111	20,298	6,810	(−)21,628	35,116	(−) 760
1989	102,872	(−)1,054	(−) 9	17,813	18,057	244	85,144	6,998	2,400	75,746	978

Notes: 1. Minus sign indicates a decrease in liabilities (capital outflow).
2. Excluding bond transactions with repurchase agreement ("gensaki").
3. Retroactive figure due to change in tabulation items.
Source: Same as Table 9-1.

ernment. Net effect was an outflow of 16.2 billion dollars in 1987 and 15.2 billion dollars in 1988.

The rapid increase in the outflow is also attributable to acquisition of stocks and bonds, which amounted to 16.8 billion dollars and 72.9 billion dollars (net basis) in 1987, respectively. The 1988 figure was smaller for the former reflecting large amount of disposal, presumably attributable to the Black Monday collapse of the New York market in October 1987 and ensuing stagnation of the market, and the net amount was recorded at 3.0 billion dollars for the former. Net purchases of bonds amounted to 85.8 billion dollars. Contributing factors were the stability in the exchange rate and the widened margin of interest differentials between Japan and foreign financial markets.

Issues of yen-denominated bonds by nonresidents showed considerable increase in recent years, but redemptions of the past issues which bore higher interest rates also increased rapidly.

The recent upsurge of outward investment can be explained by the following factors:

a. liberalization of capital market, both in Japan and in major industrial countries;

b. growing saving surplus over investment in Japan; or its reflection in the current balance surplus;

c. appreciation of the yen which made direct investment overseas more attractive by relative cheapening of labor and other inputs overseas and, at the same time, doubled the amount of available saving fund in Japan in terms of the dollar; and

d. very low interest rate which emerged in the Japanese financial market as against relatively high rate in the United States and elsewhere.

On the other hand, inward investment showed a rather complex trend. Total foreign investment in Japan, including both direct and portfolio investment, stood at 0.4 billion dollars in 1970, 13.1 billion dollars in 1980, and 17.2 billion dollars in 1985. But in subsequent years contraction has occurred in securities investment. From 16.7 billion dollars in 1985, it dropped to 0.5 billion dollars in 1986 and then to net outflow of 6.1 billion in 1987. This reversal of the flow has occurred following the collapse of the stock market in 1985 which necessitated foreign (mainly American) investors to cash in their investment. The shrinkage may also indicate pessimism among foreign investors regarding the market situation in Japan. The stock and security prices are going up but foreign investors may have noticed some unhealthy "boom" element in the market craze. The inflow of direct investment also exhibited rather irregular movement in recent years after secular gains in the early 1980s.

Short-term capital transactions show considerable fluctuation on net basis as can be observed in table 9-1.

9-6 External assets

The outstanding external assets and liabilities are shown in table 9-5-a and b. Needless to say, this table can be reached by adding up the annual flow figures concerning long-term and short-term capital transactions. In 1970, assets and liabilities almost matched at about 9 to 10 billion dollars. In 1980, assets amounted nearly double the liabilities and stood at 87.9 billion dollars. Total long-term external assets in 1988 stood at 832.7 billion dollars as compared to 311.6 billion dollar worth external liabilities. It is wrong to conclude from the developing disparity between outward investment and inward investment that access to the Japanese capital market is limited. This divergence should be interpreted as a reflection of growing investment fund in Japan.[10] When it comes to short-term capital, liabilities stand nearly double the assets. Actually this has been so as far as the period under consideration is concerned.

At the end of 1988, Japan's total outstanding external assets stood at 1469.3 billion dollars. This is 37.1% larger than the previous year when the figure first surpassed trillion dollar level. Outstanding external liabilities also rose by 41.7% to reach 1177.6 billion dollars. Thus, net external assets stood at 291.7 billion dollars at the year-end 1988. Japanese external assets had swollen from 7.0 billion dollars in 1975 and 11.5 billion dollars in 1980 to 129.8 billion dollars in 1985.

Among the asset items, short-term financial account showed an expansion of about 50% over the previous year to reach 637 billion dollars, an increase which is attributed to the opening of Tokyo offshore market at the end of 1986 which helped promote financial transactions. Security investment increased 25.8% and the total amount reached 427.2 billion dollars. Direct foreign investment showed an increase of 43.8% over 1987, totaling 110.8 billion dollars.

Among liabilities, an increase is recorded for security investment to Japanese private business. This item amounted to 298 billion dollars, or an increase of 33%. Financial account also increased 45.6% and reached 866 billion dollars.

How does this compare with other countries? The statistics for 1988 are not available except Japan, but Table 9-6 provides the clue for the conditions in 1987 when comparable figures are available. The United States has the largest assets of the four countries listed in the table but she also has the largest liabilities. In 1987, net asset was negative, showing that the United States is a net debtor.[11] The net position of the United Kingdom stood at 167.5 billion dollars and that for West Germany, 167.6

Table 9-6 External assets and liabilities in selected countries

(unit: billion dollars, %)

	Japan				U.S.	Germany	U.K.
	1980	1985	1987	1988	1987	1987	1987
Assets total	159.6	437.7	1071.6	1469.3	1167.8	663.1	1316.4
Public sector	47.0	64.5	163.3	202.4	134.2	127.5	68.1
Private sector	112.6	373.2	990.6	1267.0	1033.6	535.6	1248.3
Direct investment	19.6	44.0	77.0	110.8	308.9	65.3	171.0
Liabilities total	148.0	307.9	830.9	1177.6	1536.0	495.5	1149.0
Public sector	18.8	39.1	69.0	58.2	283.1	126.8	50.1
Private sector	129.2	268.8	761.9	1119.4	1252.9	363.3	1098.9
Direct investment	3.3	4.7	9.0	10.4	261.2	39.7	100.0
Net assets	11.5	129.8	240.7	291.7	(−)368.2	167.6	167.5

Source: Bank of Japan, *Comparative Economic and Financial Statistics, Japan and Other Major Countries*. The data for the U.S. is from *Sarvey of Current Business:* for Germany, *Monthly Report of the Deutsche Bundesbank;* for the U.K., from *Quarterly Bulletin*.

billion dollars in the same year.[12] The Japanese figure, as we have seen, stood at 240.7 billion dollars in 1987 and 291.7 billion dollars in 1988 (tables 9-5 and 9-6). The 1988 year end figures for other countries are not yet available. However, for the United States, it is estimated that net asset has expanded its negative margin judging from the current account deficit of 130 billion dollars during 1988. As for Germany, it is estimated that net asset has expanded further judging from the current account surplus of 40 billion dollars during 1988. The portion of the United Kingdom is difficult to assess from the current account balance because of the existence of international financial center. We may conclude that Japan's position as the largest net creditor remained for the four consecutive years.

Looking at the components of assets, we notice that the share of direct investment is relatively low in Japan. Despite rapid growth of direct investment, the ratio to total assets stands at 7.5% in 1988. The U.S. ratio is highest at 26.5%.

Few words of caution are in order in international comparisons of external assets and liabilities.[13] First, only limited countries publish statistics on external assets and liabilities. They include the United States, the United Kingdom, Germany, and Japan. Second, the contents of assets and liabilities may differ among countries. Unlike the balance of payments statistics which are compiled according to the IMF manual, there is no uniform standard which is accepted worldwide for the compilation of data concerning external assets and liabilities. Nor there is no obligation for its compilation. These factors make international comparisons on uniform basis rather difficult. It should be noted in this connection that the asset figures are the accumulated sum of current price flows over the years, implying that in the case of a long-standing investor such as the United States and the United Kingdom, outstanding overseas investment tend to be understated in real values. The liabilities on the other hand were accumulated fairly recently and may reflect the current value.

9-7 Japan's posture in foreign economic cooperation

The unrequited transfers which appear in the balance of payments statistics (table 9-1) show consistent and expanding deficit for Japan. The 1970 figure stood at 0.2 billion dollars, which rose to 1.5 billion dollars in 1980 and 4.1 billion dollars in 1988. This item is related to foreign economic cooperation to a large degree in the case of Japan. Other items related to foreign economic cooperation are "subscription to international institutions" and a part of direct investment and loans and credits which involve grant element.

In order to focus on the aspect of foreign assistance in a consistent manner, we prepared tables 9-6 and 9-7 which show Japan's economic cooperation statistics according to the definition of the Development Assistance Committee of the OECD.

There are several factors to which we should address ourselves. First is the ratio of development assistance to GNP which is reported in table 9-8. This ratio is in general interpreted as an indicator of a country's effort in economic cooperation. The ratio has been high in the Netherlands and Nordic countries such as Sweden and Denmark where the ratio exceeds 2% and even approached 3% in some instances. The same can be said for the United Kingdom and France, presumably reflecting strong ties which exist with former colonies, and the ratio generally stands above 1%. The record for the U.S. has been mixed, and the latest figure (1987) stood at 0.29% (table 9-8). The Japanese record has not been particularly impressive in the past, but more recently, it is around 0.8% to 0.9% of the GNP. The DAC average ranged around 0.5 to 0.7% in recent years.

Second is the official flows as opposed to private flows. The latter is interpreted to represent market transactions rather than pure economic aid. The ratio of official development assistance (ODA) to GNP stood at 0.29% in 1986 and 0.31% in 1988, slightly below the DAC average of 0.35%. The U.S. figure stood at 0.23%.

Third is the total magnitude. In 1987, Japan turned to be the largest provider of economic cooperation.[14] The Japanese aid amounts to about 22.7% of the DAC total.

Japan adopted a policy of increasing economic cooperation in the 1980s. There can be various means of contributing to the world community. Some countries do that by providing defense umbrella, but Japan's

Table 9-7 Economic cooperation

(unit: million dollars)

	Total	Total official flows	Official development assistance (ODA)	Bilateral official development assistance	Contributions to multilateral institutions	Others official flows (OOF)	Private flows at market terms (PF)
1970	1,824	1,152	458	372	87	694	669
1971	2,141	1,162	511	432	79	651	976
1972	2,725	1,468	611	478	133	856	1,252
1973	5,844	2,190	1,011	765	246	1,179	3,648
1974	2,962	1,915	1,126	880	246	789	1,039
1975	2,880	2,517	1,148	850	297	1,369	352
1976	4,003	2,438	1,105	753	352	1,333	1,548
1977	5,535	3,047	1,424	899	525	1,623	2,470
1978	10,704	4,368	2,215	1,531	684	2,153	6,317
1979	7,556	2,848	2,638	1,921	716	210	4,689
1980	6,766	4,782	3,304	1,961	1,343	1,478	1,958
1981	12,231	6,194	3,171	2,260	911	3,023	6,011
1982	8,768	5,814	3,023	2,367	656	2,791	2,928
1983	8,663	5,715	3,761	2,425	1,336	1,954	2,918
1984	16,049	5,062	4,319	2,427	1,064	743	10,946
1985	11,619	3,495	3,797	2,557	1,240	(−) 302	7,646
1986	14,578	4,910	5,634	3,846	1,788	(−) 724	9,586
1987	20,462	5,647	7,454	5,248	2,207	(−)1,808	14,723
1988	21,423	8,495	9,134	6,422	2,712	(−) 639	12,822

Note: Total includes grants by private voluntary agencies.
Source: Development Assistance Committee, *Development Cooperation.*

Table 9-8 Economic cooperation in selected countries

(unit: million dollars, %)

Year	1970	1980	1985	1986	1987	1988
Total						
Japan	1,824	6,815	11,619	14,578	20,349	21,424
United Stated	6,304	13,852	1,816	18,231	13,193	17,505
F.R.Germany	1,487	10,633	5,749	7,889	8,843	11,811
France	1,835	11,631	8,874	9,176	8,671	n.a.
United Kingdom	1,247	11,989	2,463	6,697	3,430	2,952
DAC total	15,755	75,303	45,163	68,845	65,743	n.a.
Percent of GNP						
Japan	0.92	0.66	0.87	0.74	0.85	0.75
United Stated	0.62	0.53	0.05	0.43	0.29	0.36
F.R.Germany	0.79	1.30	0.92	0.88	0.79	0.98
France	1.24	1.78	1.74	1.27	0.99	n.a.
United Kingdom	1.01	2.28	0.54	1.21	0.50	0.36
DAC total	0.78	1.04	0.53	0.66	0.55	n.a.

Notes: Figures refer to net disbursements. Total amount is the sum of official development assistance (ODA), other official flows (OOF), and private flows (PF).
Source: Development Assistance Committee, Organisation for Economic Cooperation and Development, *Development Cooperation.*

military capability is a very limited one and public opinion also does not support this approach. Another form of contribution is through economic aid which by easing the burden of economic development would help ease political and economic tension. Conceived this way, the government has allocated increasing share of the resources at disposal to economic cooperation even at a time of budget squeeze.[15]

Economic cooperation includes flows of private funds such as export credit exceeding one year, direct investment, other bilateral securities investment, lending to international institutions, etc. In order to reconcile economic assistance data with those in the balance of payments statistics, we list below the amounts of export credit and direct investment included in economic cooperation statistics.[16] Figures are in net disbursement basis. The difference between total and private flows is attributable "official" flows which are listed among "other official flows" in table 9-7.

(in billion dollars)

	Export credits		Direct investment	
	Total	Private	Total	Private
1970[17]	737	387	408	265
1975	422	83	1249	233
1980	897	74	1673	906
1985	−1146	−994	1044	1046
1986	−659	199	3093	2761
1987	−966	1081	7703	7421

In this respect, one can not neglect the role played by private flows. Especially noteworthy is the rapid increase in direct investment which is now comparable to official development assistance in its magnitude. Such trend is closely related to the fact that the recipient countries of Japanese aid, namely Asian NIEs, have graduated from the state of less developedness. There are increasing number of cases where they do not require economic aid as such. Even direct investment is being redirected from those countries to ASEAN (and China before the stalemate in 1989). For those countries where industrialization is already underway, it is probably more important for Japan to accept their exports, supplemented by development assistance where required.

As for official development assistance (ODA), the growth in the recent past has been cited as "outstanding" by the DAC. This refers to the annual growth of 32.3% during 1987 to reach 7.5 billion dollars. As a result, Japan's share in total ODA has risen from 15.4% in 1986 to 17.9% in 1987. Japan's ODA has been directed toward Asian countries for historical and geographical reasons, and about 65% of total ODA is distributed to this region. The importance for directing more funds to Africa is well recognized and bilateral grant for this region has increased. However, lending stagnated due to worsening debt-service problem.

The share of the region in total ODA has decreased from 15.4% in 1986 to 13.4% in 1987.

The share of Latin America also continued to decline. It now stands at around 8% compared to 10% in 1983. This is also a reflection of debt problem among Latin American countries where rescheduling is contemplated in many cases. The income level in this region is relatively high compared to other developing areas, and there are not many countries amenable for economic aid.

Contribution to multilateral institutions is a preferred way of distributing aid because it guarantees neutrality from the donor countries and because it enables to utilize the speciality and know-how of the international institutions. About 30% of Japan's ODA is distributed through this channel. Of the 2.2 billion dollar aid through multilateral institutions in 1987, 359 million dollars went to UN organizations and 1.816 billion dollars to development financing organizations such as IDA and ADB.[18]

Japan implemented a 30 billion-dollar recycling plan for LDCs for the purpose of correcting the deficient flow of funds. As far as the record in the 1980s is concerned, we may say that Japan's role in economic cooperation has been strengthened considerably.

9-8 Determination of the exchange rate

The performance of the Japanese economy with respect to foreign investment as well as trade in goods and services has been one of the focal points in the world economy in the 1980s. Sometimes it is regarded as a dynamic factor stimulating global economy, and sometimes it is condemned as a disturbance to the stability of the existing world economic regime. The examination of the structure of the balance of payments in this chapter revealed the magnitude of the change that have occurred in recent years.

Let us now turn to the determination of the exchange rate. Exchange rate has been subject to policy discussion, although exchange rates among major currencies have been freely flexible through the market. The agreement among G5 countries in 1985 is a typical example. The agreement marked the termination of the years of dollar appreciation which continued during the 1981–1985 period. Even on daily basis, central banks are concerned about keeping the exchange rate at an 'appropriate' level by manipulating the interest rates. There is no denying the fact, however, that the exchange rate determination in the long-run reflects economic fundamentals.

Radical change in the exchange rates in the 1980s is a testimony of

Figure 9-2 Exchange rate determination, simulation result

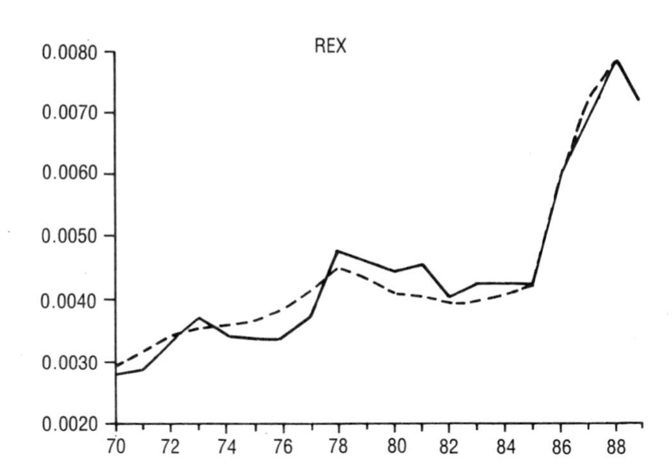

Note: Exchange rate is the period average, and is expressed in terms of dollar per yen. Solid line represents actual and dotted line simulated values.
Source: COMPASS simulation result.

equally radical changes in the economic reality, which include the following.
(1) Macroeconomic saving-investment balance: Savings in Japan has been strong mainly reflecting life-cycle of the population whereas investment tended to stagnate pending structural change of the economy from heavy industry to electronics and services, then activated toward the end of the 1980s reflecting innovation. Government investment was also constrained during most of the period under consideration due to budgetary deficit; but this also improved more recently.[19]
(2) Decline in oil prices: Official price of Arabian light now stands at around 18 to 19 dollars, compared to 32 dollars in 1980 and 34 dollars in 1981. Coupled with energy conservation effort and structural change of the economy, this resulted in a sharp decline in Japanese oil imports. Mineral fuels and related materials share nearly 1/2 of total Japanese imports, thus, the impact was rather marked.[20] It should be noted that price elasticity of demand for this category of products is rather low.
(3) Surge of technology-intensive exports: Technological change attributable to the electronics revolution gave a distinct advantage to Japanese exports in recent years. New products incorporating C-C-C technology enjoy competitiveness in the world market.[21] Here too, it is noted that technology factor tends to make the product immune to price

change in the sense that the product in question is not available from other countries.

(4) Huge capital outflows: Particularly marked is an increase in the acquisition of bonds induced by the liberalization of foreign investment in December 1980, both inward and outward.[22] High interest rate abroad, especially in the United States, prompted capital outflows. Direct foreign investment is also increasing at a rapid pace from around 1985, after suffering a slight setback in 1982–1983.

In examining the determination of the exchange rate, therefore, we have looked at both economic fundamentals and policy changes. Our exchange rate equation is as follows (observation period is from 1970 to 1988).

$$
\begin{aligned}
REX = {} & 0.000000019 \text{ BPCURRENT\$} - 0.000000004 \text{ KOUTLONG\$} \\
& (1.91) \qquad\qquad\qquad\qquad\quad (-1.55) \\
& + 1.081227 \text{ REX}(-1) + 0.0151941 \text{ XG5} - 0.000070996 \\
& (4.53) \qquad\qquad\qquad\quad (3.03) \qquad\qquad\quad (-0.09) \\
& \text{S.E.}=0.3033 \quad \text{ADJ R-SQ}=0.9462 \quad \text{D.W.}=2.1910
\end{aligned}
$$

where REX: Exchange rate (dollar per yen)
BPCURRENT$: Current balance
KOUTLONG$: Long-term assets
XG5: Dummy variable representing G5 agreement, 1 for 1985 and after, 0 otherwise.

Of these explanatory variables, current balance and long-term assets are each composed of various variables which are dependent on real as well as monetary factors. Therefore, we constructed a model containing main variables in the balance of payments. The result of final test regarding the exchange rate is shown in figure 9-2.

9-9 Implication to the world community

Is Japan a cause of world economic disorder? Trade friction, investment friction, and technology friction with Japan beleaguered her partners. Liberalization of foreign trade and investment has proceeded according to the GATT framework, but the Japanese market remains untractable while Japanese penetration into the world market continues. Thus, Japan is being accused of being "unfair" because many outside observers see conspiracy against foreign competitors.

This is admittedly so in the fields which are under government regulation. Agriculture is one example. Public construction is another.

Government procurement also falls under this category. Large-scale retail outlets are also regulated rather rigidly. Strong foreign pressure is being exerted on these fields.

Some observers believe that government control should be installed to regulate Japanese trade instead of free market (although many products are already under 'voluntary restriction') because the latter is not likely to bring about balanced results. They also claim that private investment in plant and equipment in Japan need be put under government guidance in order to stem build up of potential export capabilities. In addition, outward direct foreign investment should be regulated to prevent Japan from buying up foreign countries. It may even become necessary to discourage household savings in order to dry up investment fund. These beliefs are misguided.

Japanese inventiveness is behind the competitive edge of her products. This may create displacement of labor in some sectors, but the world economy as a whole gains from increased efficiency and better consumer satisfaction. In other words, technological progress is the dynamism of our global society, and it benefits us all wherever it is coming from. Persistent trade imbalance is unlikely under flexible exchange rate system, and the exchange rates have been adjusted reflecting economic fundamentals.[23] With the termination of a strong dollar policy in 1985 which was symbolized by the G5 agreement, the yen has appreciated against the dollar, which in turn triggered a series of structural adjustment. One concerns the increased imports of finished goods into the Japanese market.[24] The other is the expansion of direct foreign investment. The latter creates new employment in host countries while facilitating technology transfer. With the diffusion of new technology overseas, it becomes easier for Japan to increase imports further. Portfolio investment is filling the saving-investment gap overseas and help overcome the shortage of investment funds there.

Thus, from the point of view of Japan's trading partners, there seems to be no cause for concern in the long-run. On the Japanese part, especially for the household sector which is the main supplier of savings, appreciation of the yen currency means capital loss for the dollar-denominated assets. We have to assume that Japanese investors believe that the dollar would provide a secure hedge against possibly turbulent world political scene, or that the foreign assets provide better long-term returns. Many countries in Asia emerged as strong growth axis, and the structural adjustment involving Japan, the United States and Europe, and Asian NIEs do seem to provide a good chance of success for all the parties concerned.[25]

There are, however, unanswered questions. These include the question of political stability in the transition from the state of a less-developed economy to a developing one. It it known that this phase involves inherent tendency for widening income disparities and rapid urbanization. Although East Europe and the Soviet Union are not 'less developed' in their technological sophistication and income levels, difficulty in shifting to market economies poses similar transition problem.[26]

There is the question of conservation of resources and safeguarding global environment. The growth path emerging in the Pacific rim seems to be compatible with such policy aims. These problems lie outside the scope of the current study. It is hoped that the Japanese scenario is checked within the enlarged framework for its compatibility with the policy goals of other members of the global community.

Footnotes:

1 See Uno [1987] for cost structure and price trends, including the relation between domestic industrial price and export price.

2 See chapter 8 for details of trade in goods. See also Uno [1987].

3 *The Japan Economic Journal* (in Japanese), February 4, 1989; the Ministry of Finance and the Bank of Japan, "The State of Balance of Payments in December 1988 (Quick Estimate) (Showa 63nen 12gatsuchu Kokusai Shushi Jokyo, Sokuho)," February 3, 1989.

4 *Monthly Report on Fiscal and Financial Statistics*, August 1989, p.58.

5 For details, see Tanaka and Tahiro [1989].

6 See, for example, Aho and Levinson [1987] who argue that "Many problems now troubling U.S. trade relations—subsidies, restrictions on trade in services, investment restraints, agricultural policies, concessional financing, limited market access, protection of intellectual property rights—are not treated adequately under existing international agreements. ... By approaching the Canadian trade talks as a test case, the administration can begin to correct this shortcomings and also to learn the limit of the possible in the trade field."

7 For detailed discussion on service orientation of the economy both from production and employment point of view, see Uno [1989a].

8 For details of the policy measures which followed, see Tanaka and Tahiro [1989].

9 The two sources differ in the following points. (a) The method of compilation of data: The Bank of Japan figures refer to foreign exchange transactions purpose of which concerns payments or receipts of patent royalties. The Bureau of Statistics data refer to all cases where patents, know-hows, technological collaboration, etc. are transacted between Japanese firms and foreign entities. Thus, the former excludes technology component accompanying, for example, exports of plants. (b) The Bank of Japan figures cover all cases involving foreign exchange transactions, in contrast to the Bureau of Statistics figures which cover the business firms engaged in R&D. Thus, the latter

excludes technology imports by nonprofit research institutions, retail and wholesale, and business and personal services which are increasingly engaged in such activity. Thus, the Bank of Japan tends to understate technology exports whereas the Bureau of Statistics tends to understate technology imports. Science and Technology Agency, *Indicators of Science and Technology 1990*, p. 19.

10 This point is discussed in chapter 6 based on flow of fund statistics.

11 The net asset for the U.S. was –110.7 billion dollars in 1985, –269.2 billion dollars in 1986, and –368.2 billion dollars in 1987.

12 The figures here are cited from Bank of Japan, *Comparative Economic and Financial Statistics, Japan and Other Major Countries*, 1989 edition. Ministry of Finance [1989], p.25, gives slightly different figures. The U.K. figure is given as 168.9 billion dollars and the German figure as 179.4 billion dollars at the end of 1987, respectively. The figure for the U.S. is identical.

13 Ministry of Finance, International Finance Bureau [1989].

14 A Japanese government document says that Japanese economic cooperation has been the world's largest since 1985. See MITI *Current States and Problems of Economic Cooperation, Summary Report, 1988*, p.80.

15 Actually, military spending also expanded at a rate far exceeding the general expansion of the central government budget. The stringent budget policy was required after general stagnation of the economy after the two Oil Crises and the government deficit exceeded 5% of the GNP for nearly a decade.

16 Data from *Current States and Problems of Economic Cooperation, Summary Report, 1988*, p.81. There are slight differences in some years between the figures given in this source and the ones in table 9-7 regarding the private flows, although both cites DAC's *Development Cooperation* as the data source.

17 The 1970 figure includes bilateral securities investment in addition to direct investment.

18 For details, see ibid., pp.82–106.

19 See discussion in chapters 2 and 6. In particular, refer to table 6-4 for narrowing government deficit in Japan.

20 See Uno [1987], particularly chapter 19, for the structure of Japanese imports.

21 See discussion in chapter 8.

22 "What marked an important turning point in liberalization and internationalization of money and capital market in Japan was the wholesale revision of the Foreign Exchange and Foreign Trade Control Law in December 1980. Under the revised law, liberalization of external transactions and simplification of administrative processes were carried out. Specifically, this included, among others, liberalization of foreign currency savings and impact loans for residents, a shift from permission system to reporting system in the case of acquisition of foreign securities (reporting is not required when the transaction is carried out through designated security firms), and relaxation of regulations pertinent to acquisition of Japanese securities by foreign nationals." For detailed description of policy measures in recent years, see Tanaka and Tahiro [1989].

23 Exception is the strong dollar during the 1980–1985 period which was induced by deliberate policy of the U.S. government. One standard macroeconomic

textbook writes as follows. "In the period 1980–1985 the dollar appreciated strongly in world currency markets. The explanation for the dollar appreciation must be seen in tight monetary policy and expansionary fiscal policy followed in the United States beginning in 1981. The effects of the strong dollar were felt in a loss of competitiveness and a large increase in imports. The United States was becoming a net debtor."

"Table shows some of the data. The real exchange rate (R=ePf/P) appreciated more than 30 percent. Net exports declined from plus 1.2 percent of GNP in 1980 to –2.0 percent in 1985."

Effects of the strong dollar

	1980	*1981*	*1982*	*1983*	*1984*	*1985*
Real exchange rate (index 1980–1982=100)	111	100	91	88	82	78
Net exports (percent of GNP)	1.2	1.1	0.8	−0.2	−1.7	−2.0
Import penetration (%)						
Capital goods	14.6	17.0	19.7	24.6	29.6	29.2
Consumer goods	6.9	7.4	7.7	8.7	10.7	10.8
Net investment position ($U.S.billion)	106	141	147	106	28	−60

Source: Cited from Dornbusch and Fischer [1987].

"The effects of the real appreciation can be seen in the change in import penetration. Import penetration is defined as the fraction of domestic spending that is met by imports. In the 1980–1985 period import penetration in the area of capital goods (investment goods) doubled: in that area nearly 30 cents of every dollar spent is on imports. even in the area of consumer goods, import penetration rose sharply. Whereas in 1980 less than 7 cents of every dollar spent on consumer goods was for imports, in 1985 nearly 11 cents per dollar was on imports. This is an extraordinary change. Business responded to the import invasion by calling for protection from foreign producers through tariffs or quotas." Dornbusch and Fisher [1987], p.755.

24 See discussion in chapters 2 and 8.

25 See chapter 2 for detailed discussion.

26 Among various papers on the economic transition of formerly-planned economies, systematic approach is seen in *Economic Reform and Integration*, IIASA collaborative paper, July 1990. As for author's own view on the topic, see Kimio Uno, "Capital Market and Privatization (second draft)," paper prepared based on discussion at the ERI meeting in Sopron, Hungary, July–August 1990, revised for authors' meeting in New Haven, U.S.A., November 1990, and Kimio Uno, "Economic Transition and Structural Statistics—Money, Investment, Technology, and Employment—," paper presented at an International Forum: Economies in Transition, Statistical Measures Now and in the Future, Sochi, U.S.S.R., October 1990.

Part 5

Analytical framework

Chapter 10. Framework of the model COMPASS

10-1 The scope of the model

Japan's investment in plant and equipment surpassed that of the United States and Japan's standing in patent acquisition and R&D activities has improved considerably. Japan seems to have overcome energy constraint and has coped with pollution problem rather successfully. On the other hand, however, closedness of the Japanese market is being accused internationally. Despite its apparent openness as judged from the removal of trade restriction on manufactured goods, the Japanese market is difficult to penetrate for foreign producers. Possible explanation lies in emerging technological differentials as a result of innovation both in terms of new products and new production processes which are made possible through active capital formation. In order to arrive at policy prescription, we need to tackle such complex problems as:

(1) R&D activities and the flow of benefits, which result in patent acquisition, quality improvement, decreasing cost, etc.,
(2) money and banking, such as represented in flow of funds, and its relation to fixed capital formation,
(3) diffusion of industrial robots, NC metalworking machines, flexible manufacturing system (FMS), etc. and the relation with wage rate, employment, etc.,
(4) capital stock vintage and technological progress,
(5) international competitiveness and high-tech diffusion,
(6) social impact of technological change such as changing industry-occupation profile, educational and skill requirement,
(7) environmental impact such as energy conservation and pollution prevention, and
(8) exchange rate determination and the balance of payments which reflects direct foreign investment, investment revenues, technology balance of payments, among others.

These policy issues are 'messy' in the sense that they are all interrelated. In addition, the assumed relationship is quite often difficult to quantify. A multi-sector industry model is developed for the purpose of serving as a test bed for policy experiments encompassing various aspects of the economic system. The model is disaggregated to 25 industrial sectors in order to trace structural change of the economy.

The original version which was published in Uno [1987] purposefully had a fairly general specification based on established economic theories. Named Comprehensive Model for Policy Assessment (COM-

Table 10-1 Industrial classification in COMPASS

Sector Number	Modified JSIC Codes	Industrial Sectors
[1]	01&	Agriculture, forestry, and fisheries
[2]	10&	Mining
[3]	18	Food processing
[4]	20&	Textiles
[5]	(22)	Lumber and wood products (included in 38&)
[6]	(23)	Furniture and fixture (included in 38&)
[7]	24	Pulp, paper, and paper products
[8]	(25)	Printing and publishing (included in 38&)
[9]	(29)	Leather and leather products (included in 38&)
[10]	(28)	Rubber products (included in 38&)
[11]	26	Chemicals
[12]	27	Petroleum and coal products
[13]	30	Nonmetalic mineral products
[14]	31A	Iron and steel material
[15]	31B	Basic iron and steel products
[16]	32	Basic nonferrous metal products
[17]	33	Fabricated metals
[18]	34	General machinery
[19]	35	Electrical machinery
[20]	36M	Transport equipment, motor vehicles
[21]	36S	Transport equipment, others
[22]	37	Precision instrument
[23]	38&	Other manufacturing
[24]	15	Construction
[25]	70	Electric power, gas, and water
[26]	40	Wholesale and retail trade
[27]	50&	Finance, insurance, and real estate
[28]	(50R)	Real estate rent
[29]	60T	Transportation
[30]	60C	Communication
[31]	97	Public administration
[32]	75P	Public services
[33]	75M	Business and personal services
[34]	( )	Office Supplies
[35]	( )	Packing materials
[36]	( )	Activities not elsewhere classified

Note: The classification scheme corresponds to the stardardized time-series input-output tables in Uno [1989a]. Parenthesis indicates that the corresponding sector is not included in the model. Sector code 38&& indicates that "other" includes sectors 22, 23, 25, 28, and 29 together with 38&. Sectors 31A and 31B, and 75P and 75M are lumped together in the model COMPASS.

PASS), it was used in various policy simulations including the examination of the effectiveness of the appreciation of the yen currency since 1985.[1] The industrial classification in COMPASS is identical to the one adopted in the historical series of input-output tables and industry-occupation matrices which were compiled concomitantly based on a 36-sector classification, its only difference being that some minor sectors within manufacturing have been included in the "other manufacturing" and dummy sectors omitted.[2]

The model includes sources-of-growth analysis within its framework which endogenizes capital stock vintage at the disaggregated level. This makes it particularly suitable for medium- to long-term growth analysis.

In the current version, the model COMPASS has been extended to include five major aspects in order to accomodate the experimental design. First, R&D activities and their feedback to the economy is considered explicitly, including its effect on investment in high-tech, external trade, etc. Second, diffusion of C-C-C (computer, communication, control) technology is explicitly included together with its effect on employment. Third, balance of payments and external assets and liabilities accounts have been included fully. The purpose of course is to reflect Japan's international economic relations in detail. Fourth, labor supply block has been developed consisting of demographic variables, school attendance, and labor force participation ratio by sex and age bracket. The purpose of this segment is to obtain information on the labor market from both demand (which is already in the existing model) and supply sides. Fifth, quality of life block is added which is comprised of damages caused by environmental pollution and urbanization, imputed services of consumer durables, housing, and social capital, imputed values of leisure and household production, etc.

10-2 The structure of the model

Thus, the model now consists of eleven blocks which include the following.

(1) Capital stock block
(2) R&D and diffusion of C-C-C
(3) Labor demand block
(4) Technological progress and sources of growth block
(5) Final demand and macroeconomic balance block
(6) Wages and prices block
(7) Energy block
(8) Foreign trade block
(9) Balance of payments block
(10) Labor supply block
(11) Quality of life block

According to purpose of the policy experiments, pertinent blocks can be chosen and linked to form a submodel.

Capital stock block: The model includes capital stock vintage as a key variable explaining the technological progress. The capital stock block calculates the average age of the capital stock for individual sectors, based on the capital formation which takes place within a particular year and the vintage of the existing capital stock.

One of the features of the model is an attempt to include the converter for private capital formation in its specification. From the view point of describing technological progress, particularly interesting is the industrial breakdown of supplying sectors for private investment in plant and equipment.[3] Our model COMPASS has investment function for individual sectors. The sectoral investment can then be broken down to supplying sectors by use of fixed capital formation matrices which are compiled for four points in time covering 1970 to 1985 [Uno, 1990c]. The latter contains information on the sectoral composition of investment in plant and equipment for individual sectors. For example, investment in automobile industry is composed of so much of electronic machinery, so much of general machinery, so much of structure, etc. Therefore, by explicitly incorporating the information from time-series of fixed capital formation matrices, we are able to trace the shifts in supplying sectors of capital formation. For brevity, we collapse the matrix into a vector by taking the sum of the supplying sectors. This comes close to explaining the shifts of converters for investment in plant and equipment, although the fixed capital formation matrices themselves are treated as exogenously determined. Conceptually at least, this is related to the diffusion of new technology, but its inclusion in the model seems to be too deterministic at this stage.

R&D and diffusion of C-C-C: In this block, we first derive R&D expenditures and R&D personnel based on empirically determined share functions. These are then employed in explaining the production of technological knowledge, which in this model is assumed to be reflected in the number of application for patents. There are limitations in using this variable as a proxy for technological knowledge being produced. For one thing, there is the difference between application and registration, the latter takes place with considerable lags reflecting scrutiny by the Patent Agency. Real problem for us lies in the fact that this lag is not uniform: there has been cumulative delays in the registration process as well as attempts to shorten it in recent years. Another problem is the fact that the acceptance ratio has been changing over time. More serious accusation for the use of the number of patents as a proxy is that there are cases when applications are made around a core invention for the purpose of preventing cases of by-passing by other firms (protective application), and that they cannot constitute invention in the true sense of the word. However, number of patents seem to serve our purpose better than any other statistics which are readily available.

We then proceed to estimate the patent application in major industrial countries, based on which stock of industrial patents in Japan and other major countries are derived. These numbers represent interesting aspects of the performance of our economy because production of knowledge is becoming an important economic activity in itself. Through direct investment and other channels of technological diffusion across national boundaries, advanced industrial countries are gradually moving out of production of goods and shifting toward production of services, including knowledge. We need to take account of computer software, database, scientific articles, design, and other kinds of assets which have been treated as intangible assets but increasingly becoming integral part of tangible assets. Before we learn how to cope with the measurement problem in a more satisfactory manner, we have to be content by what we already have in the form of solid statistical data set. In this sense, we have to admit that the number of patents will be the most widely accepted proxy variable.

This block is now extended to include capital formation related to electronic technology, namely, main frame computers, industrial robots, numerically controlled metalworking machines, and automatic vending machines. They do not exhaust the list of electronics revolution that is encompassing computer-communication-control spheres but are considered to represent typical devices. It can be confirmed that these sectors are the main recipients of the benefits of R&D. The stocks of these items are then calculated based on the estimated life-expectancy.

In view of the labor-augmenting nature of some of these devices, an attempt is made to explain capital formation related to these items by the relative price of labor and capital, which is endogenously determined in the labor demand block. Another explanatory variable is the capital formation in the purchasing sectors, representing the ability to buy in the pertinent sectors.

Labor demand block: The labor demand block includes employment function for each sector which is explained by neo-classical variables such as production level and relative price of labor and capital.

Two alternative specification of labor demand have been attempted as a part of the research plan in order to capture the changing occupational profile as a reflection of technological change. One is the labor demand by occupation and sex, based on the identical specification as above by including standard variables and the one which represents the diffusion of electronics technology. The occupational category considered includes professional and technical workers, managers and officials, clerical and related workers, sales workers, transportation and communication workers, production process workers, and service workers. These sets of equations allow us to evaluate the varying degree of impact on different job categories and has relevant implications of our educational program for the youths as well as for retraining of the work force.[4]

Second is the industry-occupation matrices which show the detailed composition of workers within each industrial sector. Historical series of such matrices have been compiled since 1950 till the present in five year intervals.[5] The labor input coefficients, which are obtained by dividing the labor inputs by industrial outputs (in constant prices), allow us to obtain detailed information as to the occupation composition for each sector. It is noted that the first approach mentioned above amounts to providing economic explanation on the time-series changes in the column sum and the row sum of industry-occupation matrices.

This block calculates working hours consistent with the capacity utilization of the capital stock, productivity, and the tightness of the labor market. The productivity variables take care of the usual income-leisure preference. Then the model calculates relative price of labor and capital based on the hourly wage rate (which differs from one sector to another) and the price of capital goods. This variable is important not only in explaining labor demand but also in explaining the diffusion of electronics-related technology which are of labor-augmenting nature.

Technological progress and sources of growth block: The fourth block of the model is named technological progress and sources of growth. The model COMPASS is rather unique in that it provides detailed account on sources of growth for each of the 25 sectors. The sources of growth explicitly considered include the following 6 factors:
(1) number of workers,
(2) working hours,
(3) capital stock,
(4) the rate of capacity utilization,
(5) capital stock vintage, and
(6) technological progress embodied in capital.

All of the sources of growth except the last one are endogenous to the system according to the specification of the existing model. The rate of embodied technological progress is peculiar to each sector and is considered to be exogenously given.[6]

This block also calculates potential output level for each sector based on the full capacity utilization of capital and estimated working hours consistent with such capacity utilization. This is followed up by calculation of demand-supply gap ratio for each sector (final demand and macroeconomic balance block) and the estimation of the rate of capacity utilization.[7]

Finally, gross domestic product is derived based on the production levels on the disaggregated level.

Final demand and macroeconomic balance block: In this block, we first derive final demand. Of the final demand items, private investment in plant and equipment is obtained as the sum of sectoral figures calculated in capital stock block, and macroeconomic exports figures are obtained similarly as the sum of exports of individual commodity category in foreign trade block. Demand for individual industry is then derived using converters and multipliers for each sector. These parameters have been obtained from time-series input-output tables. In other words, total demand for each sector is calculated as a multiple of sectoral final demand, with due consideration for the interindustry repercussion.

The rest of this block consists of equations and definitions dealing with demand-supply gap ratio and saving-investment balance, and other macroeconomic balances. The saving-investment balance is calculated for household sector, corporate sector, government sector, and the rest-of-the-world sector. Needless to say, disaggregated figures lie at the basis of aggregated corporate investment, exports, and imports so that macroeconomic figures would reflect the structural change of the economy as much as possible. This block is analytically important because the savings and investment have to balance for the whole economy, and dealing with trade surplus problem and government deficit as a separate issue will not simply work.[8]

Wages and prices block: In the wages and prices block which follows, wage rate is calculated for each sector based on productivity in that sector and economy-wide effects of consumer prices and labor market conditions. On the other hand, unit material cost is expressed as a function of sectoral prices and import prices which constitute main inputs to the sector in question, in addition to capital stock vintage representing the technological shift in the input structure.

Producer prices by industrial sector then are calculated based on the factor prices calculated above, namely wages and unit material cost. In addition, due consideration is given to the tightness of the market, which is represented in the model by the rate of capacity utilization pertinent to that sector. Deflators of final demand items are then derived as the weighted average of sectoral prices, the weights being the share of each sector in the converters corresponding to each final demand item. In other words, in the case of deflator for private investment in plant and equipment, sectoral producer prices are bundled together employing the relative importance of individual sectors in the converters. Thus, any movements of sectoral prices, either due to changes in labor input, material input, or market conditions are reflected in final demand deflators.

Energy block: The energy block specifies consumption of energy in individual sectors as the function of output levels and relative prices of fuels to sectoral prices. The latter is to consider the fact that, if energy price hikes can be passed on to the product price, there would be no reason for that industry to save energy consumption, and vice versa. Lagged variable is employed to take account of technological inertia concerning energy-related technology. The capital stock already in place, there is little room for energy conservation in a short period. Energy demand for the economy as a whole is calculated as the sum of sectoral figures.

Foreign trade block: Foreign trade block consists of export and import functions at a disaggregated level, and in each case, the explanatory variables consist of an income term and a relative price term, a standard procedure. The latter is adjusted by the rate of exchange. The rate of exchange, in turn, can be conceived as a function of current balance of payments and demand for the currency based largely on portfolio investment motives, this will be discussed in the balance of payments block below.

Among imports, fuel is explained by the aggregate demand for energy obtained above.

Japanese exports continued to exhibit steady expansion after 1985 despite the yen exchange rate appreciation induced by the G-5 agreement. Contributing factors to such trend apparently include non-price competitiveness such as quality improvement and flexible adoptation to changing market conditions. In fact, various surveys reveal that the introduction of high-tech equipment such as computers, industrial robots, NC metalworking machines, etc., is motivated by labor saving, quality improvement of products, increase in production capacity, shortening of lead-time, flexibility in design and production, among others. In order to examine the impact of high-tech diffusion on export performance, an attempt was made to include variables representing the diffusion of C-C-C (computer, communication, and control) technology in export functions of relevant sectors.

This block also includes trade matrices designated for each of SITC one digit level. This enables to disaggregate the estimated value of exports and imports by the major trading partners. Thus, it is possible to calculate trade balance for each trading partner. The trade matrices are treated as exogenous variables in this version of the model, and, as it stands, is not capable to endogenously reproduce dynamic shift of international trade structure.

The balance of payments block: This block takes into accounts the following.

(1) Merchandise trade (where trade figures in yen terms are converted to

dollar terms)
(2) Service trade
(3) Unrequited transfers
(4) Long-term capital transactions
(5) Short-term capital transactions

One notable point is the explicit treatment of trade in services. Trade in services, including transportation, insurance, travel, investment income, patent royalties, etc., have gained importance in the world economy. In fact, this will be the focal point in the coming round of GATT negotiations.

One of the interesting technological indicators is the balance of technological trade. The model includes patent royalties income (i.e., Japan's export) and payments (import) as a function of stock of patents. In calculating the stock, due consideration is given to the "life expectancy" of patents based on survey data.

Investment income is calculated based on the outstanding amount of direct investment, loans, and trade credit. Transportation, travel, etc., are calculated based on pertinent economic activities to which they are directly related.

One the basis of flow figures on capital transactions, external assets and liabilities are then derived. The cases in question include direct investment, trade credit, loans, and securities. Finally, net external assets are derived based on the estimated assets and liabilities.

The rate of exchange can be conceived of as being determined by economic fundamentals, and the demand for currency based on portfolio investment motives. An attempt is made in this block to explain the yen-dollar exchange rate based on the current balance and capital transactions. Needless to say, current account balance reflects one country's competitiveness in the world market of goods and services, which in turn reflects diffusion of C-C-C technology and R&D activities.

Labor supply block: Labor demand is determined above according to neo-classical specification where employment is explained by production level and relative factor prices. Due to differential effects of high-tech diffusion among occupations, and between male and female work-force, it is essential to keep track of possible mismatch between demand and supply of labor. This block is designed to fulfill that purpose. Its chief objective is to calculate labor supply for male and female. The key variable therefore is the labor force participation rate which in this block is estimated based on per capita GNP, school attendance rate (for younger age brackets only), the rate of child birth, and urbanization. Birth rate is endogenously explained as well as death rates, determining the population size for each age bracket by sex. Thus, this block provides a population pyramid and distinguishes working age population as well as actual labor supply. This can then be compared with the labor demand figures available from labor demand block.

Quality of life block: This is a subsidiary block to the model which calculates an aggregate measure of economic well-being of the population.[9] The indicator which is tagged as Net National Welfare (NNW) inherits the framework adopted by the NNW Development Committee of the Japanese Government. The framework closely follows the Measures of Economic Welfare (MEW) proposed by Nordhaus and Tobin. This line of approach has its origin in the 1970s when the quality of life was questioned in the face of mounting environmental disruption. It should be noted, in addition, that recent attempt at 'environmentally adjusted GNP' can actually be interpreted to follow the earlier work in this field.

In our case, following factors are accounted for:

(1) Government consumption (including only the portion pertinent to quality of life and excludes the portion which represents 'defensive' expenditures)
(2) Personal consumption (also excludes 'defensive' expenditures and purchase of consumer durables, the latter is considered under item 4 below)
(3) Imputed flow of services attributable to household-related social capital stock
(4) Imputed flow of services attributable to durable consumer goods and housing
(5) Imputed value of leisure time
(6) Extra-market activities such as housewives' domestic services
(7) Damages caused by environmental pollution (deduction)
(8) Loss due to urbanization (deduction)

NNW is derived as the total of these items.[10]

10-3 Technology and the economy

Industrialized countries and industrializing countries, market economies and (former) planned economies are all connected by international trade, direct foreign investment, technology flows, population migration, and global environment. We are living in an age where we have witnessed the emergence of a global market for goods and services, capital flows, and technology. The functioning of such a global market is guaranteed by global rules. Developing economies and planned economies have found it difficult to be detached from this trend. Even among industrialized market economies, however, differences in "rules of the game" are constantly being watched and adjusted. Nonetheless, the cases of trade, investment, and technology frictions abound. The differentials in the diffusion of high-tech lie at the basis of such frictions.

If this supposition is true, the cure for the international frictions has to be technology transfer which is often facilitated by direct foreign investment. If the root of such frictions lies in sinister intention of one country or the other, as is sometimes alleged, the prescription has to be altogether different. Research and development (R&D), technological progress, capital formation, production, exports, direct foreign investment, employment, environmental impact, etc. are interwoven. For example, if new technology emerges as a result of R&D effort, existing production facility will become obsolete and new capital formation will be carried out. As a consequence, production will become more efficient, due, for example, to labor saving and/or resource saving, resulting in lower prices. At the same time, quality of the products will be improved. This in turn may mean export promotion. Increased production and employment will eventually make the labor market tighter, inviting wage hikes. Changes in factor prices signal the direction of desirable technological change. Labor is a scarce factor of production in industrialized countries; so is the environment in a wide sense including not only raw materials but also clean air and water. Technological progress will be induced in the direction of conservation of these scarce factors.

The purpose of this section is to demonstrate the feasibility of empirical examination within our model framework. In the following, some of the key factors are discussed which link C-C-C related technology with the performance of an economy.

R&D and machinery sectors: Research and development (R&D) is an important economic activity in today's economy. Production of technological knowledge is undoubtedly a key factor for an economy in order to gain production efficiency while achieving resource conservation. However, economic theory and statistical accounts have not dealt with R&D in a systematic manner.[11] One difficulty is the fact that the benefit of R&D activity does not remain totally within a sector which undertakes it. Rather, the benefit spills over to the entire economy through improved quality and/or lower prices of intermediate inputs and capital equipment for other industrial sectors.

A practical method was proposed by Terlecskyj [1980, 1982]. Starting from the R&D expenditures undertaken in individual industrial sectors, he tried to distribute the benefit to the purchasing sectors by the use of information obtained from input-output tables.

Based on Terlecskyj's methodology and empirical data from Japan which include annual R&D data, annual input-output tables, and fixed capital formation matrixes from 1970, 1975, 1980, and 1985, an estimation was made on the annual flow of R&D benefits accrueing to industry and final demand.[12] Industry is divided into standardized 36 sectors and final demand in broken down into private consumption, government consumption, private investment, government investment, exports, etc. Fixed capital formation matrix is employed in order to distinguish the sector where capital formation is carried out. This process is needed because fixed capital formation among final demand items in the input-output tables only shows the amount of output of a particular sector going into investment.

In addition, due consideration is given to the technology imports. Both domestic R&D and technology imports are appropriately lagged in order to take into account of the time required for R&D to meterialize in the form of new products and new production processes.[13]

Comparisons of R&D activities and benefits received reveal that precision instrument, electrical machinery, and general machinery sectors are typical examples of net provider of R&D benefit to other industrial sectors. The flow of R&D benefit among industrial sectors is taken up in chapter 4.

Diffusion of C-C-C: Electronics technology is already having a tremendous impact on our society, and yet full impact is yet to unfold toward the 21st century and beyond. As an indicator of such development, one can look at production statistics of semiconductors, the progress of digital communication, or the development of database technology. They all represent electronics revolution. In this section, we examine the diffusion process of mainframe computers, NC metalworking machines, industrial robots, and automatic vending machines as representing C-C-C technology. Figure 5-2 in chapter 5 above represents the result of simulation of C-C-C diffusion based on the multisectoral industry model COMPASS. Represented on the vertical axis is the share of C-C-C related machinery and equipment in total capital stock in respective industrial sectors.

In the model, diffusion rates (RK—i) in respective sectors are explained by the relative price of labor and capital (WHRi) and the real capital formation (IPi).

$$\left.\begin{array}{l}\text{RKROBOi}\\ \text{RKNCi}\\ \text{RKCOMi}\\ \text{RKVENDi}\end{array}\right\} = \text{f (WHRi, IPi)}$$

The reasoning behind the specification is that the diffusion of new technology would be accelerated as the relative price of capital becomes lower, either due to appreciation of wage level or cheapening of capital equipment prices. Also, it can be assumed that the introduction of new technology would be easier when investment is being carried out in order to expand productive capacity. Empirical examination of the function gave fairly good results. For details, refer to chapter 5.

In the case of industrial robots, the 1987 Survey reports that there exist 47,308 units in Japanese industry. The 1973 figure stood at 3,058 (of which 2,735 were in machinery sectors) and the 1981 figure stood at 14,158. The same source reveals that Japanese industry posessed 259 FMSs as of 1987.

The Survey also reveals vintage of metalworking machinery. The units installed within the last three years stood as follows.

NC metal cutting machines	37.4%
NC secondary metalworking machinery	35.9%
Industrial robots	46.6%
Flexible manufacturing system	47.1%

The figures indicates how rapid the diffusion of new technology has been. At the same time, such trend seems to justify the use of average age of capital stock as a proxy for quality improvement of production equipment.

Structural change of capital formation: New technology is embodied in new capital equipment. The diffusion of C-C-C has its impact on an economy through fixed capital formation. Thus, we turn to private fixed capital formation, and examine the changes in sectoral composition of the supplying sector for this particular demand category. The basis of our analysis is the annual input-output tables for the Japanese economy in the past 10 years.[14] The sectoral ratio of a supplying sector for final demand is sometimes called converter. Table 6-9 in chapter 6 shows converters for private fixed capital formation, focusing on machinery sectors including general machinery, electrical machinery, motor vehicles, other transport equipment, and precison instrument. Construction sector is also listed for comparison. Needless to say, the table shows the share of each sector, the total being unity.

A firm evidence of the nature of technological change can be found in the table. The table reveals that the total share of machinery sectors has steadily increased during the 1980–1985 period. The figures for 1975 and 1980 are not particularly different, and closer examination of annual figures confirms this point. We may say that the structural change of private fixed capital formation started around 1980 in Japan. What characterizes the new trend is the rising share of machinery sectors, especially electrical machinery and general machinery. The share of precision instrument has also risen steadily. Thus, during 1980 and 1985, the share of machinery sectors total has risen nearly ten percentage points, from 28.7% to 38.3%. During the same period, electrical machinery has gained most, expanding its share from 8.7% to 13.2%. General machinery sector increased its share from 12.3% to 16.7%. The precision instrument has also increased from 0.9% to 1.3%. In constrast, the construction sector dropped its share from around 60% in 1975 and 1980 to less than 50% in 1985. Chapter 6 looks into technological change and capital formation in detail.

High-tech and exports: The model explains exports (in real terms) in each industry (ERi) in terms of the world industrial production (YWORLD), relative prices which is the ratio of export prices adjusted for the exchange rate fluctuation (REX*PEi) and the world price (PUNi), and proxy variables describing the diffusion of mainframe computers, NC machines, and industrial robots (RKCOMi+RKNCi+RKROBOi). Exchange rate in this specification is represented by dollar per yen.

$$ERi = f\,(YWORLD,\ REX*PEi/PUNi,\ RKCOMi+RKNCi+RKROBOi)$$

The function was tested for general machinery, electrical machinery, motor vehicles, and precision instrument and the results were good. Details are reported in chapter 8 above.

It should be noted that the movement of prices already captures the effects of high-tech diffusion. That is, export price in model COMPASS is obtained as a function of the corresponding producing sector price. This in turn is explained as a function of unit labor cost and unit material cost.[15] Material cost is then specified reflecting the input structure of respective industrial sector. When C-C-C related prices go down, benefit accrues to the sectors which use these products in their production processes and intermediate inputs. The effect of lower prices of electronics-related goods thus spreads to other sectors of the economy.

In addition, as the significance of C-C-C technology becomes widely recognized internationally, countries not only import C-C-C related goods but also try to initiate their production. This means that Japan's position as a supplier of these goods and technology is even more hightened. This is reflected in the high elasticity of Japanese exports vis-a-vis the growth of world economy. The causal chain is closed by referring to the fact that R&D in Japan is quite active, especially in civilian C-C-C related sectors. It is shown that R&D expenditures by electric machinery sector have expanded quite rapidly and exceed one quarter of total R&D spending, and that large portion is going into the electronics field.

10-4 Further remarks

From the above discussion which focused on the possibility of incorporating C-C-C related variables in a framework of a multisectoral industrial model, we may say that such attempt is indeed feasible. That is to say, one can construct an econometric model which is suitable for analysing the CIM diffusion and its economic and social impact. This is important because then we will be able to analyse the CIM diffusion in a dynamic context, simultaneously and consistently taking into account other important variables such as wage level, prices, investment trend, rate of interest, input structure, exports, exchange rate, world economy, just to name a few.

Footnotes:

1 Kimio Uno, "Appreciation of the Yen and the Structural Adjustment," in Uno et al. [1988a].
2 Uno [1989b].
3 Needless to say, private investment includes housing in addition to plant and equipment. For the moment, housing investment is outside our focal point.
4 Uno [1989b], pp.145–164.
5 Uno [1989b], pp.109–144, pp.331–379.
6 We have attempted in extending the model to explain this by the benefit of R&D and imported tecnology falling onto particular sector. If this experiment is even partly successful, it provides a means of closing the causal link between research activities and the gains in productive efficiency within a sector. It should be noted that the benefit of R&D and imported technology is generated not only from an industry's effort but by the effort of the other sectors via purchases of intermediate inputs and capital goods.
7 In the simulation experiment, the rate of capacity utilization is treated as exogenous in order to increase the operationality of the model.
8 This is because we have the relation
$S - I = (G + TR - TA) + (E - M)$
where S: saving in the private sector
I: investment in the private sector
G: government spending on goods and services
TR: transfer to the private sector
TA: taxes
E: exports
M: imports.
9 Uno, "Economic Growth and Environmental Change in Japan: Net National Welfare and Beyond." Franco Archibugi and Peter Nijkamp, eds. *Economy and Ecology: Towards Sustainable Growth?"* Dordrecht, the Netherlands: Kluwer Academic Publishers, 1989.
10 There are, of course, pros and cons to such an approach. As for the opinion of

the present author, see my comment on Hisao Kanamori's paper entitled "Japanese Economic Growth and Economic Welfare" in Shigeto Tsuru, ed. *Growth and Resources Problems Related to Japan*, The Macmillan Press, 1980.

11 Uno [1989], pp.212–213, discusses some of the deficiencies in the current treatment of R&D.

12 See Uno [1990c].

13 According to a survey by the Science and Technology Agency of the Japanese government, the gestation period is 3.54 years on the average, with considerable differentials among industrial sectors. See Uno [1989a], pp.232–234.

14 Uno [1990b], pp.56–66 and pp.195–205.

15 See Uno [1987], pp.233–256.

Appendix

Table A-1 R&D expenditures by industry and product field, 1970

Sector name \ Product field	1) Total	2) Agricul-ture, etc.	3) Mining	4) Construc-tion	5) Food	6) Textiles	7) Pulp & Paper
1) Total	690,409	2,423	1,052	10,780	14,211	5,230	4,568
2) Manufacturing	665,391	1,871	41	2,442	13,898	5,230	4,568
3) Foods	17,914	622	—	—	11,772	—	26
4) Textiles	10,319	121	—	11	58	4,804	29
5) Paper & Pulp	5,438	75	—	47	—	1	4,053
6) Printing	1,470	—	—	—	—	—	21
7) Chemicals	158,765	591	19	342	1,937	230	373
8) Petroleum & Coal	9,224	—	—	—	93	—	—
9) Rubber	8,710	—	—	11	—	—	6
10) Ceramics & Cement	14,652	—	17	543	—	5	—
11) Iron & Steel	35,934	—	—	910	—	—	—
12) Nonferrous Metals	17,191	—	—	—	—	—	—
13) Metal Products	7,417	111	—	116	—	—	—
14) Machinery	51,076	230	—	56	4	82	22
15) Electric Machinery	213,377	—	—	9	—	—	—
16) Motor Vehicles	75,864	—	—	—	1	88	2
17) Other Trans.	15,496	5	—	102	—	—	—
18) Precision Instrument	11,833	—	—	—	—	—	—
19) Other Manu	10,711	117	5	295	33	19	36
20) Trans Com	7,837	—	—	157	—	—	—

	17) Iron & Steel	18) Nonferrous Matels	19) Metal products	20) Machinery	21) Household appliances	22) Com & Electronics	23) Other Electric	24) Motor Vehicles
1)	28,812	19,199	9,531	71,250	65,274	106,417	27,485	74,747
2)	28,782	16,431	9,221	69,821	65,271	105,729	27,322	74,735
3)	—	—	—	51	—	—	—	—
4)	—	—	24	79	—	5	—	8
5)	—	—	—	134	—	—	—	—
6)	—	—	—	22	—	254	—	—
7)	244	1,190	121	965	178	283	17	91
8)	—	—	—	9	—	7	—	—
9)	—	12	12	1	—	—	—	—
10)	—	315	206	205	—	162	453	—
11)	26,778	959	1,572	4,694	81	80	47	68
12)	247	13,134	835	47	38	521	732	115
13)	154	382	4,296	474	437	44	33	300
14)	385	79	1,205	39,370	315	250	769	1,165
15)	172	138	298	12,372	64,169	101,297	24,445	3,822
16)	590	131	220	2,050	34	354	178	67,882
17)	212	26	104	8,193	—	—	374	662
18)	—	—	19	1,040	2	2,302	193	533
19)	—	65	309	113	18	171	82	89
20)	—	—	—	17	—	504	47	12

Note: The survey is taken as of April 1 each year. In the tables presented here, the figures are regarded pertinent to the previous year (e.g., 1989 survey figures are listed as 1988 data) because they refer to the fiscal year ending March 31.

Source: Statistical Bureau, Management and Coordination Agency, *Report on the Survey of Research and Development.*

(unit: million yen)

8) Printing	9) Chemicals	10) Chemical Fiber	11) Oils & Paints	12) Drugs	13) Mis. Chemicals	14) Petroleum Prod.	15) Rubber	16) Ceramics
1,245	69,958	17,223	9,673	41,395	31,951	9,195	9,270	13,919
1,243	69,470	17,223	9,656	41,395	31,089	8,540	9,270	13,669
—	549	—	495	4,032	206	—	—	—
—	94	3,573	6	—	1,052	—	19	141
59	141	164	—	118	533	—	—	—
1,145	14	—	—	—	8	—	—	—
37	61,195	13,448	8,778	36,792	26,030	2,041	1,102	1,147
—	2,221	—	32	—	119	6,369	—	273
—	293	2	8	1	233	48	7,629	—
—	1,264	—	—	—	25	—	—	11,335
—	219	—	—	—	2	—	—	35
—	238	—	16	—	17	—	187	3
—	367	10	66	—	188	—	—	5
1	615	15	22	—	95	32	166	—
—	620	—	24	372	967	—	6	457
0	117	4	53	11	107	14	1	64
—	41	—	10	—	11	37	—	—
—	8	—	—	18	—	—	—	151
—	1,473	8	145	52	1,495	—	159	57
—	41	—	—	—	—	14	—	36

25) Ships	26) Aircrafts	27) Rolling Stock	28) Other Trans.	29) Precision Instrument	30) Oother Manufac-turing	31) Electricity & Gas	32) Others
5,477	4,124	1,682	511	13,029	7,860	6,354	1,963
5,449	4,124	1,654	4,947	13,024	7,697	113	1,467
—	—	—	—	159	—	—	—
—	—	—	31	22	241	—	—
—	—	—	—	—	113	—	—
—	—	—	—	7	—	—	—
—	134	—	—	862	559	—	59
—	—	—	—	—	101	—	—
—	—	—	—	—	455	—	—
—	—	—	—	—	70	52	2
440	23	—	4	—	6	12	6
—	—	—	—	2	247	—	812
9	5	19	14	137	149	—	100
1,819	1,430	57	709	1,705	113	—	128
133	115	1,216	128	2,377	108	—	126
16	824	109	2,544	360	30	5	—
3,026	1,507	176	917	—	—	13	48
—	74	—	101	7,282	5,156	—	111
6	12	77	499	112	113	31	76
—	—	26	156	—	—	6,220	494

Table A-2 R&D expenditures by industry and product field, 1975

Sector name / Product field	1) Total	2) Agricul-ture, etc.	3) Mining	4) Construc-tion	5) Food	6) Textiles	7) Pulp & Paper
1) Total	1,519,483	4,425	2,826	58,478	30,347	8,161	11,954
2) Manufacturing	1,377,452	3,028	628	15,614	29,935	8,157	11,954
3) Foods	37,268	1,603	—	—	25,448	10	69
4) Textiles	15,947	456	—	444	345	6,583	24
5) Paper & Pulp	10,841	105	—	245	—	14	8,594
6) Printing	5,130	—	—	66	52	31	82
7) Chemicals	297,539	286	414	1,827	3,381	1,062	1,189
8) Petroleum & Coal	16,061	14	3	21	462	—	—
9) Rubber	25,742	—	—	—	—	—	—
10) Ceramics & Cement	36,206	35	191	850	58	63	24
11) Iron & Steel	88,588	49	—	4,893	—	44	—
12) Nonferrous Metals	24,732	36	11	8	—	—	58
13) Metal Products	20,469	102	—	885	35	—	—
14) Machinery	96,051	40	10	606	—	143	346
15) Electric Machinery	383,914	42	—	—	—	—	1
16) Motor Vehicles	193,512	43	—	3,117	69	145	—
17) Other Trans.	55,923	—	—	678	—	—	18
18) Precision Instrument	30,441	—	—	—	—	32	—
19) Other Manu	39,089	217	—	1,974	85	31	1,550
20) Trans Com	78,506	1	—	4,783	—	—	—

	17) Iron & Steel	18) Nonferrous Matels	19) Metal products	20) Machinery	21) Household appliances	22) Com & Electronics	23) Other Electric	24) Motor Vehicles
1)	73,405	29,795	22,916	149,593	125,078	231,568	67,820	187,222
2)	73,150	25,380	21,260	143,329	124,969	178,923	65,602	187,180
3)	3	2	—	252	—	—	—	—
4)	—	—	46	434	4	90	52	169
5)	—	—	—	29	—	49	—	—
6)	—	—	16	31	—	803	113	—
7)	568	1,835	878	1,840	161	75	834	166
8)	107	1	—	34	4	39	—	23
9)	—	—	85	50	40	—	36	1,930
10)	49	22	200	653	—	134	756	—
11)	68,673	1,232	2,821	8,276	39	454	285	174
12)	565	18,878	1,221	195	293	1,493	224	288
13)	339	579	12,030	1,917	1,939	133	410	109
14)	2,193	135	1,965	72,693	4,142	4,721	2,477	1,239
15)	26	769	734	15,776	118,057	165,240	58,877	11,190
16)	345	179	216	4,555	37	734	589	169,381
17)	172	43	253	33,607	—	24	260	1,350
18)	109	—	—	2,446	64	4,849	610	16
19)	—	1,706	797	541	190	84	80	1145
20)	165	102	224	1,701	—	52,235	1,410	14

(unit: million yen)

8) Printing	9) Chemicals	10) Chemical Fiber	11) Oils & Paints	12) Drugs	13) Mis. Chemicals	14) Petroleum Prod.	15) Rubber	16) Ceramics
5,230	109,303	19,074	20,327	96,505	83,841	17,498	24,646	28,178
5,230	108,406	19,074	20,302	96,505	82,285	12,031	24,640	27,976
2	522	4	760	5,651	2,820	10	2	69
0	246	3,693	7	721	1,941	—	35	557
8	141	0	—	—	1,378	3	—	—
3,835	—	—	—	10	—	—	—	—
615	88,355	15,175	18,605	89,997	64,303	1,360	1,014	1,823
—	2,119	17	103	—	1,916	9,709	47	491
3	286	—	—	20	449	460	22,068	—
53	7,852	151	428	—	1,050	191	307	22,587
—	50	—	—	—	82	—	31	88
32	642	—	49	—	2	—	274	150
—	536	—	6	—	121	31	15	174
32	920	—	—	—	651	71	108	187
—	2,143	2	66	—	1,025	3	25	1,002
—	159	—	67	—	0	20	77	106
—	100	—	—	—	62	173	—	—
0	237	9	—	11	185	—	33	145
651	4,097	22	211	96	6,300	—	605	599
—	42	—	25	—	2	—	6	—

25) Ships	26) Aircrafts	27) Rolling Stock	28) Other Trans.	29) Precision Instrument	30) Oother Manufac-turing	31) Electricity & Gas	32) Others
14,711	9,194	6,090	4,128	25,220	33,961	13,243	4,746
14,581	8,708	2,428	3,965	25,220	33,356	396	3,242
—	—	—	—	—	11	—	32
—	—	—	—	—	99	2	—
—	—	—	—	—	275	—	—
—	—	—	—	66	26	—	—
—	125	—	—	567	833	15	236
—	—	2	—	—	914	36	—
—	—	—	—	—	313	—	—
—	—	—	—	6	542	3	—
1,275	64	—	4	—	53	—	—
17	—	—	9	—	3	—	285
17	—	16	143	73	616	110	134
194	101	151	633	1,403	786	—	104
247	286	1,093	64	4,502	352	208	2,185
462	2,853	222	1,524	370	8,243	0	—
12,031	4,772	943	1,277	2	128	—	31
337	503	—	96	17,920	2,632	—	209
2	4	—	216	311	17,529	22	26
66	485	3,662	85	—	320	12,405	773

Table A-3 R&D expenditures by industry and product field, 1980

Product field / Sector name	1) Total	2) Agricul-ture, etc.	3) Mining	4) Construc-tion	5) Food	6) Textiles	7) Pulp & Paper
1) Total	2,913,583	6,091	27,523	54,816	60,212	10,728	16,591
2) Manufacturing	2,688,741	3,376	22,166	13,536	59,843	10,728	16,115
3) Foods	70,336	1,357	—	—	47,028	—	79
4) Textiles	31,413	558	—	300	33	9,329	106
5) Paper & Pulp	13,720	15	—	—	—	63	10,906
6) Printing	5,697	—	—	128	202	38	—
7) Chemicals	517,164	574	440	3,375	5,029	1,047	1,064
8) Petroleum & Coal	59,919	—	21,358	—	—	—	—
9) Rubber	47,057	—	—	275	—	37	—
10) Ceramics & Cement	70,979	105	36	3,164	33	13	80
11) Iron & Steel	144,856	—	94	3,118	19	28	21
12) Nonferrous Metals	52,469	122	196	115	—	—	7
13) Metal Products	38,987	102	—	525	64	10	—
14) Machinery	183,389	354	—	501	—	32	3,653
15) Electric Machinery	788,585	—	—	—	—	—	—
16) Motor Vehicles	417,230	—	—	3,878	—	—	—
17) Other Trans.	90,152	—	44	131	—	—	31
18) Precision Instrument	84,085	—	—	—	—	—	—
19) Other Manu	72,704	189	—	1,517	7,435	130	169
20) Trans Com	152,850	6	—	5,535	—	—	230

	17) Iron & Steel	18) Nonferrous Matels	19) Metal products	20) Machinery	21) Household appliances	22) Com & Electronics	23) Other Electric	24) Motor Vehicles
1)	120,551	47,228	36,347	282,889	216,386	503,948	138,102	428,436
2)	120,268	43,150	35,939	274,176	216,386	412,935	133,886	428,240
3)	11	—	—	316	—	8	—	—
4)	—	—	17	578	29	408	18	405
5)	—	—	—	39	—	—	—	—
6)	—	—	39	481	—	101	12	—
7)	194	337	425	896	28	1,975	1,741	273
8)	—	4,450	—	—	—	—	—	—
9)	—	—	83	—	103	—	—	2,102
10)	—	329	249	2,647	52	1,027	3,846	131
11)	114,434	1,862	3,063	14,267	83	219	827	930
12)	284	33,709	3,622	187	100	6,289	659	1,464
13)	1,371	1,056	17,794	4,527	7,209	142	653	1,718
14)	2,612	180	5,344	135,554	775	8,255	6,931	7,925
15)	1,106	749	2,336	38,627	204,113	389,214	113,092	19,825
16)	—	8	1,052	6,328	1,141	209	419	587,641
17)	254	72	279	61,083	—	195	1,155	843
18)	—	56	95	7,900	622	4,072	2,922	2,633
19)	—	341	1,542	740	2,132	821	1,612	2,351
20)	250	135	3	2,224	—	88,745	1,969	19

(unit: million yen)

8) Printing	9) Chemicals	10) Chemical Fiber	11) Oils & Paints	12) Drugs	13) Mis. Chemicals	14) Petroleum Prod.	15) Rubber	16) Ceramics
5,766	182,405	24,082	34,902	207,949	140,785	28,035	45,562	49,874
5,766	181,621	24,082	34,777	207,928	139,528	27,838	46,555	49,562
1	1,239	—	1,256	16,286	1,468	4	7	149
248	5,342	7,291	61	3,705	1,905	—	255	420
606	104	59	—	63	1,630	—	—	5
3,686	202	—	—	—	59	—	—	47
1,101	135,549	16,469	30,544	186,810	115,301	2,502	1,792	2,703
—	6,070	57	708	—	714	24,689	—	855
—	674	47	20	12	1,075	13	41,574	16
—	15,593	89	401	229	1,197	—	42	40,186
56	723	—	—	14	85	196	—	666
59	601	—	87	34	1,091	—	666	1,105
—	921	—	392	—	329	—	531	111
10	1,094	—	—	—	2,082	42	319	1,329
—	3,388	—	473	—	2,103	—	116	335
—	—	—	—	—	—	—	32	—
—	74	—	15	—	825	119	—	—
—	122	—	—	527	390	—	—	389
—	9,925	70	821	248	9,273	272	1,221	747
—	61	—	33	—	2	—	7	—

25) Ships	26) Aircrafts	27) Rolling Stock	28) Other Trans.	29) Precision Instrument	30) Oother Manufac-turing	31) Electricity & Gas	32) Others
11,180	18,950	9,835	19,261	79,480	38,575	49,075	17,021
10,830	18,950	4,684	19,087	79,276	38,500	2,111	6,903
—	—	—	—	26	43	—	1,058
—	—	—	—	—	306	—	100
—	—	—	—	—	231	—	—
—	—	—	—	—	701	—	—
—	358	26	395	3,427	1,455	73	1259
—	—	—	—	—	1,014	4	—
—	760	10	30	8	219	—	—
—	9	12	27	93	1,240	12	137
1,658	122	64	289	442	364	376	832
42	14	226	67	54	265	8	1,399
85	4	113	219	70	968	43	29
569	265	196	1,272	3,433	664	—	—
25	748	2,266	243	6,197	2,542	120	467
552	3,745	422	14,086	157	979	3	69
7,897	12,387	1,350	2,358	2	160	—	873
—	538	—	—	63,713	—	—	107
2	—	—	99	1,653	27,348	1,472	572
288	—	5,151	94	8	—	46,555	1,535

Table A-4 R&D expenditures by industry and product field, 1985

Product field / Sector name	1) Total	2) Agricul-ture, etc.	3) Mining	4) Construc-tion	5) Food	6) Textiles	7) Pulp & Paper
1) Total	5,635,399	16,220	6,828	105,843	81,131	17,258	23,069
2) Manufacturing	5,247,946	13,976	2,653	23,492	79,466	17,258	28,069
3) Foods	115,485	4,752	—	28	71,209	—	193
4) Textiles	50,379	451	—	477	74	14,339	212
5) Paper & Pulp	28,076	300	—	237	—	49	23,043
6) Printing	18,406	15	—	—	30	15	76
7) Chemicals	883,561	7,397	13	5,169	7,472	1,883	2,562
8) Petroleum & Coal	66,654	28	1,365	75	—	—	—
9) Rubber	75,744	—	—	298	—	68	22
10) Ceramics & Cement	153,805	138	382	5,484	25	183	92
11) Iron & Steel	239,553	—	777	7,212	17	23	21
12) Nonferrous Metals	96,037	80	116	273	—	—	73
13) Metal Products	87,392	91	—	2,118	113	—	—
14) Machinery	332,869	285	—	791	111	—	1,632
15) Electric Machinery	1,875,312	—	—	487	—	—	22
16) Motor Vehicles	785,273	—	—	625	—	—	—
17) Other Trans.	136,954	242	—	443	351	—	—
18) Precision Instrument	180,382	—	—	59	—	—	—
19) Other Manu	62,892	159	—	1,077	55	—	26
20) Trans Com	259,316	—	—	5,856	—	—	—

	17) Iron & Steel	18) Nonferrous Matels	19) Metal products	20) Machinery	21) Household appliances	22) Com & Electronics	23) Other Electric	24) Motor Vehicles
1)	164,783	68,742	68,173	496,757	423,479	1,372,511	264,006	853,317
2)	164,390	62,117	66,702	483,113	423,479	1,189,232	261,100	853,175
3)	—	—	81	1,271	—	34	—	—
4)	—	—	9	190	5	915	1,820	276
5)	—	—	—	46	—	—	—	—
6)	76	—	83	1,559	—	2,187	113	61
7)	138	839	666	7,041	401	10,537	7,872	1,261
8)	—	9,442	—	23	756	95	—	—
9)	—	—	—	160	30	65	30	5,111
10)	360	527	126	4,201	—	16,213	1,429	794
11)	158,494	6,555	10,080	21,703	48	5,589	494	2,061
12)	465	40,718	8,083	325	358	23,974	4,783	5,688
13)	1,899	1,872	29,550	7,231	12,356	955	3,582	20,767
14)	1,898	852	8,560	222,332	3,387	30,002	6,066	16,850
15)	698	189	4,175	83,131	392,485	1,065,567	224,027	64,656
16)	—	—	119	14,009	1,904	1,138	877	727,640
17)	338	161	1,953	95,581	—	592	153	960
18)	—	213	135	22,997	9,983	25,142	7,620	4,138
19)	24	484	2,503	915	1,225	4,988	431	1,636
20)	199	126	2	1,269	—	178,596	2,551	—

(unit: million yen)

8) Printing	9) Chemicals	10) Chemical Fiber	11) Oils & Paints	12) Drugs	13) Mis. Chemicals	14) Petroleum Prod.	15) Rubber	16) Ceramics
14,588	264,606	39,419	53,094	386,281	252,496	34,846	72,057	104,992
14,192	259,674	39,419	52,899	385,973	251,485	34,635	72,024	103,326
6	340	—	1,061	33,028	2,682	—	—	43
186	6,743	10,627	54	8,175	2,648	5	195	424
33	208	—	—	339	3,083	—	—	—
11,351	—	—	—	—	41	—	—	84
2,094	192,934	18,946	47,944	339,687	205,351	1,188	2,306	5,921
300	5,692	—	1,280	447	8,339	32,509	40	2,372
55	172	5	164	15	1,897	243	65,387	95
—	18,189	6,551	288	2,034	3,074	17	326	84,788
—	4,427	51	286	—	1,960	139	7	3,092
—	1,597	—	421	33	1,430	—	965	1,571
—	1,775	9	418	—	843	—	21	53
166	1,504	—	—	2	533	60	59	1,174
—	5,410	115	81	—	3,457	—	—	2,360
—	—	—	—	—	—	—	—	—
—	—	—	73	—	294	—	—	—
—	448	35	—	1,131	2,467	—	—	681
—	359	—	53	—	1,250	24	1,666	544
—	275	—	94	—	—	102	33	—

25) Ships	26) Aircrafts	27) Rolling Stock	28) Other Trans.	29) Precision Instrument	30) Oother Manufac-turing	31) Electricity & Gas	32) Others
16,280	23,715	13,211	40,028	154,064	97,500	69,554	31,503
15,848	23,715	7,716	39,763	152,668	96,695	6,032	18,659
—	—	—	—	43	13	—	701
7	5	3	—	514	2,024	—	—
—	—	—	—	29	619	3	81
8	—	—	—	28	1,500	—	549
—	155	82	830	6,649	3,077	479	2,667
—	—	—	—	3	2,039	1,158	690
6	1,189	12	66	10	623	—	31
—	—	11	45	3,361	4,870	22	274
3,660	228	79	—	1,129	5,439	930	5,052
155	7	320	75	195	566	—	3,773
—	—	58	185	98	3,197	170	30
805	311	107	4,734	19,326	10,691	162	470
80	355	3,901	220	21,163	2,660	—	72
1,911	4,871	2,013	28,185	1,426	449	—	105
9,170	15,932	1,046	4,836	696	1,497	579	2,059
—	582	—	—	96,063	7,784	813	127
41	29	69	538	421	43,541	—	800
217	—	5,494	192	29	—	63,077	1,205

Table A-5 R&D expenditures by industry and product field, 1987

Sector name / Product field	1) Total	2) Agricul-ture, etc.	3) Mining	4) Construc-tion	5) Food	6) Textiles	7) Pulp & Paper
1) Total	6,194,632	17,155	8,960	141,393	99,056	21,993	30,092
2) Manufacturing	5,804,866	13,040	3,053	33,690	97,742	21,993	30,016
3) Foods	153,759	5,909	—	1	86,183	—	302
4) Textiles	55,536	464	—	301	713	17,365	174
5) Paper & Pulp	31,374	641	—	46	86	5	23,219
6) Printing	21,574	—	—	—	32	—	128
7) Chemicals	1,041,220	3,877	8	6,053	10,094	3,695	3,625
8) Petroleum & Coal	68,706	421	77	53	87	—	—
9) Rubber	81,802	—	—	358	—	80	7
10) Ceramics & Cement	168,405	122	704	5,071	26	157	43
11) Iron & Steel	241,242	300	2,052	10,918	55	59	16
12) Nonferrous Metals	97,944	44	202	392	52	—	—
13) Metal Products	77,177	129	—	1,401	178	—	—
14) Machinery	374,788	512	10	1,108	144	—	2,416
15) Electric Machinery	2,089,472	—	—	—	52	5	23
16) Motor Vehicles	810,612	—	—	548	—	28	—
17) Other Trans.	154,051	259	—	1,033	26	—	19
18) Precision Instrument	184,250	—	—	123	—	—	—
19) Other Manu	74,416	346	—	1,214	—	—	21
20) Trans Com	239,445	26	—	2,921	—	—	—

	17) Iron & Steel	18) Nonferrous Matels	19) Metal products	20) Machinery	21) Household appliances	22) Com & Electronics	23) Other Electric	24) Motor Vehicles
1)	136,031	78,750	75,309	521,239	394,629	1,613,089	303,516	890,673
2)	135,829	73,969	74,368	511,869	394,594	1,442,043	302,731	890,673
3)	—	—	48	1,512	—	22	46	—
4)	—	—	12	86	5	1,935	1,352	1,571
5)	—	—	—	45	—	—	—	210
6)	—	—	96	2,145	63	3,016	119	52
7)	531	948	820	7,715	3,374	17,187	10,863	1,690
8)	119	8,731	—	709	—	620	—	—
9)	272	—	—	193	24	407	13	5,175
10)	10	163	494	5,094	31	24,328	1,154	1,130
11)	128,004	8,050	12,190	24,995	13	19,876	1,024	1,197
12)	229	49,054	3,921	233	151	23,791	5,529	3,448
13)	816	2,912	42,994	3,018	12,104	438	2,460	5,328
14)	3,954	1,369	4,347	244,349	3,090	36,991	11,924	20,599
15)	1,045	1,870	3,442	62,952	364,312	1,285,951	252,627	72,172
16)	—	—	84	12,140	2,173	1,826	638	767,932
17)	803	48	1,928	105,530	—	519	161	998
18)	—	85	166	39,887	6,509	15,692	6,174	3,532
19)	47	740	3,050	980	2,238	6,451	2,024	2,507
20)	—	—	—	20	—	165,908	14	—

(unit: million yen)

8) Printing	9) Chemicals	10) Chemical Fiber	11) Oils & Paints	12) Drugs	13) Mis. Chemicals	14) Petroleum Prod.	15) Rubber	16) Ceramics
14,284	331,854	26,093	61,265	460,189	299,150	40,644	76,267	111,071
14,198	327,874	25,895	61,160	459,740	299,044	40,267	76,267	108,183
4	471	—	1,206	49,071	8,713	—	—	16
210	9,588	5,966	62	8,841	3,598	—	89	601
397	700	—	—	469	4,296	—	—	67
10,188	—	—	192	—	683	—	—	160
2,476	233,596	19,337	56,491	394,227	236,785	4,407	2,221	6,135
—	9,214	—	297	1,650	8,024	35,609	—	1,503
100	512	8	222	22	2,548	201	69,286	33
—	22,447	91	1,227	2,239	2,505	5	236	87,048
—	9,481	220	38	—	5,678	7	6	5,122
—	1,193	—	525	—	1,960	—	713	1,155
—	1,958	—	266	—	266	—	2,341	25
308	2,712	—	—	—	2,049	14	466	2,116
—	7,627	20	63	—	4,389	—	37	1,895
—	—	—	—	—	—	—	—	—
—	19	—	—	—	369	—	—	214
325	395	—	—	1,074	2,954	—	—	1,257
—	495	150	121	—	958	25	140	808
—	155	—	—	—	—	—	—	1,698

25) Ships	26) Aircrafts	27) Rolling Stock	28) Other Trans.	29) Precision Instrument	30) Oother Manufac-turing	31) Electricity & Gas	32) Others
11,187	37,841	7,454	26,240	170,217	101,190	67,307	20,492
10,830	35,941	7,151	25,980	169,990	99,533	2,391	14,812
—	—	—	—	—	192	—	61
20	8	1	1,364	450	382	—	379
—	—	—	—	—	1,190	3	—
—	—	—	—	898	2,313	—	1,490
—	217	170	1,161	7,247	3,967	—	2,303
—	—	—	—	29	517	156	889
137	1,291	14	76	116	702	—	—
—	—	13	77	4,058	8,146	10	1,776
1,349	58	4	265	452	7,304	726	1,783
53	9	319	16	560	982	3	3,411
30	1	6	43	161	303	2	—
366	1,173	102	4,500	24,135	5,734	14	285
41	551	3,235	85	23,138	2,353	—	1,589
1,436	6,842	1,965	13,008	1,505	487	—	—
7,368	25,115	1,150	4,804	629	2,380	55	626
—	560	—	4	104,983	30	441	58
8	70	149	475	495	50,839	—	65
225	1,900	302	—	71	30	64,579	1,595

Table B-1 R&D benefit received, time series, intermediate demand

Sector name	Year 1975	1976	1977	1978	1979
01 Agriculture, etc.	4939.6	5130.3	4634.3	4278.4	5430.7
02 Mining	4737.9	3900.8	3953.7	4861.3	3620.4
03 Food Processing	13661.8	13369.1	13136.7	11839.7	
04 Textiles	7805.9	8175.2	6840.0	5225.3	4551.9
05 Lumber and Wood	0.0	0.0	0.0	0.0	0.0
06 Furniture, Fixtures	0.0	0.0	0.0	0.0	0.0
07 Pulp and Paper	12642.9	14961.0	35716.2	17026.0	15730.4
08 Printing, Publish	3278.2	4069.0	4285.2	4706.0	4667.6
09 Leather & Prod.	0.0	0.0	0.0	0.0	0.0
10 Rubber Products	20870.3	23151.2	23067.8	23792.0	28081.4
11 Chemicals	335495.6	344836.2	359902.1	356860.5	358539.6
12 Petroleum & Coal	24222.8	19179.3	13282.1	17629.7	19916.8
13 Nonmetal Minerals	33606.2	30779.9	31428.3	34848.6	36887.3
14 Iron & Steel Mat.	64989.2	72650.1	86727.8	94552.4	89231.1
15 Iron & Steel Prod.	0.0	0.0	0.0	0.0	0.0
16 Nonferrous Metals	42591.0	45033.2	44523.6	40582.2	38501.7
17 Fabricated Metals	19359.4	25131.7	21748.0	23699.9	26845.4
18 General Machinery	96737.6	115513.4	115633.4	100684.3	118058.5
19 Electrical Mach.	261968.5	275432.7	2570853.5	235460.2	239435.5
20 Motor Vehicles	87418.1	92802.8	99522.1	90795.9	93791.4
21 Other Transport	44025.9	26433.4	27515.8	32276.1	35895.8
22 Precision Inst.	13300.4	13374.7	12091.9	12464.8	16640.3
23 Manufacturing nec	13757.5	16424.7	17638.9	30125.9	23296.6
24 Construction	4358.6	4103.0	4330.8	6260.8	5871.7
25 El., Gas, Water	11908.2	11621.7	13419.3	12773.7	13309.0
26 Wholesale Retail	0.0	0.0	0.0	0.0	0.0
27 Fin., Ins., Estate	0.0	0.0	0.0	0.0	0.0
28 Real Estate Rent	0.0	0.0	0.0	0.0	0.0
29 Transportation	123.7	9.3	19.6	0.0	0.0
30 Communication	0.0	0.0	0.0	0.0	0.0
31 Public Admin.	0.0	0.0	0.0	0.0	0.0
32 Public Services	0.0	0.0	0.0	0.0	0.0
33 Private Services	0.0	0.0	0.0	0.0	0.0
34 Office Supplies	0.0	0.0	0.0	0.0	0.0
35 Packing Materials	0.0	0.0	0.0	0.0	0.0
36 Activities nec	9334.9	11059.3	5918.5	5024.4	4345.0
Total	1131124.2	1177292.0	1207439.9	1165768.1	1200312.5

Source: Kimio Uno, *Fixed Capital Formation Matrix and R&D Benefit.*

(unit: million yen)

1980	1981	1982	1983	1984	1985	1986	1987
9763.9	4530.1	4727.8	6081.8	6006.7	6356.2	6247.4	10788.4
3445.5	3696.3	4425.2	16746.2	17712.6	8739.5	9071.0	8551.5
14873.8	14422.7	15590.8	16333.1	15761.5	16671.1	18994.7	20846.9
4151.4	5413.8	5023.2	6040.8	6414.5	5705.1	6412.9	6903.2
0.0	0.0	0.0	0.0	0.0	0.0	0.0	0.0
0.0	0.0	0.0	0.0	0.0	0.0	0.0	0.0
13618.7	13242.4	12574.0	14520.1	16159.7	13450.5	14256.7	15179.3
4688.6	4364.3	3697.7	4282.3	4333.8	7290.6	10308.2	12364.1
0.0	0.0	0.0	0.0	0.0	0.0	0.0	0.0
30465.2	28388.3	32727.9	32637.4	31059.3	33238.5	35956.9	44104.3
377503.1	367123.7	357759.3	376775.1	398099.0	422866.4	466299.6	514882.1
13923.0	15656.6	19512.4	13468.8	18830.0	21226.4	20988.3	23558.0
37245.1	38926.1	41151.6	44796.0	46687.7	50914.7	58313.1	64100.9
89743.9	89801.3	9948.0	113169.3	126954.7	124281.2	119579.1	116007.7
0.0	0.0	0.0	0.0	0.0	0.0	0.0	0.0
15181.9	35140.6	33197.0	33140.8	43812.0	47071.1	51446.0	47410.3
23004.1	25340.6	26475.2	23462.5	48608.1	41179.6	39798.2	40942.2
122919.1	120584.9	136305.4	151322.3	159259.3	178446.7	200900.7	221869.0
258134.3	266360.4	309629.3	337940.1	401751.9	457312.3	514091.1	592378.4
117713.5	125595.1	133295.1	145991.8	173818.8	195557.7	215013.9	233246.0
43536.6	40439.0	25865.7	23681.5	31510.6	34576.2	41704.2	35261.4
19215.7	19555.1	23139.5	27190.4	27175.3	30440.7	35631.3	39670.2
29554.0	28249.6	29327.8	25357.4	33099.8	38810.1	43231.1	43237.0
5130.6	4402.8	4941.7	3898.4	5114.2	5499.0	6011.2	7003.2
16196.7	19710.2	25303.2	31187.7	34937.1	34558.0	34915.5	36736.7
0.0	0.0	0.0	0.0	0.0	0.0	0.0	0.0
0.0	0.0	0.0	0.0	0.0	0.0	0.0	0.0
0.0	0.0	0.0	0.0	0.0	0.0	0.0	0.0
0.0	4.7	120.3	190.8	61.2	755.3	3.5	104.4
0.0	0.0	0.0	0.0	0.0	0.0	0.0	0.0
0.0	0.0	0.0	0.0	0.0	0.0	0.0	0.0
0.0	0.0	0.0	0.0	0.0	0.0	0.0	0.0
0.0	0.0	0.0	0.0	0.0	0.0	0.0	0.0
0.0	0.0	0.0	0.0	0.0	0.0	0.0	0.0
0.0	0.0	0.0	0.0	0.0	0.0	0.0	0.0
0.0	2904.2	3853.9	9977.3	12180.7	11630.6	15381.5	35779.8
1280059.2	1273862.8	1343628.9	1468069.8	1659347.0	1736577.1	1963557.1	2171423.3

Table B-2 R&D benefit received, time series, final demand total

Sector name	Year	1975	1976	1977	1978	1979
01	Agriculture, etc.	1496.4	1556.7	1319.7	1387.6	1621.3
02	Mining	−70.9	−5.8	18.3	−21.3	33.6
03	Food Processing	32997.2	32446.9	31561.3	31355.3	32337.2
04	Textiles	9649.1	10320.8	8510.0	6490.7	5552.1
05	Lumber and Wood	0.0	0.0	0.0	0.0	0.0
06	Furniture, Fixtures	0.0	0.0	0.0	0.0	0.0
07	Pulp and Paper	229.1	728.0	1565.8	581.0	720.6
08	Printing, Publish	1039.8	1357.0	1168.8	1440.0	1368.4
09	Leather & Prod.	0.0	0.0	0.0	0.0	0.0
10	Rubber Products	11411.7	11573.8	10451.2	10250.0	12207.6
11	Chemicals	92432.4	96130.8	81478.9	71381.5	83883.4
12	Petroleum & Coal	1995.2	4434.7	1475.9	1123.3	1812.2
13	Nonmetal Minerals	3025.8	3261.1	3100.7	2752.4	3042.7
14	Iron & Steel Mat.	11414.8	12300.9	11181.2	8704.6	10518.9
15	Iron & Steel Prod.	0.0	0.0	0.0	0.0	0.0
16	Nonferrous Metals	2171.0	1274.8	1792.4	1121.8	2379.8
17	Fabricated Metals	6133.6	7688.3	5844.0	7554.1	8109.6
18	General Machinery	104643.4	115282.6	114528.6	104500.7	120443.5
19	Electrical Mach.	375114.5	377939.3	368076.5	362002.8	372149.5
20	Motor Vehicles	162776.9	192393.2	175248.9	164034.1	181660.6
21	Other Transport	34234.1	37554.6	20732.2	17105.9	15020.2
22	Precision Inst.	27089.6	26502.3	24539.1	26573.2	36574.7
23	Manufacturing nec	8810.5	15046.3	9821.1	17602.1	15882.4
24	Construction	55230.4	61651.0	51550.2	74628.2	67433.3
25	El., Gas, Water	5460.8	6949.3	6082.7	6069.3	5957.0
26	Wholesale Retail	0.0	0.0	0.0	0.0	0.0
27	Fin., Ins., Estate	0.0	0.0	0.0	0.0	0.0
28	Real Estate Rent	0.0	0.0	0.0	0.0	0.0
29	Transportation	38.3	8.7	13.4	0.0	0.0
30	Communication	0.0	0.0	0.0	0.0	0.0
31	Public Admin.	0.0	0.0	0.0	0.0	0.0
32	Public Services	0.0	0.0	0.0	0.0	0.0
33	Private Services	0.0	0.0	0.0	0.0	0.0
34	Office Supplies	0.0	0.0	0.0	0.0	0.0
35	Packing Materials	0.0	0.0	0.0	0.0	0.0
36	Activities nec	2109.1	2404.7	1231.2	1019.6	1059.4
	Total	949532.8	1013800.0	931292.1	927656.9	979817.5

(unit: million yen)

1980	1981	1982	1983	1984	1985	1986	1987
2611.1	1282.9	1363.2	1836.2	2046.3	2229.8	2191.6	3784.6
41.5	−3.3	−13.2	−413.2	−133.6	−92.5	−96.0	−90.5
36309.2	35848.3	40290.2	41421.9	39834.5	41967.9	47817.3	52480.1
4964.6	7003.2	6249.8	7470.2	7789.5	6989.8	7857.1	8457.8
0.0	0.0	0.0	0.0	0.0	0.0	0.0	0.0
0.0	0.0	0.0	0.0	0.0	0.0	0.0	0.0
447.3	307.6	337.0	422.9	496.3	447.5	474.3	505.1
1147.4	1300.7	969.3	981.7	914.2	1252.4	1770.8	2123.9
0.0	0.0	0.0	0.0	0.0	0.0	0.0	0.0
13218.8	14866.7	13873.1	13369.6	14150.7	15634.5	16913.1	20745.5
80020.9	79227.3	84191.7	86548.9	93928.0	96306.6	106198.4	117269.2
1095.0	1386.4	4627.6	3151.2	4125.0	4773.6	4720.2	5298.0
4032.9	3430.9	4415.4	4834.0	5268.3	5764.3	6601.9	7257.1
10149.1	11451.7	13425.0	11315.7	12863.3	13106.8	12610.9	12234.3
0.0	0.0	0.0	0.0	0.0	0.0	0.0	0.0
3633.1	2857.4	3746.0	3035.2	3655.0	3164.9	3459.0	3187.7
6999.9	7745.4	7712.8	7990.5	13170.9	10867.4	10502.8	10804.8
121890.9	120923.1	124366.6	133064.7	137478.7	157991.3	177371.3	196436.0
372149.5	440728.6	467747.7	500620.9	587541.1	689408.7	775003.9	893777.6
212349.5	268737.9	276087.9	282891.2	332646.2	354534.3	389807.1	422861.0
30966.4	22335.0	32933.3	32682.5	37576.4	33945.8	40943.8	34618.6
45072.3	47185.9	50788.5	55505.6	58417.2	69858.3	81771.2	91038.8
15809.0	15298.4	16418.2	14121.6	17581.2	19445.9	21660.9	21664.0
61848.8	58674.2	66059.3	52436.6	65425.9	70559.0	77130.3	89859.8
6402.3	9738.8	11898.8	13920.3	16622.9	16390.0	16559.5	17423.3
0.0	0.0	0.0	0.0	0.0	0.0	0.0	0.0
0.0	0.0	0.0	0.0	0.0	0.0	0.0	0.0
0.0	0.0	0.0	0.0	0.0	0.0	0.0	0.0
0.0	3.3	113.7	177.2	58.3	735.7	3.5	101.6
0.0	0.0	0.0	0.0	0.0	0.0	0.0	0.0
0.0	0.0	0.0	0.0	0.0	0.0	0.0	0.0
0.0	0.0	0.0	0.0	0.0	0.0	0.0	0.0
0.0	0.0	0.0	0.0	0.0	0.0	0.0	0.0
0.0	0.0	0.0	0.0	0.0	0.0	0.0	0.0
0.0	0.0	0.0	0.0	0.0	0.0	0.0	0.0
0.0	876.8	356.2	1114.7	1228.3	1259.4	1665.5	3874.2
1033665.8	1151207.2	1227958.1	1268500.1	1452685.1	1616541.5	1803438.9	2015706.2

Table B-3 R&D benefit received, time series, private consumption

Sector name / Year	1975	1976	1977	1978	1979
01 Agriculture, etc.	1252.7	1419.7	1156.4	1192.1	1447.1
02 Mining	1.4	1.9	2.4	4.4	2.6
03 Food Processing	31630.1	30302.7	30104.1	29968.7	30699.7
04 Textiles	7641.8	3058.7	6916.7	5303.8	4629.7
05 Lumber and Wood	0.0	0.0	0.0	0.0	0.0
06 Furniture, Fixtures	0.0	0.0	0.0	0.0	0.0
07 Pulp and Paper	69.5	98.8	212.5	160.2	146.4
08 Printing, Publish	930.1	1163.9	1058.6	1328.8	1259.1
09 Leather & Prod.	0.0	0.0	0.0	0.0	0.0
10 Rubber Products	5807.5	5108.0	6784.2	6342.0	7530.0
11 Chemicals	38513.5	40436.7	35133.9	40668.9	38225.3
12 Petroleum & Coal	1080.2	3249.3	912.8	857.0	1060.4
13 Nonmetal Minerals	600.8	878.3	521.4	624.2	583.0
14 Iron & Steel Mat.	−107.0	−51.0	−146.9	−144.6	−149.7
15 Iron & Steel Prod.	0.0	0.0	0.0	0.0	0.0
16 Nonferrous Metals	−17.9	−46.4	−18.5	−20.9	−16.4
17 Fabricated Metals	1825.3	2310.8	1741.1	2306.5	2513.3
18 General Machinery	725.2	4939.0	805.6	738.7	882.5
19 Electrical Mach.	73297.5	58285.2	59137.3	57834.4	55470.8
20 Motor Vehicles	23772.4	15942.5	28960.9	26502.3	27435.0
21 Other Transport	2075.2	12426.5	1109.7	1353.1	1726.1
22 Precision Inst.	9265.5	11329.1	6967.2	7893.5	11132.6
23 Manufacturing nec	5037.2	3736.3	5392.0	10113.6	9153.9
24 Construction	0.0	0.0	0.0	0.0	0.0
25 El., Gas, Water	4304.0	5796.0	4813.1	4852.1	4704.8
26 Wholesale Retail	0.0	0.0	0.0	0.0	0.0
27 Fin., Ins., Estate	0.0	0.0	0.0	0.0	0.0
28 Real Estate Rent	0.0	0.0	0.0	0.0	0.0
29 Transportation	63.1	5.5	10.0	0.0	0.0
30 Communication	0.0	0.0	0.0	0.0	0.0
31 Public Admin.	0.0	0.0	0.0	0.0	0.0
32 Public Services	0.0	0.0	0.0	0.0	0.0
33 Private Services	0.0	0.0	0.0	0.0	0.0
34 Office Supplies	0.0	0.0	0.0	0.0	0.0
35 Packing Materials	0.0	0.0	0.0	0.0	0.0
36 Activities nec	236.9	24.2	109.4	117.3	105.9
Total	218015.0	210415.5	191633.9	197996.1	198542.1

(unit: million yen)

1980	1981	1982	1983	1984	1985	1986	1987
25654.1	1248.1	1303.5	1753.0	1736.2	1893.2	1860.8	3213.3
1.0	6.6	1.8	8.2	10.5	4.3	4.5	4.2
34804.4	33807.2	38021.4	39227.2	37594.0	39333.5	45385.4	49811.0
3953.6	5615.0	5000.7	5951.6	6204.3	5719.1	6428.6	6920.1
0.0	0.0	0.0	0.0	0.0	0.0	0.0	0.0
0.0	0.0	0.0	0.0	0.0	0.0	0.0	0.0
−119.6	−14.9	−51.6	−38.9	−58.3	−77.8	−82.5	−87.8
1065.1	1184.0	909.6	905.4	828.1	1124.3	1589.6	1906.6
0.0	0.0	0.0	0.0	0.0	0.0	0.0	0.0
6854.0	7699.4	7209.2	6859.6	7265.2	8499.0	9194.1	11277.4
36281.7	35217.1	41985.3	43042.8	45807.7	50360.0	55532.3	61318.1
922.8	934.5	4130.4	2925.1	3993.3	4690.4	4637.9	5205.6
606.8	427.8	688.1	739.5	711.8	759.5	869.9	956.2
−149.8	−111.4	−101.6	−99.6	−167.8	−137.4	−132.2	−128.2
0.0	0.0	0.0	0.0	0.0	0.0	0.0	0.0
337.7	−22.8	325.1	340.1	522.1	522.5	571.0	526.2
2064.3	1932.2	2311.1	2522.5	4441.3	3346.3	3717.2	3824.1
391.7	579.6	312.8	398.1	325.4	471.0	530.3	585.6
58238.6	44638.0	62967.5	62724.4	64205.1	79926.5	89849.9	103619.9
29651.5	30008.7	33446.6	41730.3	43049.5	40596.8	44635.8	48420.7
2607.7	2159.4	11859.8	12604.2	13499.5	13560.5	16356.0	13829.3
11854.7	12447.2	12065.0	16043.0	14251.2	16158.2	18913.6	21057.2
9195.1	7964.9	9446.5	8030.0	9393.0	10596.3	11803.9	11805.5
0.0	0.0	0.0	0.0	0.0	0.0	0.0	0.0
5335.6	7827.5	9806.3	11425.9	13797.5	13694.3	13836.5	14558.2
0.0	0.0	0.0	0.0	0.0	0.0	0.0	0.0
0.0	0.0	0.0	0.0	0.0	0.0	0.0	0.0
0.0	0.0	0.0	0.0	0.0	0.0	0.0	0.0
0.0	2.5	75.2	122.1	40.1	505.9	2.4	69.9
0.0	0.0	0.0	0.0	0.0	0.0	0.0	0.0
0.0	0.0	0.0	0.0	0.0	0.0	0.0	0.0
0.0	0.0	0.0	0.0	0.0	0.0	0.0	0.0
0.0	0.0	0.0	0.0	0.0	0.0	0.0	0.0
0.0	0.0	0.0	0.0	0.0	0.0	0.0	0.0
0.0	0.0	0.0	0.0	0.0	0.0	0.0	0.0
0.0	75.2	0.0	0.0	0.0	0.0	0.0	0.0
206461.0	193675.8	241712.7	257214.5	267961.3	292547.4	325505.0	358693.1

Table B-4 R&D benefit received, time series, fixed capital formation

Sector name	Year 1975	1976	1977	1978	1979
01 Agriculture, etc.	36.0	47.5	34.2	41.9	37.4
02 Mining	0.0	0.0	0.0	0.0	0.0
03 Food Processing	0.0	0.0	0.0	0.0	0.0
04 Textiles	110.0	75.8	98.2	75.0	64.7
05 Lumber and Wood	0.0	0.0	0.0	0.0	0.0
06 Furniture, Fixtures	0.0	0.0	0.0	0.0	0.0
07 Pulp and Paper	0.0	0.0	0.0	0.0	0.0
08 Printing, Publish	0.0	0.0	0.0	0.0	0.0
09 Leather & Prod.	0.0	0.0	0.0	0.0	0.0
10 Rubber Products	0.0	0.0	0.0	0.0	0.0
11 Chemicals	0.0	0.0	0.0	0.0	0.0
12 Petroleum & Coal	0.0	0.0	0.0	0.0	0.0
13 Nonmetal Minerals	0.0	0.0	0.0	0.0	0.0
14 Iron & Steel Mat.	−275.1	−186.9	−372.1	−361.4	−369.3
15 Iron & Steel Prod.	0.0	0.0	0.0	0.0	0.0
16 Nonferrous Metals	−1539.8	−982.8	−1736.9	−1301.2	−1062.98
17 Fabricated Metals	1343.5	759.6	847.1	1459.6	1800.2
18 General Machinery	69252.0	63745.9	71350.2	65310.4	76630.7
19 Electrical Mach.	161182.0	86121.0	140279.2	150082.7	153385.5
20 Motor Vehicles	53892.0	51449.0	43221.5	45920.4	53933.5
21 Other Transport	4495.0	3877.7	2412.4	2039.5	4322.8
22 Precision Inst.	5073.0	2572.1	4512.9	5024.2	6987.1
23 Manufacturing nec	1117.1	1126.7	1254.5	2023.7	1935.0
24 Construction	36611.7	40682.0	31829.8	46778.1	42729.5
25 El., Gas, Water	0.0	0.0	0.0	0.0	0.0
26 Wholesale Retail	0.0	0.0	0.0	0.0	0.0
27 Fin., Ins., Estate	0.0	0.0	0.0	0.0	0.0
28 Real Estate Rent	0.0	0.0	0.0	0.0	0.0
29 Transportation	2.1	0.2	0.3	0.0	0.0
30 Communication	0.0	0.0	0.0	0.0	0.0
31 Public Admin.	0.0	0.0	0.0	0.0	0.0
32 Public Services	0.0	0.0	0.0	0.0	0.0
33 Private Services	0.0	0.0	0.0	0.0	0.0
34 Office Supplies	0.0	0.0	0.0	0.0	0.0
35 Packing Materials	0.0	0.0	0.0	0.0	0.0
36 Activities nec	341.0	0.0	130.1	131.2	116.7
Total	331640.5	249267.8	293861.4	317224.1	340510.9

(unit: million yen)

1980	1981	1982	1983	1984	1985	1986	1987
112.6	36.0	46.3	57.8	57.2	65.3	64.1	110.8
0.0	0.0	0.0	0.0	0.0	0.0	0.0	0.0
0.0	0.0	0.0	0.0	0.0	0.0	0.0	0.0
57.4	69.5	66.5	75.7	79.5	69.8	78.5	84.5
0.0	0.0	0.0	0.0	0.0	0.0	0.0	0.0
0.0	0.0	0.0	0.0	0.0	0.0	0.0	0.0
0.0	0.0	0.0	0.0	0.0	0.0	0.0	0.0
0.0	0.0	0.0	0.0	0.0	0.0	0.0	0.0
0.0	0.0	0.0	0.0	0.0	0.0	0.0	0.0
0.0	0.0	0.0	0.0	0.0	0.0	0.0	0.0
0.0	0.0	0.0	0.0	0.0	0.0	0.0	0.0
0.0	0.0	0.0	0.0	0.0	0.0	0.0	0.0
0.0	0.0	0.0	0.0	0.0	0.0	0.0	0.0
−369.6	−101.3	−248.4	−697.1	−601.2	−467.1	−449.4	−436.0
0.0	0.0	0.0	0.0	0.0	0.0	0.0	0.0
−271.7	−691.6	661.3	560.7	1115.5	999.7	1092.6	1006.9
1287.2	1836.3	1316.2	1571.1	2607.0	2102.7	2032.2	2090.6
67420.7	67284.1	69025.9	74651.6	78131.1	84816.0	95488.4	105454.7
118627.2	183418.9	154620.3	170982.6	198452.2	24660.0	277284.3	319779.7
55799.0	67036.6	72215.2	70379.7	82047.3	81523.6	89634.5	97235.1
7870.8	3314.5	5491.8	5565.7	5976.0	5886.0	7099.5	6002.7
8576.0	8683.0	10335.1	11536.1	12839.0	14623.6	17117.4	19057.4
1846.3	2090.3	1930.5	1575.2	1986.7	2231.2	2485.4	2485.7
38928.2	36124.2	41031.5	32347.6	41569.2	46463.8	50791.4	59173.6
0.0	0.0	0.0	0.0	0.0	0.0	0.0	0.0
0.0	0.0	0.0	0.0	0.0	0.0	0.0	0.0
0.0	0.0	0.0	0.0	0.0	0.0	0.0	0.0
0.0	0.0	0.0	0.0	0.0	0.0	0.0	0.0
0.0	0.1	2.3	3.0	1.3	17.9	0.1	2.5
0.0	0.0	0.0	0.0	0.0	0.0	0.0	0.0
0.0	0.0	0.0	0.0	0.0	0.0	0.0	0.0
0.0	0.0	0.0	0.0	0.0	0.0	0.0	0.0
0.0	0.0	0.0	0.0	0.0	0.0	0.0	0.0
0.0	0.0	0.0	0.0	0.0	0.0	0.0	0.0
0.0	0.0	0.0	0.0	0.0	0.0	0.0	0.0
0.0	78.3	0.0	0.0	0.0	0.0	0.0	0.0
299884.1	369178.9	356494.5	368609.7	424260.8	484992.5	542719.0	612048.2

Table B-5 R&D benefit received, time series, exports

Sector name	Year 1975	1976	1977	1978	1979
01 Agriculture, etc.	18.7	19.4	13.2	14.7	23.3
02 Mining	5.1	6.2	4.8	7.7	5.5
03 Food Processing	452.6	458.2	397.8	354.2	382.5
04 Textiles	1398.1	1557.4	1243.4	744.0	598.2
05 Lumber and Wood	0.0	0.0	0.0	0.0	0.0
06 Furniture, Fixtures	0.0	0.0	0.0	0.0	0.0
07 Pulp and Paper	347.5	370.3	868.7	362.7	403.0
08 Printing, Publish	20.7	32.0	28.9	28.9	28.4
09 Leather & Prod.	0.0	0.0	0.0	0.0	0.0
10 Rubber Products	4832.6	5417.1	4330.7	3625.5	4653.4
11 Chemicals	4750.0	40216.2	40827.7	35629.1	36942.3
12 Petroleum & Coal	721.0	420.3	335.9	273.8	391.1
13 Nonmetal Minerals	1868.0	1834.8	1874.9	1688.3	1900.7
14 Iron & Steel Mat.	11384.2	12105.5	11739.3	10532.2	11007.9
15 Iron & Steel Prod.	0.0	0.0	0.0	0.0	0.0
16 Nonferrous Metals	2882.7	2535.8	3367.2	2869.2	2726.8
17 Fabricated Metals	2266.3	2892.6	2626.8	2769.1	2639.1
18 General Machinery	27716.9	36119.6	35007.6	31495.9	34678.2
19 Electrical Mach.	106711.4	149633.6	127714.1	114234.9	116690.4
20 Motor Vehicles	58370.5	89551.5	80562.9	70587.9	76740.9
21 Other Transport	26139.9	17609.5	16013.5	12217.1	8248.4
22 Precision Inst.	10804.3	11281.2	11311.7	10958.0	15176.9
23 Manufacturing nec	1523.3	2505.1	2148.5	2983.0	2681.7
24 Construction	0.0	0.0	0.0	0.0	0.0
25 El., Gas, Water	6.9	7.4	17.6	15.1	13.5
26 Wholesale Retail	0.0	0.0	0.0	0.0	0.0
27 Fin., Ins., Estate	0.0	0.0	0.0	0.0	0.0
28 Real Estate Rent	0.0	0.0	0.0	0.0	0.0
29 Transportation	22.2	2.7	2.8	0.0	0.0
30 Communication	0.0	0.0	0.0	0.0	0.0
31 Public Admin.	0.0	0.0	0.0	0.0	0.0
32 Public Services	0.0	0.0	0.0	0.0	0.0
33 Private Services	0.0	0.0	0.0	0.0	0.0
34 Office Supplies	0.0	0.0	0.0	0.0	0.0
35 Packing Materials	0.0	0.0	0.0	0.0	0.0
36 Activities nec	1360.7	871.1	903.8	690.8	767.5
Total	306353.6	375447.5	341341.8	302082.1	316699.7

(unit: million yen)

1980	1981	1982	1983	1984	1985	1986	1987
45.8	30.8	17.7	26.9	26.6	26.6	26.2	45.2
3.8	4.1	4.0	18.0	22.9	11.2	11.7	11.0
568.1	477.6	592.3	566.0	567.1	545.3	621.4	581.9
726.5	1062.9	943.6	1195.7	1207.3	980.1	1101.6	1185.9
0.0	0.0	0.0	0.0	0.0	0.0	0.0	0.0
0.0	0.0	0.0	0.0	0.0	0.0	0.0	0.0
336.2	334.7	335.7	370.6	434.7	366.9	388.9	414.1
35.6	35.1	28.0	32.6	39.9	67.5	95.4	114.5
0.0	0.0	0.0	0.0	0.0	0.0	0.0	0.0
6059.0	7193.3	6640.6	6450.2	6510.2	6793.3	7348.9	9014.2
38294.8	38654.0	38405.5	40726.2	44134.8	46102.6	50837.8	56134.5
362.3	405.9	453.8	307.5	431.6	494.0	488.5	548.3
2352.8	2405.9	2952.7	3350.0	3574.6	3876.8	4440.2	4880.9
11367.8	12778.1	15220.3	13678.0	15030.4	14645.6	14091.5	13670.6
0.0	0.0	0.0	0.0	0.0	0.0	0.0	0.0
3097.4	2910.6	2948.1	2818.1	3075.9	3390.9	3706.1	3415.4
2787.4	3096.8	3206.8	3018.3	4670.3	3518.4	3400.3	3498.1
41642.2	43254.1	45591.5	49341.1	53056.8	60289.7	67875.9	74960.3
132096.0	162347.6	172189.0	190521.1	235550.7	259961.7	292237.8	337024.9
109185.0	140303.7	147336.9	150666.6	188354.3	214645.9	236001.2	256013.0
15964.2	14670.3	13229.8	12285.1	15641.3	13341.2	16091.6	13605.6
19183.5	21877.7	21779.2	25114.8	26619.4	30400.6	35584.8	39617.9
3252.5	3361.9	3549.9	239.8	3644.0	4107.0	4574.9	4575.5
0.0	0.0	0.0	0.0	0.0	0.0	0.0	0.0
6.8	14.78	15.1	18.0	20.6	20.4	20.6	21.7
0.0	0.0	0.0	0.0	0.0	0.0	0.0	0.0
0.0	0.0	0.0	0.0	0.0	0.0	0.0	0.0
0.0	0.0	0.0	0.0	0.0	0.0	0.0	0.0
0.0	0.7	32.2	46.0	15.4	185.9	0.9	25.7
0.0	0.0	0.0	0.0	0.0	0.0	0.0	0.0
0.0	0.0	0.0	0.0	0.0	0.0	0.0	0.0
0.0	0.0	0.0	0.0	0.0	0.0	0.0	0.0
0.0	0.0	0.0	0.0	0.0	0.0	0.0	0.0
0.0	0.0	0.0	0.0	0.0	0.0	0.0	0.0
0.0	0.0	0.0	0.0	0.0	0.0	0.0	0.0
0.0	677.6	370.5	1062.6	1292.6	1258.1	1663.8	3870.2
387367.7	455898.1	475843.2	504443.2	603921.4	665029.7	740610.0	823329.4

Table C-1 World patent application matrix, 1970

From: / To:	1) Australia	2) Austria	3) Belgium	4) Canada	5) Czecho-slovakia	6) Denmark	7) France	8) East Germany	9) West Germany
1) Australia	3984	8	41	149	1	14	89	n.a.	127
2) Austria	48	2,267	130	128	95	49	317	n.a.	638
3) Belgium	60	78	1,339	163	32	49	485	n.a.	310
4) Canada	331	28	71	1,986	7	35	256	n.a.	318
5) Czechoslovakia	28	140	38	54	5,702	23	226	n.a.	361
6) Denmark	50	61	88	99	17	815	152	n.a.	266
7) France	375	351	1,767	1,105	143	268	14,106	n.a.	3,040
8) East Germany	0	0	0	0	0	0	0	n.a.	0
9) West Germany	1,153	4,468	3,906	2,404	725	1,372	8,416	n.a.	32,772
10) Italy	171	323	465	403	75	147	1,226	n.a.	1,149
11) Japan	857	147	593	1,766	119	253	2,526	n.a.	3,838
12) Netherlands	486	427	844	557	62	302	1,134	n.a.	1,334
13) Norway	26	18	28	64	5	102	65	n.a.	114
14) USSR	28	67	125	150	92	32	542	n.a.	569
15) Spain	11	21	64	47	7	19	171	n.a.	115
16) Sweden	208	180	227	454	72	458	630	n.a.	971
17) Switzerland	535	1,264	1,434	848	327	539	2,041	n.a.	2,890
18) UK	1,981	413	1,153	2,123	216	527	3,072	n.a.	3,623
19) USA	5,504	1,125	4,607	17,636	360	1,344	11,538	n.a.	12,618
20) Others	549	380	237	499	896	289	199	n.a.	1,079
21) Foreign Application (A)	12,459	9,519	15,848	28,524	3,251	5,822	33,177	n.a.	33,360
22) Total Application (B)	16,443	11,786	17,187	30,510	8,953	6,637	47,263	n.a.	66,132
23) A/B (in percent)	76	81	92	94	36	88	70	n.a.	50

Source: World Intellectual Property Organization (WIPO), *Industrial Property Statistics* as reported in Patent Agency, *Annual Report of the Patent Agency*.

(unit: number of cases)

	10) Italy	11) Japan	12) Netherlands	13) Norway	14) USSR	15) Spain	16) Swedem	17) Switzerland	18) UK	19) USA	20) Others
1)	57	133	45	17	10	28	39	20	258	285	937
2)	258	233	105	36	92	98	144	344	294	322	620
3)	253	200	310	53	59	127	108	143	348	291	768
4)	144	308	85	45	25	43	133	57	677	1,535	591
5)	141	130	71	7	32	20	80	102	232	108	369
6)	116	141	141	107	17	57	232	93	369	211	353
7)	2,292	1,354	1,383	200	489	1,181	729	1,086	2,546	2,375	3,132
8)	0	0	0	0	0	0	0	0	0	0	0
9)	6,276	5,901	4,107	767	869	1,802	3,112	4,920	7,895	6,808	4,615
10)	7,241	604	502	101	144	560	248	496	958	1,017	1,648
11)	1,443	100,511	1,233	164	438	265	567	661	3,592	5,295	1,661
12)	870	985	2,462	156	83	353	658	513	819	738	1,484
13)	41	34	46	938	19	22	155	34	123	114	176
14)	338	546	78	32	7	10	206	87	506	403	502
15)	128	47	44	13	13	2,966	33	51	117	115	371
16)	403	592	330	482	185	139	4,343	319	843	806	1,144
17)	1,418	1,744	1,162	303	581	876	971	5,927	2,000	1,506	4,952
18)	2,156	2,485	1,486	375	394	769	1,276	855	25,227	4,133	6,442
19)	7,723	13,805	4,951	988	512	2,283	4,062	3,067	14,057	76,195	15,141
20)	530	1,076	513	201	984	211	762	631	1,240	938	
21)	24,587	30,318	16,647	4,069	4,946	8,844	13,515	13,479	36,374	26,980	
22)	31,828	130,829	19,109	5,007	4,953	11,810	17,858	19,403	62,101	103,175	
23)	77	23	87	81	100	75	76	70	59	26	

Table C-2 World patent application matrix, 1975

From: / To:	1) Australia	2) Austria	3) Belgium	4) Canada	5) Czecho-slovakia	6) Denmark	7) France	8) East Germany	9) West Germany
1) Australia	4,311	14	39	158	9	24	130	5	153
2) Austria	27	2,525	116	134	78	40	266	55	554
3) Belgium	60	57	1,060	153	20	52	401	34	307
4) Canada	186	45	79	1,853	7	48	250	8	322
5) Czechoslovakia	18	39	26	31	20	12	112	115	230
6) Denmark	38	49	66	80	17	828	149	29	240
7) France	398	353	1,583	1,057	141	472	12,110	177	2,789
8) East Germany	2	42	139	28	22	13	189	4,559	442
9) West Germany	916	3,268	3,056	2,055	697	1,240	7,181	822	30,198
10) Italy	158	230	414	407	112	165	1,020	110	1,088
11) Japan	839	228	423	1,752	106	176	2,424	78	4,322
12) Netherlands	372	286	646	517	39	230	1,163	55	1,235
13) Norway	35	16	25	76	7	65	74	11	112
14) USSR	56	52	42	154	1	34	466	214	481
15) Spain	25	39	80	48	12	28	223	10	193
16) Sweden	228	204	270	521	78	426	794	84	1,108
17) Switzerland	412	1,014	764	638	231	392	1,843	235	2,647
18) UK	1,262	264	818	1,432	178	447	2,297	100	2,650
19) USA	4,227	841	3,293	14,070	350	1,077	8,521	337	9,938
20) Others	512	345	285	488	190	189	824	235	1,086
21) Foreign Application (A)	9,771	7,386	12,164	23,799	2,295	5,130	26,327	2,714	29,897
22) Total Application (B)	14,082	9,911	13,224	25,652	2,315	5,958	40,437	7,273	60,095
23) A/B (in percent)	69	75	92	93	99	86	70	37	50

(unit: number of cases)

	10) Italy	11) Japan	12) Netherlands	13) Norway	14) USSR	15) Spain	16) Swedem	17) Switzerland	18) UK	19) USA	20) Others
1)	—	186	44	17	19	31	54	30	291	415	512
2)	—	159	101	33	91	75	139	348	245	370	446
3)	—	185	236	34	47	91	68	96	315	445	596
4)	—	301	99	64	48	59	179	57	629	2,127	555
5)	—	86	38	7	9	15	55	77	145	142	219
6)	—	112	101	93	30	48	159	83	464	242	297
7)	—	1,539	1,252	279	456	1,250	783	1,067	2,536	3,048	4,240
8)	—	35	36	5	17	2	51	58	163	13	1,065
9)	—	4,778	3,475	567	957	1,757	2,434	4,066	6,368	8,258	8,915
10)	—	527	417	127	190	461	245	419	884	1,164	1,942
11)	—	135,118	979	127	338	358	582	694	3,611	8,566	2,063
12)	—	994	1,966	148	112	375	496	344	626	1,040	1,030
13)	—	67	51	752	20	35	120	21	124	156	237
14)	—	401	64	13	11	21	196	95	378	696	592
15)	—	83	65	12	19	1,903	40	89	163	182	448
16)	—	701	354	510	213	180	4,042	292	943	1,359	1,063
17)	—	1,386	797	235	410	680	773	5,834	1,696	2,131	3,445
18)	—	1,901	1,044	328	231	750	828	563	20,642	4,566	4,741
19)	—	10,490	3,819	917	1,149	2,158	3,081	2,206	11,485	64,445	15,066
20)	—	772	331	163	352	273	474	501	1,292	1,647	
21)	—	24,703	13,301	3,679	4,708	8,619	10,757	11,106	32,558	36,569	
22)	—	159,821	15,267	4,431	4,719	10,522	14,799	16,940	53,400	101,014	
23)	—	15	87	83	100	82	73	66	61	36	

Table C-3 World patent application matrix, 1980

From: / To:	1) Australia	2) Austria	3) Belgium	4) Canada	5) Czecho-slovakia	6) Denmark	7) France	8) East Germany	9) West Germany
1) Australia	6,582	5	21	233	4	12	58	3	92
2) Austria	64	2,327	45	161	69	36	142	41	487
3) Belgium	42	30	865	182	9	31	173	12	123
4) Canada	183	26	42	1,785	5	20	119	2	172
5) Czechoslovakia	6	28	5	16	57	4	68	88	130
6) Denmark	32	30	53	78	14	964	74	13	174
7) France	396	178	626	1,203	70	312	11,000	83	1,252
8) East Germany	0	43	10	3	0	16	127	6,599	483
9) West Germany	1,003	1,602	860	2,148	423	1,065	4,082	559	28,683
10) Italy	174	195	329	405	69	154	1,059	58	974
11) Japan	1,015	184	288	2,018	50	171	2,498	32	5,267
12) Netherlands	353	153	320	512	15	210	577	40	618
13) Norway	20	5	10	57	2	49	25	5	44
14) USSR	74	51	11	146	1	16	439	280	363
15) Spain	17	16	40	34	1	18	169	2	86
16) Sweden	152	98	127	472	23	342	405	18	665
17) Switzerland	357	526	258	630	147	318	872	97	1,481
18) UK	1,011	100	209	1,194	87	401	818	43	1,013
19) USA	3883	599	1,617	13,125	282	1,184	4,644	305	5,606
20) Others	572	297	233	572	224	246	640	210	870
21) Foreign Application (A)	9,354	4,166	5,104	23,189	1,495	4,605	16,939	1,891	19,900
22) Total Application (B)	15,936	6,493	5,969	24,947	1,552	5,569	27,969	8,490	48,533
23) A/B (in percent)	59	64	36	93	96	83	61	22	41

(unit: number of cases)

	10) Italy	11) Japan	12) Netherlands	13) Norway	14) USSR	15) Spain	16) Swedem	17) Switzerland	18) UK	19) USA	20) Others
1)	43	154	18	8	13	44	20	18	214	517	490
2)	112	191	32	26	51	99	54	173	146	410	357
3)	73	163	87	30	19	79	29	30	185	388	434
4)	66	271	40	37	15	54	80	24	346	1,969	265
5)	58	45	5	1	0	7	22	32	74	90	78
6)	58	119	64	59	23	45	96	40	151	217	265
7)	991	1,674	387	260	266	1,312	233	407	1,085	3,331	3,550
8)	48	93	29	3	0	1	73	90	141	96	276
9)	2,309	5,761	1,086	542	642	1,792	1,124	1,837	3,560	9,669	6,125
10)	6,369	663	292	94	145	541	193	327	904	1,501	1,456
11)	947	165,730	785	90	276	407	365	552	4,223	12,951	3,135
12)	322	944	1,826	106	68	404	179	154	781	1,025	1,104
13)	18	45	10	716	7	14	57	7	51	104	136
14)	155	327	49	9	3	18	132	80	152	338	193
15)	113	45	36	11	8	1,876	21	30	101	142	389
16)	239	598	158	350	117	155	4,106	163	560	1,207	834
17)	585	1,392	269	206	264	579	295	4,049	1,068	1,975	2,651
18)	535	1,571	241	264	152	645	261	176	19,612	4,178	2,985
19)	2,912	10,391	1,688	944	679	2,475	1,445	1,139	6,953	62,098	13,885
20)	382	343	256	207	385	330	407	334	1,333	2,123	
21)	9,971	25,290	5,532	3,247	3,130	9,001	5,086	5,613	22,028	42,231	
22)	16,340	191,020	7,358	3,963	3,133	10,377	9,192	9,662	41,640	104,329	
21)	61	13	75	82	99	83	55	58	53	40	

Table C-4 World patent application matrix, 1985

From: \ To:	1) Australia	2) Austria	3) Belgium	4) Canada	5) Czecho-slovakia	6) Denmark	7) France	8) East Germany	9) West Germany
1) Australia	7,078	15	9	330	6	154	32	3	80
2) Austria	74	2,273	8	177	25	77	80	58	427
3) Belgium	69	10	775	205	1	46	106	4	75
4) Canada	186	9	9	2,092	1	43	42	—	56
5) Czechoslovakia	6	8	3	18	8,692	4	39	136	105
6) Denmark	110	40	3	103	2	917	30	10	147
7) France	519	75	196	1,412	46	457	12,050	55	552
8) East Germany	3	40	6	12	323	31	101	11,790	632
9) West Germany	1,327	639	232	2,270	245	1,341	1,926	449	32,243
10) Italy	235	90	136	518	39	183	560	34	500
11) Japan	1,714	64	82	3,051	29	342	1,332	55	4,149
12) Netherlands	320	26	63	538	11	215	145	37	236
13) Norway	51	11	5	79	3	123	15	2	58
14) USSR	33	65	3	65	627	34	161	776	230
15) Spain	29	8	16	51	3	17	143	3	92
16) Sweden	387	63	17	477	13	674	94	21	349
17) Switzerland	479	158	86	636	62	408	371	99	937
18) UK	1,248	38	66	1,575	63	631	329	40	467
19) USA	5,438	314	404	13,128	144	2,193	1,639	172	2,706
20) Others	542	220	160	767	324	401	390	267	829
21) Foreign Application (A)	12,892	1,895	1,506	25,482	1,967	7,376	7,543	2,221	12,656
22) Total Application (B)	19,970	4,168	2,281	27,574	10,659	8,293	19,593	14,011	44,899
23) A/B (in percent)	65	45	66	92	18	89	38	16	28

(unit: number of cases)

	10) Italy	11) Japan	12) Netherlands	13) Norway	14) USSR	15) Spain	16) Swedem	17) Switzerland	18) UK	19) USA	20) Others
1)	—	267	22	110	63	63	33	26	250	739	1,118
2)	—	200	23	66	85	80	38	125	92	498	493
3)	—	177	57	43	29	109	16	14	106	450	540
4)	—	338	11	62	9	83	22	5	271	2,270	415
5)	—	39	8	—	186	4	15	27	60	68	170
6)	—	134	53	141	63	47	90	47	142	282	704
7)	—	1,874	138	369	195	1,073	90	185	403	3,605	3,008
8)	—	103	15	7	392	3	41	84	123	80	447
9)	—	5,847	372	850	635	1,676	470	860	1,812	10,452	5,763
10)	2,000	672	112	162	101	486	115	147	476	1,628	1,601
11)	—	274,373	225	201	192	612	171	193	2,919	21,431	3,477
12)	—	1,097	1,938	139	78	330	25	13	338	1,221	1,175
13)	—	58	26	938	34	18	76	10	90	160	288
14)	—	141	20	23	165,648	15	128	68	217	145	985
15)	—	65	14	10	2	2,149	10	20	105	207	288
16)	—	613	91	609	164	179	3,879	80	295	1,239	1,348
17)	—	1,330	87	301	169	561	180	3,211	638	1,894	2,992
18)	—	1,817	91	508	197	661	105	59	19,785	3,825	3,987
19)	—	12,637	567	1,858	689	2,831	773	485	3,733	63,874	19,507
20)	—	1,180	172	334	614	297	403	230	1,089	2,711	—
21)	7,851	28,622	2,105	5,796	3,892	9,149	2,808	2,682	13,219	53,132	—
22)	9,851	302,995	4,043	6,796	169,540	11,298	6,687	5,893	33,004	117,006	—
23)	80	9	52	86	2	81	42	46	40	45	—

Table C-5 World patent application matrix, 1987

From: \ To:	1) Australia	2) Austria	3) Belgium	4) Canada	5) Czecho-slovakia	6) Denmark	7) France	8) East Germany	9) West Germany
1) Australia	7,161	58	8	431	2	185	35	7	113
2) Austria	88	2,254	4	171	40	67	45	45	395
3) Belgium	65	5	548	247	5	51	111	3	55
4) Canada	193	2	3	2,527	5	45	30	1	38
5) Czechoslovakia	1	7	2	14	8,866	5	22	59	72
6) Denmark	124	54	5	117	4	1,090	31	11	126
7) France	588	84	122	1,554	49	461	12,695	54	381
8) East Germany	2	49	11	3	289	21	101	11,180	585
9) West Germany	1,330	541	133	2,400	208	1,339	1,465	432	31,663
10) Italy	296	67	65	549	46	229	461	41	419
11) Japan	1,606	64	53	3,714	39	371	1,098	40	3,635
12) Netherlands	377	17	26	556	21	249	66	39	143
13) Norway	52	7	2	95	4	116	15	4	31
14) USSR	50	47	8	89	715	31	156	397	222
15) Spain	12	5	11	48	5	25	118	3	67
16) Sweden	457	121	2	398	16	569	51	16	271
17) Switzerland	502	122	76	626	65	436	314	103	848
18) UK	1,481	103	46	1,658	61	742	226	59	383
19) USA	6,038	324	206	13,426	151	2,407	1,145	163	2,022
20) Others	642	165	104	405	244	320	372	206	728
21) Foreign Application (A)	14,036	1,844	889	26,598	1,969	7,670	5,875	1,683	10,562
22) Total Application (B)	21,197	4,098	1,437	29,125	10,835	8,760	18,570	12,863	42,225
23) A/B (in percent)	66.2	45.0	61.9	91.3	18.2	87.6	31.6	13.1	25.0

(unit: number of cases)

	10) Italy	11) Japan	12) Netherlands	13) Norway	14) USSR	15) Spain	16) Swedem	17) Switzerland	18) UK	19) USA	20) Others
1)	—	333	75	210	118	49	83	64	334	1,249	2,252
2)	—	209	12	70	69	17	35	72	63	584	501
3)	—	209	44	54	23	29	14	15	82	539	377
4)	—	318	5	65	23	12	11	5	364	2,791	495
5)	—	20	2	1	70	—	1	21	9	50	1,576
6)	—	154	69	191	67	25	82	55	140	457	720
7)	—	1,950	117	459	235	257	104	181	325	4,331	3,986
8)	—	68	21	4	168	2	40	97	93	47	330
9)	—	5,841	262	966	624	408	366	690	1,367	11,878	8,162
10)	—	777	90	205	218	183	68	108	370	1,985	2,437
11)	—	311,006	138	215	212	189	149	184	2,432	25,526	2,909
12)	—	1,278	1,971	172	83	24	28	20	354	1,387	1,372
13)	—	69	16	907	33	13	60	9	81	260	413
14)	—	195	16	35	178,082	34	88	39	174	279	1,412
15)	—	83	13	12	4	1,720	11	14	84	228	269
16)	—	583	113	824	24	63	3,614	112	134	1,716	3,531
17)	—	1,332	99	337	182	155	107	3,310	579	2,086	3,151
18)	—	1,927	151	668	317	168	145	128	20,193	5,773	5,537
19)	—	12,843	515	2,463	786	812	607	425	2,976	68,671	22,547
20)	—	1,853	126	419	655	146	339	196	1,333	3,731	—
21)	—	30,089	1,906	7,403	3,912	2,590	2,346	2,438	11,372	65,136	
22)	—	341,095	3,877	8,310	181,994	4,310	5,960	5,748	31,505	133,807	
23)	—	8.8	49.2	89.1	2.1	60.1	39.4	42.4	36.0	48.7	—

Table D-1 Flow of funds, 1970

	Financial institutions		The Bank of Japan		Private financial institutions		Public financial institutions	
	Assets	Lia-bilities	Assets	Lia-bilities	Assets	Lia-bilities	Assets	Lia-bilities
1) Deposits with The Bank of J.	812	812		812	812			
2) Currency		7,550		[(a)]7,990	325		115	
3) Demand Deposits		25,589				25,740	198	47
4) Time Deposits		72,767				59,058		13,709
5) Certificates of Deposits								
6) Non-Resident Yen Deposits & Foreign Currency Deposits		690				690		
7) Government Current Deposits		−49		−49				
8) Trust		8,121				8,121		
9) Insurance		15,567				11,967		3,600
10) Securities	21,914	13,306	[(b)]2,127		10,725	12,151	9,062	1,155
11) Short-Term Gov't Securities	1,260		1,513		−1,800		1,547	
12) Government Bonds	2,755		4,086		−2,168		837	
13) Local Government Bonds	1,739				1,639		100	
14) Public Corporation Bonds	4,719	1,137	−2,235		2,199		4,755	1,137
15) Bank Debentures	4,378	8,275	−1,237		3,776	8,275	1,839	
16) Industrial Bonds	2,452				2,472		−20	
17) Stocks	4,554	1,166			4,550	1,166	4	
18) Securities Investment Trust	57	2,572			57	2,572		
19) Bonds in Foreign Currency		156				138		18
20) The Bank of Japan Loans	4,116	4,116	4,116			4,116		
21) Call Money	4,287	4,287			4,287	4,287		
22) Bills Bought & Sold								
23) Loans	134,925				113,448		21,477	
24) Loans by Private Fin. Insts.	113,448				113,448			
25) Loans by Public Fin. Insts.	21,477						21,477	
26) Trade Credit								
27) Trust Fund Bureau deposits		11,513						11,513
28) Gold & Foreign Exchange	—		—					
29) Foreign Trade Credits	5,306	979			5,306	979		
30) Foreign Direct Investment								
31) Other Foreign Claims & Debts	1,412	2,580			772	2,653	640	−73
32) Others		−1,615	2,510			5,913		1,541
33) Financial Surplus or Deficit		6,559						
34) Total	172,772	172,772	8,753	8,753	135,675	135,675	31,492	31,492

Notes: (a) Including ¥ 744.8 billion of Bank of Japan Notes.
(b) Including ¥ 786.6 billion of net purchases of securities by the Bank of Japan from private financial institutions.
(c) Including ¥ 227.8 billion of Foreign Exchange Fund Bill.

Source: Bank of Japan, *Flow of Funds Accounts in Japan.*

(unit: ¥ 100 million)

Central government		Public corporation & local authorities		Corporate business		Private persons		Rest of the world		Total assets or liabilities
Assets	Lia-bilities	Assets	Lia-bilities	Assets	Lia-bilities	Assets	Lia-bilities	Assets	Lia-bilities	
										812
		8		757		6,785				7,550
		740		14,956		9,893				25,589
		1,357		20,948		50,462				72,767
										690
−49										−49
		97		1,585		6,439				8,121
						15,567				15,567
679	6,841	185	8,257	4,553	13,370	14,025		2,749		41,774
385	[c]1,917	138								1,917
241	4,969	−8				306				4,969
			1,831			34				1,831
		−71	6,486	1,490		2,040		1,896		7,623
						3,522				8,275
					3,460	775				3,460
53		126		2,963	9,803	4,933		695		10,969
				100		2,415				2,572
	−45		−60		107			158		158
										4,116
										4,287
	981		10,110		94,231		29,603			134,925
			1,696		86,175		25,577			113,448
	981		8,414		8,056		4,026			21,477
				89,119	71,780		17,339			89,119
11,513										11,513
—									2,812	2,812
				2,833	3,384			3,384	7,160	11,523
				1,278	338			338	1,278	1,616
	−131		−75	372	588	12		4,014	6,327	9,289
5,054			234	−3,297		1,512				−1,381
	9,506		−16,139		−50,587		57,753		−7,092	—
17,197	17,197	2,387	2,387	133,104	133,104	104,695	104,695	10,485	10,485	440,640

Table D-2 Flow of funds, 1975

	Financial institutions		The Bank of Japan		Private financial institutions		Public financial institutions	
	Assets	Lia-bilities	Assets	Lia-bilities	Assets	Lia-bilities	Assets	Lia-bilities
1) Deposits with The Bank of J.	−4,425	−4,425		−4,425	−4,432		7	
2) Currency		7,755		(a)10,188	1,868		565	
3) Demand Deposits		46,829				47,213	891	507
4) Time Deposits		186,034				136,612		49,422
5) Certificates of Deposits								
6) Non-Resident Yen Deposits & Foreign Currency Deposits		3,217				3,217		
7) Government Current Deposits		46		46				
8) Trust		20,103				20,103		
9) Insurance		33,385				21,900		11,485
10) Securities	99,986	34,285	(b)22,602		70,257	31,345	7,127	2,940
11) Short-Term Gov't Securities	11,567		−13,911		2		25,476	
12) Government Bonds	36,635		35,354		24,913		−23,632	
13) Local Government Bonds	12,377				12,379		−2	
14) Public Corporation Bonds	13,507	2,819	1,159		9,380		2,968	2,819
15) Bank Debentures	6,953	25,714			5,220	25,714	1,733	
16) Industrial Bonds	8,874				8,327		547	
17) Stocks	10,050	1,686			10,013	1,686	37	
18) Securities Investment Trust	23	3,568			23	3,568		
19) Bonds in Foreign Currency		498				377		121
20) The Bank of Japan Loans	992	992	992			992		
21) Call Money	2,188	2,188			2,188	2,188		
22) Bills Bought & Sold	−10,291	−10,291	−18,593		8,302	−10,291		
23) Loans	273,417				188,698		84,719	
24) Loans by Private Fin. Insts.	188,698				188,698			
25) Loans by Public Fin. Insts.	84,719						84,719	
26) Trade Credit								
27) Trust Fund Bureau deposits		28,400						28,400
28) Gold & Foreign Exchange	—		—					
29) Foreign Trade Credits	1,761	−2,404			1,761	−2,404		
30) Foreign Direct Investment								
31) Other Foreign Claims & Debts	−2,028	7,445			−4,750	7,479	2,722	−34
32) Others		−3,692	808			5,538		3,311
33) Financial Surplus or Deficit		11,733						
34) Total	361,600	361,600	5,809	5,809	263,892	263,892	96,031	96,031

Notes: (a) Including ¥ 949.3 billion of Bank of Japan Notes.
(b) Including ¥ 552.3 billion of net purchases of securities by the Bank of Japan from private financial institutions.
(c) Including ¥ 84.9 billion of Foreign Exchange Fund Bill.

(unit: ¥ 100 million)

Central government		Public corporation & local authorities		Corporate business		Private persons		Rest of the world		Total assets or liabilities
Assets	Lia-bilities	Assets	Lia-bilities	Assets	Lia-bilities	Assets	Lia-bilities	Assets	Lia-bilities	
										−4,425
				775		6,980				7,755
		915		29,023		16,891				46,829
		1,795		31,490		152,749				186,034
										3,217
46										46
		−714		2,268		18,549				20,103
						33,385				33,385
1,049	53,159	874	30,953	7,337	27,747	32,288		8,844		146,144
1,053	(c)13,451	352								13,451
	39,742	16				1,356				39,742
			15,185			1,250				15,185
		184	15,818	4,304		2,695		3,548		18,637
						16,118				25,714
					12,878	3,456				12,878
−4		322		3,023	11,619	3,878		1,632		13,305
				10		3,535				3,568
	−34		−50		3,250			3,664		3,664
										992
										2,188
										−10,291
	13,158		42,655		147,506		70,098			273,417
			4,210		128,272		56,216			188,698
	13,158		38,445		19,234		13,882			84,719
				53,282	18,106		35,176			53,282
28,400										28,400
—									−2,202	−2,202
				88	−5,472			−5,472	4,253	−3,623
				5,235	671			671	5,235	5,906
	−6		−73	1,634	−1,899			5,494	245	5,712
−3,483			−1,955	−5,842		1,071				−5,647
	−40,299		−68,710		−61,369		156,639		2,006	—
26,012	26,012	2,870	2,870	125,290	125,290	261,913	261,913	9,537	9,537	787,222

Table D-3 Flow of funds, 1980

	Financial institutions		The Bank of Japan		Private financial institutions		Public financial institutions	
	Assets	Lia-bilities	Assets	Lia-bilities	Assets	Lia-bilities	Assets	Lia-bilities
1) Deposits with The Bank of J.	10,555	10,555		10,555	10,558		−3	
2) Currency		3,607		[(a)]3,260	−793		446	
3) Demand Deposits		−26,274				−25,301	1,004	31
4) Time Deposits		270,070				175,648		94,422
5) Certificates of Deposits		6,990				6,990		
6) Non-Resident Yen Deposits & Foreign Currency Deposits		31,522				31,522		
7) Government Current Deposits		−313		−313				
8) Trust		23,309				23,309		
9) Insurance		60,021				39,841		20,180
10) Securities	147,138	27,915	[(b)]25,868		71,237	16,613	50,033	11,302
11) Short-Term Gov't Securities	24,288		18,792		−33		5,529	
12) Government Bonds	60,815		7,102		25,745		27,968	
13) Local Government Bonds	12,900				9,935		2,965	
14) Public Corporation Bonds	26,162	11,175	−26		14,742		11,446	11,175
15) Bank Debentures	6,640	16,511			5,959	16,511	681	
16) Industrial Bonds	4,674				3,389		1,285	
17) Stocks	11,090	914			10,931	914	159	
18) Securities Investment Trust	569	−1,117			569	−1,117		
19) Bonds in Foreign Currency		432				305		127
20) The Bank of Japan Loans	−1,131	−1,131	−1,131			−1,131		
21) Call Money	20,893	20,893			20,893	20,893		
22) Bills Bought & Sold	−7,049	−7,049	−3,500		−3,549	−7,049		
23) Loans	328,607				208,401		120,206	
24) Loans by Private Fin. Insts.	208,401				208,401			
25) Loans by Public Fin. Insts.	120,206						120,206	
26) Trade Credit								
27) Trust Fund Bureau deposits		44,316						44,316
28) Gold & Foreign Exchange	—		—					
29) Foreign Trade Credits	19,825	13,351			19,825	13,351		
30) Foreign Direct Investment								
31) Other Foreign Claims & Debts	40,502	52,599			36,954	52,626	3,548	−27
32) Others		6,686	−7,735			16,214		5,010
33) Financial Surplus or Deficit		22,273						
34) Total	559,340	559,340	13,502	13,502	363,526	363,526	175,234	175,234

Notes: (a) Including ¥ 278.6 billion of Bank of Japan Notes.
(b) Including ¥ 754.2 billion of net purchases of securities by the Bank of Japan from private financial institutions.
(c) Including ¥ 1,329.0 billion of Foreign Exchange Fund Bill.

(unit: ¥ 100 million)

Central government		Public corporation & local authorities		Corporate business		Private persons		Rest of the world		Total assets or liabilities
Assets	Lia-bilities	Assets	Lia-bilities	Assets	Lia-bilities	Assets	Lia-bilities	Assets	Lia-bilities	
										10,555
				361		3,246				3,607
		−2,321		−14,126		−9,827				−26,274
		4,683		39,285		226,102				270,070
		1,592		5,378		20				6,990
										31,522
−313										−313
		632		3,884		18,793				23,309
						60,021				60,021
5,120	153,031	−172	33,175	19,211	22,180	32,291		33,800		236,301
−8,335	(c)15,705	−340								15,705
13,465	137,336	62				17,063				137,336
			14,088			−121				14,088
		−61	18,974	15,044		2,572		16,615		30,149
						9,132				16,511
					5,630	967				5,630
−10		167		4,271	14,408	4,260		14,508		15,322
				−104		−1,582				−1,117
	−10		113		2,142			2,677		2,677
										−1,131
										20,893
										−7,049
	10,927		56,965		152,989		107,726			328,607
			3,321		133,596		71,484			208,401
	10,927		53,644		19,393		36,242			120,206
				94,911	62,431		32,480			94,911
44,316										44,316
—									10,376	10,376
				1,112	17,902			17,902	7,586	38,839
				5,442	633			633	5,442	6,075
			−66	2,086	−10,570			42,836	45,996	87,959
38,640			−932	4,913		5,547				5,754
	−76,195		−84,728		−83,108		195,987		25,771	—
87,763	87,763	4,414	4,414	162,457	162,457	336,193	336,193	95,171	95,171	1,245,338

Table D-4 Flow of funds, 1985

	Financial institutions		The Bank of Japan		Private financial institutions		Public financial institutions	
	Assets	Lia-bilities	Assets	Lia-bilities	Assets	Lia-bilities	Assets	Lia-bilities
1) Deposits with the Bank of J.	−1,185	−1,185		−1,185	−1,161		−24	
2) Cash Currency		12,833		[(a)]11,770	−1,385		322	
3) Demand Deposits		17,222				18,678	926	−530
4) Time Deposits		306,314				221,502		84,812
5) Certificates of Deposit		10,104				8,849	−1,255	
6) Non-Resident Yen Deposits & Foreign Currency Deposits		33,533				33,533		
7) Government Current Deposits		−60		−60				
8) Trust		61,415				61,415		
9) Insurance		114,441				84,721		29,720
10) Securities	207,693	62,763	[(b)] −29,911		130,170	51,544	107,434	11,219
11) Short-term Gov't Securities	−17,894		−15,256		2		−2,640	
12) Government Bonds	128,368		−14,654		42,742		100,280	
13) Local Government Bonds	−1,218				−4,721		3,503	
14) Public Corporation Bonds	22,359	9,717	−1		14,938		7,422	9,717
15) Bank Debentures	13,180	25,326			14,569	25,326	−1,389	
16) Industrial Bonds	9,541				9,372		169	
17) Stocks	51,473	3,711			51,384	3,711	89	
18) Securities Investment Trust	1,884	18,176			1,884	18,176		
19) External Bonds		5,833				4,331		1,502
20) The Bank of Japan Loans	11,079	11,079	11,079			11,079		
21) Call Money	42,388	42,388			42,388	42,388		
22) Bills Bought & Sold	67,019	67,019	25,932		41,087	67,019		
23) Commercial Paper								
24) Loans	381,820				312,450		69,370	
25) Loans by Private Fin. Insts.	312,450				312,450			
26) Loans by Public Fin. Insts.	69,370						69,370	
27) Trade Credit								
28) Trust Fund Bureau deposits		55,833						55,833
29) Gold Foreign Exchange	—		—					
30) Foreign Trade Credits	6,727	464			6,727	464		
31) Foreign Direct Investment	3,133				3,133			
32) Other Foreign Claims & Debts	140,425	74,817			133,396	74,817	7,029	
33) Others		−5,268	3,425			−9,204		2,748
34) Financial Surplus or Deficit		−4,613						
35) Total	859,099	859,099	10,525	10,525	666,805	666,805	183,802	183,802

Notes: (a) Including ¥ 1,018.4 billion of Bank of Japan Notes.
(b) Including ¥ 474.4 billion of net purchases of securities by the Bank of Japan from private financial institutions.
(c) Including ¥ −247.3 billion of Foreign Exchange Fund Bill.

(unit: ¥ 100 million)

Central government		Public corporation & local authorities		Corporate business		Private persons		Rest of the world		Total assets or liabilities
Assets	Lia-bilities	Assets	Lia-bilities	Assets	Lia-bilities	Assets	Lia-bilities	Assets	Liabilities	
										−1,185
				1,283		11,550				12,833
		−1,253		11,072		7,403				17,222
		9,177		87,916		209,221				306,314
		2,129		7,586		389				10,104
		4,969		19,425		1,791		7,348		33,533
−60										−60
		690		24,843		35,882				61,415
						114,441				114,441
703	122,446	48	26,485	19,751	50,459	32,019		40,361		262,153
11,945	(c)−6,153	17								−6,153
−11,241	128,624	226				8,949				128,624
			1,998			387				1,998
		108	23,586	16,909		5,509		11,309		33,303
						11,042				25,326
					6,819	−4,197				6,819
−1		−303		2,349	20,178	−5,470		−1,119		23,889
				493		15,799				18,176
	−25		901		23,462			30,171		30,171
										11,079
										42,388
										67,019
	−827		52,789		239,880		89,978			381,821
			12,852		229,779		69,819			312,450
	−827		39,937		10,101		20,159			69,370
				28,517	14,020		14,497			28,517
55,833										55,833
—									880	880
				6,988	−2,661			−2,661	13,251	11,054
				12,148	1,452			1,452	15,281	16,733
			−48	77,487	8,599			85,044	217,308	300,676
−1,770			1,362	−44,727		2,769				−3,906
	−66,913		−64,828		−59,460		310,990		−115,176	—
54,706	54,706	15,760	15,760	252,289	252,289	415,465	415,465	131,544	131,544	1,728,863

Table D-5 Flow of funds, 1988

	Financial institutions		The Bank of Japan		Private financial institutions		Public financial institutions	
	Assets	Lia-bilities	Assets	Lia-bilities	Assets	Lia-bilities	Assets	Lia-bilities
1) Deposits with the Bank of J.	12,835	12,835		12,835	12,822		13	
2) Cash Currency		28,979		[a]32,531	3,249		303	
3) Demand Deposits		65,068				63,736	61	1,393
4) Time Deposits		407,746				345,322	15,260	77,684
5) Certificates of Deposit		20,566				21,055	489	
6) Non-Resident Yen Deposits & Foreign Currency Deposits		−26,495				−26,495		
7) Government Current Deposits		129		129				
8) Trust		112,698				112,698		
9) Insurance		235,410				189,140		46,270
10) Securities	427,233	181,155	[b]28,878		325,155	170,796	73,200	10,359
11) Short-Term Gov't Securities	17,917		15,506		1,616		795	
12) Government Bonds	99,803		13,372		59,887		26,544	
13) Local government Bonds	−1,511				−9,231		7,720	
14) Public Corporation Bonds	14,791	9,468			−7,449		22,240	9,468
15) Bank Debentures	41,286	38,748			39,001	38,748	2,285	
16) Industrial Bonds	43,560	21,659			29,986	21,659	13,574	
17) Stocks	199,939	32,184			199,897	32,184	42	
18) Securities Investment Trust	11,448	77,983			11,448	77,983		
19) Exterdnal Bonds		1,113				222		891
20) The Bank of Japan Loans	19,072	19,072	19,072			19,072		
21) Call Money	−17,285	−17,285			−17,285	−17,285		
22) Bills Bought & Sold	49,168	49,168	3,007		46,161	49,168		
23) Commercial Paper	59,012				59,012			
24) Loans	584,696				473,506		111,190	
25) Loans by Private Fin. Insts.	473,506				473,503			
26) Loans by Public Fin. Insts.	111,190						111,190	
27) Trade Credit								
28) Trust Fund Bureau deposits		72,532						72,532
29) Gold & Foreign Exchange	—		—					
30) Foreign Trade Credits	1,917	−142			1,917	−142		
31) Foreign Direct Investment	11,578				11,578			
32) Other Foreign Claims & Debts	290,574	250,762			280,248	250,758	10,326	4
33) Others		54,532	−5,462			18,540		2,600
34) Financial Surplus or Deficit		−27,930						
35) Total	1,438,800	1,438,800	45,495	45,495	1,196,363	1,196,363	210,842	210,842

Notes: (a) Including ¥ 3,131.5 billion of Bank of Japan Notes.
(b) Including ¥ 421.5 billion of net purchases of securities by the Bank of Japan from private financial institutions.
(c) Including ¥ 2,285 billion of Foreign Exchange Fund Bill.

(unit: ¥ 100 million)

Central government		Public corporation & local authorities		Corporate business		Private persons		Rest of the world		Total assets or liabilities
Assets	Liabilities	Assets	Liabilities	Assets	Liabilities	Assets	Liabilities	Assets	Liabilities	
										12,835
				3,018		25,961				28,979
		−416		32,386		33,098				65,068
		39,723		166,219		201,804				407,746
		1,949		18,570		47				20,566
		−2,193		−20,441		−1,807		−2,054		−26,495
129										129
		939		49,500		62,259				112,698
						235,410				235,410
−38,937	55,912	5	12,214	21,830	111,154	29,334		40,977		360,435
−10,976	[(c)]6,580	−118								6,580
	49,336	−27				−12,727				49,336
			−4,395			−42				−4,395
		24	14,985	−15,378		4,843		−12,882		24,453
						−2,240				38,748
					16,072	−3,720				37,731
−27,961		126		29,111	52,257	−15,218		8,301		84,441
				8,097		58,438				77,983
	−4		1,624		42,825			45,558		45,558
										19,072
										−17,285
										49,168
				16,865	75,877					75,877
	−3,210		27,062		339,760		221,084			584,696
			−10,999		301,121		183,384			473,506
	−3,210		38,061		38,639		37,700			111,190
				181,613	156,277		25,336			181,613
72,532										72,532
—									20,588	20,588
				8,970	−1,234			−1,234	11,029	9,653
				32,224	−620			−620	43,802	43,182
			−58	38,930	16,993			265,432	329,005	596,702
34,224			−5,722	−20,809		−62,258				48,810
	15,246		6,511		−169,332		277,428		−101,923	—
67,948	67,948	40,007	40,007	528,875	528,875	523,848	523,848	302,501	302,501	2,901,979

Table E-1 Fixed capital formation matrix, 1970

	JSIC	Industrial Sectors	Total IP	01&	10&	18	20&
(1)	01&	Agriculture, forestry, and fisheries	94,043	80,087	0	0	0
(2)	10&	Mining					
(3)	18	Food processing					
(4)	20&	Textiles	32,377	18,486	56	311	311
(5)	22	Lumber and wood products	11,388	0	0	0	0
(6)	23	Furniture and fixtures	186,835	1,735	747	4,148	4,148
(7)	24	Pulp, paper, and paper products					
(8)	25	Printing and publishing					
(9)	29	Leather and leather products					
(10)	28	Rubber products					
(11)	26	Chemicals					
(12)	27	Petroleum and coal products					
(13)	30	Nonmetalic mineral products					
(14)	31A	Iron and steel materials					
(15)	31B	Basic iron and steel products					
(16)	32	Basic nonferrous metal products					
(17)	33	Fabricated metals	163,885	200	40	1,883	46
(18)	34	General machinery	3,444,332	414,048	53,953	133,866	175,800
(19)	35	Electrical machinery	1,697,718	22,248	11,807	13,431	15,345
(20)	36M	Transport equipment, motor vehicles	1,564,289	74,781	23,621	35,249	50,282
(21)	36S	Transport equipment, others	482,756	59,053	8,770	168	38
(22)	37	Precision instrument	101,782	534	533	2,600	2,247
(23)	38&	Other manufacturing	76,830	95	283	0	0
(24)	15	Construction	6,343,844	502,974	50,420	109,934	158,751
(25)	70	Electric power, gas, and water					
(26)	40	Wholesale and retail trade					
(27)	60T	Transportation					
		Total	14,200,079	1,174,241	150,230	301,590	406,968

	32	33	34	35	36	37	38&	15	70
(1)	0	0	0	0	0	0	0	0	0
(2)									
(3)									
(4)	24	215	395	433	317	81	125	614	195
(5)	0	0	0	11,388	0	0	0	0	0
(6)	318	2,859	5,269	5,773	4,223	1,084	1,641	8,181	1,607
(7)									
(8)									
(9)									
(10)									
(11)									
(12)									
(13)									
(14)									
(15)									
(16)									
(17)	0	0	115	6,759	586	11	0	0	2,597
(18)	47,030	38,429	173,808	133,400	207,295	15,824	127,278	345,070	106,567
(19)	13,674	14,829	39,059	129,537	91,832	7,072	6,838	11,136	229,293
(20)	5,702	19,032	26,770	14,959	7,517	4,628	26,104	325,301	47,154
(21)	275	151	259	0	6,356	0	56	13,320	268
(22)	1,402	1,714	4,953	3,572	9,796	1,128	344	985	767
(23)	0	0	0	0	281	0	0	23	0
(24)	53,048	128,870	162,854	148,519	197,359	25,086	132,065	128,160	422,343
(25)									
(26)									
(27)									
	121,473	206,099	413,482	454,340	525,562	54,914	294,451	832,790	810,791

Source: Administrative Management Agency, *1970 Input-Output Tables.*

(unit: million yen)

22	23	24	25	29	28	26	27	30	31
0		0		0		0	0	0	0
136		216		50		231	27	122	121
0		0		0		0	0	0	0
1,812		2,877		673		3,083	355	1,626	1,607
0		90		0		33,641	21,396	66	1,053
44,094		158,490		19,217		295,389	164,305	48,797	333,582
4,439		23,292		6,323		107,358	21,790	15,153	119,043
55,503		21,031		4,665		18,736	2,480	25,660	51,949
280		4,281		3		606	426	1,207	5,962
104		468		139		9,180	1,136	1,388	10,613
0		0		0		0	0	0	0
59,931		69,789		6,811		255,447	80,999	80,614	468,208
166,299		280,534		37,881		723,671	292,911	174,633	992,138

40	50&	50R	60T	60C	97	75M	NEC
0	0		0	0		13,596	0
2,982	1,855		829	0		4,245	0
0	0		0	0		0	0
63,798	24,719		11,040	0		33,512	0
0	0		24,686	0		70,716	0
146,912	20,126		80,552	0		160,500	0
41,938	70,337		69,520	0		612,424	0
416,775	30,972		99,882	0		175,536	0
44,075	0		309,452	0		26,185	1,568
0	0		1,580	0		46,599	0
17,790	0		13,583	0		44,775	0
746,396	1,319,687		205,694	11,342		797,202	21,341
1,480,666	1,467,696		816,818	11,342		1,985,650	22,909

Table E-2 Fixed capital formation matrix, 1975

	JSIC	Industrial Sectors	Total IP	01&	10&	18	20&
(1)	01&	Agriculture, forestry, and fisheries	204,800	179,696	0	0	0
(2)	10&	Mining					
(3)	18	Food processing					
(4)	20&	Textiles	62,151	32,216	121	464	670
(5)	22	Lumber and wood products	22,104	0	0	774	0
(6)	23	Furniture and fixtures	316,831	2,168	864	5,663	5,446
(7)	24	Pulp, papaer, and paper products					
(8)	25	Printing and publishing					
(9)	29	Leather and leather products					
(10)	28	Rubber products					
(11)	26	Chemicals					
(12)	27	Petroleum and coal products					
(13)	30	Nonmetallic mineral products					
(14)	31A	Iron and steel materials					
(15)	31B	Basic iron and stell products					
(16)	32	Basic nonferrous metal products					
(17)	33	Fabricated metals	332,847	409	25	3,564	20
(18)	34	General machinery	4,821,083	663,357	87,771	202,538	121,229
(19)	35	Electrical machinery	2,786,629	36,723	11,535	13,014	13,092
(20)	36M	Transport equipment, motor vehicles	1,789,754	108,670	18,373	24,945	21,272
(21)	36S	Transport equipment, others	569,923	63,752	5,942	283	25
(22)	37	Precision instrument	233,015	387	523	3,887	2,419
(23)	38&	Other manufacturing	224,680	24,207	261	0	0
(24)	15	Construction	10,249,412	830,478	32,424	169,703	212,147
(25)	70	Electric power, gas, and water					
(26)	40	Wholesale and retail trade	2,229,193	206,287	20,999	48,056	35,072
(27)	60T	Transportation	225,906	19,718	2,502	4,188	3,032
		Total	24,068,328	2,168,068	181,340	477,079	414,424

	32	33	34	35	36	37	38&	15	70
(1)	0	0	0	0	0	0	0	0	0
(2)									
(3)									
(4)	52	463	851	932	683	174	269	1,322	260
(5)	7,770	0	0	0	0	0	0	1,127	0
(6)	744	9,743	4,708	10,558	7,833	573	11,220	7,018	7,033
(7)									
(8)									
(9)									
(10)									
(11)									
(12)									
(13)									
(14)									
(15)									
(16)									
(17)	69	60	63	13,649	378	0	60	16,941	4,308
(18)	42,552	58,735	224,153	54,847	406,575	10,548	54,891	291,860	205,394
(19)	14,881	8,436	87,011	84,892	58,148	4,175	21,160	45,865	368,663
(20)	2,423	16,552	11,973	8,952	4,160	4,774	37,757	259,808	12,628
(21)	0	0	85	0	6,558	0	7	10,252	3,420
(22)	2,704	1,239	3,038	2,961	5,448	22,713	1,562	1,220	6,839
(23)	0	0	0	0	1,183	0	0	62	0
(24)	73,927	184,281	149,793	185,934	344,464	11,240	195,837	166,404	1,364,615
(25)									
(26)	11,389	21,265	62,869	31,493	99,906	8,819	27,211	130,658	83,208
(27)	1,422	1,804	5,634	3,695	7,910	856	2,635	14,269	11,725
	157,933	302,578	550,178	399,913	943,246	63,872	352,609	946,806	2,068,093

Source: Administrative Management Agency, *1975 Input-Output Tables.*

(unit: million yen)

22	23	24	25	29	28	26	27	30	31
0	0	0	0	0	0	0	0	0	0
155	293	0	465	0	108	497	58	263	261
0	0	0	0	3,500	0	0	0	0	0
383	2,232	2,189	3,641	0	703	6,683	1,040	10,259	2,570
0	0	0	0	0	0	67,542	43,855	1	1,378
42,560	2,575	64,718	125,218	1,179	26,777	302,371	225,934	78,983	471,818
904	979	19,490	6,645	0	1,410	98,260	17,616	11,267	307,860
23,987	4,524	4,921	13,553	1,924	2,690	8,467	2,213	6,945	21,533
/	0	0	10,651	0	0	50	73	9,573	5,638
0	0	436	46	10	1,129	7,027	4,864	1,608	11,999
0	0	0	0	0	0	0	0	0	0
49,583	28,890	52,036	68,979	4,668	21,266	373,058	117,596	119,813	427,083
14,450	2,880	17,181	28,748	1,507	4,702	73,310	31,942	22,892	132,080
1,388	255	1,642	2,417	221	514	8,011	4,416	1,958	14,549
133,410	41,628	162,613	260,363	13,009	59,299	945,276	449,607	263,562	1,396,769

40	50&	50R	60T	60C	97	75M	Paking	NEC
0	0	0	0	0	0	25,104	0	0
6,421	3,500	0	1,785	0	0	9,141	0	727
0	0	0	0	0	0	8,933	0	0
39,079	22,386	0	11,718	200	0	139,355	0	822
0	0	0	49,681	0	0	128,038	0	2,806
250,383	153,616	0	61,355	1,283	0	313,782	108,087	165,994
124,488	74,543	0	100,767	18,714	0	1,161,017	0	73,074
369,658	54,831	0	257,112	163	0	478,826	6,120	0
52,020	12,947	0	329,702	0	0	51,336	0	7,609
3,350	108	0	3,991	0	0	130,792	5,070	7,645
47,914	0	0	36,527	0	0	114,526	0	0
1,311,883	953,733	215,452	335,690	14,154	0	1,913,945	0	321,336
210,343	67,452	0	133,701	1,986	0	609,544	25,954	63,287
22,046	7,339	0	15,790	483	0	58,466	2,048	4,972
2,437,585	1,350,455	215,452	1,337,819	36,983	0	5,142,805	147,279	648,272

Table E-3 Fixed capital formation matrix, 1980

	JSIC	Industrial Sectors	Total IP	01&	10&	18	20&
(1)	01&	Agriculture, forestry, and fisheries	272,834	233,896	0	0	0
(2)	10&	Mining					
(3)	18	Food processing					
(4)	20&	Textiles	83,459	48,373	0	0	0
(5)	22	Lumber and wood products	26,372	0	0	527	0
(6)	23	Furniture and fixtures	459,389	2,994	753	6,014	3,633
(7)	24	Pulp, paper, and paper products					
(8)	25	Printing and publishing					
(9)	29	Leather and leather products					
(10)	28	Rubber products					
(11)	26	Chemicals					
(12)	27	Petroleum and coal products					
(13)	30	Nonmetallic mineral products					
(14)	31A	Iron and steel materials					
(15)	31B	Basic iron and steel products					
(16)	32	Basic nonferrous metal products	135,293	0	0	0	0
(17)	33	Fabricated metals	451,475	8	9,654	16,150	6
(18)	34	General machinery	6,479,724	578,609	51,789	339,490	139,666
(19)	35	Electrical machinery	4,409,233	30,660	5,904	30,240	14,243
(20)	36M	Transport equipment, motor vehicles	2,817,368	121,556	29,325	30,411	14,064
(21)	36S	Transport equipment, others	1,094,641	144,197	10,301	140	0
(22)	37	Precision instrument	497,396	141	742	8,563	997
(23)	38&	Other manufacturing	351,896	20,279	483	0	0
(24)	15	Construction	18,549,912	1,025,399	1,810	109,403	37,447
(25)	70	Electric power, gas, and water					
(26)	40	Wholesale and retail trade	3,563,048	230,817	27,291	74,049	40,608
(27)	60T	Transportation	234,595	10,908	1,435	5,197	1,744
		Total	39,426,635	2,447,840	139,487	620,184	252,408

	32	33	34	35	36	37	38&	15	70
(1)	0	0	0	0	0	0	0	0	0
(2)									
(3)									
(4)	0	0	0	0	0	0	0	0	0
(5)	3,600	0	0	0	0	0	0	0	0
(6)	714	7,635	14,730	4,589	9,420	812	11,411	58,986	9,787
(7)									
(8)									
(9)									
(10)									
(11)									
(12)									
(13)									
(14)									
(15)									
(16)	0	0	0	0	0	0	0	0	135,293
(17)	0	0	52	0	239	0	221	536	4,579
(18)	91,497	74,051	635,200	157,104	749,747	50,161	163,799	689,111	178,929
(19)	19,415	10,420	145,628	113,386	92,313	30,303	27,262	24,712	721,610
(20)	3,703	25,403	18,211	14,389	5,875	7,036	124,925	395,088	9,129
(21)	0	0	1,146	0	20,223	0	8,552	14,452	2,537
(22)	3,551	3,807	17,704	33,289	23,252	9,184	5,069	21,613	53,988
(23)	0	0	0	0	2,188	0	0	115	0
(24)	102,945	65,790	122,849	623,191	246,346	130,171	70,235	638,665	4,017,446
(25)									
(26)	27,499	29,244	165,281	60,506	178,104	19,008	81,190	336,064	121,393
(27)	1,575	1,516	10,000	4,028	10,737	1,160	4,314	14,374	14,342
	254,499	217,866	1,130,801	1,010,482	1,338,441	247,835	496,978	2,193,716	5,269,040

Source: Administrative Management Agency, *1980 Input-Output Tables*.

(unit: million yen)

22	23	24	25	29	28	26	27	30	31
0	0	0	0	0	0	0	0	0	0
0	0	0	0	0	0	0	0	0	0
0	0	0	0	0	0	0	0	0	13,542
1,061	475	1,681	2,950	0	665	5,331	762	5,344	1,727
0	0	0	0	0	0	0	0	0	0
0	0	16	0	0	0	258	23,985	40	447
51,403	36,761	82,597	166,509	835	2,533	345,189	94,218	161,227	243,484
918	2,212	29,327	11,008	86	1,942	112,723	20,316	22,388	183,077
22,215	4,128	2,503	6,459	949	1,378	4,116	1,093	3,518	32,003
0	0	0	0	0	0	13	0	16,350	1,124
44	199	833	2,293	0	2,275	41,863	5,275	4,634	11,945
0	0	0	0	0	0	0	0	0	0
10,001		31,120	31,120		27,108	187,391	96,879	93,085	296,975
16,131	8,260	16,103	33,012	457	1,874	70,322	16,476	33,667	89,654
933	496	1,394	2,147	21	121	6,123	1,876	2,523	6,735
102,706	52,531	165,574	255,498	2,348	37,896	773,329	260,880	342,776	880,713

40	50&	50R	60T	60C	97	75M	NEC
0	0	0	0	0	0	38,938	0
0	0	0	0	0	0	0	35,086
0	0	0	0	0	0	8,703	0
33,483	23,244	211	9,496	4,773	0	208,506	28,202
0	0	0	0	0	0	0	0
0	0	0	263,652	0	0	103,198	28,434
631,154	98,221	0	102,974	166	0	324,515	160,323
285,187	74,101	0	94,176	106,745	0	2,109,810	89,229
550,017	29,584	0	332,042	9,665	0	913,199	105,384
81,875	19,761	0	709,475	0	0	59,889	3,553
955	10,343	0	935	4,768	0	219,710	9,420
88,615	0	0	67,555	2,567	0	170,094	0
2,216,201	3,783,548	0	714,417	110,449	21,116	3,606,746	132,059
394,084	53,320	100	260,588	17,360	0	1,053,378	93,925
31,598	3,059	4	18,361	1,662	0	68,338	6,991
4,313,169	4,095,181	315	2,573,671	257,998	21,116	8,885,024	692,606

Table E-4 Fixed capital formation matrix, 1985

	JSIC	Industrial Sectors	Total IP	01&	10&	18	20&
(1)	01&	Agriculture, forestry, and fisheries	243,479	196,982	0	0	0
(2)	10&	Mining					
(3)	18	Food processing					
(4)	20&	Textiles	250,544	55,157	180	1,979	2,527
(5)	22	Lumber and wood products	21,128	0	0	4,385	755
(6)	23	Furniture and fixture	865,600	19,510	530	8,708	4,622
(7)	24	Pulp, paper, and paper products					
(8)	25	Printing and publishing					
(9)	29	Leather and leather products					
(10)	28	Rubber products					
(11)	26	Chemicals					
(12)	27	Petroleum and coal products					
(13)	30	Nonmetallic mineral products					
(14)	31A	Iron and steel materials					
(15)	31B	Basic iron and steel products					
(16)	32	Basic nonferrous metal products	283,089	0	0	0	0
(17)	33	Fabricated metals	422,923	784	288	4,081	3,582
(18)	34	General machinery	10,595,256	740,941	56,543	522,106	287,425
(19)	35	Electrical machinery	8,379,195	39,789	4,482	73,239	42,963
(20)	36M	Transport equipment, motor vehicles	3,148,068	28,368	8,197	17,830	13,417
(21)	36S	Transport equipment, others	1,807,568	240,043	12,622	10,869	4,482
(22)	37	Precision instrument	839,452	371	714	8,911	5,307
(23)	38&	Other manufacturing	535,702	0	0	0	0
(24)	15	Construction	31,477,811	861,373	29,871	315,805	162,127
(25)	70	Electric power, gas, and water					
(26)	40	Wholesale and retail trade	4,829,798	364,067	19,781	112,599	40,685
(27)	60T	Transportation	363,985	13,868	1,044	7,506	4,822
		Total	64,063,598	2,561,253	134,252	1,088,018	572,714

	32	33	34	35	36M	36S	37	38&	15
(1)	0	0	0	0	0	0	0	0	0
(2)									
(3)									
(4)	214	2,423	2,398	1,594	478	983	470	1,651	12,742
(5)	3,236	6,132	0	0	0	0	0	0	0
(6)	3,042	8,012	8,031	16,602	7,161	2,740	928	7,210	8,928
(7)									
(8)									
(9)									
(10)									
(11)									
(12)									
(13)									
(14)									
(15)									
(16)	0	0	0	0	0	0	0	0	0
(17)	381	3,308	3,685	2,839	1,145	1,643	738	2,471	33,736
(18)	141,793	179,724	617,316	547,832	1,179,738	308,311	94,477	900,003	622,658
(19)	36,865	49,716	651,765	1,343,215	146,453	85,091	83,061	81,405	197,555
(20)	2,794	19,962	19,292	12,790	1,953	3,498	8,000	42,259	113,421
(21)	4,267	6,978	13,415	19,862	18,581	10,456	7,009	1,465	53,148
(22)	10,312	3,955	25,527	45,819	29,208	4,886	67,466	6,651	19,021
(23)	0	0	0	0	0	0	0	0	0
(24)	117,306	233,993	285,826	680,078	315,953	121,031	31,053	261,075	284,245
(25)									
(26)	35,714	60,816	241,646	323,215	268,038	55,966	45,844	161,590	214,147
(27)	2,618	3,866	14,483	20,740	16,348	4,429	3,125	12,250	12,825
	358,542	578,885	1,883,384	3,014,586	1,985,056	599,034	342,171	1,478,030	1,572,426

Source: Management and Coordination Agency, *1985 Input-Output Tables.*

(unit: million yen)

22	23	24	25	29	28	26	27	30	31
0	0	0	0	0	0	0	0	0	0
890	717	533	2,103	208	215	296	25	828	320
0	0	0	0	1,082	0	0	0	0	5,538
1,168	1,120	2,734	2,124	443	1,844	8,097	1,392	2,669	4,923
0	0	0	0	0	0	0	0	0	0
1,153	964	873	2,906	275	349	1,080	193	1,381	677
39,423	33,039	111,094	324,987	47,477	91,468	479,315	74,070	267,145	319,028
11,250	10,589	51,195	60,843	2,743	9,019	131,286	40,363	37,459	227,298
10,803	2,662	4,750	11,948	2,052	2,653	10,374	1,521	3,888	14,305
5,612	288	6,077	7,001	407	1,493	12,015	1,996	29,101	7,730
43	852	7,737	4,820	43	4,917	60,204	7,380	10,784	24,756
0	0	0	0	0	0	0	0	0	0
56,040	53,667	133,431	60,926	12,283	51,320	317,749	59,837	132,113	346,086
17,250	12,165	30,959	82,729	7,250	15,762	92,139	18,526	56,301	115,454
933	614	2,129	4,401	591	1,278	8,255	1,458	3,880	7,336
144,565	116,677	351,512	564,788	74,854	180,318	1,120,810	206,761	545,549	1,073,451

70	40	50&	50R	60T	60C	97	75P	75M	NEC
0	0	0	0	0	0	0	0	46,497	0
487	31,408	2,499	2,564	4,067	9	0	4,151	116,077	351
0	0	0	0	0	0	0	0	0	0
9,737	146,028	139,197	3,085	15,133	4,716	0	174,137	216,021	35,008
283,089	0	0	0	0	0	0	0	0	0
18,392	95,198	25,111	75	87,548	7,675	0	679	92,146	27,567
692,997	706,186	124,441	0	161,370	16,413	0	53,092	792,237	62,607
651,260	793,170	476,546	0	139,477	721,024	0	419,045	1,728,863	32,166
10,949	345,190	29,444	0	1,224,285	6,835	0	235,900	936,599	2,129
771	16,504	147	0	1,185,256	300	0	2,657	120,723	6,293
23,981	79,921	1,050	2	1,065	936	0	305,443	69,047	8,323
0	5,961	0	0	142,526	72	0	218,397	102,963	65,783
1,583,237	1,914,784	5,608,435	401,041	777,370	608,416	0	1,736,579	2,913,638	11,011,123
155,435	416,979	142,038	7,713	368,943	117,926	0	306,726	885,435	35,960
44,492	29,276	8,339	2,377	38,432	8,779		19,425	58,504	5,562
3,474,827	4,580,605	6,557,248	416,857	4,145,472	1,493,101	0	3,476,231	8,078,750	11,292,872

Table F-1 All industries

a. Factor inputs

(unit: value in billion yen)

Year	Real output VQSNA	Capital stock KP	Labor force NL	Share of laber XWLSNA	Capital formation IP	Capacity utilization rate RHO	Working hours HX
1955	33,649.1	18,679.6	41,190.0	0.3928	1,206.6	0.7800	1.0439
1956	36,898.3	19,861.5	41,970.0	0.4024	1,678.6	0.8330	1.0681
1957	40,563.9	21,516.0	43,030.0	0.3950	2,099.7	0.8360	1.0632
1958	42,157.4	23,006.0	43,240.0	0.4141	1,988.1	0.7340	1.0611
1959	47,941.5	24,545.3	43,680.0	0.4113	2,337.0	0.8340	1.0723
1960	55,639.2	27,063.6	44,610.0	0.3941	3,309.3	0.8930	1.0863
1961	63,508.9	30,584.7	45,180.0	0.3845	4,520.0	0.9020	1.0772
1962	69,105.3	34,120.7	45,740.0	0.4050	4,651.2	0.8440	1.0600
1963	75,476.4	37,519.6	46,130.0	0.4094	4,865.7	0.8490	1.0536
1964	85,224.7	41,745.2	46,730.0	0.4102	5,802.9	0.8990	1.0488
1965	89,560.4	45,619.4	47,480.0	0.4285	5,407.5	0.8480	1.0338
1966	100,180.5	49,897.3	48,470.0	0.4283	6,065.8	0.9040	1.0354
1967	114,190.8	55,755.7	49,200.0	0.4176	7,753.3	0.9790	1.0343
1968	128,677.7	63,069.2	50,020.0	0.4128	9,869.8	1.0090	1.0327
1969	147,007.9	71,836.8	50,400.0	0.4133	12,008.2	1.0220	1.0182
1970	162,415.2	82,630.0	50,940.0	0.4209	13,882.4	1.0000	1.0000
1971	171,759.0	93,745.1	51,140.0	0.4453	14,444.2	0.9450	0.9904
1972	188,841.8	105,878.8	51,260.0	0.4482	15,257.9	0.9500	0.9850
1973	206,011.5	118,775.0	52,590.0	0.4582	18,176.5	1.0110	0.9737
1974	199,384.4	130,103.5	52,370.0	0.4885	16,220.8	0.9140	0.9405
1975	199,470.9	140,444.3	52,230.0	0.5170	14,040.3	0.7790	0.9218
1976	211,566.6	149,679.9	52,710.0	0.5220	15,774.1	0.8440	0.9352
1977	221,770.9	151,908.1	53,420.0	0.5295	16,155.0	0.8380	0.9362
1978	235,141.6	169,000.1	54,080.0	0.5207	17,262.3	0.8630	0.9389
1979	248,977.9	180,190.5	54,790.0	0.5199	19,551.3	0.9250	0.9443
1980	256,093.8	191,883.3	55,360.0	0.5238	20,860.8	0.8720	0.9415
1981	268,876.6	205,398.4	55,810.0	0.5331	22,048.9	0.8319	0.9384
1982	274,692.9	218,331.4	56,380.0	0.5340	22,562.6	0.8075	0.9362
1983	286,394.9	231,985.2	57,330.0	0.5391	23,037.4	0.8206	0.9368
1984	304,421.5	247,305.6	57,660.0	0.5347	25,704.9	0.8807	0.9448
1985	317,656.3	278,440.0	58,070.0	0.5268	28,990.3	0.8912	0.9421
1986	328,842.4	297,206.8	58,530.0	0.5317	29,210.6	0.8502	0.9389
1987	343,639.9	316,193.3	59,110.0	0.5317	32,309.8	0.8510	0.9426
1988	363,227.4	332,348.2	60,110.0	0.5317	35,124.0	0.9018	0.9426

Source: COMPASS database.

b. Sources of growth

Year	Growth of output	Labor input total	Labor	Working hours	Capital input total	Capital	Capacity utilization	Residual	Embodied technology	Capital vintage
1956	0.0965	0.0171	0.0076	0.0095	0.0809	0.0378	0.0431	−0.0014	−0.0011	−0.0003
1957	0.1017	0.0081	0.0099	−0.0018	0.0527	0.0504	0.0023	0.0400	0.0271	0.0129
1958	0.0369	0.0012	0.0020	−0.0008	−0.0358	0.0405	−0.0764	0.0714	0.0557	0.0157
1959	0.1372	0.0085	0.0041	0.0043	0.1249	0.0393	0.0855	0.0036	0.0025	0.0010
1960	0.1605	0.0136	0.0083	0.0052	0.1094	0.0621	0.0472	0.0362	0.0212	0.0149
1961	0.1414	0.0016	0.0049	−0.0032	0.0870	0.0800	0.0070	0.0524	0.0272	0.0252
1962	0.0881	−0.0015	0.0050	−0.0065	0.0261	0.0687	−0.0426	0.0637	0.0380	0.0257
1963	0.0921	0.0010	0.0034	−0.0024	0.0626	0.0588	0.0038	0.0284	0.0185	0.0099
1964	0.1291	0.0034	0.0053	−0.0018	0.1050	0.0664	0.0386	0.0204	0.0131	0.0073
1965	0.0508	0.0006	0.0068	−0.0062	0.0176	0.0530	−0.0354	0.0325	0.0253	0.0071
1966	0.1185	0.0096	0.0089	0.0006	0.0949	0.0536	0.0412	0.0137	0.0107	0.0030
1967	0.1398	0.0058	0.0062	−0.0004	0.1223	0.0683	0.0539	0.0114	0.0081	0.0033
1968	0.1268	0.0062	0.0068	−0.0006	0.0973	0.0770	0.0203	0.0229	0.0150	0.0078
1969	0.1424	−0.0027	0.0031	−0.0058	0.0901	0.0815	0.0086	0.0553	0.0359	0.0193
1970	0.1048	−0.0030	0.0045	−0.0076	0.0726	0.0870	−0.0143	0.0354	0.0245	0.0109
1971	0.0575	−0.0025	0.0017	−0.0042	0.0400	0.0746	−0.0346	0.0201	0.0158	0.0043
1972	0.0994	−0.0014	0.0010	−0.0024	0.0747	0.0714	0.0033	0.0262	0.0227	0.0035
1973	0.0909	0.0065	0.0118	−0.0053	0.1050	0.0659	0.0390	−0.0203	−0.0166	−0.0036
1974	−0.0321	−0.0186	−0.0020	−0.0165	−0.0049	0.0487	−0.0537	−0.0089	−0.0090	0.0001
1975	0.0004	−0.0116	−0.0013	−0.0102	−0.0386	0.0383	−0.0770	0.0518	0.0654	−0.0135
1976	0.0606	0.0124	0.0048	0.0076	0.0739	0.0314	0.0425	−0.0251	−0.0288	0.0037
1977	0.0482	0.0077	0.0071	0.0005	0.0036	0.0070	−0.0033	0.0363	0.0395	−0.0031
1978	0.0602	0.0079	0.0064	0.0015	0.0698	0.0539	0.0159	−0.0172	−0.0212	0.0039
1979	0.0588	0.0098	0.0068	0.0030	0.0685	0.0317	0.0367	−0.0192	−0.0204	0.0012
1980	0.0285	0.0038	0.0054	−0.0015	0.0018	0.0309	−0.0290	0.0226	0.0239	−0.0012
1981	0.0499	0.0025	0.0043	−0.0017	0.0099	0.0328	−0.0229	0.0372	0.0397	−0.0025
1982	0.0216	0.0041	0.0054	−0.0012	0.0148	0.0293	−0.0145	0.0026	0.0028	−0.0002
1983	0.0426	0.0094	0.0090	0.0003	0.0367	0.0288	0.0079	−0.0035	−0.0040	0.0004
1984	0.0629	0.0076	0.0030	0.0045	0.0670	0.0307	0.0363	−0.0116	−0.0124	0.0007
1985	0.0434	0.0022	0.0037	−0.0015	0.0659	0.0595	0.0063	−0.0245	−0.0282	0.0036
1986	0.0352	0.0023	0.0042	−0.0018	0.0085	0.0315	−0.0230	0.0241	0.0268	−0.0026
1987	0.0450	0.0073	0.0052	0.0021	0.0303	0.0299	0.0004	0.0071	0.0075	−0.0003
1988	0.0570	0.0090	0.0090	0.0000	0.0533	0.0239	0.0293	−0.0052	−0.0052	0.0000

Note: Figures are in terms of growth contribution.
Source: COMPASS simulation results.

Table F-2 Manufacturing
a. Factor inputs

Year	Real output VQSNA	Capital stock KP	Labor force NL	Share of laber XWLSNA	Capital formation IP	Capacity utilization rate RHO	Working hours HX
1955	10,738.8	5,798.8	7,560.0	0.4310	394.6	0.7800	1.0566
1956	12,732.8	6,266.1	8,050.0	0.4209	638.9	0.8330	1.0907
1957	14,613.2	7,043.1	8,530.0	0.4066	918.6	0.8360	1.0827
1958	14,566.5	7,553.4	9,000.0	0.4470	790.4	0.7340	1.0747
1959	17,469.1	8,259.7	9,010.0	0.4158	1,055.6	0.8340	1.0923
1960	21,776.3	9,692.6	9,510.0	0.3864	1,775.9	0.8930	1.1046
1961	25,981.8	11,675.9	10,160.0	0.3769	2,470.7	0.9020	1.0854
1962	28,160.3	13,628.6	10,720.0	0.4089	2,378.3	0.8440	1.0587
1963	31,783.7	15,443.6	11,120.0	0.4052	2,399.1	0.8490	1.0507
1964	36,649.1	17,663.1	11,370.0	0.3929	2,862.3	0.8990	1.0443
1965	38,613.9	19,341.0	11,570.0	0.4164	2,393.8	0.8480	1.0235
1966	43,845.6	20,987.3	11,870.0	0.4176	2,540.3	0.9040	1.0299
1967	51,936.8	23,920.5	12,520.0	0.4065	3,755.1	0.9790	1.0347
1968	59,793.2	27,904.5	13,050.0	0.4024	5,076.4	1.0090	1.0299
1969	70,351.4	32,524.3	13,450.0	0.4036	6,009.9	1.0220	1.0139
1970	80,378.5	38,090.1	13,770.0	0.4031	7,027.7	1.0000	1.0000
1971	84,368.2	43,425.6	13,810.0	0.4258	6,691.4	0.9450	0.9835
1972	91,889.3	48,373.2	13,780.0	0.4354	6,339.3	0.9500	0.9781
1973	102,185.8	53,907.4	14,360.0	0.4447	7,609.2	1.0110	0.9712
1974	98,449.7	59,071.1	14,170.0	0.4893	7,449.0	0.9140	0.9242
1975	93,708.1	62,956.6	13,340.0	0.5385	5,368.0	0.7790	0.8959
1976	83,787.7	66,118.7	13,450.0	0.5190	5,994.4	0.8440	0.9280
1977	107,717.8	69,201.6	13,400.0	0.5233	5,895.4	0.8380	0.9312
1978	113,653.2	72,009.5	13,260.0	0.5018	5,591.9	0.8630	0.9370
1979	121,753.1	75,509.8	13,330.0	0.4981	6,795.2	0.9250	0.9493
1980	127,384.0	79,435.4	13,670.0	0.5038	7,889.3	0.8720	0.9509
1981	133,880.1	84,514.1	13,850.0	0.5174	8,543.9	0.8319	0.9466
1982	136,225.7	89,203.7	13,800.0	0.5173	8,812.9	0.8075	0.9445
1983	143,248.3	94,052.9	14,060.0	0.5244	8,909.3	0.8206	0.9498
1984	156,579.1	100,106.2	14,380.0	0.5151	10,442.9	0.8807	0.9632
1985	164,843.0	108,039.4	14,530.0	0.5146	11,912.8	0.8912	0.9589
1986	167,802.3	114,521.7	14,440.0	0.5199	10,987.1	0.8502	0.9509
1987	170,118.0	120,454.7	14,250.0	0.5199	11,495.8	0.8510	0.9557
1988	186,437.4	127,369.5	14,540.0	0.5199	12,805.2	0.9018	0.9663

b. Sources of growth

Year	Growth of output	Labor input total	Labor	Working hours	Capital input total	Capital	Capacity utilization	Residual	Embodied technology	Capital vintage
1956	0.1856	0.0417	0.0272	0.0144	0.0891	0.0466	0.0425	0.0198	0.0340	0.0157
1957	0.1476	0.0210	0.0242	−0.0031	0.0759	0.0735	0.0024	0.0481	0.0275	0.0206
1958	−0.0032	0.0211	0.0246	−0.0034	−0.0322	0.0400	−0.0723	0.0075	0.0054	0.0021
1959	0.1992	0.0072	0.0004	0.0068	0.1416	0.0546	0.0870	0.0494	0.0302	0.0192
1960	0.2465	0.0260	0.0214	0.0045	0.1573	0.1064	0.0509	0.0591	0.0279	0.0312
1961	0.1931	0.0187	0.0257	−0.0070	0.1350	0.1275	0.0075	0.0374	0.0169	0.0204
1962	0.0838	0.0119	0.0225	−0.0106	0.0544	0.0988	−0.0443	0.0169	0.0102	0.0066
1963	0.1286	0.0119	0.0151	−0.0031	0.0832	0.0792	0.0039	0.0325	0.0230	0.0095
1964	0.1530	0.0063	0.0088	−0.0024	0.1281	0.0872	0.0408	0.0182	0.0130	0.0052
1965	0.0536	−0.0011	0.0073	−0.0084	0.0191	0.0554	−0.0362	0.0356	0.0336	0.0019
1966	0.1354	0.0135	0.0108	0.0026	0.0913	0.0495	0.0417	0.0297	0.0286	0.0011
1967	0.1845	0.0242	0.0222	0.0020	0.1390	0.0829	0.0561	0.0200	0.0155	0.0044
1968	0.1512	0.0150	0.0170	−0.0019	0.1208	0.0995	0.0213	0.0147	0.0103	0.0044
1969	0.1765	0.0059	0.0123	−0.0064	0.1076	0.0987	0.0089	0.0620	0.0449	0.0171
1970	0.1425	0.0039	0.0095	−0.0056	0.0871	0.1021	−0.0150	0.0510	0.0389	0.0120
1971	0.0496	−0.0058	0.0012	−0.0070	0.0444	0.0804	−0.0360	0.0111	0.0105	0.0006
1972	0.0891	−0.0033	−0.0009	−0.0023	0.0676	0.0643	0.0033	0.0250	0.0274	−0.0024
1973	0.1120	0.0154	0.0187	−0.0032	0.1032	0.0635	0.0397	−0.0064	−0.0064	0.0000
1974	−0.0365	−0.0298	−0.0064	−0.0233	−0.0047	0.0489	−0.0536	−0.0020	−0.0023	0.0002
1975	−0.0481	−0.0470	−0.0315	−0.0155	−0.0422	0.0303	−0.0726	0.0451	0.0720	−0.0269
1976	0.0932	0.0230	0.0042	0.0187	0.0663	0.0241	0.0421	0.0037	0.0052	−0.0015
1977	0.0515	−0.0001	−0.0019	0.0018	0.0186	0.0222	−0.0035	0.0329	0.0475	−0.0145
1978	0.0551	−0.0021	−0.0052	0.0030	0.0356	0.0202	0.0154	0.0216	0.0329	−0.0112
1979	0.0712	0.0092	0.0026	0.0065	0.0622	0.0244	0.0378	−0.0001	−0.0001	0.0000
1980	0.0462	0.0137	0.0128	0.0008	−0.0041	0.0258	−0.0299	0.0356	0.0400	−0.0043
1981	0.0510	0.0044	0.0068	−0.0023	0.0072	0.0308	−0.0236	0.0389	0.0428	−0.0039
1982	0.0177	−0.0030	−0.0018	−0.0011	0.0118	0.0267	−0.0149	0.0089	0.0099	−0.0009
1983	0.0513	0.0128	0.0098	0.0030	0.0339	0.0258	0.0081	0.0043	0.0049	−0.0006
1984	0.0930	0.0191	0.0117	0.0074	0.0690	0.0312	0.0378	0.0047	0.0048	−0.0001
1985	0.0527	0.0030	0.0053	−0.0023	0.0447	0.0384	0.0062	0.0049	0.0049	0.0000
1986	0.0179	−0.0075	−0.0032	−0.0043	0.0053	0.0288	−0.0234	0.0203	0.0227	−0.0024
1987	0.0138	−0.0042	−0.0068	0.0025	0.0253	0.0248	0.0004	−0.0073	−0.0081	0.0007
1988	0.0959	0.0164	0.0105	0.0058	0.0578	0.0275	0.0303	0.0209	0.0217	−0.0008

Table F-3 Iron and steel
a. Factor inputs

Year	Real output VQSNA	Capital stock KP	Labor force NL	Share of laber XWLSNA	Capital formation IP	Capacity utilization rate RHO	Working hours HX
1955	1,341.0	939.2	274.9	0.4074	34.6	0.7040	1.0312
1956	1,600.2	966.3	302.4	0.2687	54.5	0.7260	1.0582
1957	1,907.6	1,061.0	331.8	0.2257	136.5	0.7540	1.0442
1958	1,794.0	1,109.9	317.4	0.4513	143.1	0.4980	1.0457
1959	2,444.2	1,188.8	361.0	0.3519	202.0	0.7780	1.0764
1960	3,234.0	1,459.1	419.9	0.3035	359.2	0.8650	1.0993
1961	4,093.6	1,834.2	473.5	0.2738	482.9	0.9140	1.0821
1962	3,962.4	2,171.2	465.5	0.4014	414.6	0.7690	1.0307
1963	4,415.4	2,446.7	478.7	0.4008	365.5	0.7760	1.0301
1964	5,334.3	2,724.8	493.1	0.3156	390.4	0.8760	1.0338
1965	5,335.7	2,952.2	475.6	0.3667	349.7	0.8080	1.0088
1966	6,007.7	3,280.9	480.6	0.3574	352.3	0.8530	1.0140
1967	7,623.3	3,757.1	498.2	0.3603	621.3	0.9400	1.0426
1968	8,545.2	4,364.7	518.3	0.3760	786.1	0.9410	1.0374
1969	10,503.4	5,309.4	535.7	0.3322	943.0	1.0010	1.0192
1970	12,065.7	6,167.6	552.3	0.2664	1,018.4	1.0000	1.0000
1971	12,073.4	7,051.7	535.1	0.3060	1,078.9	0.8780	0.9615
1972	13,284.6	7,765.9	528.6	0.2864	914.9	0.8960	0.9522
1973	15,740.6	8,373.6	528.2	0.2731	866.1	1.0110	0.9579
1974	15,140.1	9,094.3	522.0	0.2972	1,030.3	0.9270	0.9220
1975	14,313.0	9,780.1	506.3	0.3729	946.4	0.7940	0.8493
1976	15,341.9	10,457.5	478.4	0.3322	1,122.3	0.8000	0.8701
1977	15,434.3	11,016.5	467.9	0.3887	910.9	0.7450	0.8763
1978	15,161.3	11,258.6	449.1	0.3249	647.6	0.7200	0.8747
1979	16,390.0	11,476.2	438.4	0.2679	725.3	0.7840	0.8971
1980	16,669.8	12,030.8	432.7	0.2742	775.1	0.7840	0.9074
1981	16,228.3	12,331.6	428.8	0.3330	936.1	0.7087	0.8986
1982	16,112.3	12,755.4	424.0	0.3557	1,218.7	0.6727	0.8898
1983	16,070.5	13,241.7	411.9	0.4175	1,124.9	0.6727	0.8898
1984	17,588.8	13,643.3	398.9	0.3322	968.5	0.7472	0.9142
1985	17,721.8	13,960.1	395.1	0.3308	865.2	0.7699	0.9127
1986	17,166.9	14,264.4	384.0	0.3603	834.0	0.7229	0.8934
1987	17,180.1	14,557.7	362.7	0.3603	687.7	0.7360	0.8892
1988	18,813.8	14,799.5	348.5	0.3603	635.8	0.8153	0.9261

b. Sources of growth

Year	Growth of output	Labor input total	Labor	Working hours	Capital input total	Capital	Capacity utilization	Residual	Embodied technology	Capital vintage
1956	0.1932	0.0346	0.0268	0.0077	0.0446	0.0211	0.0235	0.1010	0.0996	0.0013
1957	0.1921	0.0186	0.0219	−0.0032	0.1086	0.0758	0.0327	0.0598	0.0270	0.0328
1958	−0.0595	−0.0189	−0.0195	0.0006	−0.1695	0.0252	−0.1948	0.1346	0.0623	0.0723
1959	0.3624	0.0600	0.0483	0.0117	0.4363	0.0460	0.3903	−0.1144	−0.0435	−0.0709
1960	0.3231	0.0570	0.0495	0.0075	0.2539	0.1563	0.0956	0.0102	0.0032	0.0069
1961	0.2658	0.0301	0.0349	−0.0048	0.2384	0.1866	0.0517	−0.0024	−0.0008	−0.0015
1962	−0.0320	−0.0255	−0.0067	−0.0187	−0.0024	0.1099	−0.1124	−0.0043	−0.0024	−0.0018
1963	0.1143	0.0111	0.0113	−0.0002	0.0821	0.0760	0.0061	0.0204	0.0155	0.0049
1964	0.2081	0.0106	0.0094	0.0011	0.1760	0.0777	0.0982	0.0207	0.0167	0.0039
1965	0.0002	−0.0215	−0.0130	−0.0085	−0.0004	0.0528	−0.0532	0.0236	0.0232	0.0003
1966	0.1259	0.0056	0.0037	0.0018	0.1113	0.0715	0.0397	0.0088	0.0100	−0.0012
1967	0.2689	0.0237	0.0131	0.0105	0.1675	0.0928	0.0747	0.0728	0.0528	0.0199
1968	0.1209	0.0132	0.0151	−0.0019	0.1016	0.1009	0.0007	0.0058	0.0040	0.0017
1969	0.2291	0.0051	0.0111	−0.0060	0.1963	0.1445	0.0518	0.0272	0.0218	0.0054
1970	0.1487	0.0030	0.0082	−0.0051	0.1177	0.1185	−0.0008	0.0276	0.0231	0.0044
1971	0.0006	−0.0209	−0.0095	−0.0114	0.0026	0.0994	−0.0968	0.0202	0.0185	0.0017
1972	0.1003	−0.0062	−0.0034	−0.0027	0.0883	0.0722	0.0161	0.0185	0.0217	−0.0031
1973	0.1848	0.0014	−0.0002	0.0016	0.1574	0.0568	0.1006	0.0258	0.0331	−0.0073
1974	−0.0381	−0.0145	−0.0034	−0.0110	−0.0029	0.0604	−0.0634	−0.0217	−0.0249	0.0031
1975	−0.0546	−0.0397	−0.0112	−0.0285	−0.0494	0.0472	−0.0967	0.0387	0.0509	−0.0122
1976	0.0718	0.0106	−0.0183	0.0076	0.0516	0.0462	0.0054	0.0318	0.0363	−0.0044
1977	0.0060	−0.0058	−0.0085	0.0027	−0.0116	0.0326	−0.0442	0.0238	0.0344	−0.0106
1978	−0.0176	−0.0136	−0.0130	−0.0005	−0.0083	0.0148	−0.0231	0.0044	0.0087	−0.0042
1979	0.0810	0.0003	−0.0063	0.0067	0.0804	0.0141	0.0663	0.0002	0.0004	−0.0001
1980	0.0170	−0.0004	−0.0035	0.0031	0.0350	0.0350	0.0000	−0.0175	−0.0287	0.0111
1981	−0.0264	−0.0062	−0.0030	−0.0032	−0.0489	0.0166	−0.0656	0.0292	0.0380	−0.0088
1982	−0.0071	−0.0074	−0,0039	−0.0034	−0.0117	0.0221	−0.0338	0.0122	0.0124	−0.0001
1983	−0.0025	−0.0119	−0.0119	0.0000	0.0222	0.0222	0.0000	−0.0132	−0.0151	0.0019
1984	0.0944	−0.0016	−0.0104	0.0088	0.0964	0.0202	0.0762	−0.0003	−0.0004	0.0001
1985	0.0075	−0.0036	−0.0031	−0.0005	0.0363	0.0155	0.0208	−0.0253	−0.0381	0.0127
1986	−0.0313	−0.0175	−0.0101	−0.0074	−0.0259	0.0139	−0.0399	0.0128	0.0197	−0.0069
1987	0.0007	−0.0215	−0.0199	−0.0016	0.0249	0.0131	0.0118	−0.0028	−0.0051	0.0023
1988	0.0950	0.0002	−0.0141	0.0143	0.0806	0.0106	0.0700	0.0141	0.0276	−0.0135

Table F-4 General machinery
a. Factor inputs

Year	Real output VQSNA	Capital stock KP	Labor force NL	Share of laber XWLSNA	Capital formation IP	Capacity utilization rate RHO	Working hours HX
1955	427.2	202.8	355.0	0.8123	10.7	0.6190	1.0355
1956	628.7	233.4	434.0	0.8177	34.7	0.7880	1.1025
1957	846.4	280.1	506.1	0.6301	44.8	0.8810	1.0886
1958	738.5	310.3	505.9	0.5785	41.7	0.7320	1.0669
1959	945.3	365.4	576.1	0.5331	71.5	0.8910	1.1061
1960	1,453.0	459.6	712.3	0.4358	118.9	0.9250	1.1267
1961	1,979.6	659.1	815.9	0.4027	227.4	0.9350	1.0958
1962	2,143.0	871.8	839.2	0.4630	256.3	0.9020	1.0489
1963	2,286.3	1,018.8	881.1	0.5309	217.5	0.8820	1.0427
1964	2,688.1	1,194.3	886.1	0.5159	232.7	0.9160	1.0381
1965	2,611.6	1,307.7	864.4	0.5497	179.5	0.8330	0.9990
1966	3,022.5	1,437.3	894.1	0.5620	203.6	0.9430	1.0180
1967	3,973.8	1,655.9	946.8	0.5120	309.1	1.0260	1.0309
1968	5,109.5	2,006.8	1,013.6	0.4425	465.5	1.0980	1.0263
1969	6,397.9	2,503.8	1,101.5	0.4257	658.4	1.0580	1.0051
1970	7,865.7	3,026.7	1,178.3	0.4738	729.1	1.0000	1.0000
1971	7,886.2	3,483.1	1,154.8	0.4983	611.7	0.9560	0.9624
1972	7,908.8	3,874.1	1,156.7	0.5782	611.7	0.9790	0.9578
1973	9,596.2	4,274.9	1,190.9	0.6194	708.7	1.0250	0.9578
1974	9,500.7	4,701.3	1,177.5	0.6218	685.6	0.9300	0.9068
1975	8,157.6	5,008.7	1,101.7	0.6739	453.8	0.7780	0.8496
1976	9,094.4	5,231.2	1,081.0	0.6771	462.8	0.8820	0.8986
1977	9,653.4	5,384.2	1,047.8	0.7337	553.7	0.8850	0.9109
1978	10,464.5	5,644.9	1,053.6	0.6888	559.1	0.9210	0.9109
1979	11,479.6	5,921.9	1,061.6	0.6974	666.8	0.9960	0.9253
1980	12,004.0	6,230.2	1,080.5	0.7111	774.2	1.0330	0.9325
1981	16,432.8	6,847.1	1,105.4	0.5878	932.7	1.0123	0.9325
1982	16,846.3	7,364.0	1,150.7	0.5948	922.2	0.9575	0.9346
1983	17,198.1	7,827.2	1,144.0	0.6443	823.4	0.9596	0.9341
1984	19,091.4	8,361.4	1,155.1	0.6311	971.6	1.0970	0.9542
1985	20,748.3	9,236.7	1,176.1	0.5962	1,158.3	1.1073	0.9516
1986	20,467.8	9,797.3	1,204.3	0.6335	863.0	0.9711	0.9361
1987	19,897.6	10,214.9	1,178.5	0.6335	797.8	0.9202	0.9438
1988	22,823.1	10,600.9	1,182.0	0.6335	1,065.5	1.0475	0.9567

b. Sources of growth

Year	Growth of output	Labor input total	Labor	Working hours	Capital input total	Capital	Capacity utilization	Residual	Embodied technology	Capital vintage
1956	0.4716	0.2466	0.1819	0.0646	0.0847	0.0275	0.0572	0.1077	0.0477	0.0599
1957	0.3462	0.0954	0.1046	−0.0092	0.1264	0.0740	0.0523	0.1080	0.0509	0.0571
1958	−0.1274	−0.0117	−0.0002	−0.0115	−0.0335	0.0454	−0.0789	−0.0839	−0.0459	−0.0379
1959	0.2800	0.0962	0.0739	0.0223	0.2023	0.0829	0.1194	−0.0157	−0.0065	−0.0092
1960	0.5370	0.1130	0.1030	0.0100	0.1725	0.1454	0.0270	0.1996	0.0721	0.1275
1961	0.3624	0.0459	0.0585	−0.0126	0.2685	0.2592	0.0092	0.0430	0.0147	0.0283
1962	0.0825	−0.0071	0.0132	−0.0203	0.1482	0.1733	−0.0250	−0.0594	−0.0278	−0.0315
1963	0.0668	0.0232	0.0265	−0.0032	0.0669	0.0791	−0.0121	−0.0223	−0.0152	−0.0070
1964	0.1757	0.0006	0.0029	−0.0022	0.1052	0.0833	0.0218	0.0697	0.0566	0.0131
1965	−0.0284	−0.0336	−0.0134	−0.0202	−0.0019	0.0427	−0.0446	0.0075	0.0086	−0.0010
1966	0.1573	0.0303	0.0193	0.0110	0.1069	0.0434	0.0635	0.0189	0.0205	−0.0016
1967	0.3147	0.0370	0.0301	0.0068	0.1237	0.0742	0.0494	0.1435	0.1203	0.0232
1968	0.2858	0.0291	0.0312	−0.0021	0.1655	0.1181	0.0474	0.0855	0.0611	0.0243
1969	0.2521	0.0273	0.0369	−0.0095	0.1161	0.1422	−0.0261	0.1021	0.0692	0.0328
1970	0.2294	0.0304	0.0330	−0.0025	0.0750	0.1098	−0.0348	0.1164	0.0913	0.0250
1971	0.0026	−0.0283	−0.0099	−0.0183	0.0502	0.0756	−0.0254	−0.0205	−0.0227	0.0022
1972	0.0028	−0.0018	0.0009	−0.0027	0.0586	0.0473	0.0112	−0.0541	−0.0638	0.0096
1973	0.2133	0.0183	0.0183	0.0000	0.0591	0.0393	0.0197	0.1320	0.1428	−0.0108
1974	−0.0099	−0.0397	−0.0070	−0.0327	−0.0008	0.0377	−0.0385	0.0327	0.0398	−0.0071
1975	−0.1413	−0.0831	−0.0433	−0.0397	−0.0354	0.0213	−0.0567	−0.0259	−0.0488	0.0229
1976	0.1148	0.0256	−0.0127	0.0383	0.0594	0.0143	0.0450	0.0287	0.0504	−0.0217
1977	0.0614	−0.0128	−0.0225	0.0097	0.0087	0.0077	0.0009	0.0667	0.0934	−0.0267
1978	0.0840	0.0038	0.0038	0.0000	0.0283	0.0150	0.0132	0.0515	0.0729	−0.0214
1979	0.0970	0.0164	0.0053	0.0111	0.0407	0.0148	0.0258	0.0389	0.0465	−0.0075
1980	0.0456	0.0182	0.0126	0.0056	0.0263	0.0150	0.0112	0.0010	0.0010	−0.0000
1981	0.3689	0.0135	0.0135	0.0000	0.0317	0.0408	−0.0090	0.3163	0.3145	0.0018
1982	0.0251	0.0257	0.0243	0.0013	0.0070	0.0305	−0.0235	−0.0072	−0.0077	0.0004
1983	0.0208	−0.0040	−0.0037	−0.0003	0.0232	0.0223	0.0008	0.0017	0.0022	−0.0004
1984	0.1100	0.0198	0.0061	0.0137	0.0816	0.0251	0.0564	0.0083	0.0092	−0.0008
1985	0.0867	0.0091	0.0108	−0.0016	0.0464	0.0422	0.0041	0.0306	0.0320	−0.0014
1986	−0.0135	0.0046	0.0151	−0.0105	−0.0255	0.0222	−0.0478	0.0073	0.0106	−0.0032
1987	−0.0278	−0.0084	−0.0135	0.0051	−0.0044	0.0156	−0.0200	−0.0151	−0.0233	0.0081
1988	0.1470	0.0105	0.0018	0.0086	0.0664	0.0138	0.0526	0.0688	0.0784	−0.0096

Table F-5 Electrical machinery
a. Factor inputs

Year	Real output VQSNA	Capital stock KP	Labor force NL	Share of laber XWLSNA	Capital formation IP	Capacity utilization rate RHO	Working hours HX
1955	377.6	184.0	232.7	0.8142	24.9	0.6190	1.0688
1956	601.5	194.6	308.8	0.7674	34.3	0.7880	1.1331
1957	798.5	263.4	358.4	0.7034	76.0	0.8810	1.1270
1958	825.6	327.6	409.7	0.6721	74.9	0.7320	1.1104
1959	1,210.3	405.4	533.3	0.6279	97.2	0.8910	1.1309
1960	1,697.9	555.3	668.5	0.5264	176.8	0.9250	1.1403
1961	2,096.8	732.8	771.2	0.4195	244.4	0.9350	1.1082
1962	2,325.1	940.2	806.0	0.3850	251.5	0.9020	1.0810
1963	2,354.5	1,064.7	852.9	0.3958	192.4	0.8820	1.0704
1964	2,878.3	1,218.0	893.1	0.3559	188.6	0.9160	1.0560
1965	2,788.7	1,306.4	851.4	0.4198	137.5	0.8330	1.0238
1966	3,315.5	1,413.1	926.4	0.4364	167.0	0.9430	1.0388
1967	4,354.3	1,610.9	1,011.2	0.3606	261.3	1.0260	1.0444
1968	5,482.4	1,841.6	1,100.3	0.3843	337.9	1.0980	1.0416
1969	6,959.0	2,059.6	1,268.2	0.3901	493.5	1.0580	1.0250
1970	8,080.0	2,462.7	1,341.0	0.4136	542.6	1.0000	1.0000
1971	8,284.6	2,681.5	1,271.4	0.4415	392.5	0.9560	0.9762
1972	9,639.6	2,880.5	1,329.2	0.4277	383.1	0.9790	0.9800
1973	11,677.8	3,260.0	1,398.7	0.4595	623.4	1.0250	0.9778
1974	10.948.4	3,542.3	1,270.4	0.5194	525.9	0.9300	0.9212
1975	9,276.4	3,648.3	1,214.0	0.6149	265.8	0.7780	0.9035
1976	12,083.8	3,838.9	1,279.2	0.5388	513.2	0.8820	0.9578
1977	13,225.9	4,111.5	1,235.6	0.5545	505.9	0.8850	0.9529
1978	14,783.7	4,405.0	1,239.9	0.5344	545.8	0.9210	0.9673
1979	17,187.6	4,828.5	1,272.1	0.4991	707.5	0.9960	0.9823
1980	20,788.8	5,088.1	1,357.6	0.4903	821.7	1.0330	0.9811
1981	25,149.2	5,703.9	1,439.1	0.5647	1,058.5	0.9937	0.9811
1982	27,710.0	6,353.0	1,497.4	0.5563	1,023.9	0.9865	0.9717
1983	34,422.9	7,070.6	1,531.4	0.5394	1,171.8	1.0453	0.9878
1984	45,116.9	8,431.9	1,672.6	0.4969	1,974.9	1.1404	1.0006
1985	45,609.4	9,945.7	1,792.0	0.5099	2,091.4	1.0847	0.9817
1986	52,761.2	10,841.8	1,847.6	0.5348	1,812.3	1.0489	0.9772
1987	56,570.9	11,618.3	1,804.5	0.5348	1,822.9	1.0228	0.9855
1988	66,132.0	12,399.2	1,829.6	0.5348	2,300.5	1.0409	0.9916

b. Sources of growth

Year	Growth of output	Labor input total	Labor	Working hours	Capital input total	Capital	Capacity utilization	Residual	Embodied technology	Capital vintage
1956	0.5929	0.3122	0.2509	0.0612	0.0805	0.0134	0.0671	0.1422	0.0428	0.0994
1957	0.3275	0.1085	0.1129	−0.0043	0.1522	0.1048	0.0473	0.0577	0.0145	0.0432
1958	0.0339	0.0848	0.0962	−0.0113	0.0109	0.0799	−0.0689	−0.0549	−0.0201	−0.0348
1959	0.4659	0.2045	0.1894	0.0150	0.1883	0.0883	0.1000	0.0551	0.0216	0.0334
1960	0.4028	0.1389	0.1334	0.0054	0.1998	0.1751	0.0247	0.0506	0.0181	0.0325
1961	0.2349	0.0508	0.0644	−0.0136	0.1938	0.1855	0.0082	−0.0086	−0.0033	−0.0052
1962	0.1088	0.0075	0.0173	−0.0098	0.1462	0.1740	−0.0278	−0.0439	−0.0265	−0.0174
1963	0.0126	0.0189	0.0230	−0.0041	0.0648	0.0800	−0.0151	−0.0678	−0.0612	−0.0065
1964	0.2224	0.0117	0.0167	−0.0050	0.1211	0.0927	0.0284	0.0867	0.0954	−0.0087
1965	−0.0311	−0.0318	−0.0196	−0.0122	−0.0142	0.0421	−0.0563	0.0161	0.0245	−0.0083
1966	0.1889	0.0454	0.0384	0.0096	0.1265	0.0460	0.0805	0.0153	0.0198	−0.0044
1967	0.3133	0.0351	0.0330	0.0021	0.1536	0.0895	0.0641	0.1134	0.1071	0.0063
1968	0.2590	0.0327	0.0338	−0.0011	0.1375	0.0881	0.0493	0.0818	0.0682	0.0135
1969	0.2693	0.0523	0.0595	−0.0071	0.0473	0.0722	−0.0248	0.1495	0.0947	0.0547
1970	0.1610	0.0130	0.0237	−0.0106	0.0763	0.1147	−0.0384	0.0694	0.0558	0.0136
1971	0.0253	−0.0328	−0.0229	−0.0099	0.0228	0.0496	−0.0267	0.0381	0.0451	−0.0069
1972	0.1635	0.0211	0.0194	0.0017	0.0572	0.0424	0.0147	0.0810	0.1021	−0.0210
1973	0.2114	0.0229	0.0240	−0.0010	0.0999	0.0712	0.0287	0.0843	0.0735	0.0108
1974	−0.0624	−0.0749	−0.0476	−0.0273	−0.0067	0.0416	−0.0484	0.0225	0.0253	−0.0027
1975	−0.1527	−0.0385	−0.0273	−0.0112	−0.0533	0.0115	−0.0648	−0.0649	−0.1421	0.0773
1976	0.3026	0.0630	0.0289	0.0341	0.0889	0.0240	0.0648	0.1348	0.1490	−0.0142
1977	0.0945	−0.0216	−0.0189	−0.0027	0.0332	0.0316	0.0016	0.0862	0.1038	−0.0175
1978	0.1177	0.0099	0.0018	0.0081	0.0535	0.0332	0.0202	0.0533	0.0622	−0.0089
1979	0.1626	0.0209	0.0129	0.0079	0.0928	0.0481	0.0447	0.0468	0.0459	0.0008
1980	0.2095	0.0323	0.0329	−0.0006	0.0473	0.0274	0.0199	0.1218	0.1052	0.0165
1981	0.2097	0.0339	0.0339	0.0000	0.0341	0.0526	−0.0185	0.1337	0.1069	0.0268
1982	0.1018	0.0169	0.0225	−0.0055	0.0469	0.0504	−0.0035	0.0368	0.0352	0.0015
1983	0.2422	0.0213	0.0122	0.0091	0.0825	0.0520	0.0305	0.1330	0.1243	0.0086
1984	0.3106	0.0528	0.0458	0.0070	0.1514	0.0968	0.0545	0.0961	0.0667	0.0294
1985	0.0109	0.0260	0.0364	−0.0103	0.0597	0.0879	−0.0282	−0.0712	−0.0590	−0.0122
1986	0.1568	0.0140	0.0165	−0.0025	0.0251	0.0419	−0.0167	0.1145	0.1164	−0.0018
1987	0.0722	−0.0080	−0.0124	0.0044	0.0209	0.0333	−0.0124	0.0602	0.0643	−0.0041
1988	0.1690	0.0108	0.0074	0.0033	0.0400	0.0312	0.0087	0.1158	0.1029	0.0129

Table F-6 Transport equipment, motor vehicles
a. Factor inputs

Year	Real output VQSNA	Capital stock KP	Labor force NL	Share of laber XWLSNA	Capital formation IP	Capacity utilization rate RHO	Working hours HX
1955	136.1	206.7	129.4	0.5329	13.8	0.6190	1.0281
1956	204.1	210.1	142.9	0.4721	19.3	0.7880	1.0852
1957	282.7	211.2	162.9	0.4063	33.4	0.8810	1.0769
1958	307.5	208.0	171.0	0.4799	25.2	0.7320	1.0374
1959	366.0	287.0	211.6	0.4115	44.6	0.8910	1.0660
1960	517.6	449.6	275.4	0.3101	130.7	0.9250	1.0987
1961	701.4	539.0	310.1	0.4030	191.0	0.9350	1.0800
1962	848.3	700.2	327.4	0.3815	153.5	0.9020	1.0384
1963	1,030.0	815.2	366.0	0.3593	144.1	0.8820	1.0369
1964	1,359.2	994.7	401.9	0.3598	250.5	0.9160	1.0431
1965	1,625.2	1,155.6	416.4	0.3908	203.8	0.8330	1.0145
1966	1,931.2	1,207.9	455.6	0.4033	185.0	0.9430	1.0306
1967	2,555.1	1,442.9	501.1	0.3668	316.2	1.0260	1.0405
1968	3,238.5	1,860.2	538.2	0.3518	472.9	1.0980	1.0296
1969	3,920.5	2,271.4	560.7	0.3875	444.0	1.0580	1.0083
1970	4,736.6	2,641.7	579.9	0.3795	563.5	1.0000	1.0000
1971	5,121.9	2,896.0	574.8	0.4432	482.0	0.9560	0.9818
1972	5,581.7	3,017.5	607.1	0.4600	462.4	0.9790	0.9761
1973	6,126.7	3,508.4	634.4	0.4795	703.5	1.0250	0.9782
1974	6,190.7	3,816.7	614.7	0.5560	576.1	0.9300	0.9210
1975	6,248.6	3,482.2	601.1	0.5542	238.9	0.7780	0.8790
1976	6,966.8	4,051.2	622.2	0.4964	349.8	0.8820	0.9143
1977	7,889.3	4,731.3	629.4	0.4796	573.3	0.8850	0.9278
1978	8,844.7	5,459.0	637.8	0.4957	657.9	0.9210	0.9200
1979	9,914.5	5,949.1	651.3	0.4813	668.3	0.9960	0.9382
1980	11,798.6	6,246.1	682.8	0.5015	794.7	1.0330	0.9590
1981	11,189.4	7,341.0	712.1	0.4893	1,051.4	1,0206	0.9506
1982	11,178.6	8,184.5	714.1	0.4771	1,073.0	0.9586	0.9318
1983	11,888.9	9,034.9	725.0	0.4649	982.6	0.9555	0.9382
1984	13,045.4	9,164.1	730.5	0.4527	917.4	0.9596	0.9600
1985	14,426.6	9,295.1	743.7	0.4403	1,173.4	0.9813	0.9662
1986	15,015.7	10,114.3	735.0	0.4403	1,086.0	0.9411	0.9387
1987	14,180.1	10,660.0	730.4	0.4403	958.2	0.9322	0.9438
1988	15,601.3	11,239.6	728.1	0.4403	1,029.6	0.9676	0.9771

b. Sources of growth

Year	Growth of output	Labor input total	Labor	Working hours	Capital input total	Capital	Capacity utilization	Residual	Embodied technology	Capital vintage
1956	0.4996	0.0782	0.0492	0.0289	0.1551	0.0086	0.1465	0.2284	0.1569	0.0714
1957	0.3851	0.0533	0.0568	−0.0035	0.0735	0.0031	0.0704	0.2282	0.0935	0.1346
1958	0.0877	0.0053	0.0238	−0.0184	−0.0945	−0.0078	−0.0866	0.1748	0.1033	0.0715
1959	0.1902	0.1117	0.0977	0.0140	0.3999	0.2235	0.1763	−0.2527	−0.2206	−0.0321
1960	0.4142	0.1058	0.0935	0.0123	0.4321	0.3908	0.0412	−0.0922	−0.0381	−0.0541
1961	0.3551	0.0430	0.0507	−0.0077	0.1264	0.1187	0.0077	0.1676	0.0425	0.1251
1962	0.2094	0.0057	0.0212	−0.0155	0.1566	0.1849	−0.0283	0.0463	0.0300	0.0163
1963	0.2141	0.0417	0.0423	−0.0005	0.0886	0.1052	−0.0165	0.0750	0.0568	0.0181
1964	0.3196	0.0376	0.0352	0.0023	0.1710	0.1409	0.0301	0.1003	0.0558	0.0445
1965	0.1957	0.0030	0.0141	−0.0111	0.0344	0.0985	−0.0641	0.1570	0.1376	0.0194
1966	0.1882	0.0449	0.0379	0.0070	0.1093	0.0270	0.0823	0.0305	0.0288	0.0017
1967	0.3230	0.0405	0.0366	0.0038	0.1897	0.1231	0.0665	0.0835	0.0609	0.0226
1968	0.2674	0.0220	0.0260	−0.0039	0.2461	0.1874	0.0586	−0.0006	−0.0004	−0.0002
1969	0.2105	0.0078	0.0162	−0.0083	0.1081	0.1353	−0.0272	0.0927	0.0896	0.0030
1970	0.2081	0.0097	0.0130	0.0032	0.0616	0.1011	−0.0395	0.1333	0.1104	0.0229
1971	0.0813	−0.0118	−0.0039	−0.0080	0.0267	0.0536	−0.0268	0.0683	0.0723	−0.0039
1972	0.0897	0.0230	0.0258	−0.0028	0.0361	0.0226	0.0135	0.0290	0.0321	−0.0030
1973	0.0976	0.0226	0.0215	0.0010	0.1131	0.0846	0.0284	−0.0363	−0.0325	−0.0038
1974	0.0104	−0.0487	−0.0172	−0.0315	−0.0057	0.0390	−0.0447	0.0712	0.0824	−0.0112
1975	0.0093	−0.0369	−0.0122	−0.0247	−0.0703	0.0029	−0.0733	0.1250	0.3312	−0.2061
1976	0.1149	0.0380	0.0174	0.0206	0.0983	0.0273	0.0709	−0.0199	−0.0355	0.0155
1977	0.1324	0.0127	0.0055	0.0071	0.0894	0.0873	0.0020	0.0294	0.0402	−0.0107
1978	0.1211	0.0023	0.0066	−0.0042	0.1012	0.0775	0.0236	0.0173	0.0224	−0.0050
1979	0.1209	0.0199	0.0101	0.0097	0.0926	0.0465	0.0460	0.0081	0.0100	−0.0018
1980	0.1900	0.0359	0.0242	0.0116	0.0443	0.0248	0.0194	0.1024	0.1046	−0.0021
1981	−0.0516	0.0165	0.0210	−0.0044	0.0823	0.0895	−0.0072	−0.1455	−0.1500	0.0045
1982	−0.0009	−0.0080	0.0013	−0.0094	0.0246	0.0600	−0.0354	−0.0178	−0.0186	0.0007
1983	0.0635	0.0102	0.0071	0.0031	0.0536	0.0556	−0.0019	−0.0004	−0.0005	0.0001
1984	0.0972	0.0140	0.0034	0.0106	0.0102	0.0078	0.0023	0.0708	0.0873	−0.0165
1985	0.1058	0.0108	0.0079	0.0028	0.0208	0.0080	0.0128	0.0724	0.0691	0.0032
1986	0.0408	−0.0175	−0.0051	−0.0123	0.0180	0.0427	−0.0246	0.0420	0.0489	−0.0068
1987	−0.0556	−0.0003	−0.0027	0.0023	0.0310	0.0367	−0.0056	−0.0864	−0.1190	0.0326
1988	0.1002	0.0141	−0.0013	0.0154	0.0528	0.0304	0.0224	0.0322	0.0417	−0.0094

Table F-7 Precision instrument
a. Factor inputs

Year	Real output VQSNA	Capital stock KP	Labor force NL	Share of laber XWLSNA	Capital formation IP	Capacity utilization rate RHO	Working hours HX
1955	85.1	15.9	78.8	0.5480	4.3	0.6190	1.0861
1956	105.1	20.2	93.5	0.5349	6.9	0.7880	1.1266
1957	138.4	27.7	116.4	0.4528	11.3	0.8810	1.1033
1958	155.1	35.4	124.8	0.4310	9.0	0.7320	1.1166
1959	181.8	44.2	137.3	0.4242	12.5	0.8910	1.1294
1960	235.9	52.9	147.3	0.4418	16.2	0.9250	1.1327
1961	282.4	67.0	163.5	0.4778	27.3	0.9350	1.1044
1962	339.1	84.6	171.7	0.5737	24.8	0.9020	1.0838
1963	391.5	107.2	187.0	0.5490	33.0	0.8820	1.0689
1964	483.6	126.2	187.7	0.5077	32.2	0.9160	1.0650
1965	508.9	140.3	193.2	0.5414	21.9	0.8330	1.0422
1966	566.5	152.9	200.5	0.5414	21.8	0.9430	1.0439
1967	663.6	171.4	207.6	0.5272	35.0	1.0260	1.0272
1968	805.8	201.5	214.7	0.5261	52.6	1.0980	1.0250
1969	960.8	239.1	228.5	0.5333	65.3	1.0580	1.0050
1970	1,084.6	291.8	240.7	0.5697	86.2	1.0000	1.0000
1971	1,201.6	326.0	242.1	0.5779	70.5	0.9560	0.9850
1972	1,293.6	354.5	249.8	0.6266	63.6	0.9790	0.9700
1973	1,562.5	430.7	260.8	0.5824	90.8	1.0250	0.9628
1974	1,646.2	488.5	256.2	0.5689	91.5	0.9300	0.9300
1975	1,192.4	467.7	239.0	0.7327	50.5	0.7780	0.9023
1976	1,370.2	499.2	247.4	0.7243	68.0	0.8820	0.9411
1977	1,644.7	542.1	251.7	0.6683	83.9	0.8850	0.9428
1978	1,896.9	627.8	257.8	0.6517	102.5	0.9210	0.9395
1979	2,112.2	690.9	261.3	0.6527	130.0	0.9960	0.9561
1980	2,494.3	785.6	275.9	0.5971	164.3	1.0330	0.9611
1981	2,873.6	916.4	289.1	0.6854	186.7	1.0144	0.9534
1982	2,779.4	1,039.0	293.0	0.7354	186.4	0.9235	0.9511
1983	2,971.4	1,187.9	298.2	0.7341	226.3	0.9555	0.9672
1984	3,225.0	1,346.9	306.8	0.7812	226.3	1.1094	0.9789
1985	3,678.8	1,554.8	319.5	0.7193	319.0	1.2303	0.9756
1986	3,598.4	1,704.8	317.9	0.7542	279.6	1.1713	0.9627
1987	3,877.5	1,836.2	304.5	0.7542	283.5	1.0925	0.9605
1988	4,212.3	1,969.5	301.3	0.7542	377.0	1.1786	0.9727

b. Sources of growth

Year	Growth of output	Labor input total	Labor	Working hours	Capital input total	Capital	Capacity utilization	Residual	Embodied technology	Capital vintage
1956	0.2350	0.1241	0.1004	0.0236	0.2871	0.1257	0.1613	−0.1430	−0.0277	−0.1153
1957	0.3168	0.0986	0.1103	−0.0116	0.2917	0.2031	0.0885	−0.0603	−0.0134	−0.0469
1958	0.1206	0.0366	0.0311	0.0055	0.0351	0.1581	−0.1229	0.0449	0.0231	0.0218
1959	0.1721	0.0478	0.0424	0.0053	0.2993	0.1431	0.1561	−0.1572	−0.0775	−0.0797
1960	0.2975	0.0335	0.0321	0.0013	0.1353	0.1098	0.0254	0.1195	0.0596	0.0599
1961	0.1971	0.0393	0.0525	−0.0132	0.1463	0.1391	0.0071	0.0106	0.0046	0.0059
1962	0.2007	0.0175	0.0287	−0.0112	0.0929	0.1119	−0.0190	0.0875	0.0712	0.0163
1963	0.1545	0.0407	0.0489	−0.0082	0.1078	0.1204	−0.0126	0.0056	0.0045	0.0010
1964	0.2352	0.0000	0.0019	−0.0018	0.1096	0.0872	0.0223	0.1256	0.1244	0.0011
1965	0.0523	0.0039	0.0158	−0.0119	0.0050	0.0512	−0.0462	0.0430	0.0689	−0.0258
1966	0.1131	0.0213	0.0204	0.0009	0.1071	0.0411	0.0660	−0.0147	−0.0234	0.0086
1967	0.1714	0.0099	0.0186	−0.0087	0.1038	0.0572	0.0466	0.0565	0.0582	−0.0017
1968	0.2142	0.0168	0.0179	−0.0011	0.1223	0.0832	0.0391	0.0728	0.0595	0.0132
1969	0.1923	0.0232	0.0342	−0.0110	0.0669	0.0870	−0.0201	0.0979	0.0803	0.0176
1970	0.1288	0.0274	0.0304	−0.0029	0.0660	0.0948	−0.0287	0.0337	0.0271	0.0065
1971	0.1078	−0.0053	0.0033	−0.0087	0.0287	0.0494	−0.0207	0.0853	0.0950	−0.0097
1972	0.0765	0.0100	0.0199	−0.0098	0.0424	0.0326	0.0097	0.0236	0.0307	−0.0070
1973	0.2078	0.0211	0.0256	−0.0045	0.1136	0.0897	0.0238	0.0705	0.0817	−0.0111
1974	0.0535	−0.0290	−0.0100	−0.0190	0.0125	0.0578	−0.0453	0.0738	0.0876	−0.0137
1975	−0.2756	−0.0695	−0.0491	−0.0203	−0.0532	−0.0113	−0.0418	−0.1689	−0.3212	0.1522
1976	0.1491	0.0577	0.0254	0.0322	0.0579	0.0185	0.0393	0.0310	0.0430	−0.0120
1977	0.2003	0.0128	0.0116	0.0012	0.0297	0.0285	0.0012	0.1547	0.1815	−0.0267
1978	0.1533	0.0134	0.0157	−0.0023	0.0714	0.0550	0.0164	0.0670	0.0777	−0.0106
1979	0.1135	0.0205	0.0088	0.0116	0.0660	0.0349	0.0311	0.0261	0.0240	0.0020
1980	0.1809	0.0366	0.0333	0.0033	0.0722	0.0552	0.0170	0.0678	0.0581	0.0096
1981	0.1520	0.0270	0.0327	−0.0057	0.0457	0.0523	−0.0066	0.0762	0.0709	0.0052
1982	−0.0327	0.0081	0.0099	−0.0018	0.0085	0.0354	−0.0268	−0.0488	−0.0514	0.0025
1983	0.0726	0.0256	0.0130	0.0126	0.0486	0.0381	0.0105	−0.0015	−0.0015	−0.0000
1984	0.0817	0.0322	0.0225	0.0097	0.0692	0.0292	0.0399	−0.0190	−0.0213	0.0023
1985	0.1407	0.0272	0.0297	−0.0025	0.0786	0.0433	0.0353	0.0335	0.0302	0.0032
1986	−0.0218	−0.0137	−0.0037	−0.0099	0.0107	0.0237	−0.0129	−0.0192	−0.0214	0.0022
1987	0.0775	−0.0334	−0.0317	−0.0016	0.0011	0.0189	−0.0478	0.1149	0.1320	−0.0170
1988	0.0863	0.0015	−0.0079	0.0094	0.0386	0.0178	0.0207	0.0460	0.0413	0.0047

Table F-8 Wholesale and retail trade
a. Factor inputs

Year	Real output VQSNA	Capital stock KP	Labor force NL	Share of laber XWLSNA	Capital formation IP	Capacity utilization rate RHO	Working hours HX
1955	2,962.8	3,948.6	5,993.0	0.4398	103.9	1.0000	1.0280
1956	3,210.5	4,007.1	6,236.0	0.4272	168.6	1.0000	1.0468
1957	3,648.6	4,070.0	6,488.0	0.3981	162.6	1.0000	1.0398
1958	3,828.6	4,100.2	6,706.0	0.4353	123.4	1.0000	1.0592
1959	4,365.9	4,139.2	6,915.0	0.4554	140.1	1.0000	1.0560
1960	4,751.2	4,210.9	7,117.0	0.4172	176.3	1.0000	1.0630
1961	5,530.1	4,272.7	7,058.0	0.3873	212.8	1.0000	1.0630
1962	6,097.4	4,393.5	7,100.0	0.4225	264.1	1.0000	1.0522
1963	6,841.8	4,556.1	7,502.0	0.4431	324.1	1.0000	1.0485
1964	7,949.2	4,753.2	7,770.0	0.4306	406.0	1.0000	1.0452
1965	8,350.6	4,988.3	8,013.0	0.4656	377.5	1.0000	1.0339
1966	9,687.8	5,272.5	8,382.0	0.4447	461.5	1.0000	1.0323
1967	10,927.9	5,561.8	9,095.0	0.4461	501.3	1.0000	1.0296
1968	12,647.4	5,993.6	9,313.0	0.4381	652.0	1.0000	1.0296
1969	14,341.6	6,714.8	9,497.0	0.4521	920.3	1.0000	1.0140
1970	15,925.8	7,537.9	9,589.0	0.4499	1,070.5	1.0000	1.0000
1971	16,927.0	8,382.5	9,874.0	0.4762	1,125.8	1.0000	0.9930
1972	18,955.5	9,474.8	10,034.0	0.4639	1,437.3	1.0000	0.9833
1973	19,876.0	11,005.1	10,360.0	0.4854	2,000.6	1.0000	0.9634
1974	19,746.3	12,279.6	10,495.0	0.4827	1,735.6	1.0000	0.9316
1975	19,990.3	13,802.8	10,780.0	0.5240	1,744.7	1.0000	0.9235
1976	20,983.1	14,887.4	11,090.0	0.5616	1,690.5	1.0000	0.9321
1977	21,853.8	16,091.5	11,500.0	0.5961	1,916.4	1.0000	0.9348
1978	22,867.6	17,600.5	11,651.0	0.6100	1,958.3	1.0000	0.9354
1979	23,985.9	18,917.5	12,280.0	0.6118	2,209.0	1.0000	0.9295
1980	24,030.5	20,405.7	12,480.0	0.6748	2,294.5	1.0000	0.9262
1981	30,173.9	21,848.0	12,740.0	0.5529	2,204.2	1.0000	0.9208
1982	30,933.7	23,230.2	12,960.0	0.5456	2,182.3	1.0000	0.9176
1983	32,084.0	24,593.8	13,130.0	0.5499	2,128.9	1.0000	0.9133
1984	32,586.8	25,989.4	13,190.0	0.5763	2,226.2	1.0000	0.9176
1985	32,887.8	27,379.0	13,180.0	0.5754	2,234.9	1.0000	0.9090
1986	34,619.6	28,920.4	13,390.0	0.6015	2,397.8	1.0000	0.9089
1987	32,197.2	30,574.1	13,660.0	0.6015	2,722.0	1.0000	0.9084
1988	34,334.9	33,451.1	13,890.0	0.6015	2,792.5	1.0000	0.8852

b. Sources of growth

Year	Growth of output	Labor input total	Labor	Working hours	Capital input total	Capital	Capacity utilization	Residual	Embodied technology	Capital vintage
1956	0.0836	0.0254	0.0173	0.0081	0.0084	0.0084	0.0000	0.0468	0.0891	−0.0423
1957	0.1364	0.0133	0.0160	−0.0027	0.0094	0.0094	0.0000	0.1100	0.2125	−0.1025
1958	0.0493	0.0230	0.0146	0.0083	0.0041	0.0041	0.0000	0.0210	0.0517	−0.0307
1959	0.1403	0.0127	0.0141	−0.0014	0.0051	0.0051	0.0000	0.1190	0.2499	−0.1307
1960	0.0882	0.0150	0.0121	0.0028	0.0101	0.0101	0.0000	0.0609	0.1001	−0.0392
1961	0.1639	−0.0032	−0.0032	0.0000	0.0089	0.0089	0.0000	0.1594	0.2140	−0.0545
1962	0.1025	−0.0018	0.0025	−0.0043	0.0163	0.0163	0.0000	0.0884	0.0974	−0.0090
1963	0.1220	0.0234	0.0250	−0.0016	0.0206	0.0206	0.0000	0.0741	0.0689	0.0051
1964	0.1618	0.0139	0.0153	−0.0014	0.0246	0.0246	0.0000	0.1193	0.0931	0.0262
1965	0.0505	0.0093	0.0145	−0.0051	0.0264	0.0264	0.0000	0.0144	0.0130	0.0013
1966	0.1601	0.0197	0.0204	−0.0007	0.0316	0.0316	0.0000	0.1041	0.0823	0.0218
1967	0.1280	0.0366	0.0379	−0.0012	0.0303	0.0303	0.0000	0.0563	0.0438	0.0124
1968	0.1573	0.0100	0.0105	−0.0004	0.0436	0.0436	0.0000	0.0652	0.0370	0.0335
1969	0.1339	0.0024	0.0089	−0.0065	0.0659	0.0659	0.0000	0.0652	0.0370	0.0281
1970	0.1104	−0.0019	0.0043	−0,0062	0.0674	0.0674	0.0000	0.0451	0.0261	0.0189
1971	0.0628	0.0107	0.0141	−0.0034	0.0586	0.0586	0.0000	−0.0064	−0.0041	−0.0022
1972	0.1198	0.0029	0.0075	−0.0046	0.0698	0.0698	0.0000	0.0467	0.0282	0.0185
1973	0.0485	0.0056	0.0157	−0.0101	0.0831	0.0831	0.0000	−0.0397	−0.0214	−0.0182
1974	−0.0065	−0.0098	0.0062	0.0161	0.0599	0.0599	0.0000	−0.0577	−0.0424	−0.0153
1975	0.0123	0.0095	0.0142	−0.0046	0.0590	0.0590	0.0000	−0.0552	−0.0479	−0.0072
1976	0.0496	0.0215	0.0161	0.0053	0.0344	0.0344	0.0000	−0.0060	−0.0057	−0.0003
1977	0.0415	0.0238	0.0220	0.0017	0.0326	0.0326	0.0000	−0.0144	−0.0129	−0.0014
1978	0.0463	0.0084	0.0080	0.0004	0.0365	0.0365	0.0000	0.0013	0.0013	0.0000
1979	0.0489	0.0289	0.0330	−0.0040	0.0290	0.0290	0.0000	−0.0087	−0.0080	−0.0006
1980	0.0018	0.0085	0.0109	−0.0024	0.0255	0.0255	0.0000	−0.0318	−0.0310	−0.0008
1981	0.2556	0.0082	0.0115	−0.0032	0.0316	0.0316	0.0000	0.2126	0.2306	−0.0180
1982	0.0251	0.0074	0.0094	−0.0019	0.0287	0.0287	0.0000	−0.0109	−0.0125	0.0016
1983	0.0371	0.0046	0.0072	−0.0026	0.0264	0.0264	0.0000	0.0061	0.0075	−0.0014
1984	0.0156	0.0053	0.0026	0.0027	0.0240	0.0240	0.0000	−0.0136	−0.0165	0.0029
1985	0.0092	−0.0058	−0.0004	−0.0053	0.0227	0.0227	0.0000	−0.0077	−0.0096	0.0019
1986	0.0526	0.0095	0.0095	−0.0000	0.0224	0.0224	0.0000	0.0203	0.0246	−0.0043
1987	−0.0699	0.0117	0.0121	−0.0003	0.0227	0.0227	0.0000	−0.1025	−0.1135	0.0110
1988	0.0663	−0.0054	0.0101	−0.0156	0.0244	0.0244	0.0000	0.0478	0.0546	−0.0067

Table F-9 Private services
a. Factor inputs

Year	Real output VQSNA	Capital stock KP	Labor force NL	Share of laber XWLSNA	Capital formation IP	Capacity utilization rate RHO	Working hours HX
1955	3,245.3	908.8	4,500.0	0.2303	48.0	1.0000	1.0810
1956	3,611.2	950.3	4,850.0	0.3841	57.7	1.0000	1.1060
1957	4,056.8	1,008.4	5,100.0	0.2961	71.5	1.0000	1.1010
1958	4,488.6	1,061.3	5,040.0	0.3081	12.5	1.0000	1.0990
1959	4,944.2	1,119.1	5,310.0	0.3407	79.4	1.0000	1.1100
1960	5,751.7	1,195.4	5,520.0	0.3278	92.6	1.0000	1.1250
1961	6,206.2	1,308.6	5,600.0	0.3041	127.8	1.0000	1.1150
1962	6,694.9	1,423.5	5,630.0	0.2998	134.1	1.0000	1.0980
1963	7,000.9	1,551.5	5,720.0	0.3056	161.4	1.0000	1.0910
1964	7,564.3	1,789.2	5,900.0	0.3085	279.4	1.0000	1.0860
1965	7,810.6	1,975.4	6,270.0	0.3237	255.3	1.0000	1.0700
1966	8,796.6	2,254.3	6,600.0	0.3459	341.2	1.0000	1.0720
1967	10,276.1	2,612.7	6,890.0	0.3086	425.2	1.0000	1.0710
1968	11,618.4	2,816.5	7,130.0	0.3153	375.4	1.0000	1.0690
1969	13,249.9	3,325.8	7,220.0	0.3122	600.4	1.0000	1.0540
1970	13,880.5	3,979.7	7,510.0	0.3549	791.2	1.0000	1.0000
1971	14,846.7	4,729.4	7,740.0	0.4130	905.3	1.0000	0.9970
1972	16,546.6	5,658.5	7,970.0	0.4013	1,129.9	1.0000	0.9910
1973	17,453.9	6,672.9	8,220.0	0.4367	1,376.8	1.0000	0.9780
1974	16,840.0	7,519.3	8,250.0	0.4511	1,206.0	1.0000	0.9520
1975	17,201.7	8,379.6	8,490.0	0.4584	1,222.9	1.0000	0.9430
1976	17,557.1	9,132.1	8,910.0	0.4813	1,275.0	1.0000	0.9500
1977	18,643.3	10,136.8	9,180.0	0.5155	1,477.0	1.0000	0.9510
1978	20,069.2	11,644.0	9,430.0	0.5174	1,785.4	1.0000	0.9520
1979	21,370.8	13,112.1	9,800.0	0.5211	2,136.8	1.0000	0.9530
1980	21,897.2	14,773.4	10,010.0	0.4997	2,361.8	1.0000	0.9460
1981	22,917.9	17,002.6	10,300.0	0.5545	2,874.4	1.0000	0.9420
1982	24,450.9	19,270.8	10,650.0	0.5472	3,139.9	1.0000	0.9390
1983	25,967.8	22,022.0	11,220.0	0.5550	3,677.2	1.0000	0.9370
1984	27,503.3	25,721.8	11,540.0	0.5541	4,690.8	1.0000	0.9490
1985	29,129.8	30,079.4	11,730.0	0.5093	5,769.3	1.0000	0.9420
1986	30,946.4	34,407.8	12,050.0	0.5142	6,098.8	1.0000	0.9456
1987	32,870.0	41,072.4	12,550.0	0.5142	7,125.1	1.0000	0.9445
1988	34,914.5	46,417.6	12,840.0	0.5142	7,893.9	1.0000	0.9378

b. Sources of growth

Year	Growth of output	Labor input total	Labor	Working hours	Capital input total	Capital	Capacity utilization	Residual	Embodied technology	Capital vintage
1956	0.1127	0.0394	0.0298	0.0095	0.0281	0.0281	0.0000	0.0409	0.0319	0.0090
1957	0.1233	0.0138	0.0152	−0.0014	0.0430	0.0430	0.0000	0.0635	0.0435	0.0199
1958	0.1064	−0.0041	−0.0036	−0.0005	0.0363	0.0363	0.0000	0.0753	0.3842	−0.3089
1959	0.1015	0.0218	0.0182	0.0035	0.0359	0.0359	0.0000	0.0411	0.0274	0.0136
1960	0.1633	0.0175	0.0129	0.0046	0.0458	0.0458	0.0000	0.0943	0.0602	0.0345
1961	0.0790	0.0016	0.0044	−0.0027	0.0659	0.0659	0.0000	0.0113	0.0060	0.0053
1962	0.0787	−0.0029	0.0016	−0.0046	0.0614	0.0614	0.0000	0.0204	0.0116	0.0088
1963	0.0457	0.0029	0.0048	−0.0019	0.0624	0.0624	0.0000	−0.0194	−0.0103	−0.0090
1964	0.0804	0.0082	0.0097	−0.0014	0.1059	0.1059	0.0000	−0.0328	−0.0127	−0.0200
1965	0.0325	0.0152	0.0203	−0.0050	0.0703	0.0703	0.0000	−0.0506	−0.0250	−0.0256
1966	0.1262	0.0188	0.0182	0.0006	0.0923	0.0923	0.0000	0.0142	0.0065	0.0076
1967	0.1681	0.0132	0.0135	−0.0003	0.1099	0.1099	0.0000	0.0431	0.0202	0.0228
1968	0.1306	0.0103	0.0109	−0.0006	0.0534	0.0534	0.0000	0.0647	0.0376	0.0271
1969	0.1404	−0.0005	0.0039	−0.0044	0.1243	0.1243	0.0000	0.0165	0.0081	0.0084
1970	0.0475	−0.0046	0.0142	−0.0189	0.1268	0.1268	0.0000	−0.0755	−0.0368	−0.0387
1971	0.0696	0.0113	0.0126	−0.0012	0.1105	0.1105	0.0000	−0.0509	−0.0282	−0.0226
1972	0.1145	0.0094	0.0119	−0.0024	0.1176	0.1176	0.0000	−0.0122	−0.0070	−0.0051
1973	0.0548	0.0077	0.0137	−0.0059	0.1009	0.1009	0.0000	−0.0529	−0.0312	−0.0217
1974	−0.0351	−0.0103	0.0016	−0.0120	0.0696	0.0696	0.0000	−0.0966	−0.0774	−0.0191
1975	0.0214	0.0088	0.0133	−0.0044	0.0619	0.0619	0.0000	−0.0484	−0.0437	−0.0046
1976	0.0206	0.0275	0.0238	0.0037	0.0465	0.0465	0.0000	−0.0505	−0.0473	−0.0032
1977	0.0618	0.0161	0.0156	0.0005	0.0533	0.0533	0.0000	−0.0073	−0.0068	−0.0005
1978	0.0764	0.0146	0.0140	0.0005	0.0717	0.0717	0.0000	−0.0096	−0.0088	−0.0007
1979	0.0648	0.0210	0.0204	0.0005	0.0603	0.0603	0.0000	−0.0159	−0.0134	−0.0024
1980	0.0246	0.0069	0.0107	−0.0037	0.0633	0.0633	0.0000	−0.0450	−0.0399	−0.0051
1981	0.0466	0.0136	0.0160	−0.0024	0.0672	0.0672	0.0000	−0.0334	−0.0291	−0.0043
1982	0.0668	0.0167	0.0185	−0.0018	0.0604	0.0604	0.0000	−0.0100	−0.0090	−0.0009
1983	0.0620	0.0284	0.0297	−0.0012	0.0635	0.0635	0.0000	−0.0284	−0.0257	−0.0027
1984	0.0591	0.0231	0.0158	0.0073	0.0749	0.0749	0.0000	−0.0373	−0.0319	−0.0053
1985	0.0591	0.0045	0.0083	−0.0038	0.0831	0.0831	0.0000	−0.0283	−0.0234	−0.0048
1986	0.0623	0.0160	0.0140	0.0020	0.0699	0.0699	0.0000	−0.0228	−0.0208	−0.0020
1987	0.0621	0.0207	0.0213	−0.0006	0.0941	0.0941	0.0000	−0.0506	−0.0507	0.0000
1988	0.0622	0.0081	0.0118	−0.0037	0.0632	0.0632	0.0000	−0.0090	−0.0086	−0.0004

Table G-1 World trade matrix of machinery and transport equipment, 1970

(unit: billion dollars)

Export from: / Export to:	1) World	2) Developed market	3) Developing market	4) Developed OPEC	5) Centrally planned economies	Developed market: 6) Europe	7) South Africa	8) Canada	9) USA
1 World	89.720	59.450	19.450	3.850	10.140	35.980	1.720	5.840	11.610
2 Developed market	78.620	58.060	17.260	3.410	2.640	35.220	1.720	5.820	11.080
3 Developing market	1.420	0.760	0.640	0.108	0.008	0.165	0.005	0.012	0.520
4 Centrally planned economies	9.670	0.630	1.540	0.325	7.490	0.590	0.001	0.006	0.012
5 Developed market: Europe	47.180	36.330	8.500	1.980	2.310	28.390	1.180	0.720	4.150
6 " Canada	5.250	4.900	0.350	0.100	0.004	0.290	0.031	0	4.490
7 " USA	17.880	12.250	4.940	0.970	0.069	5.190	0.305	4.870	0
8 " Japan	7.830	4.380	3.200	0.340	0.250	1.310	0.145	0.230	2.420
9 " Australia & New Zealand	0.275	0.155	0.120	0.017	0	0.017	0.053	0.002	0.008
10 Developing market: Africa	0.058	0.021	0.032	0.004	0.004	0.019	0.001	0	0.001
11 " America	0.385	0.190	0.195	0.022	0	0.041	0.002	0.001	0.145
12 " Mid. East	0.077	0.022	0.043	0.028	0	0.020	0	0	0.001
13 " Other Asia	0.890	0.520	0.370	0.053	0.004	0.085	0.002	0.010	0.370
14 Centrally planned: Asia	0.069	0.002	0.047	0.007	0.020	0.001	0	0	0
15 " Europe and USSR	9.600	0.630	1.500	0.320	7.470	0.590	0.001	0.006	0.012
16 " USSR	2.780	0.145	0.900	0.235	1.730	0.140	0	0	0

Source: Compiled from United Nations, *Yearbook of International Trade Statistics.*

	10) Japan	11) Aust. & N.Z.	Developing market				Centrally planned		
			12) Africa	13) America total	14) Asia Mid. East	15) Asia other	16) Asia	17) Europe & USSR	18) USSR
1	1.820	2.040	4.580	6.840	2.520	5.280	0.750	9.390	4.330
2	1.760	2.010	3.910	6.260	2.020	4.710	0.255	2.380	1.120
3	0.043	0.019	0.097	0.200	0.057	0.280	0.003	0.005	0.001
4	0.016	0.005	0.440	0.375	0.440	0.285	0.490	7.000	3.210
5	0.590	1.010	2.660	2.690	1.370	1.680	0.130	2.180	0.970
6	0.014	0.080	0.020	0.240	0.023	0.066	0	0.004	0.001
7	1.150	0.580	0.455	2.850	0.440	1.160	0	0.069	0.045
8	0	0.265	0.750	0.480	0.175	1.750	0.125	0.125	0.105
9	0.002	0.073	0.006	0.010	0.003	0.063	0	0	0
10	0	0	0.028	0.001	0.002	0	0.003	0.001	0
11	0	0.001	0.004	0.185	0	0.005	0	0	0
12	0	0	0.009	0	0.003	0	0	0	0
13	0.043	0.009	0.056	0.015	0.022	0.275	0.001	0.003	0.001
14	0.001	0	0.015	0.006	0.005	0.021	0	0.020	0.009
15	0.015	0.005	0.425	0.370	0.435	0.265	0.490	6.980	3.200
16	0.003	0.001	0.250	0.240	0.285	0.130	0.300	1.430	0

Table G-2 World trade matrix of machinery and transport equipment, 1975

(unit: billion dollars)

Export from: / Export to:	1) World	2) Developed market	3) Developing market	4) Developed OPEC	5) Centrally planned economies	Developed market: 6) Europe	Developed market: 7) South Africa	Developed market: 8) Canada	Developed market: 9) USA
1 World	244.444	140.989	70.649	25.868	30.940	88.470	4.240	14.788	24.202
2 Developed market	212.665	135.284	63.910	23.613	11.817	85.358	4.211	14.593	22.380
3 Developing market	7.119	3.503	3.491	0.983	0.054	1.029	0.029	0.162	1.767
4 Centrally planned economies	24.659	2.202	3.248	1.272	19.069	2.083	0	0.033	0.055
5 Developed market: Europe	128.670	86.975	32.439	13.872	9.214	70.361	2.793	1.646	8.386
6 " Canada	9.683	8.641	0.993	0.443	0.049	0.484	0.073	0	7.922
7 " USA	45.710	26.641	16.550	5.700	0.915	10.120	0.784	12.360	0
8 " Japan	27.405	12.502	13.265	3.462	1.638	4.242	0.503	0.577	5.972
9 " Australia & New Zealand	0.750	0.371	0.378	0.070	0.001	0.066	0.052	0.005	0.050
10 Developing market: Africa	0.191	0.081	0.097	0.026	0.009	0.069	0.001	0.002	0.009
11 " America	1.778	0.590	1.180	0.248	0.007	0.167	0.018	0.058	0.288
12 " Mid. East	0.613	0.115	0.432	0.319	0.002	0.092	0	0	0.023
13 " Other Asia	4.529	2.711	1.778	0.390	0.036	0.697	0.010	0.102	1.447
14 Centrally planned: Asia	0.129	0.012	0.081	0.013	0.037	0.008	0	0.001	0.001
15 " Europe and USSR	24.530	2.191	3.167	1.259	19.032	2.074	0	0.032	0.054
16 " USSR	6.378	0.547	1.524	0.561	4.307	0.526	0	0.010	0.006

	10) Japan	11) Aust. & N.Z.	Developing market				Centrally planned		
			12) Africa	13) America total	14) Asia Mid. East	15) Asia other	16) Asia	17) Europe & USSR	18) USSR
1	3.147	4.969	17.125	19.508	18.582	15.079	2.935	28.005	12.660
2	2.787	4.788	15.947	17.595	16.673	13.359	1.962	9.855	4.840
3	0.345	0.168	0.495	1.107	0.615	1.257	0.011	0.043	0.025
4	0.015	0.013	0.684	0.806	1.294	0.464	0.962	18.107	7.795
5	1.027	2.072	10.656	6.953	10.238	4.481	1.007	8.208	3.703
6	0.048	0.097	0.101	0.549	0.185	0.155	0.005	0.044	0.033
7	1.698	1.235	1.472	7.490	4.022	3.519	0.148	0.767	0.547
8	0	1.192	3.509	2.540	2.142	4.991	0.802	0.835	0.558
9	0.012	0.185	0.025	0.035	0.030	0.198	0	0	0
10	0.001	0	0.080	0	0.014	0.002	0	0.009	0.004
11	0.049	0.010	0.098	1.032	0.024	0.026	0	0.007	0.001
12	0	0	0.061	0.001	0.363	0.008	0.001	0.001	0
13	0.295	0.158	0.255	0.074	0.214	1.221	0.010	0.026	0.020
14	0	0.001	0.015	0.011	0.007	0.048	0	0.037	0.016
15	0.014	0.011	0.669	0.795	1.287	0.416	0.962	18.071	7.780
16	0.004	0.001	0.240	0.474	0.613	0.197	0.598	3.709	0

Table G-3 World trade matrix of machinery and transport equipment, 1980

(unit: billion dollars)

Export from: / Export to:	1) World	2) Developed market	3) Developing market	4) Developed OPEC	5) Centrally planned economies	6) Europe (Developed market)	7) South Africa (Developed market)	8) Canada (Developed market)	9) USA (Developed market)
1 World	13.081	309.694	149.422	51.781	51.128	199.710	7.526	22.301	62.549
2 Developed market	38.861	291.728	129.278	46.036	16.425	191.908	7.402	21.868	54.594
3 Developing market	27.518	14.138	12.617	3.499	0.583	4.398	0.123	0.357	7.691
4 Centrally planned economies	46.701	3.829	7.528	2.245	34.120	3.404	0.001	0.076	0.264
5 Developed market: Europe	59.263	186.004	61.210	26.291	11.967	154.255	4.715	2.334	18.820
6 " Canada	16.675	14.587	1.869	0.840	0.219	0.900	0.056	0	13.387
7 " USA	84.512	48.835	33.678	8.763	0.824	22.541	1.334	18.009	0
8 " Japan	75.870	41.131	31.332	10.020	3.407	13.884	1.236	1.500	22.008
9 " Australia & New Zealand	1.336	0.676	0.654	0.074	0.003	0.101	0.042	0.015	0.163
10 Developing market: Africa	0.337	0.231	0.098	0.023	0.002	0.211	0.011	0.001	0.008
11 " America	5.178	1.989	3.185	0.594	0.004	0.686	0.036	0.067	1.000
12 " Mid. East	1.750	0.258	1.424	0.933	0.003	0.196	0	0	0.055
13 " Other Asia	20.243	11.654	7.906	1.949	0.574	3.300	0.075	0.289	6.627
14 Centrally planned: Asia	0.580	0.041	0.478	0.106	0.061	0.026	0	0.002	0.006
15 " Europe and USSR	46.121	3.788	7.050	2.139	34.060	3.378	0.001	0.074	0.258
16 " USSR	12.227	0.781	3.407	0.854	8.039	0.734	0	0.027	0.007

			Developing market				Centrally planned		
	10) Japan	11) Aust. & N.Z.	12) Africa	13) America total	14) Asia Mid. East	15) Asia other	16) Asia	17) Europe & USSR	18) USSR
1	7.303	8.702	31.592	40.073	35.236	41.766	6.723	44.406	21.034
2	6.159	8.204	27.864	34.770	30.585	35.338	4.202	12.222	6.164
3	1.095	0.466	1.787	3.267	2.303	5.226	0.516	0.067	0.051
4	0.049	0.033	1.940	2.036	2.347	1.202	2.004	32.116	14.819
5	2.250	2.824	20.773	12.113	17.703	10.425	1.590	10.377	4.991
6	0.058	0.165	0.204	1.048	0.333	0.276	0.006	0.213	0.072
7	3.786	2.452	2.320	15.928	5.427	9.937	0.358	0.466	0.269
8	0	2.450	4.127	5.513	7.077	14.370	2.245	1.162	0.832
9	0.061	0.294	0.079	0.040	0.040	0.289	0.001	0.001	0
10	0	0	0.087	0.004	0.006	0.002	0.001	0.001	0
11	0.148	0.051	0.427	2.549	0.110	0.093	0.001	0.003	0.001
12	0.005	0.001	0.147	0.002	1.244	0.031	0.002	0.001	0
13	0.941	0.413	1.126	0.713	0.943	5.099	0.512	0.062	0.050
14	0.004	0.003	0.116	0.044	0.062	0.255	0	0.061	0.024
15	0.045	0.029	1.824	1.992	2.285	0.948	2.004	32.055	14.796
16	0.009	0.004	0.710	1.305	0.814	0.578	1.281	6.758	0

Table G-4 World trade matrix of machinery and transport equipment, 1985

(unit: billion dollars)

Export from: / Export to:	1) World	2) Developed market	3) Developing market	4) Developed OPEC	5) Centrally planned economies	Developed market: 6) Europe	Developed market: 7) South Africa	Developed market: 8) Canada	Developed market: 9) USA
1 World	600.633	394.613	136.284	36.384	65.862	195.462	4.033	34.688	134.989
2 Developed market	494.875	359.238	111.901	30.550	20.993	184.879	3.953	33.414	114.550
3 Developing market	55.062	32.836	15.894	3.855	5.899	8.347	0.079	1.228	20.248
4 Centrally planned economies	50.695	2.539	8.489	1.979	38.969	2.236	0	0.046	0.190
5 Developed market: Europe	244.717	186.456	47.746	16.767	10.411	142.359	2.636	3.014	31.398
6 " Canada	34.142	32.646	1.303	0.273	0.192	0.815	0.020	0	31.500
7 " USA	94.303	60.610	29.178	5.726	2.167	23.087	0.573	27.033	0
8 " Japan	119.199	77.849	33.142	7.712	8.208	18.133	0.695	3.345	50.906
9 " Australia & New Zealand	0.971	0.706	0.250	0.034	0.014	0.185	0.012	0.010	0.135
10 Developing market: Africa	0.373	0.190	0.174	0.026	0.005	0.159	0.010	0.001	0.020
11 " America	8.949	6.448	2.373	0.800	0.118	0.919	0.015	0.120	5.170
12 " Mid. East	2.655	0.697	1.936	1.465	0.008	0.652	0	0.003	0.040
13 " Other Asia	39.550	24.827	10.791	1.291	3.525	6.029	0.054	1.100	14.950
14 Centrally planned: Asia	0.911	0.092	0.654	0.034	0.165	0.030	0	0.004	0.043
15 " Europe and USSR	49.785	2.447	7.836	1.945	38.804	2.206	0	0.042	0.147
16 " USSR	11.812	0.433	4.184	0.542	7.195	0.399	0	0.009	0.009

			Developing market				Centrally planned		
	10) Japan	11) Aust. & N.Z.	12) Africa	13) America total	14) Asia Mid. East	15) Asia other	16) Asia	17) Europe & USSR	18) USSR
1	10.263	12.915	22.084	31.363	30.450	48.321	17.992	47.868	27.743
2	8.069	12.133	18.581	26.792	24.855	38.668	12.069	8.925	5.148
3	2.147	0.764	1.932	2.731	3.286	7.886	3.537	2.362	1.762
4	0.047	0.018	1.571	1.840	2.309	1.766	2.386	36.581	20.833
5	2.452	3.503	13.714	7.685	13.612	10.607	3.087	7.324	4.001
6	0.067	0.220	0.159	0.543	0.232	0.362	0.123	0.069	0.034
7	5.501	3.396	1.966	12.304	4.177	10.374	1.921	0.246	0.112
8	0	4.670	2.584	6.171	6.803	17.158	6.926	1.282	0.999
9	0.042	0.321	0.013	0.014	0.020	0.116	0.011	0.003	0.003
10	0	0	0.158	0.001	0.009	0.002	0.002	0.003	0
11	0.127	0.092	0.448	1.427	0.371	0.128	0.026	0.092	0.009
12	0	0.002	0.147	0.001	1.698	0.088	0	0.008	0.008
13	2.019	0.659	0.913	1.196	0.990	7.652	3.451	0.073	0.057
14	0.010	0.005	0.095	0.014	0.075	0.468	0.007	0.159	0.105
15	0.038	0.013	1.476	1.826	2.234	1.298	2.379	36.422	20.727
16	0.010	0.005	0.684	1.351	0.658	1.073	1.587	5.605	0

Table H-1 Machinery and transport equipment exports, time series, world

(unit: billion dollars)

Export to: / Year:	1) World	2) Developed market	3) Developing market	4) Developed OPEC	5) Centrally planned economies	Developed market: 6) Europe	7) South Africa	8) Canada	9) USA
1965	46.087	27.773	11.349	2.143	6.540	17.924	1.059	3.095	3.293
1970	89.720	59.450	19.450	3.850	10.140	35.980	1.720	5.840	11.610
1971	103.930	69.590	22.410	4.680	11.110	41.020	1.990	7.210	14.710
1972	124.980	83.410	26.530	6.100	14.370	50.200	1.860	8.770	17.750
1973	164.270	108.850	35.060	8.210	19.190	67.490	2.140	10.520	21.860
1974	205.651	129.879	50.722	13.436	23.462	78.696	3.357	13.188	24.936
1975	244.444	140.989	70.649	25.868	30.940	88.470	4.240	14.788	24.202
1976	277.021	161.961	81.185	32.374	32.182	101.544	3.847	16.185	30.736
1977	317.501	186.109	93.509	38.805	36.025	117.755	3.324	17.147	37.593
1978	379.685	224.912	108.815	44.408	43.134	141.368	4.215	19.301	47.259
1979	439.831	270.764	119.185	41.408	48.071	174.445	4.429	21.795	54.058
1980	513.081	309.694	149.422	51,781	51.128	199.710	7.526	22.301	62.549
1981	522.522	304.541	165.761	63.876	49.384	181.075	8.843	25.809	67.843
1982	512.111	301.631	157.676	62.654	48.062	179.664	7.188	22.173	72.361
1983	520.001	323.182	140.504	51.198	52.227	179.235	5.834	26.129	91.569
1984	565.392	366.877	140.591	42.676	54.614	182.225	6.199	32.231	123.147
1985	600.633	394.613	136.284	36.384	65.862	195.462	4.033	34.688	134.989
1986	721.057	497.674	148.992	34.292	71.094	267.356	4.371	35.430	162.208

			Developing market				Centrally planned		
	10) Japan	11) Aust. & N.Z.	12) Africa	13) America total	14) Asia Mid. East	15) Asia other	16) Asia	17) Europe & USSR	18) USSR
1965	0.665	1.506	2.783	3.758	1.266	3.454	0.571	5.969	3.097
1970	1.820	2.040	4.580	6.840	2.520	5.280	0.750	9.390	4.330
1971	1.840	2.250	5.540	7.410	2.990	6.240	0.830	10.280	4.260
1972	2.090	2.110	6.330	8.800	4.200	6.920	0.920	13.440	5.860
1973	2.750	2.960	8.780	10.740	5.620	9.680	1.310	17.880	7.430
1974	3.770	4.900	11.782	15.482	9.478	13.671	2.451	21.010	8.436
1975	3.147	4.969	17.125	19.508	18.582	15.079	2.935	28.005	12.660
1976	3.364	5.261	19.476	20.685	23.623	17.055	2.564	29.618	13.326
1977	3.552	5.757	23.456	23.425	26.267	19.951	2.113	33.912	15.482
1978	4.778	6.633	25.019	26.871	30.173	26.229	3.117	40.017	18.757
1979	6.593	7.489	25.102	31.599	29.292	32.584	5.129	42.942	20.817
1980	7.303	8.702	31.592	40.073	35.236	41.766	6.723	44.406	21.034
1981	8.022	11.049	34.943	44.935	42.456	42.681	6.168	43.217	22.284
1982	7.378	10.769	30.023	35.682	45.410	45.913	4.816	43.246	24.345
1982	8.251	9.471	25.044	25.622	41.973	47.202	5.716	46.511	27.203
1984	9.440	11.276	24.111	30.035	34.063	51.606	9.071	45.543	26.712
1985	10.263	12.915	22.084	31.363	30.450	48.321	17.992	47.868	27.743
1986	12.360	13.236	21.622	35.916	28.181	58.119	16.649	54.443	29.498

Table H-2 Machinery and transport equipment exports, time series, Japan

(unit: billion dollars)

Export to: / Year:	1) World	2) Developed market	3) Developing market	4) Developed OPEC	5) Centrally planned economies	Developed market			
						6) Europe	7) South Africa	8) Canada	9) USA
1965	2.643	1.086	1.402	0.149	0.155	0.325	0.042	0.039	0.574
1970	7.830	4.380	3.200	0.340	0.250	1.310	0.145	0.230	2.420
1971	10.590	6.070	4.250	0.495	0.275	1.550	0.190	0.400	3.600
1972	13.650	8.110	5.120	0.720	0.420	2.470	0.190	0.600	4.480
1973	18.200	10.120	7.540	1.050	0.540	3.590	0.320	0.520	5.070
1974	25.230	12.810	11.340	1.890	1.080	4.170	0.455	0.750	6.310
1975	27.405	12.502	13.265	3.462	1.638	4.242	0.503	0.577	5.972
1976	35.917	18.266	16.263	4.540	1.388	6.246	0.418	0.850	9.192
1977	44.737	22.918	20.333	6.568	1.486	8.124	0.470	0.917	11.807
1978	55.511	28.413	24.821	7.891	2.276	9.122	0.665	1.023	15.719
1979	55.259	29.655	23.210	6.735	2.394	9.520	0.634	0.871	16.767
1980	75.870	41.131	31.332	10.020	3.407	13.884	1.236	1.500	22.008
1981	86.341	44.978	37.487	12.966	3.876	13.888	1.510	2.013	24.064
1982	78.043	41.372	33.805	12.176	2.864	11.693	1.082	1.764	23.415
1983	93.691	56.101	34.800	11.257	2.790	16.595	1.224	2.710	31.809
1984	113.252	72.056	37.310	9.635	3.886	17.426	1.329	3.239	45.556
1985	119.199	77.849	33.142	7.712	8.208	18.133	0.695	3.345	50.906
1986	146.366	102.432	37.478	6.924	6.451	27.446	1.003	4.332	65.000

			Developing market				Centrally planned		
	10) Japan	11) Aust. & N.Z.	12) Africa	13) America total	14) Asia Mid. East	15) Asia other	16) Asia	17) Europe & USSR	18) USSR
1965	0	0.092	0.429	0.172	0.061	0.732	0.072	0.082	0.060
1970	0	0.265	0.750	0.480	0.175	1.750	0.125	0.125	0.105
1971	0	0.320	1.240	0.650	0.200	2.100	0.105	0.170	0.115
1972	0	0.355	1.270	1.010	0.375	2.410	0.120	0.300	0.195
1973	0	0.600	1.980	1.510	0.600	3.370	0.210	0.335	0.170
1974	0	1.100	3.000	2.400	1.040	4.810	0.660	0.420	0.230
1975	0	1.192	3.509	2.540	2.142	4.991	0.802	0.835	0.558
1976	0	1.537	4.064	3.019	3.218	5.853	0.470	0.918	0.682
1977	0	1.574	4.442	3.952	4.375	7.419	0.305	1.181	0.769
1978	0	1.840	3.868	4.284	5.416	11.080	0.729	1.548	1.168
1979	0	1.793	2.755	3.750	4.846	11.666	1.225	1.168	0.773
1980	0	2.450	4.127	5.513	7.077	14.370	2.245	1.162	0.832
1981	0	3.429	5.460	6.875	8.841	16.072	2.476	1.400	1.018
1982	0	3.315	3.509	6.166	9.175	14.745	1.127	1.738	1.433
1983	0	3.574	2.971	4.611	9.484	17.450	1.430	1.361	0.905
1984	0	4.400	3.368	6.427	7.863	19.263	2.908	0.978	0.724
1985	0	4.670	2.584	6.171	6.803	17.158	6.926	1.282	0.999
1986	0	4.470	2.089	7.024	5.647	22.186	4.827	1.624	1.266

Table H-3 Machinery and transport equipment exports, time series, United States

(unit: billion dollars)

Export to: / Year:	1) World	2) Developed market	3) Developing market	4) Developed OPEC	5) Centrally planned economies	Developed market: 6) Europe	7) South Africa	8) Canada	9) USA
1965	10.016	6.363	3.194	0.700	0.056	2.562	0.247	2.608	0
1970	17.880	12.250	4.940	0.970	0.069	5.190	0.305	4.870	0
1971	19.460	13.370	5.260	1.130	0.089	5.130	0.375	5.880	0
1972	21.530	14.940	5.940	1.390	0.105	5.550	0.370	7.110	0
1973	27.870	18.900	7.720	1.700	0.340	7.320	0.375	8.730	0
1974	38.190	24.670	11.760	2.790	0.530	9.410	0.550	10.940	0
1975	45.710	26.641	16.550	5.700	0.915	10.120	0.784	12.360	0
1976	49.510	28.395	19.015	7.720	0.828	10.442	0.885	13.537	0
1977	51.027	29.628	19.270	7.826	0.606	11.077	0.599	14.410	0
1978	60.156	35.378	21.617	8.660	0.687	14.054	0.583	16.104	0
1979	71.507	43.623	25.947	7.989	0.850	18.199	0.736	18.257	0
1980	84.512	48.835	33.678	8.763	0.824	22.541	1.334	18.009	0
1981	96.960	56.370	37.921	11.488	0.694	24.595	1.639	21.084	0
1982	90.249	50.194	36.223	11.784	0.619	22.396	1.418	18.070	0
1983	82.417	51.185	27.822	7.641	0.806	21.387	1.102	20.653	0
1984	89.855	58.210	28.689	6.171	1.082	22.506	0.969	25.608	0
1985	94.303	60.610	29.178	5.726	2.167	23.087	0.573	27.033	0
1986	95.422	62.168	29.484	5.214	2.004	25.209	0.546	25.606	0

	10) Japan	11) Aust. & N.Z.	Developing market				Centrally planned		
			12) Africa	13) America total	14) Asia Mid. East	15) Asia other	16) Asia	17) Europe & USSR	18) USSR
1965	0.416	0.468	0.297	1.821	0.372	0.697	0.046	0.011	0.005
1970	1.150	0.580	0.455	2.850	0.440	1.160	0	0.069	0.045
1971	1.130	0.630	0.490	2.820	0.580	1.340	0	0.089	0.063
1972	1.250	0.490	0.435	3.210	0.810	1.460	0.002	0.105	0.062
1973	1.490	0.730	0.690	3.990	0.990	2.040	0.069	0.270	0.205
1974	2.120	1.310	0.810	6.010	1.840	3.080	0.105	0.425	0.225
1975	1.698	1.235	1.472	7.490	4.022	3.519	0.148	0.767	0.547
1976	1.727	1.360	1.864	7.904	5.233	3.981	0.065	0.763	0.605
1977	1.679	1.481	2.013	7.994	5.016	4.205	0.052	0.554	0.374
1978	2.373	1.707	2.033	9.820	5.379	4.330	0.102	0.585	0.317
1979	3.477	2.101	1.998	12.324	5.032	6.536	0.268	0.582	0.384
1980	3.786	2.452	2.320	15.928	5.427	9.937	0.358	0.466	0.269
1981	4.738	3.535	3.315	18.840	7.349	8.309	0.254	0.440	0.310
1982	4.433	3.044	2.967	14.232	7.597	11.356	0.265	0.354	0.229
1983	4.780	2.231	2.182	8.994	5.895	10.683	0.577	0.229	0.149
1984	5.206	2.752	2.043	10.818	4.670	11.106	0.897	0.185	0.110
1985	5.501	3.396	1.966	12.304	4.177	10.374	1.921	0.246	0.112
1986	6.213	3.647	1.409	12.975	3.686	11.068	1.705	0.298	0.156

Table H-4 Machinery and transport equipment exports, time series, Europe

(unit: billion dollars)

Export to: / Year:	1) World	2) Developed market	3) Developing market	4) Developed OPEC	5) Centrally planned economies	Developed market: 6) Europe	7) South Africa	8) Canada	9) USA
1965	25.210	18.740	5.242	1.085	1.216	14.519	0.730	0.442	1.838
1970	47.180	36.330	8.500	1.980	2.310	28.390	1.180	0.720	4.150
1971	54.680	42.400	9.870	2.460	2.390	33.090	1.330	0.890	5.030
1972	65.940	50.980	11.800	3.210	3.070	40.580	1.210	1.000	6.020
1973	87.230	67.560	15.200	4.380	4.370	45.230	1.590	1.160	7.750
1974	105.950	78.380	21.220	7.020	6.230	62.220	2.210	1.320	8.730
1975	128.670	86.975	32.439	13.872	9.214	70.361	2.793	1.646	8.386
1976	141.903	96.356	36.230	16.712	9.201	80.585	2.417	1.512	8.429
1977	163.739	111.597	42.314	20.416	9.733	93.465	2.167	1.575	10.445
1978	194.425	135.303	47.924	22.923	11.151	112.021	2.860	1.893	13.647
1979	231.341	166.635	52.458	21.409	12.189	138.995	2.928	2.246	16.577
1980	259.263	186.004	61.210	26.291	11.967	154.255	4.715	2.334	18.820
1981	240.089	164.869	64.734	30.479	10.432	133.410	5.357	2.118	18.196
1982	238.701	165.180	62.852	30.015	10.605	134.229	4.411	2.018	18.325
1983	226.051	161.757	52.971	24.286	11.270	130.320	3.272	2.070	19.973
1984	228.112	169.292	48.419	20.452	10.337	130.608	3.644	2.423	26.656
1985	244.717	186.456	47.746	16.767	10.411	142.359	2.636	3.014	31.398
1986	323.880	255.342	54.187	16.368	14.214	201.097	2.611	4.007	38.892

	10) Japan	11) Aust. & N.Z.	Developing market					Centrally planned		
			12) Africa	13) America total	14) Asia Mid. East	15) Asia other		16) Asia	17) Europe & USSR	18) USSR
1965	0.232	0.828	1.626	1.405	0.714	1.451		0.133	1.083	0.472
1970	0.590	1.010	2.660	2.690	1.370	1.680		0.130	2.180	0.970
1971	0.630	1.090	3.090	3.090	1.620	1.980		0.175	2.210	0.800
1972	0.710	1.030	3.770	3.560	2.280	2.090		0.180	2.900	1.020
1973	1.000	1.260	5.180	4.050	3.040	2.840		0.280	4.090	1.460
1974	1.250	2.010	6.810	5.160	5.180	3.970		0.730	5.490	2.010
1975	1.027	2.072	10.656	6.953	10.238	4.481		1.007	8.208	3.703
1976	1.052	1.825	11.985	6.966	12.254	4.924		0.840	8.361	3.994
1977	1.306	2.100	15.080	7.955	13.679	5.485		0.528	9.205	4.638
1978	1.731	2.437	16.442	8.539	15.563	7.227		0.712	10.438	5.075
1979	2.169	2.741	17.489	10.527	15.002	9.190		1.568	10.621	5.153
1980	2.250	2.824	20.773	12.113	17.703	10.425		1.590	10.377	4.991
1981	1.984	2.836	21.484	12.238	20.268	10.588		1.099	9.333	4.644
1982	1.962	3.109	18.899	9.802	22.256	11.714		1.033	9.572	5.793
1983	2.007	2.712	15.502	7.426	19.845	10.038		0.958	10.311	6.935
1984	2.090	2.850	14.594	7.462	16.261	9.915		1.214	9.123	5.839
1985	2.452	3.503	13.714	7.685	13.612	10.607		3.087	7.324	4.001
1986	3.583	3.657	14.623	9.742	13.609	13.139		4.527	9.688	5.060

Table H-5 Machinery and transport equipment exports, time series, Asia

(unit: billion dollars)

Export to: / Year:	1) World	2) Developed market	3) Developing market	4) Developed OPEC	5) Centrally planned economies	6) Europe (Developed market)	7) South Africa (Developed market)	8) Canada (Developed market)	9) USA (Developed market)
1965	0.239	0.063	0.162	0.013	0.007	0.017	0	0.001	0.038
1970	0.890	0.520	0.370	0.053	0.004	0.085	0.002	0.010	0.370
1971	1.170	0.520	0.470	0.064	0.012	0.100	0.003	0.023	0.500
1972	1.860	1.220	0.620	0.080	0.013	0.185	0.003	0.038	0.880
1973	3.100	2.130	0.950	0.130	0.017	0.390	0.004	0.083	1.410
1974	4.471	2.931	1.515	0.260	0.024	0.604	0.010	0.115	1.784
1975	4.529	2.711	1.778	0.390	0.036	0.697	0.010	0.102	1.447
1976	6.773	4.264	2.426	0.598	0.049	1.056	0.012	0.178	2.370
1977	8.471	5.266	3.131	0.841	0.063	1.440	0.013	0.148	3.032
1978	11.287	7.118	4.096	1.134	0.046	1.957	0.017	0.186	4.189
1979	15.056	9.170	5.641	1.330	0.212	2.511	0.039	0.252	5.300
1980	20.243	11.654	7.906	1.949	0.574	3.300	0.075	0.289	6.627
1981	22.857	13.117	8.842	2.319	0.677	3.390	0.110	0.374	7.700
1982	24.739	14.795	9.070	2.218	0.697	4.213	0.091	0.356	8.505
1983	30.272	19.643	9.592	2.056	0.835	4.704	0.103	0.555	12.610
1984	39.094	25.301	11.251	1.428	2.248	5.792	0.102	0.777	16.115
1985	39.550	24.827	10.791	1.291	3.525	6.029	0.054	1.100	14.950
1986	45.102	31.049	11.352	1.234	2.508	7.313	0.116	1.096	19.422

Note: Asia here refers to developing market Asia other than Mid. East.

			Developing market				Centrally planned		
	10) Japan	11) Aust. & N.Z.	12) Africa	13) America total	14) Asia Mid. East	15) Asia other	16) Asia	17) Europe & USSR	18) USSR
1965	0.005	0.002	0.009	0.002	0.010	0.139	0.006	0.001	0
1970	0.043	0.009	0.056	0.015	0.022	0.275	0.001	0.003	0.001
1971	0.043	0.014	0.051	0.017	0.027	0.370	0.005	0.007	0.003
1972	0.078	0.032	0.051	0.027	0.036	0.500	0.002	0.011	0.005
1973	0.175	0.063	0.062	0.045	0.053	0.790	0.006	0.011	0.004
1974	0.288	0.126	0.168	0.094	0.129	1.115	0.009	0.015	0.011
1975	0.295	0.158	0.255	0.074	0.214	1.221	0.010	0.026	0.020
1976	0.487	0.157	0.321	0.132	0.460	1.499	0.016	0.032	0.025
1977	0.428	0.199	0.389	0.248	0.563	1.921	0.029	0.034	0.026
1978	0.504	0.256	0.491	0.290	0.758	2.541	0.010	0.036	0.029
1979	0.750	0.301	0.638	0.501	0.812	3.674	0.179	0.034	0.026
1980	0.941	0.413	1.126	0.713	0.943	5.099	0.512	0.062	0.050
1981	1.029	0.495	1.168	0.951	1.015	5.675	0.594	0.083	0.064
1982	1.098	0.515	1.201	0.766	1.222	5.850	0.559	0.139	0.125
1983	1.162	0.482	0.731	0.601	1.571	6.655	0.761	0.074	0.066
1984	1.875	0.625	0.749	1.055	0.906	8.500	2.041	0.206	0.192
1985	2.019	0.659	0.913	1.196	0.990	7.652	3.451	0.073	0.057
1986	2.183	0.861	0.671	1.092	0.958	8.568	2.414	0.094	0.065

Appendix I Balance of payments by trading partner

	Goods	Exports	Imports	Services
a. 1970 Total	3,963	18,969	15,006	(–) 1,785
U.S.A.	1,465	6,000	4,535	(–) 644
E.C. member countries	303	1,289	986	(–) 235
Other OECD members	495	1,593	1,098	(–) 302
Australia, N.Z., S.Africa, Finland	(–) 569	1,019	1,588	(–) 18
Centrally planned economies	309	1,036	727	12
Other countries	1,896	7,545	5,649	(–) 103
Internation institutions	—	—	—	0
Unclassified	8	11	3	—
b. 1975 Total	5,028	54,734	49,706	(–) 5,354
U.S.A.	1,045	10,930	9,885	(–) 1,907
E.C. member countries	2,500	5,492	2,992	(–) 1,987
Other OECD members	371	3,436	3,065	(–) 450
Australia, N.Z., S.Africa, Finland	(–) 1,539	2,934	4,473	40
Centrally planned economies	2,062	4,597	2,535	99
Other countries	516	27,261	26,745	(–) 1,242
Internation institutions	—	—	—	93
Unclassified	73	84	11	—
c. 1980 Total	2,125	126,736	124,611	(–) 11,343
U.S.A.	9,486	31,351	21,505	(–) 3,376
E.C. member countries	9,313	16,032	6,719	(–) 4,311
Other OECD members	296	6,940	6,644	(–) 767
Australia, N.Z., S.Africa, Finland	(–) 2,888	5,821	8,709	263
Centrally planned economies	3,110	8,887	5,777	370
Other countries	(–) 17,409	57,705	75,114	(–) 3,662
Internation institutions	—	—	—	140
Unclassified	(–) 143	—	143	—
d. 1985 Total	55,986	174,015	118,029	(–) 5,165
OECD member countries	55,206	101,646	46,440	(–) 3,826
U.S.A.	42,988	65,617	22,629	(–) 1,012
E.C. member countries	11,089	19,859	8,770	(–) 3,077
Other OECD members	1,129	16,170	15,041	263
Centrally planned economies	8,680	15,736	7,056	818
Other countries	(–) 7,942	56,587	64,529	(–) 3,427
Internation institutions	—	—	—	1,270
Unclassified	42	46	4	—
e. 1988 Total	95,012	259,765	164,753	(–) 11,263
OECD member countries	76,987	158,041	81,054	(–) 5,297
U.S.A.	52,448	89,146	36,698	115
E.C. member countries	24,604	46,120	21,516	(–) 4,828
Other OECD members	(–) 65	22,775	22,840	(–) 584
Centrally planned economies	1,356	13,497	12,141	452
Other countries	16,669	88,227	71,558	(–) 8,434
Internation institutions	—	—	—	2,016
Unclassified	—	—	—	—

Notes: 1. Trade balance excludes processing fees and net receipts on merchanting transactions from 1980.
2. Services include processing fees and net receipts on merchanting transactions from 1980.
3. Bond transactions with repurchase agreement ("gensaki") are included in short-term capital.
4. Short-term capital excludes those belonging to balance of monetary movement.
5. E.C. member countries include, as of 1988, the Netherlands, Belgium, Luxembourg, France, Germany, Italy, Denmark, the United kingdom, Ireland, Greece, Portugal and Spain.

(unit: million dollars)

Transfers	Long-term capital	Short-term capital	Errors and omissions	Current balance	Basic balance	Overall balance
(−) 208	(−) 1,591	724	271	1,970	379	1,374
36	(−) 218	—	—	857	639	—
1	171	—	—	69	240	—
1	(−) 41	—	—	194	153	—
1	(−) 91	—	—	(−) 586	(−) 677	—
1	(−) 32	—	—	322	290	—
(−) 238	(−) 1,088	—	—	1,555	467	—
(−) 11	(−) 330	—	—	(−) 11	(−) 341	—
—	—	—	—	8	8	—
(−) 356	(−) 272	(−) 1,138	(−) 584	(−) 682	(−) 954	(−) 2,676
(−) 73	(−) 37	—	—	(−) 935	(−) 972	—
(−) 13	1,306	—	—	500	1,806	—
(−) 10	492	—	—	(−) 89	403	—
(−) 1	(−) 78	—	—	(−) 1,500	(−) 1,578	—
(−) 1	(−) 417	—	—	2,160	1,743	—
(−) 158	(−) 1,472	—	—	(−) 884	(−) 2,356	—
(−) 111	(−) 66	—	—	(−) 18	(−) 84	—
11	—	—	—	84	84	—
(−) 1,528	2,394	3,071	(−) 3,155	(−) 10,746	(−) 8,352	(−) 8,396
(−) 219	1,654	—	—	6,251	7,905	—
(−) 43	4,220	—	—	4,959	9,179	—
(−) 9	(−) 1,851	—	—	(−) 480	(−) 2,331	—
(−) 12	(−) 374	—	—	(−) 2,637	(−) 3,011	—
(−) 3	(−) 531	—	—	3,477	2,946	—
(−) 887	443	—	—	(−) 21,958	(−) 21,515	—
(−) 381	(−) 1,167	—	—	(−) 241	(−) 1,408	—
26	—	—	—	(−) 117	(−) 117	—
(−) 1,652	(−) 64,542	(−) 936	3,991	49,169	(−) 15,373	(−) 12,318
(−) 313	(−) 47,780	—	—	51,067	3,287	—
(−) 249	(−) 33,163	—	—	41,727	8,564	—
(−) 19	(−) 9,628	—	—	7,993	(−) 1,635	—
(−) 45	(−) 4,989	—	—	1,347	(−) 3,642	—
(−) 24	(−) 384	—	—	9,474	9,090	—
(−) 979	(−) 12,385	—	—	(−) 12,348	(−) 24,733	—
(−) 348	(−) 4,006	—	—	922	(−) 3,084	—
12	13	—	—	54	67	—
(−) 4,118	(−)130,930	19,521	2,796	79,631	(−) 51,299	(−) 28,982
(−) 1,562	(−) 99,505	—	—	70,128	(−) 29,377	—
(−) 1,243	(−) 59,260	—	—	51,320	(−) 7,940	—
(−) 20	(−) 34,114	—	—	19,756	(−) 14,358	—
(−) 229	(−) 6,131	—	—	(−) 948	(−) 7,079	—
(−) 76	(−) 2,491	—	—	1,732	(−) 759	—
(−) 1,726	(−) 18,887	—	—	6,509	(−) 12,378	—
(−) 754	(−) 5,364	—	—	1,262	(−) 4,102	—
—	(−) 4,683	—	—	—	(−) 4,683	—

6. Other OECD members include Norway, Sweden, Switzerland, Austria, Iceland, Finland, Australia, Canada, New Zealand, and Turkey.
7. Figures not classified by territories are recorded in "unallocated," which include such things as receipts having occured from intermediary trade transactions, non-monetary gold transactions, etc.

Source: Bank of Japan, *Economic Statistics Annual.*

References

An asterisk (*) indicates that the title is the translation by the present writer. Otherwise, the English title is from the original publication.

Adams, F. Gerard and Gagnes, Byron. 1987. "Macroeconomic Impacts of US-Japan Trade Linkages with Linked Econometric Models." Working Paper. Philadelphia: Economic Research Unit, University of Pennsylvania.

———. and Shishido, Shuntaro. 1988. *Structure of Trade and Industry in the US-Japan Economy*. Tokyo: National Institute for Research Advancement.

Administrative Management Agency. Various issues. *Input-Output Tables*. Tokyo: Zenkoku Tokei Kyokai Rengokai.

———. 1979. "Survey on the Installation and Management of Automatic Vending Machines* (Jido Hanbaikino Secchi oyobi Kanrini Kansuru Chosa)." *Annual Report on Administrative Management** (Gyosei Kansatsu Nenpo). Tokyo: Gyosei Kanri Kenkyu Center.

Advisory Group on Economic Structural Adjustment for International Harmony. 1986. *The Report of the Advisory Group on Economic Structural Adjustment for International Harmony*.

Aghevli, Bijan B., et al. 1990. *The Role of National Saving in the World Economy, Recent Trends and Prospects*. Occasional Paper 67. Washington, D.C.: International Monetary Fund.

Aho, C. Michael, and Aronson, Jonathan David. 1985. *Trade Talks, America Better Listen*. New York: The Council on Foreign Relations, Inc.

———. and Levinson, Marc. 1987. "A Canadian Opportunity." *Foreign Policy*. Number 66. Spring.

Akashi, Yoshihiko. 1987. "A Quantitative Analysis of the Post-war Japanese Patent System* (Sengo Nihonno Tokkyo Seidono Suryoteki Bunseki)." *Hikone Ronso*. No.245. Aug.

Akino, Yutaka. 1987. "Gorbachev's New Policy towards Asia." *The Indonesian Quarterly*. XV/3.

Allen, Mark, et al. 1990. *International Capital Markets, Developments and Prospects*. World Economic and Financial Surveys. Washington, D.C.: International Monetary Fund.

Amamo, Akihiro. 1988. "Japan's External Imbalance and Exchange Rates." *Statistical Data Bank Systems, Socio-Economic Database and Model Building in Japan*. Amsterdam: Elsevier Science Publishers, B.V.

Aoki, Masahiko. 1987. "The State and Markets: A Bargaining Game

Theoretic Implication." *The State and the Private Enterprise in a Global Society*. Tokyo: Japan Association for Planning Association and National Institute for Research Advancement.

Arrow, K.J.; Chenery, H.B.; Minhas, B.S.; and Solow, R.M. 1961. "Capital-Labor Substitution and Economic Efficiency." *The Review of Economics and Statistics*. Vol.XLIII No.3. August.

Ayres, Robert U. (forthcoming). *CIM: Revolution in Progress*. Volume I of IIASA's CIM Project Report. London: Chapman & Hall.

______. et al. (forthcoming). *The Diffusion of Computer Integrated Manufacturing Technologies: Models, Case Studies, and Forecasts*. Volume III of IIASA's CIM Project Report. London: Chapman & Hall.

______. Dobrinsky, R.; Haywood, W.; Uno, K.; and Zuscovitch, E. (forthcoming). *CIM: Economic and Social Impacts*. Volume IV of IIASA's CIM Project Report. London: Chapman & Hall.

The Bank of Japan. Various issues. *Economic Statistics Annual* (Keizai Tokei Nenpo). Tokyo.

______. Various issues. *Flow of Funds Accounts in Japan*. Tokyo.

______. Various issues. *Price Indexes Annual*. (Bukka Shisu Nenpo). Tokyo: The Credit Information Company of Japan.

______. Various issues. *Comparative Economic and Financial Statistics, Japan and Other Major Countries* (Nihono Chushintosuru Kokusai Hikaku Tokei). Tokyo.

Barker, Betty L. 1986. "U.S. Merchandise Trade Associated with U.S. Multinational Companies." *Survey of Current Business*. Vol.66 No.5, May.

Beckman, M., and Sato, R. 1969. "Aggregate Production Functions and Types of Technical Progress: A Statistical Survey." *American Economic Review*. 59. March.

Bergsten, C. Fred, and Cline, William R. 1985. Revised 1987. *The United States-Japan Economic Problem*. Washington, D.C.: Institute for International Economics.

______. 1987. "Economic Imbalances and World Politics." *Foreign Affairs*. Issue 4.

Berndt, E., and Khaled, M. 1979. "Parametric Productivity Measurement and Choice Among Flexible Functional Forms." *Journal of Political Economy*. 87. Dec.

Bieshaar, H. and Kleinknecht, A. 1984. "Kondratieff Long Waves in Aggregate Output? An econometric test." *Konjukturpolitik*. Vol.30 No.5. October.

______. and ______. 1986. "Kondratieff Long Waves? Reply to S. Solomou." Konjukturpolitik. Vol.32 No.5. October.

Black, S.W., and Russell, R.R. 1969. "An Alternative Estimates of Potential GNP." *Review of Economics and Statistics*. February.

Bollino, C. Andrea; Pauly, Peter; and Petersen, Christian E. 1983. "Tariffs and Global Development: Further Results from Project LINK." Paper presented at the Project LINK Meeting.

Brereton, Barbara F. 1987. "U.S. Multinational Companies: Operations in 1985." *Survey of Current Business*. Vol.67 No.6, June.

Bryant, Ralph C.; Currie, David A.; Frenkel, Jacob A.; Masson, Paul R.; and Portes, Richard. 1989. *Macroeconomic Policies in an Interdependent World*. Washington, D.C.: International Monetary Fund.

Buffa, Elwood S. 1984. "Making American Manufacturing Competitive." *California Management Review*. Vol.XXVI, No.3, Spring.

Buiter, Willem H. 1987. "Does an Improvement in the Current Account or the Trade Balance at Full Employment Require a Depreciation of the Real Exchange Rate?" *The State and the Private Enterprise in a Global Society. Tokyo: Japan Association for Planning Administrtion and National Institute for Research Advancement.*

Bureau of Economic Analysis, United States Department of Commerce. 1987. *"U.S. Direct Investment Abroad: Detail for Position and Balance of Payments Flows, 1986." Survey of Current Business*. Vol.67 No.8, August.

———. 1987 "Foreign Direct Investment in the United States: Details for Position and Balance of Payments Flows, 1986." *Survey of Current Business*. Vol.67 No.8, August.

Bureau of Statistics. Various Issues. *Report on the Survey of Research and Development*. (Kagaku Gijutsu Kenkyu Chosa Hokoku). Tokyo: Nihon Tokei Kyokai.

———. Various issues. *Japan Statistical Yearbook* (Nihon Tokei Nenkan). Tokyo: Japan Statistical Association and the Maichichi Newspapers.

———. Various issues. *Monthly Statistics of Japan* (Nihon Tokei Geppo). Tokyo: Japan Statistical Association.

The Business Roundtable. 1987. *American Excellence in a World Economy: A Summary of the Report*. New York and Washington, D.C.

Business Week. 1982. *The Reindustrialization of America*. New York: McGraw-Hill, Inc. Japanese translation by Nikkei Business. Tokyo: The Japan Economic Journal.

Cadiou, Jean-Marie. 1986. "ESPRIT in Action." Paper present to the conference on High Technology, Security and Economic Growth, Brussels.

Cartwright, David W. 1986. "Improved Deflation of Purchases of Computers." *Survey of Current Business*. Mar.

———. and Smith, Scott D. 1988. "Deflators for Purchases of Computers in GNP: Revised and Extended Estimates, 1983–1988." *Survey of Current Business*. Vol.68 No.11. November.

Clark, Peter K. 1979. "Potential GNP in the United States, 1948–1980." *The Review of Income and Wealth*. Series 25 Number 2. June .

Cole, Rosanne; Chen, Y.C.; Barquin-Stolleman, Joan A.; Dulberger, Ellen; Helvacian, Nurhan; and Hodge, James H. 1986. "Quality-Adjusted Price Indexes for Computer Processors and Selected Peripheral Equipment." *Survey of Current Business*. Jan.

The Committee for Economic Development and Keizai Doyukai (Japan Association of Corporate Executives). 1987. *United States-Japan Trade Relations: A Critical Juncture.*

Coombs, Rod; Savioti, Paolo; and Walsh, Vivien. 1987. *Economics and Technological Change*. London: The Macmillan Publishers, Ltd.

Database Promotion Center. Various issues. *Database White Paper** (Detabesu Hakusho). Tokyo: Database Promotion Center.

Denison, Edward F. 1967. *Why Growth Rates Differ: Postwar Experience in Nine Western Countries*. Washington, D.C.: The Brookings Institution.

———. 1979. *Accounting for United States Economic Growth, 1929–1969*. Washington, D.C.: The Brookings Institution.

———. and Chung, William K. 1976. *How Japan's Economy Grew So Fast, The Sources of Postwar Expansion*. Washington, D.C.: The Brookings Institution.

———. 1979. *Accounting for Slower Economic Growth, The United States in the 1970s*. Washington, D.C.: The Brookings Institution.

Dicken, Peter. 1986. *Global Shift, Industrial Change in a Turbulent World*. London: Harper & Row.

Dornbusch, Rudiger, and Fischer, Stanley. 1987. *Macroeconomics*. Fourth Edition. New York: McGraw-Hill, Inc.

Economic Council, ed. 1990. *Econometric Analysis of Structural Adjustment of the Economy—The 9th Report of the Econometric Committee—** (Keizai Kozo Choseino Keiryo Bunseki). Tokyo: Ministry of Finance Printing Bureau.

Economic Planning Agency. Various issues. *Annual Report on National Accounts* (Kokumin Keizai Keisan Nenpo). Tokyo: Ministry of Finance Printing Bureau.

———. Various issues. *Economic White Paper** (Keizai Hakusho). Tokyo: Ministry of Finance Printing Bureau.

———. Various issues. *Economic Survey of Japan*. Tokyo: Ministry of Finance Printing Bureau.

———. Various issues. *World Economic White Paper** (Sekai Keizai Hakusho). Tokyo: Ministry of Finance Printing Bureau.

———. ed. 1982a. *Japan in the Year 2000—The World Economy, a Milestone for Multipolar Stability—** (2000nenno Nihon—Sekai Keizai, Takyoku Anteieno Dohyo—). Tokyo: Ministry of Finance Printing

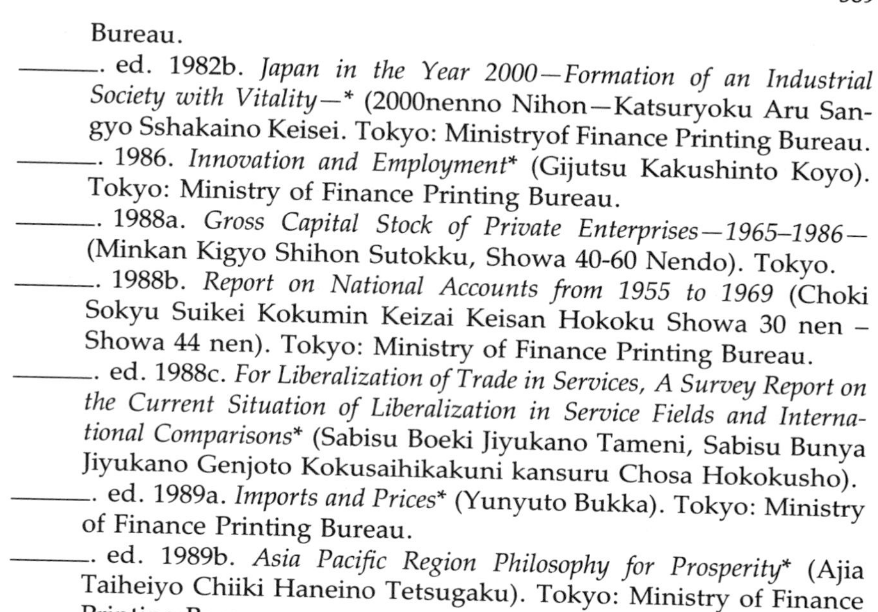

Bureau.

———. ed. 1982b. *Japan in the Year 2000—Formation of an Industrial Society with Vitality—** (2000nenno Nihon—Katsuryoku Aru Sangyo Sshakaino Keisei. Tokyo: Ministryof Finance Printing Bureau.

———. 1986. *Innovation and Employment** (Gijutsu Kakushinto Koyo). Tokyo: Ministry of Finance Printing Bureau.

———. 1988a. *Gross Capital Stock of Private Enterprises—1965–1986—* (Minkan Kigyo Shihon Sutokku, Showa 40-60 Nendo). Tokyo.

———. 1988b. *Report on National Accounts from 1955 to 1969* (Choki Sokyu Suikei Kokumin Keizai Keisan Hokoku Showa 30 nen – Showa 44 nen). Tokyo: Ministry of Finance Printing Bureau.

———. ed. 1988c. *For Liberalization of Trade in Services, A Survey Report on the Current Situation of Liberalization in Service Fields and International Comparisons** (Sabisu Boeki Jiyukano Tameni, Sabisu Bunya Jiyukano Genjoto Kokusaihikakuni kansuru Chosa Hokokusho).

———. ed. 1989a. *Imports and Prices** (Yunyuto Bukka). Tokyo: Ministry of Finance Printing Bureau.

———. ed. 1989b. *Asia Pacific Region Philosophy for Prosperity** (Ajia Taiheiyo Chiiki Haneino Tetsugaku). Tokyo: Ministry of Finance Printing Bureau.

———. ed. 1989c. *Corporate Behavior Aiming at Promotion of Domestic Demand and Horizontal Division of Labor** (Naijuno Kaitakuto Suihei Bungyoni Torikumu Kigyo Kodo). Tokyo: Ministry of Finance Printing Bureau.

———. ed. 1989d. *The Pacific Economy in the 1990s—The Birth of Bush Administration and the Issues in the Pacific Economy** (90nendaino Taiheiyo Keizai—Busshu Seikenno Tanjoto Taiheiyo Keizaino Kadai). Tokyo: Ministry of Finance Printing Bureau.

———. ed. 1990. *Globalization of the Monetary System** (Gurobarukasuru Kinyu Shisutemu). Tokyo: Ministry of Finance Printing Bureau.

Edler, Dietmar. 1989. "Modelling the Impact of Selected Technologies within a Dynamic Input-Output Framework: Industrial Robots in the Federal Republic of Germany." Paper presented at the Ninth International Conference on Input-Output Techniques.

The Edwin O. Reischauer Center for East Asian Studies. 1989. *The United States and Japan in 1989: Managing Interdependence*. Tokyo: The Japan Times.

Encarnation, Dennis J. 1986. "Cross-investment: A Second Front of Economic Rivalry." McCraw, Thomas K. ed. *America versus Japan*. Boston: Harvard Business School Press.

The Federation of Economic Organizations. 1986. "Our Proposal on Structural Adjustment of the Economy* (Keizai Kozo Choseini Taisuru Warewareno Kangaekata." (Mimeo.)

Fukushima, Kiyohiko. 1985. "Japan's Real Trade Policy." *Foreign Policy*. Summer.

Furukawa, Shunichi. 1986. *International Input-Output Analysis, Compilation and Case Studies of Interaction between ASEAN, Korea, Japan, and the United STates, 1975*. I.D.E. Occasional Papers Series No.21. Tokyo: Institute of Developing Economies.

General Agreement on Tariffs and Trade. Various issues. *News of the Uruguay Round of Multilateral Trade Negotiations*. Geneva.

Goerzig, Bernd. 1989. "Estimation of Potential GNP in the Federal Republic of Germany." Paper presented at the 21st General Conference of the International Association for Research in Income and Wealth.

Goto, Akira; Honjo, Noboru; Suzuki, Kazuyuki; and Takinosawa, Mamoru. 1986. "An Economic Analysis of Research and Development and Technical Progress* (Kenkyu Kaihatsuto Gijutsu Shinpono Keizai Bunseki)." *Keizai Bunseki*. No.103. Sept.

Goto, Osamu. 1989. "Increased Diffusion of Microelectronics in the Economy and Factors Behind It* (Keizaino Maikuro Erekutoronikkusukano Shintento sono Yoin)." *Keizai Geppo*. Oct.

Governments of Japan and the United States of America. 1986. "Arrangement between the Government of Japan and the Government of the United States of America concerning Trade in Semiconductor Products." (Mimeo.)

Green, Robert T., and Larsen Trina, L. 1988. "Only Retaliation will Open Up Japan." *Harvard Business Review*. November–December.

Griliches, Zvi. 1979. "Issues in Assessing the Contribution of Research and Development to Productivity Growth." *The Bell Journal of Economics*. 10. Spring.

______. 1980. "R&D and the Productivity Slowdown." *The American Economic Review*. 70. May.

Gruber, William; Mehta, Dileep; and Vernon, Raymond. 1967. "The R&D Factor in International Trade and International Investment of United States Industries." *Journal of Political Economy*. vol ???

Haigh, Robert W.; Gerbner, George; and Byrne, Richard B. 1981. *Communications in the Twenty-First Century*. New York: John Wiley & Sons.

Haywood, W., ed. 1990. *CIM: Revolution in Progress, Proceedings of the Final IIASA Conference on Computer Integrated Manufacturing: Technologies, Organizations, and People in Transition*. WP-90-32. Laxenburg: International Institute for Applied Systems Analysis.

Herr, Ellen M. 1987a. "U.S. Business Enterprises Acquired or Established by Foreign Direct Investors in 1986." *Survey of Current Business*. Vol.67 No.5, May.

———. 1987b. "Capital Expenditures by Majority-Owned Foreign Affiliates of U.S. Companies, 1987–1988." *Survey of Current Business*. Vol.67 No.9, September.

Houthakker, H.S., and Magee, P. 1969. "Income and Price Elasticities in World Trade." *The Review of Economics and Statistics*. Vol.LI No.2. May.

Howestine, Ned G. 1987. "U.S. Affiliates of Foreign Companies: Operations in 1985." *Survey of Current Business*. Vol.67 No.5, May.

Hughes, Alan, and Singh, Ajit. 1988. "The World Economic Slowdown and the Asian and Latin American Economies: A Comparative Analysis of Economic Structure, Policy and Performance." WP42. Helsinki: World Institute for Development Economic Research.

Institute of Developing Economies. 1982. *International Input-Output Table for ASEAN Countries, 1975*. I.D.E. Statistical Data Series No.39. Tokyo: Institute of Developing Economies.

The Institute for International Economics. 1987. "Resolving the Global Economic Crisis: A Statement by Thirty-three Economists from Thirteen Countries." (Mimeo.)

The Institute of Statistical Research. 1984. *Dynamic Development of the World Economy—NICs, Innovation, and Inflation—** (Sekai Keizaino Dotaitki Tenkai—NICs, Inobeshon, Infureshon—). Tokyo.

International Monetary Fund. Various issues. *International Financial Statistics*.

Ishiguro, Kazunori. 1987. "Expansion of Global Business Activities and Intensified International Economic Frictions—Their Legal Aspects." *The State and the Private Enterprise in a Global Society*. Tokyo: Japan Association for Planning Administration and National Institute for Research Advancement.

Ito, Kenichi. 1988. "Japan and the Soviet Union—Entangled in the Deadlock of the Northern Territories." *The Washington Quarterly*. Winter.

Iwata, Kazumasa. 1987. "Post Venice Summit Policy Coordination—Convergence of Tax Policy and Establishment of Multiple Key Currency System." *The State and the Private Enterprise in a Global Society*. Tokyo: Japan Association for Planning Association and National Institute for Research Advancement.

Japan Association for Planning Administration (JAPA) and National Institute for Research Advancement (NIRA). 1987. *The State and the Private Enterprise in a Global Society*. Tokyo.

Japan Association for Trade with Soviet Union and Socialist Countries of Europe. Various issues. *Monthly bulletin on Trade with USSR & East Europe*. Tokyo.

The Japan Development Bank. 1984. "On Capital Stock Vintage—A

Comparison of U.S. and Japanese Manufacturing Industry* (Setsubi Vintejini Tsuite—Nichibei Seizogyo Hikakuo Chushinto Shite)." *Chosa*. No.78. December.

Japan External Trade Organization. 1990. *World Trade Forecast and Economic and Trade Projectin for Selected Countries** (1990nenno Sekai Boeki Yosokuto Kakkoku Keizai Boeki Mitoshi). Tokyo.

Japan Forum on International Relations, Inc. 1988. *The Policy Recommendations on the Structural Adjustment of Economies of Japan, U.S. and Asian NICs*. JF-PR-1. Tokyo.

The Japan Industrial Robot Association (Nihon Sangyoyo Robotto Kyokai). Various issues. *Report on a Survey of Business Firms concerning Industrial Robots** (Sangyoyo Robottoni Kansuru Kigyo Jittai Chosa Hokokusho). Tokyo.

The Japan Information Processing Development Center (Nihon Joho Shori Kaihatsu Kyokai). Various issues. *Informatization Whitepaper** (Johoka Hakusho). Tokyo: Konpyuta Eiji Sha.

The Japan Institute of International Affairs. 1987. *The Development of World Trade and Intellectual Property Rights** (Sekai Boekino Hattento Chiteki Shoyuken). Tokyo.

Japan Tariff Association. Various issues. *The Summary Report on Trade of Japan*. (Gaikoku Boeki Gaikyo). Tokyo.

The Japan-Unikted States Economic Relations Group. 1981. *Report of the Japan-United States Economic Relations Group*. Prepared for the President of the United States and the Prime Minister of Japan.

Johnston, J. 1963. *Econometric Methods*. New York: McGraw-Hill Book Company, Inc.

Joint Economic Committee, Congress of the United States. 1982a. *East-West Trade: The Prospects to 1985*. Washington, D.C.: U.S. Government Printing Office.

______. 1982b. *Soviet Economy in the 1980s: Problems and Prospects*. Washington, D.C.: U.S. Government Printing Office.

Jorgenson, Dale W. 1966. "The Embodiment Hypothesis." *Journal of Political Economy*. Vol.74 No.1. February.

______. and Grililiches, Z. 1967. "The Explanation of Productivity Change." *Review of Economic Studies*, 34 (99).

______. and Gollop, F.M. 1980. "Productivity Growth by Industry, 1947–1973." Kendrick and Vaccara, eds. *New Developments in Productivity Measurement and Analysis*. Chicago: University of Chicago Press.

Jorgenson, D. and Griliches, Z. 1972. "Issues in Growth Accounting: A Reply to Edward F. Denison." *Survey of Current Business*. 52. May.

Kase, Hiroshi. 1989. "The Current Situation of Database Services in Japan." *Database Forum*. Vol.3 No.2.

Katsuhara, Ken. 1985. "The Trends in Iron and Steel Industry in South-East Asia* (Tonan Ajia Tekkogyono Doko)." Shinohara, M. ed. *A Future Scenario for the Asia-Pacific Region*. Tokyo: The Institute for Statistical Research.

Kaya, Yoichi, et al. 1988. *The Impact of Robotics and Related Technology on Industry and Economy and the Policy Options** (Robotto Kanren Gijutsuno Sangyo oyobi Keizaini Ataeru Eikyoto Taio Senryaku). Tokyo: National Institute for Research Advancement.

Kendrick, J. 1973. *Postwar Productivity Trends in the United States, 1948–1969*. New York: National Bureau of Economic Research.

———. nd Vaccara, B., eds. 1980. *New Developments in Productivity Measurements*. Chicago: University of Chicago Press.

Kinoshita, Soshichi, and Yamada, Mitsuo. 1988. "The Impact of Robotization on International Economy* (Robottokano Kokusai Keizaieno Eikyo)." Kaya, Y., ed. *The Impact of Robots and Related Technology on Industry and Economy and the Policy Options*. Tokyo: National Institute for Research Advancement.

———. and ———. 1989. "The Impact of Robotization on Macro and Sectoral Economies with a World Econometric Model." Ranta, J. ed. *Trends and Impacts of Computer Integrated Manufacturing*. Laxemburg: International Institute of Applied Systems Analysis.

Kleinknecht, A. 1987a. *Innovation Patterns and Prosperity. Schumpeter's Long Cycle Reconsidered.* London: Macmillan and New York: St. Martin's Press.

———. 1987b. "Are There Schumpeterian Waves of Innovation?" WP-87-076. Laxenburg: International Institute for Applied Systems Analysis.

Kodama, Fumio. 1990. "R&D in the Past and Future Transition: Analyzing the Japanese Post-War Development." Paper presented at International Forum on Economies in Transition: Statistical Measures Now and in the Future, organized by International Institute for Applied Systems Analysis and Academy of Sciences of the USSR, Sochi, USSR.

Komiya, Ryutaro. 1988. *Contemporary Japanese Economy, Macroeconomic Development and International Economic Relations** (Gendai Nihon Keizai, Makuroteki Tenkaito Kokusai Keizai Kankei). Tokyo: Tokyo University Press.

Krelle, Wilhelm, ed. 1989. *The Future of the World Economy, Economic Growth and Structural Change*. Berlin: Springer-Verlag.

Krugman, Paul. 1987. "Is the Japan Problem Over?" Sato, R. and Watchtel, P., eds. *Trade Friction and Economic Policy*. Cambridge and New York: Cambridge University Press.

Kuramata, Takashi; Miyashita, Hideo; and Masuda, Tomoaki. 1986. *A*

*Study on the Relationship between Technological Innovation and Economic Growth** (Gijutsu Kakushinto Keizai Seichono Sogokankeini kansuru Kenkyu). Kamakura: The Nomura Research Institute.

Kuroda, Makoto. 1989. *A View on U.S.-Japan Relations: Living through Trade Frictions** (Nichibei Kankeino Kangaekata, Boeki Masatsuo Ikite). Tokyo: Yuhikaku.

Kuwahara, Yasuo, and Umezawa, Yakashi. 1982. "The Recent Technological Progress and Industrial Relations—The Impact of Micro-electronics on Employment and its Evaluation (Saikinno Gijutsushinpoto Rodo Mondai—Maikuro Erekutoronikkusu no Koyo Rodoeno Eikyoto Hyoka)." *The Monthly Journal of the Japan Institute of Labour*. Vol.24 No.1. Jan.

Leibfritz, W. 1987. "Demand Management and Supply Side Policies in West Germany, Past Experience and Prospects for the Future." *The State and the Private Enterprise in a Global Society*. Tokyo: Japan Association for Planning Administration and National Institute for Research Advancement.

Levitt, Theodore. 1976. "The Industrialization of Service." *Harvard Business Review*. Sept.–Oct.

Loong-Hoe, Tan, and Akrasanee, Narongchai. 1988. *ASEAN-U.S. Economic Relations: Changes in the Economic Environment and Opportunities*. Singapore: Institute of Southeast Asian Studies.

Maddison, Angus. 1989. *The World Economy in the 20th Century*. Paris: The Organisation for Economic Co-operation and Development.

Mansfield, E.; Rappaport, J.; Schnee, J.; Wagner, S.; and Hamburger, M. 1971. *Research and Innovation in the Modern Corporation*New York: Norton.

Marengo, Luigi, and Sterlacchini, Alessandro. 1989. "Intersectoral Technology Flows—Methodological Aspects and Empirical Applications." Paper presetned at the Ninth International Conference on Input-Output Techniques.

Massel, B.F. 1961. "A Disaggregated View of Technical Change." *Journal of Political Economy*. Dec.

McCraw, Thomas K., ed. 1986. *America versus Japan*. Boston: harvard Business School Press.

Mensch, G. 1975. 1979. *Das Technologische Patt*. Frankfurt: Umschau (English: *Stalemate in Technology*. Cambridge, MA.)

Merritt, Giles. 1986. "The current State of Western High Technology: Does a Technology Gap Really Exist?" Paper present to the Conference on High Technology, Western Security and Economic Growth, Brussels.

Meyer, Bernd. 1989. "The Dollar and the Structure of Production of the

FRG: Simulations with a Multisectoral Econometric Model." Paper presented at the Ninth International Conference on Input-Output Techniques.

Miller, Edward M. 1983. "Capital Aggregation in the Presence of Obsolescence-Inducing Technical Change." *The Review of Income and Wealth*. Series 29 Number 3. Sept.

Minasian, J. 1969. "Research and Development, Production Functions and Rates of Return." *American Economic Review*. 59. May.

Ministry of Finance. Various issues. *Monthly Report on Fiscal and Financial Statistics** (Zaisei Kinyu Tokei Geppo). Tokyo.

———. International Finance Bureau. 1989. "Current States of External Debit and Credit of Japan* (Wagakunino Taigaino Taishakuno Genjo)." *Monthly Report on Fiscal and Financial Statistics*. August.

Ministry of International Trade and Industry. Various issues. *International Trade White Paper** (Tsusho Hakusho). Tokyo: Ministry of Finance Printing Office.

———. Various issues. *Annual Report on Indexes on Mining and Manufacturing** (Kokogyo Shisu Nenpo). Tokyo.

———. Various issues. *Input-Output Tables (Extension Tables)* (Sangyo Renkanhyo Enchohyo). Tokyo.

———. Various issues. *Business and Investment Survey of Incorporated Enterprises** (Shuyo Sangyono Setsubi Toshi Keikaku). Tokyo: Ministry of Finance Printing Bureau.

———. Various issues. *Current States and Problems of Economic Cooperation** (Keizai Kyoryokuno Genjoto Mondaiten). Tokyo: Tsusho Sangyo Chosakai.

———. Various issues. *Overseas Operation of Japanese Business** (Wagakuni Kigyono Kaigai Jigyo Katsudo). Tokyo: Ministry of Finance Printing Bureau.

———. Various issues. *Activities of Foreign-Affiliated Business Firms** (Gaishikei Kigyono Doko). Tokyo: Ministry of Finance Printing Bureau.

———. Various issues. *Survey on Machine Tools Installation* (Kosaku Kikai Setsubito Tokei Chosa Hokokusho). Tokyo.

———. Various issues. *Census of Manufactures* (Kogyo Tokeihyo). Tokyo: Ministry of Finance Printing Bureau.

———. Various issues. *Trends in Tertiary Industry Activities** (Daisanji Sangyo Katsudo Doko). Tokyo.

———. Various issues. *Plant and Equipment Investment Plans in Major Industries** (Shuyo Sangyono Setsubi Toshi Keikaku). Tokyo: Ministry of Finance Printing Bureau.

———. 1984. *Management Analysis of Enterprises of the World.** (Sekaino Kigyono Keiei Bunseki) 1984 edition. Tokyo: Ministry of Finance

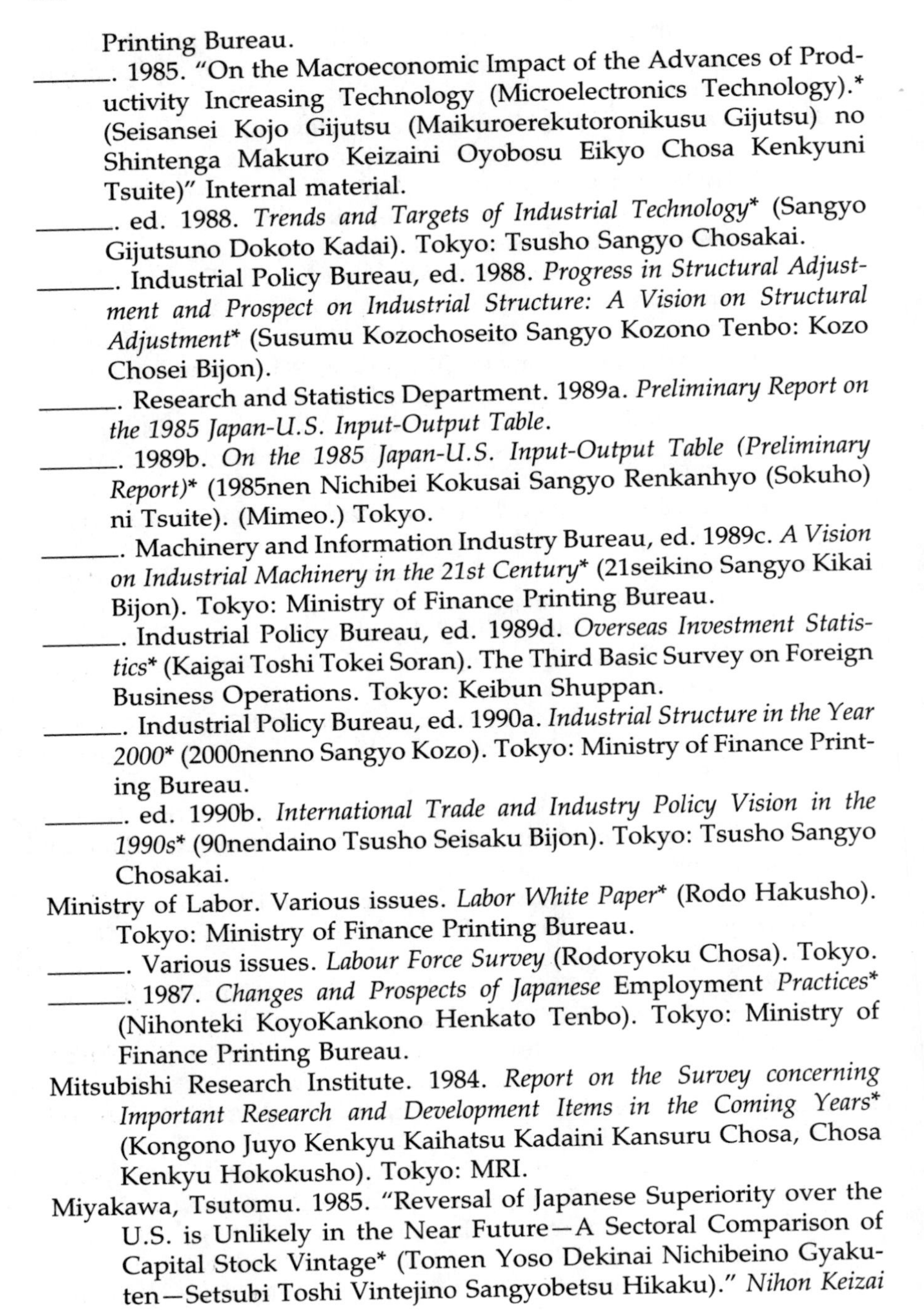

Printing Bureau.

______. 1985. "On the Macroeconomic Impact of the Advances of Productivity Increasing Technology (Microelectronics Technology).* (Seisansei Kojo Gijutsu (Maikuroerekutoronikusu Gijutsu) no Shintenga Makuro Keizaini Oyobosu Eikyo Chosa Kenkyuni Tsuite)" Internal material.

______. ed. 1988. *Trends and Targets of Industrial Technology** (Sangyo Gijutsuno Dokoto Kadai). Tokyo: Tsusho Sangyo Chosakai.

______. Industrial Policy Bureau, ed. 1988. *Progress in Structural Adjustment and Prospect on Industrial Structure: A Vision on Structural Adjustment** (Susumu Kozochoseito Sangyo Kozono Tenbo: Kozo Chosei Bijon).

______. Research and Statistics Department. 1989a. *Preliminary Report on the 1985 Japan-U.S. Input-Output Table.*

______. 1989b. *On the 1985 Japan-U.S. Input-Output Table (Preliminary Report)** (1985nen Nichibei Kokusai Sangyo Renkanhyo (Sokuho) ni Tsuite). (Mimeo.) Tokyo.

______. Machinery and Information Industry Bureau, ed. 1989c. *A Vision on Industrial Machinery in the 21st Century** (21seikino Sangyo Kikai Bijon). Tokyo: Ministry of Finance Printing Bureau.

______. Industrial Policy Bureau, ed. 1989d. *Overseas Investment Statistics** (Kaigai Toshi Tokei Soran). The Third Basic Survey on Foreign Business Operations. Tokyo: Keibun Shuppan.

______. Industrial Policy Bureau, ed. 1990a. *Industrial Structure in the Year 2000** (2000nenno Sangyo Kozo). Tokyo: Ministry of Finance Printing Bureau.

______. ed. 1990b. *International Trade and Industry Policy Vision in the 1990s** (90nendaino Tsusho Seisaku Bijon). Tokyo: Tsusho Sangyo Chosakai.

Ministry of Labor. Various issues. *Labor White Paper** (Rodo Hakusho). Tokyo: Ministry of Finance Printing Bureau.

______. Various issues. *Labour Force Survey* (Rodoryoku Chosa). Tokyo.

______. 1987. *Changes and Prospects of Japanese* Employment *Practices** (Nihonteki KoyoKankono Henkato Tenbo). Tokyo: Ministry of Finance Printing Bureau.

Mitsubishi Research Institute. 1984. *Report on the Survey concerning Important Research and Development Items in the Coming Years** (Kongono Juyo Kenkyu Kaihatsu Kadaini Kansuru Chosa, Chosa Kenkyu Hokokusho). Tokyo: MRI.

Miyakawa, Tsutomu. 1985. "Reversal of Japanese Superiority over the U.S. is Unlikely in the Near Future—A Sectoral Comparison of Capital Stock Vintage* (Tomen Yoso Dekinai Nichibeino Gyakuten—Setsubi Toshi Vintejino Sangyobetsu Hikaku)." *Nihon Keizai*

Kenkyu Senta Kaiho. No.479 and 480 joint issue. Jan.15.

Mizuno, Shoichi; Matsugu, Takashi; and Dams, Theodore, eds. 1986. *Microelectronics and Employment** (ME-kano Genjoto Koyo Mondai). Nagoya: Nagoya University Printing Office.

Mohnen, Pierre and Ducharme, Louis-Marc. 1989. "R&D Spillovers and Social Rate of Return on R&D." Paper presented at the Ninth International Conference on Input-Output Techniques.

Moran, Larry R. 1987. "Motor Vehicles, Model Year 1987." *Survey of Current Business*. Vol.67 No.11, November.

Mori, Shunsuke. 1987. "Social Benefits of CIM: Labor and Capital Augmentation by Industrial Robots and NC Machine Tools in the Japanese Manufacturing Industry." EP-87-40. Laxemburg: International Institute for Applied Systems Analysis.

———. 1989. "Trends and Problems of CIM in Japanese Manufacturing Industries—From Recent Surveys in Japan." Ranta, J., ed. *Trends and Impacts of Computer Integrated Manufacturing*. Laxenburg: International Institute for Applied Systems Analysis.

Moriguchi, Chikashi. 1988. "Robotization and Macroeconomic Problems* (Robottokato Makuro Keizai Mondai)." Kaya, Y., ed. *The Impact of Robots and Related Technology on Industry and Economy and the Policy Options*. Tokyo: National Institute for Research Advancement.

Moriya, Yuichi and Uno, Kimio, eds. 1975. *Searching for the Future Growth Path—An Interim Report of the Second Medium Range Economic Projection—** (Mosakuno Nakano Shinroo Motomete—Dainikai Chuki Keizai Yosoku Chukan Hokoku—). Tokyo: The Japan Economic Research Center.

Nadiri, Ishaq. 1980. "Contributions and Determinents of Research and Development Expenditures in the U.S. Manufacturing Industries." George M. von Furstenberg, ed. *Capital, Efficiency, and Growth*. Cambridge, Mass.: Ballinger Publishing Company.

Nagai, Yonosuke and Rosovsky, Henry, eds. 1973. Communications Gap between Japan and the United States (Nichibei Komyunikeshon Gyappu). Tokyo: The Simul Press, Inc.

Nakamura, Yoichi. 1983. "An Investigation into Structural Change in the World Trade Network." Paper presented at Project LINK Meeting.

Nakamura, Shinichiro. 1988. "The Measurement of Aggregate Robot Population and the Quality Change* (Robotto Shukeiryono Keisokuto Shitsuno Henka.)." Kaya, Yoichi, ed. *The Impact of Robots and Related Technology on Industry and Economy and the Policy Options*. Tokyo: National Institute for Research Advancement.

Nadiri, M.I. 1970. "Some Approahes to the Theory and Measurement of

Total Factor Productivity: A Survey." *Journal of Economic Literature*. 8. Dec.

Nau, Henry R. 1990. *The Myth of America's Decline, Leading the World Economy into the 1990s*. New York, Oxford: Oxford University Press.

Nelson, Richard. 1964. "Aggregate Production Functions and Medium-range Growth Projections." *The American Economic Review*. Vol-.LIV No.5. Sept.

______. Peck, M.; and Kalacheck, E. 1967. *Technology, Economic Growth, and Public Policy*. New York: Brookings.

Nihon Applied Research Kenkyujo. 1986. *Research Report on the Trends and Prospects of Industrial Structural Change, Economic Growth, and Information Orientation Index accompanying Information Orientation** (Johokani Tomonau Sangyo Kozo Henka, Keizai Seicho, oyobi Johoka Shisuno Doko narabini Shorai Tenboni kansuru Chosa Hokokusho). Tokyo.

Nihon Shinyo Chosa. 1990. *External Disequilibrium Problem and Economic Structure in Japan and the United States** (Nichibeino Taigai Fukinko Mondaito Keizai Kozo). Tokyo.

Norsworthy, J.R. 1984. "Growth Accounting and Productivity Measurement." *The Review of Income and Wealth*. Series 30 Number 3. Sept.

Norton, R.D. 1986. "Industrial Policy and American Renewal." *Journal of American Literature*. Vol.XXIV, March.

Oborne, Michael West, and Fourt, Nicolas. 1983. *Pacific Basin Economic Cooperation*. Paris: OECD.

Office of the United States Trade Representative; Department of Agriculture; Department of Commerce. Various issues. *National Trade Estimate Report on Foreign Trade Barriers*. Washington, D.C.: U.S. Government Printing Office.

Ohmae, Kenichi. 1987. "Don't Blame it on Tokyo." *New Perspectives Quarterly*. Vol.4 No.3. Fall.

Okawara, Nobuhiko et al. 1988. "The Cohabitation Era for Japan and the United States: What Can Japan Offer?* (Nichibei Kyosei Jidai, Nihonwa Nanio Ataerareruka." *Nikkei Business*.

Okita, Saburo; Jayawardena, Lal; and Sengupta, Arjun K. 1986. *The Potential of the Japanese Surplus for World Economic Development*. Helsinki: World Institute for Development Economics Research.

______. ______. and______. 1987. *Mobilizing International Surpluses for World Development: A Wider Plan for a Japanese Initiative*. Helsinki: World Institute for Development Economic Research.

Okun, A.M. 1962. "Potential GNP: Its Measurement and Significance." American Statistical Association. *Proceedings of the Business and*

Economics Section. Reprinted in Okun, A.M. *The Political Economy of Prosperity* New York: Norton. 1970.

Oniki, Hajime. 1990. "Communication Infrastructure and Socio-Economic Development." Institute of Social and Economic Research, Osaka University. (Unpublished).

Organisation for Economic Cooperation and Development. 1981a. *Information Activities, Electronics and Telecommunications Technologies, Impact on Employment, Growth and Trade*. Vol.1. Information, Computer, Communications Policy 6. Paris.

———. 1981b. *Information Activities, Electronics and Telecommunications Technologies, Vol.II, Expert Reports*. Information, Computer, Communications Policy 6. Paris.

———. 1981c. *North/South Technology Transfer, the Adjustments Ahead*. Paris.

———. 1982a. *Micro-electronics, Robotics and Jobs*. Information, Computer, Communication Policy 7. Paris.

———. 1982b. *North/South Technology Transfer, The Adjustments Ahead*. Paris.

———. 1983a. *Industrial Robots, Their Role in Manufacturing Industry*. Paris.

———. 1983b. *Long Term Outlook for the World Automobile Industry*. Paris.

———. 1984. *The Employment and Unemployment of Women in OECD Countries*. Paris.

———. 1985a. *Twenty-five Years of Development Cooperation, a Review*. Paris.

———. 1985b. *Employment Growth and Structural Change*. Paris.

———. 1985c. *Software: An Emerging Industry*. Information, Computer, Communications Policy 9. Paris.

———. 1985d. *The Semiconductor Industry, Trade Related Issues*. Paris.

———. 1985e. *Structural Adjustment and Multinational Enterprises*. Paris.

———. 1986a. *Selected Science and Technology Indicators, Recent Results, 1979–1986*. Paris.

———. 1986b. *Trends in the Information Economy*. Information, Computer, Communications Policy 11. Paris.

———. 1986c. *Code of Liberalisation of Capital Movements*. Paris.

———. 1987a. *Structural Adjustment and Economic Performance*. Paris.

———. 1987b. *Information Technology and Economic Prospects*. Paris.

———. 1987c. *External Debt Statistics, the Debt and Other External Liabilities of Developing, CMEA and Certain Other Countries and Territories at End-December 1985 and End-December 1986*. Paris.

———. 1987d. *Recent Trends in International Direct Investment*. Paris.

———. 1987e. *Controls and Impediments Affecting Inward Direct Investment in OECD Member Countries*. Paris.

______. 1987f. *The Cost of Restricting Imports: The Automobile Industry*. Paris.

______. 1988. *Geographical Distribution of Financial Flows to Developing Countries, Disbursements, Commitments, Economic Indicators*. Paris.

Otaka, Yoshiho. 1988. "Trends in the Technological Innovation of Metal Working Machinery* (Kosaku Kikaino Gijutsu Kakushinno Doko)." *Research on the Methodology for Quantitative Measurement of Productive Activity under Technological Change—Sensor Innovation Committee, Product Subcommittee Report*—(J). Tokyo: Sangyo Kenkyujo.

Patent Agency. Various issues. *Annual Report of the Patent Agency** (Tokkyocho Nenpo). Tokyo.

Patrick, Hugh. 1982. "The Economic Dimensions of the U.S.-Japan Alliance: An Overview." Center Paper No.327. Economic Growth Center, Yale University.

______. and Tachi, Ryuichiro, eds. 1986. *Japan and the United States Today: Exchange Rates, Macroeconomic Policies, and Financial Market Innovations*. New York: Center on Japanese Economy and Business, Columbia University.

Peterson, Peter G. 1987. "The Morning After." *The Atlantic Monthly*. Oct.

Pepper, Thomas; Janow, Merit E.; and Wheeler, Jimmy W. 1985. *The Competition: Dealing with Japan*. New York: Praeger Publishers.

Petri, Peter A. 1984. *Modeling Japanese-American Trade*. Cambridge, MA: Harvard University Press.

Pomfret, Richard. 1988. "Trade Policy for the 1990s: Multilateralism or Bilateralism?" *SAIS Review*.

Posner, M.V. 1961. "International Trade and Technical Change." *Oxford Economic Papers*. Oct.

Pugel, Thomas A. 1987. "Limits of Trade Policy Toward High Technology Industries: The Case of Semiconductors." Sato, Ryuzo and Wachtel, Paul, eds. *Trade Friction and Economic Policy, Problems and Prospects for Japan and the United States*. Cambridge, New York, New Rochelle, Melbourne, Sydney: Cambridge University Press.

Ranta, Jukka-Pekka, and Wandel, Sten. 1988. "Economies of Scope and Design of Flexibility in Manufacturing Logistic Systems." Paper presented at the Fifth International Working Seminar on Production Economics. Inssbruck.

______. ed. 1989. *Trends and Impacts of Computer Integrated Manufacturing*. Proceedings of the Second IIASA Annual Workshop on Computer Integrated Manufacturing: Future Trends and Impacts, and the IIASA Workshop on Technological Factors in the Diffusion of CIM Technologies. WP-89-1. Laxenburg: International Institute for Applied Systems Analysis.

Reich, Robert B. 1987. "The Rise of Techno-Nationalism." *The Atlantic Monthly*. May. Sato, R. and Wachtel, P., eds. *Trade Friction and Economic Policy*. Cambridge and New York: Cambridge University Press.

Saito, Mitsuo. 1988. "The Impact of Robotization on the Japanese Economy* (Robottokano Nihon Keizaieno Eikyo)." Kaya, Y., ed. *The Impact of Robotics and Related Technology on Industry and Economy and the Policy Options*. Tokyo: National Institute for Research Advancement.

Sakurai, Makoto, and Sadahiro, Akira. 1987. "Developing Countries' Economic Issues and International Coordination." *The State and the Private Enterprise in a Global Society*. Tokyo: Japan Association for Planning Administration and National Institute for Research Advancement.

Sangyo Kenkyujo. 1988a. *Research on the Methodology for Quantitative Measurement of Productive Activity under Technological Change—Sensor Innovation Committee Report—** (Gijutsu Kakushinkano Seisan Katsudono Keiryoteki Haaku Hohoni Kansuru Chosa Kenkyu, Sensa Inobeshon Iinkai Hokoku). Tokyo: Sangyo Kenkyujo.

———. 1988b. *Research on the Methodology for Quantitative Measurement of Productive Activity under Technological Change—Sensor Innovation Committee, Product Subcommittee Report—** (Gijutsu Kakushinkano Seisan Katsudono Keiryoteki Haaku Hohoni Kansuru Chosa Kenkyu, Sensa Inobeshon Iinkai Hinmoku Bukai Hokoku). Tokyo: Sangyo Kenkyujo.

Sato, Ryuzo, and Wachtel, Paul. 1987. *Trade Friction and Economic Policy, Problems and Prospects for Japan and the United States*. Cambridge, New York, New Rochelle, Melbourne, Sydney: Cambridge University Press.

Sautter, Christian. 1987. "A Social Compromise for Competitive Growth: French Socialist Economic Policy (1981–1986)." *The State and the Private Enterprise in a Global Society*. Tokyo: Japan Association for Planning Association and National Institute for Research Advancement.

Scherer, F.M. 1982. "Inter-industry Technology Flows in the United States." *Research Policy* 11. Autumn.

Scholl, Russell B. 1987. "The International Investment Position of the United States in 1986." *Survey of Current Business*. Vol.67 No.6, June.

Schumpeter, Joseph A. 1950. *Capitalism, Socialism, and Democracy*. Third Edition. New York: Harper & Row, Publishers, Inc.

Science and Technology Agency. Various issues. *Indicators of Science and Technology* (Kagaku Gijutsu Yoran). Tokyo: Ministry of Finance

Printing Bureau.

______. Various issues. *Science and Technology White Paper** (Kagaku Gijutsu Hakuksho). Tokyo: Ministry of Finance Printing Bureau.

Scott, Bruce R. 1984. "National Strategy for Stronger U.S. Competitiveness." *Harvard Business Review*. March–April.

Shinohara, Miyohei, ed. 1985. *Future Scenario for the Asia-Pacific Region* (Ajia Taiheiyo Chiikino Shorai Shinario). Tokyo: The Institute of Statistical Research.

Shioda, Nagahide, and Yamada, Takeshi. 1985. *A Study on the Internationalization of Industrial Policy on Advanced Technology** (Sentan Gijutsu Sangyo Seisakuno Kokusaikani Kansuru Kenkyu). Tokyo: Nihon Sogo Kenkyujo.

Shishido, Shuntaro. 1986. *An Analysis of International Repercussion stemming from Advanced Science and Technology** (Sentan Kagaku Gijutsuga Ataeru Kokusaiteki Hakyu Kokano bunseki). NIRA Output NRS-84-13. Sakura, Ibaragi: Foundation for Advancement of International Sciences.

______. 1988. "The Japanese Growth Alternatives and the World Economy: Simulations with Tsukuba-FAIS World Econometric Model." Uno, K. and Shishido, S., eds. 1988. *Statistical Data Bank Systems, Socio-Economic Database and Model Building in Japan*. Amsterdam: Elsevier Science Publishers B.V., North-Holland.

Solow, Robert. 1957. "Technical Change and the Aggregate Production Function." *Review of Economics and Statistics*. Vol.XXXIX No.3. Aug.

Smith, Gordon B. 1987. "Recent Trends in Japanese-Soviet Trade." *Problems of Communism*. January–February.

Smith, Roy C. 1987. "New Financial Aspects of the U.S.-Japan Trade Relationship." Sato, R. and Wachtel, P. *Trade Friction and Economic Policy*. Cambridge and New York: Cambridge University Press.

Stern, Robert M.; Deardorff, Alan V.; Jackson, John H.; Saxonhouse, Gary; Bornstein, Morris; Jacobson, and Harold K. 1982. *The United States in the World Economy: Adaptations to Changes in Trade, Trade Policies, and Technology Transfer*. Report prepared for National Science Foundation. Ann Arbor: The University of Michigan.

Suzumura, Kotaro, and Okuno-Fujiwara, Masahiro. 1987. "Industrial Policy in Japan: Overview and Evaluation." Sato, R. and Wachtel, P., eds. *Trade Friction and Economic Policy*. Cambridge and New York: Cambridge University Press.

Takagi, Shintaro. 1985. *An Exploration of Statistical Information regarding the National Income and the Balance of Payments** (Kokumin Shotoku Tokeito Kokusai Shushihyoni kansuru Tokei Johono Tansaku). Occasional Papers No.1. Tokyo: The Institute of Statistical Re search.

Takenaka, Heizo, and Ishii, Naoko. 1988. *Japan-U.S. Economic Controversy—The Era of 'Apologizing' is Over** (Nichibei Keizai Ronso—'Iiwake'no Jidaiwa Owatta). Tokyo: TBS Britanica.

Tanaka, Yasumasa, and Tahiro, Masuo. 1989. "Progress of Liberalization and Internationalization in Money and Capital Market and the Trends in Foreign Capital Transactions* (Kinyu Shihon Shijono Jiyuka, Kokusaikano Shintento Taigai Shihon Torihikino Doko)." Monthly Report on Fiscal and Financial Statistics, August.

Tani, Akira. 1987. "Future Penetration of Advanced Industrial Robots in the Japanese Manufacturing Industry: An Econometric Forecasting Model." WP-87-095. Laxenburg: International Institute for Applied Systems Analysis.

———. 1989a. "International Comparisons of Industrial Robot Penetration." Ranta, J., ed. *Trends and Impacts of Computer Integrated Manufacturing*. Laxenburg: International Institute for Applied Systems Analysis.

———. 1989b. "Saturation Level of NC Machine-tool Diffusion." Ranta, J., ed. *Trends and Impacts of Computer Integrated Manufacturing*. Laxenburg: International Institute for Applied Systems Analysis.

Tarr, David G. 1987. "Costs and Benefits to the United States of the 1985 Steel Import Quota Program." Sato, R. and Wachtel, P., eds. *Trade Friction and Economic Policy*. Cambridge and New York: Cambridge University Press.

Tchijov, Iouri. 1987. "The Cyclical Dynamics of Diffusion Rates." WP-87-014. Laxenburg: International Institute for Applied Systems Analysis.

———. 1989. "Economic Structural Changes: The Problems of Forecasting." Krelle, Wilhelm, ed. *The Future of the World Economy, Economic Growth and Structural Change*. Berlin: Springer-Verlag.

———. and Sheinin, Roman. 1989. "Flexible Manufacturing Systems (FMS): Current Diffusion and Main Advantages." Ranta, J., ed. *Trends and Impacts of Computer Integrated Manufacturing*. Laxenburg: International Institute for Applied Systems Analysis.

Terlecskyj, Nestor E. 1980. "Direct and Indirect Effects of Industrial Research and Development of the Productivity Growth of Industries." John W. Kendrick and Beatrice N. Vaccara, eds. *New Developments in Productivity Measurement and Analysis*. Chicago and London: The University of Chicago Press.

———. 1982. "R&D and U.S. Industrial Productivity in the 1970s." Devendra Sahal, ed. *The Transfer and Utilization of Technical Knowledge*. Lexington: Lexington Books.

Thurow, L.C. and Taylor, L.D. 1966. "The Interaction between Actual and

Potential Rates of Growth." *Review of Economics and Statistics*. Nov.

Thurow, Lester. 1984. "Revitalizing American Industry: Managing in a Competitive World Economy." *California Management Review*. Vol.XXVII, No.1, Fall.

Torre, Andre. 1989. "Technical Change and Technological Complementarities: In Search of New Tools." Paper presented at the Ninth International Conference on Input-Output Techniques.

Toyoda, Toshihisa; Ohtani, Kazuhiro; and Katayama, Sei-ichi. 1988. "Estimation of Structural Change in the Import and Export Equations: An International Comparison." Uno, K. and Shishido, S., eds. 1988. *Statistical Data Bank Systems, Socio-Economic Database and Model Building in Japan*. Amsterdam: Elsevier Science Publishers B.V., North-Holland.

Triplett, Jack E. 1986. "The Economic Interpretation of Hedonic Methods." *Survey of Current Business*. Jan.

Tsusan Tokei Kyokai, ed. 1982. *The Census of Manufactures since the World War II** (Sengono Kogyo Tokeihyo). Tokyo: Ministry of Finance Printing Bureau.

Tsusho Sangyo Chosakai, ed. 1990. *Final Report on the Japan-U.S. Structural Impediments Initiative** (Nichibei Kozo Mondai Kyogi Saishu Hokoku). Tokyo.

Tyson, Laura, and Zysman, John, eds. 1983. *American Industry in International Competition: Government Policies and Corporate Strategies*. Ithaca: Cornell University Press.

Ueda, Kazuo. 1987. "Japanese-U.S. Current Accounts and Exchange Rates before and after the G5 Agreement." Sato, R. and Wachtel, P. *Trade Friction and Economic Policy*. Cambridge and New York: Cambridge University Press.

United Nations Statistical Office. Various Issues. *Yearbook of International Trade Statistics*. New York.

United Nations Industrial Development Organization. 1984. *World Non-electrical Machinery, An Empiraical Study of the Machine-Tool Industry*. New York: United Nations.

United Nations Economic Commission for Europe. 1988. *Engineering Industries, Dynamics of the Eighties*. New York: United Nations.

United States Department of Commerce. Bureau of Economic Analysis. 1987. *Fixed Reproducible Tangible Wealth in the United States, 1925–1985*. Washington, D.C.: U.S. Government Printing Office.

Unkovic, Dennis. 1990. *Revisioning Japan: Inside the American Mind* (Amerikano Iradachi). Japanese translation by Koichi Hori and Teruhisa Akai. Tokyo: Diamond Inc.

Uno, Kimio. 1981a. "Preparing for the New Era in Communications: A Japanese Perspective." Robert W. Haigh, George Gerbner, and

Richard B. Byrne, eds. *Communications in the Twenty-First Century*. New York: John Wiley & Sons.

———. 1983a. "The Energy Situation in the Soviet Union and East Europe—An Estimation of Production Efficiency—." (in Japanese) *Communism and International Politics*. Vol.8 No.1. June.

———. 1983b. "The System of a Soviet-East European Link Model and Some Findings." (in Japanese) *Annals of the Japanese Association for Soviet and East European Studies*. No.12.

———. 1987. *Japanese Industrial Performance*. Amsterdam: Elsevier Science Publishers B.V., North-Holland.

———. 1988a. "Appreciation of the Yen and the Structural Adjustment—A Multisectoral Industry Analysis of the Japanese Economy—." Uno, K. and Shishido, S., eds. 1988. *Statistical Data Bank Systems, Socio-Economic Database and Model Building in Japan*. Amsterdam: Elsevier Science Publishers B.V., North-Holland.

———. 1988b. "The State and Private Enterprise in a Global Society: Points at Issue and Their Future Outlook." National Institute for Research Advancement. *International Symposium on the State and the Private Enterprise in a Global Society*. Tokyo.

———. 1988c. "The World Economy and Japan—Focusing on New Trends in Europe* (Sekai Keizaito Nihon—Oushu Keizaino Shinchoryuo Chushinni)." *The Future of the Advanced Economies: Towards a New Leap Forward** (Keizai Senshinkokuno Yukue: Aratana Hiyakuni Mukete). Tokyo: Social and Economic Council of Japan.

———. 1988d. "An Overview of Soviet Exports to Japan—A Japanese Perspective." Paper presetned at the 20th National Convention, American Association for Advancement of Slavic Studies. Revised and presented at the US-Japan Joint Study on the Soviet Union, Hokkaido University, June 1989.

———. 1989a. *Measurement of Services in an Input-Output Framework*. Amsterdam: Elsevier Science Publishers B.V., North-Holland.

———. 1989b. "Input-Output Tables in Japan, 1951–1985." Statistical Data Bank Project Report No. 61. Tsukuba: Institute of Socio-Economic Planning, the University of Tsukuba.

———. 1990a. "International Flow of Patents." (Release 2). Statistical Data Bank Report No.57 R.2. Tsukuba: Institute of Socio-Economic Planning, The University of Tsukuba.

———. 1990b. "Annual Input-Output Tables in Japan, 1975–1985." Statistical Data Bank Report No.63. Tsukuba: Institute of Socio-Economic Planning, The Univeristy of Tsukuba.

———. 1990c. "Fixed Capital Formation Matrix and R&D Benefit." Statistical Data Bank Report No.65. Tsukuba: Institute of Socio-Economic Planning, The University of Tsukuba.

Vuorinen, Pentti. 1988. "Flexible Automation and Less Developed Countries: Is CIM Only a Threat to the LDCs?" WP-88-85. Laxemburg: International Institute for Applied Systems Analysis.

Watanabe, Toshio. 1985. "The Emergence of Horizontal Division of Labor in Asia—A Scenario* (Ajia Suihei Bungyokenno Seisei—Hitotsuno Shinario). Shinohara, M. ed. *A Future Scenario for the Asia-Pacific Region*. Tokyo: The Institute of Statistical Research.

William, B.R. 1973. *Science and Technology in Economic Growth*. New York: Halstead Press.

Whichard, Obie G. 1985. "Measuring U.S. International Services Transactions. Paper presented at 19th General Conference of International Association for Research in Income and Wealth.

______. 1987. "U.S. Sales of Services to Foreigners." *Survey of Current Business*. Vol.67 No.1, January.

World Institute for Development Economics Research (WIDER). 1986. *The Potential of the Japanese Surplus for World Economic Development*. WIDER Study Group Series No.1. Helsinki.

______. 1987. *Mobilizing International Surpluses for World Development: A WIDER plan for a Japanese Initiative*. WIDER Study Group Series No.2. Helsinki.

______. 1989a. *Debt Reduction*. WIDER Study Group Series No.3. Helsinki.

______. 1989b. *World Economic Summits: The Role of Representative Groups in the Governance of the World Economy*. WIDER Study Group Series No.4. Helsinki.

______. 1990. *Foreign Portfolio Investment in Emerging Equity Markets*. WIDER Study Group Series No.5. Helsinki.

Yamamoto, Iwao, and Matsuura, Tetsu. 1985. "Automobile Industry in Asia—Present Status and the Prospects—*(Ajiano Jidosha Sangyo)." Shinohara, M., ed. *A Future Scenario for the Asia-Pacific Region*. Tokyo: The Institute of Statistical Research.

Yamazawa, Ippei, and Tanaka, Takuo. 1985. "Trade and Industrial Adjustment in Asia—A Scenario for the Year 2000—* (Ajiano Boekito Sangyo Chosei—2000nenno Shinario)." Shinohara, M., ed. *A Future Scenario for the Asia-Pacific Region*. Tokyo: The Institute of Statistical Research.

Yochelson, John N. 1986. "Internationalization of the U.S. Economy: Implications in the West-West Context." Paper presented to the conference on High Technology, Western Security and Economic Growth, Brussels.

Yoshitomi, Masaru. 1985. *Japan as Capital Exporter and the World Economy*. New York: Group of Thirty.

Yu, Yongding. 1987. "International Imbalance and International Cooperation." *The State and the Private Enterprise in a Global Society*. Tokyo: Japan Association for Planning Administration and National Institute for Research Advancement.

Index

H

I

N

O

P

Q

R

T

Y